Thomas Livius

S. Peter, bishop of Rome

The Roman episcopate of the prince of the apostles

Thomas Livius

S. Peter, bishop of Rome
The Roman episcopate of the prince of the apostles

ISBN/EAN: 9783743304390

Manufactured in Europe, USA, Canada, Australia, Japa

Cover: Foto ©ninafisch / pixelio.de

Manufactured and distributed by brebook publishing software (www.brebook.com)

Thomas Livius

S. Peter, bishop of Rome

Permissu Superiorum.

Nihil obstat.
   T. E. Bridgett, C.SS.R.,
       Censor Deputatus.

Imprimatur.
   Henricus Eduardus,
       Card. Archiepiscopus.

In Festo Purificationis B.M.V., 1888.

S. PETER, BISHOP OF ROME;

OR,

THE ROMAN EPISCOPATE OF THE PRINCE OF THE APOSTLES.

PROVED FROM

THE FATHERS, HISTORY, AND ARCHÆOLOGY,

AND ILLUSTRATED BY

ARGUMENTS FROM OTHER SOURCES.

BY THE

Rev. T. LIVIUS, C.SS.R.,

M.A. ORIEL COLLEGE, OXFORD.

Dedicated to

HIS EMINENCE CARDINAL NEWMAN.

LONDON: BURNS & OATES, Limited.
NEW YORK: CATHOLIC PUBLICATION SOCIETY CO.

1888.

Dedication

TO

HIS EMINENCE JOHN HENRY CARDINAL NEWMAN.

My Lord Cardinal,

It is to me a subject of very grateful satisfaction that I am allowed to dedicate this volume on S. Peter's Roman Episcopate to your Eminence, not only on account of your exalted dignity, which, by associating you with the Sovereign Pontiff in the Sacred College, brings nigh to us, in your person, the supreme pastorate of our Holy Father Leo the Thirteenth; but also, and especially, because it is mainly through your lifelong work and influence that the mind and heart of England—if not yet drawn into sympathy with the Catholic Church and the Chair of Peter—have at least been led to kindlier sentiments in that direction, and to lay aside much of old-standing prejudice and antipathy towards the ancient Faith.

It must be most consoling to your Eminence, at your venerable age, to feel that, after so many long past years of combat and misunderstanding, you have succeeded in winning for yourself not alone the esteem and confidence, but also, I may say, the affection, perhaps more than any living man, of your countrymen at large. Still much more may you be assured of having gained the love and veneration of all English-speaking Catholics, and, in particular, of that large band who, by your writings and example, have been so much helped, through the mercy and grace of God, to find their home in His one true Church. And here, amongst this number, even though mine be the last place, yet am I bold to claim in that bond of attachment a share that is not the least.

  I remain,
    My Lord Cardinal,
      With much respect,
        Your devoted Servant,
         T. LIVIUS, C.SS.R.

INTRODUCTION.

My original and principal object in writing this volume was positive and not controversial. It was undertaken with the hope that whatever polemics I might be drawn into should be in the field of history rather than that of religious doctrine. For, after all, the question of S. Peter's Roman Episcopate is one of much interest to Catholics for its own sake, and well worthy of the investigation of students of history quite independently of its theological bearings.

Nevertheless, the Catholic tradition that S. Peter was Bishop of Rome is of importance not only from an historical point of view, but also in the province of dogma within the Church, and of controversy with those outside its pale. For, as held by Catholics, in correlation with the succession of the Roman Pontiffs, it is in its theological aspect a great fact intimately bound up with what is of revealed faith— viz., the permanent institution by our Lord Jesus Christ of the Primacy in His Church. It forms, indeed, the actual verification in all time of that wondrous promise recorded in the Gospels which our Divine Lord made to S. Peter: "Thou art Peter: and upon this rock I will build My Church."* Whilst, as regards controversy, it is a matter of vital moment to Protestants; and one which they have ever most strenuously assailed, driven thereto by the very necessity of their position as opponents of the Catholic Faith. Hence, in spite of my general aim, I have found it impossible to avoid treating the subject to a large extent apologetically, and in its theological aspect.

* *Matt.* xvi. 18, 19.

The one historical point which, above all, I desire to prove and elucidate in this work is the Roman Episcopate of S. Peter. In the course of my argument I have been obliged to touch at some length on the collateral facts of his journey to Rome, his residence there, the part that he took with S. Paul in founding and consolidating the Roman Church, and the martyrdom of the two Apostles together in the Eternal City. I have, however, treated of these and other matters only as subsidiary to that which is the main and central fact of my inquiry, S. Peter's Roman Episcopate. My reason was, because this is the one point in his history of most importance to Catholic theology, and most commonly impugned by Protestant historians and controversialists. Many of these will concede the probability, at least, of the other events, but all, with very few exceptions, are unanimous in denying that S. Peter was ever Bishop of Rome.

Of course, it was not for its own sake principally that I set out to treat of this point of history. I did so on account of its important bearing on the Succession of the Roman Pontiffs to the See of Peter, and their inheritance of his Primacy. Consequently, once drawn within the sphere of theology, I determined to enter fully into the relations that exist between the See of Rome and the Primacy in the Catholic Church conferred by our Lord on S. Peter. This subject occupies an important place in my work.

It is true, as I endeavour to show in these pages, that S. Peter's Roman Episcopate was not intrinsically and antecedently necessary for the legitimate succession of the Bishops of Rome to his Primacy. For—on the proof from revelation, that our Lord conferred the Primacy on Peter with the intention of its being perpetual in His Church—it is at once clear that the Bishops of Rome alone are the *de facto* rightful inheritors of that prerogative, and that their title of succession to Peter therein is of Divine origin and institution. For this, however, there was no intrinsic or absolute need that S. Peter should have been Bishop of Rome; since it is quite conceivable that the Primacy might, by some other mode of Divine appointment, have passed from that Apostle to the line of Roman Pontiffs without his ever having been himself Bishop of the See. Still, though this was evidently antecedently possible, there can be no doubt that S. Peter's Roman Episcopate was, in the order of actual fact, the means chosen by Divine Providence for the transmission of the Primacy, and for its perpetual permanence in the See of Rome. This is, certainly, involved in the whole Catholic tradition and belief. Hence S. Peter's Roman Episcopate forms a subject of deep theological interest to which no one could adequately do justice, should he treat it merely as a historical fact, and apart from its doctrinal character.

The admission that S. Peter was really Bishop of Rome, on the part of such non-Catholics as hold the Primacy of Peter in any sense to be of Divine institution, should, I am of opinion, lead them, by strict logical sequence, to concede the truth of what are commonly called the Papal claims, and by consequence to the acknowledgment of the Catholic Faith as a whole. But, even so, I incline to doubt whether the simple intellectual admission of a fact of this sort—however cogent, strictly speaking, it may be for the logical conviction also of its consequences—would, apart by itself, as a rule at least, morally suffice to form the requisite natural constituent or accompaniment of that supernatural preparation of the mind and will which is a necessary condition for the assent of faith. Men are not wont to be practically convinced, or persuaded to believe, by arguments of bare logic. And mere intellectual conviction on such a matter-of-fact truth as that S. Peter was Bishop of Rome—however evident its apprehension, and however pregnant with further important consequences it might be seen to be—would scarcely lead to an acceptance of those other doctrinal facts and truths which it directly, or indirectly, involves. Since faith, albeit an intellectual faculty, depends principally for its exercise on some bias of the will; and the will is attracted and biassed by moral, rather than by merely speculative, truths.

Hence, I should conceive, in the case of a non-Catholic, that his intellectual apprehension of the divinity of the Church as a whole—obtained by the spectacle of her ceaseless activity; her combats and triumphs in every age; her universality; her visible unity of doctrine, government, and communion; her Religious Orders, and her influence for holiness; her perpetual self-assertion, and her exclusive claims on the submission of all men to her teaching and commands, as the one only true Church of Christ—would have persuasiveness far more potent to elicit the mind's assent to her Faith, than any simple conviction that S. Peter was Bishop of Rome.

I have made the above remarks, lest, on the one hand, the controversial value of S. Peter's Roman Episcopate should seem to be over-rated; and, on the other hand, as an apology in some sort—if such were needed—for having supplemented the treatment of a strictly historical question with various arguments and discussions of a moral and theological character.

So far, however, from deeming that any apology is really required for the course I have taken, I hold that any other treatment would be wholly inadequate for the purpose in hand, and philosophically untrue. For the question of S. Peter's Roman Episcopate is one not merely as to the bare actual occurrence of something alleged to have happened in the past,—as is that of every other historical event,—but is also one of a great *moral* fact. In treating of this question, we have to deal, not with some still-born and lifeless occurrence without results, which is no more heard of, but with a complex living fact, informed with moral principle and vitality, that enters into the order of thought and of theological truth, and into the domain of practical conduct, religion, and politics. It purports to have its original source in Divine revelation, to be the result and realisation of an express promise of Christ through Peter to His Church, or, rather, to be the divinely-appointed mode whereby that promise, which affects the essential constitution of the

Church, is carried into actual effect. Its energy as a living moral fact is manifest, in all time since its first origin, both from the results of its own active operation, and from the constantly prevalent belief of Christendom, both as to its material occurrence and its formal character. It is ever big with great consequences, momentous to the doctrine, religion, and discipline of the Church, as well as to the political principles and action of the entire Christian society. Throughout successive ages it has held its place in the minds and hearts of millions of the faithful,—as still with all Catholics at the present day,—not as though it were simply some isolated, material event of past history that happened on a time and once for all, but as an ever-present principle, influential for religious belief and practice. Hence, the conviction of its reality as an objective truth is as often and as much based on grounds of moral persuasion, as on the definite historical arguments and proofs that are brought forward in its support.

Regarded simply as an event of past history, S. Peter's Roman Episcopate, like other such events, is a matter for historical evidence. If judged by this test alone, we claim for it a more ample and precise verification than usually obtains for most of those events which learned impartial criticism has pronounced to be historically true. But in a question of a complex moral fact such as that under present consideration, a historian possessed of the true critical sense and of sound historical science is, I hold, bound to go beyond such direct and explicit proofs as are extant from authors who lived at or near to the time of the alleged event. Through various accidental causes and extrinsic circumstances, testimonies of this positive sort may, or may not, be now forthcoming—they may have perished, or they may have survived, in more or less number. Hence the historian will, in his investigation, bring other arguments to bear, whether for vindication or disproof of the occurrence, of a like moral character, proportioned to the fact in question, and consonant with its origin, surroundings, and results. This treatment appertains, I conceive, to that Philosophy of History which, not content with simply taking cognisance of the material facts on record, deals also with their several causes and effects, since these often form the best criterion for judging of the real truth or falsity of the events narrated, as also for determining their formal character or significance, and their relative importance.

The method employed so generally by German rationalists in dealing with history, whether sacred or profane, which may be termed the mythical or legendary system, might at first sight seem to bear a certain analogy with what is here propounded as the true philosophy of the really scientific and critical historian. But the two methods are diametrically opposed both in principle and result.

Genuine philosophical science deals with recorded past events, that *prima facie* are extrinsically probable, and provable by well-grounded testimony, as the first premisses and most important elements of all history, in order to preserve, substantiate, and build upon them; it investigates them in their causes and effects with a view to explain and confirm them; and aims at clothing each material event with its own proper form, and giving to it its own due import and value. But it does not compass the death of the fact itself in its desire to animate the letter thereof with spirit and life.

The rationalistic method, contrariwise, starts with denying or explaining away the actual past existence of the alleged fact, cuts at once from under it the ground whereon it rests, hardly caring to weigh at all whatever authority there may be in its support. Then, after having displaced or obliterated the recorded event, it makes its bare record serve as a symbolical element of some myth or legendary theory of its own elaboration, arbitrarily adopted, and destitute of any authenticated historical facts in its behalf. It is in such sort that German rationalism travesties S. Peter's Roman Episcopate: transmuting what is a question of historical fact into a legend or myth, symbolical of certain doctrinal tendencies which, it pretends, were at work within the bosom of the primitive Church.

It is, on the other hand, equally opposed to the true philosophical method for writers of history, whilst preserving the facts that have come down from antiquity, to seek arbitrarily to form therefrom new theories, and to draw conclusions of their own, other than such as the general intelligent sense of mankind has inherited, and understood to be their legitimate inference and result. This, unhappily, is too often the tendency of men of much erudition and research. No sooner have they made some fresh discovery in past history, and brought to light by their studies some new facts, than at once they seem to think it their business to disturb everything that was before held to be settled. Instead of letting the gain they have made to knowledge tell simply its own story—whatever that be worth—or using it, so far as may be, to illustrate and explain what has been already ascertained, they are at once in hot haste to make their discoveries so many starting-points and materials for novel speculations and crude theories, which, ere long, a deeper investigation often shows to be utterly baseless. Authors, such as these, seem ever bent on striking out for themselves some original course, and deviating from what is traditional and of common belief; as though all that has been handed down and generally received must, on that very account, be of little value, and may be lightly set aside. But it is certainly quite as much opposed to sound common-sense and the true philosophy of history to weave new historical theories from some scanty, partial, and fragmentary details, which one has recovered from antiquity—and it is really as great a folly to generalise from particular facts or statements, and then to set up such theories as the true account of history in opposition to the past general and settled belief—as it is, first to destroy or explain away the facts and statements, and then to build new theories out of their ruins. We may hold, in truth, as a first principle, that no novel historical theory that is formed exclusively from one or other isolated fact or statement is worth any serious consideration. For any such new theory to be probable, or even plausible—especially should it run counter to what is already in possession of the general human intelligence—it must rise from a wide field that is fairly exhaustive of the relevant facts. For the presumption in sound common-sense and true philosophy will always remain in favour of the theory already in possession; since this had its origin and growth when there was a more ample command of the whole range of phenomena. If, however, some newly discovered fact or statement seems really opposed to a solidly grounded theory in general acceptance, and cannot be brought into harmony with it, such fact or statement may well remain unexplained, since philosophy itself teaches us that, with all our learning and research, we are incompetent to clear up everything. This tendency to innovate and theorise is especially noticeable in some recent Anglican works bearing on the subject of this volume, and particularly in Mr. Homersham Cox's *First Century of Christianity*, and in the writings of the learned Dr. Lightfoot on the Epistles of S. Clement and S. Ignatius, in connection with the Primacy of the Roman Church, and the evolution, and position in Rome, of the Episcopate.*

As an illustration of a moral fact, and to compare great things with small, I may take that of the validity of Anglican Orders in their origin at Parker's consecration,—a fact which stands to the whole Anglican communion in much the same relation, and with at least as important consequences to that body, as the Roman Episcopate of S. Peter does to the Catholic Church.

On this question of fact there are many conflicting historical testimonies, and it is, perhaps, at the present day impossible impartially to decide the precise truth of the matter on the sole issue of these testimonies. But besides such direct evidences against the fact as Catholics are used to adduce from defects in the consecrator and the ritual

---

* See Part III. Ch. xviii. and xix.

form, there are many other arguments, of an indirect and moral character, which are with good reason brought to bear on the question. These are derived from the antecedent circumstances which, during the Reformation period, gave the fact its origin, from its concomitant circumstances and surrounding influences, and also from its consequent results.

Amongst these, I allude, in general, to the whole drift and bias of the English Reformation, which was in close alliance with that on the Continent; and to the recklessness with which, in order to do away with all vestige of Catholic priesthood and sacrifice, it made havoc of the altars, vestments, and missals, seized on the sacred vessels for profane uses, and obliterated from the new Communion Service the sacrificial character of Holy Mass, together finally with its very name; to the notorious views and conduct of the Fathers of the English Reformation with regard to Ordination and its sacramental nature; to the expressed sentiments and attitude of the Catholic party hostile to the new religion, and their constant denial from the first of the validity of Anglican Orders; to the uniform repudiation of all Anglican claims to a true priesthood, sustained even to the present time, by the whole of Catholic Christendom, and the general disavowal of them on the part of all Eastern schismatics; to the instinctive and abiding aversion of the Anglican flock, that is to say, of the Protestant English people as a body, to anything that might in their minds savour of sacerdotalism, and their shrinking from the mere name of Priest and Sacrifice; to the natural genesis and evolution of the principles of Anglicanism, shown by its disintegration, to so large an extent, into the now recognised systems of Evangelicanism, Low Church, Broad Church, multiform "orthodox" and "unorthodox" Dissent, which all unite together in disclaiming the priestly character and office; to the thinly-disguised state-craft and court policy which prompted the prudent advisability of maintaining the exterior form of hierarchical order and ecclesiastical discipline for a Church which was to serve as a support and appanage of the throne, and of which the Sovereign was to be the head and supreme governor; to the certainty that would follow such semblance of an ecclesiastical hierarchy, of claims being set up in assertion of its reality, and of a school of Anglicanism being ere long formed,—from amongst those who, from their associations or education, should have greater leanings towards the ancient Catholic tradition and doctrines, or more zeal for their clerical order,—with a view to support these claims on various grounds, and to inculcate a belief in them amongst the people. Hence the traditional Anglican or High Church party, and its more recent phases of Tractarianism and Ritualism.

These are some only of the circumstances appertaining to the origin, surroundings, and results of the controverted fact of Parker's consecration and its questioned validity, that have supplied the premisses for those moral arguments which, more than any direct historical testimonies, have served to maintain the whole Christian world—with the exception of a certain portion of Anglicans themselves—in the constant disbelief of the validity of Anglican Orders.

Here we might bring into striking contrast the corresponding circumstances of the fact of S. Peter's Roman Episcopate, the moral arguments thence derived, and the traditional belief of the fact itself. In the case of both one and the other, that saying of S. Augustine is aptly verified, "Securus judicat orbis terrarum."

I cannot refrain from here quoting, in abridged form, a passage from the illustrious Cardinal Newman on this very point. He had said in his *Apologia* * of the Anglican Church: "As to its possession of an episcopal succession from the "time of the Apostles, well, it may have it; and, if the Holy "See ever so decided, I will believe it, as being the decision "of a higher judgment than my own; but for myself, I must "have S. Philip's gift, who saw the sacerdotal character on "the forehead of a gaily-attired youngster, before I can by

* Appendix 3, *The Anglican Church.*

"my own wit acquiesce in it; for antiquarian arguments
"are altogether unequal to the urgency of visible facts."
Explaining the last clause in a letter to Fr. Coleridge,* he
writes: "By 'visible facts,' I mean such definite facts as
"throw a broad antecedent light upon what may be pre-
"sumed, in a case in which sufficient evidence is not forth-
"coming: for instance—(1) The Apostolical Succession, its
"necessity and its grace, is not an Anglican tradition,
"though it is a tradition found in the Anglican Church. . . .
"(2) If there is a true Succession, there is a true Eucha-
"rist; if there is not a true Eucharist, there is no true
"Succession. . . . If so great a gift be given, it must have
"a rite, (and) . . . a *custos* of the rite. . . . Inasmuch as
"'the Sacrament of the body and blood of Christ,' in the
"Anglican communion, is without protective ritual and
"jealous guardianship, there seems a strong presumption
"that neither the real gift, nor its appointed guardians,
"are to be found in that communion. (3) Previous bap-
"tism is the condition of the valid administration of the
"other sacraments. . . . There is much reason to believe
"that some consecrators were not Bishops for the simple
"reason that, formally speaking, they were not Christians.
"But, at least, there is a great presumption that where
"evidently our Lord has not provided a rigid rule of bap-
"tism, He has not provided valid ordination. By the light
"of such presumptions as these I interpret the doubtful
"issues of the antiquarian argument, and I feel deeply
"that if Anglican Orders are unsafe with reference to the
"actual evidence producible for their validity, much more
"are they when considered in their surroundings." †

The Book is divided into Three Parts. The First Part
comprises historical testimonies to the fact of S. Peter's
Roman Episcopate from Fathers and writers of the first

* To be found in *Characteristics from the Writings of J. H. Newman*, by W. S. Lilly, 1875.
† See further on Anglican Orders—*Essays Critical and Historical*, vol. ii. p. 76.

four centuries, and other matter that serves to illustrate this evidence. This First Part is almost entirely a translation from the Latin of Professor Jungmann's *Dissertatio Prima, De Sede Romana S. Petri Principis Apostolorum*.[*] A very few passages I have either somewhat amplified or abridged: several of the footnotes are my own.

I must here express my sense of very grateful indebtedness to the learned author for having most kindly given his sanction to whatever use I might think best to make of this Dissertation, and for having otherwise afforded me very valuable assistance on various points of my inquiry. I had previously read historical treatises on S. Peter's Roman Episcopate by other learned authors, but none of these gave me at all the same satisfaction as that of Professor Jungmann. His method of investigation, starting, as he does, from a period removed by some distance from the event, when the traditional belief is seen in more full statement, and then tracing it back step by step to its first source, approved itself to my judgment as more reasonable and better adapted to elicit the real truth, than the more ordinary inverse method. His arguments appeared to me well-weighed, solid, and precise; his criticisms sound; and generally there was evinced a spirit of moderation, a freedom from exaggeration, from unsupported assertion and theorising, joined with a reasonableness, a due consideration of the objections or arguments of opponents, and a painstaking care fully to explain difficulties and to clear up obscurities, which one does not meet with in every historian. This treatise thus commending itself to my own mind and judgment, I resolved to adopt it in its entirety as the basis of my historical agreement. I felt, moreover, that the name and authority of the learned Canon would give weight to my own work.

I have quoted the passages from the Fathers at length, because I think it necessary, in these days of historical

---

[*] *Dissertationes Selectæ in Historiam Ecclesiasticam.* Auctore Bernardo Jungmann, &c., 1880. Ratisbonæ, Pustet.

inquiry, to set before readers the words of testimony in full, if one is to have any good hope of convincing them of the truth of some controverted point. A mere argumentative essay, however learned or profound, will not suffice for conviction on questions of historical fact, for there may be suspicion of one-sidedness and partiality; nor is a summary of authorities enough, and much less so are bare references to authors. With the precise evidence before him the reader can see and judge for himself. It was necessary to give the several passages in the vernacular, as the book is intended principally for general readers of the more educated class. The work would, no doubt, have been more scholarly and complete had the original text been uniformly added. Obvious reasons of convenience forbade this as a rule: and the more learned student has ready access to the Fathers themselves, and to the Latin treatises of Sanguinetti, Jungmann, and so many more on the subject. When, however, there was some special reason, and the matter seemed to demand the original, it has been largely given. Several of the quotations are borrowed from translators of repute after having been compared with the original text.

The Second Part sets forth the evidences of S. Peter's Roman Episcopate, derived from Archaeology. Here I have availed myself with utmost freedom of the generous permission granted me by the Very Rev. Provost Northcote and the Very Rev. Canon Brownlow, to make whatever use I pleased of their well-known work *Roma Sotterranea*. This is almost the exclusive source of the first four Chapters of the Second Part.

The Third Part contains a series of Chapters occupied with discussions and arguments of a more general character on various topics relative to S. Peter's Roman Episcopate. This I may call in some sense my own work. But from such claim I must, as is plain, make large deductions, and must except the lengthened extracts I have made from the Blessed John Cardinal Fisher, Baronius, Murray, Döllinger, Cajetan, Franzelin, from the admirable volumes of Mr.

Allies, and other authors, references to whose writings are given in foot-notes. I should except also the Chapter on the Legendary Theory, which, with the kind sanction of Père Guilleux, is compiled in great measure from his Article on this subject in *La Controverse et Le Contemporain* of February, 1886. I beg to tender my best thanks to Mr. Allies and to Mr. Oxenham for kindly allowing me thus to make use of their works.

My desire has been to render this work fairly exhaustive, as it is, I believe, the only attempt as yet made in the English language to treat at any length the question of S. Peter's Roman Episcopate *ex professo*, and to set forth, at one view and *in extenso*, the various testimonies and arguments in proof of that important historical fact. Thus, however imperfect in achievement, it serves to fill a gap in English literature. I am, in truth, fully conscious of its many faults [*] and defects, especially a want of unity, owing, in part, to its composite character, and the diversity of materials with which it has to deal. Such as it is, and however unworthy of its theme, it is published in earnest hope that its perusal may dissipate the error of some of those who are fraudulently told by charlatan teachers that the venerable world-wide tradition of the Church, that S. Peter was the first Bishop of Rome, is but guess-work, or a contemptible fable unworthy of credit; and that it may serve, at the same time, to increase the loving devotion of English-speaking Catholics to the Prince of the Apostles, and strengthen their attachment to the Sovereign Pontiff, now happily reigning, Leo the Thirteenth, Supreme Pastor and Head of the universal Church, Father and infallible Teacher of all the Faithful, Vicar of Jesus Christ on earth, as successor to S. Peter in his Holy Roman See.

℣. Oremus pro Pontifice nostro Leone.

---

[*] I take the opportunity of here noting three errors, which are from no fault of the printer—(1) P. 32, for Bressel, *read* Dressel; (2) p. 46, foot-note for Ch. ii., Appendix, *read* Ch. xvi., Appendix; (3) p. 69, Patrizzi is wrongly called Cardinal; the Scripturistic author there quoted being Padre Patrizzi, S.J., brother of Cardinal Patrizzi, Vicar-General of Rome under Pius IX.

℞. Dominus conservet eum, et vivificet eum, et beatum faciat eum in terra, et non tradat eum in animam inimicorum ejus.

THE FEAST OF S. PETER'S CHAIR AT ROME, Jan. 18, 1888—THE JUBILEE YEAR OF PRIESTHOOD OF OUR HOLY FATHER, POPE LEO XIII.

CONTENTS.

	PAGE
Dedication to His Eminence Cardinal Newman,	v
Introduction,	vii

S. PETER, BISHOP OF ROME.

PART I.

PATRISTIC AND HISTORICAL EVIDENCE.

SECTION I.

Testimonies of Fathers and Writers of the First Four Centuries,	1-65
§ 1. Preliminary,	1
§ 2. General Argument,	5
§ 3. Testimonies of Fathers and Writers in the Fourth Century,	11
§ 4. Testimonies from the Third Century,	19
§ 5. Testimonies from the Second Century,	24
§ 6. Testimonies from the First Century,	33
§ 7. Scriptural Exegesis—Babylon—Roman Monuments,	37
§ 8. The Length of Duration of S. Peter's Episcopate,	39
§ 9. Answer to Objections against the Twenty-five years,	46
§ 10. Answer to Objections against the Roman Episcopate of S. Peter,	50
Babylon,	56
Simon Magus,	59
The Roman Clergy—Rationalistic Theory,	63

xxiv   CONTENTS.

Section II.
                                                              PAGE
The Chronology of the Acts of the Apostles in relation to S.
  Peter's Roman Episcopate, ...   66-81
    § 1. Preliminary—the Date of our Lord Jesus Christ's
         Birth and Death, ...   66
    § 2. Chronology of the Acts of the Apostles, . .   67
    § 3. Reply to certain Chronological Objections, .. 77
         S. Paul's journey from Troas to Jerusalem
         according to Patrizzi's Chronology, .   80

Section III.

Notices of the Bishops of Rome and their times until the close
  of the Sub-Apostolic Age, ... 82-102
    S. PETER—Condition of Jews and Christians in Rome
      —Propagation of Christianity abroad—Origin
      of Patriarchs and Metropolitans—Persecution
      of Roman Christians under Nero, . .   83
    S. LINUS—first Bishop of Rome after S. Peter, .   89
    S. CLETUS—Anacletus, ...   91
    S. CLEMENT—Persecution under Domitian—S. Cle-
      ment's Epistle to the Corinthians—His
      martyrdom, ...   92
    S. EVARISTUS—Persecution under Trajan—Pliny's
      letter—the Emperor's reply, . . .   97
    SS. ALEXANDER, SIXTUS, TELESPHORUS, HYGINUS, PIUS,   101
    S. ANICETUS—S. Polycarp's visit to Rome, ...

PART II.

Archæological.

Chapter I.

The Cemeteries of the Vatican—S. Paul on the Via Ostiensis—
  S. Priscilla and the Ostrianum, ... 105-118
    1. The Crypts of the Vatican, ... 106
    2. The Cemetery of S. Paul, ... 107
    3. The Cemetery of Priscilla, ... 108
    4. Ostrianum, ...

Chapter II.

The Cemetery of S. Domitilla, ... 114
The Cemetery of S. Sebastian, ... 125

CONTENTS. xxv

CHAPTER III.

	PAGE
The Gilded Glasses found in the Catacombs,	131
Sculpture on Christian Sarcophagi,	135
Paintings in the Catacombs,	139
Allies, on the Symbolism of the representations of S. Peter in the Catacombs,	144

CHAPTER IV.

The Chair of S. Peter in the Vatican:
The Chair of S. Peter in the Vatican not the same as that venerated in the Cœmeterium Ostrianum—The Vatican Chair recently exposed—Description of it—Its parts and ornamentation—Its Origin—Historical Notices of it—The two Feasts of S. Peter's Chair, . . 148-159
1. Description of the Chair, ... 149
2. Historical Notices of S. Peter's Chair, . . 151
3. The two Feasts of S. Peter's Chair, . . . 159

CHAPTER V.

Monuments of S. Peter's residence and Apostolate in Rome—
Notice of his work and memorials of his martyrdom there, 160
The Pallium, ... 172

CHAPTER VI.

General Reflections, ... 176
NOTE. On the loss and destruction of monuments in the Catacombs, ... 181

PART III.

DISCUSSIONS AND ARGUMENTS BEARING ON S. PETER'S ROMAN EPISCOPATE.

CHAPTER I.

On the traditional belief of S. Peter's Roman Episcopate, . 187

CHAPTER II.

Certain Objections to the Argument from Tradition considered, 198

CHAPTER III.

S. Peter's Roman Episcopate and the New Testament, . . 208
Appendix. From Dr. Döllinger, . . . 221

CHAPTER IV.

Reflections on some of the consequences involved in the question of S. Peter's Roman Episcopate, . . . 229
    Appendix—
        1. From the Blessed Martyr John Cardinal Fisher, Bishop of Rochester, . . 244
        2. From Cardinal Allen, ... 248
        3. From Dr. Döllinger, ... 249

CHAPTER V.

S. Peter's Apostleship compared with and distinguished from his Primacy, ... 251

CHAPTER VI.

The relation of the Apostolate to the Episcopate, 261

CHAPTER VII.

The historical fact of S. Peter's Roman Episcopate in relation to the dogma of the Primacy, and to its succession in the Bishops of Rome, ... 269

CHAPTER VIII.

The nature and right of the Primacy and its succession, as connected with the See of Rome, . . . 278

CHAPTER IX.

S. Peter and S. Paul—Union and Subordination, . 297

CHAPTER X.

The relation of S. Paul's work at Rome to S. Peter's Roman Episcopate and Universal Primacy, ... 307

CHAPTER XI.

S. Peter Apostle of the Circumcision, S. Paul of the Uncircumcision, ... 321

CHAPTER XII.

S. Peter's reprehension by S. Paul at Antioch, . 334

CHAPTER XIII.

Evidence of S. Peter's Roman Episcopate, Primacy, and relation to S. Paul from the Greek Liturgical Offices, . 349

CONTENTS. xxvii

Chapter XIV.

	PAGE
The succession of the Roman Pontiffs to S. Peter's Episcopate and Primacy in the See of Rome illustrated from the Greek Liturgy and other Greek sources, . . .	378
Addenda—Neale on the Eastern Liturgical languages,	385

Chapter XV.

The testimony of Eusebius to S. Peter's Roman Episcopate, .	388

Chapter XVI.

The Legendary Theory of Modern German Rationalists,	412

Appendix.

From the Preface of Rufinus to Clement's "Recognitions,"	428
From the Epistle of Clement to James, . . .	429
From the Clementine Recognitions and Homilies, . .	430
Critical remarks on the Clementines, . . .	433

Chapter XVII.

Statements and views of Anglican Authors, .	437
Cave, 442; Pearson, 447; Neale, 449.	

Chapter XVIII.

Statements and views of Anglican Authors—*Continued*,. .	451
Dr. Farrar, 451; *The Speaker's Commentary*, 453; Bishop Ellicott's *Commentary*, 453; Homersham Cox, 456; Neale, 458; Palmer, 461.	

Chapter XIX.

Statements and views of Anglican Authors—*Continued*,. .	462
Lightfoot.	
1. On Ebionism and Judaising tendencies in the Roman Church—its Orthodoxy—the Clementines, . .	465
2. On S. Clement's Epistle to the Corinthians, . .	471
3. On the Epistle of S. Ignatius to the Romans, . .	490

Chapter XX.

The Roman Episcopate of S. Peter and his Successors the chief monument of Historical Christianity, and the realisation of the Divine idea in the two Dispensations, . .	507

Appendix to Chapters VII. and VIII.

From Cardinal Franzelin, ...	534
Index, ...	547

S. PETER, BISHOP OF ROME.

PART I.

PATRISTIC AND HISTORICAL EVIDENCE OF S. PETER'S ROMAN EPISCOPATE.

SECTION I.

TESTIMONIES OF FATHERS AND WRITERS OF THE FIRST FOUR CENTURIES.

§ 1.—PRELIMINARY.

1. THAT S. PETER, Prince of the Apostles, whom Jesus Christ made Head of the whole Church, *went to Rome, was Bishop of Rome until his death, and suffered martyrdom in that city*, is a historical fact which all must allow to be of the utmost importance to entire Christendom. And as we now propose to enter into a careful and minute examination of this fact, it is well first to say a few words on its nature and bearing, as intimately connected with the Faith and Constitution of the Catholic Church.

2. That our Lord Jesus Christ instituted the Primacy to be perpetual in His Church, and that by His institution Peter, on whom He first conferred it, was to have successors, is a truth which belongs to the holy Catholic Faith. "Surely no one doubts," says the Vatican Council, "what is well known, forsooth, in all ages, that the holy and most blessed Peter, the prince and head of the Apostles, the pillar of faith, and the foundation of the Catholic Church, received the keys of the Kingdom from our Lord Jesus Christ, the Saviour and Redeemer of mankind: and that even to the present time he ever lives, presides, and exercises judgment in his successors, the Bishops of the Holy Roman See, founded by himself and consecrated with his blood." Now, S. Peter's dying Bishop of

Rome is, historically speaking, that precise fact which fixes the legitimate line of his successors in the episcopate of Rome, as also in the prerogatives of the primacy attached to that See. Hence, with good reason, theologians in treating of this question draw a distinction between *the law of succession* and its *conditions*.

By the law of succession is meant the *title* which settles the succession, and thereby is denoted the juridical decree which determines an office to be not merely and simply personal, but personal in such sense as to be at the same time real and perpetual. In virtue of the *law* of succession, by which Christ Himself conferred on Peter the primacy, and willed it to be perpetual, there will always be chief Pontiffs, universal bishops in His Church. Consequently the law of succession, whereby Peter has successors in his primacy, being made by our Lord Himself, is not a law of ecclesiastical origin, but of divine right.

3. Under the conditions of succession is comprised whatever makes this one rather than another the rightful successor, and regulates the particular place and time where and when he is to succeed. Hence, for the Bishops of Rome to be successors of S. Peter must depend on certain facts: (1) that S. Peter was himself Bishop of Rome; (2) that he was so until his death; (3) that he did not before his death resign to another his ecumenical authority; (4) that he left his supreme authority and prerogatives to the See of Rome.

Now, we may call these four points combined, *the original fact of Peter*, or *the Petrine fact;* and we claim that, with the demonstration of this quadruple *Petrine fact*, and the verification of the conditions, the Roman Pontiffs are proved to be the successors of Peter in his primacy: and since the law of succession is *de jure divino*, it thence follows that the Roman Pontiffs succeed to Peter's primacy also by divine right.*

---

* The distinction between the *law* of succession and its *condition* holds also in other cases. Thus the form of government amongst the Romans was, that supreme power should be in the hands of the Consuls. Consequently, the *law* of succession to the Consulship was held to be one of the fundamental laws of the republic. But that at such a time Pompey was Consul rather than Antony would result from the *condition* of the succession. This condition was a certain kind of election. If, then, it were asked, by what right Pompey succeeded to the Consulship, the answer would be, by right of Roman law; and if it were asked by what condition, the answer would be, by the condition of legitimate election. (See on this question, Cajetan, Opusc. III., *De Rom. Pontificis institutione*, c. xiii.; *Rom. Pontificem succedere Petro in Pontificatu totius Ecclesiæ*.) With good reason, then, the Master General of the Order of Preachers thus spoke in the Council of Florence: "Hence it is plain why the See of Peter, the Roman Church, is said to have the primacy *ratione*

4. From this we see at once of what all-importance is this question of *S. Peter, Bishop of Rome*. And here it is well to remark, that the truth of this fact, viz., Peter's Roman Episcopate, is certain with the certitude of infallibility. There are, in relation to theology, two classes of facts: some of no great importance, their existence being unconnected with revealed doctrine; others so bound up with truths of revelation, that together with their denial the deposit of faith is brought into question; and such is the fact we are now considering. For we profess as a truth of faith that the Bishops of Rome are supreme Pontiffs over the whole Church, and this precisely because they are successors of S. Peter in the Roman See. Consequently, the fact in question is one that necessarily underlies the dogma itself, or, in other words, is a *dogmatic fact*. And facts of this nature are certain with the certitude of infallibility. For the *Ecclesia docens* is assisted by the light of the Holy Ghost in the understanding and setting forth of all such matters as must needs be held settled and accepted as true, for the protection and security of the faith itself; and what is thus affirmed in consequence of such assistance of the Holy Ghost has the guarantee of infallible certitude. But still, true though all this may be, it is only most right and fitting that such dogmatic facts should be shown capable of proof by solid and convincing arguments; and it is the work of the ecclesiastical historian to find out, set forth, and unfold these arguments, and to vindicate the truth of the facts against heretical or infidel assailers.*

5. Before entering upon our subject we would say a brief word on what may be called the LITERATURE of the controversy raised by non-Catholics concerning S. Peter's going to Rome, and his being Bishop of that See.

Petri; for, through the words, 'Thou art Peter,' &c., all power is derived to the Apostolic See by the succession of those who are therein seated." (See Phillips, *K. R. I.* p. 147.)

* Moreover, many opponents of the Catholic Church, who assail the journey of S. Peter to Rome with the greatest vehemence, acknowledge that the question is ohe of great importance, and that Catholics, if once they prove that S. Peter was at Rome, can thence deduce an argument for the primacy of the Apostolic See that is by no means to be slighted. Thus Lipsius says: "The Roman Papacy bases its claim to the primacy upon the fact alleged; and it cannot be denied that if ever the Prince of the Apostles set his foot in the Eternal City, he did not go there as a simple traveller, but in virtue of his apostolic power. . . . Hence the claim of the Roman Church to trace back her bishops to Peter does not seem so absurd. . . . Anyhow, the Roman Episcopate would rest on the power conferred by Peter." (*Jahrbücher für Protest. Theologie*, 1876, ap. Schmid; *Petrus in Roma.* Luzern, 1879.)

This fact was first denied in the thirteenth century by the Waldenses,* whose sole argument was the silence of the New Testament on the matter. But the first who formally opposed the historical fact by his writings was MARSILIUS PATAVINUS, a most depraved heretic, who in the fourteenth century had espoused the cause of the schismatical Emperor Louis of Bavaria against Pope John XXII. In his book entitled *Defensor pacis* he endeavours to throw doubt on S. Peter's having ever been in Rome at all; but his chief attack is directed against the Apostle's episcopate there, in order thus more effectually to impugn the primacy of the Roman Pontiff.

"As to S. Peter," he writes, "I say that it cannot be proved from Holy Scripture that he was Bishop of Rome; nay more, that he was ever in Rome at all. Wonderful, indeed, it seems, that according to some ecclesiastical legend . . . such things are to be said of Peter, and that Luke and Paul should make no mention of them."

Others, as Bellarmine, say that William, the master of Wickliff, was the first to assail the Roman Episcopate of S. Peter. His words are much like those of Marsilius, from whom, perhaps, he borrowed them:

"Holy Scripture," he says, "does not teach this (that Peter ever went to Rome), but some apocryphal legend." †

6. From Luther until the present time many Protestants have written against the fact of S. Peter's going to Rome, and his episcopate there, chief amongst whom is FREDERICK SPANHEIM, whose Dissertation is divided into four parts. In the first part he reviews the writings and arguments in defence of the tradition; in the second he strives to show the worthlessness of such tradition, from the silence of Paul and Luke, and other like arguments; in the third he discusses and refutes the authority of those who bear witness to it; and in the fourth he essays to show the origin and occasion of the said tradition.

What subsequent Protestant authors have done has been simply to re-hash what Spanheim had written: and in this they have found meet helpers in several German Rationalists, as Baur, Weiner, and Lipsius, who have ended in relegating the historical Peter, together with all the facts of the Gospel and of early Christianity, to the region of myths and fables.

Lastly, we may note the public disputation, *De Romano Petri*

---

* According to the testimony of Moneta, O.P., an author of that time, in his work against the Cathari and Waldenses.

† From Thomas Waldensis, *Doctrin. Fidei*, t. l. l. ii. c. vii. a. 1.

Itinere, which was held in Rome (Feb. 9th and 10th, 1872), between some Catholic priests on the one side, and certain Protestant ministers on the other, one of whom was the apostate priest, Gavazzi.

7. It would be too long to mention even the names of the more celebrated Catholic authors of past and recent time who have vindicated the fact of S. Peter's Roman Episcopate against the cavils and sophistical arguments of Protestants and Rationalists. Amongst those who wrote against the Protestants are Cardinal Gregory Cortesius, the Blessed Cardinal John Fisher, Bishop of Rochester, Bellarmine, and Foggini; and during the present century many theologians and ecclesiastical historians in Germany and elsewhere have written as well against the Rationalists as the Protestants. Amongst the modern German authors especially are De Smedt, S.J., Windischmann, Herbst, Stenglein, Hagemann, Hundhausen; and amongst Italians, Perrone, Aloysius Ado, and P. Sebastian Sanguinetti, S.J., whose book is the most notable of those written professedly on this subject.*

So strong are the arguments adduced by Catholics, that many of the more celebrated learned Protestants have been convinced by them, and have held the fact of S. Peter's Roman Episcopate to be most certain on historical grounds; and some of these have written in its defence, as Cave, Pearson, Grotius, Usher, Blondell, and Basnage.† Many Anglicans, on the other hand, do not deny that S. Peter went to Rome, was martyred there, and that he even took part in preaching the faith and settling the affairs of the Church in Rome. All this they will allow to be more or less probable. But here they stop short, stoutly maintaining that he was never Bishop of Rome.

§ 2.—General Argument.

8. Before drawing out in full detail the proofs that S. Peter went to Rome and was Bishop of that See, we should say something of our proposed plan. First, we shall simply indicate, rather than expose with development, a sort of general argument derived from what is obvious and incontestable—viz.,

---

* *De Sede Romana B. Petri Principis Apostolorum. Commentarius historicus criticus.* Romæ, 1867.

† Some of those here mentioned do not, perhaps, go further than to maintain that S. Peter went to Rome and founded the Church there. We shall examine the statements of Anglican authors later on. So far as we are aware, no non-Catholic writer allows the twenty-five years of S. Peter's Roman Episcopate.

the popular recognition, at any rate in some broad sense, of the Papal Primacy, together with the *prima facie* presumption in men's minds that this primacy is intimately connected with what we have termed "*the original fact of Peter;*" and then from this being a persuasion common in all times throughout Christendom, we shall go on to prove with careful detail, from historical documents of antiquity, that S. Peter's journey to Rome and his episcopate there until death are most certain facts.

9. With regard to our first point, it is most evident from the history of Christianity in every age and country, that the relation between the Roman Pontiff and the whole Christian world is such that (1) the Pope, the Bishop of Rome, is throughout the whole history of Christianity the centre of all Churches and of the whole body of the Faithful; and (2) that the reason why he is so, and is believed so to be, is because he is always looked upon as S. Peter's successor in the Roman See. For the present we keep aloof from the question whether, rightly or wrongly, such authority is attached to the See of Rome, and whether it is due to divine institution or to human industry. All we now say is, that it is incontestably certain, from the facts of history, that the Roman See has been ever held to be the one centre of Christendom.* We are at the same time perfectly aware that, strictly speaking, this is the very point that has to be proved, especially with regard to the first centuries of Christianity, and that only when such proof has been given will the argument we now indicate be complete and have force of conviction.

* In other words, we affirm, on the one hand, as incontestable, and quite patent on the very surface of history, that the Bishop of Rome has, all along from the beginning of the Christian Church, claimed for himself and for his See a superior authority and the first place in Christendom; that such superior authority or primacy has been all along from the beginning asserted for, and conceded to, him by others, and has, in manifold ways and times, all along been put into practical exercise by him. We are not now saying what is the nature or extent of the authority thus claimed, nor that it has not been questioned, denied, opposed, and set at nought. We affirm, moreover, that the sole and exclusive ground for such assertion of superiority for the See of Rome and its Bishops, is the presumed fact that S. Peter was the first Bishop of Rome, and that the Roman Pontiffs are his successors in that See, and inherit his apostolic authority. We affirm, on the other hand, as equally incontestable, and patent on the very surface of history, that the Bishops and See of Rome have never had any rivals in the assertion of the primacy—for that no such claim to superiority and to the first place in Christendom has ever been made, or so much as thought of, in behalf of any other see or bishop in the Christian world; and that no other ground for such superiority, than succession to S. Peter, the Prince of the Apostles, has ever been imagined. So that, failing the Bishop and See of Rome, there is no such thing as a centre of Christendom at all. It is *Petrus aut nullus—Papa aut nullus.*

It is worth while to quote here a passage from Dean Milman on the influence of the Roman See.

"Latin Christianity, from its commencement, in its character and in all the circumstances of its development, had an irresistible tendency to monarchy. Its capital had for ages been the capital of the world, and it still remained that of Western Europe. This monarchy reached its height under Hildebrand and Innocent III.; the history of the Roman Pontificate thus becomes the centre of Latin Christian History. The controversies of the East, in which Occidental or Roman Christianity mingled with a lofty dictation sometimes so unimpassioned that it might seem as though the establishment of its own supremacy was its ultimate aim; the conversion of the different races of barbarians who constituted the world of Latin Christendom; monasticism, with the forms which it assumed in its successive orders; the rise and conquests of Mahommedanism, with which Latin religion came at length into direct conflict, at first in Spain and Gaul, in Sicily and Italy; afterwards when the Popes placed themselves at the head of the Crusades, and Islam and Latin Christianity might seem to contest the dominion of the human race; the restoration of the Western empire beyond the Alps; the feudal systems of which the Pope aspired to be, as it were, the Spiritual Suzerain; the long and obstinate conflicts with the temporal power; the origin and tenets of the sects which attempted to withdraw from the unity of the Church, and to retire into independent communities; the first struggles of the human mind for freedom within Latin Christendom; the gradual growth of Christian literature, Christian art, and Christian philosophy—all these momentous subjects range themselves as episodes in the chronicle of the Roman Bishops." *

10. Now, if it be asked how was it the See of Rome came thus to be regarded as the centre of Christendom, history again will unhesitatingly answer, it was so, *because the Bishop of Rome was believed to be the successor of S. Peter in the Roman Pontificate.* Certainly, if you were to ask the Catholics of all times why they held the Roman Pontiff before all others to be the centre and head of the Church, their answer would be, because he is the successor of S. Peter, who was constituted by Christ to be the head of the Church, who was, moreover, Bishop of Rome at the time of his death, and who thus fixed in the Roman See the rights of the primacy. Heretics and schismatics will themselves confess that this was the reason Catholics always had for looking on the Roman Pontiff as head of the Church, and most of them will allow that the Bishops of Rome did in fact succeed to Peter in that See, and on that account claimed for themselves supreme authority, though they would say that the Popes had no right to

---

* *History of Latin Christianity*, vol. i. book i. ch. i. pp. 20, 21. Third edition, 1872. The author's tendencies, as is well known, were rationalistic. He holds the absurd theory that the Church of Christ is a congeries of the several Christian communities. Sanguinetti, who quotes this passage, develops the argument more at length.

assume such primacy. This, at any rate, no one can deny—viz., that the historical development of Christianity was fundamentally based on the belief that the Roman Pontiff was the successor of S. Peter in the See of Rome.

11. But if S. Peter was never in Rome, and if his going there and his being Bishop of Rome are to be regarded as mere fables, it would follow that the whole of that huge mass of facts which comprises the historical development of Christianity, under the preponderating influence of the Roman Pontiff as its centre, is based on some idle legend or some absurd fabricated forgery.

Now this, we say, would be utterly opposed to all those laws which regulate and determine man's moral conduct. For, granting that there are such laws, it is impossible that an entire society should so depend on some false and baseless legend as to make it the very foundation for its whole reason of existence at all, and of all its entire course and method of action; and that the members of such society should, forsooth, depend so completely upon an empty fable of this kind, as all of them willingly and of free choice, to abdicate their own rights and subject themselves to the unjustly assumed authority of another, because of the credence given to the idle story. Historical Christianity would be, verily, but a manifest mockery and sham if that fundamental fact which, more than aught else, is the key to its whole historical evolution is to be set down as, after all, but an idle tale. This, moreover, is utterly repugnant to all our notions of Divine Providence.*

12. Now just as the whole history of Christianity *objectively* considered, as a vast series of multiplied facts, demands that that fact on which, more than on any other, it is based, should be admitted to be true; so, too, its truth may be inferred from the universal *subjective* persuasion of Christians, since such persuasion can only be explained by the reality of the fact. That this persuasion has existed all along from the first centuries of Christi-

---

* See Sanguinetti, cc. ii. and iii. It is well to remark that we are not now touching on the controversy with Protestants about *the divine right* of the primacy. What we here say is, that the *historical fact* of an existing primacy, and its influence on the Christian society cannot be denied; nor either can be denied the intimate connection in the mind of Christian society, between this primacy as exercised by the Roman Pontiffs and the fundamental and crucial fact of S. Peter's Roman Episcopate. Consequently, even though it be alleged that the Bishops of Rome have unjustly *usurped* the primacy, yet to deny altogether that underlying fact which alone could have given plausible colour for such usurpation, that is to say, S. Peter's going to Rome and being Bishop of that See, is utterly to set at nought all the laws which direct man's moral conduct, and to do away with the Providence of God and His overruling care of the Christian religion.

anity cannot be denied. Milman says that at the beginning of the fifth century the lineal succession of the Bishop of Rome from Peter was universally believed throughout Christendom.* It is easy to show—and, indeed, it necessarily follows, as we shall distinctly prove later on—that the same persuasion was no less prevalent in the fourth century. We say that here this is shown to follow necessarily. For no persuasion universally prevalent in the fifth century could have sprung up, as it were, spontaneously in that century; especially when the existing records of the same age have handed it down as received from antiquity. We must, moreover, bear in mind that we are here dealing with something which would have the effect of lowering the other Churches in favour of one alone, to which all the rest are made subordinate; and it is absurd to suppose that this could have been universally prevalent in the fifth century without being common in the fourth. And what would be the case in the fourth century would be the same likewise in the centuries preceding.

13. Now, one of two things: either so constant and universal a persuasion was founded on unmistakable evidence brought home by continuous testimony of the fact being really true,—in which case we have all we want. And this is the only hypothesis satisfactory to right reason and common sense; since a universal and constant persuasion in a matter such as this is an effect, which demands for itself a proportionate cause; and there is here no other proportionate cause save the acknowledged truth and reality of the fact. Or,—and here is the only alternative,—it is for those who contend that it was not from the real truth of the fact that the persuasion had its origin, but from some other cause, it is for them, we say, to *positively* assign the real reason or cause which gave rise to this false persuasion, and such a reason, too, as is proportioned to that effect. As it is, they can only devise hypotheses which are evidently absurd. Thus Spanheim gives out with wondrous assurance that this universal persuasion owed its origin (1) to the occurrence of the word *Babylon* in S. Peter's I. Epistle, and to the mistake some persons (notably Papias of Hierapolis) in their ignorance made, of understanding this name

---

* "At the commencement of the fifth century, the lineal descent of the Pope from S. Peter was an accredited tenet of Christianity." (Vol. i. book ii. p. 106.) Still more to the point he says: "The succession of the Bishop of Rome from S. Peter was now, near 200 years after his death, an accredited tradition." (P. 66.)

to be used by the Apostle allegorically for Rome; (2) to the circumstance that in some early apocryphal books certain things are said to have been wrought by S. Peter in relation to Simon Magus. We shall see, indeed, later on that both one and the other of these are true, and confirm our "Petrine fact." But let us suppose them to be false: and we say that—whilst one can very well understand, supposing S. Peter's journey to Rome, and his being Bishop of that See, were notorious and well attested facts, how such an interpretation of Babylon should come to be started, and that some extraordinary incidents, insufficiently authenticated, should be recorded of the Apostle during his abode in Rome,—it is absurd and simply ridiculous to pretend that a persuasion so universal, the results of which are closely bound up with the whole Church's history, had its origin in a legendary story and in the chance interpretation of a word gratuitously set forth by certain individuals.

14. To set the full force of the argument in a clearer light, we sum it up thus in few words. If some constant and universal fact cannot otherwise be satisfactorily and adequately accounted for than by recognising and affirming the truth of another fact as its foundation, then the testimony to the truth of this original and causal fact is not less a matter for current recognition and common acceptance, than is the truth of the fact which results from it. Now to apply this principle: the whole life and development of the Roman Catholic Church, together with the pre-eminent influence of the Roman See, is a universal fact, unquestionably great and manifest. Moreover, during fifteen centuries the foundation of this well-known and great fact was acknowledged and admitted by all, to be the Roman Episcopate of S. Peter, and from this Episcopate, as from a source, the Doctors of the Church were all used to derive the constitution and magisterial authority of the Church, and to vindicate these against heretics and schismatics (and this so early as Irenæus and Tertullian); whilst heretics and schismatics on their side never ventured to deny or to call in question *this fact* when opposed to them as being fundamental, but strove to defend their errors by other devices. Consequently, with the very same certitude that we have of the historical existence, continued life, and strikingly manifest development of the Roman Catholic Church, depending as these do on the Roman Episcopate of S. Peter as their *causal* fact—with the very same certitude are we certain of this fact itself. And since the Roman Episcopate of S. Peter was believed

with universal persuasion for fifteen centuries, and admitted even by heretics and schismatics, it is absolutely repugnant to sound reason now, after all those centuries, to deny or to call that fact in question.

§ 3.—Testimonies of Fathers and Writers in the Fourth Century.

15. We now proceed to a more exact and detailed proof of S. Peter's Roman Episcopate from testimonies of antiquity.

In order to anticipate sundry captious objections and cavils, and to determine more precisely the force of our argument, we think it well to make first the following remarks:

(1) The question of the Roman Episcopate of S. Peter until his death is not to be confounded with that of its *duration*, or the length of time his episcopate lasted. That S. Peter was Bishop of Rome twenty-five years is demonstrable by solid arguments, and this is the opinion which we defend. But because some Catholic authors differ on this point, such difference cannot be objected, as rendering the fact of S. Peter's Roman Episcopate itself doubtful. As to this fact, at any rate, there is amongst Catholics an unanimous consent, which is quite unaffected by any difference of opinion about the length of its duration. There is, therefore, no sense or meaning in the attempts of Protestants to confuse the question, by making the most of some difference of opinion amongst Catholic writers as to the length of time the episcopate lasted.

(2) It is very evident from the general argument we have already given, that the reason why the fact of S. Peter's going to Rome and abode in that city received the universal assent that it did, and was affirmed in the way it was by united Christendom, and why it had such an immense weight and influence on Christianity, was not so much on account of the fact itself, but because of its necessary subsidiary relation to another fact, which was alike held with settled conviction throughout the Christian world —viz., that the Roman Pontiffs were the successors of S. Peter in his See. Now it is at once evident that, to account for this, not any sort of journey of S. Peter to Rome, nor any sort of residence of the Apostle in that city, nor his bare martyrdom there, whether these be taken singly or altogether, would of themselves be enough; and that nothing short of S. Peter's having been actually Bishop of Rome until his death could adequately suffice. For the

recognition and proof in testimony which the Christian society would have of the fact must needs correspond, and be in proportion to its nature and character.

Hence, in reviewing the testimonies of various writers through a course of centuries, it is absurd to regard these testimonies *singly and apart* in such sense, that, whilst some of these authors testify expressly to S. Peter's Roman Episcopate, those others who bear witness only to his journey to Rome, or to his martyrdom there, are to be considered as ignorant of what related to his episcopate. From the very nature of the fact itself, as well as from the way in which the Christian society has always held it as the most important foundation of its constitution and life, it is clear that all these several testimonies taken singly point *implicitly* to the whole complex fact, and that writers who make incidental mention simply of S. Peter's going to Rome, or of his martyrdom there, nevertheless, speak *in concreto* of that journey and of that martyrdom which are bound up with S. Peter's episcopate, and thus indicate that one integral fact, on the strength of which the Roman Pontiffs are successors of Peter. We say this, because some heretics with presumptuous sophistry and cunning fraud have endeavoured so to divide and classify the various testimonies, as to set aside entirely, as of no importance, those in which the episcopate of Peter until his death is not expressly mentioned. But it is simply absurd to admit one part of the fact —S. Peter's going to Rome for instance—and to deny the rest; for the fact in question, though composed, so to say, of several elements, is yet one single whole, and this or that part of it cannot be denied or conceded at will.

(3) The testimonies are manifold, and may be divided into different classes, so far as some are *verbal* records, others *real*, consisting of facts and things; some again are *explicit*, others *implicit* or *complex*. But not to let our dissertation run to too great length, we shall keep little to this division; and it may suffice to have noticed it.

In order to demonstrate what we have in hand solidly, yet without great prolixity, the following method has seemed to us the best:

We shall begin with a century more remote from the apostolic age, and shall prove from testimonies thoroughly patent the universal persuasion then existing, that S. Peter was Bishop of Rome. We shall next descend to a century less remote, and shall show that then also this fact was held as certain and beyond all question. Thus, at length, we shall arrive at the times joining on to those of the Apostles, and shall follow the testimonies down to their days. And in this way it will be fully apparent that the persuasion prevalent throughout Christendom had its foundation in the unquestionable truth and objective reality of the fact itself.

16. It would be quite superfluous to bring testimonies from the fifth century in proof of our thesis; since even Protestants are agreed that in that age the persuasion of S. Peter's Roman Episcopate was universal throughout Christendom. It is enough to recall what we quoted above from Dean Milman. "At the commencement of the fifth century the lineal descent of the Pope from S. Peter was an accredited tenet of Christianity." Nay, even with regard to the fourth century, it would seem that all, generally speaking, are agreed in admitting that this was the opinion commonly prevalent in that age also. It is well, however, here to give the testimony of some of the most eminent Fathers and Doctors of the Church in proof that this was no mere chance, stray, or vague opinion, but a most firm and universal persuasion.

17. Let us listen, then, to S. JOHN CHRYSOSTOM of Antioch (A.D. 387), and afterwards Patriarch of Constantinople. We quote his testimony especially, because (1) as a native of Antioch, and living in Syria, not far from the confines of Babylonia, he would have more easily known, and better than anyone else, of any traditions still existing in those parts—if, as some of our opponents maintain, Babylon had been the place of S. Peter's episcopate and martyrdom; (2) because, were not S. Peter's Roman journey and episcopate a matter quite certain and well known to everybody, he would, on account of the jealous rivalry between the Easterns and Westerns, have been less express in what he asserts; (3) and lastly, because S. Chrysostom is so eminent both for sanctity and learning, that all will agree in accepting the utterance of this great Doctor as the voice of the entire East.

He says, then, in his *Second Homily on the Inscription of the Acts of the Apostles* which he delivered in Antioch:

"For Peter himself received this very name, not from wonders and signs, but from zeal and sincere love. For not because he raised the dead or made straight the lame was he so named; but because he manifested sincere faith, together with that confession he had that name allotted to him. 'Thou art Peter, and upon this rock I will build My Church.' And as I have named Peter, I am reminded of another Peter also (Flavian, Bishop of Antioch), our common father and teacher, who, having succeeded to his virtue, has also allotted to him his chair. For this is also one privilege of our city, that it received in the beginning for its teacher the Chief of the Apostles. For it was befitting that that city which, before the rest of the world, was crowned with the name of Christian, should receive as shepherd the first of the Apostles. But after having had him as our teacher, we did not keep him, but surrendered him to imperial Rome. Nay, but we have ever kept him. For though we did not keep Peter's body, we kept Peter's faith in Peter's stead: and having the faith of Peter we have Peter himself."

And in his *Thirty-second Homily on the Epistle to the Romans* is that celebrated eulogy of Rome:

"As a body great and strong she has two shining eyes—the bodies of these saints. Not so bright is the heaven when the sun sends forth it rays, as is the city of the Romans, which diffuses these two lights over every part of the habitable globe. Thence shall Paul be caught up; thence Peter. Think and tremble at the sight which Rome shall see—Paul raised of a sudden from that deposit with Peter, and borne up to meet the Lord. . . . This same body is a wall to that city, a greater security than any tower, and than thousands of fortifications; and with it is that of Peter; since him in life he honoured, for, said he, 'I went up to see Peter' (*Gal.* i. 18). Wherefore grace vouchsafes to make him companion of Peter in departing thence."

18. With Chrysostom let us join S. JEROME (A.D. 390), another Doctor of the Church, one who passed part of his life in the East, and part in the West, and *that* at Rome: a man who excelled in critical skill, and possessed, one might say, in his own person, all the learning of antiquity. Many testimonies, indeed, with regard to S. Peter's Roman Episcopate might be gathered from his writings—for example, from his Epistle to Damasus," the Successor of the Fisherman"; but it is enough to quote what he says of S. Peter in his *Catalogue of Ecclesiastical Writers:*

"Simon Peter, son of John, of the Province of Galilee, of the town of Bethsaida, brother of Andrew the Apostle, himself Prince of the Apostles, after being Bishop of the Church of Antioch, and preaching to those of the circumcision who believed, dispersed in Pontus, Galatia, Cappadocia, Asia, and Bythinia, proceeded in the second year of Claudius to Rome to confound Simon Magus; and there held for twenty-five years the sacerdotal See until the last year, that is the fourteenth of Nero, by whom he was crowned with martyrdom, being crucified with his head downwards and his feet raised upwards, saying that he was not worthy to be crucified as his Lord was. . . . He was buried at Rome in the Vatican, near the Triumphal Way, where he is had in public veneration of the whole city."

Thus pithily does S. Jerome set forth what was held as certain about S. Peter from the trustworthy traditions and testimony of antiquity.

19. Passing over many others, let us come to EUSEBIUS (A.D. 325), who used the greatest diligence with regard to the facts he

narrates, and was most careful to separate things doubtful from what were certain. In his Chronicle then, after giving an account of the murder of the Emperor Caius, and the beginning of the reign of Claudius, he writes at the second year of that Emperor (according to the paraphrase of S. Jerome) :

"Peter the Apostle, Galilæan by birth, the first Pontiff of Christians, having first founded the Church at Antioch (πρώτην θεμελιώσας ἐκκλησίαν), goes to Rome, and there preaching the Gospel for twenty-five years, continued bishop of that city." *

And at the thirteenth year of Nero he writes :

"Nero was the first, above all his other crimes, to raise a persecution against the Christians, in which Peter and Paul suffered a glorious death in Rome."

In various places of his Ecclesiastical History, Eusebius speaks of S. Peter's episcopate and death at Rome: *v.g.*, b. ii. ch. xxv., when, after quoting Tertullian, he says :

"Thus Nero, publicly announcing himself as the chief enemy of God, was led on in his fury to slaughter the Apostles. It is related, therefore, that Paul was beheaded in Rome, and Peter crucified under him. And this account is attested by the fact that the titles of Peter and Paul still remain in the cemeteries of that city even to this day."

He then confirms the statement by the testimony of Caius, of which we shall speak again later on. Of the coming to Rome of Peter he writes thus :

"Immediately (*i.e.*, after the arrival of Simon Magus, which Eusebius has just narrated), under the reign of Claudius, by the benign and gracious providence of God, Peter, that powerful and great Apostle, who by his excellence took the lead of all the rest, was conducted to Rome against this pest of mankind. He, like a noble commander of God, fortified with divine armour, bore the precious merchandise of the revealed light from the East to those of the West, announcing the light itself and salutary doctrine of the soul, the proclamation of the kingdom of God." †

And in the next chapter, amongst other records of S. Peter's residence at Rome, he makes mention of the Gospel set to writing by S. Mark in that city. Here too we may quote what he says, speaking of the Jew Philo :

---

* "Peter, that Coryphæus, having first founded the Church at Antioch, went away to Rome, preaching the Gospel; and, after the Church in Antioch, he also presided over that of Rome until his death." (Euseb. t. i. *Chron. ad ann. 44* (*Sync.*), pp. 539, 40. Edit. Migne.) Later on in this work we treat at length of the testimony of Eusebius to S. Peter's Roman Episcopate.

† B. ii. ch. xiv.

"The same author, in the reign of Claudius, is also said to have had familiar converse with Peter at Rome, whilst he was proclaiming the Gospel to the inhabitants of that city. Nor is this at all improbable. . . ." *

20. Our opponents have sought to raise much difficulty from the fact of the original Greek text of Eusebius' Chronicle not being still extant, and because S. Jerome confesses that he made various changes in his paraphrase,† also because in Syncellus (eighth century), who has preserved the Greek Chronicle of Eusebius in his Chronography, no mention is found of the twenty-five years. To all this we reply that, besides S. Jerome's paraphrase, there is extant also an Armenian version of Eusebius' Chronicle; here, it is true, the passage in question has its place under the reign of Caligula; this, however, is easy to explain from the subject matter of the passage being the foundation of the Church at Antioch which took place in that reign, whereas Eusebius, in his History, tells us expressly that S. Peter went to Rome in the reign of Claudius. In the Armenian version the passage runs thus:

"The Apostle Peter, having first founded the Church at Antioch, goes to the city of the Romans, and there preaches the Gospel, and remains Bishop of the Church there twenty years."

This version, we see, is in substantial accord with the text of S. Jerome; the mention of twenty years being probably attributable to an error of the copyists. It appears, however, that the learned are not agreed whether mention was made of the twenty-five years in the Greek text of Eusebius. Sanguinetti supports the affirmative opinion, whilst Fr. Pius Gams, from the Greek text of Syncellus, concludes the contrary. The question after all, as regards Eusebius, seems to be of no great moment, since, as is clear from his History, he places S. Peter's arrival in Rome at the commencement of the reign of Claudius,‡ and his martyrdom about the fourteenth year of Nero; and this of itself would give the twenty-five years. Consequently, it matters little whether the mention of the twenty-five years were an addition made by S. Jerome to the Chronicle or not.

We may hence, know, what to think of the impudence of

* Euseb. ii. 17.

† "Sciendum etenim est, me et interpretis et scriptoris ex parte officio usum esse." (*Prolog. ad Chronicum.*)

‡ Philo, it is to be remarked, came twice to Rome, as we learn from other historians, first under Caligula, A.D. 40, and again in the second year of Claudius. (See Joseph. *Antiq.* l. xviii. c. xi.; and S. Jerome, *Script. Eccl.* PHILO.)

Gavazzi, who, in the Roman disputation, strove to put the testimony of Eusebius out of court, and had the face to assert that no argument could be drawn from his Chronicle, on the ground that we did not possess his Greek original, that the extant Greek text of Syncellus was of the eleventh century(!), that S. Jerome's paraphrase is not genuine, and that nowhere in his History does Eusebius affirm that S. Peter ever went to Rome at all. Assertions such as these are very easy to refute. Besides the first and second chapters in the III. Book of his History, there is ch. vi. of Book V., where he sets forth the list of Roman Pontiffs given by S. Irenæus, and says that it agrees with "the same order and the same succession in which the traditions of the Apostles in the Church and the promulgation of the truth have descended to us."

21. It is, then, evident from what we have seen, that in the fourth century the Roman Episcopate of S. Peter was affirmed by men of the highest note in the Church for sanctity and erudition as a most certain fact, based on historical documents. Consequently, from these testimonies of the fourth century, together with the way in which they are given, there results clearly the historical proof of the fact.

It is superfluous here to remark that we might have greatly multiplied our authorities, and have cited, for example, S. Epiphanius,* S. Athanasius,† S. Ambrose,‡ S. Augustine,§ Lactantius,|| Orosius,¶ S. Optatus of Milevis,** S. Peter of Alexandria,†† and many others to be found in Sanguinetti‡‡ and Foggini.§§

22. We think it well to give here another solid argument drawn *from the agreement of all the Eastern Churches*, including those of schismatics, with regard to this fact. Everyone knows how, in all times and countries, men are naturally eager to claim persons of note and renown for their own nation or state, and deem it no little glory to themselves to reckon such heroes amongst their own fellow-citizens—that they were born or died, or that their sepulchres remain, in their midst. This sentiment prevailed amongst the heathen of old, and is set forth in the couplet:

---

* *Hæres.* 27. † *Apol. de fuga sua.*
‡ *Serm. de basilicis hæreticis non tradendis,* &c.
§ *Lib. de hæres.* c. 1.; *Epist.* 165, &c.
|| *Institut.* l. vi. c. xi., *et De Mortibus Persec.* c. ii.
¶ *Histor.* l. vii. cc. vi. vii.
** L. ii. c. *Parmenionem.* †† *Serm. de Pænit. can.* 9.
‡‡ P. ii. §§ *Exercitatio tertia.*

"Smyrna, Rhodus, Colophon, Salamis, Chios, Argos, Athenæ,
Siderei certant vatis de patria Homeri."

All know, too, how many religious contests there have been amongst Christians respecting the country, birthplace, tombs, and relics of saints. Thus it is in pious rivalry Palermo and Catana lay claim to S. Agatha. Now, if S. Peter, the Prince of the Apostles, had died in some city of the East, the tradition of this event would most surely have survived amongst the Orientals; and supposing it were not quite certain in what city Peter's death took place, or where was his sepulchre, different cities would be sure to have disputed such an honour.* And the Orientals would have been all the more careful to claim for themselves such honour, from their zealous attachment to the glories of their native land, and from the old and constant jealousy they have of the Westerns. Now, so far from any city of the East laying claim to the martyrdom and tomb of S. Peter, or any cities contesting together for this honour, all the Orientals agree with the Westerns, that Peter was Bishop of Rome, was there martyred, and that there his sacred body is preserved. And not only do the Catholic Orientals hold this, but also those ancient sects that separated from the Church many centuries ago. Thus in the Office for SS. Peter and Paul, in use amongst the Nestorians, which is thought to date from the fourth century, the preaching and martyrdom at Rome of those two Apostles form several times the subject of thanksgiving and praise.† Here, again, we see the fact in question

---

* In the case of all the Apostles, with the single exception of Peter, there is found a like difference of opinion. Whence we infer that there has ever existed a perfect agreement as to the place of death of the Prince of the Apostles. Père Martin, on this subject, says: "How strange that, amidst all the different opinions to be found in ancient documents concerning the Apostles, S. Peter is the only one about whom history has never varied in any of the records it has left us." This cannot be said with respect to the other Apostles: there prevails so much uncertainty about the sphere of their apostolate, that one cannot be always sure of the place of their death. Thus, S. Paul, whose name and memory, martyrdom and death, one would have thought, could not possibly be separated from those of S. Peter, has furnished matter for more than one mistake. We read for instance in the Karkaphia MS. in Paris: "Peter, chief of the Apostles, was crucified at Rome with his head downwards. Paul was beheaded in the land of Patras, where Andrew had been already crucified, and Thomas was thrust through with a spear at Laquimoum in India." (*Revue des Questions Historiques*, 1873; *S. Pierre, sa venuee et son martyre à Rome*, p. 14.)

† See P. Martin, "S. Pierre et S. Paul dans l'Eglise Nestorienne." *Revue des sciences ecclésiastiques*, 1875, pag. 153 *seq*. The following is from the Night Office, as translated by P. Martin: "Les chefs du bataillon des douze choisis par Jésus notre roi victorieux, Pierre et Paul, étant fortifiés par la vertu de l'Esprit Saint, sont entrés dans l'opulente Rome, en portant l'étandard de la

most conclusively proved by this agreement of the Eastern Churches and sects.*

§ 4.—Testimonies from the Third Century.

23. We come now to the witnesses of the third century: who, we shall see, speak in the same way of S. Peter's going to Rome and his episcopate there as a matter most certain and thoroughly well-known. Just as in the present day we call the Roman Pontiffs successors of Peter, so S. ANATOLIUS OF ALEXANDRIA (A.D. 276) designates them briefly as the *Successors of Peter and Paul* (inasmuch as both Apostles founded the Roman Church). Speaking in the *Paschal Canon*, n. 10, of the Asiatic Churches, he says:

> "They did not yield acquiescence to the authority of certain persons, to wit, the successors of Peter and Paul, who instructed all the Churches, in which they sowed the spiritual seeds of the Gospel, that the solemnity of the Lord's Resurrection could be celebrated on the Lord's day only. Hence also a certain contention arose among the successors of these, Victor, that is, who was at that time Bishop of the city of Rome, and Polycrates, who seemed to bear the primacy amongst the bishops of Asia, a contention which was, with great propriety, brought to a peaceful issue by Irenæus, a bishop (præsule) of a part of Gaul. . . ."

From this we see that it was recognised as a thoroughly ascertained fact that the Roman Pontiffs, who urged their authority in the Paschal question, were the successors of Peter and Paul.

S. CYPRIAN (A.D. 248) clearly bears witness to the universally received opinion concerning the episcopate of S. Peter at Rome, in these words:

> "Cornelius was made bishop by very many of our colleagues then present in the city of Rome . . . when the place of Fabian—that is, when the place of Peter and the rank of the sacerdotal chair—was vacant."†

---

croix. Dans la plus parfaite concorde ils ont semé la vie sur cette terre, qui n'avait jamais donné de fruits de gloire au Dieu de toutes choses. Ils y ont extirpé la doctrine des démons, renversé les idoles de Jupiter et d'Apollon, de Simon le prêtre impur. (*l. c.* p. 408.) Pierre évangélisa Rome, Paul les Juifs et les Gentils, mais tous deux ont terminé leur vie en combattant pour la vérité. Pierre a obtenu par la mort de la croix, la gloire qui ne passe point, et Paul a été frappé par l'épée, avant de recevoir la couronne de la victoire." (*Ib.* p. 411.)

* Later on we show how the entire *Petrine fact*, with the express mention of the Roman Episcopate, is witnessed to in the Liturgy of the Greek Church.

† Epist. 51, *ad Antonianum de Cornelio*.

And in another place he writes:

> "After all this, too, having got a pseudo-bishop set up for themselves by heretics, they dare to make sail, and to take letters from schismatics and profane persons to the Chair of Peter, and to the principal Church, whence the unity of the priesthood took its rise."*

What can be plainer and more express than this testimony?

24. It is important here to show also what S. FIRMILIAN (A.D. 257), Bishop of Cæsarea in Cappadocia, writes to his friend S. Cyprian, in a tone of bitterness and offence towards the Pope, S. Stephen. After saying that there is a diversity in some of the traditions observed at Rome and Jerusalem, and yet that there has not been on that account any breach of peace and unity, he continues:

> "This (breach) Stephen has now dared to make, breaking the peace with you, which his predecessors ever maintained with you in mutual affection and respect . . . besides defaming also Peter and Paul, as though they had handed this down. . . . And here, in this matter, I am justly indignant at this so open and manifest folly in Stephen, that he who so boasts of the place of his episcopate, and contends that he holds the succession of Peter, upon whom the foundations of the Church were laid, introduces many other *rocks*, and sets up the new buildings of many Churches, in that, by his authority, he maintains that there is baptism among them. . . . The Apostle acknowledges that the Jews, though blind through ignorance and bound down through their most grievous crime, have yet *a zeal for God* (*Rom.* x. 2), but Stephen, who proclaims that he occupies by succession the Chair of Peter, is roused by no zeal against heretics."†

In these words Firmilian, carried away by passion, unjustly attacks S. Stephen for his letter to S. Cyprian: whereupon we make the following remarks: The letter of S. Stephen has not, indeed, come down to us; but it is evident that he must have written to S. Cyprian with great authority, deciding as Pope, and as he who *holds the succession of Peter upon whom the foundations of the Church were laid*, what from ancient tradition was the course to be taken with regard to converted heretics. And thus we see that S. Stephen asserted, as a fact beyond dispute, S. Peter's Roman Episcopate and his own succession, no less emphatically and solemnly than did S. Leo two centuries later in his well-known Sermons. Firmilian could not but recognise that herein lay the foundation of Stephen's authority; yet how displeasing to him were the Pontiff's words is evident enough from the bitter way in which he repeats them. Were he able to deny or call in question the Roman Episcopate of Peter and Stephen's succession

---

* Epist. 55, *ad Cornelium*.   † Ep. 75.

therefrom, this certainly would have been the readiest and most efficacious means of breaking the force of that authority; and, from the bitter vehemence with which he asperses S. Stephen, it is only reasonable to suppose that, had he been able, he would have made use even of that means. But this he does not do: he neither denies, nor calls in question, S. Peter's Roman Episcopate and Stephen's succession. And hence it is clear that here was a fact universally held as certain. The cutting expressions of Firmilian prove only how deeply wounded he felt at the words used by Stephen in setting forth his authority as S. Peter's successor in the Roman See.

25. Let us now come to the beginning of the third century. TERTULLIAN (A.D. 195) frequently in his writings refers and bears witness to the fact of which we treat. Thus, when in opposition to the profane novelties of heretics he sets forth the primitive apostolic doctrine, and the legitimate succession preserved in the Churches founded by the Apostles, he says of the Church of Rome:

"But if thou art near to Italy, thou hast Rome, whence we also have an authority near at hand. That Church, how happy! into which the Apostles poured out all their doctrine with their blood, where Peter had a like passion with the Lord: where Paul is crowned with an end like the Baptist's." *

Again, in other places:

"Peter and Paul left to the Romans the Gospel sealed also with their blood." †

"We read the lives of the Cæsars. Nero first stained with blood the Eastern Faith at Rome. Then Peter is girded by another, when he is fastened to the cross." ‡

"There is no difference whether anyone is washed in a pond, river, or fountain, lake or tub, nor is their any distinction between those whom John bathed in the Jordan and Peter in the Tiber." §

On this last passage Sanguinetti remarks (p. 67):

"We should here carefully note this comparison between the baptism of John in the Jordan and the baptism of Peter in the Tiber; for when something perfectly well-known to everybody is compared with something else on the ground of their equality, this latter is supposed to be equally well-known. Now what is better known than that John baptised people in the Jordan? Whence it follows that Tertullian supposed it equally notorious that Peter baptised the faithful at Rome."

ORIGEN (A.D. 216), so celebrated for his great erudition, and who himself came to Rome under Zephyrinus, gives similar

---

* *De Præscript.* 36. † *Contra Marcion.* l. iv. c. v.
‡ *Scorpiac. cap. ult.* § *De Baptismo*, c. iv.

testimony concerning S. Peter in his third volume of *Commentaries on Genesis*, as Eusebius tells us:

"Peter is held to have preached through Pontus, Galatia, Bithynia, Cappadocia, and Asia, to the Jews that were scattered abroad, who, also finally being in Rome, was crucified with his head downward, having requested himself to suffer in this way." *

26. We should here note that the fact in question receives confirmation from all those Fathers and early writers who make mention of the conflict at Rome between S. Peter and Simon Magus; for, without now going into the truth of what they record as to the doings of Simon, his flight in the air and his death, we can say at any rate that they take for granted, and testify to Peter's abode in Rome as a well-known fact. Such authors are Arnobius, who wrote towards the close of the third century,† Epiphanius,‡ Eusebius,§ Philastrius Brixiensis,|| Sulpitius Severus,¶ Maximus Taurinensis,** and others.††

The following citation is from the Author of the PHILOSOPHUMENA, a man greatly opposed to the legitimate Roman Pontiffs:

"Simon, then, having again entered upon his course of attack, came to Rome, where he contended against the Apostles. It was Peter who

---

* iii. 1. See vi. 14. † *Advers. gent.* l. ii.
‡ *Hær.* xxi. 5. § *H. E.* ii. 12, 13.
|| *Hær.* xxix. ap. Galland. tom. vii. p. 485. ¶ *Hist. Sacr.* ii. 28.
** *Hom. v. in Natal. SS. Petri et Pauli.*

†† That Simon Magus was at Rome and perverted many, is recorded also by Justin, Irenæus, and Tertullian.

In giving the testimonies of the third century to the fact of S. Peter's Roman Episcopate, we should not pass over the *Clementines*, which bear witness thereto in most direct and express terms, and consequently reflect the common belief and persuasion of that age (*Ep. Clem. ad Jacob*, pp. 611-12; Galland. ii.), and also to the conflict of St. Peter with Simon Magus: "Against me, who am a solid rock and foundation of the Church, thou (Simon Magus) hast resisted as mine adversary." (*Hom.* 17, n. 19, p. 758, *ib.*) "The *Clementines* as well as the *Recognitions*," writes Dr. Waterworth (*The Fathers on S. Peter and his Successors*, 1881, pp. 9-11), "are now universally acknowledged not to be by S. Clement of Rome, but it is also pretty generally admitted that as a whole they date from about A.D. 230; and it is on this account, and also for the completeness of this essay, that they are quoted. The first extract is from the much debated letter of Clement to James. Besides Rufinus's translation of that piece (A.D. 410), Gallandius's edition gives us the Greek." In a later part of this work we have given the passage referred to in full from the Epistle to James, as well as other extracts from the *Clementines*. We have here mentioned the latest date assigned to the *Clementines* by authors. But now it is more commonly held by the learned that they were written in the second century. This Dr. Lightfoot considers certain, and that, perhaps, they were composed in quite the earlier years of the second century.

principally resisted him, because, by his evil arts, he was deceiving very many."*

27. We now produce the celebrated testimony of the presbyter Caius (a.d. 214) to the Tombs of the Apostles at Rome. After showing that the records of history prove the martyrdom under Nero of SS. Peter and Paul at Rome, Eusebius goes on to say: †

"And the titles of Peter and Paul, which have continued to this day, in the cemeteries there, lend their evidence to this account.‡ And nothing less is recorded by an ecclesiastical man, named Caius, who lived when Zephyrinus was Bishop of the Romans. He, in a writing addressed to Proclus, a leader of the Phrygian sect, uses these words concerning the places where the sacred bodies (tabernacles) of the aforesaid Apostles are deposited: 'But I have it in my power to show the trophies of the Apostles. For if you will go to the Vatican, or to the Ostian Way, you will find the trophies of those who founded this Church.'"

Caius, it is evident, is speaking of their very bodies buried at Rome; and to express this Eusebius uses the word σκηνώματα (earthly *tabernacles*) adverting probably to 2 *Pet.* i. 14, where the Apostle employs the same word in the same sense: "Being assured that the putting off of this my tabernacle (σκηνώματος) is at hand according as our Lord Jesus Christ also hath signified to me." The tombs of SS. Peter and Paul, Caius calls *trophies:* and in this sense Eusebius understood the word, as is clearly implied from the context, so that it is simply absurd for Lipsius and the anonymous Waldensis to maintain that thereby is meant memorials of these Apostles of any sort, and not their sepulchres.

We must pass over other testimonies of the third century; but it is evident from those we have already given, that in that century no less than in the fourth, there was a common consent as to the Roman Episcopate of S. Peter, and that the writers of that age, when they have occasion to refer to it, speak in such a way as shows that it was considered a thoroughly well ascertained and notorious fact.

* L. vi. c. 20. † *H. E.* ii. 25.

‡ Such is the sense, according to the rendering of Valesius. In the Greek the words of Eusebius are: καὶ πιστοῦται γε τὴν ἱστορίαν ἡ Πέτρου καὶ Παύλου εἰς δεῦρο κρατήσασα ἐπὶ τῶν αὐτόθι κοιμητηρίων πρόσρησις, which might be translated thus: "And what history thus records is confirmed by the salutation (veneration) of Peter and Paul, which has prevailed till the present day in the cemeteries that are there." Thus implying that the historical account receives confirmation from the traditional practice of the faithful who, when visiting the cemeteries, were wont to venerate the sacred bodies of the Apostles buried there.

§ 5.—Testimonies from the Second Century.

28. We come now to the *Second Century*, and here we have, in the first place, S. Irenæus (A.D. 178), that renowned Father of the Church, who composed his great work, *Contra Hæreses*, in the last decades of this century. The testimony of S. Irenæus is of quite exceptional value, for he was Bishop of one of the Gallic Churches, was wont to have recourse to the Roman See in matters of grave importance, and was thoroughly well acquainted with other Churches, from Asia in the East to Gaul in the West; for, whilst still under the discipline of Polycarp, he had lived amongst the Churches of Asia; and S. Polycarp had in his earlier days seen the Apostles themselves, particularly S. John. S. Irenæus thus writes:

"So also Polycarp, who not only had been instructed by Apostles, and had been brought up with many who had seen the Lord, but had also been appointed by the Apostles Bishop of Smyrna, in Asia. Him also we saw in our early youth,—for he endured long, and in extreme old age departed this life, yielding his testimony (martyred) most gloriously and nobly." *

It would therefore be most unreasonable and absurd to suppose that Irenæus was ignorant of the doings of SS. Peter and Paul, the sphere of their apostolic labours, and how and where they ended their life; or that he should rashly set forth as facts matters which had their foundation only in rumour and legend. Let us see then what he himself writes. There is that remarkable and well-known passage in which this holy Father shows

---

* *Contra Hær.* iii. 4. Not only had Irenæus seen Polycarp, but had enjoyed with him familiar intercourse as his disciple. This appears from what Eusebius relates (*H. E.* v. 20) from the Epistle of Irenæus *De Monarchia* to Florinus. Addressing Florinus, Irenæus thus writes: "These doctrines were never delivered to thee by presbyters before us, who were themselves the immediate disciples of the Apostles. For I saw thee when I was yet a boy in Lower Asia with Polycarp, moving in great splendour at Court, and endeavouring by all means to gain his esteem. I remember the events of those times much better than those of more recent occurrence. For what we learn to know in our youth so grows up with our minds as to become one with them; and so I can tell even the very place where the blessed Polycarp was wont to sit and discourse; and also his comings in, his walks, the complexion of his life, and the form of his body, and his conversations with the people, and his familiar intercourse with John, as he was used to tell of it, as also his intimacy with those that had seen the Lord. How also he used to relate their discourses, and what things he had heard from them concerning the Lord. Also concerning His miracles, His doctrines: all these were told by Polycarp, in consistency with the Holy Scriptures, as he had received them from the eye-witnesses of the doctrine of salvation. These things, by the mercy of God, and the opportunity then afforded me, I attentively heard, noting them down, not on paper, but in my heart: and these same facts I am always in the habit, by the grace of God, of recalling faithfully to mind."

how we are to ascertain surely what is true and apostolic doctrine. We may know it, he says, by its coming from the authentic teaching (magisterium) of the pastors of the Church holding together in unity. He then proceeds:

"But as it would be very long, in a volume like this, to give the successions of all the Churches,—by pointing out that tradition which it (the Roman Church) has from the Apostles, and the faith announced to men that is come down even to us by the successions of bishops, of that Church which is the greatest, most ancient, and known to all, the Church founded and constituted at Rome by the two most glorious Apostles Peter and Paul, we confound all those who in any way, whether by things pleasing to themselves, or by vain-glory, or blindness and evil sentiment, assemble otherwise than they ought. For to this Church, on account of a more powerful principality, it is necessary that every Church, that is, the faithful on every side, meet together (convenire, have recourse, resort to, concur, agree with); in which (same Church) always, by those who are on every side, has been preserved that tradition which is from the Apostles. The blessed Apostles, therefore, having founded and built up that Church, committed the sacred office (or ministry, λειτουργίαν) of the episcopacy to Linus. Of this Linus Paul makes mention in his Epistles to Timothy. To him succeeded Anacletus, and after him, in the third place from the Apostles, to Clement is allotted the episcopacy; who, as he had both seen and conferred with the blessed Apostle, still also had the preaching of the Apostles ringing (in his ears), and their tradition before his eyes. And not he alone, but many were still left, who had been taught by the Apostles. Wherefore under this Clement, a no slight dissension having taken place amongst the brethren at Corinth, the Church in Rome sent a most powerful epistle to the Corinthians, confirming them together into peace, and renewing their faith, and announcing the tradition which it had recently received from the Apostles. . . . But to this Clement succeeded Evaristus, and to Evaristus, Alexander. Then—thus the sixth from the Apostles—Sixtus was appointed; and after him Telesphorus, who underwent a glorious martyrdom; next Hyginus, then Pius; after whom was Anicetus. To Anicetus succeeded Soter, and to him, now in the twelfth place, Eleutherus holds the inheritance of the episcopate from the Apostles. By this same order, and by this same succession, both that tradition, which is in the Church from the Apostles, and the preaching of the truth, have come down to us. And this is the fullest proof that it is the one and the same life-giving faith which has been preserved in the Church, and handed down in truth from the Apostles even till now." *

In these words S. Irenæus declares so emphatically and decidedly that the Church at Rome was founded by SS. Peter and Paul, that to add any comment would only weaken their force. This Father is, as we have already remarked, a witness of such exceptional worth, that his authority of itself alone may be considered as proving beyond all question the fact we treat of. But one

* *Contra Hæreses*, iii. 3.

thing we would add: that the testimony of Irenæus is *polemical*, its immediate purpose being to explain the principle by which he sought to refute the heretics; and that in giving it he is led to make only casual mention that the Roman Church was founded by the Apostles Peter and Paul; and this as a simple matter of fact thoroughly well-known to all Christendom.*

29. There is also another passage (l. iii. 1) wherein S. Irenæus testifies to S. Peter at Rome, which we think well to adduce here, because it has been singularly abused by opponents. The Saint in this Third Book refutes the Gnostics, who made pretension to a secret knowledge such as not even the Apostles possessed. In order to confute these heretics on the twofold ground of the *oral preaching* of the Apostles preserved in the Churches, and of the *Sacred Scriptures*, he commences his argument, by first laying down the principle that the Apostles had a perfect knowledge of the truth, and that they delivered this to the Churches both by oral preaching, and afterwards by the Scriptures:

"By means of no others, says he, have we known the economy of our salvation, than those through whom the Gospel came to us, which then indeed they proclaimed orally, and afterwards, by the will of God, delivered to us in writing. For after the Lord rose from the dead, and they were endued with the power of the Holy Ghost coming upon them from on high, they were complete in all things, and had perfect knowledge; they (the Apostles) went forth to the ends of the earth preaching the good tidings of God's benefits to us, and announcing heavenly peace to men; each and all of them alike having the Gospel of God."

Then, going more into detail, he explains how all and each had

---

* At the time that S. Polycarp, the master of Irenæus, was enjoying the familiar intercourse of S. John, and of others who had seen the Lord, it is evident, from S. John's Gospel, that the circumstances of the Apostle Peter's death were perfectly well-known. The Evangelist (*S. John*, xxi. 18, 19) records the words which Jesus Christ, after His resurrection, spoke to Peter: "Amen, amen, I say to thee: when thou wast younger, thou didst gird thyself, and didst walk where thou wouldst. But when thou shalt be old, thou shalt stretch forth thy hands, and another shall gird thee, and lead thee whither thou wouldst not." He then adds: "And this He said, signifying by what death he should glorify God." Here both our Lord and the Evangelist distinctly allude to S. Peter's crucifixion (see Beelen here). It hence follows that S. John, who wrote his Gospel after S. Peter's death, was well acquainted with all its circumstances, and amongst these, in what city the Prince of the Apostles suffered martyrdom. Again, these circumstances were, of course, well-known to Polycarp, the disciple of S. John; so that we need not go far to find the source whence S. Irenæus was able to derive his knowledge of what he writes with so much care concerning S. Peter, his Roman Episcopate, and martyrdom;—facts which, we hold, were, also from other sources, thoroughly well-known. We here repeat again that the testimony of Irenæus is of such strength that the argument, based upon it alone, is of itself sufficient peremptorily to decide the fact in question.

equally the Gospel of God, and that it was announced both by oral preaching and by the Scriptures. But we will give the Greek text as it is in Eusebius (*H. E.* v. 8):

Ὁ μὲν δὴ Ματθαῖος ἐν τοῖς Ἑβραίοις τῇ ἰδίᾳ αὐτῶν διαλέκτῳ καὶ γραφὴν ἐξήνεγκεν Εὐαγγελίον, τοῦ Πέτρου καὶ τοῦ Παύλου ἐν Ῥώμῃ εὐαγγελιζομένων καὶ θεμελιούντων τὴν ἐκκλησίαν. Μετὰ δὲ τὴν τούτων ἔξοδον Μάρκος ὁ μαθητὴς καὶ ἑρμηνευτὴς Πέτρου καὶ αὐτὸς, τὰ ὑπὸ Πέτρου κηρυσσόμενα ἐγγράφως ἡμῖν παραδέδωκε, καὶ Λουκᾶς δὲ ὁ ἀκόλουθος Παύλου τὸ ὑπ' ἐκείνου κηρυσσόμενον εὐαγγέλιον ἐν βιβλίῳ κατέθετο. Ἔπειτα Ἰωάννης κ. τ. λ.

"Matthew, indeed, produced his Gospel written among the Hebrews in their own dialect, whilst Peter and Paul proclaimed the Gospel and founded the Church at Rome. After the departure of these, Mark, the disciple and interpreter of Peter, also translated to us in writing what had been preached by Peter. And Luke, the companion of Paul, committed to writing the Gospel preached by him (Paul). Afterwards John, the disciple of our Lord, the same that lay upon His bosom, also published the Gospel, whilst he was yet at Ephesus in Asia."

30. From these words of Irenæus this much at least is certain, that *the Apostles Peter and Paul proclaimed the Gospel at Rome, and founded there the Church;* and it would have been enough for our purpose to have noted the holy Father's express testimony here given to this fact. But the anonymous Waldensis [*] groundlessly assails this very testimony. From Irenæus, he says, we gather that *S. Matthew wrote his Gospel among the Hebrews whilst Peter and Paul were preaching at Rome, and there founding the Church.* But at the time S. Matthew wrote his Gospel among the Hebrews (which, according to antiquity, cannot be assigned to a later date than A.D. 39), Peter and Paul were certainly not in Rome; consequently, he says, we must either confess that Irenæus has been interpolated, or admit that he attributes the preaching and the founding the Church at Rome to those Apostles, because they did this by means of others, namely, their disciples. Now we know, he continues, that there were present *strangers from Rome* when S. Peter was preaching at Jerusalem on the day of Pentecost, and it was these disciples of Peter who founded the Roman Church; but that Peter himself was at Rome cannot be proved at all from Irenæus.

31. We reply, in the first place, that Irenæus, both here and in the other passage we before cited, most clearly assigns the preaching and founding the Church in Rome to the two Apostles in person, and not to others. The forced interpretation of the

[*] *Impossibiliù, &c.,* pp. 98, 99.

anonymous writer is utterly absurd: and even supposing that S. Irenæus had here made a mistake in chronology, that would be no good reason for rejecting his testimony on this point. But we hold that the holy Father made no such mistake at all, and we cannot agree with certain more modern authors who refer the writing of S. Matthew's Gospel to the last years of SS. Peter and Paul, and make use of this passage of Irenæus to support their opinion. We maintain that his words here are in full accord with the commonly received opinion as to S. Matthew's Gospel, if only they are rightly understood. Thus, by the genitive absolute, Πέτρου καὶ Παύλου ἐν ʿΡώμῃ εὐαγγελιζομένων, is not meant relation of time, as though Matthew is said to have written his Gospel at the same time that SS. Peter and Paul were preaching and founding the Church in Rome; but in the one and other clauses Irenæus intended to express the difference, both as to the place and the manner in which S. Matthew, on the one hand, and S. Peter and S. Paul on the other, delivered the Gospel. Hence, the passage may be fitly rendered as follows: "Matthew, indeed (δή), amongst the Hebrews, published in their own tongue the writing also of his Gospel (and not only preached it orally), whereas Peter and Paul in Rome preached the Gospel by word of mouth and founded the Church there." The word ἔξοδος in the next sentence is not to be understood of the death of SS. Peter and Paul, but of their celebrated *going forth*, as also of that of the other Apostles, to teach all nations. Having said that Matthew wrote his Gospel whilst still living *amongst the Hebrews*,—that is, before the *going forth*,—with this previous writing of Matthew S. Irenæus in the next clause contrasts the later writing of Mark and Luke, by saying that they wrote after *the going forth* of the Apostles to all nations. S. Irenæus had before made mention of this same going forth of the Apostles: "They went forth" (ἐξῆλθον), he writes, "to the ends of the earth proclaiming the Gospel of those good things which are from God to us."* He indicates particularly the going forth of the Apostles Peter and Paul (τούτων), because he had just before specially made mention of them, and because Mark and Luke were their companions. It is in this way Cardinal Franzelin lucidly explains the passage.†

---

* In allusion to *Romans*, x. 18. εἰς πᾶσαν τὴν γῆν ἐξῆλθεν ὁ φθόγγος αὐτῶν, καὶ εἰς τὰ πέρατα τῆς οἰκουμένης τὰ ῥήματα αὐτῶν. See also v. 15.

† *Introd. in S. Scripturam;* there is another explanation given by Patrizzi. *De Evang.* l. i. c. 2.

It should be, however, remarked that the value of the testimony of S. Irenæus, so far as he affirms expressly that SS. Peter and Paul preached in Rome and founded the Church there, is wholly independent of these interpretations.

32. Besides S. Irenæus we have, in the second century, a most convincing witness in S. DIONYSIUS, BISHOP OF CORINTH (A.D. 170), and of much note in the Church. S. Jerome says of him:

"Dionysius, Bishop of the Corinthians, was a man of so great eloquence and industry, as not only to instruct the people of his own city and province, but also, by his Epistles, the bishops of other cities and provinces."*

The testimony of S. Dionysius concerning the preaching of SS. Peter and Paul in Rome and their martyrdom in that city has been preserved by Eusebius, who, after recording the death of the Apostles, and giving in confirmation the words of Caius before quoted, adds:

"And that both suffered martyrdom at the same time, Dionysius, Bishop of Corinth, bears this testimony: 'So also you, by an admonition so valuable, have again united the planting of the Romans and Corinthians, which was by the hands of Peter and Paul. For both came to our Corinth, and, planting us, both alike (ὁμοίως) taught; and alike going to Italy also, and having taught together (ὁμοίως καὶ εἰς τὴν Ἰταλίαν ὁμόσε διδάξαντες), they gave their testimony (by martyrdom) at (or about) the same time.'" †

These words of S. Dionysius show clearly the unanimous consent of the Churches to the fact in question, as to something thoroughly well-known and certain.

33. But here again opponents have raised a number of frivolous objections, in order to make out that what Dionysius says is but after all a fictitious legend. It is evident, from the Acts of the Apostles and Paul's Epistles, they say, that Peter was never at Corinth, and that he did not found the Church there; and, consequently, what Dionysius says about the two Apostles setting off together from Corinth to Italy must be only a pious legend. We reply that, because there is no mention, in the Acts of the Apostles nor in S. Paul's Epistles to the Corinthians, of S. Peter's having been at Corinth, it does not at all follow that he never visited that city and did not preach there. That, on the contrary, he really did so, we learn expressly from Dionysius, who, though not an immediate witness, is one quite reliable and trustworthy. We are not bound, moreover, to understand the words of Dionysius as implying that the Apostles set out for Italy *at the*

---

* *Catalog. de Script. illustr.* † *H. E.* ii. 25.

same time (the meaning of ὁμοίως being *equally* or *similarly*), or that they *set out together* for Italy ; for, as Stenglein explains the passage, ὁμοίως ὅμοσε may be understood to mean that the Apostles were alike in both of them teaching in Italy (in Rome), or simply in their being together in Italy.

34. There is nothing, however, to hinder us from taking the words of Dionysius to mean, that the Apostles Peter and Paul did at one time both preach together at Corinth, and thence together departed,—Peter, straight for Italy,—Paul not, indeed, straight or at once, but with the already formed intention of visiting Italy later on. Such a time for the meeting of the two Apostles at Corinth (according to Franzelin) is aptly supposed to be the year 53. According to this reckoning, the Council of Jerusalem would be in 47: after which, since the Jews at Rome were being disturbed, and even expelled from the city by Claudius, S. Peter for some years was abroad in various regions. S. Paul at that time was making an apostolic journey. From the autumn of 48 until the spring of 50 he remained at Corinth, and seems, in the February of that year, to have gone to Jerusalem, where he was at the time of Easter. He soon went on his third apostolic journey. From Ephesus, in the winter of 51 (or at the beginning of 52), he wrote his First Epistle to the Corinthians. Towards the close of 52 he went once more to Corinth, and at the beginning of 53 wrote thence his Epistle to the Romans. Peter, as we have said, was not then at Rome, but came that same year (53) to Corinth, now about to return to Rome, where, shortly before, Aquila and Priscilla had arrived, and whom Paul salutes as thither returned, in his Epistle to the Romans. (From this it is inferred that the edict of expulsion of the Jews did not remain in force more than four years.) It was then, when Peter was come to Corinth, and after S. Paul had written his Epistle to the Romans, that the two Apostles taught together in that city, but for a short time only. S. Paul, in that Epistle, expressly mentions his purpose of going to Jerusalem with the alms he had collected, and his intention of afterwards visiting Rome. From this we may very well suppose that both Apostles left Corinth together, or much about the same time, as Dionysius seems to imply.

35. Whatever view we may prefer to take, it is very evident how silly and indecently bold are those praters, who pretend that through this letter of Dionysius, and some chance words therein contained, it has come to pass that the fabulous legend (as they

term it) of S. Peter's going to Rome, and of his Roman Episcopate, was bruited abroad and believed. For obviously Dionysius is speaking of the martyrdom of SS. Peter and Paul at Rome as of something quite notorious and absolutely certain, and is led only incidentally to mention certain circumstances of their lives, for the simple purpose of reminding the Roman faithful of what was already known to them—viz., the intimate relation which existed between the two Churches of Rome and Corinth. What then can be more absurd than to assert that, from what Dionysius here says, the idea of S. Peter's Roman journey and episcopate was first broached, and that then by degrees it came to be regarded as a certain and universally admitted fact? Dionysius, we repeat, is not relating anything new or strange, but is bringing to remembrance what was old and well-known: had he been inventing what was new, or relating what was doubtful and legendary, neither the Romans nor anyone else would have received it.

36. Another witness is CLEMENT OF ALEXANDRIA (A.D. 190), born in the middle of the second century, and a contemporary of Dionysius of Corinth. Eusebius, speaking of his work, called *Hypotyposes*, says amongst other things:

> "Again, in the same work, Clement also gives the tradition respecting the order of the Gospels, as derived from the oldest presbyters, as follows: He says that those which contain the genealogies were written first, but that the Gospel of Mark was occasioned in the following manner: 'When Peter had proclaimed the word publicly at Rome, and declared the Gospel under the influence of the Holy Spirit: as there was a great number present, they requested Mark, as one who had long followed him, and remembered well what he had said, to reduce what had been preached by the Apostle to writing, &c.'" *

Here Clement incidentally speaks of the preaching of S. Peter at Rome as of something notorious, and says that what he records respecting the origin of S. Mark's Gospel, he had received from the most ancient presbyters: "This account given by Clement," Eusebius adds, "is corroborated also by Papias, Bishop of Hierapolis." † Early tradition, moreover, records generally that S. Mark was sent by S. Peter to Alexandria from Rome.

37. S. IGNATIUS, Martyr (A.D. 107), in his Epistle to the Roman Church, testifies implicitly to the dwelling of Peter and Paul in Rome, as well-known to all:

* *H. E.* vi. 14.   † *H. E.* ii. 15.

32   TESTIMONIES FROM THE SECOND CENTURY: S. IGNATIUS.

"I am writing, says he, to the Churches, and am enjoining on all, that gladly I shall die for God, if only you do not hinder me. I beseech you not to show to me any unseasonable kindness. Suffer me to be the food of wild beasts, whereby I may attain to God. I am the wheat of God, and shall be ground by the teeth of the wild beasts, that I may be found the pure bread of Christ. . . . Pray to Christ for me that thus I may be found a victim. Not as Peter and Paul do I command you (οὐχ ὡς Πέτρος καὶ Παῦλος διατάσσομαι ὑμῖν). They were Apostles, I one condemned; they are free, I till now a slave. But if I suffer, I shall be the freedman of Jesus, and in Him I shall rise again free." (iv.)

In order to anticipate foolish and captious objections, it is well to note that, in this passage, S. Ignatius is occupied with what exclusively concerns the faithful of Rome: he entreats them, we see, not to hinder his martyrdom, which was to take place in that city. When, then, he adds: "Not as Peter and Paul do I command you," he is certainly alluding to the peculiar relation of these Apostles to the Romans, which tradition has in all ages everywhere affirmed with regard to the preaching of SS. Peter and Paul in Rome. Even sincere Protestants have acknowledged this, as Cave, Jacobson, and Baratier, who writes:

"Why does Ignatius name together Peter and Paul, unless both of them had been at Rome? Why Peter, if he had no connection with the Romans? For if he never went to Rome, since he did not write to the Romans, he had nought more in common with them, nor commanded them any more than James, or Jude, or John. It is evident here that Ignatius knew of S. Peter's journey to Rome." *

We can only put it down to prejudice, that Bressel, a modern Protestant author, expresses a contrary opinion:

"Ignatius, he writes, mentions Peter and Paul because they were pre-eminent amongst all the disciples and followers of Christ for preaching the Gospel and teaching; and being thus distinguished by a certain authority they took the lead of the rest. Hence, I marvel at Jacobson saying that Ignatius makes mention of them, because they alone of the holy Apostles had been with the Roman Christians." †

But this is arbitrarily to set aside the obvious and natural meaning of the passage, and, for the sake of preconceived opinions, to thrust on the reader a forced interpretation. For Ignatius is not here alluding to any far-fetched authority derived from some more excellent preaching of the Apostles Peter and Paul, but has in

---

* *Disquisitio chronologica de successione antiquissima Episcoporum Romanorum*, p. 3. Ultrajecti, 1740. See later on, in Part III. of this work, what the learned Dr. Lightfoot says on this point.

† *PP. Apost.* Lipsiæ, 1863.

view the submission to be paid to those who had in the Roman Church due authority to rule and command (διατάσσομαι). We may also infer, from the magnificent Inscription with which S. Ignatius has distinguished his Epistle to the Romans, that he recognised the primacy of the Roman Church. And what other reason could he have for this but the succession of its Bishop in the See of Peter? He styles the Church of Rome that Church "which has the first See (or presides ἥτις καὶ προκάθηται) in the place of the country of the Romans:" and this must evidently be understood of a presidency in the entire Christian Church, unless the sense of the whole context is unmeaningly distorted. He speaks again of that Church as "having the first place (or presiding) in charity" (προκαθημένη τῆς ἀγάπης); presiding over the confederation of charity.*

§ 6.—TESTIMONIES FROM THE FIRST CENTURY—S. CLEMENT'S EPISTLE TO THE CORINTHIANS.

38. A celebrated testimony, in fine, to the fact we are treating of, is contained in the Epistle of S. CLEMENT (A.D. 97) to the Corinthians, which he wrote on the occasion of dissensions amongst them. This Epistle has been ever held as most precious in the Church.† Therein he speaks in such wise of the martyrdom of the holy Apostles Peter and Paul, that though he does not expressly indicate Rome as the place of martyrdom, yet from the context it may be clearly gathered that it was there they suffered. In the fourth chapter S. Clement describes the evils of

* "Instead of προκάθηται, S. Ignatius, in all his other epistles, uniformly uses the word is. 'To the Church which is (τῇ οὔσῃ) in Ephesus.' 'To the Church which is (τὴν οὖσαν) in Magnesia;' and so of the rest. Προκαθημένη : this participle is used in two other places by S. Ignatius, and in each place it implies superior authority and dignity: προκαθημένου τοῦ ἐπισκόπου εἰς τόπον Θεοῦ. Ad Magnes. 6. 'Ἐνώθητε τῷ ἐπισκόπῳ καὶ τοῖς προκαθημένοις. Ib." Waterworth, pp. 180, 181.

† We are of opinion that the Epistle was written not immediately after the persecution of Nero, but towards the close of the first century after the persecution of Domitian; for it is manifest that Clement, who succeeded to Linus and Cletus, was then ruling the Church. Sufficiently clear traces occur in the Epistle itself of its having been written not at once after the death of the Apostles. For Clement speaks of presbyters cast out of the ministry *who for a long time had been approved of by all* (c. 44); he speaks of the Epistle of S. Paul to them, as written in *the beginning of the Gospel*, and calls the Church of Corinth the *most firm and ancient Church of the Corinthians*. All this shows that now some time had elapsed since the days of the Apostles. We shall return to this point later on.

hatred, envy, and jealousy, and after giving examples from the Old Testament, says:

"But to cease from ancient examples, let us come to those who have been combatants in times very near(τοὺς ἔγγιστα γενομένους ἀθλητάς); let us take the noble instances in our own age. Through jealousy and envy the greatest and most just pillars have been persecuted, and come even to their death. Let us set before our eyes also the good Apostles (τοὺς ἀγαθοὺς ἀποστόλους). Peter, through unjust jealousy, endured not one, nor two, but many painful toils, and thus martyred, went to the due place of glory. Through jealousy Paul, after having seven times borne chains, and having been banished, and stoned, received the reward of patience, and having been a herald both to the East and the West, attained to an illustrious glory of faith, having taught the whole world righteousness; and having come to the boundary of the West, and being martyred under the rulers (μαρτυρήσας ἐπὶ τῶν ἡγουμένων), departed from the world, and went to the holy place, having been the greatest example of patience. To these men who lived holily as citizens (as members of society, ὁσίως πολιτευσαμένοις) was added a great number of the elect, who, having suffered many cruelties and torments through jealousy, were, amongst ourselves (ἐν ἡμῖν), a most excellent example. Through jealousy, women suffered persecution, the Danaïdes and the Dircæ, and having undergone frightful and abominable tortures, arrived at the stable goal of faith, and, weak in body, received a noble reward." *

39. In these words Clement bears clear testimony to the martyrdom of the Apostles Peter and Paul as having taken place in Rome. For though he does not explicitly name Rome in speaking of what was so notorious, yet that this is the meaning of his words, follows from such a sense being the only one in accordance with constant tradition, and may be gathered also from the context. He joins Peter together with Paul (and his martyrdom at Rome no one denies), in the same way as Ignatius, Dionysius of Corinth, Caius, Clement of Alexandria, and Irenæus join together these two Apostles. Again, Clement speaks of the persecution under Nero, in which, according to Tacitus, a vast multitude of Christians were put to death in Rome: and to this he evidently refers in the words: "To these men who lived a life of holiness (viz., SS. Peter and Paul) was added a great multitude of the elect." He then continues: "Those elect, who were added to the Apostles, by the many cruelties and torments they suffered through jealousy, stood forth as a most noble example *amongst ourselves* (ἐν ἡμῖν)."

Here the words can have no other meaning, without wholly distorting their plain sense, than that these examples happened before the eyes of the Romans, and that Clement is proposing for the edification of the Corinthians what had taken place at Rome.

* S. Clem. Ep. 1. *ad Cor.* v. vi.

We would observe also that the word πολιτευσαμένοις may be taken in the sense of ruling, regulating, legislating, and especially of forming and establishing a society by laws and institutions. With regard to what is said of S. Paul, scil. μαρτυρήσας ἐπὶ τῶν ἡγουμενῶν, some think that hereby are meant the *Prefects*, Nymphidius Sabinus and Tigellinus, who, in the year 67, during Nero's residence in Achaia, were the Pretorian Prefects in Rome, or else Helius and Polycletus, who had the office of general governors during Nero's absence in Greece.* Others are of opinion that the word is to be understood of the Roman chief magistrates in general, or more precisely of the emperor and his council chosen from the chief men of the city.

We may note, moreover, that a sort of harmony is easily perceivable between what Clement says in his Epistle by the mention of Peter and Paul, and the words we quoted above from the Epistle of Dionysius to the Romans. For there Dionysius, alluding to this Epistle of Clement, which from time immemorial, he says, was used to be read in the Churches, speaks at the same time of SS. Peter and Paul, and gratefully records the special relation these Apostles had both with the Romans and the Corinthians. As to the *Danaülœ* and *Dircœ* mentioned by Clement, authors have laboured much to explain what these may mean, and have even proposed other readings. The explanation given by Funk,† who follows the opinion of the learned Aberle, appears very satisfactory and much to the point. He says that during Nero's persecution, many Christian women were made to act the part of the Dircæ, represented in mythology as tied to the horns of a mad bull, and thus put to a most barbarous death ; or, before they were slaughtered, in order to furnish a cruel popular spectacle, they had to represent the pains of Tartarus by being tormented as the Danaïdæ. And women, says Funk, martyred in this fashion, were known both to the Christians and Pagans under the special names of Danaïdæ and Dircæ. That Christians were put by Nero to such like tortures, and were made a sport of in their death, we also learn from Tacitus.‡

40. Opponents have striven to destroy the force of S. Clement's testimony; but from the text itself their objections are easily shown to be of no account. Thus, some pretend that it is not certain that Clement speaks here of the martyrdom of S.

---

* *Dio Cass.* l. xiii. 12, 19.   † *Patres Apostolici*, 1878, pp. 67-69.
‡ *Annal.* xv. 44.

Peter at all, because, forsooth, the word μαρτυρήσας may mean nothing more than bearing testimony to the faith: but the whole context shows that Clement is contemplating such as had suffered the martyrdom of a violent death: this is clear from his own words in the very beginning. "They suffered persecution and combated even unto death (ἕως θανάτου ἤθλησαν)."

Darby, in his attempt to make void Clement's testimony, produces so much of it only as relates in particular to SS. Peter and Paul. He then stops short, omitting all notice of the words immediately following, which clearly show that the holy Father has all along been speaking of those who had suffered martyrdom in the city of Rome. Having thus arranged his materials, he goes on to say that it is very evident that Clement (he supposes him to have written his Epistle at Rome in the year 69) was fairly acquainted with the history of Paul, of which he gives more full details, but knew nothing about Peter, except his martyrdom, but when or where this took place he was quite ignorant. And hence, says he, it may be with reason inferred that Peter was never at Rome, and could not have suffered death there.*

What we have said already is a sufficient refutation of the above. Why Clement says more about S. Paul than about S. Peter is easily explained. The observation of Funk here is much to the point:

"Clement discourses more copiously of S. Paul than of S. Peter, not because the former had 'laboured more abundantly' than the other Apostles (1 Cor. xv. 10), but because he had spent some considerable time amongst the Corinthians. For since S. Paul had founded the Church of Corinth, and had suffered martyrdom at Rome, Clement could hope that, by putting before them at some length the example of one who might be called the Apostle both of the Romans and Corinthians, he should make a great impression on the minds of the latter. In the same Epistle, too (ch. xlvii.), he appeals specially to the authority of S. Paul."

41. Now, if all the testimonies we have brought forward are well considered, together with the constant and universal belief and tradition of S. Peter's episcopate and martyrdom at Rome, no one at least who is fair and impartial can, we think, fail to see that the fact we treat of is demonstrated by most solid historical proofs such as it is simply folly to contradict.

---

* S. Peter never at Rome, 2d ed., ch. 6 (4).

§ 7.—SCRIPTURAL EXEGESIS—BABYLON—ROMAN MONUMENTS.

We must observe, in conclusion, that this persuasion of the Fathers, and of antiquity, receives additional light from various *exegetical comments* on certain texts of Holy Scripture; and also much confirmation from the *numerous monuments of the city of Rome*, which, in accordance with most ancient tradition, are associated with the memory of the holy Apostles Peter and Paul And first, with regard to Scriptural exegesis, Chrysostom, Theodoret, and Theophylact, when commenting on those texts wherein S. Paul speaks, in his Epistle to the Romans, of their faith, and of his desire to see them (*Rom.* i. 1-11; 2 *Tim.* iv. 21), remark that S. Peter preached the Gospel at Rome before S. Paul, and, in interpreting S. Paul's words, keep this fact in view. Thus, for instance, Theodoret—on the words (*Rom.* i. 11), "For I long to see you, that I may impart unto you some spiritual grace, to confirm you"—writes: "Because the great Peter first ministered to them the doctrine of the Gospel, Paul must needs add: *to confirm you.*"

All sound commentators know well the received patristic interpretation of that famous passage (1 *Pet.* vi. 13): "The Church that is in Babylon, elected together with you, saluteth you: and so doth my son Mark." For the Fathers and ancient writers affirm generally that the word Babylon is used metaphorically to mean Rome, and that S. Peter wrote that Epistle at Rome.

Eusebius, after saying that S. Mark the Evangelist, disciple of S. Peter, wrote his Gospel at Rome, and that it was approved of by S. Peter, continues:

"This account is given by Clement (of Alexandria) in the sixth book of his *Institutions*, and his testimony is corroborated also by that of Papias, Bishop of Hierapolis. Peter, moreover, makes mention of Mark in the first Epistle, which they (*i.e.*, Clement and Papias) say he wrote at Rome, and that he himself indicates this by figuratively calling Rome Babylon in these words: The Church that is in Babylon," &c.*

Here we see Eusebius speaks of this interpretation as one already set forth. And, according to the obvious sense of the words, he is to be understood as attributing what he here relates to Papias and Clement of Alexandria: for the context shows that the word

---

* Τοῦ δὲ Μάρκου μνημονεύειν τὸν Πέτρον τῇ προτέρᾳ ἐπιστολῇ ἥν καὶ συντάξαι φασὶν ἐπ' αὐτῆς 'Ρώμης, σημαίνειν τε τοῦτ' αὐτὸν τὴν πόλιν τροπικώτερον Βαβυλῶνα προσειπόντα. (*H. E.* ii. 15.)

φάσι refers to these two writers, whom he had just before named. S. Jerome likewise records this interpretation in terms which show that he himself approves of it.

"And Papias," he says, "Bishop of Hierapolis, makes mention of this Mark, as also does Peter in his first Epistle, where he signifies Rome figuratively under the name of Babylon."*

Here S. Jerome evidently alludes to the text of Eusebius. S. Chrysostom (or Severus in the Catena edited by Cramer) writes:

"He therefore metaphorically calls Rome Babylon, and the elect Church the Church of Christ constituted in the same city."†

So too Œcumenius and Bede—in fact, the old interpreters are generally agreed on this point. We shall consider the objections of opponents later on.‡

Let us here say one word respecting *the monuments of the city of Rome*. As everybody well knows, the memory of the holy Apostles Peter and Paul has from the earliest times till now been inseparably associated with many places, buildings, and other material objects in Rome: amongst these, the dungeons in which they were imprisoned, the chains of S. Peter, the place of his martyrdom, and the tombs of the Apostles, have ever been the most celebrated. Moreover, not a few churches in the very earliest times were built in some of the more famous places, where either the Apostles themselves, or their disciples, such as S. Pudens and his family, Aquila and Priscilla, and others were used to reside. And here, too, we may mention the Feast of the Chair of S. Peter, as well as the material Chair itself of the Apostle, which is preserved in Rome until the present day.§

---

* *De viris illustr. ad* MARCUM.
† *Catena in Epp. Catholicas*, edit. a J. A. Cramer. Oxonii, 1840, pp. 82.
‡ The figurative use of Babylon for Rome by S. Peter derives the greatest confirmation from the fact that the name of Babylon, that mythical city of iniquity and ungodliness so often spoken of by the Prophets (*Is.* xxi. 9; *Jer.* ll. 8), was most certainly applied to Rome in the apostolic times. All interpreters hold that in the Apocalypse S. John means by Babylon (xiv. 8, xvi. 19, xvii. 5, xviii. 2, *seqq.*), primarily and directly, heathen Rome. This is a point that has hardly been insisted upon strongly enough in the controversy. Protestants are very ready to interpret S. John's Apocalyptic Babylon of Christian Rome; surely it must be but prejudice which prevents them from seeing in S. Peter's Babylon any Rome at all.

§ The testimonies from Archæology are treated in full detail later on.

§ 8.—The Length of Duration of S. Peter's Roman Episcopate.

42. The main question of S. Peter's Roman Episcopate is, as we have already observed, entirely independent of the controversy about the length of its duration. We think good, however, to discuss this matter also; for it is a question well worth considering on its own merits, and what we shall have to say regarding it will serve very much to confirm all that we have hitherto advanced. With respect to this point, the great majority of Catholics maintain, as everyone knows, *that S. Peter held the Roman See for twenty-five years:* this, all Protestants, so far as we are aware, deny, those even who admit that S. Peter went to Rome and was Bishop of that See. Cave writes as follows:

"But even though we readily allow, with antiquity, that Peter was at Rome, and laid the foundations of the Church there, still, in opposition to more recent defenders of Papal Supremacy, we persistently deny that he held that See for twenty-five years." *

These Protestant authors are of course bound to adopt such chronological reckonings as will better help them to assail with effect the Catholic doctrine of the primacy of the Roman Pontiff. But various Catholic writers, too, dissent from the common opinion on this point; somewhat influenced, it would seem, by the idea, that if rid of the difficulties as to the duration of the episcopate, they will be able more easily and efficaciously to defend and maintain *the fact* itself. These too, consequently, deny that Peter went to Rome before the reign of Nero. Cave gives the names of several Catholic writers in favour of this negative opinion, to whom, amongst the more modern, may be added Herbst, in his *Dissertation,* to which we have already referred. No doubt the opinion which holds that S. Peter went once only to Rome, viz., under Nero, is the one more simple and free from difficulties; but the agreement of early writers to S. Peter's first going to Rome under Claudius, and to his twenty-five years' episcopate, is such as to solidly demonstrate the historical fact, and to make it impossible, on careful examination, for us to support any other view, save at the expense of reason and authority. Again, many incidents which we gather from the Acts of the Apostles fall in with this opinion; whilst all the difficulties in its way are capable of solution.

* *Hist. litt. Script. Eccles.* sæc. i. art. Petrus.

40 THE TWENTY-FIVE YEARS, IN MOST ANCIENT CATALOGUES,

We shall first, then, adduce those testimonies which *expressly* declare that S. Peter held the See of Rome for twenty-five years ; and secondly, the testimonies which determine *the time of S. Peter's arrival at Rome*, and *the year of his martyrdom*, and we shall see that all these, too, tend to the same conclusion, that S. Peter was Bishop of Rome for twenty-five years.

43. There exists, then, from the middle of the fourth century, a continuous tradition of Fathers and ecclesiastical writers—certified and attested by an unbroken series of records—as to the twenty-five years of S. Peter's Roman Episcopate. To this, in the first place, belong *the records of the Roman succession*. In the most ancient Catalogue—called the LIBERIAN CATALOGUE, because it ends with Pope Liberius (A.D. 352-366), the first part of which was composed, it seems, in the year 254—we read the following :

"In the reign of Tiberius Cæsar, our Lord Jesus Christ suffered under the two Gemini, Consuls, VIII. Kal. Aprilis.* And after His Ascension the most blessed Peter undertook the episcopate. From which time (was) by succession arranged, who bishop, and how many years he presided, or under whose reign (dispositum, quis episcopus, et quot annis præfuit, vel quo imperante). Peter twenty-five years, one month, nine days. He was in the times of Tiberius Cæsar, and Caius, and Tiberius Claudius, and Nero, from the Consulate of Vinicius and Longinus, to (that) of Nero and Vetus. He suffered, moreover, with Paul, the third day before the Kalends of July under the aforesaid Consuls, during the reign of Nero. Linus twelve years, four months, sixteen days. He was in the times of Nero, from the Consulate of Saturninus and Scipio, until Capito and Rufus."

It is true, the author of this Catalogue made a mistake in placing the martyrdom of S. Peter in the first year of Nero. This comes, however, as Bucher has already remarked,† from his reckoning the Roman Episcopate of Peter at once from our Lord's Ascension ; and since he knew as an ascertained fact that the episcopate lasted twenty-five years, he thus assigns S. Peter's death to the first year of Nero. Even from this very mistake one can judge how thoroughly universal was the persuasion that S. Peter was twenty-five years Bishop of Rome.

44. The same is attested by another Catalogue of the Roman Pontiffs, called the FELICIAN, or that of Felix IV., because it ends

---

* It is clear from ancient testimonies that Christ, Our Lord, suffered under the two Gemini, Consuls, viz., C. Fusius Geminus and S. Rubellius Geminus, in the year 29 of the vulgar era. We are of opinion that the day of our Lord's death was really XV. Kal. April, or March 16th. (See Patrizzi, *In Evang.* vol. ii. p. 536.)

† Bucher first published this Catalogue. Hence it is called also the Bucherian Catalogue.

with this Pope, compiled about the year 530, where, likewise, twenty-five years are ascribed to Peter's episcopate; and the other Popes are found in the order we now have them.

Besides the Catalogues, the Fathers, from the fourth century, unite in giving the same testimony. We have already seen what Eusebius has in his Chronicle, and from him S. Jerome, who repeats the same in the passage which we have already quoted from his *History of Illustrious Men*. And as we then observed, even supposing the twenty-five years in the Chronicle to be an addition of S. Jerome's, still Eusebius, by allotting S. Peter's coming to Rome to the first years of Claudius, and his death to the fourteenth year of Nero, gives us in this way the space of twenty-five years claimed for the episcopate. In like manner Prosper, Cassiodorus, Isidorus Hispalensis, and Bede expressly state in their Chronicles or historical works that S. Peter held the Roman See for twenty-five years. Amongst the Fathers and writers of the first centuries not one teaches the contrary.* That they should not positively affirm the fact is, indeed, nothing wonderful, since the scope of those Fathers and ecclesiastical writers who, in the first three centuries, recorded the succession of the Bishops of Rome, as Irenæus, Tertullian, the author of the Hymn against the Marcionites, and Caius, was dogmatic and polemical, and not historical. And since their whole object was to prove what was true and genuine apostolic doctrine from due order of legitimate succession, it would have been beside their purpose to set forth how many years each of the Pontiffs successively held the Roman See.

45. There is no doubt, however, that the records or catalogues drawn up in the fourth and sixth centuries were themselves derived from more ancient documents. For we may with good reason be sure, from what we know was the case later on, that in the early centuries the succession and order of the bishops, with the documents relating thereto, were kept amongst the archives of the Churches, and with all the more care on account of the importance attached to these matters. But, besides this consideration, we have clear positive traces of such earlier documents. First, there is extant a fragment of some anonymous chronographer, who wrote in the third century, at the time of Alexander Severus. Amongst other things, in a short list preserved from some lost catalogue of his, we read: "The names of the Bishops of

---

* We shall treat of Lactantius later on.

Rome. Who, How many years he presided." Now this shows that in the third century the order of the Roman succession had been drawn up, stating the number of years that the several Pontiffs held the See; and we may note how closely the wording of this fragment resembles that of the Liberian Catalogue described above. There are, moreover, in the Catalogue itself, according to the opinion of the learned, several traces showing that it was compiled from other previous catalogues; and many suppose that the Liberian Catalogue, up to the Pontificate of Pontianus, was taken from this lost earlier catalogue, composed, they think, by Hippolytus, a man of very great erudition, who wrote in the third century.*

Again, it is certain that before this, in the second century, *Hegesippus* (A.D. 178) had drawn up at Rome the succession of the Roman Pontiffs so far as Anicetus; for amongst the extracts from Hegesippus preserved by Eusebius is the following:

Γενόμενος δὲ ἐν Ῥώμῃ διαδοχὴν ἐποιησάμην μέχρις Ἀνικήτου κ. τ. λ.
"When I was in Rome, I drew up the succession as far as Anicetus, whose deacon was Eleutherus. After Anicetus Soter succeeded (διαδέχεται), and after him Eleutherus. In every succession, however, and in every city, it is just as the law proclaims, and the prophets and the Lord." †

We do not know whether Hegesippus recorded the number of years each successive Pontiff held the See, but it is probable that he did so, since he drew up the order of their succession, not with any dogmatic or polemical object, but as a historian. In any case, as he came to Rome expressly for that purpose, he would be sure to compile his catalogue from certain and reliable tradition, and from the most ancient records of the Roman Church. We thus see that the catalogues we have of the Roman Pontiffs from the fourth century, which state that S. Peter was Bishop of Rome for twenty-five years, may be traced back even to apostolic times.

46. This opinion of S. Peter's twenty-five years' episcopate

---

* Lipsius, *Chronologie der römischen Bischöfe*. Sanguinetti, pp. 184.

† *H. E.* iv. 22. It is very strange that Valesius, and also others, as the English Christophorson, translate the passage: "I made my stay with Anicetus," since immediately afterwards, in the same context, the words διαδέχεται and διαδοχή are used by Hegesippus, and are rendered even by these writers in their natural sense of *succession*. It is besides very evident, from Hegesippus' express words recorded by Eusebius (iv. 11), that he came to Rome under Anicetus, and remained in Rome until the Pontificate of Eleutherus. So also S. Jerome, writing of Hegesippus (*De viris illust.*), says: "He states that he came to Rome under Anicetus, and remained there until Eleutherus, formerly the deacon of Anicetus, was bishop of that city."

S. PETER'S COMING TO ROME UNDER CLAUDIUS. 43

receives full confirmation from all that early writers record with regard to *the date of S. Peter's first arrival in Rome, and of his death.* For they tell us that S. Peter came to Rome in the second year of Claudius (A.D. 42), and that he suffered martyrdom A.D. 67.

And first, as to the year of his arrival, we have already seen what Eusebius has in his Chronicle, and how what is found in the paraphrase of S. Jerome is in perfect accord with the Armenian version. We have seen, too, that also in his Ecclesiastical History Eusebius assigns S. Peter's going to Rome to the time of Claudius; and that he must thereby mean the first years of Claudius is evident, since he mentions the meeting together at Rome of Philo and Peter.* We have given also the words of S. Jerome. Orosius says in his History (vii. 6):

"Claudius reigned fourth in succession from Augustus. ... At the beginning of his reign, Peter, the Apostle of our Lord Jesus Christ, came to Rome; by faithful word he both taught the saving faith to all believers, and approved it by most potent virtues (*potentissimis virtutibus*). And from that time there began to be Christians in Rome."

Now, Orosius lived for a long time with S. Augustine in Africa, visited S. Jerome in Palestine, and then, on his return to Spain, about the year 416, wrote his History. With these historical writers agree also S. Isidore (Hispalensis), and the Venerable Bede. S. Leo too, in his first sermon on the Apostles SS. Peter and Paul, clearly indicates that Peter came to Rome under Claudius in those words wherewith he apostrophises S. Peter:

"Nor dost thou fear Rome, the mistress of the world, thou who in the house of Caiaphas wert greatly afraid of the maid-servant of the priest. Was then either power in Claudius, or cruelty in Nero, less than the judgment of Peter, or the rage of the Jews?"

47. There are other proofs, too, which are in full agreement with the above. And first we may mention the ancient tradition, that the dispersion of the Apostles and their going forth through-

---

* "Immediately" (*i.e.*, after the arrival of Simon Magus at Rome, just before recorded), "under the reign of Claudius, by the benign and gracious providence of God, Peter, that powerful and great Apostle who, on account of his virtue, took the lead of all the rest, was conducted to Rome against this pest of mankind." (*H. E.* ii. 14.) "Philo also, it is said, in the reign of Claudius, had at Rome familiar converse with Peter, who was then preaching there. Nor is this improbable. ..." (*Ibid.* 17.) Hence we see how entirely what Eusebius has in his Chronicle accords with what he relates in his History, and of what little importance is the objection raised as to whether the words in the former are those of S. Jerome or Eusebius. The only difference is that, in the Chronicle, as is fitting, the date of time is given more exactly.

out the world took place twelve years after the Ascension of our Lord. Eusebius (*H. E.* v. 18) thus records it on the authority of the martyr Apollonius (second century):

"Apollonius mentions also, as handed down by tradition (ὡς ἐκ παραδόσεως), that our Saviour commanded His Apostles not to depart from Jerusalem for twelve years."

Clement of Alexandria (*Strom.* vi. 6) gives somewhat more circumstantially, from the *Itinerary* of Peter, the same tradition, and in a way that shows he himself believed it:

"Peter says that the Lord said to the Apostles: After twelve years go forth into the world, that none may say: We have not heard."

Now, as our Lord's Ascension was in the year 29, we see that at the year 42 precisely the twelve years would have elapsed. The learned, moreover, conclude from the Acts of the Apostles, that the conversion of Cornelius and Peter's vision, whereby was revealed to him the admission of the Gentiles to Christianity as now near at hand, happened about the year 40.

48. We should remark, too, that no early writer records Peter's journey to Rome as taking place before his imprisonment at the time of Easter by Herod Agrippa; but this journey is supposed to have been made after his imprisonment. Now, it is certain that S. Peter's imprisonment happened in the year 42; for we learn from Josephus that some months after Claudius came to the throne (Jan. 21st, 41), Herod Agrippa, who was made by the Emperor king of all Palestine, arrived in Judæa: this then could not have been before Easter, 41. Hence we are, so to say, forced to the year 42, as the earliest date for S. Peter's setting out for Rome after his liberation from prison; and to this event S. Luke's words (*Acts*, xii. 17) may be referred καὶ ἐξελθὼν ἐπορεύθη εἰς ἕτερον τόπον. "And after his going forth he set out on a journey to another place." The death of Herod, which S. Luke goes on to relate, occurred, as we gather from Josephus, in the autumn of 43. But it would not do to place S. Peter's journey to Rome this year, because, according to the account of ancient writers (notably Eusebius in his Chronicle, and S. Jerome), S. Mark, before Herod's death in the third year of Claudius, had already been sent by S. Peter from Rome to Alexandria, after having written his Gospel in Rome. In the Chronicle of Eusebius, at the third year of Claudius, we read:

"Mark the Evangelist, interpreter of Peter, preaches Christ to Egypt and Alexandria."

Whilst S. Jerome, in his Catalogue of Writers, under the name of Mark, says:

"Taking with him, therefore, the Gospel which he had composed, he set out for Egypt."

S. Epiphanius (A.D. 385) records the same in words which imply that at once, after writing his Gospel, S. Mark was sent to Egypt:

"To Mark, who at Rome was the companion of Peter, was given the charge of writing a Gospel, and when he had written it, he was sent by Peter to Egypt." καὶ γράψας ἀποστέλλεται.*

Consequently, if S. Peter only went to Rome after Easter in 43, his journey, founding the Roman Church, and S. Mark's writing his Gospel, and then his mission and going to Egypt must have all taken place in the few months between the Easter and autumn of that year. But this interval is manifestly too short for these events, so that we are again necessarily brought back to the year 42 for S. Peter's journey and arrival at Rome.

49. The next point is the *year of S. Peter's martyrdom*. We have the testimony of very ancient records that the Apostles SS. Peter and Paul suffered martyrdom on the same day, viz., the 29th of June. Thus, for example, we read in the Liberian Catalogue of Peter: "Passus est cum Paulo die III. Kal. Julias." The martyrdom cannot be assigned to the year 68, since it is agreed on all hands that the Apostles were put to death under Nero, and Nero was slain before the middle of June that year. Some, indeed, as Prosper, speak of S. Peter's death as occurring in the thirteenth year of Nero, whilst others, as Eusebius, Jerome, and Cassiodorus, assign it to the fourteenth year, or to the last year of Nero's reign, as Bede, and again S. Jerome. But these several statements all coincide very well with the year 67. Since that year was the thirteenth year of Nero, reckoning from his accession, October 13th, 54; but was the fourteeth year, if, as was usual, the years of reign are counted from the preceding 1st day of January: it was also the last year, because there was not another year complete between the martyrdom of S. Peter and the death of Nero, and also because the year 68 was already the first year of Galba. We thus see, how entirely conclusive are the reasons for fixing the year 67 as the date of S. Peter's martyrdom; and that between his arrival at Rome in 42 and his death in 67 are reckoned the twenty-five years and some months of his episcopate.

* *Hær.* li. 6.

50. This year (67), moreover, perfectly agrees with what is narrated by the author of the book *De excidio Hierosolymarum*,* which is found among the works of S. Ambrose. It is evident from that account that Nero was in Achaia when he ordered the death of the Apostles; for he gave the command to put them to death, "when he learned that the strong hand of the Romans was brought low by the Jewish war." The defeat here referred to took place November 8th, A.D. 66;† and Nero received the news in Achaia, whither he had retired in the middle of that same year, and where he remained until the autumn of 67. Consequently Peter did not suffer martyrdom before the autumn of 66, nor after Nero's death in the middle of June, 68. And, since it is certain that the day of his martyrdom was June 29th, it necessarily must have happened in the year 67, for no other year but this remains to which it can be assigned.

§ 9.—Answers to Objections against the Twenty-Five Years.

51. And now let us deal with the objections raised against the twenty-five years of S. Peter's episcopate by those authors who, for the rest, admit that he came to Rome.

In the first place certain passages of early writers are cited, which are supposed to show that S. Peter went to Rome only under the reign of Nero. Thus, some words of *Origen*, from the third Book of his Exposition of Genesis, recorded by Eusebius:‡

"Peter appears to have preached through Pontus, Galatia, Bithynia, Cappadocia, and Asia, to the Jews that were scattered abroad; who also, finally (ἐπὶ τέλει), coming to Rome, was crucified with his head downward."

We would here first remark in general that when S. Peter is said to have been Bishop of Rome for twenty-five years, we should bear in mind, as Baronius has already observed, § that—

"This does not mean that S. Peter remained always in Rome, for, since he was charged with the care of the whole flock, he did not neglect such duties and measures as were needed for the supervision and welfare of all. Hence we see Peter at these times hardly ever remains in the same place, but whenever it may appear necessary, is traversing provinces, visiting churches, and continually exercising his pastoral solicitude." ||

---

* L. iii. c. 1. † See Joseph. *De Bello Jud.* l. iii. c. 10.
‡ *H. E.* iii. 1. § *Annal.* ad ann. 39.
|| Compare with this the words of Rufinus in his Preface to the *Recognitions*, quoted later on in Part III., ch. xvi., Appendix.

We reply, therefore, that there is nothing in these words of Origen to imply any denial on his part of another previous arrival of S. Peter at Rome, or incompatible with his belief that this in fact took place. Origen is here narrating in a brief and summary way the doings of the Apostles, their preaching, and in what countries. Then, in speaking of Peter and Paul, he mentions also the place of their death. When he says ὃς καὶ ἐπὶ τέλει ἐν 'Ρώμῃ γενόμενος, he is not asserting that this was the first time S. Peter came to Rome, but that, *after what he had just recorded, the Apostle at length, whilst he was in Rome, suffered martyrdom.* Hence no positive statement, at any rate, one way or the other, on the point can be gathered from Origen.*

52. Still easier is it to reconcile with the common opinion the words of *S. Peter of Alexandria* (A.D. 306):

"Peter, the first of the Apostles, after being often seized, thrown into prison, and treated ignominiously, was at last crucified in Rome." †

The object of the Saint was to admonish the faithful that whilst martyrdom should be endured with joy, still it is not to be voluntarily sought after; and he supports his teaching by examples. Hence, in the words quoted, the time of S. Peter's first coming to Rome is not the point in question—what is said is, that after enduring many other sufferings for Christ, he was *at last* put to death in Rome.

53. There is, no doubt, more difficulty in the passage of *Lactantius* on which Herbst most insists for the support of his opinion that S. Peter came to Rome under Nero, and there remained, at the most, a year and some months, until his martyrdom. The following are the words of Lactantius:

"In the last times of Tiberius Cæsar, as we read written, our Lord Jesus Christ was crucified by the Jews on the tenth day before the Kalends of April, in the Consulate of the two Gemini; after rising again on the third day, He gathered together His disciples, whom the fear of His apprehension had put to flight; and abiding with them for forty days, He opened their hearts, and interpreted to them the Scriptures, which until that time had been obscure and intricate; and ordained and instituted them for the preaching of His dogma and doctrine, setting in order the solemn discipline of the New Testa-

---

* We should here bear in mind who it is who preserves to us, as reliable testimony, these words of Origen. It is Eusebius, who had already stated most expressly (bk. ii. c. 14), as a great and glorious event, that S. Peter went to Rome under Claudius; and this he records again in his Chronicle. Eusebius, at any rate, saw no contradiction in the two statements, viz., that S. Peter went to Rome, first under Claudius, and again under Nero; nay, he is the voucher for both of them.

† *Serm. de Pœnit. can.* ix., ap. Harduin, Coll. Conc. i. col. 230.

ment. And having fulfilled this office, a moving cloud (*procella nubis*) encompassed Him about, and withdrawing Him from human eyes, bore Him up to heaven. And then the disciples, who at that time were eleven, having taken into Judas the traitor's place Matthias and Paul, were dispersed through all the earth to preach the Gospel, as their Lord and Master had commanded them; and during twenty-five years, until the beginning of the reign of Nero, laid the foundations of the Church through all the provinces and cities. And whilst Nero was now reigning, Peter came to Rome, and after performing certain miracles, which he wrought by virtue of God Himself, Who gave him power, he converted many to justice, and set up for God a temple faithful and stable. 'But when this was made known to Nero, and he perceived that, not only at Rome, but everywhere, day by day great numbers were leaving the worship of idols, and, condemning their old ways, were passing over to the new religion, execrable and wicked tyrant that he was, he bounded forth for the destruction of the heavenly temple, and for the overthrow of justice; and, the first of all to persecute the servants of God, he crucified Peter and slew Paul.'" *

54. This, then, is that famous passage of Lactantius, of which Protestants make so much parade, as bringing utterly to nought the assertion of Catholics, that S. Peter was Bishop of Rome for twenty-five years, and which has made some Catholics also hold it to be untenable. Well, but allowing for the sake of argument that these words of Lactantius are irreconcilable with the common Catholic opinion of the twenty-five years' episcopate, should we not rather say that it is Lactantius who has fallen into chronological error in his narrative, since the proofs we have brought forward are more than a match for Lactantius, whether we regard the weight and number of our testimonies on the one hand, or the authority of Lactantius on the other. For on our side the witnesses preponderate both in number and weight, such as Eusebius, Jerome, Orosius, Prosper, and the most ancient Catalogues; whilst Lactantius is alone by himself, and can hardly be regarded, whether relatively or absolutely, as an author of pre-eminent authority on the present question. For we should bear in mind that he was a layman, and one who, as is well known, fell into more than one error in matters relating to the Church; whilst his *rôle* is not that so much of an accurate historian as of an eloquent apologist; whereas the witnesses on our side are ecclesiastics of the greatest weight, specially versed in Church matters and in ecclesiastical history.

55. With regard to the inaccuracies in this very passage, Sanguinetti well remarks:

---

* *De Mort. Persecut.* l. i. c. 2.

"We ask in the first place, Is Lactantius exact in statement and chronology when he says: 'The disciples, who at that time were eleven, having taken into Judas the traitor's place Matthias and Paul, were dispersed,' &c., whereas we know that the election of the one and the other of these Apostles was entirely different, both as to the manner and time? We ask secondly, If what is said of Peter relates to his first arrival at Rome, is the statement accurate that during twenty-five years, until the beginning of Nero's reign, the Apostles laid the foundations of the Church through all the provinces and cities? For if so, it would thence follow that for the space of twenty-five years from all the provinces and cities an exception must be made for the capital of the world, the city of Rome alone. Is this probable, or even in the least credible? But, it will be said, the words of Lactantius do not exclude the supposition of some one else having gone to Rome and founded the Church there before S. Peter. To this we reply, that besides such a hypothesis being in the teeth of what is shown evidently to be the truth of fact, confirmed by the consent of universal tradition, it would follow therefrom that the words of Lactantius, 'And whilst Nero was now reigning,' &c., do not refer to the first founding of the Roman Church; and so the main argument of our adversaries falls to the ground: for if these words do not exclude some one else's arrival at Rome to found the Church there, prior to S. Peter, why are they to exclude a former arrival of Peter himself? We ask thirdly, whether it is consistent with accurate narrative to record abruptly the martyrdom of S. Paul, when not even a word is found in the immediate context about that Apostle, and Lactantius is altogether silent as to his coming to Rome at all?"*

56. To those, then, who believe the opinion of Lactantius to have been that S. Peter did not go to Rome until the reign of Nero, we reply, that even so, his opinion is of less value than the positive testimonies of so many grave authors.

But the words of Lactantius, we contend, are not necessarily opposed to their statements. This is evident, if we keep in view the whole context of the passage and the scope of the writer. The main object Lactantius had in his work was to treat of the deaths of persecutors, and not to compose an exact and chronological history of the lives and doings of the Apostles. With this end, before entering upon the subject of the first persecution of the Christians by Nero and his death, the author makes some prefatory remarks, wherein succinctly he gives a passing sketch of what had happened in the Church before Nero's time, viz., the preaching of the Gospel by the Apostles. This, as is evident on reflection, is but an introduction wherein the eloquent writer is hastening rapidly on to the end he has in view. But there is not a word here to say that S. Peter never went to Rome during the twenty-five years before the reign of Nero; what happened in

* Sanguinetti, p. iii. ch. 4.

50   OBJECTIONS TO S. PETER'S ROMAN EPISCOPATE.

that interval is touched on by Lactantius only in a most general way.

He makes mention of S. Peter's coming to Rome under Nero after the manner of an orator, who by a skilful and happy transition would set the reader at once on the scene of action, in the place and city where happened all those events which he is about to narrate in full detail. From the simple mention, then, by Lactantius of S. Peter's arrival at Rome under Nero, we cannot conclude that this author's narration prevents us from holding that S. Peter made other visits to Rome before Nero's time.

§ 10.—Answer to Objections against the Roman Episcopate of S. Peter.

57. In their endeavour to prove that S. Peter's going to Rome and episcopate there are unreliable legends, our Protestant and infidel opponents appeal to the silence of Holy Scripture on the matter; they, moreover, bring forward certain texts of Scripture which, they contend, positively contradict the alleged fact; and then they try to explain in various ways how the prevalent persuasion first originated. We must, then, to complete our subject, consider these several points of attack.

58. And first, with regard to the objections derived from Holy Scripture. To anticipate captious subterfuges and quibbles, we make the following remarks:—(1) When any historical fact has been proved by solid arguments of well-authenticated testimony, which is the proper source of history, its truth and certainty is noway overthrown because some points still remain obscure and less ascertained. (2) We must be careful, as we have before said, not to lose sight of the distinction between the *fact* itself and its *chronology*. All that is essential for establishing the fact is what Herbst maintains to have been the case, that S. Peter should have been at Rome, though but for a short time before his death, and there should have held the episcopate until the end of his life. And such a view as this of S. Peter's Roman Episcopate is free from nearly all the objections alleged from Scripture. We, however, shall also vindicate the position of his being Bishop of Rome for twenty-five years. (3) Our opponents must admit that the argument drawn from the silence of Scripture can be urged in reference to two books only of the New Testament with any show of difficulty—viz., the Acts of the Apostles and S. Paul's Epistle to the Romans,—since there would be no meaning in

urging, as an objection, silence in the rest of the Epistles, whether those of S. Paul or of another Apostle. Still, if one or other positive text is alleged from these, it shall receive due attention.

59. Having offered these prefatory remarks, let us now examine the line of argument of our opponents. This, then, is their contention: The scope of the writer of the Acts of the Apostles was to describe the propagation of Christianity from Jerusalem to Rome. His history ends with the two years' captivity of S. Paul in Rome, which happened, they say, at the beginning of Nero's persecution. S. Luke, however, does not make the slightest allusion to S. Peter; but he certainly would have mentioned him had that Apostle been in Rome. It is, moreover, inexplicable that S. Paul, whether in his Epistle to the Romans or in any of his Epistles written at Rome, should make no mention of Peter, friendly or any way, if Peter were Bishop of Rome.* Let us now reply to these objections.

60. First, then, with regard to the scope of the Acts of the Apostles. No doubt the immediate scope is historical; and it purports to narrate the first founding of the Church amongst the Jews, Samaritans, and Gentiles. But this immediate scope is but a means towards another and the principal end, which is to show the divine origin of Christianity and the Church. Hence it is clear we must not expect to find in the Acts an account of everything that happened, nor a complete chronological detail of what each of the Apostles did.

Now, in order to better understand the object and plan of that book, we should bear in mind that its author, S. Luke, was the companion of S. Paul, by whose counsel also he wrote his Gospel (in or after the year 48), especially *for the sake of the Gentiles.* The most prominent doctrine of S. Paul, on which he so often insists in his Epistles, is the vocation of the Gentiles to the Faith, —that, without observing the ceremonial law, they are as regards Christianity on a perfect equality with the Jews, so that the latter cannot lay claim to greater privileges in the Church than the former. This teaching, we know, was hateful not only to the Jews, but to the Judaising converts amongst Christians, who set themselves in opposition to S. Paul, and sought to destroy his influence, so that he was obliged sometimes with great vigour to uphold his authority. And since they had it in their power, by taking advantage of S. Paul's imprisonment, to prejudice the

* Lipsius, *Chronologie der Röm. Bischöfe,* 1869; Darby, *S. Peter never at Rome.*

faithful against the Apostle and his teaching, it was but natural to expect that his faithful companion and disciple, S. Luke, in writing his history whilst S. Paul was in chains, should undertake the defence of his beloved master and of his doctrine; and this we find, in fact, was the great object of S. Luke as we read his history. For the events that we see dwelt upon in the Acts with more special care and fulness of detail than others, are precisely those which make manifest the call of the Gentiles to the Faith, or have relation thereto, and such as show forth in clear light the wonderful and wholly divine vocation of S. Paul to the apostolate, or establish, not only the innocence and blamelessness, but also the glory and triumph of the imprisoned Apostle, and at the same time the obstinate impiety of the Jews, his accusers.

It being, then, S. Luke's object, as disciple and companion of S. Paul, as well as for the other reasons we have given, to record the doings of that Apostle in the conversion of the Gentiles, there is nothing strange or wonderful that he should not follow up the history and doings of S. Peter. We should remember, too, that the faithful of Rome, for whom in the first instance he wrote the Acts of the Apostles, would be already well enough acquainted with what S. Peter had been doing since his first arrival at Rome.

61. As we cannot justly argue from the silence of the Acts against the fact of S. Peter being Bishop of Rome, so neither can we do so from the silence of S. Paul's Epistles.

His Epistle to the Romans was written, we think, in Achaia, A.D. 53, when probably S. Peter was absent from Rome, since Claudius, in the ninth year of his reign, had expelled the Jews from the city, and S. Peter had not yet returned. But even supposing S. Peter was in Rome at the time when S. Paul wrote his Epistle to the Romans, there is nothing unaccountable in S. Paul's silence regarding him. For, we ask, was he *bound* to speak of S. Peter? But surely, they say, he ought to have addressed his Epistle to S. Peter, or to have at least saluted him. Not at all, we reply. S. Paul's Epistles to other churches are not addressed to their bishops, well known though these were to the Apostle, nor do we find their names amongst the salutations.*
The Epistles themselves would be carried to the bishops of the

---

* We do not find that S. Clement, in his Epistle to the Corinthians, makes any allusion to their bishop; nor is there anything to show that the Church of Corinth had in their Epistle to the Church of Rome made any direct mention of S. Clement, though certainly he was then at Rome.

several churches by trustworthy messengers, who conveyed, no doubt, at the same time to the bishop personally the Apostle's salutation, and whatever else he might wish specially to communicate to him. Thus the Epistle to the Romans was taken to Rome by Phœbe. (*Rom.* xvi. 1.) Phœbe, as we learn from S. Paul's own words, was a deaconess of the Church of Corinth, a woman of no mean authority in her own country, who was going to Rome on business; and what more natural or proper under the circumstances, than that such a woman should first have gone to see S. Peter, if he were then in Rome, have delivered to him S. Paul's Epistle, and have given him tidings of whatever was of interest to S. Peter to know about S. Paul; so that any salutation or mention of Peter in the Epistle would have been quite superfluous.*

62. Why S. Paul in the Epistles he wrote at Rome during his first and second imprisonment (to Philemon, the Colossians, the Ephesians, the Philippians, the Hebrews, first and second to Timothy), should make no mention of S. Peter, we cannot indeed exactly say; and it would be quite out of reason to expect us to do so. Our opponents, however, can, on the other hand, noway show that the Apostle *was bound* to speak in them of S. Peter; whilst there might be various good reasons for silence. Possibly S. Peter was from time to time absent from Rome: the messenger who had to convey the Epistles of S. Paul, and who could personally inform the faithful to whom he was sent more fully by word of mouth about Roman affairs, might have had special instructions to deliver to the bishop or to those presiding in the Church with regard to S. Peter, as being the Prince of the Apostles and supreme pastor; there might, too, have been reasons of prudence for avoiding the mention of Peter's name in these letters; or, in fine, it might have been judged somewhat out of place, and hardly consistent with his dignity and office to name S. Peter in common with the ordinary faithful and disciples of the Apostles who sent their salutations.

63. Our opponents allege also *certain positive statements* from the Epistles in favour of their contention that S. Peter was never at Rome; and amongst them those words (*Philip.* ii. 21), in which S. Paul complains that "all seek the things that are their own."

---

* That S. Peter was intimately conversant with all S. Paul's Epistles, and amongst them with his Epistle to the Romans, to which he makes particular allusion, that he had the greatest reverence, esteem, and special fraternal love for S. Paul, is shown by S. Peter's own words. (2 *Pet.* iii. 15, 16.)

The Apostle, they say, would not have spoken thus if Peter had been Bishop of Rome. But if we look at the context, there is here no difficulty at all. S. Paul is speaking of those who were immediately about him, ministering to him and helping him in the work of propagating the Christian religion. From amongst these, he says, he wishes to send to the Philippians Timothy; because he had no one else who was so solicitous for them: he then adds, with some fault-finding, which, however, should not be too much pressed, the words above quoted. But it is well to give the whole context:

"I hope, in the Lord Jesus, to send Timothy unto you shortly, that I also may be of good comfort, when I know the things concerning you. For I have no man so of the same mind, who, with sincere affection, is solicitous for you. For all seek the things that are their own: not the things that are Jesus Christ's. Now, know ye (γινώσκετε) the proof of him, that as a son with the father, so hath he served with me in the Gospel." (vv. 19-22.)

But what has all this to do with S. Peter? Was he to be reckoned amongst those whom S. Paul might have sent to Philippi?

64. Nor again can anything be got out of what is said (2 Tim. iv. 16):

"At my first answer no man stood with me, but all forsook me: may it not be laid to their charge." *

S. Peter was himself suffering in the same persecution: surely there is no question of him here. The question is of others, men of some influence, who might have been useful to S. Paul as witnesses before the tribunal, but who were deterred from doing anything in his behalf through fear.

65. There remains what the chief amongst the Jews at Rome, gathered together by S. Paul, say to him about the Christian religion:

"But we desire to hear of thee what thou thinkest: for as concerning this sect, we know that it is everywhere spoken against." (Acts, xxviii. 22.)

Now, say our opponents, if Peter had been at Rome, and had founded the Church there, the Christian religion would surely not have been so unknown to the principal Jews of the city as these words imply, in which they ask S. Paul to speak to them about it.

According to the showing of our opponents, then, this text

---

* See Sanguinetti, p. 137. Συμπαραγίγνομαι is a legal technical word, signifying, to take the part of another as a friend or advocate in court.

from the Acts would prove that before S. Paul went to Rome, Christianity was hardly known there at all.

To this we reply, in the first place, that the most complete refutation of such a conclusion is to be found in S. Paul's own Epistle to the Romans (i. 6-13), where it is evident that already, in the year 53, before he went to Rome, there was in that city a most flourishing Christian Church. That the Apostles, very soon after their dispersion, should preach the faith in Rome—nay, that one of the chief and foremost Apostles should do this in the world's metropolis*—is only what one would naturally, and *a priori*, expect; and that this was in fact done by S. Peter in the second year of Claudius is certain from the fullest evidence of tradition: whilst from S. Paul's Epistle, it is quite clear that faith in Christ had been already preached to the Jews in Rome, and that not a few of them were converted.

66. We reply further to the proposed objection in the words of Foggini, who, amongst other remarks, says:

"I cannot, for my part, see that the Jews, in thus speaking, show that they had never at any other time received knowledge of the Gospel: but they would seem to wish to hear S. Paul's own views regarding it, as a man who had the reputation amongst them of very great learning. Might there not, too, have been some sort of dissimulation on their part, or perhaps one might call it an inquisitive curiosity to know more distinctly, from S. Paul's own mouth, about certain points of Christian doctrine, which they had either heard of as taught by the Apostles, or read of in the Epistle which he had written to the Romans? And might not the very name of that Apostle, who by his teaching, miracles, and labours endured for Christ, was everywhere known and famous, have kindled in them a most earnest desire to hear him speak, and to listen to him with particular attention?" †

67. Or, again, there might have been special reasons why the leading Jews at Rome should have less insight than elsewhere into the doctrines and state of Christianity. Perhaps the Christian converts from Judaism still continued in many points to observe the Jewish law, and thus their separation from the Jews would not be so marked and public. We should remark also what Dio Cassius says of Claudius:

"When the Jews were again becoming so numerous in Rome, that they could not well be expelled from the city without a tumult, Claudius did not, indeed, banish them, but he would not permit them to fashion their way of living conformably with the laws of their own country." ‡

---

* 2 Cor. xi. 5; Gal. ii. 9.   † *Exercitat.* viii. See also Beelen on this passage.
‡ *Hist.* lx. 6.

From this it would appear that, previously to the edict for the expulsion of Jews from Rome in the ninth year of Claudius, they were prohibited from holding public assemblies: and so it might more easily happen that the whole distinctive manner of life of the Christians should be less known to the chief men of the Jews, if the separation of Christians from Jews was not altogether complete: for we must remember that the assemblies of the Christians were private, and held in private houses, as we know from S. Paul's Epistle to the Romans.

BABYLON.

68. Our opponents appeal, moreover, to the text (1 *Pet.* v. 13): "The Church that is in Babylon, elected together with you, saluteth you;" from which words they infer that S. Peter, when he wrote his Epistle, was at Babylon,—according to some, Babylon in Egypt, according to others, Babylon in Chaldæa, or the province of Babylon—where he found amongst the Jews a most ample field of labour; but that he never came to Rome. The tradition of Peter's Roman Episcopate arose, they say, from a false interpretation of certain persons who absurdly originated the idea that the name of Babylon was metaphorical.

To this we reply:

(1) Even though S. Peter was at Babylon, and wrote his Epistle there, no conclusion can be thence drawn against his Roman Episcopate, since a residence for some time of S. Peter at Babylon is of itself quite compatible with his being Bishop of Rome.

(2) There is absolutely no trace in tradition that S. Peter was either at the one or the other Babylon, that he wrote his Epistle, or was bishop there,—circumstances, indeed, most improbable from the fact that both these Babylons were at that time places of very little importance. There is, moreover, no small division in the adversary's camp on the matter; since those who are for Babylon in Chaldæa prove that S. Peter was not at Babylon in Egypt, while the others maintain point-blank the contrary.

(3) That Rome is signified under the name of Babylon is, as we have already seen, handed down by the consentient voice of ancient interpreters. And here holds good what Tertullian, speaking on another subject, objects against the heretics: "From the very order is manifest that that is the teaching of our Lord and true which is first handed down (prius tra-

ditum), whilst that is foreign and false which has been brought in later." *

(4) To rule that metaphor is unfit for a simple epistle written in natural style, and to apply this to a single word, is pure pretence, and throwing dust in the eyes. Such a principle might apply perhaps to whole sentences and long periods in a letter. But who would deem it out of place to use an allegorical expression in a letter, as profane authors, such as Cicero, Pliny, and others, have not hesitated to do in their epistles? To show that there would be nothing out of the way in such change of names, we may quote the words of S. Paul (2 Tim. iv. 17): "And I was delivered out of the mouth of the lion;" meaning, thereby, Nero, on account of his cruelty. Besides, S. Peter, writing as he was to Jews, might very well call heathen Rome at that time Babylon, a city by name so familiar to them, and regarded by them as the chief abode and symbol of luxury and every kind of wickedness. For Rome, we know, especially in that age of the Emperors, was given up to unbridled licentiousness, impiety, and the worship of idols—"a slave to the errors of all the nations, assuming to wear the garb of much religion, because she rejected the falsehood of none." † Orosius, too, enumerates various points of resemblance between Rome and Babylon, attributing to both cities a *like origin, like power, a like greatness, like times, like goods, and like evils.*‡ It is, moreover, easy to conjecture special reasons why S. Peter might be unwilling, from prudence, expressly to mention Rome, whereas there could be no risk of mistake for those to whom he was writing, since Sylvanus, who bore the Epistle, would tell them by word of mouth all about S. Peter and the faithful in Rome.

(5) It is worth while, again, to remark that in the very Liturgy and Office of the Syrians and Chaldeans, mention is more than once made of S. Peter's Roman Episcopate and of his martyrdom at Roma. Thus, *e.g.*, in the Chaldee Liturgy for the Feast of SS. Peter and Paul (*Noct.* ii.): "Brethren, let us adorn ourselves with praiseworthy and noble actions, in commemoration of these Apostles and Doctors, who illumined the world by their teaching; of Peter elect, Prince of the Apostles, who finished his administration at Rome." § Whilst, on the other hand, no trace

* *De Præscript.* 31.
† S. Leo, *Serm. I. de B. Ap. Pet. et Paul.*   ‡ *Hist.* ii. 2.
§ See *The Tradition of the Syrian Church of Antioch*, &c., by the Most Rev. Cyril Behnam Benni, Syrian Archbishop of Mossul (Nineveh). London, 1871.

occurs either in the Syrian and Chaldee Fathers, or in their Liturgies, that Peter was ever at Babylon.

69. The objections raised by our opponents on the score of tradition are already anticipated in our exposition; it is well, however, here to touch briefly on the nature of their attack. Following in the wake of Spanheim, they allege that the later Fathers and ecclesiastical writers rely implicitly on those who preceded them, viz., on Papias, Dionysius of Corinth, Clement of Alexandria, Origen, Irenæus, and Tertullian. Of these they say, Tertullian, Irenæus, and Origen were deceived by Papias and Clement of Alexandria, the real and sole originators of the entire tradition concerning S. Peter's Roman Episcopate; or rather, that Papias was alone responsible for it; and he, it is very evident, was a man notorious for his wonderful simplicity and credulity, as Spanheim claims to prove by several testimonies of antiquity. In this way, then, they pretend, the first origin of the whole tradition is traceable to the metaphorical interpretation of Rome for Babylon (1 *Pet.* v. 13), put forth first by Papias, and after him by Clement of Alexandria, as well as to the fabricated account of S. Peter's conflict with Simon Magus, as given in apocryphal writings. Hence, the Fathers of the fourth and following centuries were deceived by those of the third and second centuries, and these again by Clement of Alexandria and Papias, who themselves erred either through their ignorance or credulity. Here then, they say, is the real source of that huge tradition.

70. What we have already said will supply a sufficient answer to all this. But here we observe, in the first place, that when it is alleged that the Fathers of the fourth century followed the writers who went before them, this may be taken in a twofold sense. It may either mean, that this historical fact was duly authenticated in each succeeding century by an uninterrupted series of previous testimonies—and this no doubt is quite true; or it may mean, that the Fathers relied with only a blind credulity on those who had gone before them, simply repeating, without any intelligent inquiry, what they had thus received—and this is utterly false, as well as most injurious to the Fathers of the Church, who were so eminent alike for their great learning and sanctity.

What they say of the Fathers of the third and second centuries is equally false and absurd. It is, indeed, quite ridiculous to affirm that these were all taken in by Clement of Alexandria and Papias, since we have given the testimonies of Dionysius of

OBJECTIONS FROM SIMON MAGUS: HIS HISTORY.   59

Corinth, Origen, Tertullian, and Irenæus, which clearly show that they were perfectly certain as to the fact in question, and that they had not accepted it solely on the authority of Papias and Clement. The testimonies of these Fathers are, moreover, wholly independent of the interpretation of the word Babylon in S. Peter's Epistle. When we find Tertullian commemorating the Roman amongst the Apostolic Churches; Irenæus, in his contention against the heretics, recounting the succession of Roman Pontiffs from SS. Peter and Paul until his own time, saying that the greatest glory of the Roman Church is that it was founded by these Apostles, and extolling its principality; Dionysius of Corinth expressly affirming that Peter preached at Rome and was martyred in that city—what, we ask, has all this to do with Papias and Clement of Alexandria, or with their interpretation of Babylon for Rome in S. Peter's Epistle?*

SIMON MAGUS.

71. With regard to the history of Simon Magus we would observe: (1) From the evidence already given, the truth of S. Peter's Roman Episcopate is clear, and rests upon its own basis, whatever may be thought about Simon's arrival in Rome. That Simon, however, was in Rome, and that there S. Peter withstood him, is related in such a manner by several ancient writers, that we cannot prudently entertain any doubts as to the fact. In relating it, they first either presuppose or refer to S. Peter's residence at Rome as something about which there is no question, and then go on to narrate his conflict with Simon. (2) Some of the circumstances recorded of Simon may be matter for controversy, e.g., the statue erected to him, his flight through the air, and the manner of his death. Such details, however, do not affect the main fact.

72. As what is recorded of Simon Magus may not generally be well known, it will be useful to say something of his history. Justin, in his *Apology* (i. 26), writes of him as follows:

"After the Ascension of Christ into heaven, the demons instigated certain men to give themselves out to be gods. And these you not only did not oppose, but you even loaded them with honours. Thus one Simon, a Samaritan, from a town called Gittum, having wrought, by the art of the demons working in him, magic wonders in your royal city of Rome, was accounted to be God, and as God was honoured by you with a statue—which statue was erected on

---

* See later on, in Part III., the statements of modern Anglican learned authors on this question of Babylon.

an island in the Tiber between the two bridges, bearing on it this Roman inscription: SIMONI DEO SANCTO. · Him nearly all the Samaritans, and some from other nations, confess to be the first God, and adore him; and a certain Helena, who at that time followed him about everywhere, after he had first prostituted her in a brothel, they gave out to be his first notion (ἔννοιαν). One Menander, too, likewise a Samaritan, from the town of Caparetæa, a disciple of Simon, also relying on the agency of demons, when he was living at Antioch, deceived many, as we know, by his magical art." Further on, ch. 56: "Again, as we have already shown, the devils brought in others, the Samaritans Simon and Menander, who, by the magical wonders they wrought, deceived many, and keep them still deceived. For when Simon was living amongst you in the imperial city, as I have already said, in the reign of Claudius Cæsar, he struck both the sacred senate and the Roman people with so great admiration that he was thought to be a god, and was presented with a statue, as are the other gods who are worshipped by you."

S. Irenæus speaks of Simon at some length, and amongst other things as follows:

"And when still more he had disbelieved God, he became ambitious of contending against the Apostles, both that he might himself appear glorious, and that, making a still fuller investigation of the whole art of sorcery, he might strike the people with astonishment. He lived in the reign of Claudius, and is said to have been honoured by that emperor with a statue on account of his magic." *

S. Irenæus then goes on to speak of Helena, who went about with Simon, and of his doctrines. Tertullian also says:

"You inaugurated Simon Magus with a statue, and an inscription of ' Holy God.' " †

Eusebius, on the authority of Irenæus and Justin, describes the acts and doctrines of Simon, and his being overcome by S. Peter. This last circumstance Eusebius did not take from Justin and Irenæus. We find it also in the author of the *Philosophumena*, who agrees with Eusebius. ‡

73. Now it happened that in the year 1574, during the pontificate of Gregory XIII., there was dug up out of some old rubble, on that island in the Tiber, a stone, once the base of a statue; and on it was read the following inscription:

"Semoni Sanco Deo Fidio Sacrum Sex. Pompeius. Sp. F. Col. Mussianus. Quinquennalis. Decur. Bidentalis. Donum Dedit."

Baronius records § another inscription which was discovered in the Quirinal, dedicated to the same Semon Sancus: *Sango Sancto*

---

* *Contra Hæreses*, i. 23.   † *Apologet.* xiii.
‡ *H. E.* ii. 13, 14; *Philos.* l. vi. 20.   § *Ad Annum* 44. n. 54.

Semon Deo Fidio Sacrum. Semon Sancus was, it appears, a deity of the Latins, to whom statues and inscriptions were dedicated in Rome. Consequently, after the discovery of these inscriptions, many critics, most of them Protestants, and some of them Catholics, maintained, as Herbst does, that there was no reliable proof of Simon Magus having been in Rome; that Justin was deceived by seeing that monument, and wrongly supposed it was to Simon Magus, and that the other writers had blindly followed Justin.

74. Not a few, however, of the learned hold that the finding of these inscriptions does not impair the authority of Justin's narration, nor even what he says about the statue erected to Simon. They are of opinion that it was quite another statue of which Justin writes, and that we ought not to refuse credit to so grave a witness, and the less so, since the way in which S. Augustine and Theodoret speak of the statues of Simon, shows that they did not gain their knowledge from Justin alone. S. Augustine says:

"He (Simon) furnished images of himself, and of the same harlot (Helena), to his disciples for adoration, and had them set up at Rome also, by public authority, like statues of the gods. It was in this city the Apostle Peter extinguished him by the true power of Almighty God." *

Theodoret says, moreover, that that statue was of brass. The learned remark, also, that the base discovered is so small that it could not belong to the statue spoken of by Justin: and that it is quite improbable that one so well versed in Roman mythology, and in all that concerned his own Samaritan nation, should have been led into such a mistake as must have made him simply ridiculous.

75. But apart from all this (as Stenglein well shows), even though S. Justin had made a mistake through some confusion about the statue, it would no way thence follow that Simon was never in Rome at all. Nay, on the hypothesis, which we do not admit, of a mistake on the part of Justin, such a mistake would be attributable *to the certain knowledge he had* of Simon Magus having really been in Rome; and that hence he ascribed the inscription to him. For it is absurd to suppose that the mere inscription by itself should originate in S. Justin's mind the belief of Simon's visit to Rome; and equally absurd is it to suppose that Simon's disciples, still living in Rome, should have forced that belief on the Saint, through the statue that was seen there. Besides, Justin shows clearly that he derived his certainty of

* *Hæres.* i.

Simon's visit to the city from other sources, setting it down definitely as he does to the time of Claudius. S. Irenæus also records the fact of Simon's coming to Rome as one beyond all doubt, whilst he says he was told of the erection of the statue. It was, too, very natural that Simon, as he saw his influence declining in Samaria, should have turned his steps towards Rome, where, according to Tacitus, whatever elsewhere was most atrocious and shameful, met and was welcome—"cuncta undique atrocia aut pudenda confluunt celebranturque." (*Ann.* xiii. 15.) We do not hear of S. Peter's conflict with Simon in Rome from Justin, but Eusebius must have derived it from a sure source, since he records it without any hesitation or doubt; and, as we have seen, the author of the *Philosophumena* agrees with him.

76. Concerning the death of Simon, the same author, writing at an earlier date than the others who speak of it, and giving, apparently at least, a different version from them, says as follows:

"This man, coming at length to —— (the word is wanting in the Codex), sat teaching under a plane-tree. When reproached for his declining age, he said that, if buried in the tomb, he should rise again on the third day. And having bid his disciples dig a grave, he directed them to bury him in it. They did as he ordered: and there up to this day he has remained, for he was not the Christ." (L. vi. 20.)

But there are Fathers and other writers, though of a later date, yet of considerable weight, who record Simon's flight through the air and his violent death in such positive terms, that it is difficult to consider these narrations as mere fables taken from apocryphal books. Thus, *v.g.*, writes Arnobius:

"For the Romans had seen the chariot of Simon Magus and his horses of fire blown asunder by the breath of Peter, and disappear on his uttering the name of Christ. They had seen him, I say, trusting to his false gods, betrayed by them in their fear, cast down headlong through his own weight, lying on the ground with his thighs broken: then afterwards borne on to Brunda, wearied out with torments and shame, again precipitated from on high," &c.[*]

It is rather singular that in the life of Nero (ch. xii.) Suetonius writes, in reference to the scenic representations and public entertainments of the Emperor:

---

[*] Besides Arnobius, who wrote at the close of the third century (*Adv. Gent.* l. ii. n. 7), see Ephiphan. *Hær.* xxi. v. 5; Cyrill. Hieros. *Catech.* vi. n. 5; Philastrius Brix. *Hær.* xxix.; Sulpitius Severus, *Hist. Sac.* l. ii. c. 28; Maximus Taurinensis, *Hom. V. in Nat. SS. App. Petri et Pauli*; Theodoret. *Hæret. fab.* l. i. c. 1; Sanguinetti, *l. c.* p. 101.

"Icarus, in his first essay, fell at once down to the ground close to his (the Emperor's) chamber, and spattered him over with blood."

Some refer what is here noted of the new Icarus to Simon's flight through the air; whilst others wholly reject any connection between the two, and relegate whatever is said of the flight of Simon to the region of fables. Tillemont, in our opinion, writes more wisely on the matter:

"Some in the present day would dispute not only these last details which are less authentic, but everything in general that is said of the fall of Simon; not that they have any positive proof to bring against it, but because it comes, they say, originally from apocryphal writings; or they allege other reasons of still less moment. But even though it be true that the account is a fiction, we prefer, as long as there is no clear and convincing proof of its falsity, to err on this point with Arnobius, S. Cyril of Jerusalem, the Legates of Pope Liberius, S. Ambrose, S. Augustine, S. Isidore of Pelusium, Theodoret, and many others, than to be obliged to accuse of indiscreet credulity so large a number of the most illustrious and most grave Masters of the Latin and Greek Church, and on no other grounds than that it is not absolutely certain that they say the truth."*

It appears most probable from the testimonies we have given which witness to the ancient tradition, that Simon, ambitious of performing his magical wonders in presence of Nero, was confounded at the prayer of Peter, and thus met at once with the loss of his reputation and the fracture of his limbs. And if he was not, perchance, killed on that occasion, what the author of the *Philosophumena* narrates may be likewise true.

In here taking leave of Simon Magus, we remark that, so far from what is narrated of him giving rise to the witness of antiquity concerning the Roman Episcopate of S. Peter, it is on the contrary most evident that the whole story of Simon presupposes for its basis the preaching of the Gospel at Rome by S. Peter as a most certain and well-known fact.

The Roman Clergy—Rationalistic Theory.

77. A method of attack employed by some † is to make out that the first rumour of S. Peter's Roman Episcopate was got up through the cunning and ambition of the Roman clergy, and was by them more and more extensively propagated until, in the end,

---

* *Hist. Eccl.* t. i. "S. Pierre," Art. xxxiv.

† Thus Velenus, Spanheim, and, of late, Ribetti, in the Roman disputation.

it became a settled belief in the minds of the faithful generally. We do not care to answer such a wicked and shameful accusation, made without any proof whatever, against the Roman clergy in the first centuries, who were distinguished so greatly for their virtues. Besides, how could any sound criticism suppose that a persuasion so universal and popular could have had its origin, and have gained strength, from the fraud and ambition of the clergy?

78. Certain German Rationalists adopted another theory, which has revived in our own times. According to this theory, the Christian religion is a mixed compound of Jewish traditions upheld by Peter (Petrinism), and of mystic philosophy adopted by Paul (Paulinism). From the union of these tendencies resulted the Gospels which bear the names of Luke and John, and the Epistles of Peter and Paul, all of which are really the works of anonymous writers. What we have on record concerning Peter and Paul are simple myths sprung from these various tendencies. Thus, the story of Peter's Roman Episcopate arose from the tendency of Petrinism amongst the Judaising Christians, who by this means were able to make a boast of their Peter in opposition to the Gentile Christians who idolised Paul (Paulinism). Petri-Paulinism was a conciliatory compromise between these two opposite tendencies, which gave rise to the legend of the united preaching of both Peter and Paul at Rome, and of their martyrdom together in that city; and this legend is the root of the tradition borne witness to by Dionysius and Irenæus in the second century.

Lipsius further illustrates the theory thus: In the beginning, he says, the episcopal dignity did not exist, not even in the Church of Rome. But in course of time the more prominent members in the college of presbyters strove to raise themselves more and more above the other presbyters, and to rule over them, and thus arose a monarchical episcopate. The growing tendency to exalt the episcopal office led at length to the discovery or invention that its origin was derived from the Apostles. Thus it was that Hegesippus and Irenæus began soon to find out a tradition of even the first bishops after the Apostles: these were not really bishops at all, but historic persons from amongst the more eminent presbyters. The tracing back the succession to Peter was due to some chronicler about the close of the second century, who invented also the twenty-five years of S. Peter's episcopate. The legend was fully completed by the addition of two myths—one, the conflict with Simon Magus (under which name is really meant Paul) in the reign of Claudius, the other, the simultaneous martyrdom of Peter and Paul under Nero.*

79. It is beyond our purpose here to discuss these rationalist dreamings in detail.† They are refuted directly, by demonstrating the authenticity of the Books of the New Testament; and indirectly, by what we have solidly proved as true from the testimony of the Fathers. The one only thing we here remark is, how utterly contradictory one to the other is this class of opponents, and that of the followers of Velen and Spanheim. Thus Lipsius, in attributing to the second century the writing of the (so called) I. Epistle of S. Peter, says: "Babylon, where the Apostle lived when writing, can only be understood to mean Rome," and that what is written in *Acts*, xix. 21, xxiii. 11, he says, alludes to the dwelling of Peter and Paul in Rome; in other words, that there are here contained the elements of the Petri-Pauline tendency. He allows that the writers of the second century—viz., Caius, S. Dionysius of Corinth, Tertullian, and Origen—thus early acknowledged the dwelling of Peter and Paul in Rome, and their martyrdom there under Nero, but attributes this opinion of theirs to the above-mentioned pious story which these writers believed. Thus we see Lipsius, so hypercritical in other matters, accepting, without hesitation, the words of the above-named authors in their obvious and genuine sense; whilst the other class of opponents most strangely distort the same words, and strive to obscure and explain them away by what are evidently capricious and arbitrary cavils.

From what we have said it is very clear that the objections raised against the Roman Episcopate of S. Peter are devoid of all real force; and that if Protestants and unbelievers reject the historical fact, it is not on the ground of any solid arguments, but under the influence, whether of inveterate prejudice, or hatred of the Catholic Church, or impiety: and that in such opposition to truth those words of the Apostle are again verified: "Their foolish heart was darkened: for, professing themselves to be wise, they became fools." (*Rom.* i. 21, 22.)

* Lipsius, *l. c.* pp. 145, 162. See also *Stimmen aus Maria Laach*, Juni, 1872.

† We shall return to this matter later on in Part III. Ch. xvi.

SECTION II.

THE CHRONOLOGY OF THE ACTS OF THE APOSTLES IN RELATION TO S. PETER'S ROMAN EPISCOPATE.

§ 1.—PRELIMINARY—THE DATE OF OUR LORD JESUS CHRIST'S BIRTH AND DEATH.

AN objection very commonly brought against S. Peter's twenty-five years' episcopate at Rome is that the chronology of the Acts of the Apostles cannot be reconciled with such a hypothesis. It is necessary, then, in order to complete our task, to consider attentively this objection also; and with this end, we add here Professor Jungmann's Appendix, wherein he clearly proves that there is nothing in the Acts of the Apostles which militates against the Roman Episcopate of S. Peter, but that, on the contrary, there exists an entire harmony between S. Luke's history and this fact.

For the sake of brevity, and not to introduce into a book intended for popular use any recondite matter that does not bear immediately on our subject, we omit the paragraphs 80-84, which treat of other chronological *Eras* and *Epochs*, and pass at once to what is said of the Dionysian or Vulgar Era in paragraph 85. As we shall have to deal with some events in profane history, particularly that of Rome, it may be well to note that the date of the founding the city of Rome (U.C.), to which reference is sometimes made, is reckoned 754 years before Christ, according to the Vulgar Era.

85. THE DIONYSIAN, commonly called the VULGAR ERA, is the one now followed by all civilised nations. Its publication A.D. 526 was due to the studious labours of Dionysius Exiguus, from whom it receives its name. This era begins from our Lord's Incarnation, which was supposed to have taken place March 25th, U.C. 754; so that the Birth of our Lord Jesus Christ would be December 25th of that year 754. This same year, U.C. 754, is thus the first year of the Vulgar Era.

The learned are, however, now fully agreed that Dionysius

made a mistake in the year he fixed for our Lord's Birth. Since it is evident from Josephus and other writers that Herod, who massacred the Innocents, and who must consequently have been reigning at the birth of Christ, was already dead about the month of April, U.C. 750. Our Lord must therefore have been born before that year; and we hold as solid the opinion of those who fix December 25th, U.C. 747, as the date of our Lord's birth. Hence, according to this calculation, on the 1st of January, A.D. 1, of the Vulgar Era (U.C. 754), He would have already completed His sixth, and be entering upon His seventh, year.

86. The date of our Lord's Death, according to the common and constant opinion of the three first centuries, is the fifteenth year of Tiberius, under the consulate of L. Rubellius Geminus and C. Fufius Geminus, i.e., the 29th year of our Vulgar Era (U.C. 782). Here, however, many formerly found much difficulty from the words of S. Luke (iii. 1), where he says that S. John the Baptist began to exercise his ministry *in the fifteenth year of Tiberius Cæsar*, and there were consequently various opinions held as to the year of our Lord's death. This difference is now well set to right by the learned, on consideration that S. Luke does not count the years of Tiberius Cæsar's reign from his accession to the throne on the death of Augustus (A.D. 14 of the Vulgar Era), but from the year when Tiberius received from the senate the same power as Augustus over the provinces. Now, this took place in the year U.C. 764, and this year was for the provinces the first year of Tiberius Cæsar's reign. Hence the fifteenth year of Tiberius mentioned by S. Luke commenced for the Jews with the new moon of Tisri (October), U.C. 778; and with this opinion it is quite consistent to hold that our Lord suffered in the year U.C. 782, or A.D. 29 of the Vulgar Era. The day of His death was, according to Patrizzi,* March 16th (new style).

In calculating, then, the dates of events which happened in the beginning of the Church, after our Lord's death, we must bear in mind that the year of His Passion was 29, and not 33, of the Vulgar Era. Accordingly, the age of Jesus Christ A.D. 29, when He was crucified, was 34 years and some months.

§ 2.—CHRONOLOGY OF THE ACTS OF THE APOSTLES.

87. In order to arrange our chronology with greater accuracy, it is necessary to fix precisely the date of some fact, which will

* *Diss. in Evangel.* xx. li. lii.

serve as a hinge whereon the whole chronology may turn; and the fact selected should be one that has its agents and surrounding circumstances recorded by other historians also. Now, such an event is S. Paul's *imprisonment at Jerusalem*, narrated in *Acts*, xxi. 27, the date of which can be precisely determined, as occurring at the time of Pentecost, A.D. 53 (Vulgar Era).

Let us examine the proofs of this. The imprisonment of S. Paul could not have happened *before* this year, for when it took place, Drusilla, daughter of the elder Agrippa and sister of the younger, was already the wife of Felix the Procurator of Judæa.* But Felix, as is clear from Josephus,† did not marry Drusilla until after the close of the 12th year of Claudius, *i.e.*, after the autumn of 52. From this it is evident that S. Paul's imprisonment could not be earlier than 53. Nor can it be reckoned *later:* it cannot be set down to 54, for it is certain that S. Paul was imprisoned during the high-priesthood of Ananias.‡ Now, Ananias might have continued to hold that office throughout the year 53, and even somewhat longer, but certainly he was not the high priest at Pentecost 54, since by that time Ismael had succeeded him. This is evident from Josephus, who records the celebration of the Paschal Feast under Claudius and Ismael the high priest.§ Now, the one only Passover celebrated under Claudius after the year 53 must have been that of 54, since, in the month of October

---

* "And after some days, Felix coming with Drusilla his wife, who was a Jewess, sent for Paul, and heard of him the faith that is in Christ Jesus." (*Acts*, xxiv. 24.)

† Josephus writes: "Claudius sent Felix, the brother of Pallas, to assume the government of Judæa. And in the *twelfth year complete* of his reign he appointed Agrippa to the tetrarchy which Philip had held, and of Batanea, with Trachonitis and Abila... Agrippa, thus honoured and enriched by Cæsar, married his sister Drusilla to Azizus, king of the Emesenes, on his consent to embrace the Jewish religion... But soon after the marriage of Drusilla and Azizus was dissolved for this reason. Felix, when procurator of Judæa, seeing Drusilla... became enamoured of her, and sent Simon, a friend of his, a celebrated Jewish magician, to use his endeavours to prevail upon Drusilla to desert her husband and marry him... And she was prevailed upon... to renounce her religion and marry Felix." (*Ant.* b. xx. c. 7.)

‡ "And the high priest Ananias commanded them that stood by to strike him on the mouth." (*Acts*, xxiii. 2.)

§ Shortly before the war with the Romans, during *the reign of Claudius, and the high-priesthood of Ismael*, the famine was so sore in our land that an assar of corn was sold for four drachmas: yet when seventy cori of wheat were brought in for the *Feast of Azymes*, not one of the famished priests dared to eat so much as a crumb in such a time of scarcity, out of reverence for the laws and fear of the Divine anger which is wont to fall even on secret sins." (Josephus, *Antiquit.* l. iii. c. xv. n. 3.)

that same year, 54, Claudius came to his end. Since, then, Ismael had succeeded Ananias in the high-priesthood by Easter 54, it is clear that the imprisonment of S. Paul cannot be referred to the Pentecost of that year. Another proof that S. Paul's imprisonment took place in the year 53 is that Felix, whose administration of Judæa was confirmed by Nero A.D. 54,* returned to Rome whilst his brother Pallas was still high in Nero's favour.† But Pallas lost the favour of Nero shortly before the Saturnalia, *i.e.*, before the month of December 55.‡ Consequently, Felix must have returned to Rome before that date—not in 54, since he was confirmed in his government by Nero towards the close of that year, but during the course of the following year 55. Now, it is said (*Acts*, xxiv. 27) that ".when two years were ended, Felix had for successor Portius Festus," and consequently left Palestine. The imprisonment of S. Paul, therefore, happened in the year 53.

88. Although it is generally held that the imprisonment of S. Paul took place several years after 53, still we hold this opinion, which is maintained by Cardinal Patrizzi § to be *certain*. Tacitus says expressly:

"Nero, in his anger against those who supported the pride of the woman (Agrippina), removes Pallas from his office." ‖

Josephus also writes:

"Nero having now transferred the government from Felix to Portius Festus, some of the leading Jews of Cæsarea repaired to Rome in order to lay accusation against Felix for the exercise of injustice and tyranny towards the Jews: and he would inevitably have been punished but for the interference of his brother Pallas, who, being at that time high in the Emperor's favour, solicited and obtained his pardon." ¶

This, then, happened in the course of the year 55. Wieseler, too, agrees that the latest date that can be assigned to S. Paul's arrival in Rome is best determined by this passage of Josephus—that is, we may thence infer that Felix went to Rome whilst Pallas was still in Nero's favour, and that soon afterwards Paul came also to Rome. But then the learned author only remarks that Pallas perished by poison in the year 62; and, consequently, that S. Paul came to Rome in the spring at least of 63. He did not, however, advert to the fact that, according to Tacitus, Pallas had already lost Nero's favour in the year 55; and thus clearly,

---

* Josephus, *De Bello*, l. ii. c. xiii. 2.   † Josephus, *Antiq.* l. xx. c. viii. 9.
‡ Tacit. *Annal.* l. xiii. 14, 15.   § *De Evang.* l. i. c. iii. n. 23.
‖ *Annal.* xiii. n. 14, ad a. U.C. 809, A.D. 55.   ¶ *Ant.* l. xx. c. vii.

according to his own admission, Felix must have returned to Rome before the end of the year 55.*

89. Having thus ascertained the precise date of S. Paul's imprisonment, we are now able to determine the dates of certain other events, and, in the first place, that of the *Council of Jerusalem*. It seems evident from the history of the Acts of the Apostles that the Council cannot be placed later than A.D. 47.

After the Council, until his apprehension in 58, S. Paul dwelt at Corinth for a year and a half (*Acts*, xviii. 11), at Ephesus two years and three months (xix. 8-11), three months in Greece (xx. 3). This, altogether, would make up four years. If to this we add the time spent by the Apostle at Antioch (xv. 35)—in his different journeys, and in various cities, as S. Luke narrates (xv. 40, 41; xvi.-xxi.)—which, certainly, could not have been less than a year and a half—the Council would have been held five years and a half at least before Pentecost 58. And this brings it to the year 47.

We know, again, from the Epistle to the Galatians (c. i.), how many years after S. Paul's conversion the Council took place. For it is evident that the visit of Paul and Barnabas to Jerusalem for the Council recorded in the Acts,† is the same as that mentioned by S. Paul himself writing to the Galatians (c. ii.): since in either case there was the same motive and object for the journey—viz., to consult with the other Apostles on the Gospel S. Paul was preaching amongst the Gentiles, as well as to settle the question of the immunity of the Gentiles from the ceremonial observances of the Jewish law. And in both cases we find there was the same result.

Now, S. Paul clearly indicates in this same Epistle how many years it was after his conversion he made that journey to Jerusalem: for there (i. 15, *sqq.*) he purposely mentions certain events of his life in consecutive order, to prove that it was not from any of the Apostles he had received his knowledge of the Gospel; and to indicate this succession of time, he uses the word ἔπειτα (*deinde, then*), which denotes such sequence. Thus we learn from the Apostle, that between his conversion and his second journey

---

* See Wieseler, *Chronologie des apost. Zeitalter*, § 12.

† "And some coming down from Judæa, taught the brethren: That except you be circumcised after the manner of Moses, you cannot be saved. And when Paul and Barnabas had no small contest with them, they determined that Paul and Barnabas, and certain others on the other side, should go up to the Apostles and priests to Jerusalem, about this question." (*Acts*, xv. 1, 2.)

to Jerusalem (to the Council), there was an interval of seventeen years. And this is also the interpretation of the passage given by S. Jerome in his Commentary.

90. We have seen that the Council of Jerusalem cannot have been later than the year 47; we shall now show that it was not before that year. This will appear from the date we must assign to *S. Paul's conversion*.

In the first chapters of the Acts of the Apostles S. Luke records, in a summary way, the events that took place up to the conversion of S. Paul—viz., the founding the Church at Jerusalem, and the holy life of the faithful there; the founding the Church in Samaria; the election of the Deacons; the virtues and martyrdom of S. Stephen; the subsequent persecution by Saul, of which, on various occasions, S. Paul speaks himself in such a way as to imply that it lasted probably for several months. Now, a shorter time than twenty months at least, or even two years, would not have sufficed for the occurrence of all these events. Hence the date of S. Paul's conversion cannot be earlier than the first months of the year 31. This conclusion, which may be held as most certain, is confirmed by ecclesiastical records, such as various ancient martyrologies, mentioning the conversion of S. Paul as taking place in the second year after our Lord's Ascension: and the same is attested by Œcumenius. Consequently, the seventeenth year after S. Paul's conversion, when he went to the Council, is no other than A.D. 47; and in that year the Council was held.*

91. We must now endeavour to fix the date of some other events relating to SS. Peter and Paul in the early days of the Church. S. Luke says (*Acts*, xi. 19): "Now they who had been dispersed, by the persecution that arose on occasion of Stephen, went about as far as Phœnice, and Cyprus, and Antioch, speaking the word to none, but to the Jews only." Hence we see that a Church was formed at Antioch of converted Jews soon after the Ascension of Christ: of this Church, according to the testimony of antiquity, S. Peter was bishop for six or seven years: and we may suppose that he undertook the episcopate at Antioch about the year 35.

S. Peter would have understood, from his mission to Cornelius and his previous vision, that the time for preaching the Gospel to the Gentiles was now at hand. After narrating the conversion of Cornelius, S. Luke returns, in his history, to those who had been dispersed abroad through the persecution in the time of

* Patrizzi, *In Evangel*. l. iii. diss. li. 10.

Stephen, and says that now, at Antioch, the Gospel had begun to be preached also to the Greeks, "and a great number of believers was converted to the Lord." (*Acts*, xi. 20-26). On this being known in Jerusalem, Barnabas was sent to Antioch; thence, soon after his arrival, he went to Tarsus, and brought back Saul with him to Antioch. All this must have taken some months. Saul, we read, remained then a whole year at Antioch, until, with Barnabas, he went to Jerusalem for the Pasch in the year 42 (*Acts*, xi. 20). Hence it appears that the conversion of Cornelius cannot be dated later than the autumn of 40. And as we cannot suppose that after this event the Apostles would longer delay the execution of their Master's command to go and teach all nations, *the going forth of the Apostles* into the whole world may be set down to the year 41—*i.e.*, twelve years after the Ascension of our Lord.

92. As we have already seen, S. Peter's imprisonment, liberation, and journey to Rome (*Acts*, xii.), took place A.D. 42, the second year of Claudius. After Easter 42, Paul and Barnabas returned from Jerusalem to Antioch, and were there set apart for the work of the apostolate (xii. 25, xiii. 2). They then set out on their *first* apostolic journey: and on their return again to Antioch, "abode there no small time with the disciples" (xiv. 25-27). This filled up the time until the year 47. Meanwhile Peter founded the Church at Rome, wrote his first Epistle (A.D. 43), wherein is found *the salutation of Mark*, and shortly afterwards, in the same year (43), sent Mark, after he had written his Gospel, to Alexandria, where, according to the Chronicle of Eusebius and ancient tradition, he died in the eighth year of Nero, A.D. 61 or 62.

Afterwards, about the year 46, S. Peter left Rome for some time, perhaps on the publication of the edict of Claudius, which, as Dio testifies (*Hist. Rom.* l. lx. 6), prohibited the assemblies of the Jews. The Apostle, it seems, then went to Antioch, where, on the arrival of some of the Circumcision from Jerusalem, a contention arose as to the observance of Jewish ceremonies; and it was most probably on that occasion that Peter was reprehended by Paul, on account of the economy made use of by the former Apostle in his mode of action (*Gal.* ii. 11, *seqq.*). That this happened before the Council, as S. Augustine holds, is intrinsically more probable, and is confirmed by comparing *Acts*, xv. 1, with *Gal.* ii. 12. Nor does it matter that S. Paul relates this incident in his Epistle (ch. ii.) after he had spoken of the Council (ch. i.); for in doing so his object was not to give the chronological order, but to explain certain circumstances which led to the Council, and which might serve as an introduction to what he had further to say in his Epistle. The Council then, on the question of the obligation of legal ceremonies, was held at Jerusalem, it seems, about Pentecost, A.D. 47.

93. After the Council SS. Paul and Barnabas returned to Antioch, where they remained some time (*Acts*, xv. 30-35). In the autumn of 47 Paul went on his *second* apostolic journey with Silas; who soon after, A.D. 48, were joined by SS. Timothy and Luke (v. 40). After traversing several countries of Asia Minor, they passed over to Macedonia and Greece: S. Paul preached at Athens, and thence went to Corinth. Thither had already come Aquila and his wife Priscilla, lately expelled from Rome by Claudius, A.D. 48 (xviii. 1); S. Paul, who arrived towards the end of the same year, dwelt with them whilst at Corinth for a year and six months (v. 11). There the Apostle defended himself before Gallio, the Proconsul of Achaia, who was the elder brother of Seneca; and there, too, he wrote his two Epistles to the Thessalonians. From Corinth Paul departed in the spring of 50, setting sail for Syria with Aquila and Priscilla (v. 18). On their voyage they landed at Ephesus, and here Paul left Aquila and Priscilla; whilst he himself soon continued his voyage, as (according to the Greek text) he wished to be at Jerusalem in time for some Feast, most probably that of Easter. From Jerusalem the Apostle went to Antioch.

94. Soon after this S. Paul went on his *third* apostolic journey. Going through Galatia and Phrygia he arrived, not much after Pentecost, A.D. 50, again at Ephesus, where, the guest of Aquila and Priscilla,* he remained two years and three months (*Acts*, xix. 8-10). Probably from Ephesus the Apostle wrote his Epistle to the Galatians; and certainly his First Epistle to the Corinthians, before Easter, A.D. 52. Owing to the tumult excited by Demetrius the silversmith in the summer of 52, S. Paul was obliged to leave Ephesus, and passed over to Macedonia, where, only a few months after sending his first Epistle, he wrote his Second Epistle to the Corinthians. In this Second Epistle he tells them that he is making a collection through the Churches of Macedonia in behalf of the poor in Jerusalem, and that he hopes

---

* "The Churches of Asia salute you. Aquila and Priscilla salute you much in the Lord, with the Church that is in their house; with whom I also lodge." (1 *Cor*. xvi. 19.)

very soon to visit them at Corinth, and to receive their alms also. (2 *Cor.* viii. and ix.). Accordingly, from Macedonia he soon went to Corinth, where he remained three months (*Acts*, xx. 3). As subsequently to these three months, at Easter, A.D. 53, we find S. Paul again at Philippi in Macedonia (v. 6), he must have arrived at Corinth in the month of December 52 at the latest. We learn from S. Luke that, whilst still at Ephesus, the Apostle's intention was to go through Macedonia and Achaia, thence by sea to Syria, on to Jerusalem, and after that to Rome. We also find him plainly expressing the same intention in his Epistle to the Romans.* Hence we gather that this Epistle was written about the beginning of the year 53 at Corinth, as appears also from other indications, and in particular from the commendation of Phœbe (*Rom.* xvi. 1). In the same Epistle, Aquila and Priscilla, whose guest S. Paul had been at Ephesus, are specially praised and saluted: so that from this, it seems that when the Apostle was driven out of that city, they themselves returned to Rome. As S. Paul was hindered by plots of the Jews from sailing direct from Corinth to Syria and Palestine, he returned to Macedonia, and was at Philippi by Easter 53 (*Acts*, xx. 6). After Easter, he continued his journey with Luke to Jerusalem, where they arrived about Pentecost that same year (v. 16). Thus, S. Paul was at Corinth by the month of December, A.D. 52, at latest, and remained there during the first months of 53; and it was then probably, as we have already said, that Peter and Paul met at Corinth, preached together there, and left that city, though by different routes, at the same time.†

* "And when these things (at Ephesus) were ended, Paul purposed in the spirit, when he had passed through Macedonia and Achaia, to go to Jerusalem, saying: After I have been there I must see Rome also." (*Acts*, xix. 21.) "I was hindered very much from coming to you, and have been kept away till now. But now, having no more place in these countries, and having a great desire these many years past to come unto you, when I shall begin to take my journey into Spain, I hope that, as I pass, I shall see you, and be brought on my way thither by you, if first, in part, I shall have enjoyed you: but now I shall go to Jerusalem, to minister unto the saints. For it hath pleased them of Macedonia and Achaia to make a contribution for the poor of the saints that are in Jerusalem. For they have pleased them, and they are their debtors. For if the Gentiles have been made partakers of their carnal things, they ought also in carnal things to minister to them. When, therefore, I shall have accomplished this, and consigned to them this fruit, I will come by you into Spain." (*Rom.* xv. 22-28.)

† We may remark, again, how well is thus explained the silence of S. Paul in his Epistle to the Romans with regard to S. Peter, and why the name of S. Peter does not appear amongst the salutations. That Apostle from the year 46, perhaps on account of the first edict of Claudius against the Jews, had left Rome. In the year 48 there was another edict of Claudius expelling

95. About the middle of the month of May, A.D. 53, Paul was cast into prison at Jerusalem; for Pentecost that year fell on the 12th or 13th day of May. From Jerusalem, after three days, he was taken to Cæsarea, where he was detained for two years under the Procurator Antonius Felix, brother of Pallas, who up to December 55 was in great favour with Nero. At the beginning of the summer, A.D. 55, Portius Festus succeeded Felix, who returned to Rome before his brother Pallas had lost the Emperor's favour. About twenty days after the arrival of Festus, Paul made his defence before the new Governor against his Jewish accusers, and appealed to Cæsar. On this Festus determined to send him to Rome, and, shortly after, an opportunity offering, Paul set out on his voyage to Italy, which, with its perils, S. Luke describes (*Acts*, xxvii. xxviii.).

96. In the month of October 55, they arrived shipwrecked at the Island of Malta, where they passed the three winter months. In the year 56, as soon as fair weather for sailing began to set in, they completed their voyage to Italy. After some three weeks Paul arrived at Rome about the commencement of spring 56. The centurion there handed him over to the Prefect of the Pretorian guard, who at that time was Burrus, a friend of Seneca; and S. Paul was detained in free custody for two years, till the earlier part of the year 58. Whether S. Peter was at the same time in Rome cannot be gathered from the New Testament. During these two years S. Paul wrote several of his Epistles, as we have already mentioned. After his liberation from this his first imprisonment in Rome, he undertook fresh apostolic journeys. That he was again in Asia and Greece is to be plainly gathered from his second Epistle to Timothy. It is also probable enough that he made then the journey he had contemplated to Spain.

The chronological order we have followed agrees with S. Jerome's, and the Chronicle of Eusebius. Thus Jerome, in his Catalogue of Ecclesiastical Writers, on S. Paul says:

"In the twenty-fifth year after our Lord's Passion,* that is, in the second year of Nero (A.D. 55), at the time when Festus succeeded Felix as Procurator

the Jews from the city, hence S. Peter was for a considerable time absent from Rome. As Aquila and Priscilla had already returned to Rome before the beginning of the year 58, it is inferred that the decree had been withdrawn; and it is reasonable, therefore, to suppose that S. Peter returned also that same year.

* S. Jerome was of opinion that the Passion occurred in 31 or 32 of the Vulgar Era.

of Judæa, Paul is sent bound to Rome, and for two years, remaining in free custody, disputed daily against the Jews of the coming of Christ. It should be known, too, that, since at his first trial before the Roman tribunal, the reign of Nero was not yet become strong, and he had not yet broken out into those enormous crimes which history records of him, Paul was set free by the Emperor, and preached the Gospel in the regions of the West."

Concerning Mark, amongst other things, S. Jerome says:

"He died in the eighth year of Nero, and was buried at Alexandria, Anianus being his successor."

Eusebius, in his Chronicle, assigns the first imprisonment of Paul to nearly the same years—*i.e.*, to the end of the reign of Claudius, and to the beginning of that of Nero, and by no means, as some modern writers are pleased to do, to the latter years of Nero. At the last year (the fourteenth) of Claudius, Eusebius thus writes:

"Festus succeeds to Felix, before whom (Festus), in the presence of king Agrippa, the Apostle Paul, after setting forth the grounds of his religious faith, is sent bound to Rome." *

97. It is very difficult to frame the chronology of the two Apostles' history with accuracy and certainty; still we think that the order we have here exposed, following Patrizzi and other authors, rests on solid arguments, and is well suited to explain the various events in the lives of SS. Peter and Paul, and to solve certain difficulties with regard to Peter's going to Rome and being Bishop of that city. We should, moreover, bear in mind that the chronological order we have thus traced out from the inspired history itself is not one of new invention or mere arbitrary adoption, but coincides with that of the ancient authors. And hereby is conclusively shown how entirely worthless is the argument of those who assert that the chronological order of the events of S. Peter's history makes it impossible that he ever went to Rome or was Bishop of the Roman See. A certain writer of the name of Darby insists especially on this line of argument, and, with much show of learning, arranges his chronology in a very arbitrary and positive manner, to prove that S. Peter was never at Rome. At the very outset, however, of his chronology he commits a great blunder, saying, as he does, that the conversion of Paul is generally held to have occurred in the year 35, or two years after our Lord's Passion (*l. c.* p. 10, n. 5). Whereas the

---

* We have taken much in the above chronological exposition from the Prelections of the *Introduction to Holy Scripture*, delivered by His Eminence the late Cardinal Franzelin, when Professor of Theology in the Roman College. This work has not yet been published.

learned are generally agreed that Christ did not suffer in the year 33 of our era, but hold, with the ancients, that the Passion took place in the Consulate of the two Gemini—*i.e.*, in the year U.C. 782, and in the year 29 of the Vulgar Era. Hence, if S. Paul's conversion happened, as we also are of opinion, two years after the Passion, it must be assigned to the year 31, as we have dated it; and thus the chronological calculations of the learned Darby fall to the ground, and his arguments have no force.

§ 3.—REPLY TO CERTAIN CHRONOLOGICAL OBJECTIONS.

The following objections have been made to the foregoing Chronology, with reference to the year 53 assigned to S. Paul's imprisonment:

(1) The first objection is drawn from the opening words of S. Paul's address to Felix (*Acts*, xxiv. 10): "Knowing that *for many years* thou hast been judge over this nation, I will, with good courage, answer for myself." It is hence, they say, evident that when S. Paul spoke these words, Felix had been for many years Procurator of Judæa; and we know at the same time that he first entered upon that office, A.D. 52, in the twelfth year of Claudius, consequently the imprisonment of Paul could not have occurred in 53, but must have been several years later.

To rightly form an opinion on this objection we must see what Tacitus has written in his Annals:*

"But his (Pallas's) brother, Felix by name, did not act with like moderation, for having been now for a long time set over Judæa *(jam pridem* Judææ impositus), and relying on his great power, he seemed to think he might commit every crime with impunity. The Jews, it is true, gave the appearance of insurrection, when, on hearing of the murder of Caius and a rising taking place, they refused to submit. There was, moreover, an abiding fear that whoever had the rule would govern in the same way; Felix, too, *in the interim*, was fanning the flames of crime and lawlessness by his unreasonable remedies. He had, as a rival in his enormities, Ventidius Cumanus, who had part of the province. The division that had been made placed the people of Galilee under Cumanus, and those of Samaria under Felix; and these people, before at variance the one with the other, now ill-smothered their mutual hates beneath the contempt they bore to their rulers."

Here we learn that Felix had been already joint governor of the province with Cumanus; and Josephus tells us that

---

* L. xii. n. 54, ad ann. U.C. 785, A.D. 52, twelfth year of Claudius, in the Consulate of Faustus Sulla and Salvius Otho.

Cumanus entered on his office in the eighth year of Claudius, A.D. 48.

> "As successor to Tiberius Alexander came Cumanus... in the eighth year of the reign of Claudius."*

From this we see that Felix, too, had been "judge over this nation" since A.D. 48. Tacitus and Josephus record, moreover, that Cumanus, being accused by the Jews of oppression, was deposed in the twelfth year of Claudius (according to Patrizzi, A.D. 49, according to others 52), and then Felix obtained the whole province. Hence S. Paul, in the middle of the year 53, could say that Felix had been "judge over the nation many years" (as Tacitus had said "*jam pridem* Judææ impositus"), reckoning as well the years that Felix had been over Samaria. Taking, therefore, into consideration the short terms of office of the preceding Procurators—Tiberius Alexander and Cumanus—the five years at least of Felix might very well be called *many*, especially as the Apostle's words were meant to convey praise of Felix, and to make the most of whatever could be said in his favour.†

(2) Another objection is raised from the marriage of Drusilla and Felix.

It was only in the year 53 that the father of Drusilla (or rather her brother Agrippa) treated with Azizus, king of Emessa, about the marriage which he (the king) wished to contract with Drusilla; and the terms were agreed on that Azizus should be circumcised, and should conform to the religion of the Jews. And then the marriage took place. Now these preliminary arrangements and the marriage occurred in the year 53: How then could Drusilla be the wife of Felix by Pentecost that same year? It was not so soon that she left Azizus and married Felix; consequently S. Paul's imprisonment must be deferred to a later date.

After weighing well this objection, we find it to be of no force to induce us to change our chronology, for there is no difficulty in solving it. Josephus writes:

> "Claudius having now completed the twelfth year of his reign (ἤδη πεπληρώκως) gave Agrippa the Tetrarchy of Philip and Batanea, and as a further addition Trachonitis, together with Abila. Hereupon Agrippa, laden with these gifts of the Emperor, gave his sister Drusilla in marriage to Azizus, king of Emessa, on consenting to be circumcised ... Not much after, however, the marriage of Drusilla and Azizus was dissolved. ... And she, not

---

* *Antiq.* xx. v. 2.
† See Petavius, *De Doctrina tempor.* vol. ii. 1. xi. c. 11, who generally agrees with us in the chronology.

acting rightly, allowed herself to be persuaded to contravene the ordinances of her fathers, and to marry Felix."*

Now, the twelfth year of Claudius was the year 52; but, as the civil year of the Jews began with the new moon of the month Tisri (*i.e.*, September), the twelfth year of Claudius came to an end, for the Jews and Josephus, with the month of September, 52; and the remaining autumn months of 52 belonged to the thirteenth year of Claudius. We may then very well place the marriage of Drusilla with Azizus in the last quarter of 52 or the beginning of 53 : Josephus does not in any way lead us to think that the preliminary arrangements occupied much time. He says, on the other hand, that shortly after the marriage was contracted it was dissolved, and that Drusilla was married to Felix. This, certainly, might easily have taken place within the earlier months of the year 53, and, consequently, there was nothing to hinder Drusilla from being the wife of Felix shortly after Pentecost that same year.

We may remark also what Josephus says in the following chapter (n. 4):

"In the first year of the reign of Nero, Azizus, king of the Emesenes, being now dead, Soemus his brother succeeded to the throne."

With the Jews, we must remember, the first year of Nero occupied from October of the year 54 to September (Tisri) of the year 55. Now, from the fact that Josephus, when recording the dissolution of the marriage of Azizus and Drusilla, does not at once speak of the subsequent death of the king, but defers its mention to the next chapter, it is conjectured that an interval of time not altogether inconsiderable intervened between the divorce and the death of Azizus, and this would have been the case if the divorce is referred to the first months of A.D. 53.

(3) But it is still further objected : The question is absolutely decided, as Anger and Wieseler have proved, by the fact that the chronological order of the apostolic journey which S. Paul made the year of his imprisonment—with reference to his sailing from Philippi to Troas (*Acts*, xx. 6-11)—falls in only with the year 58, and with no other year; in particular, not with 53. S. Luke relates that the space of twelve days intervened between the date of leaving Philippi and again leaving Troas, and that the last day spent at Troas was a Sunday, and that the day they left Philippi was that "after the days of Azymes." Consequently, they sailed

* *Antiq.* xx. vii. 1, 2.

from Philippi on a Wednesday. Now, in the year 58 the week of Azymes was from Tuesday, March 28th, until Tuesday, April 4th. And so S. Paul left Philippi Wednesday, April 5th, arrived at Troas in five days, remained there from Monday, April 10th, until Monday, April 17th. And on Sunday, the 16th, happened what is narrated in the Acts concerning Eutyches, &c.*

To this we reply, that Wieseler, in his calculation, endeavours to prove that this voyage of S. Paul did not take place in the years 56, 57, or 59 (s. 115), but he says nothing with regard to the year 53. Von Gunpach,† on the other hand, argues against Wieseler that this apostolic journey of S. Paul is to be assigned to the year 59. Patrizzi, however, shows, in his Commentary on the Acts of the Apostles, that the whole account of S. Luke (*Acts*, xx.) is completely in accord with the year 53:

"In the year 53 the solemnity of the Pasch fell on the 24th day of March. About that day Paul arrived at Philippi. . . . The last day of the Azymes that year, Sunday, April 1st, was spent at Philippi; the next day, Monday, April 2nd, Paul and Luke left Philippi. . . . 'We came to them to Troas *in five days*' (v. 6), ἄχρις ἡμέρων πέντε. It is quite certain that the force of the preposition ἄχρις is to exclude all limit of time beyond that which is expressly mentioned. But when the limit stated is indivisible, it is undertain whether this is itself excluded or not; when it is divisible, sometimes the whole, sometimes part only, is included.‡ Now, since Paul and Luke left Philippi, Monday, April 2nd, the space of five days reckoned from the hour they went on board, ended on Saturday, April 7th. . . . 'Where we abode seven days.' The last of these seven days was April 14th. It is quite certain that this seventh day was a Saturday, for on the day following, which was Sunday (v. 7: 'On the first day of the week, v. 11, at "daylight"), Paul departed.' Consequently, this day cannot be included in the number of the seven days he remained at Troas." §

S. Paul's Journey from Troas to Jerusalem according to Patrizzi's Chronology.

A.D. 53.

April 15. The fellow-voyagers of S. Paul set out from Troas early in the morning of that day, which was Sunday, in hope of reaching Jerusalem before May 14th, on which day, that year 53, fell the Feast of Pentecost. From Troas they sail to Assos, where they take S. Paul on board, who had gone thither by land; they touch at Mitylene. (*Acts*, xx. 13, 14.)

---

* Wieseler, *Chronologie, &c.*, s. 118.

† *Ueber den altjudischen Kalender.* Brussel u. Leipzic, 1848.

‡ See examples in the Note ad *Viger. De præcip. Græcæ diction. idiotism.* c. vii. sect. ix. ed. *Herman.*

§ *In Act. Apost. Commentarium*, p. 161. Romæ 1867.

April 16. They come over against Chios. (v. 15.)
,, 17. They arrive at Samos. (Ib.)
,, 18. They came to Miletus. For Paul had determined to sail by Ephesus, lest he should be stayed any time in Asia. For he hasted, if it were possible for him, to keep the day of Pentecost at Jerusalem. And, sending from Miletus to Ephesus, he called the ancients of the Church. (vv. 15-17.)
,, 19. These meet him at Miletus. (vv. 17-38.)
,, 20. Paul and his companions leaving Miletus came to Coos. (xxi. 1.)
,, 21. They touch at Rhodes (Ib.), and
,, 22. Arrive at Patara. (Ib.)
,, 24. They sail past Cyprus. (v. 3.)
,, 26. They come to Tyre. (Ib.)
May 3. The last of the seven days they tarried at Tyre. (v. 4.)
,, 4. Sailing from Tyre, they arrive at Ptolemais. (v. 7.)
,, 5. They abide one day with the brethren at Ptolemais. (Ib.)
,, 6. From Ptolemais they come by land to Cæsarea. (v. 8.)
,, 11. The last day of their abode at Cæsarea. (8-14.)
,, 12. They leave Cæsarea for Jerusalem. (vv. 15, 16.)
,, 13. They arrive at Jerusalem. (v. 17.)
,, 14. The Feast of Pentecost. (v. 18.)

SECTION III.

NOTICES OF THE BISHOPS OF ROME AND THEIR TIMES UNTIL THE CLOSE OF THE SUB-APOSTOLIC AGE.

THE Apostle S. PETER was, from the date of our Lord's Ascension [A.D. 29], the Head of the Church on earth, the Vicar of Christ, and chief Pastor of all the faithful. He held, as we have seen, the Roman See from 42 to 67, when, on the 29th of June, he was, together with S. Paul, crowned in Rome with a glorious martyrdom. Authors are not, indeed, all agreed as to the year and day of S. Peter's martyrdom; but the opinion we have followed is the one by far most solidly founded.

We have already set forth the principal noteworthy points with regard to S. Peter's episcopate; but some others still remain to claim our attention.

That abundant fruits resulted from his preaching in the city of Rome may be inferred both from his own Epistles and those of S. Paul, and also from certain indications of profane authors. S. Paul salutes many Christians in his Epistle to the Romans, and in his Epistle to the Philippians, written from his prison in Rome, he says:

> "All the saints salute you, especially those of Cæsar's household." *

Whence we see that, even of the Emperor's household, there were some converted to the faith. According to a Roman tradition, amongst converts of high rank was eminent *S. Petronilla*, whose name, however, probably did not come, as some have supposed, from her being a spiritual daughter of S. Peter, but from Petro, her father or grandfather; for it was customary amongst the Romans to form in this way the names of females.

Pudens also, a Roman Senator, was, with his family, amongst the first to embrace the Christian religion; and in his house S. Peter is said to have lived at Rome.

We must here record what Tacitus relates in his Annals.† How a noble lady, *Pomponia Græcina*, the wife of Plautius, on his

---

* *Phil.* iv. 22.   † L. xiii. c. xxxii. A.U. 811.

return from Britain, was accused of some foreign superstition; and on the affair being left to the husband's discretion, she was, after a private investigation before members of the family, declared innocent. Pomponia lived to an advanced age, and is spoken of as spending her last forty years in a fashion of uninterrupted mourning and melancholy. The learned are generally agreed that under the term *foreign superstition* is meant the Christian religion. What is here described as forty years of mourning and melancholy may well accord with the life of a holy Christian matron, as this appeared to the eyes of a heathen. For, since in those days, lust, crime, and idolatry were everywhere prevalent, Christians lived a life of corresponding severity, absenting themselves from the public games, scandalous spectacles, unbridled feastings and banquetings so universally frequented. Christians thus came to be regarded as people living in misery and sadness, and often excited the hatred and ill-will of such as felt that their own dissolute way of living was thereby rebuked. Now Pomponia Græcina lived till the times of Domitian, that is, until the year 83, and the forty years mentioned by Tacitus will take us back to the year 43; so that shortly after S. Peter's arrival in Rome, this lady appears to have been converted to Christianity. Some think that Pomponia was identical with Lucina, a noble matron of apostolic times, after whom several cemeteries were called, and whose name many holy women adopted later on.

Acte, also a freed slave of Nero, and for a time his concubine, is thought by some, and on no slight grounds, to have been converted to Christianity after she had been cast off by the Emperor.

We do not know for certain what was the number of Christians at Rome in S. Peter's time; we may, however, suppose that it amounted to some thousands. The whole population of the city was then probably two millions.

At first the Christian religion was not legally proscribed, but its profession was quite free; for Judaism was expressly recognised by the Roman laws, and enjoyed protection, especially under Julius Cæsar and Augustus. The Jews were, indeed, persecuted from time to time, but these persecutions were but brief and passing. The Emperor Claudius, in the year 42, confirmed the privileges granted to the Jews. Some time after, however, he published edicts against the Jews, when disturbances were caused by them, perhaps on occasion of the stir that arose through the preaching of Christianity. Then again, for some years later, they dwelt at Rome in quiet, and at the beginning of Nero's reign were there in great numbers. The same legal toleration was extended to the Christians also; and this, at first, was not from arbitrary confusion with the Jews, but because the Christians, differing from the former only in their belief that the expected Messiah was come, whilst in other respects they reverenced the Jewish religion, were looked on by the Roman law as a sect of Judaism, and so enjoyed the same liberty as the Jews. This was the case, not only with the Jewish converts, but also with the Gentile Christians, though these latter did not observe the ceremonial Jewish law. For, before the preaching of Christianity, Gentiles were used not unfrequently to join themselves to the religion of the Jews, either as proselytes of righteousness (justitiæ)—and these embraced entire Judaism—or as proselytes of the gate (portæ), God-fearing men (timentes Deum, οἱ σεβόμενοι τὸν Θέον), who, though not obliged to observe the ritual law, abandoned their Gentile idolatry and embraced the monotheism of the Jews. This was not forbidden by Roman law; and the Gentiles converted to Christianity were considered as belonging to this sort of proselytes.

From what has been said, we can understand how ancient writers frequently assert that the originators of persecutions against the Christians were Jews. Thus, we find in the Acts that the Jews raised tumults against the Apostles in their preaching, and against the Christian converts, and even brought their grievances and accusations before the Roman tribunals. The disturbances at Rome under Claudius—spoken of by Suetonius as got up "by one Chrestus," but really on account of Christ, through the preaching of Christianity—were evidently of this sort. Claudius thereupon issued an edict banishing from Rome, though for a short time only, all who were reckoned as Jews. The Christians were certainly affected by this decree, not indeed as Christians, but as Jews.

Afterwards, when the Jews were now being driven from the tribunals in their prosecutions of the Christians, they excited the populace against them; striving to persuade the multitude that a new and infamous sect was sprouting forth from the bosom of Judaism, a sect utterly irreligious and atheistical, which they themselves, as Jews, altogether reprobated; protesting, at the same time, against the protection and privileges granted by Roman laws to themselves being extended to this sect.

As many more were converted to Christianity from the Gentiles than from the Jews, and the number of Christians was daily increasing through these Gentile converts, the attention of the people was soon turned to the Christian religion; and suspicions, fears, the very worst opinions, aversion, and hatred against Christians soon began to spread amongst a credulous populace. Hence the legality of Christianity did not last long. For when the Jewish Synagogue, whence Christianity took its origin, persisting in their protests against the Christian religion, cast out and persecuted its adherents, the circumstances of the times demanded that the Roman State should by law either recognise that religion and tolerate it equally with that of the Jews, or should legally proscribe it. The course that was taken by different emperors we shall see later on.

Reliable tradition testifies that during the episcopate of S. Peter at Rome disciples were sent by him also to other countries to preach the faith, and to preside over the Churches. S. Innocent I., A.D. 410, shows this in his Epistle to Decentius, Bishop of Eugubium, in the following words:

"Who knows not or does not call to mind that what was delivered by Peter, the Prince of the Apostles, to the Roman Church, and is kept to this day, ought to be preserved by all? Especially since it is manifest that no one founded Churches for all Italy, the Gauls, the Spains, in Africa, Sicily, and the adjacent isles, save those whom the venerable Apostle Peter, or his successors, constituted priests. Or let them read whether in these provinces any other of the Apostles is found, or is recorded, to have taught. But those who do not so read, because they find it nowhere, ought to follow what the Roman Church keeps, from whom it is clear they received their origin, lest by going after strange assertions they should seem to pass over the head of institutions."

Moreover, in very many parts are found traditions of the disciples sent by Peter, and of the propagation of Christianity through them. Thus in Tuscany Paulinus is said to have founded the Church at Lucca, Romulus at Fiesoli, Apollinaris at Ravenna, all disciples of S. Peter. When S. Paul was drawing near to Rome, "on the second day," says S. Luke, "we came to Puteoli, where finding brethren, we were desired to tarry with them seven days." [*] Thus so early as the year 56 the Christian religion was received at Puteoli, and the first Bishop of that town is said to have been S. Patrobas, whom S. Paul salutes in his Epistle to the Romans.[†] In Campania, also, the Christian religion was early propagated; and that there were Christians in Pompeii when that city was entombed in 79 is attested by an inscription discovered there in

---

[*] *Acts*, xxviii. 13, 14.   [†] *Rom.* xvi. 14.

our own days—*Audi Christianos sævos olores* (cygnos): by which words there is seeming allusion to the persecution of Nero. The first Bishop of Beneventum was Photinus, sent by S. Peter, as testified by all the Martyrologies; of Bari, Maurus; of Capua, Priscus; of Naples, Aspres; of Sicily, Philip Agyriensis and Marcian, all of whom trustworthy tradition records as having been appointed by S. Peter.

That S. Peter sent several disciples into Gaul is held on good grounds by many writers. Not to mention others, the following words, addressed (450) by the Gallic Bishops of the province of Vienne to S. Leo, are of the highest authority:

"It is known in all the regions of Gaul, nor is it unknown to the holy Roman Church, that the city of Arles first in all Gaul merited to have S. Trophimus as its Bishop (sacerdotem), sent thither by the most Blessed Peter, and from them the blessing of faith and religion was diffused by degrees over other regions of Gaul."*

With regard to Spain, the ancient tradition is very probable that after S. Paul himself passed a year in Spain, seven Bishops, with Torquatus at their head, were sent thither by SS. Peter and Paul, and that they preached the Gospel in that country. It would be too long to enter further into details; but so far it is clear that S. Peter, the first supreme Pontiff, propagated the kingdom of God—in other words, the Christian religion—far and wide, into many countries.

From these earliest times, too, are to be derived the distinctions of METROPOLITAN and PATRIARCHAL Churches. The civil metropolis of a province became the ecclesiastical metropolis from the institution, it seems, of the Apostles themselves, in so far as they settled that those who were Bishops in metropolitan cities of the empire should be ecclesiastical metropolitans. The Ninth Canon of the Synod of Antioch, held in the year 341,† accords with this opinion. It runs thus:

"In the several regions it is right for the Bishops to know that the metropolitan Bishop has care of the whole province, wherefore all around who may have matters to transact have recourse to the metropolis. Hence it hath seemed good that he should both excel in honour, and that henceforth the Bishops should not act independently of him, according to the ancient rule laid down by our Fathers."

* Natal. Alex. *H. E.* sæc. i. *Dissert.* xv.

† Before this date the General Council of Nice, in the Seventh Canon, whilst confirming to the Church of Jerusalem certain honours that it possessed, added "saving the rightful honour of the metropolis," that is, of the Bishop of Antioch, the Patriarch of the East, and of the Bishop of Cæsarea, the Metropolitan of Palestine. (Rohrbacher, *Histoire, &c.* 8mo, 1884, p. 207.)

Now, as we nowhere read of the ancient rule being laid down, it seems to have had no other than apostolic origin. It naturally, moreover, seems very probable that the Apostles should have made some distinction amongst the bishops, so that some should be above others, since this would avail much for putting an end to discussions, allaying strifes, destroying errors, and consulting for the needs of the Churches.

We may say much the same with regard to the origin and institution of the patriarchial dignity. For though the name of patriarchs is referred to the times of the General Council of Chalcedon, still, that their institution and rights are anterior to the First Council of Nice, held in 325, is quite clear from the Sixth Canon of that Council. For in that canon the patriarchial rights of the Bishop of Alexandria, as well as of the Bishops of Rome and Antioch, are confirmed according to ancient custom. But since the origin of this ancient custom, to which the Nicene Fathers appeal, is nowhere found, it is with good reason attributed to the Apostles. It is well, too, to note that originally there were three Patriarchal Sees — Rome, Alexandria, and Antioch; that these three sees were always had in special honour by the ancient Fathers and ecclesiastical writers, from their being founded by S. Peter, the Prince of the Apostles. Thus we see that the very ground of the patriarchal dignity and prerogatives attached to these sees is intimately associated with their apostolic origin. Concerning these patriarchs, the Roman Synod held under S. Gelasius I., A.D. 494 (n. 11), declares:

"The first, therefore, is the See of Peter, the Roman Church . . . the See at Alexandria was consecrated in the name of Blessed Peter by his disciple and evangelist Mark. The third See at Antioch is held honourable by the name of the same Blessed Peter, because he dwelt there before he came to Rome, and there first the name of Christians was given to the new people."*

In the year 64 A.D. the persecution of Nero against the Christians arose on the occasion of the burning of the city in the month of July, which Tacitus records at some length in his Annals.† The conflagration was so great that ten out of the fourteen

---

* See Wouter's *Dissert.* t. i. Diss. xxiv. See also especially *The Throne of the Fisherman*, by T. W. Allies, K.C.S.G. (Burns & Oates, 1887, pp. 47-70), where the learned author treats very profoundly and lucidly of the three Patriarchates, their origin from, and intimate union with, S. Peter, and of their signification in the idea of Providence and in the mind of the Holy Church.

† L. xv. 38-40, 44.

quarters (*regiones*) of the city were destroyed. Whether it took place by accident or by the design of the Emperor, Tacitus says is uncertain, and that both views have been given out by authors. He himself seems to hold that it was by the order and the caprice of the Emperor. He speaks of the persecution of the Christians as follows:

"But not all human efforts, nor all the largesses of the prince, nor all the means used to appease the gods before the people, could do away in popular belief with the infamous imputation that the conflagration had been pre-arranged and ordered. To make an end, therefore, of this rumour, Nero caused to be accused, and to be put to most cruel tortures, persons detested for their abominable crimes, whom the populace called Christians. Christ, the author of this name, had suffered punishment under the Procurator Pontius Pilate in the reign of Tiberius. The deadly superstition, repressed for a time, began again to break out not only in Judæa, where the evil first arose, but also in the city, where all that is everywhere else atrocious and shameful congregates and finds welcome. Those first seized turned informers, and through their evidence a vast multitude were convicted, quite as much, and more indeed, for their hatred of the human race than for the crime of the burning. And as they were dying they were made a sport of. Some had their bodies covered with the hides of wild beasts, and so perished by the mangling of dogs; or they were fastened to crosses, or set on fire, so that when the daylight failed, their burning might serve for light during the night. Nero had lent his own gardens for the spectacle, and there he exhibited the games of the circus, himself in the garb of a charioteer, either mingling with the people or driving his car. Hence though they were a pack of criminals who well deserved the worst punishment, yet their case excited pity, for people felt that it was not from any motive of the public good, but for the gratification of one man's cruelty, that they were put to death."

Suetonius also, writing on Nero (c. xvi.), speaks of the same persecution thus:

"Severe punishments were inflicted on the Christians, a set of men belonging to a new and wicked superstition."

Now it appears, from the account of Tacitus, that the Christians were at first prosecuted on the charge of causing the conflagration, but afterwards that the very profession of Christianity was held to be a crime before the tribunals. Thus, then, the Christian religion, which up to that time had been tolerated, was now legally condemned, and a distinction between Christianity and Judaism was sanctioned by the laws. Reumont[*] is of opinion that the persecution of Nero was directed against Jews as well as Christians, both being alike an object of hatred to the Roman populace, and that what Tacitus says of some of the

[*] *Gesch. d. Stadt Rom.* i. sect. 369.

accused incriminating others, refers to the Jews giving information against the Christians. It seems more probable, however, that the persecution of Nero was confined to the Christians; for by this time, owing to the accusations of the Jews, they had become odious to the credulous populace, and hence it was not difficult for Nero to make them suspected of causing the conflagration. With regard to what Tacitus says, that some of the accused gave information about others, this may have happened, from the fact that the Christian religion had been legal up to that time; and so the Christians, being too much off their guard, might have imprudently made mention of others before the judges. It is clear from Tacitus that the number of those who suffered must have been very great. The persecution went on during the years following until the death of Nero. And this is easy to understand from the fact that now the very profession of Christianity was a recognised crime; and so, when all suspicion of incendiarism was over, the reason for persecuting the Christians remained still as before. This persecution, too, appears to have spread to the regions in the neighbourhood of Rome, but not to other provinces. We have already seen that in the year 67 SS. Peter and Paul received the crown of martyrdom.

S. LINUS, writes Eusebius, succeeded to S. Peter (A.D. 67-79):

"After the martyrdom of Paul and Peter, the first to receive the episcopate of the Roman Church was Linus. Of him Paul makes mention in the Epistle he wrote from the city of Rome to Timothy, amongst the salutations which are read at the end of the Epistle: Eubulus, he says, and Pudens, and Linus, and Claudia salute thee."*

With what Eusebius here says of Linus the other early records agree. From them we learn also that he was Italian by birth, and held the See for eleven or twelve years. He had already, as is probable, assisted S. Peter in the government of the Church. Of his pontificate it is recorded that from precept of S. Peter he ordained that a woman who entered the church should have her head veiled; and an ancient anonymous author of a work against heretics, entitled *Prætextatus*, says that Linus condemned the followers of Menander, a disciple of Simon Magus, and declared that the God of the Old Testament is the Creator of all things, and that there is nothing evil in things of their own nature. Since Menander was actually at that time disseminating his doctrines, what we are thus told is exceedingly probable. During

* H. E. l. iii. c. 2. See Iren. *Adv. Hær.* l. iii. c. 3.

the pontificate of Linus occurred the destruction of Jerusalem, when the Roman Christians beheld the triumph of Vespasian and Titus over the conquered Jews, and saw the prophecies of Christ fulfilled. In the Felician Catalogue it is said of Linus: *Martyrio coronatur;* and this could well happen, since from time to time various Christians were brought before the tribunals and condemned, even under those emperors who raised no general persecution. At all events, that Linus laboured and suffered much for religion, and that he was a man of the greatest merit and sanctity, is inferred from the fact that his name is commemorated in the Canon of Mass immediately after the Apostles. In the Felician Catalogue it is said: *Qui et sepultus est juxta corpus B. Petri in Vaticano.* And as a fact, when the restoration of the Confession of S. Peter was being made under Urban VIII., a sarcophagus was found with the simple inscription: LINUS; and other arguments show how true it is that the successors of S. Peter were buried close by him.

Here we must remark that some ancient writers, and amongst them Tertullian, thought that S. Peter's first successor was Clement. S. Jerome thus refers to them when writing about Clement:

"After Peter he was the fourth Bishop of Rome, since Linus was the second, Anacletus the third, although most of the Latins suppose that Clement was second after the Apostle Peter."*

But most of the ancient Fathers and writers, as S. Irenæus, Eusebius, S. Optatus of Milevis, S. Epiphanius, S. Augustine, S. Prosper, as well as the ancient Catalogues, agree that S. Linus was the immediate successor of S. Peter. The reason, perhaps, why some reckoned Clement next after S. Peter was because Clement is made to say in his Epistle to James, that he was consecrated Bishop by S. Peter, as also Tertullian affirms (*De Præscript.*, c. 32). But though information like this, derived even from apocryphal books, such as this Epistle, is not to be despised, yet it is altogether outweighed by the testimonies above given. Still, the opinion of Baronius, Cotelier, Tillemont, Natalis Alexander, and others is not improbable—viz., that Clement was really ordained Bishop by S. Peter, and after the Apostle's martyrdom refused the pontificate out of humility, and that Linus and Cletus were successively chosen to undertake the government of the Church. Possibly not Clement only, but Linus and Cletus also,

* *De Viris illust.* CLEMENS.

were made Bishops by S. Peter, to be his coadjutors and administrators in the many difficult circumstances of the time, and on account of his own frequent absence from the city, and elected afterwards successively to rule the Church.

SS. CLETUS—ANACLETUS (A.D. 79-91). It is a matter of controversy whether the Pontiffs who, after Linus, are named Cletus and Anacletus or Anencletus, were really two successive Popes, or whether this twofold name denotes one and the same person. Before briefly touching on this point, we will first give what is said of these Pontiffs in the Felician Catalogue:

"Cletus, by country a Roman, of the region Vicus Patricii—his father Æmilianus. He held the See twelve years, one month, and six days. He was in the times of Vespasian and Titus. He was crowned with martyrdom. According to the precept of the Blessed Peter, he ordained twenty-five Presbyters in the city of Rome in the month of December, and he was buried by the side of the body of Blessed Peter in the Vatican (VI. Kal. Maias), April 26."

If what is here said of the ordination of twenty-five priests means that they were for the city of Rome, we may infer that the number of Christians was already very great.[*]

In the Liberian Catalogue Clement is put in the third place and Cletus in the fourth; whilst in the Felician it is the contrary. Here in both these Catalogues follow Anacletus; of whom the Felician speaks thus:

"Anacletus, a Greek by birth, from Athens—his father Antiochus. He held the See twelve years, ten months, and three days. He was in the times of Domitian, &c. He constructed and arranged the monument of Blessed Peter—having been himself ordained priest by Blessed Peter—where the Bishops were to be buried, and where at length he himself also was buried. He held two ordinations, five priests, three deacons, bishops for different places, seven in the month of December; and the See was vacant fifteen days."

If Cletus and Anacletus are one and the same person, the above should seem partly to be ascribed to Cletus.

With regard to the controversy on the matter, the question cannot, it appears, be decided with any certainty. We may observe the following points. Several ancient Fathers and writers

---

[*] It is not easy to form any correct idea of the number of Christians in those early days from the very vague way in which ancient writers speak on this matter. From the Epistle of Pope Cornelius to Fabian of Antioch (A.D. 252) it appears that there were then in Rome forty-four priests, seven deacons, &c. Thence, the learned infer that there were then about 50,000 Christians in the city. However, this calculation seems too small. At any rate the number of twenty-five priests in the time of S. Cletus indicates that Christianity had made great spread in Rome.

name one only, either Cletus or Anacletus: Caius, the priest mentioned by Eusebius (*H. E.* 1. v. c. 8), calls S. Victor the thirteenth Bishop of Rome from S. Peter; and S. Cyprian (Ep. 71, *ad Pompeium*) calls Hyginus the ninth Bishop of the city of Rome. Now, if Cletus and Anacletus were two distinct Pontiffs, Victor would be the fourteenth and Hyginus the tenth. Moreover, there is the greatest difficulty in arranging the chronology, if twelve years are to be reckoned separately for both one and the other; whereas there is perfect accord if these twelve years are set down for one person only. But, on the other hand, Cletus and Anacletus are found distinct in the old Catalogues, and since these are based on the Chronicle of Hippolytus, and perhaps on the writings of Hegesippus, the argument thence derived is evidently not without force. It hence would seem that such was the tradition of the Roman Church, and to this tradition much deference is due. Also the author of the *Carmen contra Marcionem* has as follows:

> "Post quem (Linum) Cletus et ipse gregem suscepit ovilis.
> Hujus Anacletus successor sorte locatus:
> Quem sequitur Clemens." *

The similarity of the name might easily be the reason why many in early times confounded Cletus and Anacletus, and left out one of them in the list of Popes. Caius and Cyprian perhaps reckoned the Pontiffs without including S. Peter. Since, then, there remain reasons of some weight for holding Cletus and Anacletus to be two distinct Popes, we leave the question undecided.†

S. CLEMENT (A.D. 91-100) succeeded to the See of Peter about A.D. 91. S. Irenæus says of him:

> "In the third place from the Apostles the episcopate falls to Clement, who both saw the Apostles themselves, and conferred with them; and he had the preaching of the Apostles still resounding in his ears, and their tradition before his eyes; and in this he was not alone, for as yet many who had been taught by the Apostles were then surviving. When, then, under the same Clement, a no small dissension had arisen amongst the brethren at Corinth, the Church of Rome wrote a most powerful letter to the Corinthians, with a view to restore them to peace, to repair their faith, and to announce to them the tradition which but recently it had received from the Apostles."‡

---

* De Rossi is of opinion that this hymn was written in the third century. (*Bullet.* v. p. 85.)

† See more at length De Smedt, *Dissert.* vii. c. i. art. 1, who holds as more probable—nay, as certain—the opinion that Cletus and Anacletus were not distinct; so also P. Columbier, "Les premiers successions de S. Pierre," *Revue des Quest. Hist.* t. xix. 1876, p. 881.

‡ *Adv. Hær.* l. iii. c. 8.

THE PONTIFICATE OF S. CLEMENT.

In the Liberian and Felician Catalogues Clement is described as "Roman by birth, of the Region, Cœlius Mons—his father Faustinus." According to one Roman tradition, Clement was of a noble family, related to Vespasian, and a relative of T. Flavius Clemens, of consular rank, who, under Domitian, with his wife Flavia Domitilla, was brought before the tribunal charged with being a Christian. The present Church of S. Clement is said to be on the site of his paternal house; and this tradition receives confirmation from the Church, being in that part of Rome where the most noble families used to reside. Of this same Church says S. Jerome:

"The Church built in Rome preserves to us his memory down to the present day." *

In the Felician Catalogue and the Liber Pontificalis is ascribed to Clement the ecclesiastical division of the city, in these words:

"He made seven regions (districts, quarters), and divided them to faithful Notaries of the Church, who should with solicitude and care make diligent inquiry concerning the acts of the martyrs, each in his own respective region."

This distribution appears, with good reason, to be assigned to Clement, for of its great antiquity there is no doubt. Rome had been divided by Augustus into fourteen civil regions: these seven ecclesiastical regions did not, however, correspond with the civil regions. The number of seven is probably in allusion to the number of the seven deacons.

During Clement's pontificate arose the second persecution of the Christians, in the last years of the Emperor Domitian.† Of this persecution Eusebius writes:

"Domitian having exercised his cruelty against many, and unjustly slain no small number of noble and illustrious men at Rome, and having, without cause, punished vast numbers of honourable men with exile and the confiscation of their property, at length established himself as the successor of Nero, in his hatred and hostility to God. He was the second that raised a persecution against us, although his father Vespasian had attempted nothing to our prejudice."‡

Dio Cassius says:

"The same year (U.C. 848) Domitian put to death, amongst many others, Flavius Clemens the Consul, although he was his cousin-german, and was

---

* *De Viris illust.* CLEMENS.
† After the death of Nero (June, A.D. 68), Galba, Otho, and Vitellius were rivals for the Empire, and soon miserably perished. In December, 69, F. Vespasian came to the throne; he was succeeded by Titus (A.D. 79), who died September, 81. To him succeeded his younger brother Tit. Fl. Domitian, killed in 96. After him reigned Nerva (96-98), and then Trajan (98-117).
‡ *H. E.* iii. 17.

married to Flavia Domitilla, also related to him (Domitian) by blood—a charge of impiety against the gods being brought against both of them. And on the same charge many others who had gone astray into Judaism were likewise condemned, some of whom were put to death, and others deprived of their property. Domitilla was only banished to Pandateria."*

The following appear to have been the causes of this persecution. Domitian was a cruel tyrant, very suspicious, and of such excessive pride as to arrogate to himself the name of Lord and God; whilst at the same time he displayed an ostentatious zeal for the national religion of the Romans. Hence, the propagation of Christianity exceedingly displeased him, and the more so, because several of the imperial family had embraced it.

It appears that many other members of the Flavian family were Christians: this fact may be due in some measure to Pomponia Græcina, who, as monuments of antiquity go to prove, was in all probability of the same family, as was also, it is said, Pope Clement himself. That Christianity had by that time made its way into many noble families is certain from tombs of that age recently discovered in the cemeteries or catacombs of S. Lucina and S. Callistus. These show that there were Christians in the families of the Octavii, Cæcilii, Æmilii, and Æmiliani; also amongst the descendants of Atticus the friend of Cicero, and of Asinius Pollio.

It is said, moreover, that the events of the life and history of Christ, His reign and kingdom, caused Domitian to entertain fears for himself; for Hegesippus, as quoted by Eusebius,† tells us that the Emperor had brought to him from Judæa the remaining descendants to be found of David, who were of the kindred of our Lord; but that when he saw that they were only poor simple labouring men he let them go.

Besides the celebrated Epistle of S. Clement to the Corinthians, which is undoubtedly authentic, there are extant also under his name a second Epistle, or rather a Homily, to the Corinthians, and two Epistles to the brethren and sisters in praise of virginity, but the genuineness of these is questioned. With regard to S. Clement's first Epistle, it is well to say something, because it is a remarkable document in vindication of the primacy and authority of the Roman Pontiff. No small disturbance had arisen in the Church of Corinth, and matters had gone so far that priests, constituted by the Apostles or by apostolic men, with the consent of the whole Church, most conspicuous, too, for the purity

---

* *Domitian*, c. 114.   † *H. E.* l. iii. cc. 19 and 20.

of their life and doctrine, had been cast out of their ministry.*
Now, to remedy this unhappy state of things, although the
Apostle S. John was still living, it was considered more advisable
to consult the Roman Apostolic See. Clement assented to the
desire of the Corinthians, and gave answer on the matter of their
consultation by a most powerful letter (ἱκανωτάτῃ, Iren.), according to the rule of the Apostles—viz., that they were unjustly cast
out, whose election had both been ratified by the unanimous
consent of the Church, and whose manner of life was pure from
all fault and blame.†

Though the Epistle is inscribed: "The Church of God which
dwells in Rome to the Church of God which dwells in Corinth,"
yet, according to the unanimous tradition of antiquity, the Epistle
is that of Clement himself.

"Clement preferred, however," remarks Constant, "to write it in the
name of his Church rather than in his own name; either because at that
time bishops were not wont to act without taking counsel of their Church, as
Cyprian recorded of himself in his Epistle v. to his clergy in these words:
'Of myself alone I could not answer; for from the beginning of my episcopate I determined to take no step of my own private judgment, without
your counsel and the consent of the people;' or, again, lest he might seem to
be partial and one-sided if, in his endeavour to restore due honour and
respect for their priests among the Corinthians, either himself alone, or together
with the clergy but without the people, he should address the Church at
Corinth. Besides, it seemed only meet and proper that as the Corinthians
had written not to Clement alone, but to the Romans, that Clement should
answer back not in his own name, but in that of the Romans."‡

As to the date of the Epistle, Cotelier, Tillemont, Funk, and
others think with good reason that it was written about the year

---

* It seems, from the words of the Epistle, that with them the Bishop of
Corinth also had been deprived of his See.

† It seems but reasonable to infer, from the nature and whole context of
the Epistle, that Clement or the Roman Church had been consulted by the
presbyters of Corinth, either by writing or by deputation, as has been hitherto
the general opinion of authors; though this cannot perhaps be conclusively
drawn from the words, βράδιον νομίζομεν ἐπιστροφὴν πεποιῆσθαι περὶ τῶν
ἐπιζητουμένων παρ' ὑμῖν πραγμάτων. (c. i.) For, as Funk remarks, it is not said
παρ' ὑμῶν, but παρ' ὑμῖν; the rendering consequently is not, as some would
have it: "We think we have too tardily turned our attention to those things
that are being asked of by you;" but: "Things that are being sought for
amongst you." However, if Clement, without their previous consultation,
took in hand the affairs of the Corinthians by means of his Epistle (ἱκανωτάτην,
Iren., μεγάλην τε καὶ θαυμασίαν, Euseb. iii. 16), his authority does not thereby
appear less. He speaks with great vigour, and c. 63 recommends obedience,
and announces his intention of sending legates for the restoration of peace.

‡ Epistolæ R. R. Pontificum, Epist. i. Clementis, n. i. nota a. We return
to this matter later on in Part III. ch. xix.

97, at the close of Domitian's persecution. For the Epistle begins with these words:

> "On account of sudden and successive calamities and misfortunes which have happened to us, too tardily, brethren, we deem we have turned our attention to those things which are desired amongst you."

Hence we may gather that at that time calamities which had recently befallen the Roman Church were now at an end. This fits in very well with the close of Domitian's persecution. Some understand the above words as referring to Nero's persecution, and would date the Epistle soon after its cessation. But against this view are arguments both intrinsic and extrinsic. First: Clement (c. 44), after commending the prudent foresight of the Apostles:

> "Those, therefore, who have been constituted by them, or in succession by other conspicuous men, and have obtained for a long time excellent testimony from all, such we consider are unjustly deposed from their office."

words which show that now some considerable time had elapsed since the Apostles.

Besides, Clement's pontificate, according to Irenæus, Eusebius, and Jerome, is to be referred to the times of Domitian; and Irenæus and Eusebius relate that it was under Clement's pontificate the schism arose at Corinth, and that the Epistle was written by him. It is arbitrary, therefore, to suppose that the Epistle was written by Clement when he was not yet Pope, but assisting Linus in the administration of the Church.

Those who contend that the Epistle was written immediately after Nero's persecution base their proof on what is found in c. 41:

> "Not everywhere, brethren, are offered continual sacrifices, whether votive, or for sin and crime, but at Jerusalem only."

From these words Grabe and Hefele consider it certain that the Temple at Jerusalem was then standing; for otherwise it would not be said "are offered," in the present tense, but "were formerly offered." These learned authors fail here to advert to the common mode of speech, whereby, with a view to set past events more graphically before others, the narrator expresses them in the present tense. The words mean no more than this: According to the prescription of the law sacrifices are not offered in every place, but only in Jerusalem. And by this comparison Clement admonishes the Corinthians that they, too, should reverently receive and keep the order of oblations and offices appointed by the Apostles. This explanation is confirmed by what follows:

"They, therefore, who do anything beyond what is in accordance with His will are punished with death;"

for certainly such severity in the Jewish laws did not continue in force until shortly before the year 70, when the Temple was destroyed. Some, perhaps, may think it strange, if the Epistle was written after the persecution of Domitian, that Clement (cc. 5 and 6) should recall to memory the persecution of Nero, rather than that of Domitian, and should say nothing of the illustrious Roman matron Domitilla, when speaking of the sufferings of the Danaïdæ and Dircæ: but we should here remember that Clement's main object was to set forth the example of the Apostles SS. Peter and Paul, on account of the special relation of Paul with the Corinthians, and that only incidentally, in speaking of women, he makes mention of the Danaïdæ and Dircæ.

Eusebius records S. Clement's death as follows: "In the third year of Trajan's reign, Clement Bishop of Rome departed this life, leaving the episcopal charge to Evarestus, after providing for the preaching of the divine word nine years." *

Trajan succeeded Nerva, January 28th, A.D. 98, so that his third year would be 100 A.D. In the Felician Catalogue, and in the *Liber Pontificalis*, Clement is said to have been crowned with martyrdom, and buried in Greece. Pope Zozimus (A.D. 418), the African bishops, Rufinus, and Gregory the Great, also call him a martyr. The Acts of his martyrdom date from the fourth century, and were afterwards arranged by Metaphrastes. According to these Acts, Clement was banished by Trajan to the Chersonese (Crimea), and there soon after was precipitated into the sea. Though these Acts of themselves have not sufficient authority, yet that he was a martyr, and died elsewhere than in Rome, is held on good grounds according to ancient tradition.

S. EVARISTUS (A.D. 100-108). In the Felician Catalogue we read:

"Evaristus, a Greek by birth, from Antioch—his father Judas, from Bethlehem—held the See nine years, ten months, and two days; he was crowned with martyrdom. He divided titles in Rome to the priests, and ordained seven deacons, who should guard the Bishop as he preached; for the sake of the style of truth. . . . He was buried near the body of Blessed Peter in the Vatican."

At this time a fresh persecution under Trajan broke out, and raged in many places, from the hatred of the heathen against the

* *H. E.* iii. 34.

Christians. Trajan put in force against them the law passed against the Hetæriæ, or secret societies. It was in this persecution that Pliny the younger, prefect of Bithynia, wrote to Trajan his celebrated letter, asking for special instructions as to how he was to deal with the Christians, and received the Emperor's reply. In order to illustrate the condition of Christians at that time we give both one and the other document:

"I have never been present," writes Pliny, "at the trials of Christians, and therefore do not know either the nature of their crime, or the degree of the punishment, or how far examination should go. And I have been in great hesitation whether age made any difference, or the tender should not be distinguished from the strong; whether they should be pardoned upon repentance, or, when once a man has been a Christian, his ceasing to be so should not profit him; or whether the mere profession without any crime, or whether the crimes involved in the profession should be punished. In the meantime, with regard to those brought before me as Christians, my practice has been this: I asked them if they were Christians? If they admitted this, I put the question a second and a third time, threatening them with death. If they persevered, I ordered them to be led away to execution. For whatever it was that they were thus confessing, I had no doubt that stubbornness and inflexible obstinacy deserved punishment. There were others of a like infatuation, but as being Roman citizens I directed them to be sent to the city. Presently the crime spreading from being under prosecution, as is usual, several incidents happened. An anonymous delation was sent in to me, containing the names of many who say that they are not Christians, nor ever were. As at my instance they invoked the gods, and made supplication with frankincense and wine to your image, which I had ordered for that purpose to be brought, together with the statues of the gods; and as, moreover, they reviled Christ, none of which things, it is said, real Christians can be induced to do, I thought they might be let go. Others, being accused by a witness, admitted that they were Christians, and presently said that they had been, some three years before, some many years, and some even twenty, but were so no longer. All venerated your image and the statues of the gods, and reviled Christ. But they alleged that the utmost of their fault or error was this: They were accustomed to meet before dawn on a stated day, and addressed themselves in a certain form to Christ as to a god, binding themselves by oath not to any crime, but not to commit theft, robbery, adultery, the breaking of their word, or the refusal to restore a deposit. After this they were wont to separate, and then reassemble to take a common and harmless meal. This, however, they had ceased to do from the publication of my edict forbidding, according to your command, private assemblies. I therefore thought it the more necessary to examine into the truth by putting to the torture two female slaves, who were said to be deaconesses among them. I found, however, nothing but a perverse and immoderate superstition, and so, adjourning the inquiry, I took refuge in consulting you. For the matter seemed to me worthy of consultation, especially on account of the number of those involved in danger. For many of every age, every rank, both sexes, have been already, and will be, endangered, since the contagion of this superstition has spread not only through cities but through villages and country. And it seems capable of being arrested and corrected. At all events, there is proof that the almost deserted temples have begun to be frequented, and the long intermitted rites renewed, and victims for sacrifice are found ready, whereof hitherto there were very few purchasers. Hence it is easy to form an opinion what a number of persons may be reclaimed if pardon be allowed."

To which the Emperor Trajan replies :

"You have pursued the right course, my dear Secundus, in examining the causes of those delated to you as Christians. For no universal rule can be laid down in a certain formula. They are not to be searched after; but if brought before you and convicted, they must be punished. Yet with this condition, that whoever denies that he is a Christian, and makes this plain in fact—that is, by supplicating our gods, even though he has been in past time suspected—shall obtain pardon for his repentance. But anonymous delations must not be admitted for any accusation. This is at once the very worst precedent, and unworthy of our time."

With regard to these letters of Pliny and Trajan, we think well to make the following remarks: 1. From Pliny's Epistle is manifest the very extensive propagation of Christianity in Bithynia. He expressly says that the contagion was widespread, not only through cities, but also through villages and country parts. And this is of special force against certain authors, who from very slight reasons make out that, though it is true that in the first centuries Christianity spread in the cities, still it had hardly any existence in the country. Whereas Tertullian also gives the same evidence as Pliny to the contrary. The heathen, he says,

"Cry out aloud that the state is overrun with us, that Christians are to be found in the country parts, in forts, in islands, and lament as a disaster that every sex, age, and condition, and rank is now going over to their religion."[*]

2. Some consider Trajan's rescript as restraining the persecution of Christians, since it says that they are not to be searched after. It is true that this might to some extent lessen the cruelty of the persecution; but, on the other hand, by the same rescript, the Emperor definitively declared that the Christian religion had no legal existence. Consequently Christians were liable to prosecution in virtue of several laws. Domitius Ulpianus, a pagan lawyer, inimical to the Christians, cites those laws which, in his opinion, might be put in force against Christians—to wit, the Julian law of high treason, laws against sacrilege, laws against magic, laws against foreign superstition and unlawful worship.[†]

[*] *Apolog.* i. 37.
[†] The Treatise of Ulpianus partly survives in the Digests of Justinian.

Even emperors, who in other respects might be fair and equitable, were henceforth unable, without rescinding Trajan's rescript, to protect Christians in any other way than by forbidding accusation.

Under Trajan occurred also the glorious martyrdom of S. IGNATIUS of Antioch, whose seven Epistles constitute so celebrated a monument of the most ancient Christian times. In his Epistle to the Romans (its magnificent inscription we have already recorded) he recommends the Church of Antioch to the Church of Rome in the following words:

"Be ye mindful in your prayers of the Church which is in Syria, which for me has God for its pastor. May Jesus Christ, in place of its bishop, alone rule it and your charity."

Doubtless Pope Evaristus responded to the desire of S. Ignatius. The holy martyr's name was received into the Canon of the Mass, and this was probably done shortly after his martyrdom.

We will briefly make mention of the successive Roman Pontiffs down to Anicetus, whose pontificate recalls to memory S. Polycarp, the disciple of S. John and Bishop of Smyrna, the last surviving on record of those who had known and conversed with any of the Apostles.

S. ALEXANDER (A.D. 108-117), Martyr. (See Euseb. *H.E.* iv. 4, and *Lib. Pontificalem*.) His name is in the Canon of the Mass after that of S. Ignatius.

S. SIXTUS (A.D. 117-127), Martyr. In the *Liber Pontificalis* it is said, amongst other things, of him:

"He ordained that if any bishop should be summoned to the Apostolic See, and return to his diocese, he was not to be received unless he brought commendatory letters with him of the (Apostolic) Patriarch..."

According to S. Irenæus the controversy about the observance of Easter first commenced under S. Sixtus.

S. TELESPHORUS (127-139), Martyr.

S. HYGINUS (139-142). It was from the time of S. Hyginus that the Gnostic heresiarchs, such as Valentinus, Cerdon, and Marcion,* began to come to Rome in order to obtain, if possible, sanction for their doctrines, and at least appearance of communion from the Roman Church, the mother and head of all other Churches; or to prefer their false pretensions and rival claims in the city of Rome. These heretics were manfully opposed by S. Hyginus and his successors.

---

* Eusebius, *H.E.* iv. 10 and 11; S. Epiphanius, *Hæres*. 42 n. 1, 2.

S. Pius (142-157), Martyr, in whose time especially flourished S. Justin Martyr and Hermas, brother of S. Pius and author of the *Pastor*.

S. Anicetus (157-168). S. Jerome thus writes:

"Polycarp, disciple of John the Apostle, and by him ordained Bishop of Smyrna, was chief of all Asia, having seen, and had for his teachers, some of the Apostles and those who had seen the Lord. On account of certain questions about the day of Easter, he came to Rome under the Emperor Antoninus Pius, whilst Anicetus ruled the Church in that city; where he brought back to the faith very many of the believers who had been deceived by the persuasions of Marcion and Valentinus." [*]

Eusebius, writing of the pontificate of S. Victor (190-200 A.D.), says:

"Victor, the Bishop of the Church of Rome, forthwith attempted to cut off from the common unity the Churches of all Asia, together with the neighbouring Churches, as heterodox, and proscribed them by letters, proclaiming all the brethren there utterly excommunicated.[†] But this did not please all the bishops, who, on the contrary, exhorted him to have sentiments of peace, and union, and love towards his neighbours. There are also extant the expressions of some of those who pressed upon Victor with greater severity. Amongst these, too, was Irenæus, who, in a letter which he wrote in the name of the brethren in Gaul over whom he ruled, whilst maintaining the obligation of celebrating the mystery of the Lord's Resurrection on a Sunday only, yet in becoming terms exhorts Victor not to cut off whole Churches who observed the tradition of an ancient custom.... 'Those presbyters (Irenæus writes in his letter to S. Victor) who, before Soter presided over the Church which thou now governest—I mean Anicetus and Pius, Hyginus, Telesphorus and Xystus—neither kept it themselves, nor permitted those with them to observe it (*i.e.*, the ancient custom of the Asian Church); yet, none the less, were they who observed it not, at peace with those who came from other Churches in which it was observed; although to observe it, among those who observed it not, was (an act) more in opposition. Neither at any time were any cast off on account of this form; but those very presbyters before thee who did not observe it sent the Eucharist to those who did observe it. And when the Blessed Polycarp had come to Rome under Anicetus, and they had some little difference between themselves respecting other matters, they immediately were at peace, not disputing much with one another on this head (Easter). For neither could Anicetus persuade Polycarp not to continue the practice which he had always observed with John the disciple of our Lord, and the other Apostles with whom he associated; nor could Polycarp persuade Anicetus to adopt his practice: Anicetus pleading that he was bound to maintain the custom of the presbyters before him. And things being so, they held communion with each other. And, by way of respect, Anicetus yielded to Polycarp (the office of consecrating) the Eucharist, and they separated from each other in peace, both those that observed, and

---

[*] *De vir. illustr.* i. 7.—See Euseb. *H. E.* iv. 14.
[†] Professor Jungmann inclines to the opinion that, most probably Victor's decree of excommunication did not actually take effect.

those that did not observe (the custom), maintaining the peace of the whole Church.' And this same Irenæus, as one whose character answered well to his name, being in this way a peacemaker, exhorted and negotiated such matters as these for the peace of the Churches. And not only to Victor, but likewise to the most of the other rulers of the Churches, he sent letters of exhortation on the agitated question."*

Hegesippus, as we have already said, came to Rome in the pontificate of Anicetus, and from this time forward we see continually bishops and illustrious men resorting from all parts to the Apostolic See, which is in itself an evident recognition of the supreme dignity and authority of the Roman Pontiff.

* Eusebius, *H. E.* v. 24. "The foregoing statement is, in its main incidents, too clear to require any lengthened comment. 1. The authority of Victor to excommunicate the Asian Churches is not denied, even by those very Churches. They resist indeed, but resistance does not imply denial; and yet denial was the readiest method, had they thought it available. 2. The Bishops, who disapproved of the Pope's conduct, reason, remonstrate, exhort, but do not go beyond this."—Waterworth, *A Commentary on the place of S. Peter and his Successors, &c.*, 1871, p. 191.

PART II.
ARCHÆOLOGICAL.

PART II.

ARCHÆOLOGICAL.

CHAPTER I.

THE CEMETERIES OF THE VATICAN, S. PAUL ON THE VIA OSTIENSIS, S. PRISCILLA, AND THE OSTRIANUM.

It must ever remain a subject of the deepest regret that nearly all Christian literature, which was contemporary with the beginning of the Catacombs, should have perished in the flames of the last terrible persecution of Diocletian. The memory of many interesting and important facts is thus lost beyond all hope of recovery. Nevertheless, with the help of the scanty records that still remain, together with meagre allusions, or brief statements in Christian and Pagan authors, but still more through means of evidence furnished in recent times by the monuments of the Catacombs themselves, it is possible to reconstruct, in great measure, the history of the primitive Church. For the proofs of this in detail we must refer our readers to De Rossi's *Roma Sotterranea*, and especially to the valuable and learned compilation of De Rossi's works by Provost Northcote and Canon Brownlow, from which we have, by their kind permission, taken nearly everything that bears upon our subject in these chapters, and have made copious literal quotations.*

Our intention is to notice, so far as may be necessary for our particular purpose, such archæological monuments at Rome, and especially in the Catacombs, as are considered to be of the

---

* *Roma Sotterranea* (Longmans, 1879), part i. book iii. ch. i. pp. 110-120. As it has been found necessary sometimes to bring together passages from different parts of this work, to make every now and then verbal changes for the sake of connection, and to use curtailment or omission, we have thought it better not to employ inverted commas even in our literal quotations, but simply to give reference to the pages in footnotes.

apostolic age; as well as those of a later date which illustrate the primitive tradition of S. Peter's residence in Rome and his Roman Episcopate. And here it will be immediately asked: Are there, then, really existing in Rome Christian cemeteries and sepulchres of the apostolic age, and if so what are their characteristics? To these questions De Rossi replies as follows:

"Precisely in those cemeteries to which history or tradition assigns apostolic origin, I see, in the light of the most searching archæological criticism, the cradle both of subterranean sepulchres, of Christian art, and of Christian inscriptions; there I find memorials of persons who appear to belong to the times of the Flavii and of Trajan; and, finally, I discover precise dates of those times."

First, then, let us see what those cemeteries are for which the Martyrologies, the Itineraries, or any other ecclesiastical traditions claim this venerable antiquity. They are those of S. Peter, on the Via Cornelia; of S. Paul, on the Via Ostiensis; of Priscilla (one of the family of Pudens), on the Via Salaria Nova; Ostrianum, where Peter is said to have baptised, on the Via Nomentana; and of Domitilla, on the Via Ardeatina, where were buried the Martyrs Nereus and Achilleus, near to S. Petronilla, all three disciples of S. Peter. To this list it would be possible to add some two or three others.

1. The CRYPTS OF THE VATICAN naturally have the first claim on our attention, but it is no longer possible to recognise in them the primitive form of a catacomb: it has been destroyed by the foundations of the vast Basilica which now guards the tomb of S. Peter. Nevertheless, there was once a general cemetery there, and the particulars which have reached us about the sepulchres that were found in it are all in harmony with the high antiquity to which it is referred. Old Martyrologies speak of the tomb of S. Peter as though it had been a public monument. The *Liber Pontificalis* states that Anacletus, the successor of Clement in the Apostolic See—

"Built and adorned the sepulchral monuments (*construxit memoriam*) of Blessed Peter, since he had been ordained priest by S. Peter, and other burial-places where the bishops might be laid."

It adds that he himself was buried there; and the same is recorded of Linus and Cletus, and of Evaristus, Sixtus I., Telesphorus, Hyginus, Pius I., Eleutherius, and Victor, the last of whom was buried A.D. 198; but after S. Victor, no other Pontiff is recorded to have been buried there until S. Leo the

Great, A.D. 461, when the series of Pontifical burials at the Vatican was renewed. Early in the seventeeth century, Urban VIII. made extensive excavations round the "Confession" of S. Peter, in the course of which several marble sarcophagi came to light. One of these may be seen in the Museo Campana in Paris; and by the character of its sculpture (mere wavy spiral lines), the simplicity of its inscription, and the symbols engraved upon it, must certainly be assigned to a very early age. Another was inscribed with the single name of LINUS, a name of extremely rare occurrence on Christian monuments; and, considering where it was found, it does not seem rash to believe, with De Rossi, that this was the sepulchre of the immediate successor of S. Peter, of whom we read : *Sepultus est juxta corpus Beati Petri.*

2. From S. Peter's on the Vatican the mind passes naturally to the resting-place of S. PAUL, the Apostle of the Gentiles, on the other side of the river and of Rome. But here, too, the hill has been cut away to make room for the magnificent Basilica of S. Paul, *extra muros;* and hence the greater part of the Catacomb of Lucina (or of Commodilla, for both these names occur in ancient records) has been destroyed, and what galleries yet remain are so choked with earth and ruins of various kinds as to be almost impassable. This, however, is of less consequence, since we know that Boldetti read within this catacomb the most ancient inscription, with a consular date, that has come down to us.* It was scratched on the mortar round one of the graves, and the consulate of *Sura et Senecio* marks the year A.D. 107. A second was also found in the same place, in marble, recording the names of *Piso et Bolanus,* consuls, A.D. 110. The same explorer discovered here also yet a third inscription, which De Rossi considers one of the most ancient of Christian Rome :

DORMITIONI T. FLA. EUTYCHIO. QUI. VIXIT. ANN. XVIIII. MES. XI. D. III. HUNC. LOCUM. DONABIT. M. ORBIUS. HELIUS. AMICUS. KARISSIMUS. KARE BALE.

"As a place of sleep for Titus Flavius Eutychius, who lived nineteen years, eleven months, three days, his dearest friend, Marcus Orbius Helius, gave this grave. Farewell, beloved."

The first word of this inscription, the place where it was found, and certain symbols rudely carved between the last two words (apparently intended to represent two loaves and two fishes),

* There is, indeed, a more ancient-dated Christian inscription of the third year of Vespasian—*i.e.*, A.D. 72—but unfortunately it is no longer possible to ascertain to what cemetery this inscription belonged.—*Inscript. Christian.* tom. i. p. 3, No. 2.

show this inscription to be Christian; while the style, the ancient nomenclature, differing from the usual Christian epitaphs, and the prænomen, T. Flavius, point to the age of the Flavian emperors—*i.e.*, the end of the first century. It can hardly be a mere accident that these rare and contemporaneous dates should have been discovered in the same place and precisely in the cemetery where, less than forty years before, had been deposited the body of the Apostle Paul. They may be taken as certain proofs that a catacomb was begun here not long after his martyrdom.

3. The CEMETERY OF PRISCILLA, on the Via Salaria Nova, is said to have been dug in the property of the family of Pudens, converted by the Apostles; and a particular chapel in the middle of it—known from the language of its inscriptions as the *Cappella Greca*—was manifestly the centre or original nucleus round which the whole cemetery was in due time developed. Everything in this chapel betokens the highest antiquity; it was clearly made before the system of excavation, which afterwards became normal, had been devised. It is not simply hewn out of the tufa, but regularly constructed with bricks and mortar. There are no graves in the walls; it was made only to receive sarcophagi, not one of which, unhappily, has survived to our time, but only numerous fragments have been collected, both by Bosio and De Rossi. It was beautifully decorated with ornamental stuccowork, worthy of being compared with some of the best work of Pagan times; with frescoes also, quite of classical style, the scenes depicted in most of them differing widely from the usual well-known subjects which, in after times, when Christian symbolism had assumed a more fixed and stereotyped character, repeat themselves so frequently. It has also a special family of inscriptions, traced in vermilion on the tiles, and quite unlike later Christian epitaphs, being sometimes bare names, or, if anything be added, it is the apostolic salutation PAX TECUM or TIBI. The only symbol used is the most ancient of all, the anchor. The characters of the incised inscriptions are classical in form. The names also are classical, such as TITUS FLAVIUS FELICISSIMUS, FELIX AMPLIATUS, and others. In a word, there are many and important variations from the uniformity of Christian subterranean cemeteries, such as we find them in the third century, and they all point to a date anterior to any such systematic arrangement.

4. In certain Acts of Pope Liberius mention is made of the

CŒMETERIUM OSTRIANUM, or FONS PETRI, as being "not far from the Cemetery of Novella, which was on the third mile of the Via Salaria." When Panvinius compiled his catalogue of the cemeteries,* he set down this as being the oldest of all, "because it was in use when S. Peter preached the Faith to the Romans." Bosio† and all other antiquaries had failed to identify it, but De Rossi's more scientific mode of procedure has been more successful. He observed that the Abbot John,‡ in the Papyrus MS. at Monza, in which he gives a list of oils from the lamps before the celebrated shrines of Rome which he visited, after "the oil of S. Agnes and many others" on the Via Nomentana, and before "the oil of S. Vitalis, S. Alexander, and others on the Via Salaria," mentions, "oil from the Chair where Peter the Apostle first sat (*prius sedit*)," as though this were situated somewhere between the roads that have been named. In like manner, in the index of the cemeteries in the *Liber Mirabilium* (of the latter half of the tenth century), between that of S. Agnes and

---

* Onophrius Panvinius, an Augustinian friar, considered the marvel of his age for learning and industry, published a work in 1568 on the *Ceremonies of Christian Burial and the Ancient Christian Cemeteries*; he could only gather their names from the Acts of the Martyrs and other ancient documents. He expressly states that only three of them were at all accessible—that at S. Sebastian's, that at San Lorenzo, and that of S. Valentine, on the Via Flaminia. (*Ibid.* p. 26.)

† Antonio Bosio (b. 1575, d. 1629) was a man of immense learning and industry. On account of his lifelong labours and successful researches in the Catacombs, he has been justly called the true Columbus of this subterranean world. The publication of his *Roma Sotterranea* was begun in 1632 and finished in 1635. (*Ibid.* pp. 32-36.)

‡ The Abbot John, in the days of S. Gregory the Great, A.D. 600, collected a number of relics, which were sent to Theodolinda, Queen of the Lombards. This list, written on papyrus, together with many of the relics themselves, and the little parchment labels attached to them, is still to be seen in the Cathedral of Monza. We must not, however, be misled by the word "relics," and picture to ourselves, according to modern custom, the bodies or portions of the bodies of Saints. S. Gregory himself specifies the only kinds of relics that in his day were permitted to be carried away by the faithful. He writes to the Empress Constantia (*Epist.* lib. iii. ep. 30): "When the Romans give the relics of the Saints, they do not touch the bodies; their custom is only to put a piece of linen in a box, which is placed near the holy body, and which they afterwards take away. . . . In the time of the Pope S. Leo, some Greeks, doubting of the virtue of these relics, brought scissors and cut the linen, from whence proceeded blood, as is reported by the ancient inhabitants." But besides these, drops of oil from the lamps which burned before the tombs of the Saints were frequently carried away as relics; and S. Gregory often sent these *olea* in little glass phials to persons at a distance. They were relics of this latter kind that were collected by John the Abbot; and in the list of them he carefully records every shrine which he visited, and this (as was natural) in the order of his visits. A comparison of this local order with the topographical notices in the Itineraries by De Rossi has been specially fruitful in important results. (*Ibid.* pp. 25, 26.)

that of S. Priscilla, that is, between the same two roads, is placed the cemetery of the Font of S. Peter (*Fontis S. Petri*—in other copies, *Ad Nymphas S. Petri*), near the Basilica of S. Emerentiana. Now, this situation exactly corresponds with that of the cemetery upon which Father Marchi bestowed his chief labours,* and which has, therefore, become so familiar to all Roman visitors under the name of the Catacomb of S. Agnes; but the galleries and chambers which he recovered there do not bear marks of greater antiquity than the third century. Bosio, however, tell us that he went down by a square hole into a crypt, which struck him as remarkable, both for the frequency of the *luminaria* and the beauty of the ornamentation. Near one of these light-holes, which he found still open, "one sees," he writes:—

"Without the aid of a candle, a large niche like a tribune, with leaves in stucco-work, and within the niche are some red letters, which are almost all obliterated and illegible, but some few which remain are beautifully formed; under that niche must anciently have been the altar, the place being sufficiently spacious."

De Rossi observes that it is now well ascertained that the ancient custom was to place in the tribune, not the altar, but the pontifical chair; and this description by Bosio seemed to him, therefore, to read like an account of the crypt where was formerly venerated on the 18th of January "the chair in which Peter first sat," and which was also known in the Martyrologies of Ado and Bede as the *Cœmeterium Majus*, or *Cœmeterium ad Nymphas*, where Peter baptised; and he expressed an earnest hope that it might be once more brought to light. Thanks to the devotion and generosity of the prelate under whose ground it happened to lie, this hope has now been realised.

Monsignor Crostarosa carried on the work of excavation at his own expense until the long-lost crypt was discovered, and the keen and practised eye of one of De Rossi's pupils deciphered a few letters of the inscription which had baffled Bosio three hundred years ago. Now that Signor Armellini has published his discovery,† others also can read the same letters, and all agree that De Rossi's conjectures have been completely verified. The first letters that are legible,

---

* The late Padre Marchi, S.J., as *custode* of the Catacombs gave the first great impulse to that lively interest in them which is now so generally felt. In 1841 he commenced a great work on the Monuments of early Christian Art in Rome. He was the precursor of his illustrious disciple De Rossi. (*Ibid.* pp. 45, 46.)

† *Scoperta della cripta di Santa Emerenziana per Mariano Armellini.* Roma, 1877.

AMAS, naturally suggest the name of Pope Damasus, who is sure to have illustrated this place in some way or other, if it be what we suppose it to be; the letters, however, are printed, not engraved, as most of the inscriptions were that were set up by that Pontiff. Presently we come upon SANC P, in which we are tempted at once to read the name of the great Apostle; possibly, however, they might have referred to the martyr Papias, who was buried in this cemetery. Other letters follow after a short interval, C EMER IANTI, and these can hardly stand for any other than S. Emerentiana.

In the English *Roma Sotterranea* an engraving is given of the chapel, but on too small a scale to exhibit the letters distinctly, though it will enable the readers to understand the general appearance of the chamber thus happily recovered. They will recognise in the round pillar, which stands opposite the chair, a clear proof of the veneration in which the chamber was once held; for this is a feature common to all the most important historical crypts, being used to support the vase of perfumed oils, in which lighted wicks were always floating, and from which drops were taken and treasured as sacred relics. It was from the vase on this pillar that the Abbot John sent to Theodolinda "oil from the chair where Peter the Apostle first sat."

This pillar and the few letters which have been deciphered in the tribune, taken together with the notices recovered from ancient documents, and the chair hewn out of the rock, tell us that this was the place where "the chair in which S. Peter first sat in Rome" was once honoured; and, indeed, a *graffito* still remains which seems almost to record as much. We can just decipher *Febras ob amor . . . . . is san . . . . Romæ*, in which it does not seem unreasonable to recognise the traces of some ancient pilgrim attracted to the spot by a love of the *sedis* SANcti *Petri, ubi prius sedit*, ROMÆ, as we still read in the description of this cemetery in the old Martyrologies, and in the parchment labels attached to the little phial of oil sent hence in S. Gregory's time to the Lombard Queen. (*Ibid.* p. 234.)

Of course, if this evidence is admitted, the primitive antiquity of this catacomb is at once established; but even before this discovery was made, it can hardly be considered to have been doubtful. For De Rossi had long since pointed out that in a particular part of it (which now proves to be close to the original centre of the whole), there was a large number of epitaphs of most ancient type, forming quite a class by themselves, not painted on tiles, as those in the Cemetery of Priscilla, but incised on marble, in letters of beautifully classical shape, bearing no Christian symbol but the anchor and (once) the fish, having only one Christian acclamation, and that the first that came into use, VIVAS IN DEO. Their style is as laconic as possible; merely the names, or with the addition, as on Pagan tombstones, of the name and relationship of those who set up the *titulus*, and the epithet *dulcissimus*, or (once or twice) *incomparabilis*. Of the men, the three names are often given; of the women, the *gentilitium* and the *cognomen*. In nearly a hundred instances the *gentilitia* are of Claudii, Flavii, Ulpii, and others, which carry us back to the period between Nero and the first of the Antonines—*i.e.*, to the age of those who either heard the Apostles themselves, or at least their first disciples. Once the deceased is stated to have been the freed-woman of Lucius Clodius Clemens.

In fact, these epitaphs vary so little from the old classical type, that had they not been seen by Marini and other competent witnesses in their original position, and had not a fresh batch of them been discovered *in situ* in our own day, and some few of them been marked with a Christian symbol, we might have hesitated whether they ought not rather to be classed among Pagan than Christian monuments. As it is, we are sure that the persons whose graves they marked must have lived in the very earliest Christian ages.*

Surely no further words of ours are needed to strengthen the force of direct proof, amounting, we might say, to ocular demonstration, that S. Peter was Bishop of Rome, which this discovery of the chapel where was "the chair in which he first sat" supplies. Taken in conjunction with the ancient and universal tradition, with the constant and deep-rooted belief of his Roman Episcopate,

* *R. S. ibid.* pp. 116-120. The gradual development of this excavation belongs no doubt to the later period of the use of the Catacombs, that is to say, to the days of Damasus, or somewhere thereabouts, though the original nucleus went back, of course, to the days of the Apostles. But the grander basilica which we have described was made all at once, and De Rossi assigns it to the very earliest years of the fourth century. It is not at all probable that it was made after the days of persecution were ended, and when it would have been so much easier to build more commodious basilicas above ground; on the other hand, its scale of grandeur, and the completeness of all its arrangements in detail, mark a late development of subterranean architecture, and forbid our assigning to it the very early date named by Father Marchi. (*Ibid.* p. 234.)

and with so many corroborative still-existing memorials and written records of antiquity, the discovery of this monument—attended by so many undesigned coincidences—is, we deem, of itself alone sufficient to settle the matter definitively, dissipate all doubt, and bring home to the conviction of everyone who honestly seeks for truth that S. Peter was really Bishop of the Roman Church. Certainly, were an analogous case made out on some point of merely secular history, where the passions of religious prejudice bore no part, and were it, in place of S. Peter, a question of some temporal sovereign, and instead of an episcopal chair a regal throne, every impartial historian or antiquary would say that the point was settled, and that there was now no room for any further dispute.

CHAPTER II.

THE CEMETERY OF S. DOMITILLA.—THE CEMETERY OF S. SEBASTIAN.

THE CEMETERY OF S. DOMITILLA, or of her chamberlains, SS. Nereus and Achilleus, on the Via Ardeatina, is the last of those we mentioned as claiming to be of the apostolic age. This cemetery deserves special notice, because it is connected with one of the most remarkable facts in the annals of the early Church, viz., the profession of the Christian faith by some of the imperial family, and also with other personages of high rank, whose names tradition has associated with S. Peter at Rome. In order, therefore, better to illustrate this part of our treatise, we shall here give some account of those more illustrious amongst them.*

Let us, then, first speak of the profession of Christianity by certain members of the family of the FLAVII AUGUSTI, which had evidently a very close connection with the Cemetery of S. Domitilla. This family gave Vespasian to the throne. The elder brother of Vespasian, Titus Flavius Sabinus, had been prefect of the city in the year in which the princes of the Apostles, SS. Peter and Paul, suffered martyrdom; it is certain, therefore, that he must have been brought into contact with them, and heard something of the Christian faith. He is described by the great historian of the empire as one whose innocence and justice were unimpeachable; a mild man, who had a horror of all unnecessary bloodshed and violence. Towards the close of his life he was accused by some of great inactivity and want of interest in public affairs;† others thought him only a man of moderation, anxious to spare the lives of his fellow-citizens; others, again, spoke of his retiring habits as the natural result of the infirmities of old age. Whilst we listen to all these conjectures as to the cause of a certain change which seems to have come upon him in his declining years, the question naturally occurs to us, whether it is possible that he can have had some leaning towards the Christian faith, or even been actually converted to it. It is a

* *Rom. Sott.* part i. pp. 83-86, 120 *sqq.*   † Tacitus, *Hist.* iii. 65.

question which cannot now be answered; but at least it is certain that the charges brought against him correspond with those which were not uncommonly urged against Christianity—viz., that its principles were prejudicial to active industry,* and its general tendency unsocial; and the fact that some of the prefect's descendants in the next generation were undoubtedly of this faith gives a certain plausibility to the conjecture.

Flavius Sabinus seems to have had four children, of whom the most conspicuous was Titus Flavius Clemens, the consul and martyr. He married the daughter of his cousin, who was sister to the Emperor Domitian, and called by the same name as her mother, Flavia Domitilla. Flavia Domitilla the younger bore to her husband, the consul, two sons, who were named respectively Vespasian junior and Domitian junior, having been intended to succeed to the throne; and the famous Quinctilian † was appointed by the Emperor himself to be their tutor. At what time their parents became Christian, and what was the history of their conversion, we do not know; but the facts of Clemens' martyrdom and Domitilla's banishment are attested by Dio Cassius. His words are, that—

"Domitian put to death several persons, and amongst them Flavius Clemens, the consul, although he was his nephew, and although he had Flavia Domitilla for his wife, who also was a relation of the Emperor's. The charge of atheism was brought against them both, on which charge many others also had been condemned, going after the manners and customs of the Jews; and some of them were put to death, and others had their goods confiscated; but Domitilla was only banished to Pandateria" (an island opposite the Gulf of Gaeta, half way between Ponza and Ischia, now known by the name of Sta. Maria).‡

The reader will observe that Christianity is not expressly mentioned in the passage; on the contrary, the crimes laid to the charge of these victims of imperial tyranny are those of atheism and conformity to Jewish manners; but most learned critics have agreed with Gibbon § that this singular association of ideas could not with any propriety have been applied to any but Christians. Of them we have abundant testimony, both that they were for some time confounded by the Pagans with the Jews, and also that they were accused of atheism.‖

Had it been handed down in any Acts of the Martyrs that,

* "Infructuosi in negotiis dicimur." Tertull. *Apol.* sec. 42.
† *Instit.* iv. 1, sec. 2. ‡ *Hist.* lxvii. 13.
§ *Decline and Fall of the Roman Empire*, ch. xvi.
‖ S. Justin, *Apol.* i. 6, ii. 8; Athanag. *Legat. pro Christ.* 8; Minut. Felix, *Octavius*, 8, 10; and Euseb. *Hist. Eccl.* iv. 15.

immediately after the death of the Apostles, Christianity was within an ace of mounting the imperial throne, that a cousin and niece of the Emperor not only professed the new religion, but also suffered exile, and even death itself, on its account, we can imagine with what vehemence the pious legend would have been laughed to scorn by some modern critics; but the testimony of Dio Cassius, to which we may add, perhaps, that of Suetonius also,[*] is generally received with greater respect.

There was yet a third lady of the same noble family, bearing the same name of Flavia Domitilla, with whom we are more nearly concerned than with either of her ancestors. She was a grand-daughter (on the mother's side) of Titus Flavius Sabinus, and consequently a niece of the consul. She, too, suffered banishment, like her aunt, and for the same cause—profession of the Christian faith. Some modern authors,[†] indeed, have insisted on identifying her with the last-mentioned lady; but Tillemont justly says, it is unreasonable to accuse of inaccuracy grave ancient authors unless necessity obliges, and in the present instance there is no such necessity. Both the weight of historical testimony and ecclesiastical tradition are in favour of distinguishing the two Christian Domitillas.[‡] In speaking of the younger lady, Eusebius has a very striking passage, which testifies clearly to the marvellous spread of the Christian religion, even before the expiration of the first century. He has just had occasion to mention the latter part of Domitian's reign, and he says:

"The teaching of our faith had by this time shone so far and wide, that even Pagan historians did not refuse to insert in their narratives some account of the persecution and the martyrdoms that were suffered in it. Some, too, have marked the time accurately, mentioning amongst many others, in the fifteenth year of Domitian (A.D. 96), Flavia Domitilla, the daughter of a sister of Flavius Clemens, one of the Roman consuls of those days, who for her testimony for Christ was punished by exile to the Island of Pontia."[§]

The same writer in his *Chronicon* ‖ gives the name of one of the authors to whom he refers, and that name is Brutius. It is

---
[*] He accuses the consul, "contemptissimæ inertiæ."
[†] Amongst them is Dr. Lightfoot.—*Ignatius*.
[‡] *Mem. d'Hist. Eccl.* tom. ii. p. 126. Scaliger was the first to suggest correction of the texts, either of Dio Cassius or Eusebius, or of both, in order to make them seem to speak of the same person. *Notæ in Euseb. Chron.;* Amstel. 1658, p. 205. Mommsen (*Corpus Inscript. Latin.* tom. vi. p. 172) has lately attempted to effect the same purpose in another way. Their arguments are fully discussed and answered by De Rossi, *Bullettino*, 1875, pp. 69-77.
[§] *H. E.* iii. 18.
‖ S. Hieron. *Interp.* A.D. 98, tom. viii. p. 605, ed. Migne.

worth mentioning, because many fragments of inscriptions belonging to the Gens Brutia have been found in the immediate neighbourhood of the Cemetery of Domitilla (the same whose exile he had recorded), as though the burial-place of these two families had been in close proximity; and the epitaph of a child (Brutius Crispinus) found within the cemetery itself would seem to indicate that some members of the historian's family had become Christians at an early period. This confirms the conjecture of Scaliger that the historian Brutius is identical with Brutius Præsens, the friend of Pliny the younger, and the ancestor of the Empress Crispina, wife of Commodus:

"It is evident, writes De Rossi, that the Brutii had lands, or at least a cemetery, adjoining the property of Flavia Domitilla, and it is natural that this circumstance should specially have drawn the attention of the historian Brutius to the noble ladies of the imperial family who were condemned on account of their profession of Christianity."

S. Jerome* tells us that in his days the island of Pontia (Ponza) was frequented by pious Christian pilgrims, "who delighted to visit with devotion the cells in which Flavia Domitilla had suffered a life-long martyrdom." † Whether she really shed her blood at the last for the faith is uncertain, the Acts of SS. Nereus and Achilleus being of doubtful authenticity. They state, however, that she and one of her female companions were buried in a sarcophagus at Terracina, but that her chamberlains (who are said to have been baptised by S. Peter) suffered death by the sword, and were buried in a cemetery about a mile and a half out of Rome on the Via Ardeatina, in a farm belonging to their mistress. The farm, now known by the name of Tor Marancia, is situated just at this distance from Rome, and on the road named; and an inscription which has been found there shows clearly that it once belonged to this very person, Flavia Domitilla. It gives the measurements of a sepulchral area of thirty-five feet in front and forty into the field, whether for a Pagan or a Christian monument we cannot say; but at all events the ground had been granted to one Sergius Cornelius Julianus, *ex indulgentia Flaviæ Domitillæ, neptis Vespasiani;* another, probably belonging to the same place, records a similar grant, *ex beneficio* of the same lady.

Anyhow, it is certain that Domitilla had property in this place; and though Bosio imagined this cemetery to be that of S. Callixtus, nobody now doubts that it is really that which in olden

* See *R. S. ib.* pp. 120-122.   † *Ep.* 108, *ad Eustoch.*

118 S. AURELIA PETRONILLA.

times was known as *Cœmeterium Domitillæ, Nerei et Achillei, ad S. Petronillam, Via Ardeatina.*

Before we descend into it, it will be well to say a few words about this new name which thus enters into the title. S. PETRONILLA is described in the Martyrologies as having been "the daughter of St. Peter," and some critics have imagined that this word denoted a real natural relationship, and not merely a spiritual one, as in the analogous case of S. Mark, whom S. Peter calls his "son."* They have even argued that the very name indicated a blood-relationship with the Prince of the Apostles. But this is a mistake. Baronius long since pointed out that Petronilla could not, according to Roman usage, be derived from Petrus, but rather from Petronius, as Priscilla from Priscus, Drusilla from Drusus, &c. Moreover, we now know that she bore another name, which connects her with a noble Roman family, and not with the poor Jewish fisherman; for on the sarcophagus in which she was buried were inscribed the two names—AURELIÆ PETRONILLÆ. Now, the name of Petro was no stranger to the family of Domitilla; for Titus Flavius Petro was the father of the first T. Flavius Sabinus; and if Petronilla was descended from this Petro, as she may have been on her mother's side, it is at once accounted for how she found her place of burial on the property of her relative Domitilla.

The Acts of SS. NEREUS and ACHILLEUS, composed originally in Greek, some say in the fourth, others in the fifth or sixth century, are considered by Baronius and Tillemont unreliable as to many details, and are to be reckoned as very much a historical romance, in which, moreover, are traceable certain Manichæan errors. Still, as Tillemont remarks, the most perverted histories have generally somewhat of truth for their groundwork.

"And this is the case," observes M. Paul Allard, "with a great number of the Acts of the Martyrs. Since the discoveries of Christian archæology have proved that, what are apparently the most legendary accounts, sometimes are based on a solid historical *substratum*, and that often the imagination of the later Martyrologists has been but embroidering on an ancient canvas. Thus, in the Acts of SS. Nereus and Achilleus, compiled at a time when the places and monuments referred to were still under the writer's eye, De Rossi has been able to disentangle from the midst of much that is doubtful a certain number of facts, which researches of more than twenty years in the Christian cemetery on the Via Ardeatina have demonstrated as true."

Here have been rediscovered, from indications in these Acts, the

* 1 *Peter*, v. 13.

very site of the sepulchre of Nereus and Achilleus, as also that of Aurelia Petronilla. It is to be well remarked, at the same time, that no trace has been found of the burial here of any Flavia Domitilla, nor is there mention made of her tomb in this cemetery in the ancient Itineraries of pilgrims. From this we may reasonably infer the correctness of the Acts in saying that the niece of Clemens was martyred and buried at Terracina.

From these Acts, compared with the inscription which S. Damasus placed on their tomb in the fourth century, we may pretty safely infer the following points in the history of SS. NEREUS and ACHILLEUS as reliable. They appear to have belonged, under Nero, to the Pretorian cohort, and even to have taken part in the bloody execution for which, to the shame of military discipline, more than once the wicked emperors employed this privileged corps. They were soldiers of rank and distinction, and had received marks of decoration for their bravery. We learn from the Acts that they were converted and baptised by S. Peter. It is certain that the Pretorian camp had relations with the Apostles, for S. Paul writes from Rome * that his chains had become the preaching of Christ ἐν ὅλῳ τῷ πραιτωρίῳ, and as S. Peter returned to Rome soon after the arrival of S. Paul, and probably resumed his former abode in the sixth region, he may have laboured, together with the Apostle of the Gentiles, in the neighbourhood of the Pretorian camp on the Via Nomentana.† After their baptism they left the military service, and, as appears, obtained some post in the house of Domitilla, possibly on the recommendation of Aurelia Petronilla, also a convert of S. Peter, and related to the imperial family. The Acts inform us that they followed their mistress in her exile at Pontia. We have thus explained how it was they were buried in the Cemetery of the Flavii; for the fact of their martyrdom and the place of their sepulture are quite certain.

In the catacomb itself are to be found abundant proofs both of its identity and its extreme antiquity. On the second level of excavation is one of the widest corridors to be seen in all the Catacombs, leading to an ante-chamber illuminated by the largest *luminare* yet discovered. Opening out of this is another chamber, unlike in many respects the ordinary family vaults of the Catacombs. Originally there were no graves dug in the walls. These were covered with the finest stucco, and then decorated with

---

* *Philip.* i. 13. † Allard, p. 34.

ornamental devices bearing so close a resemblance to the decoration of Pagan chambers of the same date, that the whole might almost be mistaken for a Pagan monument, were it not for the figure of the Good Shepherd which occupies the centre of the ceiling. The *arcosolium* is even decorated with landscape painting, such as may be seen on the walls of private houses at Pompeii, but of which only one other example, we believe, has been found in the Roman Catacombs. At no great distance, in a most ancient part of the catacomb, not far from the sepulchre of SS. Nereus and Achilleus is another chamber where may be seen an inscription: "M. Antonius Restitutus made this subterranean (sepulchre) for himself and those of his family who believe in the Lord."

More recently has been discovered in the same neighbourhood a monument which De Rossi unhesitatingly announces as belonging to some member of the Flavian family who lived and died in the days of Domitian. It is certainly one of the most ancient Christian monuments yet discovered in the Catacombs. Its position close to the highway; its front of fine brick-work, with a cornice of terra-cotta, with the usual space over the doorway for an inscription (which has now, alas! perished); the spaciousness of its gallery, with only four or five separate niches prepared for as many sarcophagi; the fine stucco on the wall; the eminently classical character of its decorations—all these particulars make it perfectly clear that it was the monument of a family of distinction, excavated at great cost, and without the slightest attempt at concealment.*

In the gallery, some tombs, still closed, bear the names of the deceased written in black on very large tiles—just like those which we have seen in the most ancient part of the catacomb of S. Priscilla; and the inscriptions on the other graves are all of the simplest and oldest form. The names may still be traced of Claudii, Flavii, Ulpii, and Aurelii. Lastly, the whole of the vaulted roof of the gallery is covered with the most exquisitely graceful designs of the branches of a vine (with birds and winged genii among them), trailing with all the freedom of nature over the whole walls, not fearing any interruption by graves, nor confined by any of those lines of geometrical symmetry which characterise similar productions in the next century. Here also is that other specimen we have alluded to of landscape painting—two persons sitting at a feast, with bread and fish only on the table; a man

---

* *R. S. ib.* pp. 122-3.

fishing; a sheep feeding near a tree; and Daniel in the lions' den, may still be seen here, or at least fragments of them may be traced.

Could we have seen these chambers in their original condition, we should have perhaps found, as De Rossi conjectures, that here was the very *memoria* of Flavius Clemens himself, the martyred consul, and husband of one of the Domitillas, whose remains are believed to have been afterwards translated to the Basilica of S. Clement within the walls. At any rate, we are quite sure that we have been here brought face to face with one of the earliest specimens of Christian subterranean burial in Rome; and it shows us the sense of liberty and security under which it was executed. Not only was there no attempt at concealment of the sepulchre, but even the paintings of Biblical subjects, which we have described, were placed close to the entrance, and where they could be seen by the light of day.*

But now to return † to the Cemetery of Domitilla itself. Here, in the year 1873, was discovered, through the labours of De Rossi, the subterranean Basilica of S. Petronilla. This had evidently been constructed after the existence of the cemetery, and was built to do honour to some part of it. We have already mentioned that the most ancient name of this catacomb was *Domitillæ Cœmeterium*, but that at a later period, when the names of the martyrs generally superseded those of the owners of the soil, it was consecrated by three names—Petronilla, Nereus, and Achilleus. And we must remember that S. Domitilla is recorded in the Acts of Nereus and Achilleus to have been buried at Terracina, and that no trace of her is to be met with in the cemetery which bears her name. Here there was found a large fragment of an inscription of eight lines, long known to scholars, and published amongst the works of S. Damasus, decided by critics as commemorating SS. Nereus and Achilleus, on the authority of more than one MS. which states that it was seen at their sepulchre. The inscription runs thus (the letters printed in italics being those which have been recovered):

MILITIÆ NOMEN DEDERANT SÆVUMQUE GEREBANT
OFFICIUM PARITER SPECTANTES JUSS*A TYR*ANNI
PRÆCEPTIS PULSANTE METU SERVI*RE P*ARATI
MIRA FIDES RERUM SUBITO POSUE*RE FUROR*EM
CONVERSI FUGIUNT DUCIS IMPIA CAST*RA RELINQUUNT*
PROJICIUNT CLYPEOS FALERAS TEL*AQ. CRUENTA*
CONFESSI GAUDENT CHRISTI PORTAR*E TRIUMFOS*
CREDITE PER DAMASUM POSSIT QUID *GLORIA CHRISTI.*

* *R. S.* part i. pp. 125-6.   † *Ib.* pp. 176 *seq.*

122 VOTIVE COLUMNS TO SS. NEREUS AND ACHILLEUS.

"They had given their names to the army, and were at the same time fulfilling a cruel office, heeding the commands of the tyrant, and prepared to obey his commands, under the influence of fear. Suddenly—wonderful to believe are these things—they laid aside their madness, are converted, and fly; they desert the wicked camp of their leader, throw away their shields, military ornaments, and blood-stained weapons. Confessing [the faith], they glory in bearing the triumphs of Christ [by martyrdom]. Believe [all ye who read], by [these verses of] Damasus, what [marvels] the glory of Christ can effect."

In order to appreciate the sense of these lines, it is well that we should remember that it was one of Nero's crimes that he employed some of his soldiers, his own body-guard, the Pretorian cohort, to be the executioners of his unjust sentences against those whom he was determined to destroy. The first lines of the inscription evidently allude to this, and it is mentioned as the justification of the act of the Saints in deserting their military office. They had obeyed through fear; now they boldly confess Christ, and suffer martyrdom for His sake. The inscription says, indeed, nothing about their having filled the post of *eunuchi cubicularii* to Domitilla, and might, at first sight, seem almost to contradict such an idea. On the other hand, the fact of their being buried in ground which belonged to that lady indicates some connection between them; and as to the precise title which is given them, the Acts from which it is taken are a work of the fifth or sixth century, confessedly translated from the Greek, and nothing is more natural than that the translator should have introduced titles, with which the Byzantine court of the day made him familiar. But setting the Acts on one side, the inscription must, at least, be admitted as evidence that this was the cemetery in which their sepulchre was shown in the fourth century.

In the year 1874 there was found, moreover, a marble column in a lower gallery of the cemetery, into which it had fallen through the pavement of the Basilica. On this column is seen carved a representation of the martyrdom of Achilleus, together with his name and the *triumphus Christi*, the crown on the top of a cross, between the executioner and his victim. The base of the corresponding pillar, then also discovered, shows that a similar representation was once to be seen there also of S. Nereus. It is impossible to doubt, then, that it was in this church that S. Gregory the Great preached that homily which appears among his works, having been taken down (as he tells us) by a shorthand writer who heard him deliver it "before the tombs of SS. Nereus and Achilleus," and that Cardinal Baronius was in error when he caused a portion of it to be engraved on the episcopal chair in the church within the city, as if it had been delivered there.

A memorial has been most happily discovered of S. Petronilla also. At the back of the apse of the Basilica is a small chamber, in which the *arcosolium* is partially blocked up with masonry; and on the plaster of this wall is represented the young Petronilla, here called a martyr, standing by the side of an elderly matron, named Veneranda, who died or was buried on the 7th of January. Doubtless she is here represented as the advocate of the deceased lady whom she is introducing into Paradise, pointing at the same time to the books of Holy Scripture in the chest by her side, which are, as it were, the proofs and token of her Christian faith. The inscription upon the stone which once closed the remainder of this *arcosolium* bore a date, of which sufficient fragments remain to enable us to say that it must have been of the year 320, 326, or 356, most probably the last, and this may very well have been the date of the painting also. By that time we know how common was the desire to be buried near the martyrs, and how general the belief that some spiritual advantage could be gained thereby. This chamber, and the whole of the *arcosolium*, even its arch, is crowded with graves—a sure evidence of the proximity of some shrine. It was for this reason that Veneranda was thus placed under the patronage, as it were, of Petronilla, viz., because she was buried in the neighbourhood of her tomb. We cannot now identify the precise site of that tomb; we only know that it was a sarcophagus engraved with the words AURELIÆ PETRONILLÆ FILIÆ DULCISSIMÆ, and that this was removed by Pope Stephen II., or his successor, to a building close to S. Peter's, which had been the mausoleum of the Emperor Honorius and his wife, but which was afterwards taken down and its site included within the present Basilica, where an altar was dedicated in her honour. Many of our readers may have admired the copy in mosaic which is placed over it of Guercino's picture of the opening of the Saint's tomb that her lover might be satisfied as to the reality of her death. For the story was that when her hand was asked in marriage by some noble Roman, she begged for a delay of three days in which she might make her decision; that these days were spent in fasting and prayer, and that on the last day, "the mysteries of the Lord's oblation having been celebrated, she received the Sacrament of Christ, lay back on her couch, and gave up her spirit."* There is nothing improbable in the hand having been sought in marriage by one of noble blood, as we have already seen that she was not the daughter of the Jewish fisherman and Christian Apostle, but must have been descended from a noble Roman family. Her names, Aurelia Petronilla, are a sufficient proof of this; and the latter name seems to indicate a connection with the very family to which Domitilla herself belonged, the family of the Flavii.

In the title given to her on the painting she is called a martyr, whereas in the legend there is not only no evidence to show that she shed her blood for the faith, but she does not seem to have been called upon to suffer anything on its account, nor even to make a public confession of it. And here De Rossi is disposed to give credence to the legend rather than to the artist. If Petronilla had really been a martyr, the Martyrologies would not have failed to give her that title, whereas they seem uniformly to withhold it. Nevertheless, she enjoyed a great celebrity, of which the way in which her name has been connected with S. Peter's is a sufficient proof; and at a time when the devotion of the faithful was so warmly and so exclusively exhibited towards the martyrs, this singular pre-eminence of Petronilla may have betrayed the artist into the blunder we are speaking of.

Though the verses in honour of SS. Nereus and Achilleus were confessedly written by Pope Damasus, it appears that they were engraved and set up in the time of his successor, Siricius. So, too, it can be proved that though this Basilica of S. Petronilla may have been begun by Damasus, yet he was certainly dead before it was finished. It must then be attributed to his successor. It was frequented as a place of public assembly in the days of S. Gregory the Great, at which time oil was taken from its shrines, and sent as a precious relic to Theodolinda, Queen of the Lombards; and the label which was sent with it may still be read in the treasury of the Cathedral at Monza, "of S. Petronilla, daughter of S. Peter the Apostle, of S. Nereus, and of S. Achilleus." The same names appear in the Itineraries compiled by pilgrims from various nations who visited it in the seventh century. Pope Gregory III. (A.D. 715-741) appointed an annual station to be held here, and made offerings of a golden crown, a silver chalice and paten, and other churc

---

* Ado, Martyr. 31 Maii. p. 241.

ornaments. At the end of the same century, we read that Pope Leo III., seeing the Church of SS. Nereus and Achilleus in danger of falling, and much injured by the inundation of waters, built another in a higher spot in the immediate neighbourhood. We do not know that any trace has yet been found of Leo's church "built in a higher place," but the situation of the Basilica we have been describing would certainly have exposed it to the inundation of the waters, and, if a new church was built very near it, we can understand the careful removal of the stone chair and benches, the *ambones*, and the pavement from the old one, and their transfer to the new, whilst all the columns of the building, its sarcophagi, and other monuments remained untouched. The very doorway was walled up, and every precaution taken that it should not be desecrated. A hundred years later, in 897, there was an earthquake, which did great damage to Rome, especially to the Lateran Basilica; and it is probable that the old Basilica of S. Petronilla was finally destroyed at the same time; the position of the columns, all lying in one direction across the floor, seems to point to some such cause of its ruin.

CEMETERY OF S. SEBASTIAN.

One of the ancient guides of the seventh and eighth centuries —the most ancient and accurate of all—describing what he himself saw and visited at some time between the years 625 and 638, writes as follows:

"Afterwards you arrive by the Via Appia at S. Sebastian, Martyr, whose body lies in a very low spot; and there are the sepulchres of the Apostles Peter and Paul, in which they rested forty years." *

He then goes on to point out the tombs of many other Popes and Martyrs. Another of these guides, who wrote not many years later, also says:

"Near the Via Appia is the Church of S. Sebastian, Martyr, where he himself sleeps; where are also the burial-places of the Apostles, in which they rested forty years."†

The Basilica of S. Sebastian, built by Constantine over the tomb where the body of this Martyr still rests, is well known to every visitor of Rome. It stands on the Appian Road, between two and three miles out of the city, where, at the

---

* *Notitia Ecclesiarum Urbis Romæ*, p. 28.
† *De locis Sanctis Martryrum quæ sunt foris Civitatis Romæ*, p. 23.

126   THE BASILICA—INSCRIPTION OF POPE DAMASUS.

back of the high altar, are still shown "the burial-places of the Apostles;" that is, the semi-subterranean building in which, according to the authorities we have quoted, the bodies of SS. Peter and Paul once found a temporary resting-place. The form of this building is so irregular that it would never have been selected by an architect for its own sake, but it was manifestly designed to enclose some particular point of interest, without interfering more than was necessary with what lay around it. It is impossible, therefore, to assent to the theory which would recognise in it some ancient heathen temple; it is clear that it was erected expressly for the sake of commemorating a spot endeared to the Church by associations connected with her days of persecution; and, in fact, it is the one only point throughout all the Catacombs of which we are sure that it continued to be visited by devout pilgrims in the fourth and fifth centuries, although the relics which had made it holy had been long since removed. Pope Damasus provided a marble pavement for its floor, and otherwise adorned it, at the same time setting up one of his usual metrical and historical inscriptions, which exists in old MSS., and an incomplete copy of which, executed in the twelfth or thirteenth century, may still be seen:

HIC HABITASSE PRIUS SANCTOS COGNOSCERE DEBES,
NOMINA QUISQUE PETRI PARITER PAULIQUE REQUIRIS,
DISCIPULOS ORIENS MISIT, QUOD SPONTE FATEMUR,
SANGUINIS OB MERITUM CHRISTUMQUE PER ASTRA SEQUUTI,
ÆTHERIOS PETIERE SINUS ET REGNA PIORUM,
ROMA SUOS POTIUS MERUIT DEFENDERE CIVES,
HÆC DAMASUS VESTRAS REFERAT NOVA SIDERA LAUDES.

"Here you must know, that Saints once dwelt. If you ask their names, they were Peter and Paul. The East sent disciples, as we willingly acknowledge. The Saints themselves had, by the merit of their blood-shedding, followed Christ to the stars, and sought the home of heaven and the kingdoms of the blest. Rome, however, obtained to defend her own citizens. May Damasus be allowed to record these things for your praise, O new stars [of the heavenly host]."

A low step, or seat of stone, runs round the interior, destined (Father Marchi conjectures) for the use of those who recited here in choir the psalms and public offices of the Church. In the middle of the area is a small, square aperture, widening at the depth of about two feet into a large pit or double grave, measuring between six and seven feet both in length, breadth, and depth. This pit is divided into two equal compartments by a slab of marble; its sides are also cased with marble to the height of three feet, and its vaulted roof is covered with paintings of our Lord and His Apostles. This, then, is the spot where, according to the testimony of both our ancient witnesses, "the bodies of S. Peter and S. Paul rested for a period of forty years."

There is some difficulty in unravelling the true history of this temporary translation of the bodies of the Apostles. Originally they were buried each near the scene of his own martyrdom; the one on the Vatican Hill, the other on the Ostian Way. But we learn from other equally authentic sources that as soon as the Oriental Christians had heard of their death, they sent some of the brethren to remove the bodies and bring them back to the East, where they claimed them as their fellow-citizens and countrymen. These messengers so far prospered in their mission as to gain a momentary possession of the sacred relics, which they carried along the Appian Way, as far as this spot which we have been just now examining, adjoining the Basilica of S. Sebastian. This was probably their appointed place of rendezvous before starting on their homeward journey by way of Brundusium; for just at this point a cross-road, coming directly from S. Paul's, joins the Appian and Ostian Ways, by which ways the bodies of S. Peter and S. Paul respectively must have been brought. What happened to them whilst they rested here we cannot exactly tell. The language of Pope Damasus, which we have given above, while it hints at the claim of the Orientals and the successful opposition of the Romans, bears evident tokens of reserve, and we can easily understand his unwillingness to perpetuate on a public monument, which would be seen by pilgrims from all parts of the world, a history that might hereafter become a subject of angry recrimination between the Eastern and Western Christians. But S. Gregory the Great, writing two centuries later, and only in a private letter, had no such motive for reticence. A chapel having been built in the Imperial Palace at Constantinople, to be dedicated to S. Paul, Constantia, wife of the Emperor Maurice, wished to enrich the altar with some considerable relics, and begged from the Sovereign Pontiff nothing less than the head of the great Apostle. S. Gregory, in justification of his refusal to comply with her request, relates the story—embellished perhaps by this time with some legendary additions—of the attempt of the Oriental Christians to carry off his relics soon after his martyrdom, and says:

"It is well known that at the time when they suffered, Christians from the East came to recover their bodies as [the relics] of their fellow-citizens, and having carried them as far as the second milestone from the city, laid them in the place which is called *ad Catacumbas*; but when the whole company of them assembled together and attempted to take them from thence, a storm of thunder and lightning so greatly terrified them, and dispersed them, that after that they durst not make any more attempts. The Romans, however, then went out and took up their bodies, having been counted worthy to do this by the goodness of the Lord, and laid them in the places where they are now buried." *

These last words of S. Gregory do not seem to be quite accurate. There is no doubt that the Romans first buried them where they recovered them, in or near the Cemetery *ad Catacumbas*, and there was an old tradition, embodied in one of the lessons formerly used on S. Peter's Feast in the French Church, which said that they were restored to their original places of sepulchre after the lapse of a year and seven months; † nor is there any reason to suppose that the body of S. Paul was ever again removed. Of the relics of S. Peter there are faint traces of a second translation, which is assigned by some writers to the first half of the third century. They are too indistinct, however, to be depended upon, and we must be content to acknowledge our ignorance as to the authority on which it was believed by the writers of the Itineraries in the seventh and eighth centuries that the bodies of the Apostles had lain near the Basilica of S. Sebastian for a period of forty years.‡

It has occurred to us that, perhaps, some one on reading this chapter of details about the Catacombs and persons connected with them in the past, may ask why it is here at all, and what special relation has it with S. Peter and his Roman Episcopate? We have had more than one reason for placing it here. First, we would represent the Catacombs in as realistic a form as is possible, and show that they are no longer that shadowy and unknown world which once they were, but have been explored, mapped out, their main features and history well ascertained, and that, consequently, they may serve to the historian as an archæological store-house, not only of probable conjectures, but also of most solid and sure proofs regarding the past. But we could only present them in this view by peopling them again with some of those whose names have been traditionally more or

---

* *Opp. S. Greg.* tom. ii. Ep. 30.
† This is the time mentioned in the apocryphal acts of SS. Peter and Paul, § 87, p. 39, ed. Tischendorf.
‡ *Rom. Sott.* part i. pp. 265-271.

less associated with them, and by surrounding them with a number of interesting details. Mere general statement, or the mention of one or other particular fact, would hardly serve our purpose here, since their force is appreciable only in their multiplicity and by means of circumstantial narrative. Those more illustrious persons, moreover, of whom this chapter has given an account, are not unconnected with S. Peter, but are associated with him in the traditional history of that Apostle in Rome. Some of them were his converts, disciples, and friends; all of them his contemporaries. To the mind of certain modern historians, scarcely anything had survived of them except their names; for what is recorded of their lives and the acts of their martyrdom—from these having been drawn up at a later date, and then filled in sometimes with romantic and improbable details—had come to be regarded as simply unreliable legends, so that even the real personal existence at all of some of them was discredited. But now that from unimpeachable evidence discovered in the Catacombs, they are, so to say, brought anew to life, and the traditional history attached to them has, in the main, as well as in many particulars, been substantiated, there is afforded at once solid ground for presuming that much else that has been handed down from antiquity, and believed with common assent with regard to the first planting of Christianity in Rome, is also historically trustworthy, and was matter of actual occurrence.

We here remark what, at first sight, seems strange, but we deem is true, that people generally, especially in these days when a lively Christian faith is less common, are much more disinclined to believe in some reported discovery with reference to those of the past, who belonged immediately to the domain and epoch of the first revelation of Christianity—and still more so should the discovery concern one who is held to be a typical representative of an unpopular religious doctrine—than they are to give credit to an alleged discovery regarding persons of the same or even greater antiquity belonging wholly to secular history. Thus, a report of the discovery by archæologists of the sepulchral urn of Seneca or Nero would, we think, meet with a more respectful hearing, more patient attention, and more ready acceptance at the hands of the general public in this country, than a similar report touching some important relic of one of the Apostles, and particularly the episcopal chair of S. Peter at Rome, even though the evidence and proofs in both cases were of equal value.

Our thought, then, was that by first producing solid proofs from the Catacombs of the past living existence of some who were more or less illustrious in antiquity on other than religious grounds, and by revindicating the claim of ancient Catholic tradition to their association with the first age of Roman Christianity, and to their character and position, in the same tradition, of patrician or senatorial rank, of military distinction, of office in a noble or princely house, or of relationship with the imperial family—we might thus, without any unfairness, insinuate into the minds of the more sceptical about S. Peter some disposition to weigh carefully, and so to believe in, the proofs also which the Catacombs afford of the life and works of that Apostle in Rome, and of the position assigned to him by ancient tradition as Bishop of the Roman Church. For we must bear in mind that the testimonies found in the Catacombs in behalf of S. Peter are of the very same nature and force as those producible for those others who have passed under our notice; with this difference, however, that the evidences in favour of S. Peter are manifold more numerous than those for the former. If then these evidences are held conclusively to prove their point in the one case, they must be held also to prove their point in the other, by those who look at the matter impartially with a spirit of candour and apart from religious prejudice. And the conclusion to which, in S. Peter's case, these evidences point is that he resided in Rome, there exercised his apostolic zeal, and ruled the Church as Bishop of that See.

CHAPTER III.

THE GILDED GLASSES FOUND IN THE CATACOMBS.—SCULPTURE ON CHRISTIAN SARCOPHAGI.—PAINTINGS IN THE CATACOMBS.

1. THE GILDED GLASSES.

THE Gilded Glasses found in the Catacombs date most probably, according to De Rossi, from the second half of the third to the beginning of the fourth century. Mr. Palmer thinks that their manufacture was commenced as early as the second century, and says that one glass shows a heap of coins, with the effigy of Heliogabulus (A.D. 218-222). Archæologists are generally of opinion that this kind of glass was made only in Rome. These glasses are, the greater part of them, evidently the bottoms of drinking cups. Their peculiarity consists in a design having been executed in gold leaf on the flat bottom of the cup in such a manner as that the figures and letters should be seen from the inside, like the designs on the glass bottoms of the ale tankards so popular at Oxford and Cambridge. The gold leaf was then protected by a plate of glass, which was welded by fire so as to form one solid mass with the cup.

The favourite subject on these glasses is the representation of the two great Apostles, SS. Peter and Paul. It is certain that their feast was observed as a general holiday in Rome during the fourth century, very much as Christmas is now kept amongst ourselves, and the representation of the two Apostles on eighty glasses out of the three hundred and forty published by Garrucci is a strong argument of their having been intended in some way to commemorate that day. The inscriptions, where they occur with the figures of the Apostles, confirm this supposition, for they are all of a convivial character. We give a few examples: "Dignitas amicorum pie zeses (for πίε ζήσης) cum tuis omnibus bibas (perhaps for vivas)." "Dignitas amicorum pie zeses cum tuis omnibus biba et propina." "Cum tuis feliciter zeses." These may be translated: "A mark of friendship, drink and long life to thee, with all thine. Mayest thou live long." "A mark of friendship, drink, and long life to thee, with all thine, drink (or live), and drink to my health." "Mayest thou live happily with thine own;" or, more freely, "Life and happiness to thee and thine." A more religious inscription is: "Hilaris vivas cum tuis omnibus feliciter semper in pace Dei zeses." That is: "Joyfully mayest thou live with all thine; happily mayest thou live for ever in the peace of God."

Doubtless, in Rome many a pious pilgrim followed the practice which S. Monica learned in Africa, of whom S. Augustine records, with the playful fondness of filial affection, that she used to bring to the festivals—

"A small cup of wine, diluted according to her own abstemious habits, which for courtesy she would taste (*unde dignationem sumeret*). And if there were many shrines of the departed Saints to be honoured in that manner, she would carry round that one same cup which she used everywhere; and this, even when it had become not only watery, but unpleasantly lukewarm, she would distribute to those about her by small sips, for she sought their devotion, not pleasure."*

De Rossi inclines to the opinion that these glasses served for these purposes at the tombs of the Apostles.

A question here naturally arises as to the representations of the Apostles, how far they may be considered to be real likenesses, or whether they were purely conventional, invented and perpetuated merely by Christian art. We have the testimony of Eusebius, who says:

"We have seen representations of the Apostles Peter and Paul, and of Christ Himself, still preserved in paintings." †

S. Augustine also says that—

"People in many places used to see them (Peter and Paul) represented in pictures with Christ. For Rome in a specially honourable and solemn manner commends the merits of Peter and Paul on account of their having suffered on the same day." ‡

S. Ambrose, in his account of the vision which he had of SS. Gervasius and Protasius, adds that—

"There appeared another third person, who seemed to be like Blessed Paul the Apostle, whose countenance I had learned from pictures." §

Moreover, it cannot be denied that there is a certain uniformity of type about the figures of these Apostles on most of the glasses

---

* *Confess.* vi. 2. † *Hist. Eccl.* vii. 18. ‡ *De Consens. Evang.* i. 10.
§ "Cujus me vultum pictura docuerat." (*Epist.* 58.)

of which we are speaking, so that they might often be distinguished, even if there were no legends over their heads.

The oldest represention of them now extant is probably that on a bronze plate preserved in the Vatican Library. This medallion is about three inches in diameter; it is cut with a die or with a hammer, and finished with a chisel. De Rossi says:

"It is certainly a work of classical type, and of a style rather Greek than Roman. . . . It is enough to say that to every eye practised in the study of Pagan and Christian art in the third century, it is evident that this bronze is not more modern than about the time of Alexander Severus (A.D. 222-230)."

Boldetti (1720) himself extracted this bronze from the Catacomb of Domitilla, and De Rossi has seen the impressions of similar medallions in the plaster of *loculi*. The portraits on this bronze are very life-like and natural, bearing a strong impress of individual character. One of the heads is covered with short curly hair, the beard clipped short and also curled, the features somewhat rough and commonplace. The features of the other are more noble, graceful, and strongly marked; the head is bald, and the beard is thick and long.* This valuable medal confirms the tradition preserved by Nicephorus † of the personal appearance of the two Apostles, the first being that of S. Peter and the latter that of S. Paul; and, as we have already said, these characteristics are in the main retained in most of the glasses, excepting a few which are of very inferior execution.

The two Apostles are represented side by side, sometimes standing and sometimes seated. In some instances Christ is represented in the air (that is, from heaven, as it were), holding over the head of each a crown of victory; or, in other instances, a single crown is suspended between the two, as if to show that "in their death they were not divided." This crown becomes sometimes a circle surrounding the *labarum* or ☧, which is often supported on a pillar, thus symbolising "the pillar and ground of the truth," which is "that very great, very ancient, and universally-known Church, founded and organised at Rome by the two most glorious Apostles Peter and Paul." ‡ For there certainly seems to be good ground for Mr. Palmer's conjecture, §

---

* Thus, on the sarcophagus of Junius Bassus, in the Lateran Museum, on one side of which the apprehension of our Saviour in the garden is represented, and the apprehension of S. Peter on the other. The Apostle is distinguished from his Lord by the beard. (*R. S.* part ii. p. 259.)

† See also S. Jerome, *in Ep. ad Galat.* i. 18.

‡ S. Irenæus, *Hær.* iii. 3.   § *Early Christian Symbolism*, p. 5.

that in some of these glasses the Roman Church is intended to be symbolised in the persons of her founders and patrons, rather than the Apostles themselves to be represented personally. In this way we can account for their being placed on either side of the Blessed Virgin, of S. Agnes, or of other Saints, who have their hands uplifted in prayer, whilst the Apostles are not in the same attitude, and, moreover, are made to appear of very diminutive stature. It can never have been intended to represent S. Agnes as superior to the chiefs of the Apostles, or as making intercession for those who had "finished their course" more than two centuries before her. Rather we understand S. Agnes, S. Peregrina, and the rest, even our Blessed Lady herself, as praying for the Roman Church which these Apostles had founded, and through it for the Church at large.

The relative positions of these two Apostles in ancient works of art have been a subject of frequent discussion, ever since the days of S. Peter Damian. It seems impossible, however, to establish any theory upon them. S. Peter is generally at the right hand, but by no means always so; and if anyone attempts to prove from this that the Roman Christians looked upon the two Apostles as in all respects equal and co-ordinate, he is met by the fact;—First, that our Lord Himself is found once standing on the left of S. Paul; S. Agnes, too, in the place of honour, where she appears with the Blessed Virgin; and husbands often placed on the left of their wives: moreover, that Pagan artists, when they placed Jupiter between Juno and Minerva, observe the same indifference as to the relative position of the two goddesses; and that the Seal of the Papal Bulls to this day represents S. Peter on the left hand. And secondly, that the primacy of S. Peter is distinctly attested in some of these glasses by another symbol which can hardly be misunderstood. We mean those in which he appears under the type of Moses striking the rock. The rock, of course, at once suggests the passage of S. Paul: "They drank of that spiritual rock that followed them, and that rock was Christ;" but we should hardly have ventured to affirm that the figure striking the rock was S. Peter, if his name had not, in two instances at least, been unmistakably given at his side.*

"In one glass, writes Mr. Palmer, a single crown of martyrdom unites the two heads of the Apostles Peter and Paul (the names being attached), to show that the two together are one joint foundation for the Roman and for

* *R. S.* part ii. p. 298 *seq.*

the whole Church. But lest anyone should wrest the sense of this painting, and argue that, therefore, the two Apostles are in all respects equal and co-ordinate, so that the Church began from a dualism, and not from unity, on another glass the figure of a man striking the rock, and the name " PETAVS " inscribed, show plainly to all such as doubt, that the Christians transferred the story of Moses striking the rock from the Old Testament to the Gospel, and that for them Moses was Peter. But if Peter strikes the rock in the New Covenant as Moses struck it in the Old, then it is clear that he represents the unity of the whole hierarchy, and communicates the grace of the Gospel to the whole spiritual Israel, S. Paul himself included. For when all were athirst in the wilderness, all the congregation, from the first to the last, and Aaron himself, however closely associated with his brother, depended on the rod of Moses. Wherefore by analogy there is no room in the new Israel any more than in the old for a dualism; but the rod of Moses in the hand of Peter is the single source of grace to the indivisible unity of the Catholic Church, both of the circumcision and of the uncircumcision. This Glass is preserved in the Vatican. It has been published by Boldetii, p. 200; and by P. Garrucci, in his pl. x. 9."*

2. CHRISTIAN SARCOPHAGI.

These invaluable Glasses thus supply us with a key to many of the sculptures on Christian sarcophagi and paintings in the Catacombs, where the same scene is so frequently repeated. They show us that S. Peter was considered to be the Moses of "the new Israel of God," as Prudentius speaks, and they explain the reason why the rod, the emblem of Divine power,† is never found except in three hands, those of Moses, Christ, and Peter. It belongs primarily, and by inherent right, to Christ, the eternal Son of God. By Him it was of old delegated to Moses, of whom God testified, "He is most faithful in all My house."‡ For a few years the rod of power was visibly wielded by the Incarnate Word; and when He withdrew His own visible presence from the earth, afterwards, to use the words of S. Macarius of Egypt:

"Moses was succeeded by Peter, to whom He committed the new Church of Christ and the new priesthood."§

What in this connection is most noteworthy and of the highest significance, as bearing immediately on the subject of S. Peter's Roman Episcopate in a historical point of view, is that in the sarcophagi the figure of Moses striking the rock is almost

* *E. C. S.* pp. 16, 17.   † See *Ps.* cix. 2; *Mich.* vii. 14.
‡ *Num.* xii. 7; compare *Heb.* iii. 5, 6.
§ *Hom.* xxvi. c. 23. S. Bernard speaks of the Pope as "primatu Abel, gubernatu Noe, patriarchatu Abraham, ordine Melchisidech, dignitate Aaron, auctoritate Moysee, judicatu Samuel, potestate Petrus, unctione Christus." (*De Consid.* lib. ii. 8.)

invariably found in immediate juxtaposition with the Prince of the Apostles led captive by the satellites of Herod Agrippa, and there is frequently a studied similarity in the features of the principal figure in both scenes. Perhaps the most striking example of this is to be found in a small sarcophagus of the fourth century, where the likeness between the two is unmistakable. This sarcophagus now stands in the principal hall of the Lateran Museum. Mr. Parker, in his collection of photographs, describes it thus : " S. Peter striking the rock and bringing out the Stream of Life, at which the Jews are drinking. The arrest of S. Peter."

Another example may be seen in the large sarcophagus which stands at the end of the same hall. This sarcophagus was recently found above the tomb of S. Paul, when the excavations were made for the construction of the magnificent Baldacchino which now covers the high altar in his basilica on the Via Ostiensis. That basilica was rebuilt by Theodosius towards the close of the fourth century, and this sarcophagus appears to have been placed there about that time. The front of the sarcophagus is divided into four compartments. On the upper one, to the left, we see our Lord with the rod of His power changing the water into wine, and multiplying the loaves, the well-known patristic symbols of the Holy Eucharist, in which the wine becomes His blood and the bread His flesh, which He gives for the life of the world. And then, as a type and foreshadowing of the power of the Holy Eucharist even upon the mortal body, according to His promise,* we have a third group that represents the raising of Lazarus.

Immediately beneath this Eucharist Series, as we may call it, we see three other groups, evidently intended to answer in some way to those above, containing an epitome of S. Peter's life. In the first he stands with the rod of power which our Lord held in the former series, already given him by his Divine Master, and yet receiving from Him the solemn warning of his fall : " Before the cock crow thou shalt deny Me thrice." The uplifted hand of our Lord, and the cock at S. Peter's feet, express this with sufficient clearness, while the rod in the Apostle's hand shows that his fall would not deprive him of his great prerogatives, but that, being converted, he should " confirm his brethren."

The next group represents the apprehension of S. Peter. The bearded face and general similarity of expression identify the

* *John*, vi. 55.

Apostle, and distinguish him from his Divine Master. The Jewish caps mark the satellites of Herod Agrippa; and it is worthy of note that, though they have power to lead the Apostle whither he would not, yet he still retains the rod, for "the Word of God is not bound," and imperial soldiers, who repeated the scene over and over again in the person of Peter's successors, have never been able to wrest from him the rod of power with which he rules the Church as Vicar of Christ.*

Another reason which probably led to the very frequent representation of this scene in S. Peter's life, is that his imprisonment and miraculous deliverance, after which "he went into another place," † was the immediate occasion and cause of his coming to Rome and founding the Church there, where the same scene was enacted again and again in the apprehension and martyrdom of so many of his successors. Thus, too, Roman Christians would see in the apprehension of S. Peter the symbol of "the Holy See of Blessed Peter, through which," in the words of S. Leo—

"Rome was made a priestly and royal city and the head of the world, extending her sway more widely by the religion of God than ever she had done by earthly domination."

The third group is a mutilated representation of Moses striking the rock, of the waters flowing, from which the people of Israel are drinking. We have seen from the glasses found in the Catacombs that this is to be interpreted as a symbol of S. Peter using the rod of power to bring from "the spiritual Rock" the streams of grace at which the Israel of God slake the thirst of

---

* Paisius Ligarides, the worthless opponent of the Muscovite Patriarch Nicon, once a student at the Greek College in Rome, says: "There is an old tradition that our Lord by His question to Peter, thrice repeated, meant to set him right of his thrice-repeated denial, saying, 'Peter, lovest thou Me?' and that as He said the words, 'Feed My lambs,' 'Feed My sheep,' He gave him a staff significative of pastoral authority. For as Moses, when constituted leader of the people of Israel, received the staff of the patriarch Jacob, which had been inherited by his son Joseph, and after his death had been taken to Pharaoh's palace, and was given by the daughter of Pharaoh, the Princess Thermoutis (wife of Thothmes), to Moses, her adopted son; so Peter also, being put forward from all the sheep of the world, and at once appearing to be, and being called and indicated as, the mouth of the whole choir of the Apostles, receives the charge of being leader of the flock, as Theophylact declares, in meet recompense for the ardour of his love. This staff of the Prince of the Apostles, the Christians living at Antioch once upon a time having set up as a conquering standard against the Hagarenes, put to flight 40,000 of them." (Palmer's *The Patriarch and the Tsar*, vol. iii. p. 109.) Whatever may be thought of this tradition, it is a curious comment on the figures under consideration.

† *Acts*, xii. 17.

their souls in all their needs; or, to use the words of S. Cyprian:

> "It is preached (by this eloquent stone) that the Jews, if they thirst and seek after Christ, shall drink together with us, that is, shall obtain the grace of baptism." *

Again, in the same hall, there is a very finely-sculptured sarcophagus, which formerly stood beneath the altar in the tribune of *S. Paolo fuori le mura*. The upper series of figures, amongst other scriptural subjects, represents Peter warned of his denial before the cock should crow, and Moses receiving the law from a hand stretched out from heaven. The interpretation of Moses as the figure of S. Peter is confirmed by this sarcophagus, on the lower portion of which, and immediately under the group just referred to, we see that Apostle in the hands of Herod's satellites still pointing to the stream which flows from the rock above his head; while Christ, or possibly S. John, is represented as also engaging the attention of the satellites, either in allusion to His own apprehension in the garden or else to teach us that He suffers still in the persecution of His Church.†

On another sarcophagus, found in the crypt of S. Peter's, which is considered perhaps to be the finest specimen of Christian sculpture of all the sarcophagi in the Lateran Museum, amongst other scenes are represented the Apostles grouped around our Lord, Who is seated in the centre as in glory. De Rossi remarks that the grace and refinement of the faces of our Lord and the Apostles would incline us to ascribe this work to the age of Septimius Severus (A.D. 194)‡ rather than to that of Constantine, did not the ☧ on one of the sides indicate the latter as its actual date. The two principal figures among the Apostles are manifestly intended for SS. Peter and Paul, and the characteristics of each Apostle are easily to be discerned here. S. Paul is on the right, distinguished by his baldness from S. Peter, who receives, with hands reverently veiled, the new law from the Mediator of the New Testament, just as heathen magistrates were wont to receive from the emperors the book of the constitutions whereby they were to govern the province committed to their charge. Often on similar representations our Lord is represented as giving the volume to the Apostle, but saying nothing. In others, again, the roll bears the inscription, DOMINUS DAT LEGEM, or PACEM,

---

* *Epist.* lxiii. 8.   † *R. S. ibid.* pp. 314, 318, 243-6, 252-3.
‡ Sickler, *Almanach aus Rom.* pp. 173-4, actually assigns to it that date.

sometimes one and sometimes the other, whence the Bishop Eribert was led to engrave on the Book of the Gospels provided for the Cathedral of Milan the words LEX ET PAX. Here again we see Peter represented as the Moses of the new dispensation, and every such discovery increases the probability that in all other representations also of Moses the chief Apostle was really meant to be understood. The two sides of this sarcophagus are covered with sculpture. On one is represented the denial of S. Peter, with a basilica and a baptistery in the background, the latter of which (no doubt by an intentional anachronism) is surmounted with the ☧. On the other side is a similar kind of background, but in front is the smitten rock and apparently the "*Noli me tangere*," although this latter group may be intended to represent the gratitude of Mary for the resurrection of her brother.*

3. PAINTINGS IN THE CATACOMBS.

The same idea, to which as we have thus seen the sculptures on the sarcophagi of the fourth and fifth centuries so frequently give expression, runs also through the paintings in the earliest cubicula of the Catacombs during the two preceding centuries. Peter is there also represented under the form of Moses striking the rock with his rod of power, to indicate that all sacramental grace flows from that one stream over which Peter presides.†

In a fresco in the Cemetery of S. Callixtus two scenes in the life of Moses are represented close together, almost as parts of the same picture; but the figure of Moses in the two is manifestly different. In one he is in the act of taking off his shoes before drawing near to witness the manifestation of the presence of God, Whose call to him is indicated by the hand issuing from the cloud; here he is young and without a beard. In the second

---

* *R. S.* pp. 254-7. Sickler, *Almanach aus Rom.* pp. 254-7.

† Early in the fifth century, S. Augustine expressed the same idea when, writing to Pope Innocent I., he said : " We do not pour back our streamlet for the purpose of increasing your great fountain, but we wish it to be decided by you whether our stream, however small, flows forth from that same head of rivers whence comes your own abundance." (*Epist.* 178.) And in his reply the Pope says of S. Peter : " . . . from whom the very episcopate and all the authority of this name (of the Apostolic See) sprung . . . that thence all other Churches might derive what they should order ; whom they should absolve ; whom, as bemired with ineffaceable pollution, the stream that is worthy only of pure bodies should avoid ; just as from their parent source all waters flow, and through the different regions of the whole world the pure streams of the fountain well forth uncorrupted." (*Inter Epist. S. Aug.* 181.) See the next chapter on the *Chair of S. Peter*, and its connection with the Baptismal Font in the Vatican.

scene, in advance of the other to the right of the spectator, he is striking the rock, and instead of being depicted, as is usual, alone in this act, one of the children of Israel stands in front of him eagerly with open hands quenching his thirst at the miraculous stream; here Moses is older and bearded, and both the general look of his hair and beard and the outline of his features seem to present a certain marked resemblance to the traditional figure of S. Peter, thus indicating the artist's desire to suggest a thought of "the leader of the new people of Israel" rather than of the old.*

Close by in the same catacomb, covering the back of the wall, above an *arcosolium*, there is a remarkable painting of the Good Shepherd, which belongs to the earlier half of the fourth century —according to Mr. Palmer to the middle of the third. The Shepherd occupies His usual position in the centre, bearing the lost sheep upon His shoulders. He stands amid trees in a garden, and has another sheep or goat on either side of Him. But because He has still other sheep also which are not yet of His fold (represented by two pairs of sheep, one at either extremity of the picture), but whom it is necessary that He should bring, and that they should hear His voice,† therefore two Apostles— probably S. Peter and S. Paul, the Apostles of the Jews and Gentiles respectively, and representing therefore the whole apostolate from the beginning to the end—are seen hurrying away from His side to fulfil the mission entrusted to them. He had said, "Going, teach all nations, baptising them in the name of the Father, and of the Son, and of the Holy Ghost;"‡ and here they are seen taking of the waters of divine grace which appear flowing from the mystical Rock of Christ to pour them on the heads of the sheep which surround them, thus illustrating in the most graphic manner the words of S. Cyprian, that it is by means of this water that we are made the sheep of Christ.§ The sheep receive the proffered gift according to their different dispositions. Whilst one obeys the call, another turns his back to it; whilst one with uplifted head drinks in the message with eager attention, another keeps his head steadily towards the ground, intent on the pasturage which is offered him in the goods of the natural world. And the water which is made to fall upon them seems to bear a certain proportion to these varieties of attitude which we have supposed to betoken a difference of inward feeling.

* *R. S.* part ii. pp. 108, 109, 178, 180.   † *John*, x. 16.   ‡ *Matt.* xxviii. 20.
§ " Hæc est aqua in Ecclesia sancta, quæ oves facit." (*Epist.* 71.)

This remarkable painting covers the back of the wall above an *arcosolium*. On one side of the same recess, to the right of the spectator, appears the figure of Moses before described, pp. 139-40.*

"In a painting from the Cemetery of SS. Nereus and Achilleus," says Mr. Palmer,† "Moses is seen with the rod striking the rock, while behind the rock are the Virgin and Child. In another similar painting Moses is striking the rock, and behind the rock Christ is touching the bread with the rod; and again, in a third variety, Moses is striking the rock, and behind the rock Christ is touching with the rod the head of Lazarus, to raise him from the dead."

These two last subjects are studiously brought together in the Catacombs, sometimes, as here, in the same compartment of a painting; sometimes roughly sketched side by side on a gravestone; and are still more often together on a sarcophagus. Most probably the two subjects are intended to represent the beginning and the end of the Christian course: "The fountain of water springing up unto life everlasting," God's grace and the gift of faith being typified by the water flowing from the rock, "which was Christ," and everlasting by the victory over death and the second life vouchsafed to Lazarus. But here again we should bear in mind Peter, symbolised by Moses, who causes the stream of grace to flow forth from the Spiritual Rock.‡

In the principal *arcosolium* of a chamber in the Catacomb of Cyriaca, which was brought to light some five-and-twenty years ago in consequence of the enlargement of the Campo Santo, a modern cemetery of Rome, amongst other paintings there is a scene in which our Lord appears with the *nimbus*. The cock on the pillar shows that He is in the act of foretelling to Peter his threefold denial of Him—a scene which, whatever may have been the motive for its selection, is continually repeated on the sarcophagi of the fourth and fifth centuries. Perhaps it was chosen from a motive of humility, according to the interpretation of the incident which we find in some of the Homilies of the Fathers, who connect very beautifully S. Peter's fall with the high office for which he was destined, in this way: they say that he was allowed to fall in a more signal manner than any other of the Apostles, because to him were to be entrusted the keys of the kingdom of heaven.§ It was necessary, therefore, that he

* *R. S.* 177-80. † *E. C. S. ibid.* p. 12. ‡ *R. S.* ii. p. 115.

§ We should have preferred to have said here, the universal pastorate. The Fathers are used to connect together very frequently the threefold denial of S. Peter with the triple questioning by our Lord of His Apostle, and the

should be a penitent, lest innocence should refuse to open the gate to those who had fallen and risen again. De Rossi, however, prefers to interpret this scene more simply as an emblem of faith. He observes that at the same time that our Blessed Lord foretold the shameful fall of Peter, He also gave an indication of his future firmness and indefectibility in the faith. "Jesus said: I have prayed for thee that thy faith fail not; and thou, being once converted, confirm thy brethren."* On the sarcophagi, S. Peter and the cock are almost always followed by S. Peter's apprehension and imprisonment by the Jews, and by Moses (or Peter) striking the mystical rock. Thus his weakness is brought into immediate juxtaposition with the strength of his faith in confessing Christ boldly before men, and with the immovable firmness of that Rock whence flows the stream of evangelical doctrine and the grace of the Sacraments.†

A striking confirmation of the interpretation of the symbol of Moses as a type of S. Peter is supplied by a large glass plate brought by M. Basilewsky from Podogoritza, the ancient Doclea in Dalmatia, and described by De Rossi with an engraving of the exact size of the original. The plate is 9¼ inches in diameter, of white transparent glass, scratched with rude figures representing Scriptural subjects, arranged in a circle round a central group of Abraham's sacrifice of Isaac. We have Daniel with a lion on each side of him, and the words: DANIEL DE LACO LEONIS (Daniel from the lion's den); then the Three Children, with the title: TRIS PUERI DE IGNE CAMINO (Three Children from the furnace of fire); next, a woman with her arms extended in prayer, and the legend: SUSANA DE FALSO CREMINE (Susanna from the false accusation); then comes a boat from which Jonas has been thrown and swallowed by a monster, who gazes at him under the gourd, with the words: DIUNAN DE VENTRE QUETI LIBERATUS EST (Jonas

---

thrice-repeated charge to be shepherd over His lambs and sheep. This is strikingly illustrated by passages from the Greek Offices (see *infra*, part iii. ch. xiii.), the word-painting of which very remarkably corresponds with these ancient paintings on the walls of the Catacombs, and affords a strong presumption for the early date of these Offices.

* *Luke*, xxii. 32.

† *R. S.* part ii. pp. 191-3. Besides the scenes of Moses and the Arrest, so frequently repeated, there are several other interesting subjects, particularly illustrating the character and position of S. Peter in early Roman painting and sculpture, such as his receiving the keys, or the roll of the New Law, from our Lord, &c. For these we must refer the reader to Palmer's *Symbolism*, and to the volumes cited above, from the pages of which we have almost exclusively formed this and the two preceding chapters by continuous and textual quotation.

from the whale's belly was delivered). Then we have the fall of our first parents, with the words: ABRAM ET FI[lius—Adam et] EVAM (Abraham and his son—Adam and Eve). The resurrection of Lazarus follows, with the words: DOMINUS LAZARUM (The Lord [raises] Lazarus). Finally, we have Peter striking the rock, with the legend in cursive characters which De Rossi has deciphered thus: PETRUS VIRGA PERQUODSET, FONTIS CIPERUNT QUORERE—that is, PETRUS VIRGA PERCUSSIT, FONTES CŒPERUNT CURRERE (Peter struck [the Rock] with the Rod, and the streams [of grace] began to flow). The rudeness of the drawing makes the rock look more like a tree, but the legend leaves no room for doubt about the meaning. De Rossi has not yet given to the world his judgment as to the exact date of this precious relic of antiquity, which the archæological zeal of M. Basilewsky succeeded in rescuing from Serajevo just at the commencement of the Eastern war, but he is justified in saying: " This testimony which comes to us from the east of Illyricum, sets the seal with dazzling clearness to the truth of the Moses-Peter, whom the Roman monuments had first revealed to Padre Marchi, of illustrious memory." *

On S. Peter's arrest Mr. Palmer says:

"This representation occurs so frequently,† as of itself to suggest the thought that something more must be meant by it than an allusion to the mere fact of the imprisonment and miraculous deliverance of the chief Apostle at Jerusalem; a fact paralleled by the imprisonment and deliverance of S. Paul at Philippi, which yet is nowhere represented. And if we consider closely the history of the first opening of the kingdom of God to the Gentile world, we shall see that the position of the Italian volunteer cohort at Cæsarea, the appointment of Herod Agrippa, a Jew, by the Emperor Claudius on his accession, to be King of Judæa, and its consequences; namely, that both Herod should take a side against the Christians, and that the Italians should evacuate Cæsarea, were designed preparations towards an end; while the imprisonment and deliverance of S. Peter, making it natural that he should leave Judæa just as his Italian converts also were returning to Italy, was the last of the series of preparations, the touch, as it were, of the spring which sent him from the heart and capital of the Hebrew to that of the Gentile world: to Rome, that is, where we find him soon after, according to the local Roman tradition, near the head of a street (*Vicus Corneliorum*) named from the Cornelii, whose clients were extremely numerous, and in the house of a Roman senator, one of the heads of the same most noble family to

---

* R. S. part ii. pp. 318-19.

‡ After the representation of Jonas, the smitten rock and the apprehension of S. Peter are the subjects most frequently found on the sarcophagi: the latter is found on twenty sarcophagi in the Lateran Museum.

144   SYMBOLISM OF PETER AS MOSES STRIKING THE ROCK.

which Rome had been so largely indebted for the extension of her empire.*
Sometimes on the sculptured sarcophagi we find a consolidation of these two
representations of S. Peter. He strikes the rock with the rod, and proselytes
converted from among the Jews run up to drink, while others are laying
hands upon him to take him to prison."

The following eloquent pages from the pen of Mr. Allies† will
form a luminous commentary on what has been the principal
subject of the present chapter :

"This work of Peter in the midst of the heathen world, and especially at
Rome, its centre and capital, was represented to Christian eyes in the ancient
paintings of the catacombs, and in the sculptures of sarcophagi, under a
symbol which cannot be mistaken. There often recurs the image of Moses
striking the rock with the rod of power, from which the streams of salvation
issue. The rock, according to the Apostle's interpretation, signifies Christ; the
stream, that one fountain of grace on which the Christian life depends, and
which, accordingly, the sheep are represented as drinking. The allusion to
the Old Testament narrative is plain, but usually no name is given to the man
striking the rock; in two instances, however, of the ancient glasses, the
name of Peter is written above this image, to signify that in the new Israel of
God he occupies the place which Moses occupied in the old. But, moreover,
this scene of Moses striking the rock is found constantly in juxtaposition with
another scene of Peter taken captive by the satellites of Herod, and the
features of the captive Peter and the man striking the rock are frequently
made with a studied similarity to each other. For the repetition of these
scenes close to each other no reason can be assigned but that Peter's imprisonment and miraculous deliverance immediately preceded that 'going
forth into another place,' in which he founded the Roman Church, the most
signal instance wherein he appeared as the Moses of the new covenant,
causing the stream of grace to flow from the rock of Christ in the very centre
and high place of Pagan idolatry. The exhibition of such paintings on the
walls of Roman catacombs, and of such sculptures on Roman sarcophagi,
conveyed a whole history to the beholder's mind. There was the local
tradition of the Roman Church, and the universal tradition of the whole
Church, embodied in colour or in stone, as to the part which Peter had taken
in founding the great See wherein he would deposit his jurisdiction; but that
jurisdiction itself is indicated in the rod, the symbol of divine power, given in
these paintings and sculptures to three persons alone—the Incarnate God

---

* The relationship of the family of Pudens with the *gens Cornelia* is proved
by a bronze diploma of the year 222, found, in 1776, near the Church of S.
Prisca on the Aventine, to one Caius Marius Pudens Cornelianus, of senatorial
rank. S. Prisca is the traditional site of the first Christian church in Rome,
in the house of Prisca and Aquila (*Rom.* xvi. 3-5). The Italian cohort, to
which Cornelius, the first Gentile convert made by S. Peter belonged (*Acts*, x.
1), was composed of volunteers from some of the noblest families in Rome.
It is styled in inscriptions: *Cohors Italica, Cohors Civium Romanorum Volun-
tariorum, Cohors Ingenuorum Civium Romanorum.* If the full name of the
convert of S. Peter was Cornelius Pudens, the account of the Apostle being
the guest of Pudens on the Viminal, as stated in the *Acts of the Martyrdom of
S. Praxedes,* is fully explained. (*Early Christian Symbolism,* pp. 12, 13.)

† *The Formation of Christendom,* part iii. pp. 44-53.

Himself; Moses, who prefigured Him; and Peter, who followed Him. And the work accomplished is conveyed under the image of Moses striking the rock, with a fulness and pregnancy of meaning such as reminds us of our Lord's own parables; for it would require a great space adequately to develop the thoughts suggested by the representation of Peter discharging to the new people of God functions which corresponded to those discharged by Moses when he led the typical nation through the desert.

"But we may fully exhibit some of the truth conveyed by this speaking symbol, and so elucidate the idea which the Christian artists of the third, fourth, and fifth centuries intended to portray; and that especially because, in their delineation of Scriptural scenes, 'they neither treated them accurately as parts of history, nor yet freely as subjects of the imagination, but strictly with a view to their spiritual or dogmatic signification.'* The transit of the Jewish people from their slavery in Egypt through the wilderness to their promised possession is the type of the Christian people delivered from their darker slavery, and led through the desert of the world to their divine inheritance. But in that transit Moses was the leader and lawgiver of his people. As their mediator with God, he received from God and gave to them a revelation of doctrine and a code of morals. Into his people, as a receptacle, he poured the knowledge of one personal God, the Creator and rewarder of men; and as a deduction from that truth, he gave them a code of duties, in which the first table contained all their relations to God, and the second all their relations to each other. Thus in the person of Moses were combined the two great powers of the Prophet or Teacher, and of the Lawgiver or King, but both as the deputy of Another, with Whom he communed on the Mount. And in the same character, as the deputy of that Other, Who was not only the Revealer of truth and the Source of authority, but the Object likewise of worship, he instituted the third great power, the priesthood—not, however, in his own person, but in his brother Aaron and Aaron's sons. It is in this triple mediation, as the instrument through whom a revelation was conveyed and a law promulgated, and a priesthood, together with its worship, instituted, that the pre-eminence of Moses consisted. He thus made a complete society, feeding his people with truth, governing them with law, and sanctifying them with sacrifice and prayer. In the union of the three he educated them for their promised possession, and constituted them a nation. For their nationality was to consist in the continued joint possession of these three things, by maintaining which they were to be distinguished from all other nations down to the coming of the great Chief Whom they expected. . . .

"But the three powers which were thus united in the mediation of Moses, while they were continued in the nation which he moulded, were not deposited in the same hands. We need not enter here into the various manners in which, during the course of fifteen hundred years, they were exercised. It is enough for the present purpose to note that in the nation as ultimately constituted we find the synagogue, the temple, and the throne of David;† that is, the teaching office, which communicates doctrine; the priesthood, which celebrates worship; the royalty, which is the guardian and transmitter of the kingdom promised to David. As Moses left these three

---

* Northcote and Brownlow, vol. ii. p. 104.
† Döllinger, *Christenthum und Kirche*, p. 228.

powers in the Jewish community, so, after all the changes through which it had passed, they were found at the time of Christ still existing. The great Council of Jerusalem sat in the seat of Moses,* guarding and applying the double code of revelation and of morals which was contained in the law and the prophets; the high priest occupied the place of Aaron, and Herod filled the throne of David. The Prophet, the Priest, and the King, three rays of the divine sovereignty, made up 'the polity of Israel;'† but they were separate and distinct in their holders, until He came unto Whom each of them pointed. The priesthood, with all the elaborate arrangement of sacrifices connected with it, was instituted only to mark out the office and prepare the way for the great High Priest. The prophet who had established the law, both as the disclosure of divine truth and the rule of life, gave it as the image of that Prophet like unto him who was to be raised up among his brethren. The throne had only been consecrated in David's person as the typical seat of the Eternal King. The whole polity which contained these three powers had been prepared during so many ages, to be taken up and transmitted by Him Who should unite all these offices in His own Person.

"But these offices, upon their being received by Him, acquired an augmentation of dignity proportionate to His Person. The bearer of them being divine, the things borne rose to His height. The Incarnate God willed that the law should prefigure His truth, the priesthood His atonement, the seat of David His royal power; that thus there should be continuity between the Jewish type and Christian antitype, but continuity attended by an immeasurable exaltation. First He joined together in Himself these powers which make the perfect kingdom; then He imparted them so joined to the apostolate which He created, and especially to Peter, whom alone He made the Rock, the Foundation, and the Doorkeeper, the Confirmer of his brethren, the Shepherd and the Ruler of the Fold. He extended that which had been confined within the limits of a nation to the whole race of man: He detached the carnal covering which veiled the promises, and disclosed them in their full spiritual light. For the priesthood, which offered the sacrifices of bulls and sheep, He instituted the priesthood which offered at His own table the sacrifice offered by Himself; and He made it a royal priesthood, ordering that its possessors should sit upon twelve thrones judging the twelve tribes of Israel, and so be perpetual guardians and maintainers of the law of truth and charity which He left in that new Israel. Thus He disposed to them the kingdom which had been disposed to Him.‡ In this manner the covenant, the legislation, the worship, the adoption, the glory, and the promises, which made, according to S. Paul, the distinction of the Jewish Church, passed over to the Christian, which became in a higher sense than the former, in the words of S. Peter, 'a chosen race, a royal priesthood, a holy nation, a purchased people.' Moses, Aaron, and David having been gathered up into the one Christ, the race of Abraham became the race of the God-man.

"Now, what Moses did in the type, Peter did in the antitype. As Moses drew out the life of the Jewish people as a personal relation to God in what

---

* *Matt.* xxiii. 2. † *Ephes.* ii. 12.

‡ *Luke*, xxii. 29, 30, in which passage, as Döllinger notes, while creating the royal priesthood in the apostolate, He marks that there should be one that is greater among them.

they believed, in what they worshipped, in what they did, which made up the adoption of sons, so the Christian life which Peter set up at Rome was the establishment of the same relation to Christ in doctrine, worship, and morals. Obedience to Him in these three things formed His kingdom. The whole domain of truth was guaranteed to the Christian as the illumination given by the one Prophet. His worship was the perpetual recognition of the Redeemer in the very act of His Sacrifice; while His morality was summed up in charity, the filial spirit which raised the cardinal virtues to the level of divine gifts, and was thus 'the fulfilment of the law' as perfected by Christ. The painter in the catacombs of the second and third centuries, the sculptor on the monuments of the fourth and fifth, conveyed all this when they represented Peter on the very scene of his spiritual triumph, the centre of the world's power, and the seat of idolatry, striking with the rod of divine power which he alone received from the hands of his Lord, that Rock which is Christ, and so drawing forth the one stream of salvation, the grace which works in the great Christian priesthood, which conveys to the sheep the faith and the Sacraments, the whole supernatural life. In their eyes, as but one Moses was the mediator of the old covenant, so but one Peter was the masterbuilder of the Church, the deriver of the stream to the sheep. They anticipated in colour and on stone what S. Leo, at the same spot, has set forth so powerfully and distinctly in language. The living mind of the Church in their day, as seen in their works and in his words, is the same, which he declares to his brethren, the Bishops of Italy: 'Whatever we do rightly and discern clearly is of his own working and his merit, whose power lives and whose authority is pre-eminent in his own See; for throughout the whole Church Peter is daily saying, Thou art Christ, the Son of the living God, and every tongue confessing the Lord is imbued with the teaching of that Word of His.' For 'out of the whole world Peter alone is chosen to preside over the calling of all the nations, over the whole number of the Apostles, and all the Fathers of the Church; so that though there be in the people of God many priests and many shepherds, yet Peter rules all with ordinary, whom Christ rules with sovereign, power.'"*

* S. Leo, *Serm.* iii. 3, iv. 2.

CHAPTER IV.

THE CHAIR OF S. PETER IN THE VATICAN.*

THE CHAIR OF S. PETER IN THE VATICAN NOT THE SAME AS THAT VENERATED IN THE CÆMETERIUM OSTRIANUM—THE VATICAN CHAIR RECENTLY EXPOSED—DESCRIPTION OF IT—ITS PARTS AND ORNAMENTATION—ITS ORIGIN—HISTORICAL NOTICES OF IT—THE TWO FEASTS OF S. PETER'S CHAIR.

IN our account of the Catacombs of the first century we have described the Cæmeterium Ostrianum, in which Signor Armellini has recently identified the chapel where was once venerated "the Chair where Peter the Apostle first sat"—*Sedes ubi prius sedit Petrus Apostolus.* The Hieronymian Martyrology marks January 18 as "*Dedicatio Cathedræ S. Petri Apostoli, qua primum Romæ sedit.*" This same day is marked as the Feast of S. Peter's Chair at Rome in the Martyrologies of Ado and Bede, and in other ancient records, and it is never said *ubi primus* or *prior*, but always the adverb *prius* or *primum*, so that the reference is evidently not to the line of Roman Pontiffs of whom he was the first, but to some other Chair in which he afterwards sat at Rome. All ancient authors record two journeys of the Apostle to Rome, one in the time of Claudius, and another in the reign of Nero; and these two journeys afford an easy explanation of his having had two well-remembered places of abode, and two Chairs treasured up with affection and veneration by his children in the Gospel. All trace of the Chair from which the Abbot John brought the *olea* to Queen Theodolinda has now disappeared, but another Chair of S. Peter is still preserved in the Vatican Basilica, and we propose to supplement our notice of the Chair that is lost† by an account of the venerable relic that still exists.

Everyone knows the magnificent monument of gilded bronze erected by Bernini over the altar at the extremity of the tribune

* This chapter is found in *Roma Sotterranea*, Appendix II. to Part i. pp. 483-491.
† Pp. 109-113.

of S. Peter's. The four Latin and Greek Doctors of the Church support a gigantic seat about sixteen feet in height, within which is enclosed an ancient chair, affirmed by Roman tradition to have been actually used by the Prince of the Apostles. Among the Essays of the late Cardinal Wiseman is a learned and interesting paper, which exposes the absurdity of Lady Morgan's amusing blunder in confusing this venerable relic with an ancient chair at Venice, and so pretending that on the Chair of S. Peter was to be found the Mussulman formula. The Cardinal, however, was obliged to be content with descriptions and drawings of the true chair which were two hundred years old, as the relic had never been seen by man since Alexander VII. had placed it in its present position. Commendatore De Rossi has been more fortunate; for, at the eighteen hundredth anniversary of the Martyrdom of the Apostles, in 1867, Pope Pius IX. commanded this venerable relic to be exposed for the veneration of the faithful, and full opportunities were given for a close and scientific examination of it from every point of view. We shall follow De Rossi in his description of the chair.

1. DESCRIPTION OF THE CHAIR.

The chair is about 4 feet 9 inches high and 2 feet 10 inches wide. The depth from the front to the back is about 2 feet 2 inches, while the seat is about 2 feet $1\frac{1}{4}$ inches from the ground. The seat itself is gone. The chair has four solid legs composed of yellow oak, united by horizontal bars of the same material. In these legs are fixed the iron rings which make the whole a *sella gestatoria*, such as that in which the Sovereign Pontiff is now carried on state occasions, and such as those which the Roman senators began to use in the time of Claudius. The four oak legs were evidently once square, but they are much eaten away by age, and have also had pieces cut from them as relics. These time-worn portions have been strengthened and rendered more ornamental by pieces of dark acacia wood, which form the whole interior part of the chair, and which appear to have hardly suffered at all from the same causes which have so altered the appearance of the oak legs. The panels of the front and sides, and the row of arches with the tympanum above them, which forms the back, are also composed of this wood. But the most remarkable circumstance about these two different kinds of material is, that all the ivory ornaments which cover the front and back of the chair are attached to the acacia portions alone, and never to the parts composed of oak. Thus the oak framework, with its rings, appears to be of quite a distinct antiquity from that of the acacia portions with their ivory decorations.... The ivory ornaments themselves, again, are of two distinct kinds of workmanship. Those which cover the front panel of the chair are square plates of ivory, disposed in three rows, six in a row. The two upper rows have the Labours of Hercules engraved upon them, with thin *laminæ* of gold let into the lines of the engraving. The six lower plates have figures probably intended for constellations. Some of them are put on upside down, and their present use is evidently not that for which they were originally intended. The other ivories, on the contrary, fit exactly the portions of acacia which they cover, with the architecture of which they correspond, and they appear to have been made on purpose, and never to have been used for ornamenting any other article. They consist of bands of ivory, not engraved, but sculptured in relief, and represent combats of beasts, centaurs, and men; and in the middle of the horizontal bar of the tympanum is a figure of a crowned emperor, holding in his right hand a sceptre, which is broken, and in his left a globe; he has a moustache, but no beard, and De Rossi conjectures he may be intended for Charlemagne, or one of his successors. Garrucci speaks of it as a portrait of Charles the Bald. Two angels, one on either side, offer him crowns, and the two others bear palms. The style of the carving and of the arabesques corresponds to the age of Charlemagne. The Labours of Hercules are of a much more ancient date, but De Rossi does not think them as old as the first century. Mr. Nesbitt says: "They are no doubt Byzantine, and probably date from the eleventh century." In this date he agrees with P. Garrucci.

Mr. Nesbitt gives many learned reasons to support his hypothesis that the main portion of the chair, *i.e.*, the acacia additions, was originally an imperial throne of Byzantine manufacture. We know that several of the marks of dignity with which the Sovereign Pontiffs are surrounded, such as the *flabella*, have an Oriental origin; and there is no difficulty in supposing that an imperial throne was sent by the Byzantine Emperor to one of the Popes of the ninth century, and that its amalgamation with the Chair of S. Peter rendered it a more fitting symbol of the authority of the Pope. Cardinal Wiseman adopted the theory that this chair had once been the ivory curule-chair of the Senator

Pudens. But, though the more precise examination of it that has taken place in our day prevents our accepting this hypothesis, yet archæological criticism by no means contradicts the traditional antiquity of the oak framework of the chair. The mythological figures on the ivories need not surprise us. At the time when the inner part of acacia was added, and adorned with bands of ivory, the ancient ivories which cover the front appear to have been put on, and it is not at all uncommon to meet with copies of the Gospels, reliquaries, and other valuable works of the early mediæval period, which are ornamented with ivories representing subjects of Pagan mythology. At that time Paganism was dead in Europe, and its treasures of art were transferred to innocent and often to sacred uses; but when the struggle between the infant Church and the dominant power of heathen idolatry was still raging, the Christians were extremely cautious in their admission of scenes of Pagan mythology, and would not have been likely to allow them to remain undefaced on so sacred an object as the Chair of S. Peter. On the other hand, all that the Cardinal urges as to the introduction of the use of the *sella gestatoria* by the senators, precisely in the reign of Claudius, is most valuable, as showing what was regarded in those days as a special honour, and therefore one antecedently probable to have been conferred by a convert of senatorial rank upon the Chief Pastor of the Church, to whom, in the words of the *Liber Pontificalis*, "the chair was delivered or committed by our Lord Jesus Christ."*

2. HISTORICAL NOTICES OF S. PETER'S CHAIR.

In order to prove satisfactorily from historical sources that the relic now venerated as the Chair of S. Peter was so regarded from the earliest ages of the Roman Church, it will be necessary not only to trace a chain of testimonies up to apostolic or quasi-apostolic times to the *cathedra Petri*, but also to produce good evidence that the expression *cathedra* or *sedes Petri* is to be understood not merely in a metaphorical and moral, but also in a literal and physical sense. For instance, when we read in the pages of Bede (*H. E.* v. 8) that Ceadwalla, king of the West Saxons, converted by S. Wilfrid, went to Rome to be baptised, and died there

* "Hic (Clemens) ex præcepto Beati Petri suscepit Ecclesiam, et Pontificatum gubernandum, sicut ei fuerat a Domino Jesu Christo cathedra tradita, vel commissa." (*Lib. Pont.* c. iv.)

A.D. 689, and that Pope Sergius I. put up in S. Peter's an epitaph which stated:

> "King Ceadwalla, the powerful in war, for love of God left all, that he might visit and see Peter and Peter's chair, and humbly receive from his font the cleansing waters,"

we might reasonably think that as "Peter" is put metaphorically for his successor, Pope Sergius, so "Peter's Chair" might not improbably be a metaphorical expression for Rome, the seat of his jurisdiction; and hence we could not from such passages as this conclude that any certain reference was intended to a visible material chair, such as that of which we have given a description.

Our first authority, then, shall be one who leaves us in no doubt upon this point. Ennodius of Pavia, who flourished at the end of the fifth and beginning of the sixth centuries, introduces Rome as rejoicing in having become Christian, and puts into her mouth the following words:

> "Ecce nunc ad gestatoriam sellam apostolicæ confessionis uda mittunt limina candidatos: et uberibus gaudio exactore fletibus collata Dei beneficio dona geminantur." *

> "See now the dripping thresholds send forth the white-robed (neophytes) to the *sella gestatoria* of the Apostle's Confession; and amid floods of joyous tears the gifts conferred by the kindness of God are doubled," *i.e.*, in the two Sacraments of Baptism and Confirmation.

In this passage Ennodius brings vividly before us the scene presented by the Baptistery of the Vatican, when the newly-baptised, with joyful emotion, passed at once from the font to receive confirmation from the Bishop seated in the *sella gestatoria*, which appears to have been then a conspicuous object at S. Peter's shrine.

This passage is illustrated by some lines from the Codex of Verdun, a fragment of the fourth or fifth century:

> "Istic insontes cœlesti flumine lotas
> Pastoris Summi dextera signat oves.
> Huc undis generate veni quo Sanctus ad unum
> Spiritus ut capias te sua dona vocat."

> "In this place the right hand of the Chief Pastor seals the innocent sheep, who have been washed in the heavenly stream. O thou who hast been born again in the waters, come to that one place whither the Holy Ghost calls thee to receive His gifts."

* *Apol. pro Synodo*, apud Sirmond. Opp. tom. i. p. 1647.

The lines preceding these in the same Codex were written at the entrance of the Baptistery:

> "Sumite perpetuam sancto de gurgite vitam
> Cursus hic est fidei, mors ubi sola perit.
> Roborat hic animos divino fonte lavacrum,
> Et dum membra madent, mens solidatur aquis.
> Auxit apostolicæ geminatum sedis honorem
> Christus et ad cœlos hunc dedit esse viam:
> Nam cui siderei commisit limina regni
> Hic habet in templis altera claustra poli."

"From this sacred font draw everlasting life; for this is the stream of faith in which death alone is destroyed. Here the washing in the font of God gives strength to souls, and while the limbs are moistened, the mind is made strong by the waters. Christ has added double honour to the Chair of the Apostle, and given him to be the way to heaven; for he to whom He committed the portals of the kingdom above has here in the churches another gate of heaven."

From these lines we gather that the Baptistery of the Vatican in which they were inscribed, was "an honour doubled by Christ to Peter, and to the Chair of the Apostle," and that there was in that Baptistery a distinct place where the neophytes were sealed and enriched with the gifts of the Holy Ghost by the hand of the Supreme Pastor. Now, comparing this with the passage of Ennodius, we perceive that the *sedes apostolica* is not mentioned only in its moral, but also in its literal and material sense; and that in the fifth century at least there was solemnly preserved in the Baptistery of the Vatican a *sella gestatoria*, upon which, or in front of which, the Pope used to sit when he conferred the Sacrament of Confirmation.

A remarkable testimony to the same fact is the evident allusion to it in the inscription which S. Damasus put up in the Baptistery which he had built:

"UNA PETRI SEDES UNUM VERUMQUE LAVACRUM."

Again, in the inscription on the tomb of the immediate successor of Damasus, we read that Pope Siricius—

"FONTE SACRO MAGNUS MERUIT SEDERE SACERDOS." *

Now, the usual place for the Bishop's throne was in the *apse* of the Basilica, and therefore if it is recorded that Siricius "was counted worthy to sit as High Priest at the Sacred Font," it is

---

* Gruter, *Inscr.* pp. 1168, 10, and 1171, 16.

clear that "in the Sacred Font," *i.e.*, in the Baptistery,* was placed the Chair to which the Bishop of Rome owed his pre-eminent rank as the *Sacerdos Magnus;* and, in fact, the magnificent Baptistery of S. Damasus is described by Prudentius as "the Apostolic Chair."

With these authorities to guide us, we read the epitaph of Ceadwalla in an entirely new light, and we cannot doubt that the "Chair of Peter," which he is described as leaving home to see, was none other than the famous *sella gestatoria* which the Saxon king could not fail to visit when he received the sacrament of regeneration in "Peter's Font."

Our next authority shall be S. Optatus of Milevis, who published the first edition of his work against the Donatists during the Pontificate of S. Damasus, and the second during that of S. Siricius. The Donatists boasted of having in Rome a bishop of their sect. Optatus opposed to them the line of Roman Pontiffs from Peter to Damasus and to Siricius, "all occupiers," as he pointed out, "of the same Chair": and proceeded—

"In fact, if Macrobius" (the Donatist bishop) "be asked where he sits in Rome, can he say, In the chair of Peter? (*in cathedra Petri*); which I am not aware that he has ever seen with his eyes, and to whose shrine he, as a schismatic, has not approached." †

The Chair, therefore, on which Damasus and afterwards Siricius sat as Pontiffs was in the time of S. Optatus regarded not only morally but materially as the Chair of S. Peter, and was seen by the eyes of those who approached *ad Petri memoriam, i.e.,* to his Basilica on the Vatican.

Now, it is impossible that this Chair could have been so generally regarded in the fourth century as having belonged to the Apostle S. Peter and his successors, unless there had been at the time an ancient tradition to that effect. Before S. Damasus placed it in the Baptistery of the Vatican, it must have been preserved elsewhere, perhaps in the very crypt of S. Peter's tomb, or in the Basilica of Constantine. At any rate, before the Diocletian persecution, and in the course of the third century, Catholics professed, in the presence of heretics who did not attempt to

---

* We cannot but be struck with the coincidence that both chairs should be thus connected with *Fons Petri*—the chair in the Ostrianum in which Peter first sat, *ad Fontem* or *ad Nymphas Petri* where he baptised; and this other chair at the font, in the Baptistery of the Vatican—serving to illustrate, as it does, the symbolical representation so frequently repeated of Peter striking the rock with the rod to cause the saving waters to flow forth.

† S. Optat. *ad Parmen.* ii. 4.

deny it, the same tradition which S. Optatus opposed to the Donatists concerning the Chair in which the successors of S. Peter presided over the Church. This comes out with striking clearness in the Poem against Marcion usually appended to the works of Tertullian, and which from internal evidence clearly belongs to the third century. Towards the end of Book III. this ancient author enumerates the Bishops of Rome, and commences the list with these lines:

> "Hac cathedra Petrus, qua sederat ipse, locatum
> Maxima Roma Linum primum considere jussit."

"In this chair, in which Peter himself had sat, he ordained Linus first to sit with him (as bishop) established in Great Rome."*

These words certainly suggest the idea of a material chair, and this literal sense becomes still more certain when we recall the language of S. Optatus and Ennodius. In fact, with the light thrown upon the expression *cathedra Petri* by the passages of these authors, it is impossible to avoid observing, that in many of the works of the early Fathers in which that expression occurs, its force is immensely increased, if we suppose them to have used it with a full knowledge that the very Chair of the Apostle was preserved in Rome as the visible witness to, and symbol of, the apostolic foundation of her line of Pontiffs. Thus, when S. Cyprian wrote of the Roman See being vacant by the martyrdom of S. Fabian, "*cum locus Fabiani, id est locus Petri et gradus cathedra sacerdotalis vacaret,*"† the force of the expression is greatly increased, if we understand him to have had in view the venerable Chair " in which Peter himself had sat," and on which his successors, down to S. Fabian, were enthroned.

The celebrated passage of Tertullian, *De Præscript.* c. 36, loses much of its significance if we regard him as ignorant of the existence of this venerable relic. He invites all heretics to test their doctrines by the living tradition of the Apostolic Churches:

> "Percurre ecclesias apostolicas, apud quas ipsæ adhuc cathedræ apostolorum suis locis præsident. ... Si Italiæ adjaces, habes Romam."

> "Go through the Apostolic Churches, where the very chairs of the Apostles still preside in their places. ... If you are near Italy, you have Rome."

---

* Thus Oehler's punctuation renders it, and thus it is given in the metrical translation of the *Ante-Nicene Library*, "Writings of Tertullian," vol. iii. p. 357. The laws of prosody are no guide in determining the case of words in compositions of this date. Witness the epitaph of Severus, *Rom. Sotterran.* part i. p. 350.

† Epist. 59.

The Church of Jerusalem preserved the *ipsa cathedra* of S. James;[*] Alexandria venerated the *ipsa cathedra* of S. Mark;[†] and Tertullian's long residence in Rome must have familiarised him with the *ipsa cathedra* "in which Peter himself had sat."

Another passage of the same work of Tertullian states: "Romanorum [ecclesia] Clementem a Petro ordinatum edit." "The Church of the Romans proclaims Clement to have been ordained by Peter." Yet the ancient Catalogues place both Linus and Cletus before Clement. At any rate, this passage of Tertullian shows the antiquity of the account afterwards inserted in the *Liber Pontificalis*, that Linus and Cletus had governed the Roman Church while the Apostles were living, and that Clement had been ordained by Peter himself as his successor, and had been enthroned by him in his own chair. This tradition forms the subject of one of the frescoes recently brought to light by Father Mullooly in the subterranean Church of San Clemente. It is true that a full account of it is found in the apocryphal Clementines, but it does not therefore follow that the whole story is fabulous,[‡] for these pages abound in examples of valuable historical truths having been buried under a mass of doubtful and sometimes fictitious stories.

We have now traced up the testimonies to this celebrated relic, from the fifth century to the age when men were living who had conversed with the contemporaries of the Apostles themselves. All this time it was regarded by Christians in various parts of the world as the very pledge and symbol of apostolic succession and of true dogmatic teaching. It was the object of a festival, celebrated alike by S. Ambrose at Milan and S. Augustine in Africa; and the relic itself was deposited by S. Damasus in the Basilica of the Vatican, where it remained throughout the fifth and at the beginning of the sixth centuries; and there is every probability that it is directly alluded to in the epitaph of Ceadwalla at the close of the seventh century. Pope Adrian I. (772-779) made a richly ornamented marble repository for its reception. During the Middle Ages the mention of it becomes merely incidental, principally in accounts of the enthronisations of the Pope, and in liturgical books; so that instead of this Chair

---

[*] Euseb. *H. E.* vii. 19, 32.   [†] Vales. *in ibid.*

[‡] Nay, the fact that the material chair of S. Peter is expressly mentioned and that S. Clement is represented as seated in it, in the letter to S. James; which is now held by the learned to have been written certainly some time in the second century, is a direct testimony to what is here the matter of proof.

of S. Peter having been an invention of the credulity of the barbarous ages, it barely maintained, during these ages, the veneration paid to it from apostolic times, and was never adduced, as in earlier days, as an important weapon for the confusion of heretics. We learn from incidental notices that every year, on the 22nd of February, it used to be solemnly carried to the high altar of S. Peter's, and that the Pope was then seated in it. The historians of the Vatican relate that it was translated from one chapel of the Basilica to another, until Alexander VII., two centuries ago, enclosed it in the bronze monument, where it remained concealed from the eyes of all until the summer of 1867. It is impossible, or, to say the least, in the highest degree improbable, that a new chair could have been surreptitiously substituted for that mentioned by Ennodius, and placed by S. Damasus in the Vatican Baptistery. The *sella gestatoria* exposed for veneration in 1867 corresponds exactly with Ennodius' description, for the rings which render it *gestatoria* are fixed in a portion clearly distinguishable from the more modern additions to the chair; wherefore we conclude that, from a historical and archæological point of view, we are justified in regarding as true the venerable title which a living tradition has never failed to give to the Chair of S. Peter.

3. THE TWO FEASTS OF S. PETER'S CHAIR.

The establishment of the Roman Church by S. Peter as the perpetual seat of his divinely-received primacy was never disputed until the sixteenth century, when the straits to which the clear teaching of Holy Scripture and the Fathers reduced Protestant controversialists impelled some of the more unscrupulous of them boldly to assert that S. Peter was never at Rome at all, that he never made it the seat of his apostolic jurisdiction, and never watered with his blood the foundations of that long line of Pontiffs whose history is the history of Christianity.

"It was," says the Abbé Gueranger, "in order to nullify, by the authority of the Liturgy, this strange pretension of Protestants, that Pope Paul IV., in 1558, restored the ancient Feast of S. Peter's Chair at Rome, and fixed it on the 18th of January. For many centuries the Church had not solemnised the mystery of the Pontificate of the Prince of the Apostles on any distinct feast, but had made the single feast of February 22nd serve for both the *Chair at Antioch* and the *Chair at Rome*. From that time forward the 22nd of February has been kept for the *Chair at Antioch*, which was the first occupied by the Apostle."*

* *Liturgical Year*, Christmas, vol. ii. p. 331, Jan. 18. Duffy, 1868.

And in fact all the Martyrologies, from the eighth century downwards, mark that day as "*Cathedra Petri in Antiochia*," or "*apud Antiochiam*," or "*qua sedit apud Antiochiam.*" De Rossi, however, observes that ancient documents, anterior to the eighth century, make no allusion to Antioch in connection with the feast of February 22nd. Thus the Gregorian Liturgy simply marks that day as "*Cathedra S. Petri*,"* and in one MS. of that book it is expressly added *in Roma*. In the times of S. Leo the Great this day was celebrated in the Vatican Basilica with a large concourse of bishops, and was called "*dies Apostoli;*" while in the Bucherian Calendar, which marks the greater feasts of the Roman Church restored after the Diocletian persecution, we find it noted as "*Natale Petri de cathedra.*" The sermon attributed to S. Augustine on this festival makes no mention of Antioch, but states:

> "The institution of to-day's solemnity received from our forefathers the name of the Chair (*cathedræ*), because Peter, the first of the Apostles, is said to have received on this day the chair of the episcopate. Rightly, therefore, do the churches venerate the feast of that See (*sedis*), which the Apostle undertook for the salvation of the churches."†

S. Ambrose, in his sermon for this feast, merely expounds the Gospel, without any allusion to the special object of the festival. Ptolemæus Silvius, in the fifth century, registers the Feast of S. Peter as on the 22nd of February; and the Gothic-Gallican Sacramentary assigns to the same day a Mass, the collect of which begins:

> "O God, Who on this day didst give blessed Peter to be after Thyself the head of the Church," &c. ‡

The same Mass, however, in the later edition of this Sacramentary, reformed in the eighth century, was transferred to the 18th of January. §

We gather from these authorities that an ancient tradition existed in the Church that the famous words, "Thou art Peter, and upon this rock," &c., were addressed by our Lord to His chief Apostle in the month of February, and that the 22nd of that month was especially dedicated to the celebration of the insti-

---

* S. Greg. *Mag. Opp.* iii. p. 311; ed. Maur.
† S. Aug. *Serm.* 15, *De Sanctis.*
‡ Mabillon, *Liturgia Gallicana*, p. 266. "Deus qui *hodierna die* beatum Petrum post te dedisti caput ecclesiæ, cum te ille vere confessus sit et a te digne prælatus sit," &c.
§ *Ibid.* p. 121.

tution of the Primacy of S. Peter, and that in Rome this festival was made still more marked by the solemn enthronisation of the supreme Pontiff in the very chair which the Apostle himself had once used. This is confirmed by the words of the Gothic Liturgy, which declare:

"God committed the keys of heaven to a man compacted of the earth . . . and set on high the throne of the supreme See. The episcopal chair of blessed Peter, this day exposed [for veneration], is the witness."*

It is equally clear that there is no mention of Antioch, as connected with this feast, until the eighth century. Two difficulties, however, remain to be cleared up, viz., How did the idea of Antioch become connected with the feast of February 22nd? and also, How did the Feast of S. Peter's Chair in Rome, on the 18th of January, find its way into the Martyrologies of the eighth and ninth centuries?

The latter question appears to be satisfactorily answered by the supposition of the chair, which, we have shown, was venerated at the Cemetery of Ostrianus. This chair did not, indeed, like that in the Vatican, symbolise S. Peter's Primacy, but it did symbolise his first coming to Rome [and the inauguration of his Roman episcopate], whatever may have determined the particular day on which that chair was venerated. The other question it is impossible to determine with any certainty, but the suggestion of De Rossi commends itself as probable, viz., that the copyist of the ancient Roman calendar finding the 18th of January marked as "*cathedra S. Petri qua primum Romæ sedit,*" and not understanding why another Feast of S. Peter's Chair at Rome should be kept on February 22nd, inserted the words "*apud Antiochiam*" in order to explain the anomaly. The Feast of S. Thecla, with the title of *discipula Pauli Apostoli*, who went to Antioch in Pisidia to hear S. Paul, and a certain S. Gallus, a martyr of Antioch, being celebrated on the same day, may have led to the insertion of the word which has perplexed so many antiquaries, and which receives no explanation from any records of the Church of Antioch which have come down to us.†

* Mabillon, *l. c.* p. 298.
† Mr. Wright has published a valuable Syriac Martyrology of the fourth century, from a MS. of the year 412, in which the martyrdom "in the city of Rome of Paul the Apostle, and of Simon Peter, the Prince of the Apostles," is commemorated on the 28th of December. (*Journal of Sacred Literature and Biblical Records*, for January, 1869.) S. Gregory of Nyssa and S. Sophronius of Jerusalem assign the same date to the festival of the two Apostles.

CHAPTER V.

MONUMENTS OF S. PETER'S RESIDENCE AND APOSTOLATE IN ROME—NOTICE OF HIS WORK AND MEMORIALS OF HIS MARTYRDOM THERE—THE PALLIUM.

THE residence and work of S. Peter in Rome are, in the mind of Catholic antiquity, closely bound up with his episcopate. Being accessory constituent parts of one and the same tradition, they form together a single concrete whole. It is in this sense, and on this account especially, we treasure up all that survives concerning S. Peter in his relation to Rome, as serving to illustrate and confirm the prime and central fact of his Roman Episcopate. These traces of S. Peter's life in Rome, consisting for the most part of isolated details and minute fragmentary circumstances, sometimes of merely passing allusion, are, no doubt, comparatively few, incomplete, and partial: hence it would be impossible, at this date, to construct from them any consecutive history which, as a whole, would be more than probable. Still, we should bear in mind that these several details regarded singly, and, so to say, held in solution, are, of themselves, in the historical and moral order, fully trustworthy and reliable, based as they are on sure testimony and solid proof. Their force of conviction is, moreover, strengthened by their accumulation, as well as by the many undesigned coincidences that are found to attend them.

In the preceding chapters of this Second Part we were looking for the footprints of S. Peter in Rome one by one, and we found them, though few and far between, still distinctly traceable; indeed, the marks of his former presence are to this day clearly visible, and matter of ocular demonstration to everybody in the many monumental records that witness to him. We now propose to view these discovered vestiges collectively, and to form from them something like a continuous route: gathering together the principal disjointed details, we shall endeavour to devise therefrom in some sort a connected series.

The chief object, then, of this chapter is to indicate summarily and at one view the various places in Rome which tradition and archæological research have assigned to S. Peter, as hallowed by memories of his residence and apostolic labours. And, as before, when appraising the evidential value of positive facts and matters of certainty, we implicitly followed the opinion of guides versed in antiquarian science; so now, too, in blending together these facts and certainties with what is more or less only matter of probable conjecture, we shall avail ourselves of the mature and solid judgment of learned authors.

We shall, at the same time, take some notice of the results of S. Peter's work in Rome, and then conclude the chapter by treating of one or other matter which, from an archæological point of view, bears on our main subject.

The authors we follow, and from whom we shall largely quote, are Northcote and Brownlow, Allies, Paul Allard, and Fouard.

"The first sowing of the seed of the Gospel in the metropolis of the ancient Pagan world is involved in some obscurity. It is certain, however, that it must have been almost simultaneous with the birth of Christianity. For we know that among the witnesses of the miracle on the Day of Pentecost were 'strangers of Rome, Jews and proselytes;' and on the return of the strangers to their homes, the wonderful sight they had witnessed would be at once communicated to others, and the solemn tidings they had heard would be circulated from mouth to mouth among the Jews of the capital. These, then, were probably the first preachers of the Gospel in the Eternal City. But they had not been 'sent;' they were not apostles, and were, therefore, incapable of founding a church.

"For twelve years after the Ascension, in obedience (as we are told) to an express command of Christ, the Apostles had preached only to the Jews. At the end of this time, the chief Apostle was chosen by Divine Providence to admit the Gentile Cornelius into the bosom of the Church, thereby teaching that the restriction was now removed, and that henceforward the whole Gentile world was opened to the preaching of the Gospel. The imperial city of Rome, the capital of the known world, the very heart and centre of heathendom, was manifestly the chief field for such a work. The name of Cornelius, 'a centurion of the Italian band,' pointed Romewards; and circumstances soon occurred which obliged S. Peter to fly from Judæa, and so led him to bend his steps in that direction. He had been seized by Herod Agrippa, and was in imminent danger of death, when he was miraculously delivered out of prison; whereupon the inspired writer says, 'he departed and went into another place;' and ancient writers tell us that this 'other place' was the city of Rome."[*]

"It is remarkable that the 'Italian band,' in consequence of Herod's accession, was ordered back to Rome just at this time, so that there were special facilities for the Apostle to have accompanied Cornelius to the capital. That the kingdom in which Herod ruled would henceforth, so

[*] Euseb. ii. 14; Oros. vii. 6; S. Leo, *Serm.* 82, 4.

long as Herod was its ruler, be unsafe for him is plain; and probably S. Luke was unwilling to disclose the name of the place whither he went, because S. Paul was, at this very time when the Evangelist wrote, a prisoner in Rome, and would presently be called to justify his conduct before Nero, so that it was not desirable to record anything about the foundation of a Christian Church in that city." *

"It appears," writes Allies, "that Peter came to Rome to do exactly that which the Roman law most expressly forbade, since it looked with the utmost jealousy upon any college or fellowship of men bound together by rules of its own, and not recognised by the Senate. This suggests a sufficient reason why the Evangelist, writing while Peter was still alive, what would fall into the hands of foes as well as friends, passed over in silence both the sphere of his action and all that he accomplished in it. Again, the narrative of S. Luke ends with the appearance of S. Paul at Rome to justify his conduct before the Emperor Nero, which would supply a further adequate reason for passing over all mention of the founding a Church at Rome. But it is a fact that S. Luke is silent about S. Peter's acts for a period of several years after his delivery from prison, and this period exactly corresponds with the historical statement of the Roman Church's foundation. It is only after S. Peter had been driven out of Rome by the edict of the Emperor Claudius (A.D. 47) banishing the Jews who had raised tumults concerning Christ, that S. Luke makes him reappear at the Council of Jerusalem. The mention of this tumult, and of the Emperor's decree arising out of it by his heathen biographer, gives us another assurance that at this time the Christian faith had been planted in Rome. His words: *Judæos impulsore Christo assidue tumultuantes Roma expulit* (Suet. *Claudius*, 25.), point evidently to the stir created among the Jewish residents at Rome by that event, which broke them up into antagonistic parties, some accepting some rejecting the Messiah declared to them. Hence would follow naturally the expulsion of foreign Jews from Rome, who would be represented as the cause of the tumult."†

It seems obvious to suppose that S. Peter on his arrival at Rome first took up his abode in the Transtiberine region, where dwelt a very large population of Jews,‡ and that there he began

* *Roma Sotterranea*, part i. bk. ii. ch. iii.   † *Form. of Christ.* part iii. p. 18.

‡ "The Jews had a particular quarter in the Transtiberine region of the city of Rome, where they had lived in part since 63 B.C., when Pompey brought thousands of them there as prisoners of war, and gave them their freedom. It was they who afterwards established the Synagogue of the Libertines at Jerusalem. At the death of the first Herod eight thousand of their fellow-countrymen living in Rome had joined the deputies sent from Jerusalem. Since then the number had increased, and many proselytes of the gate were added to it. In 49 A.D. they were banished from Rome, because, in the words of the Roman historian, 'they excited an incessant disturbance instigated by one Chrestus.' (Suet. *Claud.* 25.) That quarrels about the Messiahship of Christ and the disturbance caused by the formation of a Christian community are here meant, is so obvious an explanation that it is sure to be always recurred to. At the death of Claudius soon afterwards, the exiles returned. When S. Paul wrote to the Romans, Aquila and Priscilla, who had been expelled by the Edict, were again there. But when he

his apostolic ministry by preaching Christ to his own fellow-countrymen in their synagogues. This we know was the invariable practice of S. Paul, and with still greater reason should we expect it to be that of S. Peter, who was especially the Apostle of the Circumcision. Here, too, it is probable were some Christians whom he had before known from among those "Strangers of Rome, Jews and Proselytes," converted at Jerusalem by his preaching on the day of Pentecost. Of these might be Andronicus and Junias whom S. Paul salutes in his Epistle,[*] and mentioned as "of note among the Apostles," and as having been converts to Christianity before himself. But this is only matter of conjecture, more or less probable: since, so far as we are aware, no positive traces are found in tradition of S. Peter's residence or work in Transtevere. In any case, it would seem he did not remain there long, for tradition gives evidence of his early residence and work in other parts of Rome to the north of the Tiber. Perhaps—and indeed very probably—the turbulence of his compatriots was the reason for his dwelling at a distance from their quarters.

"The doctrine of the Gospel," observes M. Paul Allard, "brought into the midst of the Roman Jews from Jerusalem by devout pilgrims to the Temple, or by some of the traders and hawkers who were continually journeying to and fro between Rome and Syria, had probably not passed as yet beyond the sphere of individual propagandism: some souls had been won over without the Jewish population being stirred to its depths. The preaching of Peter, however, would be just that leaven which would cause the mass to ferment. The presence of an Apostle, and intimate friend of Jesus Christ, the visible Head of His Church, and the continuer of His work, one till recently obscure and unknown, but now famous, at whose voice thousands had been converted in Judæa—this was calculated to excite all their passions, and soon the Jewish quarters, that is to say, a great portion of the Roman suburbs, became full of trouble and tumult. We learn from S. Justin, that soon after the death of Christ there came men, sent from Jerusalem, to stir up all the Jews against came to Rome, about the year 62, in consequence of his appeal to Cæsar, the chief men among the Roman Jews expressed themselves with evident reserve about the Christian community: 'We wish to hear what thou thinkest, for this sect is known to us to be everywhere spoken against.' (*Acts*, xxviii. 22.) They had evidently been frightened, and made cautious by the previous events and their sufferings under Claudius, and were unwilling to give any weapons against themselves to the man who was soon to be heard before the Emperor or his delegates, protected by his Roman citizenship. S. Paul himself seems to have seen through their mistrust, for he assures them that, in appealing to the Emperor, he has no intention of accusing his own people. (*Acts*, xxviii. 17-19.) S. Peter's journey to Rome must, then, have preceded Claudius' decree of banishment. . . . That S. Luke omits S. Peter's journey to Rome will surprise no one who remembers his omissions in the history of S. Paul." (Döllinger's *First Age of the Church*, vol. i. pp. 160, 161.)

[*] *Rom.* xvi. 7.

those who professed the new doctrine; and we may, therefore, well suppose that the journey of S. Peter did not long pass without notice, but that messengers followed his steps to put the Jews in Rome on their guard against his coming. Hence, the Apostle, if he thought at first of permanently taking up his quarters on the other side of the Tiber, had soon to seek an asylum elsewhere."*

Tradition assigns to what seems an early period of S. Peter's Roman sojourn the hospitality he received on the Aventine in the house of Aquila and Priscilla, where, it is said, the Apostle was wont to celebrate the Sacred Mysteries, to preach and baptise. S. Paul saluting Aquila and Priscilla in his Epistle to the Romans† speaks of "the Church which is in their house." We know too that when they were driven out from Rome by the edict of Claudius they gave the same hospitality to himself at Ephesus and Corinth as they showed to S. Peter in Rome—and that at Ephesus they again opened their house for the assembly of the faithful.‡ The present Church of S. Prisca, originally called the Church of the Pastor, afterwards that of S. Aquila, or of SS. Aquila and Priscilla, marks the spot on the Aventine thus consecrated by ancient tradition to the memory of S. Peter. In the fifteenth century there was still seen over the door of this sanctuary the following inscription:

"Hæc domus est Aquilæ, seu Priscæ, virginis almæ;
Quos.... Paule, tuo ore vehis Domino,
Hic, Petre, divini tribuebas ferculа verbi
Sæpius hocce loco sacrificans Domino."

"This is the house of Aquila, or of Prisca, beneficent virgin, whom by thy word, O Paul, thou dost bring to the Lord. Here, Peter, didst thou distribute the food of the Divine Word, often in this place offering up sacrifice to the Lord."

The ancient apocryphal letters of Pastor and Timothy record that Pudens had a relation named Priscilla, who gave her name to the Cemetery on the Via Salaria, constructed, it is said, on the property of Pudens. Here were discovered the bodies of Pudens and his two daughters, Pudentiana and Praxedes. This same catacomb contained also sepulchres bearing the names of Aquila and Prisca. These De Rossi identifies as the two Saints whose dwelling is venerated on the Aventine: and the great antiquity of the catacomb of Priscilla renders this very probable. But how, we may ask, did these persons of Jewish extraction and humble circumstances come to be buried in this cemetery of Roman

* *Les Persécutions des deux premiers siècles.* † *Rom.* xvi. 3-5.
‡ *Acts,* xviii. 3. 1 *Cor.* xvi. 19.

nobles? For Aquila and Priscilla belonged to the industrial class: their occupation was tent-making, and it is probable that they had on the Aventine a workshop for their manufacture, as they had at Corinth. It seems probable, says De Rossi, that they were freedmen of Pudens. Slaves were often used to take the name of their masters who had given them freedom: and so the Jewess Prisca adopted that of the matron Priscilla, and obtained a place for herself and her family in the Christian burying-place of her noble patrons.*

We do not know whether Aquila and Priscilla were among the early converts of S. Peter at Rome, or whether they were already Christians before his arrival: but it is not unlikely that through them he was introduced to the noble family of Pudens, who according to tradition was together with his household baptised by the Apostle. Pudens was of senatorial rank: his house was situated on the Viminal, in the aristocratic quarter of the "Vicus Patricius." Here S. Peter is said to have dwelt as the guest of Pudens, and to have exercised his sacred ministry. The ancient Church of S. Pudentiana (daughter of Pudens) stands on the site of this sanctuary of the Prince of the Apostles.† It

---

* De Rossi (*Bulletino*, 1880, p. 5) says of the Cemetery of Priscilla: "Here probably rested Priscilla, the foundress of the cemetery, mother of Pudens, contemporary of the Apostles. Here the topographists, the letters extant under the names of Pastor and Timothy, the compilers of the historical martyrologies place the sepulchres of Pudens, of his daughters Pudentiana and Praxedes, of Symetrius the priest, with other martyrs whose burial, they say, was looked after by these holy sisters in the time of Antoninus Pius. Here is a Prisca, whom some indications make me suspect to be connected with the couple Aquila and Prisca, or Priscilla, named by S. Paul in his Epistles and by S. Luke in the Acts," &c. . . .

† De Rossi (*Bulletino*, 1867, p. 43) gives an account of the Oratory in the house of Pudens, and (p. 44) a picture copied from Ciacconio of a Mosaic of the fourth century which was there in his time representing S. Peter in a chair surrounded by the lambs of Christ. It is most probable that in this Oratory was that chair of S. Peter which is now venerated in the Vatican. De Rossi (p. 37) declines to "examine the conjectures of some moderns who would attribute the chair now venerated in the Vatican to the domestic furniture of Pudens." We think, as the more probable conjecture, that S. Peter was the guest of Pudens subsequently to his abode near Ostrianum, and particularly when he came the second time to Rome in Nero's reign. The tradition of the second chair, and the salutation of Pudens mentioned by S. Paul (2 *Tim.* iv. 21) would seem to bear out this view. What has been considered a serious objection against the ancient tradition that SS. Praxedes and Pudentiana were daughters of the Pudens in apostolic times is that, according to ancient documents, these two Saints were still living in the days of S. Pius I. Hence the Bollandists suppose a Pudens senior and a Pudens junior, and that this latter lived in the second century and was the father of the two sisters. To this De Rossi replies, that as S. Pius was Pope from about 140-150, the two Saints might still be living at an advanced age under his Pontificate: that S. Paul in his Epistle (written about 67), in speaking of

is impossible now to say precisely in which of the several places in Rome, traditionally hallowed by memories of S. Peter, the Apostle first or successively made his abode. M. Paul Allard seems to be of opinion that the Apostle at once on his arrival went to settle in the environs of the Via Nomentana, and there first exercised his ministry some two miles distant from the city, on the very spot where, as De Rossi has shown, Romulus reviewed his army for the last time and then mysteriously disappeared. Here there was in the first century a burial-ground (*prædium funerarium*), which some ancient documents call the Cemetery of Ostrianus, and others "the Great Cemetery" (*cemeterium majus*). An abundant spring, or more probably a marshy sheet of water from which the place was called *ad Nymphas*, and soon by a singular combination *ad Nymphas Petri*, and *Fons Petri*, served for the baptism of the neophytes brought forth to Christ by the preaching of the Apostle. Here too he gave his instructions; and here modern archæologists have discovered his subterranean Oratory, and the site of "that chair where Peter first sat."

Why S. Peter should settle in the environs of the Via Nomentana outside the city to the north, is explained by his desire to be at a distance from the turbulence of the Jews in Trastevere; whereas around the Ostrianum public tranquillity was guaranteed by the Pretorian camp recently constructed in its vicinity. There were probably, moreover, some Christians of position and influence residing in that quarter, since already they possessed there a place of sepulture.

But besides all this, the relations that had existed between S. Peter and the centurion Cornelius—and especially if they came to Rome together—would make it probable that the Apostle's first abode at Rome should be near this military camp. It is not unlikely that Cornelius and some of those "kinsmen, special friends,"[*] and fellow-soldiers converted with him by S. Peter

Pudens and Claudia (2 *Tim.* iv. 21), makes no mention of the daughters, who might then be infants or not yet born. The Bollandists, moreover, adopted a text according to which S. Pudentiana died under S. Pius I. at the age of sixteen. De Rossi replies that "the best MSS. say that the Saint had been in retirement or shut up in her house for sixteen years." He compares with the age of these Saints the long life of S. Polycarp, extending to A.D. 155, and says that "the monuments of the fourth century relating to the holy virgins Pudentiana and Praxedes contradict that youthfulness of age, and give them grey hairs" (p. 50). And thus they are represented in the Mosaic in the Apse of the S. Pudenziana Basilica (see p. 59). This mosaic was put up between 390 and 398. The objection consequently falls, and there is no reason for questioning the ancient tradition.

[*] *Acts*, x. 24.

would be quartered there. There is evidence that a great work was being done from the first days of Christianity amongst the Roman soldiers. Nereus and Achilleus, officers of rank, were amongst S. Peter's converts. It seems that S. Paul later on had his abode near or within the precincts of this same Pretorian camp, and found there a fruitful field for his apostolic labour. We may gather as much from what he says in his Epistle to the Philippians (i. 13).

It might be that through Cornelius S. Peter first made the acquaintance of Pudens. We have given evidence in a preceding chapter of the relationship between the family of Pudens and the *gens Cornelia*. If, as has been conjectured, the full name of S. Peter's convert was Cornelius Pudens, the account of the Apostle's being the guest of Pudens on the Viminal, whose house was near the head of a street (*vicus Corneliorum*) named after the Cornelii, and also of his being the guest of Aquila and Priscilla on the Aventine, is adequately explained.

It is said that here, near the Via Nomentana, S. Peter preached the Gospel for several years, baptising in the water " of the fountain of Peter," for so the old *Nymphæum* of Ostrianus was called in the succeeding centuries.

"In the year 53, at the end of eleven years from the first preaching of S. Peter," writes Mr. Allies, "we have a very striking testimony to the work which he had done in the capital of the Roman Empire, and the chief seat of idol worship. S. Paul, writing to the Roman Christians at that time, renders thanks to God for their 'faith being spoken of throughout the whole world,' and that 'their obedience had reached all men,' terms which carry with them the meaning of a completely constituted and very flourishing Church. He calls them, besides, 'full of goodness and all knowledge, and able to admonish others,' and 'desires much to see them, that he might impart some gratuitous spiritual gift, to confirm them,' that is, to console himself and them with their mutual faith,'* language, again, which implies the complete formation of a Church. But he, moreover, alleges a very remarkable reason why he had not hitherto visited them. He states that it had been his object, while labouring at the publication of the gospel-kingdom from Jerusalem all round in a circle to Illyricum, and there planting churches, not to build on another man's foundation.† Here he uses

* *Rom.* i. 8, xvi. 19, xv. 14, i. 11.

† xv. 20. ἵνα μὴ ἐπ᾽ ἀλλότριον θεμέλιον οἰκοδομῶ. "In the second year of the Emperor Claudius, Peter laid the foundation and organised the construction of the Roman Church. The double term used of this event by ancient writers is one of great significance and pregnant meaning. As a house is not a chance collection of stones and mortar, but is constructed on a definite plan for a preconceived use, so when they say that Peter founded and constructed the Roman Church, θεμελιώσαντες οὖν καὶ οἰκοδομήσαντες οἱ

exactly the two words applied by ancient writers to Peter's work at Rome, that is, founding and building; and he adds, 'for this reason I have been many times prevented coming to see you,' that is, because you were already founded and built by another. But when S. Paul uses such language, it is evident that this other must be at least of equal rank with himself. Nor did he, indeed, avoid simple preaching where other Apostles preached, for this he had done in Judæa, but he avoided founding a Church on another's foundation; and he goes on to say that he will take the opportunity of his going into Spain to visit them, words again implying that they did not need his work as an Apostle to found their Church, because it had already been done by another. And, in fact, five years later his own appeal to Cæsar led him as it were incidentally to Rome, where he was destined to do a great work, to be associated in labour and in martyrdom with Peter, and so, notwithstanding his own words, to have his authority from age to age appealed to, as deposited in the superior principate of the Roman Church. If, however, we put these several expressions of his letters together, they intimate not only that the Roman Church had been already founded and built, that is, organised, but that it had attained so great a distinction that its faith and obedience were spoken of among Christians all over the world." *

M. Paul Allard writes:—

"That the seed of the word sown by S. Peter bore much fruit, we may gather from the great number of faithful at Rome, whose names were known to S. Paul, and are mentioned by him at the end of his Epistle to the Romans. Amongst the women are Mary, Junia, Tryphena, Tryphosa, Persis, Julia, Olympias. Amongst the men, Epenetus, Andronicus, Ampliatus, Urbanus, Stachys, Apelles, Herodion, Rufus, Asyncritus, Phlegon, Hermas, Patrobas, Hermes, Philologus, Nereus; the anonymous groups 'them that are of Aristobulus's household,' 'them that are of Narcissus's household,' and others whom the Apostle designates without naming them. This nomenclature leads us to infer the humble condition of these first Roman Christians. Many bear servile *cognomina*. Those of 'the households of Aristobulus and of Narcissus' were probably slaves or freedmen of some great families. The master or patron of the first, Aristobulus, may have been a rich Jew on terms of intimacy with the imperial court, conversant with the government and manners of Rome, perhaps that descendant of Herod whom Nero made king of Lesser Armenia.† The others may have belonged to the household of that Narcissus who was enfranchised by Nero and put to death by Galba. One of the Christians named by S. Paul should to all appearance be identified with the slave of that name whose magnificent tomb has recently been discovered in one of the most ancient catacombs. It would, however, be a mistake to suppose that the Gospel had not penetrated at this epoch the higher state of Roman society. We have already narrated the interesting episode recorded by

μακάριοι ἀπόστολοι τὴν ἐκκλησίαν—S. Irenæus, iii. 8—they mean that he instituted a society with the principle of life in itself, exerting definite action on its members, and possessing a definite government." (*Formation, &c., ib.* p. 16.)

* *Ib.* pp. 19-21.   † Joseph. *Ant. Jud.* xx. 5.

Tacitus of the conversion of Pomponia Græcina (A.D. 58), the wife of Aulus Plautius, one of the first personages of the empire.... It has been conjectured, and not without reason, that Pomponia was the great lady known only by her *agnomen*, probably symbolical and baptismal, Lucina, who opened in a *prædium* on the Via Appia one of the most ancient Christian catacombs, near, perhaps underneath, land that belonged to the Pomponii Bassi. In this truly aristocratic cemetery are found epitaphs of the Cæcilii, Cæciliani, Attici, and Annii, noble families related to one another, and also to that of the Pomponii. Hence we see that at the commencement of Nero's reign the Church in Rome was composed of very different elements. There were rich and poor, slaves and nobles; Christians of Jewish origin, spirit, and manners, and also of Greek or Roman birth and education. S. Paul, in his Epistle, seems to have in view both the Jewish and Hellenic element, which could not fail to coexist in the bosom of a Church such as that of Rome; like two parallel currents flowing down the bed of a single stream without mutual opposition and yet without intermingling their waters.

"The Apostle frequently in this Epistle addresses the Gentile faithful, and dilates in the first chapter on the horrible corruption of Pagan morality, whilst the long doctrinal exposition which follows seems to be more specially directed to the Jewish Christians. Moreover, several of his practical counsels in the later chapters appear to be particularly addressed to them, those, namely, that regard submission to established authority, and the duty of paying taxes and customs." [*]

On the same subject Mr. Allies says:

"Six years later, in the year 64, we have the unimpeachable witness of Tacitus to the greatness of the work accomplished by S. Peter and S. Paul in the twenty-two years which had elapsed since the first coming of the former to Rome. When the persecution of Nero broke out, he records that a 'vast multitude' gave the testimony of martyrdom to their belief.[†] We may thus compute what had been the growth of a community which, so few years after its first origin, was strong enough to render such a proof of its faith. We may note at the same time how, in the centre of heathenism, under the eyes of Nero, amid a society eaten out with the most profligate corruption, a work had been accomplished unheard of upon the earth before. It was not merely among Jews, prepared by the knowledge of the one true God, and by the expectation of a Messiah, but out of the Gentiles in their worst stage of moral decline, that a spiritual community had been founded, which could pass through such a shock, and, far from losing, transmit its life onwards with a yet more vigorous growth. Such a result supposes a vast work of previous charity, the work of converting soul by soul, of instructing, catechising, baptising, holding assemblies for preaching and for worship within the precincts of private houses, which alone were in a measure safe under the protection of domestic liberty. In this manner the whole sacramental life had to be transfused by the daily operation of its powers with a mass of converts, partly Jewish, partly heathen, and with regard to all these latter, it was requisite to implant the new principle of obedience to foreign teachers without public warrant, and to make the new principle of faith in the unseen the spring of every action.

[*] Allard, *Persécutions des deux premiers siècles*.   [†] *Annal.* 15, 44.

"We see, then, that the Church, which, in its eleventh year, was already renowned among all Christians for such a faith and such an obedience, was, after another eleven years, and before the episcopate of its founder had terminated, the first to incur persecution from the emperor, in which its witnesses, enduring every extreme of mockery and cruelty, amounted to a vast multitude, as attested by one who denounced their belief as a pernicious superstition, and declared their crimes to merit the severest punishment." *

We cannot forego presenting to our readers another very striking passage from the same writer, which enables us to appreciate the nature of S. Peter's work during his Roman Episcopate:

"The conversion of the centurion Cornelius, the first fruit of the Gentiles, was accompanied by a visible descent of the Holy Ghost, which recalled to mind, in its chief circumstances, the day of Pentecost itself; for indeed it betokened no less an event than the actual extension of the kingdom of God from Jewish converts to the whole world of the Gentiles. It had been preluded by a vision in which Peter, praying at noon-day on the top of the house of Simon at Joppa, had seen 'the heavens open and a vessel like a great sheet descending upon him, bound at its four corners and let down upon the earth, in which were all four-footed creatures of the earth, wild beasts, reptiles, and birds, and a voice was heard saying, Arise, Peter, kill and eat.' Such was the Divine instruction of what was presently to be. There followed immediately upon this vision the conversion of Cornelius, his kinsmen, and particular friends. But the Apostles at Jerusalem recognised in this act the opening up of the whole Gentile world to their preaching. Peter's imprisonment by Herod, and miraculous delivery by the Angel, happened shortly afterwards, upon which he forthwith 'departed into another place.' And in this other place it was that the vision, in all its exactness, was accomplished. In Rome, the seat of power, the capital of all the subject provinces, whither congregated all that was rich, ambitious, distinguished, but likewise the central slave-market of the world, the sink of the nations, whither drained all that was vile and suffering—in Rome Peter was to find the four-footed creatures of the earth, its wild beasts, reptiles, and birds, whom he should spiritually kill and eat, that is, amalgamate into one community. What image could more clearly represent the variety of Peter's Gentile converts, here and there a senator, such as Cornelius Pudens, here and there a high-born lady, such as Pomponia Græcina, but many freedmen and slaves from the household of Narcissus, from the imperial palace itself, from hundreds of other houses, whose domestics were like a nation, women of all ranks, the unlearned and the poor. Add to these the foreigners of all nations and all religions, of all climates and of every temperament from the extreme of Eastern superstition to that of Western barbarism, who were to be found at Rome, and from whom the preaching of the Apostle would select the recipients of Divine grace. The population of Rome at this time represented all the diversities of human nature, and all the various trials which the vitality of the Gospel-seed was to experience in future

* *Annal.* pp. 22-24.

times, and distant regions were collected here, so that its Church would be an epitome of the Church in the whole world. There were they who had been all in their natural condition, 'common and unclean,' sunk in the impurities of heathenism, though diverse in their qualities, but whom the mouth of Peter was to cleanse by the Word and the power following on that Word, and then to offer up in mystical sacrifice to God; and the Holy Ghost came down visibly to signify and commence a work which had had no parallel since the beginning of the world." *

For the further development of this subject, and for the influence which the work of S. Peter's episcopate had on the Jewish element in Rome, we must refer our readers to the gifted author's own pages.

Let us now resume our notice of the memorials of S. Peter's life and episcopate in Rome.

Besides the churches of S. Prisca on the Aventine, of S. Pudentiana on the Viminal, and the Cemetery of Ostrianus, which testify to his apostolic labours, there is also his celebrated Chair in the Vatican, of which we have already given the full history and description; when we, at the same time, treated of the two Feasts in commemoration of his double Chair at Rome.

There remains then to speak of the churches in Rome that are specially dedicated in honour of the Prince of the Apostles, and after that of his Pallium.

These churches are few in number, and of very ancient foundation; all of them, save one, bear testimony in various ways to the martyrdom of S. Peter, in Rome, as handed down by universal tradition. They are: the *Vatican Basilica* of S. Peter where rests his sacred body; *S. Peter in Carcere* in the Mamertine Prison, where, with S. Paul, he was confined before being led to death; *S. Peter in Montorio*, which stands on the site of the ancient fortress of the Janiculum, where S. Peter is said to have been crucified; and *S. Peter in Vinculis* on the Esquiline, where are venerated the two chains with which S. Peter was bound when in prison at Jerusalem, on his apprehension there by order of Herod Agrippa. This church of S. Peter's, though it does not bear upon any circumstance of his presence in Rome, has a very fitting significance as commemorating by these chains the event of his imprisonment and miraculous delivery, which, from the earliest days of the Church was, as we have seen, ever associated in Catholic tradition and Christian symbolism with his first coming to Rome, his episcopate, and his primacy.

* *Annal.* pp. 25 *seq.*

The following words of Dom Gueranger may here be aptly cited:

"We know," he says,[*] "that the churches erected in the capital of the Christian world in honour of the Martyrs of Rome, when they did not contain their relics, or, at any rate, were not built at the entrance of the Cemeteries where they were buried, served to mark the very places they had sanctified by their residence, or by their sufferings. This custom was observed not only in the Church of Rome. We find it laid down as a point of discipline in the Church of Africa, by the fourteenth Canon of the Fourth Council of Carthage in 398,[†] and this Canon has its place in the *Corpus Juris*.[‡] Later on, this discipline was mitigated, but, nevertheless, it prevailed in Rome for many centuries. It is for this reason that the churches in honour of S. Peter are so few there, although the holy Apostle is the Patron of the city. Four churches only are dedicated to him, and all the four are so many monuments of his history. The Vatican Basilica, which contains his body; the Eudoxian Basilica or S. Peter *in Vincoli*, because there are preserved his chains; the Mamertine Prison, or S. Peter *in Carcere*, erected over the dungeon in which he was imprisoned with S. Paul; and lastly, S. Peter *in Montorio*, on the site where he was said to have been crucified: whilst this last is not of the highest antiquity."

THE PALLIUM.

Amongst the ancient monuments which bear witness to the Roman Episcopate of S. Peter, and of his succession in the Roman Pontiffs, we may reckon the Roman Pallium. It is a band of white wool worn on the shoulders, with two strings of the same material, and with four purple crosses worked on it.[§] It is worn by the Pope in token of the plenary jurisdiction he possesses as Supreme Pontiff by virtue of his succession to the Primacy of S. Peter, and to the See of Rome, of which he was the first Bishop.

It is sent by the Pope to Patriarchs, Primates, and Archbishops, in token of his own universal jurisdiction, and is a symbol of a special share in his authority, and of the fulness of their episcopal jurisdiction, which, with its grant, they receive.

---

[*] *Histoire de S. Cécile*, ch. xiv.

[†] Et omnino nulla memoria Martyrum probabiliter acceptetur, nisi aut ibi corpus, aut aliquae certae reliquiae sint, aut ubi origo alicujus habitationis, vel possessionis, vel passionis, fidelissima origine traditur. (Labbe, *Concilia*, t. ii. p. 1218.)

[‡] *De Consecratione Distinct.* i. Can. xxvi. *Placuit ut altaria.*

[§] Formerly the Good Shepherd seems to have been represented upon the *pallium*; and S. Isidore, of Pelusium (L. i. Ep. 136, ad Herm.), speaks of it as an ornament worn on the shoulders of bishops, made, not of linen, but of wool, to denote the wandering sheep whom the Lord went in quest of and brought home on His shoulders. The bishop wears it, he says, to show to all the people by this very dress that he fulfils the office of Christ the Good Shepherd. Baronius (ad Ann. 216), and, many authors of weight, adopt this explanation. (See Martigny's *Étude Archéologique sur l'Agneau et le Bon Pasteur*, p. 68.)

The origin of the *pallium* is most probably to be sought in the ancient and widespread custom of disciples adopting the dress as well as the principles of their masters; whilst the handing on to another of the master's own mantle significantly served to designate his legitimate successor.

This custom obtained in the schools of famous heathen philosophers; and we find the same principle in use amongst the prophets of the Old Testament, where we read that the mantle (*pallium*) of Elias fell upon Eliseus in token that Eliseus was the successor of Elias in the prophetic office, and inherited the fulness of his master's spirit and power.*

It was the same amongst the early Christian ascetics. Thus S. Antony received from S. Athanasius the mantle of that great Doctor, and after he had buried the hermit Paul in it, at the dying Saint's request, he took the hermit's mantle in exchange, and was ever afterwards wont to wear it at the more solemn festivals.

In ancient times the ecclesiastical *pallium* was not exclusively confined to Rome. All the Patriarchal Churches, and some of the other greater Sees, seem to have had their own *pallium*: and the Patriarchs gave a sort of *pallium*, ὠμοφόριον, to their Metropolitans.

Thus it is recorded that when S. Ignatius, Patriarch of Constantinople, was habited in the episcopal vestments,

"They reverently put on him the venerable cloak of S. James, the brother of our Lord, which had lately been brought from Jerusalem, and which Ignatius received with the same respect and veneration as though he had recognised in it its former apostolic owner."

But more important examples are recorded which clearly involve the principle of succession to office by him to whom the *pallium* was transferred. Thus we read that Metrophanes, who occupied the See of Byzantium in the time of Constantine, took off his *pallium*, and laid it on the altar, charging that it should be preserved and delivered to his successor. And still more distinctly, Liberatus the Deacon, in his history of the Nestorian and Eutychian heresies, testifies to it as an essential part of the ceremony of consecrating and enthroning the Patriarchs of Alexandria.

"It is the custom at Alexandria," he says, "for him who succeeds to the deceased bishop to keep a vigil by the corpse of the deceased, to lay the dead man's hand upon his own head, and then, having buried him with his own

* 4 *Kings*, ii. 9, 13, 14.

hands, to take the *pallium*, or mantle of S. Mark, and to place it on his own neck, after which he is held legitimately to occupy his place."

Thus the *pallium*, or mantle of S. Mark, was religiously handed on from one of his successors to another in the See of Alexandria, and its possession was accounted an important token of the legitimate possession of that dignity and office.

We may hence, then, infer that the origin of the Roman Pallium was precisely the same, that it was in fact the cloak of S. Peter. The oldest writers agree in referring the first use of the *pallium* at Rome to Linus, the immediate successor of S. Peter, and speak of it as implying legitimate succession to Peter's Primacy and Roman See. What confirms this conclusion is that it has always been described, and is still described, as *pallium de corpore Sancti Petri*. It is always blessed on the Feast of his Martyrdom—the very day, that is, on which its first transfer was made, if not materially, yet morally—and at the lower altar of "the Confession," *i.e.*, at the Apostle's tomb. It used to remain there for one night, and then to be preserved in a small chest over the Apostle's chair; but since that relic was enclosed in bronze and elevated to its present position, the *pallium* remains at the tomb. It is always assumed by each successive Pontiff at the altar above that tomb, and used to be delivered to archbishops on their promotions, only at the same place.* When it was conferred upon anyone, it was always given as to a person holding the place of the Pope for the time being, acting as his deputy and representative within certain limits. Rupertus,† an author of the twelfth century, says that S. Peter not only wore the *pallium* himself, but gave it to Maternus, the first Bishop of Treves. This assertion of so early a date for the use and grant of the *pallium*, has been impugned.

"But Lupus," writes Catalani, "replies very ably and much to the point, that Rupertus has the entire support of irrefragable testimonies of antiquity, and especially in the conduct of S. Mark: since that Evangelist founded, was bishop of, and ruled the Church of Alexandria, not so much in his own name, as in the name and place of the Apostle Peter. For Alexandria was certainly a Patriarchal and Apostolic Church, the second See, too, of all Christendom, founded by the Prince of the Apostles himself, through means of S. Mark: and consequently whatever points of sacred discipline he there instituted, he, no doubt, received them from S. Peter.‡ And this S. Leo

* *R. S.* part i. pp. 477-9.
† Abbas Tuitensis, l. i.; *De Divinis Officiis*, c. xxii.
‡ *Opera*, tom. viii.; *De Africanæ Ecclesiæ Romanis Appellationibus*, c. xiii. ap. Catalani, *Cæremoniale Episcoporum*, p. 852.

most lucidly declares in a letter to Dioscorus, newly appointed Patriarch of Alexandria, in the following words: 'It behoves us to be at one in thought and action. For since the most blessed Peter received the Apostolic Primacy from the Lord, and the Roman Church holds fast to its institutions, it is criminal to believe that his holy disciple Mark, who was the first that governed the Church of Alexandria, formed decrees by the rules of his own traditions; since, without doubt, from the same source of grace, the spirit of the disciple and of his master was one; neither could the ordained deliver other than that which he received from him who ordained him.'" [*]

Whoever receives the *pallium* from the Pope cannot transfer it to his successor, or wear it out of his own patriarchate, province, &c., or on other than specified occasions. If translated, he must ask for another *pallium*. The *pallium*, or *pallia*, if he has received more than one, are buried with the bishop to whom they are given. The Pope receives but one *pallium*, thus showing that his Roman Episcopate and his supreme Pontificate of the universal Church are but one and the same. He wears it in all sacred functions, always and everywhere, in token of his supreme and universal authority, as Innocent III. declares:

"Sane solus Romanus Pontifex in Missarum solemniis et in aliis ecclesiasticis functionibus pallio semper utitur, et ubique, quoniam assumptus est in plenitudinem ecclesiasticæ potestatis, quæ per pallium significatur." [†]

[*] *Epist.* 81.
[†] Catalani. *Ib.*

CHAPTER VI.

GENERAL REFLECTIONS.

Our research into the works of archæologists on the first age of Christianity in Rome, the sum of which we have now given, has forced upon us many reflections.

First, we are struck with wonder at the comparative wealth of testimony which from the relics of antiquity accrues to S. Peter in relation to his work and position in the Roman Church; for we have by no means exhausted all that might be produced. Is there, we would ask, any other single fact, of the same personal character, in ancient history, whether sacred or profane, that can claim such abundant and various witnesses for itself as this? And here we should not fail gratefully to admire that overruling providence of God, whereby it happened that the first works of Christian art during the apostolic and primitive age of the Church were wrought and found their place underground in the Catacombs, and were thus in great measure kept safe from effacement and decay, so that many of them have survived even to the present day, as testimonies in confirmation of the Catholic faith and tradition of S. Peter's primacy and Roman episcopate; whilst the remains of monumental architecture above ground, of a somewhat later date, giving a similar witness, that have been re-discovered in the non-subterranean cemeteries, owe their preservation very much to the fact of their having so long lain buried beneath their own ruins.

We have, moreover, to bear in mind that the memorials which are preserved to us form but a small part of the original whole; since the Catacombs, together with their paintings and other decorations, have suffered great losses not only from neglect and natural causes, such as decay of time during so many ages, inundation, and earthquake; but also from the indiscreet piety of the faithful who, coveting for themselves a place of burial close to the bodies of the martyrs, effected their purpose, often greatly to the injury of the sacred shrines. Besides this, the Catacombs were subjected, during the first seven or eight centuries, to frequent desecration and spoliation in the successive devastations of Rome by barbarians; whilst considerable injury was also doubtless done to them, and many losses sustained, by the wholesale translation of the martyrs' relics to the churches in the city. Hence we may count it a special and blessed providence, for us at least in these later days, that the Catacombs found at length a time of rest and seclusion, during those many centuries when they were deserted, forgotten, and unknown; for otherwise their whole aspect and character, as first they were, might have become entirely changed, and hardly anything of original interest in them might now be left. But even as it was, unhappily on their rediscovery in the sixteenth century, they had to suffer yet more than they had done before—ransacked, as at once they began to be, and pillaged of their treasures, whether through the eager but ill-regulated devotion of the faithful for holy relics, or the misdirected zeal and efforts of antiquarians to obtain for themselves specimens of early Christian art.* Amongst the great number of monuments thus lost or destroyed must doubtless be reckoned many memorials of S. Peter.

But if records, naturally so enduring as those hewn from stone or chiselled and painted on the living rock, have thus perished, how must it have fared with others,—ecclesiastical furniture wrought in wood, sacred ornaments, vestments, books, registers, archives, and such-like? These were, in all probability, for the most part destroyed and given to the flames in the successive persecutions (especially the last and longest under Diocletian) that swept over the Roman Church during the first three centuries. The scanty vestiges of them, however, that still remain, and what is recorded by early writers, tell us how much there was in them that bore upon S. Peter as Bishop of Rome and his succession in the Episcopate.

But to our mind, we confess, it is not so much the direct witness which these ancient monuments bear to S. Peter at Rome, whether regarded in their aggregate, or looked at one by one, that is of most evidential value, but rather what they represent, and the tale that they tell of all the energy and work, both physical and mental, expended in their elaboration; of lavish pouring forth of all that there then was of genius and talent, of

---

* See *Note* A. at the end of this Chapter, where what has been here summarily recorded is illustrated in detail from passages collected from *Roma Sotterranea*. Some abridgment has been made in their quotation.

imagination, poetic invention, artistic taste and skill; of cost of time, industrious toil, and pecuniary sacrifice; of sacred study, and use of Scriptural lore; of sound theological judgment; of right discernment in true symbolism and æsthetic combination, on the part of the clergy and laity of the primitive Roman Church: and all this, we should note, in the midst of so many and great disadvantages, arising from their being for the most part of poor and humble condition, from the persecution to which they were continually exposed, from the danger of being informed against and the consequent secrecy which they had to observe, and from the dark and confined places in which they had to work. We must consider, moreover, the long persevering constancy and persistence wherewith, not for a few years, nor within one generation only, but during several centuries and for many generations, they prosecuted their labours. Taking, then, all this into account, herein, we say, consists the highest and greatest evidential value of these ancient monuments, viz., that throughout this lengthened period all those of them that relate to S. Peter endure as standing proofs of the active self-sacrificing zeal and devotion which the first Roman Christians had for the Prince of the Apostles, and are still so many living witnesses to their firm and lively faith in the primacy bestowed upon him by Jesus Christ, whereby he was constituted, as they themselves represented him, a second Moses in the New Dispensation, the supreme legislator, ruler, and pastor of the whole Christian flock, and, at the same time, the chief founder and the first Bishop of the Church of Rome.

Those ancient monuments testify, also, to the primitive faith and practice on many other points: such as the sacred mysteries of the Blessed Trinity and the Incarnation; the doctrines of man's fall, and his redemption by Jesus Christ; the revealed historical truths of our Lord's birth, life, death, resurrection, and ascension; His gift of the Holy Ghost to His Church; His divine commission to His Apostles; His real presence in the Eucharist, the Sacrifice of the Altar, Baptism, and Sacramental Grace; honour and devotion to the Blessed Virgin, and the Saints; the power of their intercession; the veneration of their relics; and prayer for the faithful departed.

Anglicans, for the most part, profess to follow as their guide the teaching of the early Church, and do so on the ground that what was of primitive belief and practice, so far as this is ascertainable, forms the best and safest criterion of genuine apostolic truth. Now, if from the evidence in the Catacombs, they apply this principle to other matters of primitive Christianity, they are bound, would they be consistent, on the same grounds, and by the same process of reasoning, to apply it also to the doctrine regarding S. Peter: for the monuments of Christian antiquity in Rome bear witness, at least, as clear and explicit to the early belief of S. Peter's Primacy and Roman Episcopate as they do to that of any other of the points enumerated, and, so far, by consequence, are proofs of the real objective truth of these doctrinal facts.

This same belief, embodied, as we have seen, in so many material memorials of active zeal, piety, and devotion, during the first centuries, shows itself so sturdy and vigorous a stem, as to make us quite sure, on the one hand, that its roots lie deep down, and that it can have derived its origin from nought else but the Divine word of Christ Himself; and to secure us from much wonder, on the other hand, when ere long this same stem is seen grown up into the trunk of a great tree, stretching forth its branches to the ends of the earth, and yielding its fruit in all generations for the healing of the nations. It rises as a firm column based upon a foundation so solid, even upon a rock, that we marvel not when we behold it bearing up not only the whole building of the Church's faith and ecclesiastical polity, but sustaining also the thrones of temporal princes, and the entire edifice of social order and Christian civilisation, by reason of its strength.

In truth, the evidences that now shine forth from the darkness of the Catacombs, where they for so long lay buried, are to our mind so clear and conclusive that, were there no written testimony of antiquity still surviving, these alone would suffice for confirmations and proofs, in the historical order, of the objective reality of the Petrine facts, as they have been handed down and believed through Catholic tradition.

How utterly insignificant and of no account, light and imponderable, even as the very dust in the balance, are the speculative objections and difficulties raised by the learned, together with all their counter theories and hypotheses, when set against the original, continuously enduring, still living faith and tradition of the Catholic Church, who in her life of ages remains always the same, ever fresh in her pristine youth and vigour, knowing neither old age, decline, nor decay; and when, too, this her faith and tradition, after the lapse of so many centuries, are found witnessed to, and palpably demonstrated, by the imperishable memorials that were contemporary with her birth and surrounded her cradle.

Let them with their vaunted "legal evidence" convict the whole Petrine doctrine to be but matter of "guess-work" or of inextricable confusion if they will. Let them stoutly deny that in the earliest times there was a primacy at all or that any "such authority as the Papacy existed in the Church." Or let them start the novel theory, still more singularly grotesque, that in the apostolic and sub-apostolic times a primacy certainly did exist—one, too, of the Church of Rome—but that this was independent of the "presbyter-bishop" of Rome, whose personality and authority were absorbed in the body of the Church; and that in this primacy " the idea of the *Cathedra Petri* had no place."

Well, after all, what boots it? Even as they have done with others, others will, in their turn, do with them. Men of learning, and their generations, pass away like the rest. A new generation of the erudite will arise to controvert and demolish these ingenious theorisings, and will put forth new views to supply their place. And thus it will go on. Meanwhile, outside the Church, no gain will be made to true knowledge, nor any nearer approach either to theological or historical certainty, but only a greater advance in scepticism and more room and occasion for fresh disputes. All their more learned men—rejecting that knowledge and information which the Catholic Church alone can give as the one, sole, ever-living witness from the beginning until now of her past history and of its real facts; and even refusing in their historical researches to apply the first natural principle of cause and effect to the question at issue—will go on groping in the dark; they will study and toil in vain, continually overreaching themselves and one another in their theories, with their doubts, subtle questionings, and minute investigations; they will fail of ever arriving at a satisfactory conclusion. *Defecerunt scrutantes scrutinio;** and thus whilst "ever learning they will never come to the knowledge of the truth."

Whereas, within the Catholic Church, the ancient truth, handed down by divine tradition, will abide secure, receiving continually fresh illustration from her theologians, historians, and archæologists; confirmation, too, from non-Catholic erudition; nay, even from the variations and contradictions of error itself. And still the belief of Peter's Primacy, as derived from Christ

* *Ps.* lxiii. 7

Himself, and by His will incorporated in the Roman Episcopate, together with the exercise of that Primacy by Peter's successor, the Bishop of Rome, will continue, as they have ever done, to go on hand in hand; since both of these have been from the beginning, and are at all times, in intimate correlation, the one the counterpart and fellow-witness of the other, both equally strong and mutually self-sustaining, both alike the effects of one Divine cause, even the word of the Lord, in the power of Whose word they abide ever immanent, and are of the same power perpetual emanations—that word, we mean, that was spoken of old by Christ to His Apostle: "I say to thee: that thou art Peter; and upon this rock I will build My Church."*

NOTE A.

Christians were extremely anxious to be buried as near as possible to the tombs of the martyrs; and to gratify this desire they excavated graves at the back of the *arcosolia*, leaving a very insufficient interval of rock between them: not sparing even the paintings with which their forefathers had adorned them. They spoilt the symmetry of the chapels and destroyed their decorations by introducing new monuments and sarcophagi into the area, or making *loculi* in the walls, and often endangered the safety of the constructions by indiscreet excavations.†

The Goths had made attacks upon Rome as early as the fourth century; but it was during their irruption under Vitiges, A.D. 539, that they did the greatest injury to the Catacombs. After the peace of the Church, basilicas and monasteries began to be erected near the cemeteries, to which other buildings were added for pilgrims, &c. These grew into suburban villages and towns. It can therefore be no matter of surprise that the cemeteries should have attracted the attention of the barbarians as they drew near the city. In the churches they might hope to find silver and golden vessels; and from the churches it was easy to gain access to the Catacombs, in which they might not unreasonably suspect more treasure to be hid. That they effected an entrance there we cannot doubt; for there is evidence that as soon as the storm had passed, both the clergy and the people set themselves to work to repair the mischief that had been done. In two different catacombs fragments have been found of a metrical inscription by Pope Vigilius, A.D. 538-555, declaring how it had grieved him to see the memorials of the martyrs sacrilegiously broken, and how he had done his best to restore them; whilst in a third catacomb has been found another like inscription, showing that the people had borne their share in the good work. Again, another notice has been preserved recording that Pope John III., A.D. 560-574, after the devastation of Rome by Totila, "restored the cemeteries of the holy martyrs."

During this period the disturbed state of the country rendered it inconvenient and unsafe—indeed practically impossible—that the dead should be

---

* *Matt.* xvi.8.1·   † *Roma Sotterranea*, part i. pp. 170-173.

carried so far beyond the walls of the city for the purpose of burial, and henceforth intramural burial became common.

There is reason to believe that some few bodies of the martyrs had been removed from their original resting-places to churches prepared for their reception even as early as the fifth century; but it had not been done often. It was not until after the devastations and sacrileges committed by the Lombards under Astolphus, A.D. 756, that Paul I., elected in the following year, resolved upon translating on a large scale the relics of the Saints, in order to save them from profanation.

In a Constitution, dated June 2, 761, he complains that whereas, even before the siege of Rome by Astolphus, some of these subterranean cemeteries had been neglected and ruined, yet by the impious Lombards this ruin had now been made more complete; for they had broken open the graves and carried off some bodies of the Saints. "From that time forward," he says, "people have been very slothful and negligent in paying due honour to the cemeteries; animals have been allowed to have access to them; even folds have been purposely set up in them, so that they have been defiled with all sorts of corruption." He had therefore thought it good, he continues, to remove the bodies of martyrs and other Saints to the church he had built in honour of S. Stephen and S. Sylvester on the site of his own paternal house. Lists of the Saints whose relics were thus translated have come down to us, and there must have been more than a hundred in all.

Notwithstanding the efforts made by Paul's immediate successors to bring back the ancient honour and magnificence of the cemeteries by restorations, and to revive the interest in the crypts of the martyrs, Paschal I. was constrained to imitate the example of Paul, because they were being destroyed and abandoned. The inscription in Sta. Prassede still attests how he translated thither two thousand three hundred bodies on 20th July, 817. Sergius II. and Leo IV. continued the same work. We read, however, of no more translations of relics from the Catacombs in ancient times after the days of Leo IV., A.D. 848.

All the documents which mention these translations assign the cause of them to the abandonment and ruin of the cemeteries; and of course the translations, in their turn, still further hurried forward and completed the work of ruin and abandonment. The sacred treasures which had caused these places to be regarded with so much love and veneration having been removed, there was no longer the same motive for protecting or ornamenting them; and thus the first half of the ninth century may be said to have ended the history of the Catacombs as shrines or places of pilgrimage, just as the beginning of the fifth had ended their history as cemeteries. Henceforth they have no history; they were soon forgotten and practically unknown. In the eleventh and twelfth centuries we read of an occasional visitor to four or five cemeteries, the immediate neighbourhood of which to churches or monasteries had saved them from falling into utter oblivion.*

Certain partial discoveries of the Catacombs were made in the fifteenth century by some Franciscan Friars, and also by Roman Academicians, chief of whom was Pomponio Leto. But whatever researches they made, the former attracted by motives of piety, the latter by enthusiasm only for what was Pagan, were without result, and fruitless for historical or antiquarian science.

* *Roma Sotterranea*, part i. pp. 248-9, 252-61.

The date of the re-discovery of the Catacombs was May 31st, 1578, when some labourers, who were digging *pozzolana* in a vineyard on the Via Salaria, about two miles beyond the walls, happened to break into a gallery of graves, ornamented with Christian paintings, Greek and Latin inscriptions, and two or three sculptured sarcophagi. The discovery at once attracted universal attention, and persons of all classes flocked to see it. "Rome was amazed," writes a contemporary author, "at finding that she had other cities, unknown to her, concealed beneath her own suburbs, beginning now to understand what she had before only heard or read of;" and "In that day," says De Rossi, was born the name and the knowledge of *Roma Sotterranea*."

The Catacombs at once excited the interest of men of holiness and learning then in Rome, such as S. Philip Neri and Baronius; whilst archæologists, such as Ciacconio, De Winghe, and above all, Antonio Bosio, actively prosecuted their researches with immense industry. But the re-discovery of the Catacombs was not a matter of merely archæological interest; the devotion of the faithful was excited by the report that in those dark recesses might still be lying concealed the remains of saints and martyrs; and the concessions made to the piety of individuals to search for, and extract, these relics proved in the end most disastrous to the cemeteries as authentic records of the early Roman Church. Thus, though the rules laid down for the identification and translation of the relics may have been scrupulously observed, a number of private persons acting independently of each other were permitted to make excavations, who, alas for Christian archæology! in their search, had no regard for the preservation of monuments, whether of painting, sculpture, or inscriptions which came in their way. They did not even care to keep a record of what they had seen, which would at least have provided materials for future authors. Many of these permissions to extract relics were given to religious communities. None of them followed any systematic and comprehensive plan; and soon afterwards the permissions were revoked and vigorously repressed by successive Popes—definitely by Clement IX. about A.D. 1668. The loss, however, sustained by Christian archæology in the interval is incalculable. We learn something of the nature and extent of our loss from the incidental notices which occur in the writings of the archæologists of the seventeenth century; thus, we hear of a sepulchre all covered with gold, of a superb cameo, a series of the rarest coins and medals, various ornaments in crystal and metal, &c., besides a multitude of other objects, which were secretly sold by the labourers engaged in the excavations. But we are told nothing as to the precise localities in which any of these things were found. Had but an accurate record been kept of all discoveries, the work of reconstructing the history and topography of these cemeteries would have been comparatively easy and certain. Truly nothing is so vexatious, as a modern historian has justly remarked, "as the constantly recurring fact, that the most precious relics of antiquity, having lasted through centuries of neglect and oblivion, are destroyed when they are on the point of coming within the grasp of modern research." (*Roma Sotterranea*, part i. pp. 27-38.)

PART III.

DISCUSSIONS AND ARGUMENTS BEARING ON S. PETER'S ROMAN EPISCOPATE.

PART III.

DISCUSSIONS AND ARGUMENTS BEARING ON S. PETER'S ROMAN EPISCOPATE.

CHAPTER I.

ON THE TRADITIONAL BELIEF OF S. PETER'S ROMAN EPISCOPATE.

THAT S. Peter was the first Bishop of Rome, and that the Roman Pontiffs are his successors in that See, is still, as it has ever been since the earliest ages of the Church, the firmly-rooted conviction and belief of all the Catholic Faithful. No time can be named from the days of the Apostles until now when a contrary view was ever held, or so much as heard of, within the bosom of the Catholic Church. For some fourteen centuries the fact of S. Peter's Roman Episcopate was never denied or brought into question even by heretics or schismatics. The Papal Primacy being an article of Faith intimately bound up with the whole Christian religion, essential to the unity, strength, and permanence of the Catholic Church, and underlying her entire visible polity and superstructure, the fact of Peter's See, and of Peter's succession, whereby that Primacy is externally manifested and brought into exercise, was to the mind of the faithful as a first principle of Christianity, the simple and obvious historical realisation of our Lord's promise that the rock of Peter should be the firm and abiding foundation on which He would build His Church.

From the intimate relation that exists between the fact of Peter's Roman Episcopate, and the continued succession of the Roman Pontiffs to his Primacy, which is a matter of Faith, the former is more than a merely human historical fact, but partakes of the nature of a "dogmatic fact" (using this term in a wide sense, for a fact closely bound up with dogma), which, as such, has for Catholics the same divine infallible certainty as the Faith itself.

Hence it is quite evident that the primary and formal grounds for a Catholic's assent to it cannot be any mere human testimony to be gathered from antiquity, but must be the divine witness of the Church herself, and of Catholic tradition. The persuasion, therefore, in the Church, so constant and universal, is of itself an adequate and decisive proof for Catholics of the truth of this fact; and, strictly speaking, they do not need any direct and positive evidence from antiquity in support of their belief. And the less is such evidence required, because the actual exercise of the Papal Primacy (which the fact in question symbolises and connotes) in the unbroken succession of the Roman Pontiffs is an ever-living and standing witness, visible and patent to all in every generation of the faithful, that S. Peter held the See of Rome until his death; since these two facts are in the mind of Catholics counterparts the one of the other, bearing the correlation of necessary cause and effect.

But besides being in this sense a dogmatic fact, the Roman Episcopate of S. Peter is also a historical fact in the natural order; and consequently, as any other event of history, even that of Christianity itself, may well form a fit subject for the investigation of the historian, and is here amenable to the criterion and proof of testimony. And it has been our purpose to set forth and carefully to examine the evidences which antiquity furnishes of S. Peter's Episcopate at Rome as a historical fact.

If we were to judge *a priori*, we might reasonably presume that a fact so long, so constantly, and universally believed by the faithful, would have left some traces in the early records of Christianity. And though we may well suppose that many, perhaps even most of these records, have perished, whether in the times of Pagan persecution and barbarian invasion or through other causes, during the lapse of so many centuries; yet it would not be unreasonable to believe that, through the over-ruling Providence of God, an event so vitally important to His Church and to the Catholic religion would not be left without surviving witness in the first ages of Christianity, for the greater confirmation of the Faith, and its more effectual defence against the assaults of unbelievers.

All learned Catholic historians have maintained unanimously, since the question was first raised,* that the Roman Episcopate of S. Peter is clearly and strictly capable of historical proof: and that the testimonies and evidences, both direct and indirect, when taken together, are so strong as to be quite decisive, and to leave no doubt on the matter, for all the earlier evidence in surviving records is in support of the fact, whilst there is absolutely no shadow of historical testimony against it. It is witnessed to by a continuous stream of trustworthy testimony and intelligent assent in each succeeding century from the apostolic age.

"That S. Peter," says S. Alphonsus, "was at Rome several years—twenty-five, it is computed—and there died, has been always, whatever the innovators may say, the common opinion of all the holy Fathers and of all historians. The only difference amongst authors is as to the precise date when S. Peter arrived in Rome; but this does not do away with the fact of his residence in that city for many years, and until his death. Besides, independently of the testimony of a host of authors who affirm it, this fact results also from S. Peter's First Epistle, where we read: 'The Church which is at Babylon salutes you.' By Babylon the Apostle beyond doubt means the city of Rome, as Papias, a disciple of the Apostle, testifies according to the statement of Eusebius. This testimony agrees with the Apocalypse, where the city of Rome is called Babylon, on account of the many superstitions which the heathen there practised. And S. John, in the same book, foretells that this Babylon was one day to fall, which is to be understood of the paganism and temporal power of that city." †

So closely was S. Peter's Roman Episcopate bound up and identified in the minds of the early Christians with the idea of a first principle essential to the Church, and with belief in the fulfilment of Christ's promise to Peter, that the faithful in the first ages needed no elaborate proofs or argument to convince them of its reality as a historical fact. It was a part of the received tradition, and, whilst fully capable of attestation, was

---

* The learned Anglican bishop Pearson appositely remarks: "Although in this age a dissertation treating of this apostolical succession (whether namely the first bishop of Rome had some one of the Apostles as author and predecessor) may be called *a question*"—he soon goes on to prove that it was from S. Peter alone the Roman Bishops derived their succession—"yet in the primitive Church, it was never looked upon as a question, but as a real and indubitable truth." (Pearson's *Minor Theological Works*. Edited by Churton, Oxford, 1844, vol. ii. cap. vi. p. 323.)

† *Verità della Fede*, part iii. c. viii. 7. In affirming S. Peter's residence in Rome for many years, S. Alphonsus means also that the Apostle was Bishop of Rome during that time. This is plain from what he had said just before when speaking expressly of the Roman Episcopate. On the other hand, the holy Doctor does not mean thereby to imply that S. Peter's residence was continuous during those years.

doubtless, for the most part, taken for granted. But as soon as the Church was able, in any way, to form for itself a literature, all those who can be named as most renowned of old in Christendom, whether for genius, talent, profound learning, critical research in history, Canon Law and ecclesiastical science, or for doctrine and sanctity, are found to speak, as occasion offered, of the Roman Episcopate of S. Peter, and of the succession of the Roman Pontiffs to him in that See, as of something that was certain, universally accepted from the beginning, and about which there was no dispute or question.

The first age of Christianity was not occupied in writing history, but in preaching Christian doctrine, in spreading and establishing the Faith, and in converting the nations. We find indeed some of the earliest Fathers, as Justin, Tertullian, Irenæus, and Cyprian, in their Christian Apologies, or when combating heretics and schismatics, referring to the facts of S. Peter's preaching at Rome, his founding the Church there, as well as to his Episcopate and the succession to him in that See. They do not, however, treat of these matters *ex professo*, or as historians, but write in order to show where was to be found the genuine and primitive apostolic teaching, and to enforce the principle and necessity of unity in the Church. Hence, the testimonies they afford to S. Peter, whether as Apostle, Bishop, or Martyr in Rome, are, for the most part, but brief, fragmentary, indirect, implicit allusions, made off-hand and in passing, by those who had at the time no thought that facts so patent, notorious, and vital to the Catholic Church, stood in need of proof, or would one day be denied, and made a subject of controversy.

No one who reads impartially the works of the early Fathers and ecclesiastical writers can, we think, fail to see that the fact of S. Peter's having been Bishop of Rome, as we have already remarked, is looked upon by them as something taken for granted, and about which there is no second opinion. With them it is an already settled matter of fact to be built upon, and from which doctrinal and disciplinary conclusions are to be gathered for insistence, rather than a historical event requiring to be laid down with particular statement and explicit proof. It is less important with them in its historical than in its doctrinal aspect and bearing; embodying and symbolising, as it does, all that is most vital to the Church, that is, the Primacy, which forms at once the keystone and Divine principle of its unity, the centre and source of its jurisdiction, and the guarantee for the truth of its teaching. It is, no doubt, important also as a historical fact, but it is so especially as being the historical interpretation and the actual accomplishment before the world of that Primacy and of those prerogatives which Christ had promised to Peter, and which, in the *Romana Cathedra Petri*, were to remain a permanent and fundamental institution of His Church. It is in this light that the early Fathers treasure up and record the connection of S. Peter with Rome: and, hence, whatever mention they make of him in this relation, whether of his journey to Rome, his preaching and founding the Church there, his being Bishop of that See, or his martyrdom in that city, is made with a view to illustrate the same one fundamental doctrinal fact, viz., the Primacy of S. Peter and of his successors in the Roman See. Consequently whatever arguments or testimony the writings of the early Fathers supply in proof that S. Peter went to Rome at all, go also to prove his Episcopate and martyrdom in Rome. It is in this concrete, collective sense antiquity understood these several facts, which must stand or fall together.*

What we have hitherto said will account for the fact, that in the earlier ecclesiastical writers there are found comparatively so few direct and explicit testimonies to S. Peter's Episcopate at Rome. It was only later on, after the lapse of some time, when the Church was able to enjoy, so to say, more quiet leisure, that she began to exercise her memory and to recall the circumstances of her origin, engaging her wise and learned to collect the past traditions and ancient records, diligently to examine and sift them with critical care, and to compose chronicles and histories of the earlier times.

There was, moreover, another reason why the historical fact of S. Peter's Roman Episcopate and succession less needed the testimony of written statement for obtaining the credence of all

---

* In this light, so far as we have been able to judge from the objections and counter-arguments of Protestants, they, as a rule at any rate, regard the matter; though some, we are aware, separate these facts, as though they have no necessary bearing on one another; contending that whilst the evidence for some residence of S. Peter at Rome, and for his martyrdom there, may be sufficient to render these very probable, or even certain, yet that there is none at all, or what there is entirely fails, to prove his Episcopate. Many eminent Protestant writers and modern learned authors of the German critical school do not distinguish between these facts, but treat of them as one integral whole, and they say that perhaps no fact in ancient history is so placed beyond all question through the unanimous testimony of early Christian Doctors, and is so full of historical certainty, as what is recorded of S. Peter's dwelling and martyrdom in Rome; so much so, that we must give up faith in all history whatsoever, or admit this as historic truth.

the faithful, and this was that Peter's See (*Cathedra Petri*) was itself a visible, ever-present fact before their eyes, and that the principle it involved was continually living, active, and being brought into constant practical exercise. For it was precisely on the ground that S. Peter, chosen by Christ to be Prince of the Apostles and supreme Pastor of His Church, had been the first Bishop of Rome, and still lived in his successors to that See, that the Roman Pontiffs claimed authority over other Churches in their numerous epistles and by so many acts of their administration; and it was because Rome was universally held to have been Peter's See that such special honour and deference was paid to the Bishop and Church of Rome. Hence also it was that other Bishops from all parts of Christendom, in East and West, came to consult him, or sent to ask his advice or mediation in matters of greater importance; hence so many appeals were made to him, and so many persons of repute for learning or sanctity, heretics too amongst the number, resorted to Rome—whether for approbation of their doctrine, for admission to communion, or for redress of their grievances—as to the See of Peter, the chief Chair of teaching, and the centre of unity. It will suffice simply to recall the names of Clement and the Church of Corinth, of Anicetus and Polycarp, of Soter and Dionysius of Corinth, of Irenæus and the Churches of Gaul and Asia, of Victor and Polycrates, of Cornelius and Cyprian, of Marcion, Montanus, and Praxeas, in order to understand how great was the influence of the Bishop and See of Rome in the earliest times of Christianity. And herein lies a proof of the Roman Episcopate of Peter and of his succession in the Roman Pontiffs, more real and stable than any testimony contained simply in written documents.

"Who," writes S. Alphonsus, "can imagine the Bishops, Princes, the Holy Fathers, Doctors, and the rest of the faithful (all indeed except heretics who have ever sought to withdraw themselves from obedience to the Pope) from the earliest time blinded to such a degree as to have been willing to submit for so many centuries to the Bishop of Rome, venerating him as the Head of the Church, and obliging themselves to observe his definitions and ordinances as Divine utterances, had they not been fully assured by the teaching of Jesus Christ, that the Roman Pontiffs are the true successors of S. Peter in the Primacy and in the supreme power which they have over the Church? All in fact have looked upon the Bishop of Rome as the head of the Church; and consequently the Roman Pontiffs, after the death of S. Peter, continued always to ordain bishops for other Churches (S. Linus we read ordained fifteen), whilst they deposed others who misgoverned their flocks. Thus Bellarmine relates the deposition of eight Patriarchs in the Church of Constantinople alone. It is in like manner notorious from the whole *Corpus*

Juris Canonici that the Bishops in their doubts had recourse continually to the Roman Pontiffs, whose answers were held as so many laws. It is, moreover, certain, as we shall see later on in Chapter X., that from the beginning these same Pontiffs condemned various heresies for several centuries, during which no council was held."*

It is strange indeed, on the face of it, that what purports thus to be a historical fact, based all along from the beginning on trustworthy testimony without a single dissentient voice against it, confirmed by so many patent circumstantial evidences, accepted as absolutely certain, with the assent of universal Christendom for so many centuries, by all those most eminent for holiness, intelligence, and learning, and by the whole Catholic faithful throughout the world, up to the present time,—by the schismatical churches, too, of the East—it is strange, we say, that such a fact should in these days be passed over with indifference, or be disbelieved as devoid of credit, by all English-speaking Christians who are outside the Catholic Church; nay, that even some of them professing to be learned and critical scholars, should presume peremptorily to decide that it is supported by no argument or testimony worthy the serious consideration of a historian. One would have thought that a fact of this nature, which has proved to be pregnant with so many great practical issues vital to the whole of Christendom, bore with it its own credentials, and that the very universality and constancy of its belief was at once sufficient argument and proof of its real objective truth; and that all might safely take on trust such evidence of Peter's Roman Episcopate as was enough for the conviction of men like Cyprian, Jerome, Rufinus, Augustine, Eusebius, Chrysostom, Ambrose, Optatus, Gregory of Nyssa, Leo, and so many more.

With regard to this strange divergence of opinion, it is well to remark that Catholics, who universally, from the beginning of Christianity, believed S. Peter to have been the first Bishop of Rome and that the Popes were his successors in that See, held this to be true, not on any polemical or controversial grounds, but for its own sake, both as the embodiment and realisation of a positive doctrinal promise made by Christ to His Church, and also on its own merits as a historical fact.

For several centuries Christendom was united under the Primacy of the Roman Pontiff, who was acknowledged in the East, as well as in the West, to be the successor of Peter in his See; for on this point there was never any controversy at all.

* *Verità della Fede*, part ii. cap. viii. n. 5.

Remonstrances and resistance were indeed offered from time to time to the Bishop of Rome against the exercise he made of his authority; and he was charged by some as arrogating powers and prerogatives that did not belong to him, and exceeding the claims of Peter. But none ever denied or questioned the fact that Rome was Peter's See, or that the Bishop of Rome was Peter's successor, though not unfrequently it would have been the interest of some to deny this, and—so bitter were at times the disputes—they would not have shrunk from the denial had it been possible. Not even when the breach between the East and West was at length consummated, did any of the schismatical churches ever deny the fact of S. Peter's Roman Episcopate or the succession to him in that See of the Roman Pontiffs. Their sole accusation was that the Bishops of Rome unduly magnified Peter's Primacy, or exercised unjustly their authority and prerogatives. The historical fact was in possession, and the line of argument in support of the fact used by all, whether Catholics or others, who have held to the prescriptive persuasion of Christendom has, we say, uniformly been of a positive and uncontroversial character; whilst, on the other hand, those who have opposed the prescriptive belief of Catholics in this matter have done so, not on the simple merits of the question, but on controversial grounds, and for the sake of other points of doctrine that belonged to the religious system they had adopted, and in order to justify their rejection of Catholic faith and authority. But this they were unable to do without first discrediting the authority of the Roman Pontiff, and his claim to inherit the Primacy promised by Christ to Peter as successor of that Apostle in the Roman See. They took, then, at once the shortest and readiest way, which was to deny that Peter was ever Bishop of Rome, or even ever at Rome at all. Such a denial, they saw, would make a clean sweep of all Papal claims, and was, indeed, necessary for the position and for the cause of Protestantism.

Hence, the arguments of Protestants against the ancient prescriptive belief can hardly be impartial, or free from the taint and suspicion of self-interest. The furious prejudice that, at the time of the Reformation, raged against the Pope, on whom Luther and his adherents poured all the vilest epithets, necessitated the denial of the historical fact: and though the fierce heat of prejudice has since cooled down, still antipathy to Rome is hereditary amongst Protestants, and prevents, for the most part, even their learned and otherwise candid men from judging impartially and dispassionately on any historical question or fact which concerns the claims of the Pope or the Roman See. The denial of these claims is, we must remember, still of as much consequence to them as ever, constituting at once their most serviceable weapon of attack, and being made to form, with ingenious plausibility, their most convenient defence of the entire Protestant superstition.

Some few, it is true, of the more eminent and learned Protestants, especially amongst Anglicans, have shown themselves superior to the vulgar prejudice, and have affirmed, as an incontestable truth, that S. Peter held the Episcopal See of Rome. But these are rare exceptions.

We believe that, generally speaking, English Protestants in the present day hardly care to cast a thought on the question, regarding it as one unworthy of their notice; whilst Anglicans of the ritualistic type, in their superficial, but artfully concocted textbooks, and in their hebdomadal literature, are taught by their flippant Doctors, who affect to be learned, that the Episcopate of S. Peter at Rome is mere guess-work, a legend undeserving of serious credence, and to be looked on simply as a Popish myth.

We know not whether any of the really more learned Anglicans of the present day have written *ex professo*, or what they may generally hold, on this particular question. But we observe that one, at least, who has the repute of being a theologian of eminence amongst them, Dr. E. H. Browne, Bishop of Winchester, when formerly at Ely, wrote as follows:

"I think it may fairly be said, that if twelve judges in law or equity, of unprejudiced minds, were called on to decide from testimony of primitive Fathers and early history, whether S. Peter was ever truly Bishop of Rome, their unanimous judgment would be, that there was no sufficient evidence that he was so." And again, "The Bishops of Rome are no more successors of S. Peter than other Bishops ordained by him."*

And we know that he has expressed his opinion, that if any one fact of history is more certain than another, it is that S. Peter was never Bishop of Rome. That whilst it is only probable, but by no means certain, that S. Peter was ever in Rome at all, it is utterly improbable that he was there for more than a very short time. And that no evidence worth weighing in a historical balance can be produced to show that he was Bishop of Rome; for that all the earlier evidence is against it: and that no Roman Catholic

* *A Charge to the Clergy and Churchwardens of Ely*, 1869, pp. 67, 68. Longmans & Co.

writer has given even an approximate argument in proof of such a thesis.

So far as we have been able to gather, whatever arguments Protestants bring against S. Peter's Roman Episcopate are exclusively of the negative kind; thus, they allege that the testimonies produced by Catholics in its behalf are inconclusive, whether from insufficient directness and explicitness, some being only second-hand, others too vague and general, and others, again, derived from authors of spurious or doubtful authority. Then again, they insist much on certain real or apparent discrepancies in the various testimonies; and most especially on difficulties with regard to chronology. Thus the argument of Protestants is one wholly of negation and objections; they leave out of sight and ignore, as though of no account, the incontestable fact which itself forms the strongest argument of all, and is worth more than a whole host of extrinsic testimonies, namely, that belief in S. Peter's Roman Episcopate has been from time immemorial in unbroken possession throughout all Christendom. For from the days of the Apostle S. Peter himself it is impossible, on the one hand, to lay one's finger on any intervening date of time, or on any one surviving testimony from antiquity, and to affirm with any reasonable claim to probability, not to say certainty, "This is the origin of the belief, here it first began;" whilst, on the other hand, not a single item of positive evidence to the contrary is producible from ancient records.

By confession of a learned Protestant historian, before the close of the third century of the Christian era, belief in the Roman Episcopate of Peter, and that the Popes were his successors and heirs to his apostolic supremacy, was universal and the most dominant principle throughout Christendom.*

This belief appeared, even at that early epoch, like some broad majestic river bearing on its full tide all the fortunes and treasures of the Church, irrigating either shore of Christendom, which was now enlarging its borders in East and West. We follow it upwards towards its rising along the two centuries that divide it from its source. Ever lessening in breadth the stream appears, but still on Eastern and Western shores the narrowing bounds of Christendom are washed by its salutary wave. And

---

* "Before the end of the third century, the lineal descent of Rome's bishops from S. Peter was unhesitatingly claimed and obsequiously admitted by the Christian world."—Milman's *History of Early Christianity*, vol. iii. p. 370, ed. 1840.

just as the river when nearing its source shows its surface broken and rugged amongst rapids and rocky steeps, so flows this stream of traditional faith, tossed confusedly at times amidst persecutions and conflicts of the Church's primitive age. We pursue still upwards its course; and ever and anon, like some tiny rivulet falling seemingly with intermittent flow, it is almost lost to view. At length we have traced back the broad river to its original fountain-head in the Rock of Peter.

CHAPTER II.

CERTAIN OBJECTIONS TO THE ARGUMENT FROM TRADITION CONSIDERED.

WHOEVER believes in the historical personality of S. Peter at all, will allow that he had a history; and that, as the foremost of Christ's Apostles, he occupied a position and a sphere of labour, and did a work in the apostolic primitive Church of importance and prominence proportionate with the place assigned to him in the Apostolic College by the Gospel narrative, and with all that is recorded of him by S. Luke in the Acts of the Apostles. After the last word was spoken of him in that Evangelist's history, he certainly had a subsequent career of apostolic toil and fruitfulness, which, we are assured by the prophetic words of our Lord Jesus Christ Himself, was to be closed by a glorious martyrdom. We have, moreover, the Evangelist S. John, who records that prophecy, at the same time witnessing to its fulfilment, and to the special kind of martyrdom by crucifixion endured by S. Peter: for S. John wrote his Gospel after that event. Thus Peter's martyrdom, alone of all the Apostles, was expressly foretold by Christ, and alone (save that of S. James) is set on record in the New Testament. And can we suppose that his memory in the pages of the early Church's history has perished with him? It would be so, indeed, if Protestants are to be listened to, and the unvarying prescriptive tradition and belief of Catholics from the beginning are to be called in question or discredited; for there is absolutely no other account or history of S. Peter's later career of apostolic labour, or of his place of martyrdom, than that which has been delivered by Catholic tradition, and accepted by universal Catholic belief—viz., that which records his journey to Rome, his preaching and founding the Church there, his episcopate of that See, and his martyrdom in that city.

Protestants choose to deny and reject this account of S. Peter's career; but with all their ingenuity they have never been able to devise any other from historical remains, nor to imagine one for substitution in its place that could have any claim to even a plausible hypothesis.

Granted, for the sake of argument, that the early testimonies to S. Peter's Roman Episcopate are few and scanty, obscure and inexplicit; that some of the witnesses are of no great, or of doubtful, authority; and that some of the proofs are mixed up with unreliable legends, or derived from spurious and apocryphal writings. This is only what might have been expected. The early Christian writers were not historians; there seemed no need of at once narrating and giving the proofs of what all knew, were familiar with, and unhesitatingly believed. The most that was done in those days, in the way of history, was to commit to brief record some acts of martyrs; to register here and there certain dates; or to chronicle, in succinct and fragmentary words, divers passing occurrences, perhaps of interest rather to individuals than to the community at large. Such is ever the way at the first rise and beginning of all institutions, before more regular system, and an appointment to particular offices, according to the growing exigencies, are recognised as necessary, and are introduced.

There were indeed Christian authors in those earlier days, some of whose writings have come down to us; as the Apostolic Fathers, Hermas, Justin, Tertullian, Irenæus, Origen, Clement of Alexandria, and Cyprian. But the object of these first Fathers was not to write history, but to teach and develop Christian doctrine; to spread and establish the faith; and to convert the people. We find nearly all of them, indeed, in their Christian Apologies, or their writings against heretics, referring in turn to one or other of the facts of S. Peter's preaching at Rome, founding the Church there, being Bishop of Rome, and there martyred, as well as of his unbroken line of successors in the Roman See. This, however, they do, not for the sake of stating these facts, the truth of which no one then sought to deny; but pointing them out, in order to show how and where primitive apostolic doctrine might be surely ascertained, and to illustrate the principle, and enforce the necessity of the Church's unity. These earlier Fathers, and those, too, who came after them, as Ambrose, Augustine, Jerome, and Chrysostom, have all of them incidentally left in their writings passages bearing direct witness to the Episcopate of S. Peter, his succession in the Roman See, and its consequent prerogatives; but these topics seem to be in their mind something quite obvious, axiomatic, and elementary, that is, rather to be taken for granted as a first principle in the Church than a matter of historical fact needing any very explicit demonstration. Hence, whilst the Fathers, in their Commentaries and Gospel Homilies, dwell largely on the special office and prerogatives of S. Peter, their wont, for the most part, is, when discoursing on our Lord's words addressed to that Apostle, to leave their literal sense, together with the truths and facts they primarily express, and to develop rather such other doctrinal, moral, or mystical applications as they are led to draw from those words and facts. They appear to dwell much on *Peter in the Gospels* as the embodiment of doctrinal and mystical teaching, with a view to illustrate this class of truth, and proportionately little on *Peter in the Church* as regards his personal office and action, in a historical aspect. But here and there, and every now and then, there is a brief word, a passing allusion, a detached sentence, luminous and startling as a direct revelation by its explicitness and pregnancy, which casts a flood of light on all the rest, showing the doctrinal or mystical Peter of the Gospels, not only in his own distinct personality, but also in his official character as Supreme Pastor, to be ever living and energising in the Church, to be still the central source and principle of unity and authority, through his successors in the *Cathedra Petri*, the See of Rome.

These express testimonies of the earlier Fathers, though comparatively few, and scattered here and there in their writings, inform with fitting coherence and significance whatever else they say, with so much diffusiveness, concerning Peter's personal office and prerogatives; and hence all this, too, is really applicable to S. Peter as he lives in his successors, and serves as matter of solid argument in proof of his Episcopate and succession in the Roman See. For, if all that the name of Peter connotes and represents, if what is embodied in, and clusters round, that Apostle were not some vital principle, something ever present to, and energising in the Church, it would seem unlikely that the Fathers should give themselves continually to develop and illustrate what pertains to S. Peter with so much fullness of doctrinal, moral, and mystical reflection as we find they do. Whereas, on the other hand, if, as we claim to be the truth, this active principle, together with what forms its material component parts, viz.: the facts of S. Peter's Primacy, *jure divino ;* his Roman Episcopate, and the supremacy inherited by his successors in the See of Rome—if, we say, all this was something considered elementary, and was commonly admitted, we may then well understand how the Fathers should make it a matter rather for doctrinal and moral discourse than one of explicit statement and proof. And whereas the express statements they actually make are quite enough to show clearly what they held on the mere matter of fact, the very fewness of their statements on this point is an evidence of the firm and prevalent belief of its historical reality, and shows that its foundation was so solid and deeply laid as to need no arguments or proofs for its confirmation.

Even though we should allow—what is in truth but an *ex parte* statement of opponents—that some of the earlier witnesses are of mean or doubtful authority, what would this prove but that the voice of unlearned and simple men reflects a generally prevalent persuasion, as much as the attestation of the more intelligent and erudite? It is, however, quite certain, on the one hand, that those particular testimonies alleged to be of little weight did not, as opponents pretend, originate the tradition; for we can trace the stream even higher still, even to its source in the very times of the Apostles themselves; and it is equally certain, on the other hand, that if they were of such little weight as is alleged, they could not of themselves have formed the authority for a belief so persistent, unbroken, and universal; a belief shared by all those most eminent, through a course of many centuries both in East and West, for learning, intelligence, doctrine, sanctity, or critical science,—a belief fraught with such momentous issues, not alone to the whole Episcopate, to all the Churches of Christendom, and to the Christian faith itself, but also to the entire fabric of the new European society and polity,—to kings and governments, and nations and peoples. For it is not too much to say that no principle was so potent a factor in the creation, formation, and conservation of Christian civilisation, as this strong, settled, and universal belief,—namely, that the Pope was successor to S. Peter in the See of Rome, and thereby, at the same time, inheritor, with sanction of Divine right, of that Apostle's prerogatives and supremacy in Christendom.

It surely needs no uncommon sagacity to see how unphilosophical, how untrue to history, as well as to all experience of human nature—not to say how unreasonable and absurd—it is, to ground a mighty belief like this, so pregnant with practical and most critical consequences, on the flimsy basis of guess-work, and the utterances of credulous ignorance, or crazy superstition.

But it may be objected: It is quite certain, and now freely admitted on all hands, that several of the early Christian writings, which embody, and witness to the tradition, are spurious and apocryphal, containing forged accounts and legends devoid of historical truth. It cannot, moreover, be denied that some of such writings, now ascertained to be unreliable, were accepted even by the learned in early times as authentic. Thus the spurious *Clementines*, a forgery of the second or third century, were a principal foundation of the growing belief in S. Peter's Roman Episcopate.

To this we reply, that neither the *Clementines* nor any other apocryphal writings were the source from which the tradition first sprang, for it is seen to be anterior to any of these. It is a commonplace of sound historical criticism that any widely prevailing traditionary belief that is persistently strong and enduring, especially one that entails important results, has its origin in historical fact; and whilst it may be fostered by legend and fiction, it is the cause of these, and not their effect. We may say generally, that when the subject-matter of a work of fiction and that of a popular belief are one and the same, it is the belief that gives rise to the fiction, not the fiction to the belief—that the production of the fiction is, so far, an evidence of the strength and prevalence of the belief; and that in proportion to the strength and universality of the belief, such fiction is an evidence also of the reality of the fact which forms the object and ground of the belief.

The disposition to invent, and the love of fiction, whether in poetry or prose, are inherent in human nature; and the tendency to romance manifests itself in varying degrees and divers ways amongst a people at different times. Fiction has its groundwork in reality: it takes up the facts and traditions of the past, whether historical or legendary, or the current associations of the present—it may be some passing event of the day, the manners and fashions of society, the tastes, the interests, the modes of thought and sentiment that are prevalent—to weave them together with the tissue of its own invention: these the imaginative faculty draws out and develops, amplifies and adorns with circumstances, details, and hues of its own creative fancy; and, just so far as the subjective accretions of imagination assimilate and are found in harmony with the groundwork of the objective reality, does the composite fabric commend itself as genuinely artistic, or, as we are wont to express it, it forms a work of fiction true to life. Works of fiction are generally intended to be taken for what they are; the author has no thought or desire that they should be considered aught else, nor are they otherwise

understood by those who read them. But there are other
fictitious works that are made to wear the face of historical
truths, perhaps by express design of the author; and these often
come to be accepted, for a time at any rate, as genuine by the
public. Written, for the most part, some time after the events
they describe—with the view of winning greater credit—they
purport to be the composition of some earlier author of trustworthy repute, and are made to bear his name. Works of this
kind have generally for their subject-matter the life of some well-
known personage, or some event of history about which no doubt
exists; and this the writer amplifies with details and circumstances of uncertain credibility, anecdotes and stories which he
has received at hearsay, and from second-hand unreliable information, or which are the pure fabrication of his own imagination.
There are several writings extant, from the early ages of the
Church, more or less of this character; as, for example, the
apocryphal Gospels and Epistles. It would seem that certain
Christians let their innate talents and their taste for fiction run
much in the line of pious frauds in those primitive days. There
was little at that time congenial to their minds in the past or
present of Paganism, or in the public life and society around
them, and they allowed their inventive faculty of imagination
to work upon what was of uppermost interest to them, and hence
its play in the sphere of Christian doctrine, the history of the
Church, the life of Jesus Christ its Divine Founder, and all that
bore upon His disciples and their immediate successors.* Hence
the various apocryphal Gospels, the spurious Epistles, and other
supposititious writings of that period which have come down to us.
We are not here passing any judgment, whether of justification
or censure, on the morality of such procedure, nor are we appraising the relative trustworthy value of such works. We are
here simply stating the fact; and we say generally that so far
from such like unauthentic works, fabrications, and forgeries
weakening or detracting in any way from the credibility of the
main history and events which form the groundwork of their

* In those early times, moreover, when as yet so many Christian doctrines had not received from the Church their formal and precise definition,
and religious speculation was everywhere so rife, many sought to blend with
some strange philosophical system on the one hand, or with Judaising tenets
on the other, more or less of Christian teaching, and found this sort of fiction,
through spurious and apocryphal writings, the most convenient mode of
ventilating, and giving a plausible colour to, their peculiar and erratic views:
by engrafting them on the main groundwork of Christianity, and associating
them with its founders and more prominent historical characters.

composition and furnish their authors with the occasion of writing at all, they are, on the contrary, the strongest confirmation of the actual truth and reality of the historical events. Thus the pseudo-Gospels would never have been written later on, had there not been the genuine Gospels already in existence; and the former would never have obtained the credit they did, had they not contained very much that was already from other sources held as certain, generally believed, and well known to be true; or had the additions made by the author's invention, or otherwise obtained, been out of harmony with what was certainly authentic, and with the current belief.

Who can read the *Gospel of Nicodemus* and not more clearly recognise in its sublime descriptions the fulness of faith prevalent amongst the primitive Christians in the descent of our Lord into hell, His delivering the souls of the just from Limbo, and His triumphant resurrection from the dead? Call it fiction and forgery if you will, still it stands out as a grand epic, illustrative of the faith of the primitive Church, and so far serves, by consequence, to confirm the truth of the revealed mysteries it embodies.

The same may be said of the supposititious Epistle of Clement to S. James the Apostle. Granted, that it is all fictitious, and that the transfer of the See of Rome and of supreme authority by S. Peter to Clement, recorded with so much dramatic circumstance, is a pure imagination of the forger, what does all this prove? but that the belief in the fact that S. Peter held the Roman See, and that the Bishops of Rome succeeding to his See inherited his supremacy, was so firmly rooted in the minds of the Christian public in the second and third centuries, that some ingenious writer could dress up this fact with certain details of interest of his own invention into a circumstantial story, which obtained credit as being *a priori* probable on account of its harmony with the traditional and current popular belief.

We have something else to remark with regard to early works of this sort. It would be a great mistake to suppose that everything recorded by apocryphal writers, over and above what is contained in the authentic and genuine works, must be valueless and without foundation. Very often much they say is found, on other independent grounds, to be true, or to have in it a substratum of truth, or what is told in anecdote and story illustrates, or approximates to, what is true. This we know is the case in secular history, that for example of our early English sovereigns, Canute and Alfred. There are many incidents recorded, which, if critically examined, might be found to rest on very slender or doubtful authority, and yet we do not on that account deem these legends and traits of personal character as idle and baseless fables, but mete to them their proportional value of more or less intrinsic and extrinsic probability, whether as themselves of real occurrence, or as illustrating what is certainly historical fact. And this we hold should be the dealing of reasonable and fair critics with regard to events of sacred and ecclesiastical history recorded by apocryphal authors.

Further: that the invention of such writers is often based on at least a substratum of truth, is illustrated by the aforementioned spurious Epistle of S. Clement to S. James. The main fact which it records is now held by critical historians of great name and weight to be most probably true, having for its support other independent and trustworthy testimony of antiquity; though the way in which that fact is related in the Epistle, and the circumstances with which it is clothed, must be set down to the pure invention of the forger. The main fact is, that S. Clement was invested with the episcopal character during the lifetime of S. Peter, and most probably by that Apostle himself, with a view to his taking part in the administration of the Church of Rome, and to his future succession to S. Peter in that See. Historians of note, we say, hold this to be most probable, since the fact of S. Clement's consecration by S. Peter is positively asserted by more than one very early writer. They are, moreover, of opinion that not Clement alone, but also Linus and Cletus were probably made bishops by S. Peter during his own Episcopate, and that these bishops assisted S. Peter in his pastoral work at Rome, and in administrating the affairs of that Church, and more especially when he himself was absent from the city engaged in his apostolic labours. This is confirmed by Rufinus in his Preface to the *Recognitions*, who, when commenting on the Epistle to James, offers with approval an explanation on this point which he had heard from others. This, whilst it does not in every respect coincide with the one just mentioned, contains the following statement:

> "Linus and Cletus were bishops in the city of Rome during the lifetime of Peter: that is, they undertook the care of the Episcopate, and he fulfilled the office of the Apostolate, as is found also to have been the case at Cæsarea, where, when he himself was present, he yet had Zacchæus ordained by himself as bishop."

There are, as is well known, various conflicting statements of early writers regarding the appointment and succession of the first bishops of Rome after S. Peter. Rufinus in his Preface adds confirmation to the universally received order of the first three, namely, Linus, Cletus, Clement. It seems to have been thought by some that Clement succeeded immediately to S. Peter; this notion probably arose from its being such a well-known fact that Clement was consecrated bishop by that Apostle, as Tertullian expressly affirms.*

It is, moreover, considered most probable by those who set store by a passage of S. Epiphanius† that Clement was really designated by S. Peter to be his immediate successor, but through humility declined the dignity, first in favour of Linus, and then of Cletus, and could not be prevailed on to accept it until after their death. Whatever may have been the actual truth of the matter, all here goes to show how large a substratum of reality there is in the account given by the writer of the supposititious Epistle of Clement to James.‡

Another kind of objection made by Protestants against S. Peter's Roman Episcopate is derived from Chronology. But where, may we ask, as to events of ancient history are there not chronological difficulties? Certainly we might expect many in this case. Since the chronological account of S. Peter—and everybody, we presume, will grant that he had some chronological history—is no simple matter, but one obviously of much complication, depending on the chronological dates and arrangement of several other series of events, themselves very difficult to determine, namely, of the Gospel record, of the Acts of the Apostles, and of contemporaneous profane history, and depending, again, on the harmony of the two former with the third. No marvel, then, that the question of S. Peter's Roman Episcopate has difficulties of chronology, since it must needs have part in the chronological intricacies of other histories besides its own. But what we hold to be in truth a marvel is, that the chronological exposition of S. Peter's Roman Episcopate and of other collateral historical events, offered by learned critical Catholic historians and Scripturists, forms not only a complete solution of the difficulties objected, but also a strong positive confirmation in proof of the whole Petrine fact itself, and as that fact has been handed down by tradition,

---

* *De Præscript.* 32.   † *Adv. Hæres.* 27.

‡ The explanation given in the text serves to conciliate the varying or discrepant statements that occur in early writers of weight with regard to the three afore-named first successors to S. Peter in the Roman See.

and generally accepted by the faithful. It was not necessary for the Catholic thesis to show that S. Peter was Bishop of Rome for twenty-five years; it was, strictly speaking, enough to prove that he held the See for some time, however short, until his death. But it is not a little remarkable that the amended date of our Lord's Crucifixion, from 33 to 29 of the Vulgar Era—now held generally by learned critics, whether Catholic or Protestant, to be certainly the true date—should not only smooth away whatever difficulties in the chronology of the Acts of the Apostles seemed to lie against the twenty-five years, but should, moreover, even enable critical interpreters to establish from S. Luke's history twenty-five years to be the exact duration of S. Peter's Roman Episcopate in accordance with a natural and unstrained computation of that chronology. Herein we have an undesigned coincidence of great importance in confirmation of the fact.

CHAPTER III.

S. PETER'S ROMAN EPISCOPATE AND THE NEW TESTAMENT.

It will, we think, be clear to anyone, who thoughtfully, and without prepossession or prejudice, peruses the page of the Gospel, seeking to understand the words of our Divine Lord in their plain and obvious meaning, that much of His moral and doctrinal teaching is also prophetic; in such sense that it reveals, insists on, or brings to prominent view certain principles, truths, qualities, and conditions, which were to be distinctly characteristic throughout future time of that Church which He came on earth to establish, and of that Divine faith and religion, which it was to be the mission of that Church to promulgate in all generations until the end of the world. We will not here delay to speak of the visibility of Christ's Church, or of what are known as her four great notes—Unity, Sanctity, Catholicity, and Apostolicity; but we shall at once illustrate what we have said, by mentioning some points of more particular detail, less frequently noticed in this relation.

We note, then, on the first page of the Gospel, that ascription of blessing to Mary, the Virgin Mother of our Lord Jesus Christ, the Divine Incarnate Word, was to be ever a characteristic mark of all generations of Christ's true faithful until the end of time.* Thus some devotion, at least, to Mary, the second Eve, the Blessed one amongst women, is set down as a note of Christ's Church, and a seal whereby "the Lord knoweth who are His,"† in contradistinction to that enmity against the Woman and her seed foretold by God Himself in the first page of Genesis, which, as a brand, was to mark, in perpetuity, the arch-deceiver and his seed of error.‡ Hence, from the Gospel, we should expect to find devotion to the Blessed Virgin to be ever a prominent feature in the true Church of Christ.

Again, our Divine Lord evidently contemplates in the future of His Church the adoption and profession, by some of its mem-

* *Luke*, i. 48.   † 2 *Tim*. ii. 19.   ‡ *Gen*. iii. 15.

bers, of a special and more strict manner of life than that of ordinary Christians—a life marked by the voluntary choice of a state of perpetual chastity, of poverty, by the renunciation of worldly possessions, and of obedience, by more complete subjection of individual self-will. His words indicating such a state are well known; and it is evident that they were not meant for His Apostles and immediate disciples alone, but were applicable to His faithful in every age; for, when speaking of voluntary chastity for the sake of the kingdom of heaven, He says generally: "All men take not this word, but they to whom it is given. He that can take, let him take it:"[*] and He extends the promised reward of voluntary poverty, and of following His footsteps by more perfect obedience, to all who should adopt these evangelical counsels. His words are emphatically universal. "And *every one* that hath left house, or brethren," &c. "Amen, I say to you there is *no man* that hath left house, or parents," &c.[†] We should expect, then, that the profession of the evangelical counsels would find a distinctive place at all times in the true Church of Jesus Christ.

We might illustrate this subject by many other instances of our Lord's doctrinal or moral teaching, which are evidently prophetic and descriptive of the future circumstances and condition of His Church: but there are three points of His teaching, about which His words are, we deem, more plain, emphatic, and explicit, than any other of His utterances recorded by the Evangelists; whilst, at the same time, they partake of that prophetic sense to which we have been directing attention. These three points are the Holy Eucharist, the power left in His Church to absolve from sin, and a very special and intimate relation of His Church with S. Peter. We shall here touch but briefly on the two first; but shall dwell at some length in the course of this chapter upon the third, as forming a very important argument in the whole inquiry we are instituting on the point of S. Peter's Roman Episcopate.

With regard to the Holy Eucharist, no words of our Lord can be cited from the Gospels more clear and emphatic than those He gave utterance to at the time of its institution, as narrated by the three first Evangelists,[‡] and in His doctrinal discourse left on record by S. John.[§] Our Lord, at the same time, clearly teaches

---

[*] *Matt.* xix. 11-13; 1 *Cor.* vii. 37, 38.
[†] *Matt.* xix. 27-29; *Luke,* xviii. 28-30.
[‡] *Matt.* xxvi. 26-28; *Mark,* xiv. 22-24; *Luke,* xxii. 19, 20; 1 *Cor.* xi. 23-29.
[§] *John,* vi. 32-72.

that the Divine gift He bestows in the Holy Eucharist is to be the heritage of His universal faithful, and the peculiar property of His Church in every age; for He insists on the obligations and responsibilities which this gift entails on all who shall believe in Him. He ordains it by solemn command to be an abiding institution in His religion, and a perpetual memorial of Himself. Surely, then, we must believe that by His true faithful this behest will be obeyed; and that nought will be so greatly treasured, so highly honoured, or frequented in His Church with so much lively faith and loving devotion, as the Holy Eucharist.

Take, again, the words of Christ as He bestows on His Church the power of the keys, whereby to absolve His people from sin. Could He speak more plainly, and in more absolute terms, or with more wide and universal application?* Oh, amazing, unimagined, yet most needful bestowal of a prerogative all-divine! And will there not be seen continually, in every age, throngs of penitents, craving the exercise of this prerogative, in witness of its abiding existence in the Church of Christ?

Before we give ourselves to consider more fully the third point, that, namely, of the special and intimate relation of the Church with S. Peter, let us sum up our argument. It is this:

We meet, so to say, on the very surface of the Gospel page certain truths, principles, and practices predicted to be characteristic of the true faithful, and distinctive of the Church of Christ, such, especially, as devotion to the Virgin Mother of our Lord; profession of the evangelical counsels; the Eucharist set forth as the highest, most prominent, and most cherished by the faithful, of Christian rites; the exercise of the power of the keys by absolution from sin. This being so, we are bound to find the continual realisation, and the actual working of these truths, principles, and practices in the true Church of Christ; otherwise His prophetic words and teaching would remain unfulfilled, and the truth of the Gospels might be, with just reason, impeached.

But what is the fact? Those several self-same points, which were thus the subject-matter of our Lord's teaching in His prevision of the future, are seen at all times in the Catholic Church, as in their proper home, to have their practical realisation and their normal development; they form so many visible and permanent institutions in her system, engaging continually her

---

* *Matt.* xviii. 18; *Mark*, ii. 5-11; *Luke*, v. 20-24; *John*, xx. 21-23.

every-day work, and the interest, activity, and zeal of her members; whilst it is these very points which distinguish, in a most marked and prominent manner, the Catholic Church from all Protestant forms of Christianity, whether of Anglicanism or of other sects.*

Hence, by necessary consequence, we conclude that the Catholic Church, in that distinctive aspect of doctrinal teaching and practice in which she has been ever actually recognisable, is the realised object of our Lord's Divine prevision, and the fulfilment of His prophetic words. Herein, moreover, we find, at

* It is true that of late years some of these doctrines and practices have been partially adopted by some amongst the Anglicans, who now have their high and low celebrations of Eucharists, their use of confession, and their convents. But it is also true, and clear as daylight, if not to themselves, at any rate to all the world besides, including the majority of "English Churchmen," in these as in past times, that the Anglican Establishment is not the proper home for such doctrines and practices; since, notoriously, "the Church of England" was built upon the ruins of altars, confessionals, and monasteries, and established in this country as a standing protest against them. Three centuries of their disuse, or rather of their repudiation, is a fair index of what is connatural and normal to the Anglican Communion, during which space its ministers and people got on very contentedly without them, neither feeling their loss, nor seeking to supply it. On the contrary, many of its most eminent worthies and divines nurtured their personal piety and won their religious fame by their earnest denial and denunciation of these very doctrines and practices, as entirely contrary to true Christianity. Departure, more or less, and in one way or other, from its first principles and from its original norm is incident to every purely human institution, which of its own nature is ever tending to disintegration. It is, therefore, no way surprising that Anglicanism, which has in the past assimilated to itself, as a religion, so many other foreign elements, should also take some from the Catholic Church, of which in England it pretends to be the representative and heir. Several adventitious causes have, moreover, in recent days helped to this adoption—for adoption, in truth, it is, and not a normal genesis. In part we welcome it, on many grounds, as a movement upwards to what is good and true; and, especially, so far as it may, in the gracious designs of God's providence, afford to sincere and earnest souls matter and motives for that pious affection and disposition towards the belief of revealed truths, which, as a preparation of heart, is the needful precursor of firm divine faith. A very simple test-mark of the different relation borne by the Catholic Church and the Anglican Communion to Catholic faith and practice is the following: an Anglican, whether he holds or denies what is of Catholic faith and practice, may be considered by his coreligionists a good and orthodox Anglican; a Catholic, if he denies or rejects the same, must thereby be reckoned a bad Catholic, or rather ceases to be a Catholic in a true sense. It is not a little remarkable that amongst Catholic accretions to modern Anglicanism devotion to the Blessed Virgin does not find its place; this, so far as we have observed, assumes no other type than a carefully guarded, cold, distant, solemn, theological reverence of S. Mary. When once, however, an Anglican has some loving, filial recognition of Mary as his mother, then another world and another spiritual life begin to open to him, and then thoughts and steps are tending homewards. We need hardly add that Anglicanism cannot admit any special acknowledgment of, or devotion to, S. Peter: this would be to subvert its whole system.

the same time, a most clear proof in confirmation of the truth of His own Divinity, and of the Divine inspiration of the Gospel record.

We might, with equal cogency, turn our argument another way, thus :—We see, as a matter of fact, certain principles of doctrine and practice at actual work in a Church which claims to be the one true Catholic Church founded by Christ Himself. These principles are connatural and necessary to its very essence and life, distinguishing it from all other religions around. Hence, naturally, and with reason, we should expect that, if its claim to be indeed the Church of Christ were good and true, distinct mention of these principles would have been made by the Divine Founder, and would be discoverable in the surviving record of His words. Such mention appears in the inspired Gospels; for there these very same principles are set forth by our Lord Himself, as characteristic of that Church which He came on earth to found. By this process, again, conclusive witness is secured to the twofold truth of the Divine inspiration of the Gospels, and of the Divine origin of the Catholic Church.

We have drawn out, with the foregoing illustrations, this general argument for its better application to the point most pertinent to our subject, which we have as yet held in reserve, namely, the special and intimate relation of Christ's true Church with S. Peter.

Now, on this head we find our Lord's words in the Gospel most plain, explicit, and emphatic. Andrew, S. John records,[*] "brought Simon to Jesus, and Jesus, looking upon him, said: Thou art Simon the son of Jona, thou shalt be called Cephas, which is interpreted Peter"—the word Cephas signifying, in the vernacular which our Lord spoke, a rock. Later on, upon the occasion of the Apostle's confession of His Divinity, Christ proclaims him to be indeed what that name imports: "I say to thee, that thou *art* Peter; and upon this rock I will build My Church."[†] Our Lord spake these words in Syro-Chaldaic: Thou art Cephas (a rock), and on this Cephas, &c.; but the Evangelist is careful in recording them to interpret the name Cephas into Peter: for by that name the Prince of the Apostles was to be designated and known throughout all future ages. "Thou art Peter, a rock." And then our Lord goes on to show the proper meaning of this his new name, and the precise import of its

---

[*] *John*, i. 42.   [†] *Matt.* xvi. 18.

bestowal, by declaring in what sense, and in what relation, he is thus a rock. For now Christ speaks for the first time explicitly of that Church which He is about to found. "I say to thee that thou art Peter—thou art Cephas, a rock; and on this rock (on thee) I will build My Church." Thou art Peter, for on thee as a strong rock, and chief foundation stone, inseparably united with Myself, I will build My Church, the House of God on earth.* Built on this foundation, based on this rock, that Church, the citadel of Divine truth, and the gathering-place of His elect, our Lord proclaims, shall abide in strength, stable and secure, until the end of time, against all deceits of error, and all assaults of wickedness. "And the gates of hell shall not prevail against it."

In this His Church, which he pronounces to be indestructible through all ages, our Lord foretells, there will be a supremacy of rule and jurisdiction, with power universal to bind and to loose; and He promises that the acts of that supremacy here on earth, whether of binding or loosing, shall be confirmed and ratified by Himself in heaven. This supremacy, divinely instituted together with the Church itself, belongs, and perpetually adheres thereto, as a part of its essential constitution; and this supremacy Christ entrusts to *one*, who personally must exercise it with exclusive individual right, as long as that Church shall endure, and her acts of binding and loosing shall need here on earth Divine sanction in heaven. Hence, in virtue of its institution, this supremacy ordained by Christ must by His own Divine law reside perpetually in His Church, in the hands of *one* who, receiving it handed down in line of legitimate succession, will by its heritage be thus supreme. This same supremacy He bestows on Peter, to be henceforth in perpetuity associated with his name, as deriving

---

* S. Alphonsus shows that these words were addressed by Christ to Peter and here apply to him alone, that they are to be understood, moreover, in their literal sense of Peter being the rock on which the Church was built according to the general interpretation of the Fathers, notably of S. Jerome, whose words he cites. "Not as though Peter has one meaning and Cephas another; but the word which we in Latin and Greek call Petra, the Hebrews and Syrians, from the affinity of their language, call Cephas." "Since, then," continues S. Alphonsus, "Peter is the rock, or the foundation of the Church, he cannot fail; otherwise if the foundation could fail, the Church too might one day fail; but this is impossible on account of the promise already made in this very place: *Et portæ inferi non prævalebunt adversus eam*. And if Peter cannot fail, neither can the Pontiffs his successors fail; because, since Jesus Christ promised that hell should never prevail against His Church, the promise must necessarily be understood as made for all time, even as long as the Church shall last." (*Verità della Fede*. p. iii. cap. ix. 4.)

its force and authority from the virtue and strength which that name of his imparts; for he has been made by Christ Peter, the rock and foundation of the Church. "Thou art Peter, and on this rock I will build My Church... and I will give to thee the keys of the kingdom of heaven, and whatever thou shalt bind on earth shall be bound in heaven, and whatever thou shalt loose on earth shall be loosed in heaven."

The sum of our contention here is, that according to the plain and obvious sense of these prophetic words of our Lord descriptive of His Church and its constitution, He portrays that Church as essentially connected with Peter as its foundation, and as containing a supremacy of jurisdiction to be ever associated with Peter's name. Consequently a continuous claim on the name of Peter for her origin and authority will be a mark, which the true Church of Christ must always wear in her forefront, and by which she must be distinctly recognisable in every age.

Let us note some other words of our Lord in the Gospel, descriptive of His future Church, and spoken in special relation to S. Peter.

On one occasion He likens His visible Church on earth to a sheep-fold, numerically one, into which all His sheep throughout the whole world shall be gathered, and shall be under the care of one chief shepherd. Contrasting this fold with that of the Jewish Church, into which His entire flock was not gathered, He says: "Other sheep I have that are not of this fold: them also I must bring, and they shall hear My voice, and there shall be one fold and one shepherd." * Later on, when He, the Divine Shepherd, had now paid the price for His sheep at the cost of His Blood and His life, and was still tarrying on earth after His Resurrection to prepare and set in order the new fold of His Church—Himself about to withdraw therefrom His visible presence—He speaks once more in words of most solemn and tender pathos. Having received the thrice-told assurance of Peter's love, the Divine Pastor requires of His Apostle, as proof of that love, that now he should take charge of His universal flock; and with thrice-repeated commission He makes Peter in His own stead Chief Shepherd of His fold and Supreme Pastor in His Church. "Simon, Son of John, lovest thou Me more than these: Feed then My lambs, feed My sheep." † Other pastors besides

---

* John, x. 16.

† John, xxi. 16, 19. Commenting on these words, S. Alphonsus cites the following passage from S. Eucherius (*Serm. in Vigil S. Petri*): "Jesus Christ

Peter He set over His flock, even His other beloved and chosen Apostles, whose pastoral office was to be perpetuated in the collective succession of bishops and priests. But Peter was made pastor supreme over all the rest, and his office of chief pastor was also to endure in the Church; for, when speaking prophetically of His visible Church, He describes it in the Gospel to be a universal Sheep-fold, numerically one, with a universal Pastor also numerically one. "There shall be one fold, and one shepherd."

Now if our Lord's words thus addressed personally to S. Peter in relation to His Church, according to their plain and obvious meaning, and as uniformly interpreted by the Fathers and Doctors, point, as we maintain, by necessary consequence to something that was to be inherent in His Church, and to an office of supreme dignity, which should be held by another in perpetual succession after Peter's death,—if we say this be so, it would be fair to presume, that whatever else in the Gospels was said of S. Peter, thus personally and individually, in distinction from the rest of the Apostles, would bear also on that special prerogative and office, which was to belong permanently to the constitution of the Church of Christ.

Considered in this relation, all the notices of S. Peter in the New Testament which serve to place him in special prominence and priority above the other Apostles have a particular meaning and import, as illustrating and confirming that supreme rank of dignity and office which, as we have seen, was by Divine institution not alone conferred personally on him, but was to devolve also on others in a line of enduring succession. These notices, we grant, taken singly by themselves, may be deemed of no decisive value; but considered in their accumulation, and especially in conjunction with our Lord's express collation to S. Peter, they will appear to all candid and unprejudiced minds of very important account. Such, for example, are the uniform

---

entrusted to Peter first the lambs and then the sheep, because He constituted him not only pastor, but pastor of pastors. Peter therefore feeds the lambs, and feeds the sheep also: he feeds the children, and feeds likewise the mothers; he governs the subjects and the prelates. Consequently he is the pastor of all, since there is nothing else in the Church besides the lambs and the sheep." Amongst many other Saints and Fathers, the holy Doctor cites also S. Bernard, *De Consid.* l. ii. c. 8, n. 15 (the passage will be found in this work later on), and S. Cyprian, who had said the same before in these few words: "The Church is the people united to the priest, the flock attached to its pastor." "Ecclesia plebs sacerdoti adunata, et pastori suo grex adhærens." (*Ep. ad Florent.*—*Verità della Fede.* p. iii. c. ix.)

first mention of S. Peter's name before that of the other Apostles; the leadership amongst them he is so frequently seen to take, and which was conceded to him by them, it would seem, as a matter of course; the particular and intimate union between Peter and his Divine Master, manifested by so many little incidents of individual interest and personal preference on record in the Gospels, wherein he appears at once as the mouthpiece of the other Apostles for what they would say to their Master, and at the same time—so often are His words addressed specially to Peter—the medium for imparting His teaching to them. How significant, when viewed in this connection, are the words spoken by Christ to Peter on the occasion of paying the tribute money: " But that we may not scandalise them. . . . Take that and give it to them for Me and thee" (*Matt.* xvii. 26). In the light of so many other of our Lord's words, it would almost seem as though He had wrought the miracle, and would have it recorded, in order to show forth the close union that linked Him with Peter, whom He had made together with Himself the rock of foundation to His Church, who was to be the chief shepherd of His flock in His own stead, and His vicar on earth, after His ascension into heaven. We might go beyond the Gospel narrative and show from the Acts of the Apostles how at once, on the withdrawal of the Divine Founder and Supreme Head of the Church from earth to heaven, the whole conduct of S. Peter serves to illustrate the Primacy he had received in the Apostolic College and the universal Church; but it is enough here to recall the election of Matthias to the Apostolate, the days of the first Pentecost, how the Gospel was preached first by Peter alike to the Jews and to the Gentiles, and the history of the Council at Jerusalem, in proof of our point. Any further witness to it that may be gathered from the Epistles will be noted later on, when we treat more particularly of S. Peter in relation to S. Paul.

There is, however, still one passage of great importance in the Gospel of S. Luke, which we have held in reserve, as demanding a notice apart. We refer to those remarkable words, addressed with so great solemnity to Peter by our Lord on the eve of His Passion after the institution of the Holy Eucharist.*

His disciples were disputing amongst themselves which of them should seem the greater. Our Lord gently rebukes them, by drawing a contrast between the way of worldly kings and

---

* *Luke*, xxii. 24-32.

potentates, and what should be their conduct. The former, He says, are accounted great and receive praise from men, because they take care to let their power continually appear by lording it over others and making a parade of their beneficence, but it must be otherwise with His Apostles. He tells them that He is making over to them a kingdom, even that same kingdom which He had Himself received from His Father, the kingdom of His Church. He tells them, moreover, that they will all alike be princes, seated in place of honour, and invested with high authority, in this kingdom. He does not deny that one will be greater than the rest. His words clearly imply that this will be the case. But what He does say, and *that* expressly, is, that he who is the greater must rule his conduct by His own example of meekness and humble service towards the others :

"But he that is the greater among you, let him become as the younger, and he that is the leader as he that serveth."

He shows, at the same time, that he who is the greater will not thus demean his authority, any more than He their Lord and Master had done, Who came not to be ministered to but to minister, and to give even His life as a sacrifice for all. Who that one of them was that was to be the greater among them, and their leader, our Lord had already made known to them, and had designated by name as first and supreme in His kingdom, by setting him to be the rock of faith and chief foundation of His Church, and by giving to him the keys of that same kingdom, of which He was now disposing to them who had remained faithful to Him in His own trials and temptations. He had before declared that not all the gates of hell should ever prevail against His Church, nor against the rock of Peter's faith whereon it was built. But now He goes on to warn them of the terrible proof to which they should all be put; for that Satan was doing his utmost for their complete ruin. Whilst intimating their partial falling away through weakness and cowardice, together with their recovery and victory in the end over Satan's assaults, our Lord reveals what was to be the secret of their power to bear up and overcome, and whence they were ever to find strength against weakness in the future. But in making known to them the remedy, He addresses His words not to them, but to Peter individually :

"Simon, Simon, behold Satan hath desired to have you (*i.e.*, all of you My Apostles), that he may sift you (all) as wheat. But (here He indicates the remedy and means of prevention) I have prayed for thee (Peter) that thy faith fail not: and thou being once converted confirm thy brethren."

That heaven-bestowed gift, then, of Peter's faith, so pure and strong, which had erst earned his beatification from his Master's lips, our Lord here declares He had specially prayed for, that it might not fail, even in the shock of his threefold denial, but remain ever as a rock, firm and immovable, for the support of the Church and confirmation of his brethren.

These words of our Lord are prophetic of what was soon to happen to the Apostles, and to Peter in particular, in the hour of His Passion; they are prophetic, too, of the availing efficaciousness of His own prayer, and by consequence of the part Peter was in the future to take as the Confirmer of his brethren; they convey an office and a charge delivered to Peter alone amongst the Apostles; and, taken in conjunction with what He had before said of Peter's place in the constitution of His Church, and in relation to the rest of the Apostles, they impart something that was to be not simply personal, but official, belonging to that office which should devolve on others in succession, so long as His Church should endure.

As the College of the Apostles was formed by Christ to be a permanent institution, and to have its succession in the whole collective Episcopate of the Church; in like manner, that particular rank and office amongst his brethren in the Apostolate, deputed by Christ to Peter, must also find its place in the future collective Episcopate: there must be still one, like Peter, greater than the rest, to lead and confirm them; and that one must be invested with Peter's jurisdiction, and be endowed with Peter's faith, in order adequately and efficaciously to discharge such office.

Here, again, the prophetic sense of these words of our Lord to Peter would lead us to expect that there would be ever in His Church one, like that Apostle, supreme in jurisdiction and infallible in faith, set over all other ecclesiastical rulers and prelates, to lead and confirm them—one professing, at the same time, to model his conduct after the example set by the Divine Lord and Master, as "*Servus servorum Dei.*"

We have now fulfilled the task we proposed of proving and illustrating from the Gospels that special relation with S. Peter, which, we affirmed, the prophetic sense of our Lord's teaching clearly indicates, as a distinctive note of His Church throughout all time.

What now remains is briefly to apply the foregoing reflections to that which is the particular object of our inquiry, namely, the Episcopate of Peter in the Roman See.

We say, then, in the first place, that the prophetic sense of our Lord's Divine teaching on this head must of necessity obtain its adequate realisation and visible accomplishment in every age of Christendom. And hence, His true Church will ever lay exclusive claim to a special relation with Peter for her Divine origin, as founded and built upon that Apostle: she will ever openly profess this relation as the charter of her rightful succession to Divine titles and prerogatives, by the acknowledgment of Peter's supreme jurisdiction, conferred by Christ Himself when founding His Church, as a part of her own constitution. She will proclaim her participation in the infallibility of Peter's faith to be the sure guarantee of the purity and integrity of her own doctrinal teaching, and Peter's universal pastorate to be her own Divine rule and government.

That alone, then, can be the Church of our Lord's Divine prevision, and the subject of His prophetic discourses in the Gospel, which ever wears in its forefront that characteristic mark of relation to Peter by which He Himself so specially distinguishes it.

There is one Church on earth that wears, and has ever worn, this mark, and one alone, in contrast with all the other so-called Churches in Christendom: and this is the Catholic Church in communion with the Roman See, and obedient to the Bishop of Rome as its supreme visible Head and universal Pastor. This communion and obedience is a necessary condition of membership with that Church, because therein Rome is held to have been Peter's See, and because the Roman Pontiff is held to be successor to Peter in that See, and inheritor thus of Peter's Divine prerogatives as the Church's supreme visible Head and universal Pastor.

Other doctrines and practices, indicated in the Gospel as belonging to Christ's Church, may be found more or less prevailing in churches and sects outside the Communion of Rome. There are in the schismatical Churches of the East devotion to the Virgin Mother of God, profession of the religious life, a true recognition of the Holy Eucharist, the sacrifice of Mass, and the practice of sacramental penance. But in none of these is there even profession made of any special relation to S. Peter: nay, their very existence as separate Churches, like that of Anglicanism and other Protestant sects, depends upon, and is bound up with, the denial of the prerogatives of Peter's Primacy, and of its succession in the Roman See. Here, then, is the crucial note which marks off the Catholic Church and the Catholic Faith from all other communions and religious beliefs throughout Christendom; and thus what was predicted of Christ Himself, Who is at once the Divine Founder of His Church and its chief corner-stone, is verified also of the rock of Peter by the rejection of Christ's Vicar, that it shall be to many "a stone of stumbling and a rock of scandal;" whereas by the true faithful it will be held in honour, elect and precious, because made honourable before God, and chosen by Him to be that living stone whereon His Church is built, and to remain ever the foundation of its stability and strength.*

The sum then of our argument is: The special relation of Christ's Church with S. Peter foretold in the Gospels must have its fulfilment in time: and it has that fulfilment in the Roman Catholic Church alone; for if not there, it remains unfulfilled. Consequently the mode of that fulfilment, as it actually exists in the Roman Catholic Church, must be that very same mode which our Lord contemplated, in His Divine prevision, as the accomplishment of His prophetic words. Now that mode consists essentially in the Roman Episcopate of S. Peter, and in there ever being a legitimate succession of chief pontiffs, who are held to be by Divine right the heirs to his Primacy. It has, moreover, been defined as a Catholic truth belonging to the Faith that these are the Bishops of the Roman See, which Peter was the first to occupy. And hence it follows that our Divine Lord, when speaking so much of the relation of His future Church with Peter, had expressly in view the Episcopate and See of Rome, both as a means and centre for the personal exercise of Peter's supreme authority, and as a place of deposit where Peter's office and prerogatives should remain for their transmission to others in the line of legitimate succession.

We have thus endeavoured to show that the fact of S. Peter's Roman Episcopate and succession in the See of Rome is implicitly demonstrable from the page of the Gospel, because in the truth of this fact exclusively is to be found the fulfilment, and consequently the veracity, of our Divine Lord's own prophetic words.

* See *Is.* viii. 14-15; *Rom.* ix. 33; *Luc.* ii. 34; *Matt.* xxi. 44; *Pet.* ii. 6-8.

APPENDIX.

We think that it will not be without interest to our readers if we supplement this chapter by the following extract from Dr. Döllinger :—

"At the turning-point, when His ministry was closing and His sufferings about to begin, Peter made confession that Jesus Christ was the Son of the living God. For this he was repaid by four closely allied promises of future power and pre-eminence in the Church. First: he should be the Rock whereon Christ would build it; secondly, the Church built on him should never fail; thirdly, Christ would give him the keys of His kingdom or Church; fourthly, what he bound or loosed on earth would be bound or loosed in heaven.*

"Peter alone here spoke; he was not commissioned by the other Apostles, and stood foremost among them through the faith given him by his heavenly Father. That faith, firm as a rock, fitted him to be the foundation of the Church which Christ had compared to a house. Now first Simon Bar Jona perceived why the Lord originally named him Cephas, the rock. And thus Christ, like S. Paul afterwards, has combined the two similes of a home and of family life. He wills to build His house, the imperishable Church, never to be overcome by the powers of death, on the believing and confessing Simon, who again is to be its foundation in the same sense as all the Apostles are according to S. Paul or S. John, though excelling all others in his speciality as chief foundation stone.† And in this house built upon him, Peter is to have the duties and powers, not of the master of the house—that Christ is, and remains—but of the steward. These were promised him under the symbol of the keys, whereby he is enabled to open the treasures of the house, to guard the spiritual stores and possessions of the Church, doctrine and means of grace.

"What is here first, according to S. Matthew's account, only *promised* to Peter was after the Resurrection bestowed upon him, at the third appearance of Jesus, to three Apostles and

---

* *Matt.* xvii. 18, 19. The Greek translator of the Aramaic text was obliged to use Πέτρος and Πέτρα; in the original, *Cephas* stood in each place without change of gender: "Thou art stone, and on this stone," &c., Cephas being both name and title.

† *Eph.* ii. 19, 20; *Apoc.* xxi. 14.

three disciples only besides himself. As He had before assured him of his future exaltation on the evidence of his divinely inspired strength of faith, so now He taught him by a question, thrice solemnly repeated, that he must also surpass the other Apostles in love to Him, and be a Rock-man in love as in faith, giving him thereby an opportunity of retracting his three denials, and adding the charge thrice repeated, 'Feed My lambs; feed My sheep.' Thereby a chief shepherd was given to the whole Church, including the Apostles, and Peter was placed in the same relation as Christ had been before to the collective body of believers, as the good shepherd who cares for his sheep and gives himself for them out of love, not like a hireling for his own advantage.*

"When Christ prophesied to S. Peter, just before the beginning of His Passion, that on the same night he would deny Him thrice, He also assured him that, by virtue of a special prayer offered for him to the Father, his weakness in faith should not sink as low as complete apostasy or determinate unbelief. And He exhorted him, when recovered from his own fall, to strengthen his brethren, the Apostles and other disciples, in their wavering faith; to sustain them in their discouragement, and console them with the hope of His sure and speedy resurrection."†

We must here, parenthetically, express our unfeigned surprise both at the sense and the restricted application which Dr. Döllinger attaches to Christ's words in this passage.

The general rule or principle of the learned author of *The First Age of Christianity*—and one which we cannot sufficiently admire, as being in full accord with the true philosophical method and critical science of a genuine historian—is, we conceive, to take the facts of his New Testament narrative simply as they stand, without any arbitrary theorising: to let them speak for themselves; and to allow the statements of the several writers, after careful collation, mutually to explain one another; making use only of such extraneous aids as might be necessary for their more complete elucidation; viewing them, withal, in the light of their realised accomplishment and results, outside which no thoughtful student of history and tradition could fail to regard or represent them to others.

But in the present instance Dr. Döllinger has, we hold,

---

* *John*, xxi. 15-17; x. 12.   † *Luke*, xxii. 31, 32.

departed from this sound principle, and has hazarded an interpretation which is gratuitous and unfounded.

For there is nothing in the consequent Gospel narrative to suggest the idea that S. Peter immediately on his conversion received, in answer to Christ's prayer, any special grant of faith and hope in the Resurrection, or fulfilled the Divine injunction to confirm his brethren, by encouraging them in those same sentiments during the interval that elapsed between his own conversion and their own assurance of the Resurrection by the actual sight of their risen Lord.

So far from this, if we are to judge from what the Evangelists themselves say on the matter, we are led to an entirely opposite conclusion. Their words are contained in the following passages :—*Mark*, xvi. 7, 11 ; *Luke*, xxiv. 9-11 ; and *John*, xx. 1-9. In the last of these it is recorded of S. John, and not of S. Peter, " He saw (the linen cloths lying), and believed."

If our Lord's words to Peter are to be interpreted by their fulfilment, and if this fulfilment is discoverable in the New Testament, we shall find it, not before the Resurrection, but after the Ascension, in the prominent part S. Peter filled in the Church and amongst the Apostles, as recorded by S. Luke in the earlier chapters of the Acts.*

Dr. Döllinger's view, besides being opposed to the Gospel narrative, has, moreover, no countenance so far as we are aware in the Fathers, and certainly is contrary to their common interpretation and to the general sense of tradition.

We are not here entering into the question of what precisely was that unfailingness of Peter's faith for which Christ prayed, or that confirmation, in its nature and extent, which Peter was enjoined to afford to his brethren. This is a matter of dogma which the Church has decided in the Vatican Council. Our present point is not doctrinal, but purely one of fact, which every ecclesiastical historian, who treated of the question at all, would be bound to take into account, at any time before that Council, and quite independently of any dogmatic definition.

And our contention is—let Peter's unfailing faith, and his obligation to confirm his brethren, in the case be what they may—they are traditionally regarded and spoken of by the Fathers as not transiently or accidentally personal to Peter, but as permanently inherent in his office of chief Pastor, and in that of his

* Dr. Döllinger himself very graphically describes this pre-eminence of S. Peter, vol. ii. pp. 115-122.

successors. We readily admit that this passage of S. Luke is not at all so often cited by the Fathers, nor explained by them with the same fulness, in relation to S. Peter's prerogatives, as the two others of S. Matthew and S. John; and, that being of general moral significance, it is frequently applied in this sense. But when they treat of these words of our Lord to Peter in their literal and historical import, they apply them not as limited to the incident of his denial and conversion,—though this was the occasion of their being spoken,—but in a sense so wide-reaching as to cover Peter's whole office as universal Pastor, and to extend also to his successors.

In proof of this we cite the following passages.

S. Ambrose writes:

"Whence also it was said to Peter, 'Simon, behold Satan hath desired to have you, that he may sift you as wheat; but I have prayed My Father, that thy faith fail not.' . . . In fine, Peter after being tempted by the devil, is set over the Church. The Lord therefore signifies beforehand what that is, that He afterwards chose him the pastor of the Lord's flock. For to him He said, 'But thou when converted confirm thy brethren.'" *

S. Chrysostom over and over again † when speaking of S. Peter's Primacy quotes, and in this relation only, the passage of S. Luke. Thus:

"He (Christ) constituted him the first of the Apostles: wherefore He said, 'Simon, Simon, behold Satan . . . that thy faith fail not.' ‡—Peter first acts with authority in this matter (the election of Matthias), as having all put into his hands; for to him Christ had said, 'And thou, being converted, confirm thy brethren.'" §

Theodoret, after quoting Christ's words (*Luke*, xxii. 31, 32), thus paraphrases them:

"'For as I,' He says, 'did not overlook thee when thou wast tottering, so do thou also become a support to thy brethren when shaken, and communicate of that help of which thou hast partaken; and do not cast down the falling, but raise up those endangered. Since for this cause do I permit thee to stumble first, and suffer thee not to fall, contriving through thee stability for the wavering.' Then did the great pillar support the tottering world, and not

---

* *In Ps.* xliii. 12.

† *De B. Paphlegonio*, n. 2; *Hom.* 8, *adv. Judæos*, n. 3; *Hom.* 3, *de Pœnitentia*, n. 4; *Hom.* 82, *in Matt.* n. 3. See also S. Cyprian, *Ep. ad Cler. et de Deprec. De Orat. Dom.*; S. Optatus of Milevis, *De Schism. Donat.* vii. 3; S. Epiphanius, *Adv. Hæres. Cathar.* 59, n. 7, 8; Hilary the Deacon, *Quæst.* 75 *ex N. Test. in App. S. August.*; S. Cyril of Alexandria, *in Luc.* t. v. p. 420, *Migne*; Arnobius Junior, *in Ps.* 138.

‡ *In Ps.* cxxix. n. 2.

§ *Hom.* 3, *in Acta*, n. 3.

suffer it to fall down utterly, but raised it up, and made it stable, and received a command 'to feed the sheep' of God."*

S. Leo says:

"When Christ's Passion which was to trouble the constancy of the disciples was now near, 'The Lord says, Simon, Simon, behold, &c. (*Luke*, xxii. 31, 32). The danger from the temptation of fear was common to all the Apostles, and they stood equally in need of the help of the Divine protection, because the devil desired to trouble all, to crush all. . . . And yet, special care of Peter is undertaken by the Lord, and for the faith of Peter in particular does He pray, as if the state of the others would be more sure, if the mind of their prince were not conquered. In Peter, therefore, the fortitude of all is defended, and the help of Divine grace is so ordered that the firmness which through Christ is given to Peter, may through Peter be conferred on the Apostles. Wherefore, most beloved, since we see that so great a safeguard has been divinely instituted for us, reasonably and justly do we rejoice in the merits and dignity of our leader, giving thanks to our everlasting King and Redeemer, the Lord Jesus Christ, Who gave so great power to him whom He made the prince of the whole Church, that if anything is rightly done and rightly ordered by us even in our days, it be referred to his doing, to his governing, unto whom was said, 'And thou converted, confirm thy brethren; and to whom, after His Resurrection, the Lord, for a triple profession of everlasting love, with a mystic meaning, thrice said, 'Feed My sheep.' Which he now also beyond doubt does, and the pious shepherd executes the mandate of the Lord, confirming us by his exhortations, and ceasing not to pray for us, that we be not overcome by any temptation. But if, as is to be believed, he everywhere extends this care of his piety to the whole people of God, how much more does he vouchsafe to bestow his aid upon us his disciples, amongst whom, in the same flesh that he presided, he rests on the sacred couch of his blessed sleep (*dormitationis*). To him, therefore, let us assign this feast, this anniversary-day (birth-day) of our servitude; to him this feast, by whose patronage we have merited to be sharers of his Chair, the grace of our Lord Jesus Christ aiding us in all things."†

The passages we have cited from the Fathers clearly show that the words of Christ (*Luke*, xxii. 31, 32) are traditionally interpreted as applicable to S. Peter, in his office of universal Pastor, and not in the limited sense attached to them by Dr. Döllinger.

We shall use some words of S. Bernard in proof that they were held in his time to be applicable also to S. Peter's successors:

"For indeed, he says, I think it meet that there, above all, the losses of faith be repaired where faith can suffer no failure. Since this is the prerogative of that See. For to whom was it once said: 'I have prayed for thee, Peter, that thy faith fail not'? Therefore, what follows is demanded of Peter's successor: 'And thou being once converted, confirm thy brethren.'"‡

* *Or. de Sanct. Carit.* See also *Hæret. Fab.* l. v. c. 28; *Ep.* 77, *Eulalio*.
† *Serm.* 4, *in Natal. Ordin.* co. i.-iv.   ‡ *Epist.* cxc. *Ad Innoc.* ii.

Pope S. Gelasius had written long before (A.D. 492):

"Though amidst the various difficulties of the times, involved in continual labours, we can scarcely breathe, yet for the government of the Apostolic See, engaged without ceasing in the care of the whole fold of the Lord, which (care) was delegated to the Blessed Peter by the voice of the Saviour Himself, 'And thou converted, confirm thy brethren;' and again, 'Peter, lovest thou Me, feed My sheep,' we neither can, nor ought to, dissemble such things as constrain our solicitude."[*]

Bossuet, in modern times, expresses the same. Speaking of Peter, he says:

"Il est donc de nouveau chargé de toute l'Eglise; il est chargé de tous ses frères, puisque Jésus-Christ lui ordonne de les affermir dans cette foi, qu'il venait de rendre invincible par sa prière."[†]

And again, applying the words to Peter's successors, he says:

"Hoc ex officio Petrus habet, hoc Petri successores in Petro acceperunt, ut fratres confirmare jubeantur."[‡]

S. Alphonsus says:

"They are equally wrong who pretend that in this passage (*Luc.* xxii. 31, 32) Jesus Christ prayed for the perseverance of Peter, since, as a fact, Peter wavered in his faith at the death of our Saviour, as is evident from the words, 'When thou shalt be converted,' and from those other words which Jesus Christ addressed to all the Apostles after the Supper: 'I shall be for you all, this very night, an occasion of scandal. Do you now believe? The time is coming, and is already come, when you will be scattered each one to his own, and when you shall leave Me alone' (*Matt.* xxvi. 31; *John,* xvi. 31, 32). It is plain, then, that in the words: 'I have prayed for thee, that thy faith fail not,' Jesus Christ was not speaking of Peter's faith as a private individual, but of that faith which was never to fail him as head of the Church, nor his successors either, who should inherit the primacy that had been conferred on him. And then follow the words: 'Confirm thy brethren.' Here let us listen to the very simple explanation which Pope Agatho gives of these words, in the letter which he addressed to the Emperor Constantine, and which was afterwards read and unanimously approved in the Sixth Ecumenical Council. § 'Here, then, is the rule of the true faith—the rule which the Apostolic Church of Christ has always kept. . . . The Lord promised that the faith of Peter should not fail, and He charged him to confirm his brethren: now it is within the knowledge of all that this is what the Apostolic (Roman) Pontiffs—whose successor I am, notwithstanding my meanness—have ever done with all confidence.'"[||]

We have been mindful all along in this lengthened digression that Dr. Döllinger does not deny the larger application of Christ's

---

[*] *Ep.* 5, *Ad Honor. Dalmat. Episc.*
[†] See Bossuet, *Méditations sur les Evangiles Jour.* lxx.
[‡] *Defens. declarat.* l. iii. c. 3.
[§] *Act.* iii.   [||] *Verità della Fede,* pt. iii. c. ix. 5.

words to Peter, which we claim to be that of Catholic tradition. Indeed, later on in the same work he expressly refers to these same words, and applies them, in our sense, to the office of S. Peter as "bidden by Christ to strengthen his brethren."* We are, therefore, the more surprised that, when professing to give the meaning of the passage, he should have explained it as he has done. We have dwelt at so great length and so strongly on this point for the sake especially of earnest-minded Anglicans who may read these pages. For there are some amongst a certain noisy ultra-Protestant clique of the High Church party who dare constantly to assert, whether from gross—we should rather say affected —ignorance, or with most mendacious recklessness, that the dogmatic interpretation which the Holy Church gives of this passage from S. Luke, as well as of the other two from S. Matthew and S. John, is new—they call it "Ultramontane"—and has no foundation or countenance in tradition and the writings of the Fathers. But enough of these false teachers, with their flippant pratings.

Let us resume our quotation from Dr. Döllinger where we had broken off.

"S. Peter is so uniformly marked out in the Gospels, and placed in such immediate proximity to Jesus, as the shadow accompanying Him, the one who possessed His confidence and mediated between Him and the other disciples, that in this respect no other Apostle comes near him. Where only the Apostles are enumerated or mentioned he always stands first. All the critical moments in the life of Jesus are placed in a certain relation to him, and to him alone. To him individually Jesus ordered his Resurrection to be made known; the New Testament narrative records only his failings and humiliations, not those of the other Apostles; while it mentions the strength of his faith and love, and the dignity conferred in return for it, it carefully marks the depth of his fall. There is no other to whose education and training Christ devoted so much labour. Much of grave import He communicated only to him directly, as his future martyrdom, and his elevation to the highest dignity. And, again, in his death he was to be like his Lord.

"It was only in common with the other Apostles that S. Peter received the remaining powers left by Christ to His Church: viz., the power to bind and loose in a manner availing in

* Vol. ii. pp. 115-120.

heaven as on earth, which means to forbid and command; and finally, after the Resurrection, the communication of the Spirit with power to remit and retain. Three prerogatives were left to him exclusively. He was chosen before all other Apostles, and in a peculiar sense, as the foundation of the Church; to him alone were the keys given in Christ's house; he alone was to have power as shepherd of the whole flock."*

* *The First Age of Christianity, &c.* Translated by H. N. Oxenham, M.A. Vol. i. pp. 47-50. Ed. 1877.

CHAPTER IV.

REFLECTIONS ON SOME OF THE CONSEQUENCES INVOLVED IN THE QUESTION OF S. PETER'S ROMAN EPISCOPATE.

LET us here pause to consider briefly the issue of the question of Peter's Roman Episcopate and succession in another light; what, namely, are some of the consequences involved on either hand in its affirmation or denial. With its affirmation the whole career of Peter's Apostolate obtains a progress and consummation in fit proportion to the high promise of its commencement. Great and marvellous, indeed, were the words spoken by Christ concerning him and his future. Elected to be chief among the Apostles, marked out for exceptional prerogative, we see him hold in all things the first and foremost place, and take the lead of all in the earliest days of the Church; and surely the course of the Prince of the Apostles will not fail of its anticipated full career and befitting consummation. The Providence of God does not suffer such falling off in the case of His choice vessels of election to whom He has thus entrusted some great and extraordinary mission: but His Wisdom "reacheth from end to end mightily, and ordereth all things sweetly,"* that in them especially His promise may be fulfilled: "The path of the just, as a shining light, goeth forwards and increaseth even to perfect day." †

And so when the Apostles divide the heathen world amongst them to conquer it to Christ, Peter, their chief, will choose for himself the first and most arduous post, and, shrinking from neither toil nor danger, will go to Rome, its mighty metropolis and seat of Empire, there, in Satan's principal stronghold of idolatry and wickedness, to preach the Gospel of Christ's kingdom, and to found a Church over which he himself will preside in person during life, and after death in a long unbroken line of heirs who shall succeed him,—a Church whose faith shall be ever celebrated throughout the world, and whose See, to be associated in perpetuity with his Name and Primacy, will hence-

---

* *Wisd.* viii. 1. † *Prov.* iv. 18.

forth be the first and above all others in rank and authority throughout universal Christendom, as the Chair of his infallible teaching and the throne of his supreme jurisdiction. Peter, being thus constituted at Rome, in his own person and in his succession, the immovable Rock of the Church's unity, faith, and permanence, and having proved himself to be indeed the Pastor of Christ's universal flock, will receive the crown of martyrdom by a death of crucifixion like to his Lord's, whose Vicar he is, in his own primatial Rome, which from his ever-enduring pontificate will be thenceforth known as the Eternal City.

Here is something that satisfies, and more than fulfils, the anticipation of our thoughts, as being verily worthy of the Prince of the Apostles, the Vicar of God, and visible Head of His Church on earth—something, we should say rather, that is worthy of Him Who shows Himself ever most admirable in His Saints, and Whose words, in their accomplishment, are found always to surpass the bounds of their promise.

Here is something so wondrously great and sublime, as far to exceed all human expectation and any earthly conception, involving, as it does, a height of dignity and power, which to claim or assume might well be accounted an extravagant folly or sacrilegious usurpation, were not its right and origin from heaven guaranteed by divine revelation;—something, for such as have eyes to see, and hearts to understand, if possible, yet more marvellous still, in its visible realisation as an accomplished fact, through the course of long centuries until the present time.

For what other principle or institution throughout the whole world's history has been so potent and influential in the sphere alike of religion and of the state—gathering round it and concentrating all that is most intense and glorious of men's love, devotion, faith, union, and support, on the one hand, and on the other, of hatred, strife, envy, contempt, and opposition—as the claim to Peter's succession in the Roman See, and the realised exercise of Papal Supremacy, whether we regard the earlier centuries of the Church, the middle age, or more modern times?

Herein, moreover, we see fulfilled so many words of Scripture and prophetic vision. That which Daniel foresaw of old is now brought to pass:

"A stone was cut out of a mountain without hands: which struck the statue upon the feet thereof, that were of iron and of clay, and broke them in pieces.... But the stone that struck the statue became a great mountain and filled the whole earth."*

That stone was, indeed, in its first and fullest sense no other than "Jesus Christ Himself, the chief Corner-stone,"† of Whom Isaias writes:

"Thus saith the Lord God: Behold I will lay a stone in the foundations of Sion, a tried stone, a corner-stone, a precious stone, founded in the foundation."‡

But it is none the less true that these prophetic words, as well as the comment S. Peter makes in quoting them:

"To you therefore that believe is honour: but to them that believe not... a stone of stumbling, and a rock of scandal, to them who stumble at the word and believe not," §

may be applied in a real and proper sense to S. Peter also as the rock and foundation united by Christ to Himself, upon which He built His Church, according to the teaching of the great S. Leo:

"*And I*, says Christ, *say to thee*: that is, as My Father has manifested to thee My divinity, so also do I make known to thee thy eminence. *For thou art Peter*, that is, whereas I am the inviolable rock, I the corner-stone, Who made both one, I the foundation, besides which no man can lay other: yet thou also art a rock, because thou art consolidated by My might, that what things are Mine alone by My power, may be common to thee by participation with Me." ∥

Hence what was said at the laying of the Chief Corner-stone of the Church, even Jesus Christ our Lord, is verified again in Peter, "to whom what things are Christ's are by participation common:"

"Behold this Child is set for the fall, and for the resurrection of many in Israel, and for a sign which shall be contradicted, ... that out of many hearts thoughts may be revealed:"¶

diverse thoughts, indeed, some of faith and attachment, some of unbelief and opposition.

Herein we see, again, a fulfilment of S. John's Apocalyptic vision, which was to receive at least its first and partial realisation from the time that the "eternal Gospel began to be preached unto them that sit upon the earth, and over every nation, and tribe, and tongue, and people;" the object of which preaching was, that "the kingdom of this world should become our Lord's

* *Dan.* ii. 34, 35.   † *Ephes.* ii. 20.   ‡ *Isa.* xxviii. 26.
§ 1 *Pet.* ii. 6-8.   ∥ *Serm.* 4, *in Natal. Ordin.*   ¶ *Luke*, ii. 34, 35.

and His Christ's." For how strikingly is this fulfilment witnessed to by the Prince of those Apostles—to whom the commission to preach that Gospel was first and immediately entrusted—proclaiming it in Rome, " the great city which had kingdom over the kings of the earth," and there in " that great city Babylon, that mighty city, seated upon the seven hills," founding the Church of Christ, wherein, as in His own kingdom, He might reign for ever.*

Babylon in the language of the Prophets was the name for Satan's central seat of empire on earth, where he held his sway of falsehood, idolatry, and wickedness; Rome was emphatically that same central seat in Apostolic times, and therefore the mystic Babylon of S. John in his Apocalypse. What marvel then — nay, how naturally fitting — that S. Peter, in an Epistle written at Rome—when, moreover, from prudence he was loth to let his residence there publicly transpire — should call that city by the name of Babylon? How wondrously significant, moreover, that the Prince of the Apostles of Christ should date his Epistle to the Faithful from Babylon, the chief seat of Satan's rule, which already the Vicar of Christ had appropriated to himself as his own See in token of its henceforth being the centre of Christ's kingdom on earth.

In fine, how entirely does what Tradition and History record of S. Peter at Rome illustrate and harmonise with all we know of his character as portrayed on the page of the Sacred Scriptures—that spirit of lively faith, of confidence, of devotion and love; that ardent, impetuous courage and active zeal, which made him be ever foremost, and urged him to attempt even the impossible for the cause of his Divine Master and the Person of his Lord whilst He was yet on earth. All these qualities we see still in S. Peter after Christ's Ascension, but dignified and sanctified by a wondrous divine enlightenment and holy prudence, together with a full sense of his authority and the responsibility of his exalted position as Prince of the Apostles and Chief Pastor of the Church. And, so, still he shows himself first and foremost to engage in labour, to encounter difficulty, to face danger for the cause of his Lord, for the salvation of souls, and for the interests of the Church. And where would labour, and difficulty, and danger be greater than in Rome, the central stronghold of a tyrannous idolatry; and what trophy more glorious to win for

---

* See *Apoc.* xiv. 6; xi. 15; xvii. 18; xviii. 10; xvii. 9.

Christ, of more importance for His Church, and more worthy of the zeal and dignity of the Prince of the Apostles, than the great imperial city of the Pagan world?

But, on the other hand, once deny the episcopate of Peter at Rome and his succession in that See, and what follows? Then those marvellous words of our Lord erst spoken to His Apostle, and which should correspondingly in their fulfilment have a like marvellous significance, were words void of meaning, and are found to have been spoken for nought, and to be of no effect. For if S. Peter did not found the Church of Rome, and was not Bishop of that Church; if what tradition reports of him be not true, then no other work commensurate with his place and office in the Gospel can be assigned to him; nay more, in that case Peter has no history at all, and his memory, after the last word was said of him in the Acts of the Apostles—if we except his own Epistles—has been clean wiped off from the face of the Church.

But here we are forgetting; for there still remains a very signal and unique record concerning Peter in the inspired Word. To Peter, alone of all the Apostles, our Lord Himself foretells that at length in old age he will receive the crown of martyrdom by a death of crucifixion like unto His own; and S. John, the last survivor of the Apostles, in whose special hearing this prediction was made, is at once the Evangelist to record the prophecy and to bear witness to its glorious accomplishment. The words of our Lord in speaking of S. Peter's martyrdom and of the mode of his death were of themselves by no means clear; and S. John, doubtless, did not apprehend their meaning as he heard them : he understood them afterwards by the actual event, and he interpreted them in his Gospel by means of that event. This he speaks of as having already taken place; for, as we know, when S. John wrote his Gospel our Lord's prediction had been long fulfilled, since the Evangelist wrote some thirty years after the death of S. Peter. It should be specially remarked that S. John, in his interpretation of our Lord's words as indicating the kind of martyrdom S. Peter was to suffer, does not enter into any explanation; he simply observes, "And this He said, signifying by what death he should glorify God." From this we gather that S. Peter's death by crucifixion was an event of such universal notoriety in the early Church, as to have rendered its explicit mention by the Evangelist unnecessary and superfluous after its occurrence, when interpreting here the Divine words which sufficiently adumbrated it. Possibly many persons who read the

Bible may deem that this passage of itself shows plainly that S. Peter was put to death by crucifixion. We are of a contrary opinion, and think that, without the testimony of tradition and history, this interpretation would hardly have been even one of conjecture, and that neither our Lord's words, nor S. John's explanation of them, would of themselves convey any definite meaning to the reader as to the mode of S. Peter's martyrdom; whereas, with the knowledge of the fact supplied through history and tradition, the true sense of both is obvious and clear. The place, moreover, where S. Peter suffered must have been equally notorious and certain amongst the early Christians as the martyrdom itself. We should remember, too, that S. John most probably wrote his Gospel not long after he himself had been in Rome, when, on the spot, he would have learned and thence borne away the still fresh memories of S. Peter's Passion. We know also how that event was attested by the earliest Christian writers, and has been a matter of unvarying and universal tradition until the present day. Hence we can appreciate the following critical statement of the Anglican Bishop of Winchester at its proper worth:

"The Church of Rome may reasonably claim to be an Apostolic Church when (*sic*) S. Paul pretty certainly, and *most probably* S. Peter, were martyred at Rome, and perhaps jointly organised the Church there." *

On this point the eminent ecclesiastical historian, Dr. Döllinger, writes as follows:

"S. Peter died as a martyr in Rome under Nero by crucifixion, and Origen mentions the special circumstance of his being nailed to the cross head downwards. This tradition is confirmed by the universal testimony of the whole ancient Church, and the grounds on which it has been assailed are not the result of historical criticism. S. John's Gospel leaves no doubt as to the Apostle's manner of death, for the Lord warned him prophetically in His last conversation with him of his end: in his old age his hands would be stretched and bound, and he would be carried whither he would not. The Evangelist adds that Jesus thereby signified by what manner of death he should glorify God.† And if, as this observation shows, S. Peter's martyrdom was a fact universally known in the Church at the end of the first century, so that the Evangelist found this mere intimation enough, it is impossible that the place where he glorified his Lord by his death, should not have been equally notorious. But no other city than Rome has ever been mentioned: there is not the least trace of any other Church having ever claimed to be the place of the Apostle's death. Dionysius of Corinth says (170 A.D.) that both the Apostles suffered martyrdom in Rome at the same time. The Roman Christian, Caius, says (A.D. 200), in his treatise against Proclus the Montanist,

* *A Charge, &c.*, p. 68, note. † *John*, xxi. 19.

that he can point out on the Vatican and on the road to Ostia the memorials (trophies) of the Apostles (Peter and Paul), who founded this Church.* His contemporary Tertullian reckons among the prerogatives of the Roman Church, that 'Peter was there conformed to the sufferings of the Lord.'†

"S. Peter suffered death either with S. Paul or after him. Clement of Rome fixes the time in saying, 'Paul was executed under the rulers,' for this points to the period of Nero's absence from Rome (A.D. 67), when the Prefect of the City, Helius Cæsarianus, and the pretorian Prefects, Nimphidius Sabinus and Tigellinus, were administering the government. The old tradition of S. Peter's twenty-five years' episcopate in Rome arose from placing his journey thither in the year 42, the second of the reign of Claudius, when he was set free from Agrippa's prison and escaped from Judæa: from then till his death in 67 is twenty-five years. But, of course, it must not be inferred that he spent all that time in Rome."‡

Returning from our digression, we now ask: Is it for a moment credible that the first and most eminent of all Christ's Apostles, whom He Himself exceptionally privileged, the beginnings and final consummation of whose glorious career are on record in the inspired Scriptures, should not have fulfilled a course in all things proportioned to, and worthy of, such a commencement and close? We ask again, is it reasonable, or rather is it not most absurd folly, to suppose that all trace of the main history of such an Apostle should have been lost in the Church of God? And not only so, but that he should have become so positively unknown, and his history have been plunged in such utter and hopeless obscurity, that an entirely false account, made up in ignorance and credulity, of legend and forgery, could have been palmed off as the true and authentic history of S. Peter on the minds of the faithful, and have obtained universal assent both of learned and simple, not merely as a theoretical belief, but as a practical truth fraught with the most momentous issues to the whole civilised world, destined to prove not only a most influential principle of religious faith, but also to form the basis of the secular as well as ecclesiastical polity of entire Christendom? *Credat Judæus.*

Again, if S. Peter was not founder and first Bishop of the Roman Church (for here both of these facts must stand or fall together, being inseparately united, and resting on the self-same authority and testimony), it must follow that that Church had no Apostle for its founder, and that its true origin is absolutely lost without record or tradition at all. The only Apostles, besides S. Peter, whose names are associated in any way with Rome

* Euseb. ii. 25.   † Tertull. *De Præscript.* 36.
‡ *First Age of the Church*, vol. ii. pp. 164-6.

are S. Paul and S. John. No one ever supposed that the latter founded the Church there; moreover, the circumstances and date of S. John's being in Rome render this impossible. It is quite certain that S. Paul was not the first founder, for, before he set foot in the city, we find him speaking in his Epistle to the Romans of their Church as having been already founded by another, and then in so settled and flourishing a state, that their faith was spoken of throughout the whole world.* Now we ask, on the one hand, can any rational man, not to say Christian, persuade himself that the Apostles in carrying out their Divine Master's command to go into all the world, and preach the Gospel to every creature, would have passed over Rome in the calculations of their zeal? If at their dispersion they went forth everywhere, even to the ends of the known world, indefatigable in preaching the word and founding Churches in all the principal cities amongst the different nations far and near, surely one of the earliest and most earnest efforts of their Apostolic enterprise would be to preach the Faith and establish Christ's kingdom in Rome, the capital of the world, and the central seat of its empire; and a work so great and glorious as this would surely devolve on one of the very first Apostles.

Then, is it credible, on the other hand, that whilst the first origin of so many Churches, in places comparatively unimportant, should be carefully preserved, Rome, which was from earliest times the chief theatre, as well for the Church's action and suffering as for the heroic conflicts and triumphs of individual Christians, should not know the first Apostle of her Faith? And can we believe that the first founder of the glorious Roman Church, which played so prominent a part in the primitive age and through all subsequent history, should have left no trace of recognition behind, and that his very name should have perished? And yet this is what follows, if the Catholic tradition and the historical witness of antiquity, concerning the first foundation of the Roman Church by Peter and his episcopate, are rejected.

We will add yet another consequence of the denial of the Catholic tradition. It is, that thence follows necessarily the negation of all unity, or bond of union, in the visible Church of Christ.

The historical fact of S. Peter's Roman Episcopate, and of his perpetual succession in the line of Roman Pontiffs, as received by the Catholic Church, is, so to say, the outside shell wherein is

* *Rom.* xv. 20-22, i. 8-12.

contained the kernel—we mean the Primacy conferred by Christ on Peter. For the sake of argument, we leave here undetermined what that primacy may be, whether supremacy of jurisdiction, or only the priority of rank and honour of one who is *primus inter pares;* whether an essential principle and source, or merely a symbol, of unity. And we say, that with the denial of the historical fact in question, significant of, and embodying such primacy, every sort of primacy, and, by consequence, all principle of unity, in the Church of Christ must be also denied.

If words have any meaning at all, it seems impossible for anyone to deny that some sort of primacy was bestowed by our Lord on S. Peter. And, as we have before seen, the primacy he did receive was, according to the obvious sense of Christ's words, something belonging to and bound up with the very constitution of His Church, and consequently, being not simply personal but official, it was to continue permanently in the Church after Peter's death.

But, without reverting again to anything from the New Testament on this matter, we will here consider it in another light.

We take for granted, then, that all who believe the Church founded by Christ on earth to be a visible, external body, hold also that it is essentially, in a real and true sense, numerically one. We need not now bring forward the many plain passages in the Gospels and Epistles which insist on this unity. Now, Christ's true Church on earth, thus visible and numerically one, is, we know, a moral body in life and action, composed of many individual members, and consequently, if thus one, it must have a living, active organisation, with due correlation of member to member, and subordination of each and all to some principle of rule or law common to the one living body. And, because the body is visible, this subordination and rule must be externally and visibly recognisable.

We might adduce many well-known passages from the New Testament in application of all this to Christ's Church; but it evidently stands to reason, as being in the very nature of things, and conformable with all human experience.

Take, for example, a political state, a particular religious body, or a business company—paramount rule and order, in some form or other, with common subordination thereto, is an essential condition for its unity and permanence, nay, for its very existence. The same principle of subordination to a common rule and law holds good also with regard to a confederation of states, and to a union of several religious bodies under one denomination, or of branch companies joined together in mutual association. Without some supreme and general rule, visibly and externally recognised, and in actual force and obligation, the union of all moral bodies will be broken up, they will fall to pieces, and be resolved into so many separate units. We would here observe that not merely union, but numerical unity in its strictest sense—that is, unicity, or a single oneness, is throughout the inspired Scriptures predicated as the distinctive quality and condition of the Church of Christ. This is to be marked everywhere, whether in Old Testament prophecy or in the figures and parables of our Lord; or in His own express teaching, or that of the sacred writers, concerning the Church. Thus the visible Church of Christ is represented as a house built together on one foundation, as a sheepfold with one chief pastor, as a living body with one head and many members, as a draught of fishes with one masterfisherman. But most frequently, and especially, the Church is spoken of as a kingdom, as the kingdom of heaven here on earth. This implies one supreme ruler or king. The Church is never set forth as a confederation of states. A union of co-ordinate churches, according to the common Anglican notion, in no way corresponds, but is utterly opposed, to the Scriptural idea of the visible Body of Christ.

We will not, however, now insist on this, though it is indisputably certain and true, but will pass it over for the sake of argument. We suppose, then, that all who believe Christ's Church to be visible and one—whether that oneness be conceived as strictly numerical unity, or merely some sort of union—must hold that it received in its original constitution, from its Divine Founder, such external law or rule as should be necessary for the establishment and permanence of its unity. As, on the one hand, the Church of Christ must, according to His assured promise, ever continue to exist, preserving that self-same unity in which He constituted it; so the law, rule, or bond of that unity must be itself Divine, and must also be ever recognisable in its visible actuality. Now, where is it found thus visible? The Catholic can point to it at once, as existing in the supreme authority of the Roman Pontiff, who is held to inherit by Divine right, through legitimate succession in Peter's See, the office and prerogatives of that primacy in the Church which our Lord Himself bestowed upon S. Peter. But outside the Communion of

Rome no one even pretends that any such Divine law and bond of unity exists. There, indeed, what is held to be Christ's visible Church is, of course, theoretically conceived as one: one, however, not with any visible or objective unity determined by a Divine rule and law common to the whole body; but one, in virtue of some invisible esoteric unity which is merely subjective, varying, both as to its nature and extension, according to the various opinions of those who believe in its existence at all. Considered in relation to the Church of Christ as a visible body, which our present argument supposes it to be, such invisible unity is really non-existent, for to thus apply it is a contradiction in terms. But taking such a visible body of the Church in its relation to such invisible unity, as the terms stand, for what it is, and so far as it is capable of outward formula, it may be described as an arbitrary enumeration together of a number of religious bodies —popularly called various Churches or denominations—with the potentiality of indefinite multiplication; each of them being entirely independent, autonomous, self-contained, and distinct from any other: and then the bestowal, on such an aggregation, of the name of Christ's one visible Church.

It must be remarked, moreover, that these separate religious bodies, so far from being bound together by any external common law or rule of visible communion, are for the most part mutually repellent, and practically excommunicate one another.* Still,

---

* These separate bodies may, it is true, be mutually non-repellent, and, like all other independent human corporations, may under certain circumstances form some sort of alliance, or at least make overtures towards an alliance. Such overtures will perhaps be more or less reciprocated and favourably entertained. Thus we see the Anglican Archbishop of Canterbury makes approaches from time to time to one or other of the Eastern schismatical Churches—Constantinople, Alexandria, or Jerusalem—with varying degrees of success. Friendly letters are interchanged full of compliments and expressions of sympathy on either side; perhaps even something like intercommunion is admitted. Other Anglican prelates will hold out the right hand of fellowship to the new-fledged Old Catholics of Germany, or to the still newer French communion of M. Loyson at Paris; whilst others, again, of the clergy take steps towards a brotherly union with Wesleyans, Presbyterians, and other Nonconformists. It is not for us to speak of the success which these well-meant advances have achieved. But however great this may be, we must bear in mind that union of this kind is, after all, merely accidental —that is, it may be, or may not be, and may come to an end any day—a change of circumstances, of time, or person may alter or efface whatever mutual arrangements have been thus formed. The allied parties are always free to withdraw, since neither justice nor any obligation of Divine law is involved in the matter, but only their own voluntary and independent choice —for they are all *sui juris*, irresponsible ecclesiastically to any external rule and authority, whether human or Divine, other than their own—save, perhaps, the political government of the particular State that controls them.

the fact of this objective disunion and exclusiveness presents no difficulty in the way of subjective unity to such minds as choose to entertain that idea.

Besides this, there exists a very wide divergence of opinion amongst non-Catholics who hold that Christ's Church is visible and one, as to what religious bodies should be included within its pale. There is the view, for example, of the Evangelical Alliance, which is diametrically opposed to that commonly held by High-Church Anglicans. According to the latter, those religious bodies that are able to claim for their bishops and clergy valid ordination, or, as they term it, apostolical succession, and these alone, are to be recognised as forming the aggregation of Christ's one visible Church. This view, generally known as the three-branch theory, or system of tripartite unity, limits the one Church to three separate groups—namely, first, that of all the Churches in communion with Rome (except, perhaps, such as are within British territory, though on this point there is difference of opinion); secondly, that of all those Churches in the East, and other episcopal Churches abroad, which have cast off the Pope's authority, and consequently are not in communion with Rome; and thirdly, the Protestant Anglican Communion, which is not in communion with either of the two former groups. It is hardly necessary to repeat, that since these three groups, or branches so called, are bound together by no common rule or law, but, on the contrary, have severally their own independent government, their own separate doctrines and standards of faith, and since they are themselves *de facto* externally divided, by mutually excommunicating one another, the unity claimed for their collection can be neither visible nor invisible, but is really non-existent, save in an impossible theory, and in some strangely

---

Any alliance of this kind is confessedly impracticable with Rome, alone of all Christian communions; and the reason of this impossibility is not far to seek. It does not lie so much in differences of faith, since, for the matter of that, the Church of England is as far removed, as regards points of doctrinal belief and religious practice, from the Churches of Constantinople or Alexandria as it is from Rome. (And here, in these unions of antagonism to the true Church, we are painfully reminded of the analogy there is between such alliances, and the friendship formed of old between Herod and Pilate in opposition to Jesus Christ, her Divine Founder.) The reason of the impossibility is to be found in the existence for the Roman Communion alone of a visible Divine law which, whilst it hedges round in unity the Vineyard of the Lord, at the same time effectually excludes and warns off all such as will not acknowledge, and submit themselves to, its obligation. We mean the Primacy bestowed by Christ upon Peter descending in the line of his successors in the Roman See.

abnormal, subjective idea. If we regard these groups or branches individually, we find that the Roman Communion alone professes to exist as autonomous and one, in virtue of claim to any Divine rule or law; and *that*, namely, of the heritage, by Divine right, of the Primacy, through succession to Peter's See. The Anglican Communion and the Eastern Church (if thus we can denote the manifold congeries of separate Oriental sects) do not claim a right to their independent existence and autonomy in virtue of any positive Divine authority or law, but precisely because they have cast away from them an authority and law which previously they had held and submitted to as Divine; or by hypocritically appealing to purely ecclesiastical arrangements of ancient patriarchates or metropolitan sees, made in virtue of that very Divine Supremacy of the Roman Pontiffs which they have rejected.

From the foregoing reflections, we conclude that the denial of the Roman Primacy, as set forth and continued historically in the fact of S. Peter's Roman Episcopate and his succession in the See of Rome, involves equally the denial of the unity of Christ's visible Church, and also its very existence; and this, whether we look at the constitution of the Church by Christ Himself, or view the question by the light of reason and the necessary nature of things, or we regard the face of Christendom as it actually exists.

We are well aware that against what we have termed the visible law of unity in the Catholic Church, viz., the Petrine succession in the Roman See, many objections and difficulties are urged, especially by certain Anglican ritualists of an extreme Protestant type. Themselves dwelling in a city of disunion, whose normal condition is discordant opinion and strife of tongues about everything religious, they would fain prove that no such thing as certainty of faith is to be found anywhere in Christendom, and that the whole history of Christ's true Church, like that of their own sect, is also one of inextricable confusion. Having no peace or security themselves, they grudge to others that which they enjoy. Hence, it is amongst their special delights to hash up again old objections many times solved; and they will gloat over, with immense satisfaction, whatever scandals, ancient or modern, they can discover, seeming failures, difficult and perplexing passages of history, in the chequered course of Christ's Catholic Church militant here on earth. Foreigners themselves to that Church, as in truth they are, and clearly show themselves to be, whilst noisily pretending to be amongst the number of her most favoured sons, they have nought of compassion or sympathy with her, but rejoice in her sorrows and disappointments; and by traducing her fair name, together with her doctrines and practices, by setting at nought her authority, and, by vilifying her cherished Saints and Doctors, they loudly proclaim their hate, and that they have neither part nor lot with her. It is such as these who, to beguile the simple and ignorant, and to hinder the wavering from entering her communion, will tell them, in the last resource, that, whatever may be the original truth of Peter's Primacy and its succession in the Bishops of Rome, all this has been long vitiated and brought to nought, whether through heresy on the part of Popes, or through broken succession by means of anti-popes and schism. It is not so long ago that these astute doctors lit upon a new mare's nest, with the discovery of which they sought to startle their hearers, proclaiming it with much parade of learning and flourish of trumpets—viz., that four hundred years ago the line of descent from Peter in the Roman See was utterly and hopelessly broken through uncanonical election; that during all that time the Papal Chair has been vacant, and is so still; that the so-called Pope has not a shadow of jurisdiction either in Rome or elsewhere; and that there is no possible way under present circumstances of ever getting a lawful Pope again. Poor silly praters! And yet so blind and infatuated as not to see that they are patently convicted of foolishness even by their own loud assertion of folly! Let the whole world be judge here, and *Securus judicat orbis terrarum*: for this truth we have the voucher of S. Augustine, re-echoed in these days by the great Cardinal Newman. Never, then, since the first age of the Gospel, the whole world will say, did the Pope wield the sceptre of his Primacy with more power and strength throughout Christendom; never were the Catholic bishops, the clergy, and the faithful more united to him as their universal Pastor in obedience and loving devotion than at the present day. Never was a Pope so much revered, nor his influence and moral force on earth so clearly recognised by those outside the Roman Communion, as at this very time in the person of Leo XIII., now happily reigning. This, the judgment of the wide world, is safe and true—for *Securus judicat orbis terrarum*.

To enter into serious argument with these false teachers on particular points of controversy is beyond our present scope, and would, moreover, lead to no good result, for they know full well that their misrepresentations and sophistries have been met and refuted over and over again by learned Catholic theologians, and to these they will not hearken.

> "They have gone astray from the womb, they have spoken false things. Their madness is according to the likeness of the serpent; like the deaf asp that stoppeth her ears; which will not hear the voice of the charmers; nor of the wizard that charmeth wisely." (*Ps.* lvii. 6.)

If, then, we quote on the above-mentioned points some brief words of S. Alphonsus—a Saint whom these writers are especially given to misrepresent and malign—we do so rather for others than for them, and to show that whatever objections are thus raised against the Petrine succession in the line of the Bishops of Rome have been already anticipated in Catholic theology. The holy Doctor writes as follows:

> "It matters not that in past centuries some Pope was illegitimately elected, or was fraudulently intruded into the Pontificate. It is enough that he was afterwards accepted as Pope by the whole Church, since by such acceptation he then became legitimate and true Pope. But if for some time he was not really accepted universally by the Church, in such case the Pontifical See was vacant during that time, as it is vacant at the death of a Pope. Again, it matters not that, in the case of schism, there should be for a considerable time doubt as to who is the true Pope, since one would then be the true Pope, even though he were insufficiently known as such; and if none of the rivals were the true Pope, then the Pontificate would simply be vacant.
>
> "Some have sought to prove that certain Popes fell into heresy, but in this they have never succeeded, and never will succeed; and we shall prove the direct contrary in the tenth chapter. If, however, God were to permit any Pope to become a notorious and contumacious heretic, he would by such fact cease to be Pope, and the Pontificate would be vacant. But were he only a secret heretic, and did not propose to the Church any false dogmas, no harm in that case would happen to the Church. But we ought, with good reason, to presume, as Cardinal Bellarmine says, that God will never allow any of the Roman Pontiffs, even as a private person, to become a heretic, either notorious or secret."[*]

As an Appendix to this Chapter we give the following passage from the Blessed John Cardinal Fisher, Cardinal Allen, and Dr. Döllinger, which bear upon our subject.

[*] *Verità della Fede*, pt. iii. c. viii. 9, 10.

APPENDIX.

1. FROM THE BLESSED MARTYR, JOHN CARDINAL FISHER, BISHOP OF ROCHESTER.

"Having proved historically the truth of the tradition that S. Peter was at Rome, and refuted all the trifles and sophisms which have been objected, my work seems to be at an end. Yet before concluding I will try to show, from what is related in the Gospel, how exactly this choice of place fitted in with the purposes of God.

"I will mention but three prerogatives of S. Peter. In the first place, that, though he was not first called, yet he was placed by our Lord first among His Apostles. Secondly, that he was called by Christ the Rock on which the building of the Church should rest. And thirdly, that Christ said to him, 'I have prayed for thee, Peter, that thy faith fail not.' These are three facts that none but the most impudent could deny.

"1. Let, then, the reader consider whether it was not fitting that, if the whole world was to become Christian, that city which is held to be the first in the whole world should be given as a See, by God's providence, to him only who was first among the Apostles. Had it been otherwise, an inferior Apostle would have occupied the first See, and S. Peter in this respect would have had one who was preferred to himself. Whence S. Leo writes as follows:—

"'When the twelve Apostles, after having received from the Holy Ghost the gift of speaking all tongues, and having divided the various parts of the earth between themselves, undertook to spread the Gospel through the world, the most blessed Peter, the Prince of the apostolic order, was reserved for the citadel of the Roman Empire, in order that the light of truth, which had been revealed for the salvation of all nations, might more efficaciously be diffused from the head throughout the whole body of the world. What nation at that time had not some of its members in that city? Or what nations could remain ignorant of what Rome had learned? It was here that the opinions of philosophers were to be trampled under foot, and the vanities of earthly wisdom to be dissipated; here the worship of demons was to be confuted; here the impiety of all sacrileges to be destroyed, since here superstition had most diligently brought together whatever in any place had been set up by foolish error.'

"Thus wrote S. Leo the First, who, in the Council of Chalcedon, by the enthusiastic admiration of the assembled Fathers, was saluted as the thrice holy Pope.

"2. Secondly, I said that Peter was made by Christ the solid Rock and principle foundation of the whole Church after Himself. Though Lutherans deny this, yet so certain is it, from the consent of the interpreters of Holy Scripture, that their objections deserve no more attention than the barking of dogs. But if Lutherans care not a straw for the sacred exponents of Scripture, Scripture itself is explicit enough. For did not Christ say to Simon, 'Thou art Simon the son of Jonas, thou shalt be called Cephas,' that is, a stone? And what difference is there between a stone and a rock? Certainly none, at least as regards the matter we have in hand. Having, then, given him this name of Cephas, or Peter, *i.e.*, stone or rock, He added: 'On this Rock I will build my Church.' And to what purpose did He give to Simon the name of Rock rather than to the other Apostles, except that on him, as on the principal foundation after Himself, the edifice of the Church should be raised? And do we not see this most evidently fulfilled at the present day? Who cannot see that the Church that now exists has come to us from no other Apostle than Peter? Where are the Christians whom Andrew converted, or John, or the rest? They exist no longer, and have left no succession. I speak, of course, of real Christians, not of heretics and schismatics, for all are not true Christians who use the name of Christ. . . . Is it not, then, evident that the historical fact that Peter erected his See in Rome is in exact accord with the promise of Christ, since it is from the Roman Church, as from a focus, that the light of the true faith has been derived to the other Churches which are dispersed throughout Christendom?

"3. Thirdly, if we consider how our Lord prayed for Peter that his faith might not fail, we shall clearly perceive that it was not fitting that Peter should have received as his principal See any of those which are now covered with the darkness of infidelity. I do not deny that the Faith once shone brightly at Antioch, where Peter first sat, but now it is in the hands of infidels; Jerusalem, too, where ruled James, the brother of the Lord, is in the power of the Sultan. Andrew won Achaia to Christ, but it is now subject to the Turks, the enemies of Christ. John conquered Asia Minor, yet there the great ruler of the Turks is also master. And most of the regions which fell to the lots of the other Apostles are now in the hands of infidels. It was, then, fitting that that part of the earth should have been allotted to Peter, in which the light of the Faith has never been extinguished. . . .

"But perhaps some one may say: 'Nowhere else is the life of

Christians more contrary to Christ than in Rome, and *that*, too, even among the prelates of the Church, whose conversation is diametrically opposed to the life of Christ. Christ loved poverty; they fly from poverty so far that their only study is to heap up riches. Christ shunned the glory of this world; they will do and suffer everything for glory. Christ afflicted Himself by frequent fasts and continual prayers; they neither fast nor pray, but give themselves up to luxury and lust. They are the greatest scandal to all who live sincere Christian lives, since their morals are so contrary to the doctrine of Christ, that through them the name of Christ is blasphemed throughout the world.' This is perhaps what an adversary might object. But all this merely confirms what I am proving. For since the Sees of other Apostles are everywhere occupied by infidels, and this one only, which belonged to Peter, yet remains under Christian rule, though, for so many crimes and such unspeakable wickedness, it has deserved like the rest to be destroyed, what must we conclude but that Christ is most faithful to His promises, since He keeps them in favour of His greatest enemies, however grievous and many may be their insults to Him?

"The faith preached by Peter at Rome has not yet failed, and the true succession of the Church which began with Peter still endures—of that Church, I say, of which he was set by Christ as the solid rock-foundation. Who then does not see how those things mutually confirm each other? The seat of Peter, which he planted at Rome, proves the veracity of Christ; and, on the other hand, the words of Christ give most certain assurance that indeed Peter placed his See in Rome. . . . Indeed, those events so moved S. Augustine, that he openly confesses that by means of them he was kept fast in the bosom of the Church:

"'The succession of priests down to the present Episcopate, in that See of the Apostle Peter, to whom our Lord after His Resurrection committed His sheep to be fed, keeps me in the Catholic Church. The name of Catholic also, which that Church alone among so many heresies not without reason has obtained, retains me.'

From these words of Augustine we understand these three things: first, the See of Peter; next, the perpetual succession of bishops from Peter downwards; and thirdly, that that Church alone which has descended from Peter has obtained the name of Catholic." *

---

* Joannis Fischerii Roffensis Opera. *Convulsio calumniarum Ulrichi Veleni quibus Petrum nunquam Romæ fuisse cavillatus est. Cavillus vii. ad fin.*

The work, of which this passage is the conclusion, was composed by Fisher in the year 1524. A very short time was to elapse before a most striking confirmation should be given to the world of the truth of his assertions regarding our Lord's special providence over Rome. If the luxury and wickedness of Rome were at that time as great as its bitterest enemies asserted, or as Fisher seems to deplore, the chastisement, which was to purify, not destroy it, was at hand. The outrages and cruelties perpetrated in Rome, in 1527, by the undisciplined hordes of German and Spanish soldiers, led on by the Constable Bourbon, not without the connivance of the master of the Holy Roman empire, are simply beyond conception, and had they not been described by eyewitnesses would be beyond belief. It was no doubt the justice of Him who wept over Jerusalem while He foretold its deserved calamities, which allowed the brutal Lutherans, who composed the mass of the German forces, and the equally brutal half-Moorish soldiers who had come from Spain, to join with wicked and apostate Italians, principally Romans, in that fearful sack of the churches and palaces of Rome, and in the slaughter of its inhabitants. Yet in His anger our Lord was faithful to His promises. He would not allow heresy or infidelity to become permanent possessors of the holy city of S. Peter. How nearly this was being accomplished in the designs of men is strikingly shown in a letter which was written to the Emperor Charles V., while the pillage of Rome was continuing, and the Pope in the Castle of S. Angelo was completely in the power of his enemies. An imperial officer of high rank thus wrote to the Emperor:

"We are expecting to hear from your Majesty how the city is to be governed, and whether the Holy See is to be retained or not. Some are of opinion it should not continue in Rome, but the French king should make a patriarch in his kingdom, and deny obedience to the said See, and the king of England and all other Christian princes do the same. The Imperialists advise that the Holy See should be kept so low that the Emperor will be able to dispose of it at his pleasure." *

So men thought, and so they advised, and they took so little heed to God's providence that one of them actually wrote to the Emperor Charles that now neither man nor God Himself could resist him. Yet more than three hundred and sixty years have passed since the Blessed John Fisher wrote, and still this spec-

---

* The whole letter is given by Mr. Brewer in his Introduction to the *Letters and Papers of Henry VIII.*, vol. iv. p. clxx., where will also be found a graphic account of those fearful scenes.

tacle, which moved S. Augustine in the fourth century, when the barbarians were about to sack Rome and overthrow the ancient Roman empire, and which moved Fisher in the sixteenth, when the armies of the Christian Roman Empire were surpassing in Rome the cruelties and sacrileges of Huns and Vandals—this spectacle, we say, is still before our eyes in the nineteenth, when another Catholic king has battered down the walls of Rome, profaned its churches, emptied its monasteries, and occupied its palaces, and another Protestant German emperor, after grievously afflicting the Catholic Church in his own realms, has at length returned to measures of peace, acknowledging the moral power and influence of the Holy See by the confidence and honour he has given to it in the person of the present reigning Pontiff, Leo XIII.—the spectacle of the uninterrupted succession in the Chair of S. Peter and of the Church against which the gates of hell cannot prevail.

2. From Cardinal Allen.

On Hatred of the Holy See of Rome.

William Allen, afterwards Cardinal, writing in 1565, in answer to the first Protestant revilers of Rome, says:

"The shrews do know full well the might of truth in that seat and succession to have beaten down all their forefathers, the heretics of all ages. They fear their fall whose steps they follow. They utter much malice and torment themselves in every sermon in vain. That Church feeleth no sore, but in sorrow of compassion towards her forsakers. She hath ridden greater storms than this—first by tyrants, then by heretics, last and most by the evil life of her own bishops. In all which she yet standeth, and ever riseth to honour as she is most impugned.

"Their own preaching (*i.e.*, that of the 'Reformers') hath singularly opened the might of God in the defence of that seat of unity. When they first began to touch and taunt the Pope in every sermon, in every play, in book and ballad, men that before living in faithful simplicity much meddled not with his matters, nor often heard of his name, began straight upon their busy railing to conceive by reasonable discretion, that there lay some great ground of matter and weight of truth upon that point which they could not digest in so many years' bawling and barking at his name. They saw the Pope ever in their way, never out of their mouth, and they doubted not but that singular hatred grew upon some great importance; and so admonished, luckily by the adversaries, they sought the bottom of that perfect and deep hatred, and found that it was the old sore of the Arians and disease of the Donatists, and common to all heretics. They perceived by S. Cyprian, that the first attempt of such men was to drive away the pastor, that they might without resistance devour and destroy the flock. And, which was the prick of all their endeavours, to take from us the acknowledging of the great and singular benefit of our conversion to the faith; that in stopping the head of that conduit and plentiful well of our faith they might, in heat of contention and heresy, dry up the whole issue thereof. And this earnest consideration causeth many at this day to forsake their heresies, and to be a great deal more at this time which know the truth of this matter than when they began first to preach thereof."*

3. From Dr. Döllinger.

"Two questions are involved in deciding S. Peter's relation to the Church of Rome: Did he found it? Did he die there? We must examine both. 1. The Roman Church must have been founded by an Apostle, and that Apostle can only have been Peter. S. Paul declares in his Epistle to the Romans that he had often withstood his longing to come to them, because he made a principle of only bringing the Gospel where Christ had not yet been preached, so as not to build on another man's foundation. But now, after the Church had been founded in the West, he was going into Spain, and would visit Rome on the way.† He was unwilling, then, at that time to undertake a regular Apostolic office in Rome, 'because the foundation was already laid.' By whom? S. Paul cannot possibly have meant by the chance visit of some nameless believer, or by those who returned from Jerusalem and related what they had heard there; he found irregular pre-announcements of that kind in most Churches, to which he none the less devoted his special energies. He cannot, in a word, mean that it was his principle only to teach where no one had preached the Gospel before him, for, on the one hand, no intelligible ground for such a rule can be imagined; on the other, the contrary is proved by his labours in Antioch and Cyprus, and his

---

* *A Defense of Purgatory*, by William Allen (1565), ch. xii. p. 235. Edited by Rev. T. E. Bridgett, C.SS.R. *Souls Departed*, pp. 323-4. Burns & Oates, 1886. † *Rom.* xv. 20-24.

anxious care and earnest exhortations written to the community of Colossæ, which was unknown to him personally. He must refer, therefore, to his former agreement with the great Apostles at Jerusalem, and the position he took towards them, according to which he desired to abstain from meddling with their work or building on a foundation laid by them. There can be no doubt, then, that it was S. Peter, perhaps accompanied by S. John,* who had laid the foundation in Rome.

"The formation of a Church at Rome, in the centre of the Empire, where the number of Jews was greater and their position more important than at any other town out of Judæa, excepting Alexandria, was far too important a matter to be left to chance. If S. Philip's work in Samaria determined the Apostles Peter and John to go there to carry on and perfect what the deacon had begun, if the example of Antioch showed them the expansive power of the Gospel and the importance and necessity of an ecclesiastical organisation in the great capital, it is inconceivable that at Jerusalem, where Jews from Rome appeared at every festival, the idea of planting the Gospel in the great capital of the world should not have been seriously entertained. While all the principal Churches have their tradition about the men to whom they owe their first foundation, Peter is marked out, both by the universal tradition of all Churches and the special tradition of the Roman, as the founder and first ruler of that Church, and is said—which comes to the same thing—to have first gone to Rome under Claudius. S. Dionysius of Corinth and S. Irenæus in the second century mention S. Peter as having laid the foundation of the Roman community. The planting of the Roman and Corinthian Churches, says the former, was by Peter and Paul†—*i.e.*, as S. Paul founded the Corinthian, S. Peter founded the Roman Church.‡ S. Irenæus likewise ascribes to the two Apostles the founding and ordering of these Churches; and since all S. Paul did at Rome occurred at a later period, it is S. Peter who always appears as the special father of the Church there." §

* We are unable to conjecture Döllinger's ground for this supposition.

† Dionysius (Eus. vi. 25) uses the word φυτείαν, and Irenæus says (Eus. v. 6) θεμελιώσαντες καὶ οἰκοδομήσαντες.—*Cf.* Eus. v. 8.

‡ We cannot agree with Dr. Döllinger in this interpretation of the words of S. Dionysius.

§ *First Age of Christianity*, vol. i. pp. 156-158.

CHAPTER V.

S. PETER'S APOSTLESHIP COMPARED WITH AND DISTINGUISHED FROM HIS PRIMACY.

In discussing the historical fact of S. Peter's Episcopate at Rome, it is not our intention to treat *ex professo* of the question of his Primacy. If we speak of this at all, it is only for the better elucidation of our main point, and so far as any arguments in proof of the Primacy may bear upon the Episcopate.

We recognise, then, in S. Peter three distinct endowments: his Apostleship, his Primacy, and his Episcopate. He is at once Apostle, Supreme Pastor of the universal Church, and Bishop of the Roman See. Hence we think it well, in order to give more completeness to our subject, and to anticipate sundry difficulties and questions which might arise in the minds of our readers, to treat of Peter's Primacy, not, indeed, as it is in itself, but relatively; comparing it first with his Apostleship, and secondly with his Episcopate, distinguishing it at the same time from both one and the other. The subject, then, of this present chapter will be: The Apostleship of S. Peter compared with and distinguished from his Primacy.*

Whatever Peter's Apostleship imported was also equally the property of each and all the twelve Apostles. So that to consider Peter's Primacy in relation to his Apostleship is one and the same thing as to compare the Apostle S. Peter with the several other members of the Apostolic College. By such comparison we shall discover what were those prerogatives, and what that office which Christ conferred on all the Apostles in common, and what it was in addition that He bestowed upon S. Peter alone.

We observe, then, in the first place—what, indeed, is self-evident—that, in order to found and constitute any new society, its first founders must have certain powers which are quite un-

---

* See Murray, *De Ecclesia Christi*, vol. iii. disp. xviii. 349-386, whence we have taken much that is in this Chapter.

necessary for those to possess who are afterwards called to rule and direct the society when it has been once established, since much that may be required for the first foundation of a state is, in great measure, wholly unneeded afterwards for preserving it in good order. And this truth holds especially with regard to the Church on account of its entirely exceptional nature.

Hence all Catholic theologians, and, so far as we are aware, Protestants also, are unanimously agreed, that, whilst some of the gifts and powers bestowed by Christ upon His Apostles were to be continued to their successors, others were not to be so continued, or, at any rate, were not to be continued in virtue of succession and vested right. Of these gifts and powers the former are called *ordinary*, the latter *extraordinary*, and in so far as they belonged to the Apostles, as such, are termed *purely Apostolic*.

We observe, in the second place, that the gifts conferred by Christ upon the Apostles were of three kinds:—(1) those which belong to the power of Order, which has its plenitude in the Episcopate; (2) those that regard the power of jurisdiction, *v.g.*, the right to teach, the power to make laws, &c.; (3) special gifts, such as personal infallibility, inspiration, the power of working miracles, &c.

Gifts of the first kind were ordinary, and to continue to those who should succeed the Apostles. This is admitted on all hands, by those, at least, who hold such gifts to have been of Divine bestowal at all.

Gifts of the third class were extraordinary, conferred specially on the Apostles for first founding the Church, and were not to pass on to their successors. This, too, is allowed by all.

The question into which we have now to inquire relates to the second sort of gifts bestowed upon the Apostles, and it is: What precisely was that jurisdiction, in its nature and extent, which each and all the Apostles, as such, received in common from Jesus Christ?

The question here is not concerning the ordinary episcopal jurisdiction which any Apostle who held a particular See; *v.g.*, S. James at Jerusalem, or S. Peter at Antioch and afterwards at Rome, would exercise as its diocesan bishop. On this point Suarez writes:—

"All the Apostles were made bishops, as regards consecration, by Jesus Christ, immediately; and thus, so far, all bishops are their successors; the Apostles, too, were made, so to say, universal bishops of the whole Church by immediate collation of Christ; and in this they have had no successors save in the case of Peter alone, who received the universal pontificate in a way above the other Apostles. Some of the Apostles, moreover (though not all), had determined episcopal Sees; but here they did not have their episcopate immediately from Christ but by human appointment. Thus James was made the first Bishop of Jerusalem by Peter, as Chrysostom testifies, *Hom.* 87, *in Joann*, and Eusebius *H. E.* ii. 1. So, too, Peter was himself the first Bishop of Antioch, which See he had not immediately from Christ but took by his own authority, whereby he also afterwards relinquished it. As regards, then, these episcopates, bishops are the successors of the Apostles; they are so, however, in a proper and strict sense, only in such Churches as had one of the Apostles for its first bishop, but in other Churches only by a certain resemblance or participation which they have with Peter, and not immediately from Christ." *

Before, in n. 21, Suarez had said:

"Paul was bishop; but we do not know that he was bishop of any certain diocese or had any special Church, as its ordinary and immediate pastor, though he had the solicitude of all the Churches and created bishops in many of them, as Titus at Crete, Timothy at Ephesus, Dionysius at Athens. Of John the Evangelist we also read that he ruled all the Churches of the East and set bishops in them, but not that he occupied as particular bishop any special See."

Our present inquiry is, we repeat, respecting the jurisdiction which each and all the Apostles had, as Apostles.

Now, it is evident from the Acts of the Apostles and the Epistles, as well as from the tradition of the Church contained in the writings of the Fathers, that each and all of the Apostles, on the one hand, had received from Christ the power, wherever they went, of doing all things necessary for their instituting, founding, governing, consolidating, and preserving the Church; and consequently of preaching, baptising, making laws, appointing bishops and other ministers, &c.

It is, moreover, certain, on the other hand, that individual Apostles were bound to exercise their power in such a manner that due order should be preserved, the preaching of the Gospel extended, and the profit of the faithful advanced. "But let all things be done decently and according to order," says the Apostle S. Paul; † and again: "Concerning our power, which the Lord hath given us unto edification, and not for your destruction." ‡

Accordingly, we have clear intimation in Scripture and tradition that the several Apostles had, for a time at least, each their own special and distinct spheres of labour; whether this was due to the appointment of S. Peter, or of the whole body of the Apostles after general consultation, or was the effect of a

* *De Legibus* l. iv. c. iv. n. 22. † 1 *Cor.* xiv. 20. ‡ 2 *Cor.* x. 8.

particular impulse of the Holy Ghost. Thus S. Peter was in a special manner the Apostle of the Jews, and S. Paul of the Gentiles :* although the former did not preach to the Jews alone, nor the latter exclusively to the Gentiles, as is clear from the Acts of the Apostles.† We know, moreover, that S. Peter went about everywhere, visiting all the Churches.‡ Commenting on this passage, S. Chrysostom thus writes :

"Like the commander of an army, he (Peter) went about inspecting the ranks : what part was compact, what in good order, what needed his presence. Behold him making his rounds on every side, and the first to be found. When an Apostle was to be chosen, he was the first : when the Jews were to be told those were not drunken : when the lame man was to be healed : when the multitude was to be addressed, he is before the rest : when they had to deal with the rulers, it is he : when with Ananias, when healings took place from the shadow, still it was he. And when there was danger, it is he ; and when there is dispensation ; but when all is tranquil, all act in common ; he sought not the greater honour. Again, when miracles are to be worked, he starts forward."§

It was competent to any of the Apostles to put forth writings for the use of all the faithful, or to address letters to them. But this they did by a special impulse of the Holy Spirit : and not only were the Apostles thus inspired to write, but S. Mark and S. Luke also, who were not Apostles.

Everyone of the Apostles could, as we have said, make laws for the provinces of which they severally had the care, but not for the whole Church ; for nowhere is there any grant of a like power extant, nor is there to be found any example of an Apostle exercising such power. Besides, such a power in each of the Apostles was noways necessary.

What was the nature and fulness of the purely Apostolic office and prerogative may be gathered, not so much from any express promise and mandate of Christ, as from its exercise, especially as shown forth in the pages of Scripture. And that this was providentially so ordered is no mere conjecture. For it was not necessary, on the one hand, that either the inspired Scriptures or tradition should contain a full and detailed exposition of gifts and offices which appertained exclusively to the Apostles, and were not to pass down to their successors, nor to continue in the Church. Indeed, if we examine the various passages of the New Testament wherein gifts and offices are

* *Galat.* ii. 7, 8. † Chapters ix. and x.
‡ *Acts*, ix. 32. § *Hom. in Act. Apost.* xxi. n. 2.

assigned to the Apostles, we shall see that they do not, in point of fact, speak of such as are purely Apostolical, and which consequently were to cease with the Apostles, but of such as are pastoral, and intended to remain in perpetuity. Thus, the power which the words import: "Whatsoever you shall bind on earth," &c.,* was given not to found the Church, but to govern the Church when already founded and constituted. Again, the power given† to convert, baptise, and teach all nations—with the promise attached, of our Lord's abiding presence until the end of the world—was a power to endure perpetually in the Church, and to be at all times exercised; as also was the commission, through the power of the Holy Ghost, to bear witness of Christ even to the uttermost part of the earth. And the same may be said of the power of remitting sins.‡

Our purport, hitherto, has been to make a brief survey of those gifts and powers bestowed by Christ upon His Apostles, which they each and all shared in common as Apostles, and equally with Peter. And we would now go on to inquire into what it was that Peter received, over and above the rest, as Prince of the Apostles and Supreme Pastor of the Church, and to consider his position, as such, in relation to them.

First, then, we remark: that the rest of the Apostles did not, and could not, make up their body corporate, properly speaking, or what is termed the Apostolic College, apart from Peter. For, since he was constituted their ruler and head, they were incapable of collective union, and of exercising jurisdiction as a body, unless united with and under him. Hence, no comparison can be instituted between the jurisdiction of S. Peter and that of the rest of the Apostles taken together as a corporate body, since, as such, without him, it had no existence.

Nor can S. Peter's jurisdiction be compared with the jurisdiction of the collective body of the Apostles, himself included; for then the corporate jurisdiction in such case would be derived from himself as head, and the comparison would be between what was, in point of fact, identical.

Since, then, S. Peter cannot be compared with the rest of the Apostles collectively, the only comparison to be drawn is by taking them singly, one by one. But here we should note, in the first place, that the preeminence and authority of S. Peter over

---

* *Matt.* xviii. 18.   † *Matt.* xxviii. 19, 20; *Mark*, xvi. 15, 16.
‡ *Acts*, i. 8; *John*, xx. 21, 22.

the other Apostles was not so great as that which he had over bishops, or as that which the Roman Pontiff has over bishops. For all alike, as much as S. Peter, were constituted Apostles by Christ Himself, and as Apostles were made by Him equal in all things, except the Primacy, which was conferred on Peter alone. Moreover, as Primate he had no power to take from them their Apostleship, or to restrict it, but only to direct its exercise, as we shall point out. Much less had he power to take away, or restrict, their divinely-imparted gifts and privileges. The reason of all this is derived from the Divine appointment of the Apostleship, according as that appointment is set forth in Scripture and tradition.

"The jurisdiction of S. Peter surpassed that of the other Apostles, says Suarez, by a two-fold title: first, because to him alone was given the ordinary power to rule and feed the universal Church of Christ, in such sense that he was to have in the Church a perpetual succession;* and this was not bestowed on the other Apostles. In their case, the power which they had throughout the Church was, so to say, delegated and by privilege. And, secondly, because the jurisdiction of S. Peter extended directly over the Apostles themselves—namely, by his power to command them, and to send them here or there."†

In the following three points, then, the Primatial authority of S. Peter excelled the purely Apostolical authority:

1. The Apostolical authority was to cease with the Apostles, and did thus actually cease with them; whilst the Primatial authority of S. Peter was to remain whole and entire in his successors, and does so remain.

2. S. Peter had supreme power to rule the universal Church; to make, for example, universal laws. The jurisdiction of the other Apostles was universal indeed, in the sense that they could severally exercise it in any place whatever. But Peter alone could rule the whole Church; whilst no other Apostle could take that office on himself—not, at least, without subordination and subjection to S. Peter.

3. S. Peter could impose a precept on the other Apostles, by assigning, for example, this or that province to one or another Apostle, whilst no other Apostle possessed any jurisdiction over a fellow-Apostle. There was however no necessity, as a rule at least, for such exercise of authority over the Apostles on the part of S. Peter.

We say *as a rule at least;* for whilst, on the one hand, it is

---

* This is *de Fide*. † *Tr. de Fide*, part i. d. 10, § 1, n. 12, 25.

THE PRIMACY NO INFRINGEMENT ON APOSTOLIC RIGHTS. 257

evident that our Lord before His Ascension, during His visible converse with His Apostles, taught and directed them Himself immediately, as He did also at times after the descent of the Holy Ghost, yet, on the other hand, it noways appears that they were regularly, much less always, thus taught and directed. On the contrary we have an example* of how S. Paul and S. Barnabas, in order to settle a dispute of dogma, went up to Jerusalem to consult the Apostles and ancients; who thereupon met together and held a great discussion on the question. It is, moreover, certain that to S. Peter was assigned by Christ the office of confirming his brother Apostles, and consequently so far of feeding and tending them as their pastor with doctrine and discipline.

Two points of difficulty might here be objected, with the consideration of which we will conclude this chapter.

1. With such jurisdiction over the rest of the Apostles, it was in S. Peter's power to infringe on the office and rights of an Apostle, should some manifest necessity arise in the Church (as Pius VII. at the beginning of this century deprived of jurisdiction the whole Episcopate of France), or on account of some fault committed.

To this we reply, in the first place, that by the special providence of God, which ruled and directed His Church and His Apostles, such a necessity could not happen, and, in fact, did not happen. We say, in the second place, that though, according to the more common teaching of theologians, the Apostles were not granted the privilege of avoiding entirely all sins, and hence fell sometimes into venial faults, not indeed fully deliberate, but what are called sins of surprise,† yet it is certain that by the descent of the Holy Ghost they were confirmed in grace, and that none of them thenceforward committed any grave fault; whilst it is certain, on the other hand, that the Apostles attained to a very great interior sanctity, since they were established in a state of the highest perfection, and were made to partake in so many ways and in such fulness of the Divine Spirit.‡

2. As a second difficulty, the question arises: Whether the Apostles who survived S. Peter were subject to the Bishop of Rome as S. Peter's successor?

We reply with Suarez:

---

* *Acts*, xv. † Suarez, *de Gratia*, l. ix. c. viii. n. 25.
‡ Suarez, *de Mysteriis Vitæ Christi*, d. viii. § 1, n. 9.

"It seems to follow from what has been said that in jurisdiction the Apostles were inferior to the Roman Pontiff, and were therefore subject to his authority, whilst they were, at the same time, superior to him in other prerogatives and excellencies."*

There is, however, nothing incongruous in the Apostles being subject to Peter's successor after Peter's death, if we bear in mind the two following points:—*First*, The Apostles would be indeed subject by right to the Roman Pontiff, but as, on account of their dignity, special gifts, and prerogatives, and their eminent virtues, there was no need for S. Peter himself to exercise jurisdiction over them, at any rate of a coercive kind, much less was there need of any such exercise on the part of the Roman Pontiff. *Secondly*, The several Apostles would retain all their Apostolic prerogatives and privileges entire; and consequently if, on the one hand, they were subject to the Roman Pontiff, he, on his part, could not infringe on their Apostolic powers, but was bound to jealously respect them, and to hold the Apostles themselves in the greatest honour and veneration.

In confirmation of what has been said in this chapter we here add the following extracts from the writings of S. Alphonsus Liguori, the latest of the Doctors of the Catholic Church:

On the words of our Lord addressed to His Apostles in common, "Amen, I say to you, whatsoever you shall bind upon earth," &c., the Saint says:

"All the Apostles were commissioned by Jesus Christ to propagate the faith, with the power to make priests, bishops, and also to found Churches, in those first days when the new law needed to be firmly established. This power, however, which was conferred on the Apostles was a power always subordinate to that of S. Peter. It was, moreover, an extraordinary power which came to an end with the Apostles, whilst the power conferred upon S. Peter was absolute, and, so to say, ordinary—a power which was to pass to his successors. Hence S. Jerome says that although at first, when the faith needed to be propagated, all the Apostles had the same power, nevertheless on Peter alone was conferred the supreme power, in order that he might preside over all the rest in quality of head.

'It is on Peter properly that the Church is founded; and though in another place of the Gospel the same is said of all the Apostles that they all received the keys of the kingdom of heaven, and that the strength of the

---

* *Tr. de Fide*, part i. x. § 1, n. 28.

Church is consolidated equally on them all, yet one alone is chosen from among the twelve, that, a head being once constituted, all occasion of schism might be taken away.'*

S. Cyprian speaks in the same sense :

'The Apostles were endowed with a like share of honour and power; but the beginning proceeds from unity, and the primacy is given to Peter that the Church may be set forth as one.'

And this agrees with what the Saint says further on :

'Just as the light of the sun is one though its rays are multiplied, so too the Church of God diffuses its rays of light over the whole world, although that light everywhere diffused is but one.... The head of the Church is one and its origin one.'†

Here he is speaking of Peter, on whom was bestowed the primacy in the Church." ‡

Again, on the words of S. Leo,§ S. Alphonsus writes :

"In these words S. Leo clearly shows that although the Apostles had by a special privilege equal plenary power with Peter of preaching everywhere, of ordaining priests, constituting bishops, of founding new Churches, and making new laws concerning the administration of the sacraments—for this was necessary, says Bellarmine, in those first days for the propagation of the faith—yet Peter received this power as the ordinary pastor, the Apostles as delegated ; and all of them were subordinate to Peter as the director of all, on whom they were to be dependent, that thus contentions might have no place, as S. Jerome teaches in the passage already quoted." ||

In the same treatise, commenting on *Matt.* xviii. 18, the Saint says :

"We have already affirmed that the Apostles received immediately from Christ a power equal to that of Peter, as the first founders of the Gospel, but that they all were subject to Peter as to their head and prince, as all the Fathers proclaim him. . . . We should, moreover, remark that this equality of power was bestowed upon the Apostles in virtue of a special privilege, and that consequently it ceased with them. Hence it is false that bishops, as successors of the Apostles, are equal to the supreme Pontiff as regards the power of the keys. They are recognised with truth as successors of the Apostles, so far as regards episcopal order and character, but not as regards

---

* *Contra Jovinian*, l. i.   † *De Unitate Ecclesiæ.*
‡ *Venità della Fede*, part iii. c. vii.   § *In anniv. assump. suæ* Serm. 3, c. 5.
|| *Vindiciæ pro suprema Pontificis potestate adv. Justin. Febron.* c. i. 12.

the power and jurisdiction which the Apostles had. It is true that Bishops are appointed by the Holy Ghost 'to rule the Church of God ;'* but they rule the Church as members, according to the portion thereof assigned to each, whilst the Pope rules it as the head, to whom the government of the whole Church has been entrusted." †

"The power to make laws was bestowed upon all the Apostles by Christ when He said to them, 'Whatsoever you shall bind on earth,' &c. ‡ For the power to bind clearly imports that of making laws and imposing an obligation, as in fact the Apostles did, and is recorded in their Acts (ch. xv. 41). But this power of binding was given principally to Peter in these words, 'And I will give to thee the keys of the kingdom of heaven, and whatsoever thou shalt bind on earth,' &c." §

"There is no force, says S. Alphonsus again, in the objection against S. Peter's Primacy that is made from the particular fact recorded in the Acts (ch. viii. 14), viz., that the Apostles sent S. Peter, together with S. John, to Samaria, since they did not send him by way of command, but only by way of counsel, just as sometimes it is said that the king is sent to the war by his ministers."

* *Acts*, xx. 28. † *Ib.* ch. ii. 8. ‡ *Matt.* xviii. 18.
§ *Ib.* vii. 12. ‖ *Verità della Fede*, part iii. c. ix. 6.

CHAPTER VI.

THE RELATION OF THE APOSTOLATE TO THE EPISCOPATE.

We have not met with any author who treats of the relation of the Apostolate to the Episcopate in such wise as to determine what would essentially constitute one of the Twelve Apostles, strictly speaking, a bishop of some particular See; or, in other words, in what a diocesan episcopate precisely consists, as distinguished from such supervision and functions of Apostolic power, whether of order or jurisdiction, as an Apostle might continue to exercise with regard to any of the Churches he had founded.

We know that the Apostles, together with the plenitude of order and jurisdiction which they received from Christ, were given whatever belongs to the episcopal character and office. For the Episcopate was contained in the Apostolate. Consequently, they could be diocesan bishops in such sense as this term is universally understood.

We know, moreover, that in the mind of the early Church a diocesan episcopate was not incompatible with the Apostolate; nor was it incongruous that an Apostle should preside as bishop over a particular See: for S. James was always accounted Bishop of Jerusalem, S. Peter Bishop, first of Antioch, and afterwards of Rome; whilst later on S. Andrew was claimed to have been Bishop of Byzantium.

On the other hand, the Apostle S. Paul was never called, nor is held to have been, Bishop of Corinth, or of Philippi, or of any other Church that he himself founded, though he continued to watch over and rule these Churches with pastoral care, and by acts of jurisdiction and legislation such as a diocesan bishop would ordinarily exercise. The same might be said of S. John's supervision over the Churches of Asia Minor; though we know from his Apocalypse that these Churches had at the same time each its own presiding bishop.

The supervision exercised, then, by S. James at Jerusalem,

and by S. Peter at Antioch or Rome, in addition to, or as distinguished from, that which belonged to their office as Apostles, was episcopal and diocesan; whilst the supervision of S. Paul and S. John over the Churches under their care was not episcopal, but purely apostolical.

What, it will be asked, makes the essential difference in the two cases? In default of any authority to guide us, we should answer, that an Apostle became also *de facto* a diocesan bishop by his appropriation to himself of some local sphere or district for the particular exercise of that episcopal power which was virtually contained in his Apostolate. For, since every Apostle was empowered by Christ to found Churches, create episcopal Sees, and appoint over them bishops whose supervision, jurisdiction, duties, and prerogatives would be localised, diocesan, and ordinary, that is, resulting from, peculiar to, and circumscribed by their office as bishops of their several Sees; so by the same Divine right every Apostle had power, if so he judged good for the Church, to appropriate any See to himself, and therein localise his episcopal jurisdiction, and this without prejudice to the higher and more extended power and dignity of the Apostolate.

The eminent Church historian, Dr. Döllinger, though he does not precisely touch the particular question here raised, goes nearer to it than any other author we have read, in his Chapter on the various orders of ministers in the early Church, where he most luminously treats of the genesis, first formation, and gradual development of the deacons, presbyters, and bishops in the Apostolic age.

As the extracts we give from this Chapter may somewhat suffer from curtailment and abridgment here and there, we refer the reader to the original work.*

"The Apostolic Church before the year 64 was by no means a lawless chaos; as the body of Christ, it was from the beginning a well-ordered whole. . . . All power and authority was lodged in the Apostolate. As long as the Apostles lived it was they who ruled the Church, and in whose hands was centred all official power. Each Apostle possessed in solidarity not a divided or partial, but a complete right of superintendence over the Christian communities; he was able and bound to use his Apostolical authority where it was needful and useful in

* *First Age of the Church*, translated by H. N. Oxenham, M.A. Vol. ii., pp. 112-115; ed. 1877.

every portion of the Church: and hence S. Paul says that the care of all the Churches was laid upon him.* ... The Twelve gave laws, as well conjointly, as at the Synod of Jerusalem, as separately, many of them not expressly ordained by Christ....

"The Apostles had their ministering disciples and subordinate helpers ... mostly younger men, as assistants. They were sent here and there on commissions between the Apostles and the various communities, and brought a report of the state of these communities. Certain duties were left to them, as of baptising, which the Apostles usually committed to others, after Christ's example, Who did not baptise Himself, but made His disciples do so.† ... Laying on of hands was a special prerogative of the Apostles, as appears from S. Paul's action at Ephesus, and the case of the Samaritans baptised by the evangelist Philip.

"S. Peter held a preeminence among the Apostles, which none of the rest contested. He received the keys of the kingdom, and is the rock on which the Church is built—that is, the continuance, increase, and growth of the Church rests on the office created in his person. To him was the charge given to strengthen his brethren and feed the flock of Christ."

After discussing the *Charismata*, which formed so distinguishing a feature of the Apostolic Church in its first years, their wide diffusion, and their influence, Dr. Döllinger goes on to treat of the origin and growth of the Diaconate and the Presbyterate, and thus continues:

"In the early years of the Apostolic Church, the office afterwards called episcopal was not, then, yet marked off—the Episcopate slept in the Apostolate. It was the last branch to grow out of the Apostolic stem. In Jerusalem it had already taken shape in the person of S. James, whose attitude towards the local Church, his renunciation of missionary work, and his remaining within the holy city, point him out as the first true and proper Bishop. The other Apostles discharged their episcopal office in superintending and guiding several com-

---

* 2 Cor. xi. 28. We may be allowed to express the distinction here intimated between the office of S. Peter and that of S. Paul, or any other of the Apostles thus: S. Paul by right of his Apostleship had the care of all the Churches distributively; S. Peter, as Prince of the Apostles and Supreme Pastor, had charge of the whole entire flock of Christ collectively. See the last chapter—"S. Peter's Apostleship compared with and distinguished from his Primacy."

† John iv. 2; Acts, x. 47, 48, xix. 5, 6, viii. 14-17; 1 Cor. i. 14-17.

munities. Tradition knows only of S. Peter and S. James—one in Jerusalem, the other in Antioch and Rome—as founders of a line of bishops, forming themselves the first link in the chain. No Pauline Church claims S. Paul as its first bishop; he belonged to all, and gave no such preeminence to any. But his martyrdom at Rome gave the Church there a right to claim him, with S. Peter, as joint-founder of the Roman See. The rest of the Apostles have not so bound themselves to any particular Church as to be called its first bishops. Ephesus was the centre from which S. John administered his Apostolic office, but he is never called its first bishop; indeed, the Apocalypse shows that there was another there under him. But the nearer came the moment for their departure, and for the complete separation of the Christian Church from Judaism, the more urgent was the call on them to provide for the continuation of their Apostolic office—that is, to appoint bishops. We saw what weighty grounds they had for delaying this step; but there were others besides. While the Temple stood, and the connection with Judaism was not finally dissolved, the organisation of the Church was in one sense incomplete and provisional. It might in the interval have presbyters, who were a common Jewish institution, and whose appointment was no sign of separation; but the appointment of bishops would certainly have been regarded by all Jews, and by Gentiles also, as an act sealing the exclusion of the Church and its definitive separation from the Israelite nation and religion.* Therefore, the Apostles retained the episcopal authority provisionally in their own hands. And again, until the two nationalities, Jewish and Gentile, were completely amalgamated, there would have been great difficulties about appointing a bishop, who must necessarily have belonged to one of the two classes, and yet have governed both. . . . The only available form of government while this division remained—in other words, while Jewish converts still observed the ritual law—was a presbyterate gathered from, and representing both classes, subjected to the authority of the Apostles and sustained by it. . . . Moreover, there was a great difficulty in finding the right men for an office doubly difficult

---

* It may be objected that S. James appeared as bishop in Jerusalem from the first, and under the very eye of the authorities there. But he, from his habit of visiting the Temple and his careful observance of the law, was peculiarly qualified to dispel in the minds of Jews all suspicion of an intended separation. It was different elsewhere.

under the then state of circumstances. S. Paul writes to the Philippians that he would shortly send them Timothy to bring him word of their condition, because he had no other equally of one heart and mind with him; the rest sought their own, not what was Christ's.* Even if this severe sentence refers only to a temporary absence of suitable helpers, still it shows how the Apostles were forced to keep the superintendence of the communities as long as they could in their own hands. S. Paul could more easily find dozens of presbyters than one bishop, one man ready to undertake this burden with entire self-denial and self-devotion. And even this one, whom he had much rather have kept by him to send here and there on commissions, he gave up as bishop to the Church of Ephesus, though bidding him take care that he be not despised on account of his youth.† So, too, S. Titus had only a charge from him in Crete to appoint presbyters in the island communities. How could men be found for bishops in those newly-formed communities, which had only temporarily enjoyed apostolical care, and all whose members were novices? Neophytes were not even to be made presbyters.‡

"But, as these hindrances to introducing the Episcopate diminished with each year, and men gradually grew ripe for the discharge of that office, so, too, as the end of the chief Apostles drew near, dangers multiplied, which forbade them to defer any longer the consolidation of the Churches. S. Peter and S. Paul saw times of persecution at hand, and also the imminent peril of false teachers rising up from within, and of a widely-spread apostasy.

"Thus we find, in the Epistle to the Philippians, that S. Paul, who at the opening addresses the community 'with the Overseers and Deacons,' afterwards speaks of some one, not named, as a 'true yoke-fellow,' and gives him a charge.§ It was he who received the Epistle and was to communicate or read it to the rest, and he is the only person in all S. Paul's Epistles to whom this honourable title is given. He elsewhere calls those who worked with and under him 'fellow-labourers,' 'fellow-soldiers,' 'fellow-servants.' ‖ All this points to a man who had no equal then in his office—to a bishop. So, again, with Archippus at

---

* *Phil.* ii. 20, 21. † 1 *Tim.* iv. 12.
‡ "The Apostles were not able to settle and arrange everything all at once, straight off," says Epiphanius quite correctly. (*Hær.* 75.)
§ *Phil.* iv. 3. ‖ *Rom.* xvi. 3, 9, 21; *Phil.* ii. 25, iv. 3; *Col.* i. 7; *Philem.* 1.

Colossæ; he is the only person there whom S. Paul exhorts to administer his office carefully.* And, when writing to Philemon, in whose house the community, or a part of it, assembled, in order to reconcile him with his slave, Onesimus, he also addresses Archippus, 'our fellow-soldier,' though the Epistle contains not a word relating to him, and is wholly occupied with the private relations of Philemon and Onesimus; and this shows that the only ground for addressing Archippus was the fact of his being the head of the Church there, who as such was to join his intercession with S. Paul's for Onesimus.†

"S. Timothy, then, was placed at Ephesus, in the Church which the Apostle of the Gentiles held dearest and most important, in a position which implied full possession of episcopal authority. He was the Apostle's favourite; S. Paul not only calls him his true and beloved son, but his brother; he six times joins him with himself in the superscription of his Epistles, and says he has no other like-minded with him.‡ He gives over to him the full Apostolical authority he had used himself at Ephesus, as well over ministers as members of the Church; he was to rule and teach those confided to him, to arrange the solemnities of worship, not to allow women to teach in public. His office is to watch over the purity of the doctrine taught and himself to appoint trustworthy men for preaching it, to ordain bishops and deacons, to judge the qualifications of men for Church offices, and not 'lay hands suddenly on any man,' which implies the further right of deposing the unworthy from the ministry. It is also his duty to provide that fitting submission and reverence be paid to the ministers of the Church, to exercise jurisdiction, to examine and decide not only about laymen, but presbyters, and to impose proportionate punishments on offences. He is to denounce sinners publicly, that others may fear, and to show strict impartiality.§ The man clothed with such ample authority is still so young, that care must be taken that his youth be not despised. He is to admonish presbyters as fathers, to judge those who are themselves rulers, and, lastly— which shows how little S. Paul thought of a mere transitory office—he is to keep the Apostle's commandment unspotted and blameless till the return of Christ, that is, of course, he and his

* *Col.* iv. 17. † *Philem.* 2.
‡ *Rom.* xvi. 21; 1 *Cor.* iv. 17; 2 *Cor.* i. 1; *Phil.* i. 1; *Col.* i. 1; 1 *Thess.* iii. 2; *Phil.* ii. 20.
§ 1 *Tim.* iv. 11, i. 3, iii. 1, 2; 2 *Tim.* ii. 2; 1 *Tim.* v. 17, 19, 21.

successors in the Episcopate.* Tradition, accordingly, makes him the first Bishop of Ephesus; those who followed are called his successors, and, at the Council of Chalcedon, twenty-seven bishops of Ephesus from him were counted up.† He has been also regarded as an Apostolic delegate, one of a special class of ecclesiastical officers, but that does not prevent his being a bishop. The authority which S. Paul gave him, unless it had a defined and permanent character within a certain sphere, would have expired with the Apostle's death. The needs of the Church would indeed have been ill-provided for by mere delegates of dead men, and that, too, at a transition period from Apostolic to post-Apostolic times, when it needed a firm authority and a universally recognised ministry of superior teachers and pastors to maintain and hold together its communities against the violent and pertinacious assaults of heretical disorder. . . .

" S. Timothy, then, was Bishop of Ephesus, though not in such sense bound to that city and community as to be incapacitated from giving apostolical assistance in the neighbourhood also. S. Paul, left almost alone, summoned him to Rome, and promised to send him to Philippi on his return to Asia. He seems once to have been sent to Judæa.‡ It was a peculiarity of this transition period that apostolic legates became bishops, and bishops on occasion became legates again, as in later times also bishops often travelled on affairs of the Church. And the powers and commissions S. Paul gave his disciple extended over all pro-consular Asia, though Ephesus continued to be his regular place of residence. . . . Thus tradition makes S. Titus, at least latterly, Bishop of Gortyna, though S. Paul gave him charge of all the communities in Crete. Hence we see why there are no precepts or intimations in the Apostolic Epistles about the Church being guided by the collegiate action of the presbytery. . . . Diotrephes, who is mentioned in the Third Epistle of S. John, seems to have been in a position which must have been that of a bishop. In his domineering pride he forbids members of the Church to receive foreign brethren, and puts those who do so out of communion; he shows contempt for the Apostle himself, and S. John saw that he must come there in person to unmask him.§ In the

* 1 *Tim.* v. 1, 17, 19; vi. 14.
† Chrys. *Ep. ad Tim.* Photius Bibl. Cod. 254; Conc. Chalc. ap. Labb, iv. 699.
‡ *Heb.* xiii. 23. § S *John,* 9, 10.

Apocalypse the Episcopate appears clearly and unmistakably. The Lord sends written messages to the presidents of the seven Asiatic Churches, who are called in prophetic language 'angels,' or messengers of God. . . . The name comes nearest that of an Apostle, and is almost synonymous with it; those so called are messengers of God, who, as successors of the Apostles, have to proclaim God's will to the people. Christ calls these angels the seven stars in His right hand; their seven churches are symbolised by seven candlesticks distinct from the stars.* . . . The angels are always spoken of in the singular number, which is then first changed into the plural when the communities are spoken of.† . . . Thus the angel or bishop is always distinguished from the community. . . . These angels are praised for the good found in their churches, and made responsible for the abuses, which last, therefore, they have authority to put down. The angel at Philadelphia is promised that, although he has little power as yet, a portion of the unbelieving Jews shall kneel before him—either to make profession of faith at baptism, or to receive confirmation. Those in whose communities are Nicolaitans or Balaamites are sharply rebuked; they ought to have thrust these men out of the Church. Here, then, are seven bearers of Apostolical, now become Episcopal authority. S. John praises, blames, and threatens them, not in his own name, but in the name of the Lord, who Himself bids him write these letters. The Church of Ephesus which, when S. Paul took leave of it at Miletus, was under the guidance of several Elders and the superintendence of the Apostle, is now under a successor of S. Timothy, who is praised for having tried and rejected the false Apostles, and for hating the deeds of the Nicolaitans."‡

* *Apoc.* i. 16, 20; ii. 1.   † *Apoc.* ii. 13, 24.   ‡ *Ib.* pp. 130-142.

CHAPTER VII.

THE HISTORICAL FACT OF S. PETER'S ROMAN EPISCOPATE, IN RELATION TO THE DOGMA OF THE PRIMACY, AND TO ITS SUCCESSION IN THE BISHOPS OF ROME.

WHOEVER is persuaded from Holy Scripture and tradition that Christ our Lord conferred the Primacy upon S. Peter, with the intention that it should be perpetual in his Church—who, in other words, believes that there must be ever in the Church a successor by Divine right to S. Peter in the Primacy—will have no reasonable doubt at all as to who that successor is, but must acknowledge as certain that he can be no other than the Roman Pontiff. This follows by necessary consequence, and is at once self-evident. For, on the one hand, no one else has been ever held, or himself has ever claimed, to be S. Peter's successor in the Primacy, except the Bishop of Rome; whilst, on the other hand, all history and tradition is loud in witness to the universality both of such belief and claim in his regard.

That the Primacy conferred by Christ on S. Peter was by Divine right to be perpetual in the Church, or, what is the same thing, that S. Peter was always to have successors in his Primacy, is a divinely revealed article of Catholic Faith; and that the Roman Pontiff, and he alone, is the true successor of S. Peter in the Primacy is a Catholic truth which all are bound to believe, being defined by the Church, and, therefore, infallibly certain. From these two truths results the theological conclusion, also infallibly certain, that the Roman Pontiff holds the Primacy by Divine right.

But around this last Catholic truth, namely, that the Bishop of Rome has S. Peter's Primacy by Divine right, is found a double group of questions, affording matter for theological discussion.

The questions in the first group concern the relation that the historical fact of S. Peter's Roman Episcopate bears to what is of Catholic dogma, viz., his Primacy and its actual succession in the line of Roman Pontiffs; that is to say, how far the verification of these dogmatic truths depends upon the reality of that fact.

The questions in the second group regard the conditions of the same succession, and the nature of the right, whether human or Divine, whereby the Primacy is attached to the Roman See. These latter questions are not concerned immediately with any dogma of Faith, but with points that are of open controversy amongst Catholic theologians.

The questions in the first group are: (1) Was S. Peter ever at Rome? (2) Did he die there? (3) Was he Bishop of Rome? (4) Did he hold the episcopate until his death?

It will, no doubt, at first sight appear strange that we should institute an inquiry here into these questions, since the answer we give to them is already known, and the very thesis we have undertaken to prove in these pages is, that the Apostle Peter went to Rome, preached and founded the Church there, was Bishop of Rome, and held the episcopate until his death, which was crowned in that city by a glorious martyrdom; and this thesis we claim to have demonstrated as certain by the testimony of history and other proofs.

We must premise, then, that, in our present discussion, we are not now viewing these questions in their material aspect as simple facts of history; but, following the teaching of approved theologians, are testing their formal import and doctrinal value in relation to the dogma of the Primacy, and their intrinsic bearing on that dogma, that thus we may ascertain whether or not their affirmation is essential, or how far necessary and important for the establishment of what may be termed the dogmatic fact that the Roman Pontiffs are *de facto* the true successors of S. Peter, and possess the Primacy by Divine right.

Some authors appear to think that all the above four questions must necessarily be affirmed, as vital to the Primacy of the Roman Pontiffs: whilst others, more generally and with better reason, are of opinion that it is enough to affirm the two last alone in order to prove that the Bishops of Rome are possessed of the Primacy by their succession to S. Peter's See. For S. Peter might, in point of fact, have been true Bishop of Rome, though he never set foot in that city; as we know was the case with several Popes—*e.g.*, Clement V., John XXII., Clement VI., and Innocent VI., who were consecrated in France, and always remained there. And still less was it necessary for S. Peter's Roman Episcopate that he should have died in Rome. Many Popes and Bishops have died away from their Sees.

But we may go yet further and say that for the Roman Pontiffs to be the true successors of S. Peter in his Primacy, strictly and absolutely speaking, there was no intrinsic reason to necessitate S. Peter's being Bishop of Rome, or indeed his holding any episcopal See at all; and still less his holding the Roman Episcopate until death.

But here it should be borne in mind that we are not adverting to such a hypothesis, as though it were even colourably probable, either in the light of history or theology. We shall appraise later on the various propositions implied in the affirmation or negation of the several questions, according to their theological value. It appears, moreover, plain to reason, that for the Bishops of Rome to succeed to S. Peter's Primacy otherwise than as they do in fact—namely, through succession to his See—would, in the actual order established in Christ's Church, be strangely incongruous and abnormal, and, consequently, too improbable to deserve any serious consideration. We mention this hypothesis here with the simple view of ascertaining what is, and what is not, intrinsically necessary to establish the fact that the Roman Pontiffs are S. Peter's successors in the Primacy, and for a well-grounded belief in that fact. For we can easily conceive the case of some one believing firmly the Catholic verities, that the Primacy conferred on Peter was by the will of Christ to be perpetual in His Church, and that the Roman Pontiffs are the actual successors of S. Peter in that Primacy, *jure divino*, who yet is ignorant, or unconvinced by historical evidence, of the fact, either that S. Peter was ever Bishop of Rome, that he was so until his death, or that he had held an episcopal See at all: and still this ignorance or scepticism might exist without any infringement on his faith. It was through some such misconception of fact that the author of the *Clementines*, whilst testifying both to the Primacy and to its succession, seemingly makes S. Peter abdicate both his episcopate and his Primacy before his death in favour of S. Clement. And many good Christians, though fully beliving in the Papal Primacy, may never have heard at all of the fact that S. Peter was Bishop of Rome. We think it well to bring this point into prominence, because its consideration may serve at once to explain a difficulty and to dissipate an error.

A difficulty sometimes arises, when it is found how comparatively very few are the direct testimonies of early Fathers to the Roman Episcopate of S. Peter, and with what little stress the fact when mentioned is insisted upon in their writings. We admit this, though we hold, at the same time, that the surviving testimony found in antiquity is amply sufficient to prove with full certainty the historical reality of the fact. But we observe that alongside of this comparative barrenness there is contrariwise a corresponding abundance. We mean, that if direct testimonies to S. Peter's Roman Episcopate in the earlier Fathers are few and scanty, still in their writings we meet with multiplied testimonies to the truth of Peter's Primacy, and manifold evidences of the fact and belief that the Roman Pontiffs were S. Peter's successors and exercised his Primacy. So that passing in review the Fathers of the three first centuries, and especially the more early of these, we discover many more proofs that the Bishops of Rome were S. Peter's successors in the Primacy than that S. Peter was himself ever Bishop of Rome. And what does all this tend to show? But that a firm belief of the former truth was quite independent, so to say, of any explicit and historical knowledge and conviction of the latter fact; or rather that belief in the Roman Pontiff's succession to Peter's Primacy does not rest for its formal and essential basis on the persuasion of the actuality of S. Peter's Roman Episcopate. The faithful of those days believed on the testimony of God's word, as delivered by the Church, that the Primacy was conferred by Christ on S. Peter, and was to remain in perpetuity; and on the same testimony they believed that the Roman Pontiff succeeded to Peter in that Primacy. On this last point, moreover, their own reason, and their personal sensible experience, came in to confirm their faith, since they were well aware that no other was ever reported, believed, or himself claimed to be successor of S. Peter and universal Primate but the Bishop of Rome. The other truth—a fact of common notoriety—that S. Peter was himself also Bishop of Rome, whilst it served to explain the mode of succession, did not necessarily enter into the proof or belief of the rightful—i.e., *jure divino*—succession itself. It was an interesting historical fact, rather than one of doctrine; and hence we may easily understand how it came to be in those early doctrinal times a matter of less frequent record and insistence.

In consequence of the Protestant denial of S. Peter's Roman Episcopate, with the view to a further denial of all else that concerns the Petrine privilege, this question has assumed a more distinctively doctrinal character, whilst, at the same time, its dogmatic value, as intrinsically bearing on what is properly of faith, has been, perhaps both on one side and the other, much over-rated. If Protestants were only more logical in their argument, and more consistent to their professed principles, they would see that the question whether or not S. Peter was Bishop of Rome had no real weight nor any vital importance in their controversy with Catholics on the Papal claims, but that it is a mere side question, non-essential to the main issue. The one point they have to determine is, What saith the Scripture on these two questions? First, did or did not Christ confer on S. Peter an office of Primacy? and secondly, was it, or was it not, His will that such office should be permanent in His Church? In other words, Was S. Peter to have successors in his Primacy? On the answer given to these two questions depends alone, so far as Protestants are concerned, the whole issue of the controversy respecting the Papal claims. If they decide the questions from Scripture negatively, then their doctrinal controversy with Catholics is at an end, and no view that may be taken of the historical question, whether S. Peter was Bishop of Rome, can afford any ground for re-opening the discussion on the score of doctrine. Should their answer to the Scripture questions be affirmative—and they are logical and honest—then there is nothing for them but to confess that the Roman Pontiff is the true successor of S. Peter in the Primacy. For since our Divine Lord willed that Peter should have a successor, and His will must needs have effect, there is necessarily, in point of fact, such a successor, and he can be no other than the Bishop of Rome, for no one else but he ever himself claimed, or was claimed by others, to be Peter's successor in the Primacy; whereas he, on his part, has ever set forth such claim, and such claim has been ever made by others in his behalf. And from these premisses, we say, it follows rigorously, as a necessary truth, naturally evident to all who can use their reason, that the Bishop of Rome, and he alone, is S. Peter's true successor, and has the Primacy. But here, let us observe, the reasoning is complete and the conclusion peremptory, without the point of S. Peter's Roman Episcopate being any factor in the argument. It is, therefore, simply to evade and obscure the main issue, and to throw dust in people's eyes, for Protestant controversialists to go off on such side questions as whether or not S. Peter was Bishop of Rome.

The question has, indeed, a certain controversial value for Catholics, though this is accidental and of a merely presumptive and confirmatory nature; for the demonstration of S. Peter's Roman Episcopate affords, on the one hand, a fair presumption that his successors in that See inherit his prerogatives; whilst, on the other hand, the Catholic demonstration from revelation and reason of the Roman Pontiff's succession to Peter's Primacy receives some confirmation from the historical fact that he was himself also Bishop of Rome. But in either case it is necessary to prove first S. Peter's Primacy, and its perpetuity by divine right, in order that the argument drawn from his episcopate should have any real force in controversy.

From what we have said, it follows, that because Protestants may hold S. Peter's Roman Episcopate to be not proven, or even disproved, they have no right thence to infer as a consequence the nullity of the Papal claims; since the Roman Primacy is a doctrinal question, the truth of which depends on Divine revelation, and, as such, is unaffected alike by the affirmation or the denial of the historical question of S. Peter's episcopate. Consequently, their refusal to affirm, or their failure to recognise, the proofs of that episcopate, as a fact of history, does not give them, either on logical or on theological grounds, any justifying plea for denying or ignoring what Catholics claim to be a truth of revelation.

Again, it follows also from our argument, that the admission on the part of Protestants of the historical fact, that S. Peter was Bishop of Rome, would not of itself afford them any sufficient or logical ground for their thence concluding either that S. Peter received the Primacy from Christ, or that the Roman Pontiffs have succeeded to it; though certainly, we think, such a persuasion should, in reason, help them towards a right conviction of the Catholic truth. For, on one side, it is clear that S. Peter might have been Bishop of Rome without having received from Christ any office of Primacy; and it is evident, on the other, that succession to Peter's Primacy by no means *of itself* follows, as a necessary consequence, from simple succession to Peter's See. For that matter, we know, many learned Protestants have maintained as indubitable, both that S. Peter was Bishop of Rome, and that the Roman Pontiffs are his successors in that See, whilst they have, at the same time, strenuously contested any right to Primacy on the part of S. Peter, or of the Roman Pontiffs.

We have made this polemical digression in order to test the real value to Protestants of the question of S. Peter's Roman Episcopate in their controversy with Catholics on the Papal claims, and we have seen that it is here of no material value at all; though, generally, very erroneously they think otherwise.*

---

* Thus, a well-known ultra-Protestant controversialist, before alluded to, with his usual great shallowness and assurance, flippantly pronounces:

What alone can avail them in their contention is to disprove the Catholic argument from Scripture, and from thence to prove its direct contrary—viz., that no office of Primacy was conferred on S. Peter by Christ to be by His will perpetual in the Church. Failing to do this, they have no other reasonable choice than to confess the Primacy by Divine right of the Roman Pontiff, since otherwise they must assert that, whilst *de facto* there ever exists, according to Christ's institution, a supreme visible head in the Church, yet that she has not only never recognised nor known him, but has continually acknowledged, in his stead, one that is false and fictitious. Another alternative, indeed, still remains—namely, for them to affirm that our Divine Lord's promise of a perpetual Primacy to His Church has been unfulfilled, and consequently that both His will and His words have proved to be of no effect.

The sum, then, of our present inquiry into the questions proposed is, that the historical facts implied therein have intrinsically no necessary connection either with S. Peter's Primacy, nor with its succession in the Roman Pontiffs. Not with his Primacy; for S. Peter had received and exercised the Primacy before his entrance upon the Roman Episcopate, and would have continued its exercise had he never been Bishop of any particular See at all. Not with the succession of the Roman Pontiffs to the Primacy; for it is quite conceivable that they might have become the *de facto* true (that is, *jure divino*) successors to S. Peter's Primacy in some other way than by succession to S. Peter's Episcopal See, and without his ever having been himself Bishop of Rome. Their legitimate succession to the Primacy might, for instance, have been consequent on the exercise of power possessed by S. Peter to determine that the Bishops of such or such a See (in the case, that of Rome) should, by the very fact of their lawful election to that See, be his true successors in the Primacy. Thus the Roman See would be the Primatial See, even though S. Peter had never himself held that See.

We must bear in mind that the whole matter of the legitimate succession to the Primacy is one of Divine positive law, depending on the Divine Will. Hence, God might have left it entirely to S. Peter to choose himself the Episcopal See to which the Primacy was to be attached, or He might have expressly intimated to him

---

"If all these points," of which ours is one, "be not clearly proved by plain and convincing Scriptural and historical evidence, there is no basis whatever for the huge fabric of Papal claims, which is, in truth, the most vague and uncertain of structures."

the particular See in which He willed it to be permanent; and in either case, all that S. Peter had to do would be to carry into effect the Divine Will.

From what we have said, it is clear that whilst the several points under discussion, regarding S. Peter's Roman Episcopate, are to be affirmed as certainly true if weighed in the balance of history, tradition, and the universal belief of the faithful; yet that these same historical facts, considered doctrinally in their intrinsic and formal relation to what is of Divine Faith and Catholic teaching, are not of essential, but only of accidental moment, and, consequently, are of no vital importance in the doctrinal controversy with Protestants on S. Peter's Primacy and its succession in the Roman Pontiffs.

If these several points, considered simply as historical facts, are weighed in the balance of Theology, and by the standard of Faith, there is no doubt at all as to their affirmation, and that such affirmation is certainly true, since it has received the sanction of the Church's teaching, if not of her express definition.

First, that S. Peter was at Rome, and, secondly, that he was martyred there, are facts in many ways expressly taught by the Church. The first proposition is necessarily included in the second, as well as (so, at least, it should seem) in the affirmation of the fact that the Church of Rome was founded by S. Peter.

Now, that S. Peter founded the Roman Church and suffered martyrdom at Rome are facts witnessed to by universal tradition from the beginning of the Church; they have their place in her Liturgy, and their truth is frequently attested in authoritative documents of Popes and Councils, and notably by the Vatican Council in the following passage:*

"Nulli sane dubium, imo sæculis omnibus notum est, quod sanctus beatissimusque Petrus, Apostolorum Princeps et Caput, fideique columna et Ecclesiæ Catholicæ fundamentum, a Domino Nostro Jesu Christo, Salvatore humani generis ac Redemptore, claves regni accepit: qui ad hoc usque tempus et semper in suis successoribus, episcopis sanctæ Romanæ Sedis, *ab ipso fundatæ, ejusque consecratæ sanguine* vivit, et præsidet, et judicium exercet."

Hence we should gather that the propositions denying that S. Peter was ever at Rome and that he suffered martyrdom there, would be branded as "scandalous, impious, and savouring of heresy."

* *Constitutio Dogmatica Prima De Ecclesia Christi.* cap. ii.

That, thirdly, S. Peter was Bishop of Rome is not only a most certain historical fact, but to be affirmed also as a truth appertaining to the Faith, so far as it has been implicitly defined by the Church; hence it cannot be denied without manifold notes of censure. The General Council of Florence thus decreed:

"We define ... that the Roman Pontiff is the successor of Blessed Peter;"

and that of the Vatican thus renews the decree:

"Si quis dixerit ... Romanum Pontificem non esse beati Petri in eodem primatu successorem: anathema sit."

Now, as theologians teach, the succession to the Primacy here spoken of is, according to the obvious and primary sense of the words, to be understood as being an episcopal succession to Peter in the Roman See. For it is defined that the Bishop of Rome, as such, is S. Peter's successor. But it is clear that there cannot be here this episcopal succession of the line of Roman Pontiffs, unless S. Peter was himself also Bishop of Rome. Hence it is held to be implicitly defined that S. Peter was Bishop of Rome, and that he fixed the Primacy in the Roman See. And whatever is thus implicitly and equivalently defined belongs, by the very fact, to the Faith, and cannot be denied without detriment to the Faith. We are of opinion, therefore, that such a denial would be censured as "savouring of heresy."

Fourthly, that S. Peter was Bishop of Rome up to the time of his death is most certain as a historical fact. To deny it would not only be a grave error in matter of history, but would be opposed to the general sense and tradition of the Church. That S. Peter died Bishop of Rome is, moreover, held to be a condition in the legitimate title of the Roman Pontiffs' true succession to him in that See,—a succession which, as we have already seen, has been implicitly defined by the Church. The denial, then, of the proposition in question would, we think, be stigmatised as at least "false and temerarious."

CHAPTER VIII.

THE NATURE AND RIGHT OF THE PRIMACY AND ITS SUCCESSION, AS CONNECTED WITH THE SEE OF ROME.

WE considered in the last Chapter those several questions of fact that group round S. Peter's Roman Episcopate as their centre, and form with it one complex whole in their relation to the Primacy and its possession by the Roman Pontiffs (S. Peter's *de facto* true successors), in order to test the theological value of these historical facts in their intrinsic bearing upon those dogmatic truths.

We have now to deal with a second series of questions which regard not the succession itself, but the conditions and right of the succession, and the precise relation that S. Peter's Primacy and its succession bear to the particular See of Rome.

1. How came it to pass that S. Peter elected Rome in particular for his own Episcopal See? Was this of his own choice, or in consequence of a Divine decree?

2. Was the fixing on Rome as the See for S. Peter's successors in the Primacy an act simply of S. Peter's own decision and free choice? Or, was it in virtue of an express Divine revelation to that effect?

3. Is the See of Rome attached to the Primacy in such sense that S. Peter's successor in the Primacy must necessarily be Bishop of Rome? In other words, does the Roman Pontiff, as such, succeed to S. Peter's Primacy by Divine right?

4. Could the Roman Pontiff in some urgent necessity validly separate the Primacy from the See and Episcopate of Rome and attach it to another See?

5. Wherein does the relation between S. Peter's Roman Episcopate and his universal Pontificate essentially consist?

The foregoing questions concerning the relation of the Roman See to the Primacy are here proposed separately, in order to give a more clear understanding in detail of the several points that enter into the whole matter of the condition and right of the

Roman Pontiff's succession; but for the sake of brevity, and because these questions run very much one into the other, we shall, with the exception of the two last, treat them collectively all together.

Before, however, we enter into our subject we think it well to make some preliminary observations.

These are not questions of faith, but are open to discussion amongst Catholic theologians. The succession, as Bellarmine says, is one thing; the reason of the succession (*ratio successionis*) another. The succession itself is of Christ's institution, and of Divine right, because Christ Himself constituted the Primacy in Peter to endure in the Church until the end of the world. Consequently, according to the institution and by the will of Christ, there must needs always actually be in the Church a true successor of S. Peter, and whoever is such receives the Primacy from Christ Himself. The Church, moreover, is both able and bound, according to Christ's institution and will, to acknowledge the true successor of S. Peter as her supreme head and infallible teacher.[*] All these are truths of revelation, and to be believed of Divine faith. But as a matter of fact, no one else is claimed to be S. Peter's successor, nor does so succeed, save the Roman Pontiff, whilst he, and he alone, is, and has ever been, acknowledged by the whole Church as S. Peter's successor; consequently, the Roman Pontiff, and he alone, is S. Peter's true successor, and as such receives the Primacy from Christ Himself. In other words, he is supreme pastor in succession to S. Peter *jure divino*, and according to Christ's institution. This is a theological conclusion whose premisses are, first, the revealed truth of the perpetual Primacy instituted by Christ Himself which the Church has formally defined, and, secondly, a necessary truth that is naturally known, and forms the subject-matter of tradition and history. This conclusion is itself, too, a Catholic truth defined by the Church in the Councils of Florence and the Vatican; and hence, whoever denies it is constructively a heretic: for, if asked why he denies it, he would have to answer either

---

[*] It is evident, and stands to reason, that since the Church is "the pillar and ground of the truth" (1 *Tim*. iii. 15), she cannot be deceived so as universally to believe and teach as true anything that is really false. But for her to err in what concerns the true visible rule of her faith, that is, in regard to her supreme pastor and infallible teacher, would be still more injurious to her than to err with regard to particular doctrines; since this would be to err in the very foundation of her faith. *De Lugo*, disp. i. n. 828; Mazzella, *De Virtut. Infusis*, disp. ii. n. 500.

that the Church has erred in defining it, or that she has no right to define it; and both one and the other of these assertions contradict the revealed truth that the Church is infallible in her teaching on what concerns the guardianship and defence of the deposit of faith.

To say, then, that the Popes are S. Peter's true successors, and have the Primacy by Divine right, is to assert a Catholic truth that has been defined by the Church and belongs to her faith.

But to say, further, that the Popes are S. Peter's true successors, and have the Primacy by Divine right, for the very reason that they are the Bishops of Rome, in other words, because as such they succeed to S. Peter by Divine right, is an affirmation that does not belong to the faith; for it cannot be certainly shown that this was in any way revealed, nor has the Church defined it as a truth.

Whilst, then, the succession itself is revealed and defined as of Christ's institution, the reason and conditions of the succession are not so revealed nor defined. What was Christ's institution and will was that Peter should have a true succession, and thereby He consequently instituted and willed that he in whom were verified the conditions of a true succession should actually be, and should be acknowledged to be, Peter's true successor; but so far as Christ's institution in the Gospel is concerned, He did not determine what were to be the conditions *in concreto* of such true succession, but left all this to the determination of S. Peter and his successors; nor can it be shown that S. Peter afterwards received any express revelation or Divine command on this matter.

Hence, so far as we know what was revealed and of Christ's institution, S. Peter might have never chosen any episcopal See at all, nor have made any special provision for his succession, in which case there would have been no particular bishop to succeed him at his death, but his successor would have been chosen by the whole Church; or, had he died in the See of Antioch, then the Bishop of Antioch would have been his successor. This, however, was not the way in which, through Divine Providence, the mode and conditions of the succession to the Primacy were actually determined, for it came to pass that S. Peter was led to found the See of Rome, and by the fact of his holding that See until his death, he showed plainly to the whole Church where his succession was to be found; and thus in the

Bishops of Rome who succeed to the See of Peter the will and institution of Christ are fully verified: they are the true successors of Peter, and, as such, have the Primacy *jure divino*.

Hence, so far as Divine revelation and the teaching of the Church discover to us, the fact of S. Peter's Roman Episcopate and of his succession in that See is due not to any positive institution of Christ, but to the action of Peter himself; and, consequently, the whole question of the conditions of the succession, that is, why the See of Rome specially, more than any other See, is the seat of the Primacy, and its bishops specially are S. Peter's successors—whether they are so precisely because they are Bishops of Rome, and whether this is of human or of Divine right—forms a moot point in Catholic theology. In other words, it is an open question amongst theologians whether, or how far, the *de facto* connection that exists between the See of Rome and the Primacy was due exclusively to the personal act of S. Peter, or whether this was also in virtue of an express revelation or Divine command made to S. Peter to that effect. For, whilst theologians are generally agreed that nothing here can be known with any certainty as revealed or defined by the Church, they have yet formed various opinions on the question, and these are held in the Schools as more or less solidly probable.

Before we propose for consideration these several theological opinions, let us first note the different ways in which the act of constituting the succession to the Primacy may be conceived as taking effect.*

1. The first way, then, would be if God had ordained that S. Peter should hold no particular See, and that on his death the Church was to have the power to choose whom it willed to succeed him in his Primacy. In this case the succession of the Popes to the Primacy would have no more necessary connection with the Roman See than with any other. This was, certainly, not the way in which the succession was settled, and we only mention it as an *a priori* conceivable hypothesis.

2. A second way would be, if S. Peter of his own will—directed, indeed, by such secret Divine influence only as God on many other occasions in His Church is wont to vouchsafe, but without any express revelation or command on His part—had chosen for himself a particular See, that, namely, of Rome, and settled at the same time, simply by his own act, that whoever should suc-

---

* See Murray, *De Ecclesia Christi*, vol. iii., for the matter here.

ceed at his death to that See, viz., the Roman Pontiff, should be also his successor in the Primacy.

On this hypothesis the Roman Pontiff might, absolutely speaking, transfer the Primatial See to another city or diocese. For he has all the jurisdiction that S. Peter had. Consequently, if S. Peter, without any Divine mandate to that effect, could of his own will alone choose the particular See of Rome and settle the succession to the Primacy in that See, by the same right any other Supreme Pontiff might take another than the Roman See, and place therein the Primatial succession. According to this hypothesis—all relation *jure divino* of succession to the Primacy with the See of Rome being excluded by the very terms—the connection is affirmed to be of purely human appointment; and hence, we say, it would be within the absolute power of the Pope to transfer the Primacy in some very extreme and urgent necessity to another See.

3. We may suppose, thirdly, that—whether or not S. Peter received a Divine command to choose Rome for his See—Christ made the succession of the Roman Pontiffs to the Primacy to depend in the last result upon the condition that S. Peter so willed and determined it. In this case the connection of the Primacy with the Roman See being mediately at least the act of Christ, would be in a true sense *jure divino*.

4. Or, again, if Christ had left it free to S. Peter to choose his own See (his actual choice being that of Rome), signifying at the same time His will that the Primacy was to pass in perpetuity to the Bishops who should succeed after his death to the See which he definitely chose for himself,—in this way, though the selection of the See of Rome would be the free act of S. Peter, the Roman Pontiffs would succeed, as such, to the Primacy in virtue of the express will of Christ Himself; that is, *jure divino*.

5. The fifth and last mode of succession would be, if Christ had not only ordained that S. Peter should have some episcopal See, but, moreover, had positively revealed to him His will that he should take the particular See of Rome, and that the bishops who should succeed him in this same See were to be his successors in the Primacy. In this case it would be of faith that the Bishop of Rome, as such, is S. Peter's successor *jure divino;* in other words, that the Primacy is attached to the Roman See by Divine right.

The opinions of theologians founded on these several hypotheses may be here summarily reduced to three.

The first is of those who maintain that the connection of the Primacy and its succession with the Roman See was a purely human act depending solely on the will of S. Peter; whence it would follow that the Primacy might, at least absolutely speaking, be transferred to some other See. This opinion is generally considered, for many grave reasons, to be void of solid probability, and, though not condemned, is held to be erroneous, as opposed to the mind and sense of the Church. All theologians of any note are agreed in holding as certain that the connection of the Primacy with the Roman See was not exclusively the act of Peter, but was also some way dependent, in a true sense, on the Divine Will.

The second opinion is of those who defend the third or fourth mode of succession; whereby, though certain acts in the process were left to the free choice of S. Peter, yet the succession to the Primacy by the Roman Pontiffs, as such, was eventually, and, regarded in the whole result, a Divine act consequent on the will of Christ, and thus *jure divino*. This opinion has several theologians of great name in its support.

The third opinion is of those who defend the fifth mode of succession, and affirm that S. Peter received by special revelation a Divine command to undertake the Roman Episcopate, and to settle the succession to his Primacy in the See of Rome. This opinion is held either as the more probable one, or even as certain, by the greater number of theologians of eminence, and is supported by most weighty arguments.

It must, however, be borne in mind that, however solidly probable on other grounds this opinion may be, no certain proof can be shown of the fact of such Divine revelation having been made to S. Peter, and that the Church has defined nothing on this particular matter. It consequently remains an open question.

What the Church has defined is the fact that the Roman Pontiff is S. Peter's true successor and has the Primacy. This is a Catholic truth of necessity to be believed by all, and infallibly certain: whence it follows that the See of Rome is the mother and mistress of all Churches.

"Item definimus Sanctam Apostolicam Sedem et Romanum Pontificem in universum orbem tenere primatum, et ipsum Pontificem Romanum successorem esse Beati Petri, principis Apostolorum, et verum Christi Vicarium, totiusque Ecclesiæ caput, . . . et ipsi in Beato Petro pascendi, regendi, et gubernandi universalem Ecclesiam a Domino Nostro Jesu Christo plenam potestatem traditam esse."*

* Conc. Flor. *Sess. ult. Def. Labb.* p. 2, *collat.* 22.

"... Unde quicumque in hac (Romana) Cathedra Petro succedit, is secundum Christi ipsius institutionem, primatum Petri in universam Ecclesiam obtinet.... Si quis ergo dixerit... Romanum Pontificem non esse Beati Petri in eodem primatu successorem, anathema sit."*

Here the questions might be raised, whether S. Peter by Divine appointment united the Primacy to Rome in perpetuity; whether in the Divine disposition was implied the promise that the Bishopric of Rome should remain always; whether, again, since the particular disposition was one of Divine positive law, made for the benefit of the Church, the Supreme Pontiff might not, as the Vicar of Christ, otherwise dispose for the good of the Church in a case of most evident grave necessity, and when such disposition ceased to be beneficial. Considering the special Divine Providence, and its manifestation in the past, with regard to the Holy See, the destruction of the Bishopric of Rome is indeed most improbable in the future. Still, it is an event within the sphere of possibility, and there does not appear to be any such certain, positive, and absolute guarantee for its perpetual permanence as there is for that of the Catholic Church itself. Hence, theologians have supposed the extreme case of the extinction both of the city and See of Rome; and here their opinions are divided. Some think that the Pope would then be bound to content himself with the title, together with the right of ruling the Roman See, should it be again revived—much the same as in the case of titular bishops *in partibus infidelium;* and that this would suffice for the actual succession of the Roman Pontiffs, as such, to the Primacy, since the title and right would still survive: so that whoever succeeded thereto would, as S. Peter's legitimate successor, have the Primacy over the universal Church. Other theologians incline to hold that, in such a case, a transfer of the Primacy to another See that the Pope might choose would be within the rights of the Vicar of Jesus Christ.

In the above Decrees, as has been before said,† it is implicitly and equivalently defined that S. Peter was himself Bishop of Rome, and that he attached his Primacy to the Roman See: and thus, so far, the Church has pronounced on the part that S. Peter bore in this act, but she has made no pronouncement as to whether it was also a positive act of the Divine Will; and, if so, in what way, or to what extent, this had effect—that is to say, whether the connection is *jure divino*.

* Concil. Vatican, *Constitut.* " Pastor æternus," cap. ii. † Ch. vii. p. 277.

Even granting that the union of the Primacy with the Roman See is *jure divino*, the particular question may still be raised: whether a Pope, in some evidently most grave and urgent necessity, could validly separate the Primacy from the See of Rome. The solution here is no easy one, and grave theologians may be cited on either side. It seems certainly to be the sentiment of the Church, that the very fact of the union made by S. Peter of the Primacy with the Roman See affords a sufficient guarantee for the perpetuity of that See to the end. Occasions, moreover, have occurred which seemed urgently to demand the removal from Rome of the Pontifical See, if that were possible; and yet no such transfer was ever contemplated by any Pope. Nevertheless, what may be the absolute power of the Supreme Pontiff in such a case must depend entirely on the nature and extent of the exercise of the Divine Will—whether, for instance, this were absolute, or anywise conditional—in that act whereby the Primacy was united to the Roman See.

Theologians, however, hesitate to express their opinion, for one side or the other, decisively on this matter; and most probably the sentiment of the Church will not be set forth more explicitly until events should render the question some way practical. As it is, we may not only piously believe that Rome and the Roman Church will continue even to the end of the world, but we may hold this, with good reason, as morally certain; especially if, with most theologians, we believe it to have been by the Divine appointment of Christ Himself that the Primacy is attached to the See of Rome.

It is here to the purpose to give the teaching on this question of Pius IX., of holy and glorious memory, in the Syllabus annexed to his celebrated Encyclical *Quanta Cura*, 8th December, 1864, in which the following proposition was condemned:

"There is nothing to prevent the transfer of the Roman Bishop and of the Church of Rome to another bishop and another city, whether (this be done) by a decree of a General Council* or by the action of all the peoples."

Before entering upon our next point, we shall offer some words of S. Alphonsus, which bear upon the matters which we have already discussed. The holy Doctor says:

"Hence God has given us a rule to know the true Church: for this Church is no other than that one whose Head descends by a legitimate succession from the Apostle Peter. It is thus the holy Fathers describe the

---

* We presume that the term "General Council" is here used in the sense of the maintainers of the proposition; *i.e.*, a General Council unratified by the Pope.

true Church of Jesus Christ... 'Thou canst not deny,' writes S. Optatus to Parmenian, 'that thou knowest that the Episcopal See in the city of Rome was first conferred on Peter, wherein sat Peter, the head of all the Apostles ... to Peter succeeded Linus,' &c.... Hence we see that the Roman Pontiff was always acknowledged to be S. Peter's successor, and consequently the Vicar of Christ and Supreme Head of the Church.... Personal residence in the Church of Rome does not belong to the essence of pontifical jurisdiction. ... The learned are not agreed on the question whether the universal Primacy of the Church is annexed by human right, or by Divine right, to the Roman Episcopate. In any case it is certain that, since the death of S. Peter, who fixed his pontificate in the See of Rome, it has never been, and never will be, lawful, not even for the whole Church, to assign the succession of S. Peter to another bishop than that of Rome, by separating the episcopal authority of Rome from the pontifical authority; since this would be to interrupt the succession of the Roman Bishops, by means of which the faithful, guided by the holy Fathers, have ever recognised the succession of the power of S. Peter."*

We now come to the question : In what does the relation between S. Peter's Roman Episcopate and his universal Pontificate essentially consist ? Here theologians hold unanimously that the Roman Episcopate and the Ecumenical Episcopate are not really two episcopates, but that the Roman Episcopate was constituted, and is, a universal episcopate, just as a simple bishopric might be made an archbishopric. Cardinal Cajetan seems to treat the subject more lucidly than perhaps other theologians. In the lengthened extracts which we here make from his treatise,† not only is the particular point in question well explained, but further light is thrown on the matters which we have already discussed.

Cajetan first, then (in Chapter vii.), lays down the principle that Christ founded His own, whole, one, only Church on the one rock of Peter ; and, in order to bring this truth out clearly, he thus comments on the words : "Upon this rock I will build my Church : " ‡

"Christ did not say My Churches, but 'My Church,' to emphasise its unicity, or oneness, and to show that He was not speaking distributively of His Church in parts, but of his entire Church as one single whole. Nor did He speak indefinitely : in the sense of 'My Church,' whatever this may be, leaving it for men to find out for themselves which that one was that should be built upon this rock ; as when at the Last Supper He said : 'One of you shall betray Me,' and then left it doubtful who that one

* *Verità della Fede*, part iii. c. viii. 3, 4, 8.
† *Opusc*. iii. *De Institutione div. Pontificatus*. ‡ *Matt*. xvi. 18.

was. But His words here assure us that His own, one, only, and entire Church (as a single unit), and this alone and exclusively, is built upon this one rock. So that, in saying 'My Church,' He would have us hereby clearly understand that one, whole, and only Church of Christ which is spoken of in the Creed, that is, the One Catholic Church; and that this Church He was to build on one rock, that is, on Peter.

"Every particular Church may, indeed, be called Christ's Church, but with some addition; as, for example, the Roman the Antiochene, the Constantinopolitan, the Corinthian Churches. Every true Church, moreover, may be said to be built on Peter, and is verified as in reality Christ's, by reason of its being thus built upon Peter; but it is both one and the other as a part only; whereas the Catholic Church is Christ's, and built on Peter as a whole. Consequently, if the Roman Church is specially and emphatically said to be built on Peter, this is because, in such case, that Church is either taken for the Catholic Church, and then it is simply a question of change of names : or the Roman Church is so spoken of by appropriation, and not in strict propriety; since, literally, the words, 'My Church built upon the rock,' are properly verified only in Christ's one entire Church, wherein all particular Churches are included, as parts are in a whole.

"But here," he says, "we should well note that the Roman Church differs from all other particular Churches, by its close and intimate relation with the Head of the Catholic Church : since its own particular head is not only united to, but identical with, the Head of the Catholic Church; for, from the fact of Peter, the Bishop of Rome and the Supreme Pontiff of the Catholic Church are one and the same person; and thus the Roman Church, considered in itself, is immediately united to the Supreme Head of the Catholic Church. Now, no other particular Church whatsoever, whether considered in itself, is thus immediately connected with the Chief Pastor of Christ's Church; nor, if regarded in its own particular head, has it one identical with the Head of the Catholic Church. By reason, then, of this close and intimate relation of the Roman Church to the Supreme Head and Pastor of the Catholic Church, the words of Christ are rightly appropriated to the Roman Church rather than to any other—not, indeed, that they are, in a strict sense, proper to it, but to the Catholic Church alone, as has been already explained."

In Chapter xii. ("Peter by Christ's institution has a successor in the Pontificate of the Catholic Church ") the learned Cardinal says :

"Catholics and schismatics agree that Peter was Prince of the Apostles, and was Bishop of Rome just as James the Apostle was Bishop of Jerusalem, and that, consequently, all the Bishops of Rome are Peter's successors in the episcopate of the Roman Church, in the same way that all the Bishops of Jerusalem are successors of James in the bishopric of Jerusalem. They agree, also, that the Bishops of Jerusalem succeeded James in the episcopate only, and not in Apostolical authority. But here at once they part company and disagree: schismatics maintaining, on the one hand, that the Bishop of Rome succeeds S. Peter in the Roman Episcopate only; whilst Catholics, on the contrary, affirm that he succeeds to Peter not only in his Episcopate, but also in his Pontificate of the Catholic Church.

"Two things have, then, to be settled : (1) that Peter had by Divine right a successor in the Pontificate of the Catholic Church ; and (2) that this successor is the Bishop of Rome. . . ."

Having proved the first point, which was the matter of Chapter xii., Cajetan, in Chapter xiii. (" The Roman Pontiff is Peter's successor in the Pontificate of the whole Church "), proposes two questions :

"(1) Whence comes it that the Roman Pontiff should be Peter's successor in his Primacy? and (2) How is it known that the Bishop of Rome is thus Peter's successor ?

"With regard to the former, we must clearly distinguish two things : first, Peter's having a successor at all ; and, secondly, Who, in point of fact, is his rightful successor?

"The first is contained in our Lord's institution recorded in the Gospels, whereby He founded in Peter the permanent office of a Supreme Pastorate over His whole Church—as was already proved. But the second point : Who Peter's successor is, is not one of Divine institution recorded in the Gospel, but appertains to a subsequent fact of Peter, whereby the Roman Church was appropriated to him by a definitive and firmly ratified appropriation.

"It is clear that the fact, and the title, of the Roman Pontiff being the successor to Peter in the Primacy are not discoverable from any Divine institution recorded in the Gospel, since we read nothing there concerning Peter's appropriation of the Roman Church, but what is there said is that the whole Church was committed to him in those words: 'Feed My sheep.' Consequently, had Peter gone on to the end as he began, without appropriating to himself any one particular Church, neither the Bishop of Rome nor the bishop of any other See would be Peter's successor as Chief Pastor; but, on Peter's going to heaven, some one would have been elected as Bishop of the Catholic Church, and he would have been Peter's successor in the Primacy. Or, if Peter had remained until his death in the See of Antioch, which he first appropriated to himself, in that case not the Bishop of Rome, but the Bishop of Antioch, would have been Peter's successor.* Or, again, if Peter had taken leave of Rome, not of the city only, but of the See, and chosen for himself some other See, then the Bishop of Rome would not have been Peter's successor any more than the Bishop of Antioch, since by such departure Peter would have changed not only his residence, but also his See. Hence, we say again, it is evident that the succession of the Bishop of Rome to Peter's Primacy is not to be attributed to the Divine institution recorded in the Gospels, since that institution was not concerned with such like changes, but left all this to be disposed of and settled by subsequent facts.

"The succession of the Bishop of Rome to the Primacy had, then, its origin in the fact of the Roman Church being annexed to Peter's universal Pontificate by his firmly settled (*firmata*) appropriation of that See. We call it a firmly settled appropriation, both because it was rendered firm and fixed by the death of Peter as both Bishop of Rome and Head of the Catholic Church, and also because it obtained the strength of firmness from the authority of Christ. . . . For, as S. Ambrose and other ancient authors relate, when Peter was on his way to leave Rome, Christ met him and bid him return thither to suffer death, saying: 'I go to Rome to be crucified again.' And this shows that not the

---

* To the objection, made sometimes by Anglicans, that Antioch or Alexandria has as much claim as Rome to the Pontificate, since S. Peter was Bishop of Antioch and, mediately at least, of Alexandria, S. Alphonsus replies, in the same sense as Cardinal Cajetan, that "though S. Peter was Bishop of these two Sees, yet he never settled his Pontificate in either of these two Churches, but bore it with him in his own person, and fixed it definitely in the See of Rome, which was raised by him to the pontifical dignity. Consequently, the Bishops of Antioch and Alexandria are successors of Peter in the Episcopate, but not in the Pontificate; whereas the bishops who succeed S. Peter in the Roman See, and they alone, are his successors in the Pontificate. For this cause all antiquity has constantly attributed the Primacy to the Bishops of Rome, and not to the Bishops of Antioch or Alexandria, which Sees have been regarded as simply patriarchal, on account of their former connection with S. Peter." (*Verità della Fede*, part iii. c. viii. 6).

bare death of Peter in Rome, but his death there commanded by Christ, was to make firm the Roman See in the succession of Peter. If, therefore, we trace to its source and first rise the Roman Pontiff's succession to Peter in his Primacy, we find the account of it to be the appropriation of the Roman Church to Peter's universal Pastorate, rendered firm and settled in perpetuity, both by the death of Peter, and by the command of Christ.

"Now, in speaking of Peter as, at one and the same time, both Pontiff of Rome and Pontiff of the Catholic Church, we are not to understand this as though there were two pontificates;* for they are not two actually, but only potentially—that is to say, they might have been two, separated the one from the other, as we have already shown; but they were never so in fact. Hence they are not in the relation of two united bishoprics : for there was no Episcopate at all in the Roman Church before Peter; but it was Peter himself who first raised up the Roman Church to an Episcopate, and that no other than his own, which he bore with him, as inherent in his own person, so that the very same one Episcopate which Peter had from Christ in relation to the whole Catholic Church, that self-same he brought personally into actual relation to the Roman See by appropriating its Episcopate to himself. This unity of the Episcopates is thus intensified by the fact that the Bishop of Rome and the Chief Bishop of the Catholic Church are one and the same, not only through unity of person, but also through the very identity of Episcopate. And, in token of this, the Roman Pontiff does not receive two Palliums, but one only : whereas it is notorious that any other bishop, in possession of more than one See, receives as many Palliums as he has Sees for which the Pallium is required.

"To sum up what has been said. The fact that some one was to succeed Peter in the Primacy has its ground and evidence in Christ's institution recorded by the Evangelists; and the Bishop of Rome who thus succeeds derives his authority from the words of our Lord in this same institution, 'Feed My sheep:' for the self-same words that Christ spoke to Peter, He spoke equally to

---

* This is implied also in the words of the Creed of Pius IV., that "the Roman Church is the Mother and Mistress of all Churches." By this expression it is not simply meant that the Bishop of Rome is Father and Master at the same time of any or of all these distributively, as well of his own Roman Church; nor does it mean that he is Head of all Churches collectively in any other real relation than that whereby he is Head of the Roman Church.

everyone of his successors, in the person of Peter. Hence, though the identity of the Apostolic See with the See of Rome had its beginning in Peter's appropriation of the Roman Church, yet, from this being firmly settled in the way we have explained, by the very fact that anyone is the true Bishop of Rome, he is at once possessed of the Supreme Pastorate instituted by Christ Himself in the person of Blessed Peter. Thus we see clearly how it is that the Bishop of Rome is Peter's successor and Pastor of the whole Church."

Cajetan next discusses the second question he had proposed: How is this known? Though this point does not directly belong to our main thesis, nor to the subject of the present Chapter, yet we cannot refrain from giving here some further extracts.

"This," he says, "is known by Divine revelation, made as well to the universal Church as to innumerable Doctors and Councils. Since no Christian is allowed to doubt that whatsoever belongs to the reason and ground of Christian faith—as from the decree *Unam Sanctam* it is certain this does—comes from Divine revelation.

"The common confession of Christians of old time, now and always, has been, is, and will be, that the See of the Bishop of Rome is alone the Apostolic See. But what else is this but to acknowledge that the Bishop of Rome is Peter's successor as ruler of the Catholic Church? For in the Apostolic See (as everybody knows, unless he is ignorant of the proper meaning of the term) resides exclusively all Apostolic authority, and in Apostolic authority is included the power of ruling the whole Church, as those who are versed in theology well understand. Nay, this is so evident, that all agree that to Apostolic authority was committed by Christ the whole world, so that everyone of the Apostles, wherever he might be, could found Churches, appoint bishops, and do everything else of this kind, as also their own acts attest. Hence in 1 *Cor.* xii. 28, where we read, 'Posuit Deus in ecclesia primum Apostolos,' the interlinear gloss is, *Omnium ordinatores et judices;* showing that this Apostolic authority is universal in what it ordains and adjudicates. In confessing, then, a See to have Apostolic authority, we necessarily confess one that can legislate for and judge all. And that this is the intention of those who thus confess is shown by the fact that the See of Peter alone is confessed to be the Apostolic See. Contrast this, for example, with the See of Jerusalem. If a See were Apostolic simply because it was founded by an Apostle, we might then have several Apostolic Sees; but the Christian world calls one alone the Apostolic See—viz., the See of Rome—and thereby acknowledges it to be the See of Apostolic authority. And as the Episcopal, Archiepiscopal, or Patriarchal authority belongs exclusively to an Episcopal, Archiepiscopal, or Patriarchal See, so is it with the Apostolic authority in the Apostolic See.

"Moreover, in the admission of the Apostolic See is necessarily implied the confession of its Divine institution. For if we look at the matter in the light of truth, an Apostolic See, just as much as Apostolic authority, is derived from Christ alone, and can come from no other than from Him, Who alone had power to make Apostles; since it is a no less thing to institute an Apostolic See and Apostolic authority, than it is to make an Apostle, just as it is a no less thing to create Episcopal authority and an Episcopal See, than to make a bishop. Consequently whoever admits the Apostolic See must needs confess that its authority is immediately from Jesus Christ, and that therefore its institution is *of Divine right*.

"Hence, when the Fathers, Saints, and Doctors of the Church speak of the See of the Bishop of Rome as Apostolic, or as an Apostolate, or as possessing Apostolic authority, they thereby mean that the Bishop of Rome is supreme ruler of the whole Church. And this is very necessary to bear in mind, both for its own sake and that we may not have to repeat it when citing their testimony and authority...."

Cajetan then proceeds to answer at length a number of objections. In reply to the last of these he says:

"By the appellation of the Roman Church may be understood either the particular body of the Church of Rome, as considered in itself or in its head. Now, though the Roman Church, if regarded in its members that compose it, is neither the first, nor the mother of all Churches, nor was immediately instituted by Christ, still the self-same Roman Church, if it be regarded in Peter its Head, and in Peter's successor, is the first, the mother, and mistress of all Churches, and has its authority and firmness from Christ immediately, by virtue of His words in the Gospel, as has been before shown. Hence the statements of the Canons, as also of the Saints, asserting that the Roman Church is the first, the mistress, and the mother of all Churches, or that it was founded by Christ our Lord in the words of the Gospel, are true and verified by reason of its Head. And that this was the meaning of those who wrote them is plain from the fact that these, their statements, are founded on the words of Christ to Peter, who was himself in person, and still is, in his successors, the Head of the Roman Church. And hence the objections made with reference to the Church of Jerusalem have no force against this Primacy of Peter; for that Church was not before, nor above, Peter (*prior Petro*), but was subject to Peter."

In Chapter xiv. Cajetan gives a host of passages from the Greek and Latin Fathers, Saints, and Doctors, as well as from Councils, affirming that in Peter, and in the Bishop of Rome as successor to Peter, was divinely instituted the Pontificate of the whole Church. Of these we cite here one only—the testimony, namely, of Theophilus, often quoted by S. Jerome—because it is perhaps less commonly known than that of many others.

On the words: "And thou being once converted, confirm thy brethren,"* he writes:

"When, after denying Me, thou shalt have wept and repented, strengthen the others, since I have appointed thee to be the Prince of the Apostles; for this befits thee, who with Me art the strength and the rock of the Church."

And further on:

"Though he was an Apostle, he denied, and again by penance obtained the prerogative to be the ruler of the world."

On *John*, xxi. 15-17:

"When dinner was ended He commends the sheep of the world to Peter, not to any other."

And on verse 22:

"Our Lord in saying to Peter, 'Follow thou Me,' institutes in him the prelacy over all the faithful."

Lastly, on the words, "Till I come," v. 22:

"This means, whilst willingly I appoint him, that is, John, for the work of preaching, thou art the one whom I now appoint for the Pastorate of the world, and in this follow thou Me."

After giving many authorities, Cardinal Cajetan thus concludes:

"I pass over a multitude of Canons and Doctors, such as no man could number, who all say the same thing. From those, however, that I have adduced it is so evidently clear that Peter's successor, the Bishop of Rome, was instituted in Peter by Christ as Pastor of the whole Church, that no room is left for

* *Luke*, xxii. 32.

doubt. And if anyone should still hesitate, he must be either extremely ignorant and wanting in brains (*rudis et ineptus*), or he takes his views from heretics and schismatics. At all events he is no Christian; for, according to the teaching of philosophers, any man is very ill-instructed who seeks in all things for mathematical certainty. It is the way of heretics and schismatics to make use of Holy Scripture, but according to that sense in which they themselves make it to sound. Whereas the wisdom of Christians, who are really Catholics, understands the Sacred Scriptures according to the sense in which the holy Doctors and the Sacred Councils, confirmed by Apostolic authority, understand them. Whoever rejects this means of knowing Christian truth is no Christian; he who departs from this way is in truth an unbeliever. For once allow the licence of going aside from this way, and it will be lawful to call into question the one substance of the Trinity with Arius, to doubt also with those of old whether the Holy Ghost proceeds from the Son, and whether bread in the Sacrament of the Altar is changed into the Body of Christ.

"For all these points are rendered certain to Christians, and tenable with an undoubting faith, in no other way than by the interpretation of Holy Scripture, according to the writings of the Saints, and the definition of the Sacred Councils that have been confirmed by Apostolical authority. Wherefore, since there are texts from the Gospel forthcoming in support of the proposition, and the teaching of the Saints is clearly conformable thereto, with absolutely not one of the Saints in opposition, and there is the definition of the Sacred Councils with Apostolic authority, and every age of Christians, from Peter until the present time, in the Catholic Church is found confessing the same, and the testimonies of the rest of the Doctors are innumerable, the fact that the Bishop of Rome as Peter's successor was by Christ instituted in Peter, the Pastor of the whole Church, is rendered so certain, that a more certain faith cannot be had. Amen.

"Rome, in the year of Christian salvation 1521, and of my own age 52, the 17th day of February."

The gist, then, of Cajetan's argument, so far as it directly bears on the subject of the present Chapter, is: Peter identified and incorporated that supreme universal Episcopate over the whole Church which he had received from Christ with the Roman Episcopate, which he made his own and administered in person. This union of the two Episcopates was made firm, and settled in perpetuity, by Peter's death: and thus, *in concreto*, on Peter's death the Roman Episcopate was one and the same with the supreme Episcopate of the Catholic Church. Consequently, whoever became Peter's rightful successor in the Roman See succeeded at once to the universal Episcopate, which was identical with that of Rome.

This explanation is held to be the true one, and most solidly founded; as being in entire harmony with what we have already seen is the doctrine of the Church and the teaching of most approved theologians on the relation of the Roman Episcopate to the Primacy, and the right of succession thereto of the Roman Pontiff.

Another question yet remains of a speculative nature, for which we deem simple advertence as sufficient. It is whether Peter, before his death, could have separated the supreme and universal Pontificate from the Roman Episcopate; or have ordained that, after his death, one should be constituted universal Supreme Pontiff, without occupying any special See, and another be the particular Bishop of Rome, subject to the former. It is, at all events, certain that Peter did not act in this way, whatever be thought of the hypothesis, but that he left his successor in full possession of his own entire office, dignity, and authority, which were to remain in perpetuity. Whilst, indeed, this was in itself but a congruous and connatural result flowing from the whole case—that is, from the connected series of providential circumstances attending S. Peter, which we may term the entire Petrine fact, or perhaps we should rather say from the positive and expressed will of Christ on the matter—we may yet reasonably suppose that Peter himself, too, made definite arrangements that, after him, the Roman Episcopate should continue to be the supreme universal Pontificate, and that no separation should be made.

Throughout the whole foregoing discussion what we before said must be borne in mind, namely, that the intimate union of the Roman Episcopate with the universal Primacy was a Divine act, as well as the act of Peter. For the sake of more distinct elucidation, we have been viewing the several steps of Peter's conduct in the matter, in great measure, as though they were all his own, but not forgetting, at the same time, that herein he was divinely directed, and was carrying out the will of Christ, whether this was explicitly revealed to him or not.

We conclude with one other remark. It was clearly of the utmost importance, nay, of necessity, that a matter of such paramount interest to the Catholic Church, and to the whole world, as the succession to the Primacy, should be publicly notified, marked out, and determined in a very striking way by some great, patent, and signal fact, distinctly conspicuous. Many such are, perhaps, antecedently conceivable. But if account be taken of the exceptional position of Rome in the whole providential history of nations, and the eminent prestige, at any rate from past associations, which that city must ever continue to hold in the world, we can conceive of no fact more adequate for the purpose, than that which thus actually has taken place, namely, the incorporation and identification of the Primacy with the Episcopate of Rome, which has resulted from the original erection and personal appropriation of that See by the Prince of the Apostles and Supreme Pastor of the Church—a union, moreover, that has been definitively fixed and made permanent by the event of S. Peter's dying, at once universal Primate and Bishop of the See of Rome, by a glorious martyrdom in that city, where, in testimony to the whole world, his sacred body has ever since been venerated. By such signal and unmistakable manifestation to all generations of men has that Primacy, instituted by Christ Himself in Blessed Peter, been firmly secured in perpetuity to his lineal successors, the Bishops of Rome, in every age until the end of time—an enduring dynasty of universal princes in the Eternal City, more venerable and truly royal than any other that the world has ever seen. In what more striking way, we ask, could the Primacy of the Catholic Church, whether as regards the person who succeeds to it or the title of his succession, be certified and published to the Church and to the world than by such a fact as this?

CHAPTER IX.

S. PETER AND S. PAUL.—UNION AND SUBORDINATION.

That which to our mind, more perhaps than anything else, distinguishes Catholicism as contrasted with Protestantism, is the breadth and comprehensiveness of the former, together with its unity in multiplicity and variety.

Let us explain our meaning. Truth to us-ward is manifold and diverse. There are truths of different kinds; whether of reason, of nature, of experience, of natural religion, or of Divine revelation. Particular truths, moreover, tend in different directions, each with its own bias and separate bearing; but all are, at the same time, connected with, and dependent on, one another, with due subordination of the less to the greater, of what is of a lower to that which is of a higher order, so as together to form a consistent whole. When particular truths are viewed in isolation, and are dwelt upon apart by themselves and to the exclusion of other truths belonging to the same order, they are liable, in this partial aspect, to become distorted and exaggerated, and so to appear mutually opposed. This, in point of fact, is what happens with religion outside the Catholic Church, where truth is to be found only in a fragmentary form, and, so to say, in solution. There, amongst the sects, certain particular portions of truth are, indeed, admitted, but with individual preference, to the exclusion of others; and such partial adoption forms the subject-matter and basis of various doctrinal systems and of the several religious persuasions. Hence truth, in this way, is made to clash with truth, and the result is division and divorce.

It is quite otherwise within the Catholic Church, which alone is the sure home and citadel of Divine truth and knowledge, through the revelation of supernatural faith, and the indwelling infallible guidance of the Holy Ghost. There all particular religious truths find their own proper place. Manifold and various, they are preserved in union and due proportion one with another, and combine together in one harmonious whole.

We might illustrate the foregoing remarks in many ways. Let us take one or other example. Thus: Protestants hold that invocation and veneration paid to the Blessed Virgin Mary and other Saints is derogatory to the supreme worship of God; the Catholic Church teaches that such cultus is a part of revealed religion, and serves greatly to enhance the Divine glory. Again: because faith and the merits of our Lord Jesus Christ are essential for justification, Protestants would exclude all works and every sort of merit on man's part; the Catholic Church insists on the necessity of both. Once more: because our Lord teaches that true worship of God must be interior and from the heart, certain Protestants hold that all exterior worship and outward forms in religion are, therefore, profitless and vain; the Catholic Church inculcates the importance and obligation of both one and the other. These are a few out of many instances in point.

We have adverted to this general principle of comprehensiveness, and unity in variety, as characteristic of Catholicism, because it has an analogous bearing upon the particular subject of the present Chapter, namely, the relation of the Apostle S. Paul to S. Peter, as Primate of the universal Church and Bishop of Rome.

We have already considered the place S. Peter held amongst the number of the Twelve Apostles; but in treating of his Roman Episcopate S. Paul claims our interest and attention far more importantly than any of these, on account of the special connection he had with Rome and the Roman Church.

What a wonderful and striking fact is the close union wherewith the names of the two Apostles SS. Peter and Paul are linked together in the mind and utterance of the Catholic Church! Tradition hands them down as together founders of the Roman Church, as having together preached the faith in Rome, as together there imprisoned, as having together in Rome on the same day received the crown of martyrdom. Early Fathers, when giving the series of the first Roman Pontiffs and deriving their Apostolic succession, place the names of SS. Peter and Paul together at the head of the list. SS. Peter and Paul united are regarded as the two principal and special patrons of the City and See of Rome and of the Roman Pontiffs, as also the two great pillars and protectors of the whole Catholic Church. Their twin names are together invoked by the faithful in the common language of popular devotion. It is as though in the name and person, with the sanction and authority of these two Apostles conjointly, that the Supreme Pontiff delivers all his most important doctrinal utterances and most solemn sentences of discipline and judgment. In the Liturgy of the Church, the intercession of both Apostles is always invoked together. If there is a Feast in honour of one, there is ever, at the same time, next following, a commemoration of the other. The sacred bodies of the two Apostles repose at Rome in one tomb, and are venerated together at the same shrine. Well, then, does the Holy Church sing during the Octave of their Festival : " Peter and Paul ... these two princes of the Church on earth ... united together in life by love, so in death they were not divided."

We remark that this intimate union of S. Peter and S. Paul in the Catholic Church is something very wonderful and lovely, contrasting strangely with what is seen outside. There these two Apostles seem to be regarded as rivals, or as typical representatives of opposing ideas. S. Paul is, so to say, pitted against S. Peter, and is wont to be exalted at the expense, and to the depreciation of, S. Peter.

Thus, a notorious ultra-Protestant controversialist has actually taken the trouble to count up the number of verses in S. Paul's and S. Peter's Epistles, thereby to found an argument for the relative excellence and superiority of the one Apostle over the other. What, otherwise, would be too trivial and absurd for notice, save as an instance of very small pedantry, raises here our indignant disgust and pity, as a trick tending to dishonour the Church of God and His Saints, as well as to mislead ignorant and simple souls. Again, in a learned and elaborate literary work on S. Paul, that Apostle is represented as a man full of independence, chafing under any restraint or authority—a sort of free-lance in the Church, and the exponent of religious ideas very different from those of S. Peter.

Independently of what we know from Catholic tradition and history of the cooperation and union that existed between these two Apostles, there is much left on record in the New Testament to show how closely S. Paul was connected with the Roman Church, which was the See of Peter the Supreme Pastor, wherein the succession to his Primacy was to remain. And here, at once, we find an explanation as to why SS. Peter and Paul are so intimately associated together in the mind of the Church.

S. Paul had already, in the course of his Apostolic journeys in Asia Minor and Greece, met with many of the Roman Christians; and reckoned some of the leading members of the Church of Rome amongst his truest and best-beloved disciples and friends. From the great interest the Apostle took in that Church he had often, and long, desired to visit Rome, and it was to satisfy, in part, his zeal and love for the faithful there, that he wrote to them the most celebrated, and what is held to be the greatest and most important, of all his Epistles. Sent to Rome, on his appeal to Cæsar, he remained there two whole years, a prisoner indeed, but in free custody, and so far at large, that he was allowed " to dwell by himself in his own hired lodgings, with a soldier that kept him,* where he received all that came in to him, preaching the kingdom of God, and teaching the things which concern the Lord Jesus Christ with all confidence, without prohibition."† During this two years' Roman sojourn he wrote several of his Epistles. We know, moreover, from the New Testament, that later on he was again at Rome; that there in prison he awaited the near approach of his martyrdom, and thence wrote some other of his Epistles. Thus we see, from the New Testament, the intimate connection of S. Paul with the Roman Church, and the claim that he consequently had to be so closely linked with S. Peter, its chief founder and first Bishop.

And here we may ask, with reverence and humility, why in the designs of Divine Providence S. Paul particularly was chosen, rather than any other Apostle, to be thus exceptionally associated with S. Peter? Why in preference to S. Andrew, S. Peter's own brother, or to S. John, the disciple whom Jesus loved, or some other one of the Twelve? What renders this union of SS. Peter and Paul all the more remarkable is, the great contrast to be found between the two Apostles in all the circumstances of their

---

* That is, after the Roman manner, S. Paul's right hand was attached to the soldier's left hand. But this would be only when he went abroad. " S. Paul," writes Dr. Döllinger, " had often felt a wish to visit the Christians in Rome, but had always abstained from doing so on his principle of not choosing a Church already founded by an Apostle as the field of his energies, not, as he says, building on another man's foundation. But though he had not himself been at Rome, he had many friends and followers there, among them Aquila and Priscilla. And so he wrote, for the first time, to a community not personally known to him. The Church there must already have been in a flourishing state, and its faith in Christ was spoken of through the whole world, as S. Paul says (*Rom.* i. 8); though it consisted, of course, of a mixed body of Gentile and Jewish Christians, there were no parties and hostile principles at work, even if the difficulties of a complete fusion of Jewish and Gentile believers were felt there as elsewhere. The chief hindrances, however, were overcome when S. Paul wrote this Epistle; he testifies to the Romans that they are full of goodness, filled with all knowledge, and able to admonish one another (*Rom.* xv. 14). He warns them not against the actual, but the possible, danger of being misled by false doctrine." (*The First Age of the Church*, vol. i. pp. 120-1.)

† *Acts*, xxviii. 16, 30, 31.

life, character, and vocation. Let us dwell a little on this point, for its consideration will help us to give an answer to the question we have just proposed.

S. Peter was a simple, unlettered fisherman, from a small, obscure town in the despised province of Galilee, whence came most of the twelve Apostles. S. Paul did not belong to Palestine at all. He was a native of Tarsus, a "no mean city" amongst the Greeks in Cilicia, born with inherited rights of Roman citizenship. He was a man of high education and culture, brought up in all the learning, sacred and profane, that was known in the schools of the most famous teachers of that time, both in his own city* and in Jerusalem. S. Peter was called by Jesus Christ, during His lifetime on earth, to the Apostleship, and made by Him the first amongst His chosen Twelve, who were to take a part in His public ministry, to be constantly with Him, to hear His words, to receive His oral teaching, to be eye-witnesses of His miracles, His life and example, and to bear personal testimony to His Passion, Resurrection, and Ascension. Together they received from their Divine Master their Apostolic authority and prerogatives, and the commission to preach His Word and establish His Church throughout the world. Their number was restricted to twelve. On the falling away of one of them another was elected in his place, and the Apostolic College was once more complete. Together they received the outpouring of the Holy Ghost and the plenitude of Pentecostal gifts.

How different was the case of S. Paul. He was converted to Christianity, by an extraordinary grace of Divine illumination, from being an arch-persecutor of the Apostles and of the infant Church. When called by our Lord Himself to be an Apostle, and a special vessel of election, he was still outside the number of the chosen Twelve. His vocation to the Apostleship was abnormal. According to his own words, he "was as one born out of due time," after the life of Jesus Christ on earth was over, after the day of Pentecost was past, after the full revelation of Divine truth had been given to the Church. The indispensable qualification for election amongst the Twelve was wanting in S. Paul: for he was not one of those who had companied with them during their Master's lifetime, listening to His words, beholding His actions, His example, His Passion and Death; and

---

* "Tarsus could even compete with Athens and Alexandria as a chief seat of Greek civilisation and science." (Döllinger, *The First Age of the Church*, vol. i. p. 84.)

consequently he could not be made, in like manner with them, a witness of His Resurrection.* Seeing, then, how different was S. Paul in all his associations and antecedents, in everything that belonged to his vocation and Apostleship, from S. Peter and the rest of the Twelve—Why, we ask again, was he thus chosen out by the Providence of God to be so marvellously united to S. Peter in the mind and thought of the Catholic Church, that one is hardly ever named without the other? Other reasons may be given: we will state what appears to us to be the chief.

By this union of S. Peter and S. Paul, God would show that all gifts, all graces, all vocations, however great and extraordinary in His Church, must be found in union with, and in submission to, that supreme authority which our Lord committed to S. Peter, and which He instituted to be the ever-abiding source and centre of all jurisdiction in the Catholic Church. For, whilst there is in the Church perfect unity, there is, at the same time, wondrous variety. Not only does the Church include every variety of country, of nation, of peoples, and tongues, differing from one another in so many points, and themselves diverse in every age and epoch: but there are also diversities of operations, of ministries, of vocations, of gifts, and graces. Some are called to the ordinary vocation of living as simple Christians in the world; others are called to the ecclesiastical state; or, as religious, to enter monasteries and convents—some to be contemplatives, some to devote themselves to a life of perfection by the exercise of active works of charity and usefulness. Some are called to show forth the gifts and power of God in a way quite extraordinary: to work miracles, to have visions and ecstasies, and revelations, to bear in their bodies the Stigmata, or marks of our Lord's own Passion, to practise unwonted austerities, and to undergo excessive suffering. Others receive gifts of sublime wisdom and knowledge, that they may be Doctors and lights in the Church. Others, again, are called to be extraordinary apostles and preachers of the Divine Word. But it is the will of Christ, the Divine Founder, that all these diversities of gifts and operations, which the One and Self-same Holy Spirit works in His Church, should be brought into union with, and be in submission to, that Chair of infallible truth and supreme authority which He has set up in S. Peter and his successors; that so in the Catholic Church, amidst this most wondrous variety, there may be ever at the same time the most perfect unity of authority and teaching.

* *Acts*, i. 21, 22.

And this is shown forth most strikingly in the whole history of S. Paul, and by his union with S. Peter.

Just consider the case of S. Paul and his history once more. Our Divine Lord had gone away to heaven: before leaving the earth He had given to His Apostles, and preeminently to S. Peter, whom He had made their Chief, and the universal Pastor, all power of government and jurisdiction: He had delivered to them His doctrine: He had poured upon them the Holy Ghost, to teach and illuminate them, so that they might more fully understand all His own words. Here was the governing and teaching body, to teach and govern all.

Some time after, Saul, a Jew, who had been a terrible persecutor of the new Christian believers, is converted directly by Jesus Christ Himself; taught the whole Christian Faith, without any intervention of man; enlightened from heaven to know the Gospel in its fulness, to understand all the deepest mysteries of revelation; given at once most marvellous powers and graces, that he may expound and teach others what he has himself received; eloquence and talents most persuasive, so that more than any man he is able to convince his hearers and convert them to the Faith; a light to see the bearings and conclusions of Christian doctrines, and to apply them to particular cases and emergencies, perhaps stronger than that given to any of the other Apostles. His first preaching has most astonishing success, both with Jews and Gentiles. He has learnt the whole Gospel, not from any man, not from any Apostle, but immediately from our Lord Jesus Christ. And he is absolutely persuaded that all this is no illusion, that he is chosen to be an Apostle by the Will of God, and that what he has received is by clear and express revelation from heaven. Three years he meditates thereon in the solitude of Arabia, where doubtless his revelations are increased. What does he then do? Has he need of anything further, having thus received his Apostolic office and authority from Jesus Christ Himself? Will he not now go forth of himself, and teach and preach everywhere, in order to convert the nations, and instruct the people in the truths he has thus learnt? No; for amongst the doctrines he had learnt as essential to the Christian Faith was that of the supreme authority and universal pastorate of S. Peter. And so his first act, on his return to Damascus from Arabia, was, as he expressly tells us, to go to Jerusalem to see Peter, and to confer with him on what he had received—not, indeed, to learn anything more from S. Peter or the other Apostles, for he had been given a full revelation from our Lord Himself: but still to lay all before S. Peter as Supreme and Universal Pastor, to acknowledge his authority, and to obtain his sanction. God gave to S. Paul lights, and a spirit of prudence and wisdom so great, as to enable him to make observations and admonitions, of profit even to the Prince of the Apostles; and such holy zeal and courage, that he did not shrink from so doing when he saw there was need: yet all the while he acted in submission to S. Peter.* Thus we see him going forth on his mission to the heathen at the bidding of S. Peter and of the Council over which S. Peter presided, though he had already received his mission from Christ Himself; carrying the resolutions and decrees, put into his hand, that emanated from that Council, of which he himself had been the most conspicuous light: and though he had already arrived at the conclusions, and recognised the truths contained in those decrees, before they were drawn up and made obligatory. He goes forth on his Apostolic journeys, and we may say he converts the world to Christ. He goes throughout Asia Minor and Greece, to the Islands, to Rome, to Spain, to the farthest bounds of the known world, preaching and labouring and suffering, witnessing everywhere to the Faith, and to the truth of that Gospel which he had received directly from Jesus Christ: vindicating his Divine vocation and his claims to be an Apostle as much as any of the chosen Twelve, and working miracles and wonders in proof and confirmation of his Apostleship. Jews and Gentiles, learned and unlearned, Greeks and barbarians, bondsmen and free citizens, princes and people fall before him, and submit to the yoke of Jesus Christ. In his humility he calls himself the least and last of the Apostles, and yet declares that, by the grace of God, he had laboured more, and with greater success, than all the rest. He writes, under inspiration of the Holy Ghost, Epistles to the Churches more profound, more burning with the love of Jesus Christ than those of others. Look at him in his history, in his whole character, in his sphere of labour, in his success, in the New Testament, and you will say that he is the greatest Apostle, the greatest Doctor, that he is conqueror of the world, that all are at his feet. And yet all the while he acts with such spirit of

---

* "What took S. Paul to Jerusalem," writes Dr. Döllinger, "was the desire to become better acquainted with the first and chiefest of the Apostles, whom Christ Himself had made the shepherd of His flock, and to hold converse with him—to show honour to his Primacy." (*The First Age of the Church*, vol. i. pp. 88-93.)

subordination and deference as is due to the supreme authority of S. Peter.

We know that it was so, and we can gather as much from his own words. But if it were otherwise, then the case would be astonishing indeed, and, we might say, incredible. For, to us at least, it appears that, had the immense influence possessed by S. Paul been of absolutely independent exercise, without subordination and submission to S. Peter, it would, considering his extraordinary Apostleship and mission, have necessarily drawn a gathering after him, created a schism, and divided the Church. We learn from his own Epistles that so great was this influence, that some who were not fully grounded in the doctrines of the Faith did, in fact, let their personal attachment to him wear the look of partisanship, and that they were ready to hail him as the leader of a party. This spirit the Apostle strongly deprecates and condemns. To those who would say: "I am of Paul," &c., he cries: "Is Christ divided? What then is Paul?" and insists on the unity of the Church, wherein all are theirs in common, whether Paul, or Apollo, or Cephas.*

S. Peter, on his part, witnesses very forcibly to the close and brotherly union which existed between himself and S. Paul. For in his Second Epistle, written at Rome shortly before his martyrdom, he singles out S. Paul from all the other Apostles, to speak of him in terms of deep and tender affection, as "our most dear brother Paul," testifying at the same time to the Divine wisdom bestowed upon him, as manifest in all his Epistles. From this we see that all S. Paul's Epistles were well-known to S. Peter; and what makes his praise and commendation of them all the more touching and remarkable is, that S. Peter was well aware that in one of these Epistles was left on record the reprehension passed by S. Paul on his own conduct at Antioch. Thus, in his humility, he confesses implicitly to the justice of S. Paul's reproof, and to the wisdom of his fraternal correction on that occasion. It is, moreover, noteworthy that S. Peter, in speaking of the Epistles of S. Paul, remarks that, through the depth and sublimity of their doctrine, certain passages in them had been wrested from their true meaning, and were perverted to an erroneous sense by the unlearned and unstable, to their souls' destruction. But whilst thus warning the faithful, and putting them on their guard against such a danger, S. Peter testifies, at the same time, that all S. Paul's Epistles were replete with wisdom and edification for

* 1 *Cor.* ii.

those who were heedful against error and solidly grounded in the faith.*

And here, in this discriminating commendation and approbation of S. Peter, we seem to see the exercise already of that judicious supervision and discernment which the Supreme Pastor must constantly exercise in what concerns the doctrinal food and spiritual nourishment of the universal flock committed to his trust. But, in saying this, we would not have our words misinterpreted, or pressed too far; for we are not forgetting that, if S. Peter here sets, so to say, his seal of sanction on all the Epistles of S. Paul, he knew full well that the Divine signet had been already set to them, forasmuch as they were the Word of God written under the inspiration of the Holy Ghost. And if we have here S. Peter's authoritative *imprimatur*, so to say, for S. Paul's Epistles, it is given, at the same time, as a solemn declaration that they all form part of the Canon of the Sacred Scriptures.

* 2 *Pet.* iii. 15-17.

CHAPTER X.

THE RELATION OF S. PAUL'S WORK AT ROME TO S. PETER'S ROMAN EPISCOPATE AND UNIVERSAL PRIMACY.

Our object in the last Chapter was to show in general the union and concord that existed between the two Apostles, together with the due subordination of S. Paul to S. Peter. We would now consider more in detail the several facts and data which form the material and groundwork for the part ascribed to S. Paul as co-founder with S. Peter of the Church at Rome; and thus we shall, at the same time, see more precisely what relation this bore to S. Peter's Roman Episcopate and universal Primacy.

With regard to the share S. Paul had in founding the Roman Church, the facts which, as we think, should especially and principally be taken into account are, his celebrated Epistle to the Romans, his two years' imprisonment at Rome, his successful preaching during that time and conversion of persons there of high position, even "*de domo Cæsaris*," and the great fame that must have thence resulted. The Church of Rome was, evidently, already, as compared with other Churches, in a very flourishing state when, in the first months of A.D. 53, before S. Peter had yet returned to the City, S. Paul wrote from Corinth his Epistle to the Romans.* The Edict of Claudius having been lately repealed,

---

* "The Roman Church when S. Paul wrote his Epistle," says Dr. Döllinger, "was in a different state, and is addressed by him in a different tone, from other Churches. It was already complete, so to speak, and its faith spoken of over all the world (*Rom.* i. 8, xvi. 19). There were no quarrels and party-strifes, Jews and Gentiles lived together in the Church as brethren, and S. Paul speaks in turn to the one and the other, but he speaks with an apologetic respectfulness, found in none of his other Epistles;—he excuses his 'boldness' in admonishing them, appealing to his lofty mission as a minister of Christ among the Gentiles, although the main contents of the Epistle concern the Jews more than the Gentiles. He knows well that the Roman Christians are already filled with all knowledge. It is impossible he could have written in such terms at a time when the most imperfect knowledge of the new doctrine was found in many communities, and among individuals, like Apollos, unless he had recognised in the person of its founder and first preacher a guarantee for the purity and perfection of the Gospel planted

Aquila and Priscilla had returned a short time before. S. Paul salutes them in his Epistle; and we see from the other salutations that the Apostle knew already a considerable number of the Roman faithful, probably Jewish converts, whose acquaintance he had made in Asia during the four years they had been absent from Rome on account of the Edict of Claudius. The return from banishment of so many Christians to Rome would naturally have given a new life, and increased vigour and strength, to the Roman Church; and this would result in discussions more frequent, and of more lively interest, between the Christians, whether Jewish or Gentile converts on the one hand, and the unconverted Jews and Pagans on the other.

When S. Paul was brought to Rome as a prisoner in the spring of A.D. 56, we find that his fame and the news of his coming had preceded his arrival, for the brethren went out to meet him on his near approach to the city. During his two years' imprisonment at Rome he enjoyed considerable liberty: all persons had easy access to him; and he seems to have preached especially to the Gentiles. Thus he was brought into relation with Romans of distinction; and, amongst others, it is thought more than probable that he made the acquaintance of Seneca, brother of Gallio, Proconsul of Achaia;* and, not improbably, Acte, the Emperor Nero's cast-off concubine, was one of S. Paul's converts. S. Luke, who accompanied S. Paul to Rome, and remained with him during his two years' imprisonment, wrote there his *Acts of the Apostles*, principally for the Gentile converts, and also for such unconverted Gentiles as were of good will, in order to vindicate and make manifest the mission and Apostleship of S. Paul. The way in which S. Luke speaks of S. Peter, describing, as he does, with so much detail and care, the leadership of S. Peter amongst the Apostles and in the Church, his activity, discourses, and miracles—these are all so many further proofs of the complete union that existed between SS. Peter and Paul.†

there. It is only at the end that he introduces a very short and generally-worded warning against divisions (*Rom.* xvi. 17, 18). Neither, again, had he any Judaising opponents at Rome, as in so many other communities; and if we consider that the Church there was clearly not founded by his disciples, while yet its unity implied a well-ordered ecclesiastical organisation, such as then could only be set up by an Apostle, we are brought back to Peter as the only founder who can be imagined. The notion of a gradual origin of the community without any particular founder, or of Aquila and Priscilla being its founders, or S. Paul himself, is self-evidently untenable." (*First Age of the Church*, vol. i. pp. 158-160.)

* *Acts*, xviii. 12.   † See P. Allard's *Les Persécutions, &c.*

The very position of S. Paul at Rome as a prisoner, in the way we have mentioned above, could hardly accord with the supposition that he shared with S. Peter during those two years in the active administration of the Roman Church. He would no doubt have frequent conferences with S. Peter and the other Roman ecclesiastics for mutual consultation on the affairs of the Church, and on the means to be employed for the spread of the faith. But it seems to be especially the propagation of Christianity in Rome through his preaching and personal influence that merited for him his exceptional claim to share with S. Peter the title of Founder of the Roman Church. We see from the Epistles which S. Paul wrote towards the end of his two years' imprisonment that he was then anticipating his near release, and that he had the intention, on obtaining his liberty, of leaving Rome, and of soon returning to Macedonia and Asia Minor.*

Hence we gather that S. Paul, on obtaining his release A.D. 58, left Rome to make fresh Apostolic journeys in Europe and Asia, to Crete also, where he left Titus, whom he sent for later on to come to him at Nicopolis in Epirus, where he then was.† Perhaps, too, he accomplished his long projected missionary journey to Spain, and evangelised other distant countries also.

What is at any rate certain,—we find him at last, at the end of his course, again at Rome, and a second time a prisoner there. It was then he wrote his Second Epistle to S. Timothy; and from it we learn that he was in great danger, and expecting his death to be near at hand.‡ This was in A.D. 67. We do not know whether between the years 58 and 67 S. Paul made any visit to Rome; no traces at any rate are to be found of his having done so. It would appear that he had not been long in Rome when he wrote this Second Epistle to Timothy.§ S. Peter was probably then already in Rome, but not yet in prison.

It is here worth remarking that at the end of his Epistle S. Paul writes: "Eubulus and *Pudens* and *Linus* and *Claudia* and all the brethren salute thee." Pudens is the Senator in whose house, according to tradition, S. Peter dwelt at Rome. His daughters

---

* "I trust in the Lord that I myself also shall come to you shortly." (*Philip.* ii. 24.) "But withal prepare me also a lodging; for I hope that through your prayers I shall be given unto you." (*Philem.* 22.)

† *Titus*, iii. 12.

‡ "I am even now ready to be sacrificed; and the time of my dissolution is at hand." (2 *Tim.* iv. 6.)

§ We gather so much at least from what he says. (2 *Tim.* v. 13.) "The cloak that I left at Troas with Carpus, when thou comest, bring with thee, and the books, especially the parchments."

were S. Pudentiana and S. Praxedes. Claudia is thought to have been his wife. Linus was the immediate successor of S. Peter, and probably had now a chief part in the direction of ecclesiastical affairs at Rome. From the close union that hence appears to have existed between S. Paul and S. Peter's special friends, we may gather an additional proof of the accord there was between the two Apostles. The persecution under Nero was now raging, and if, as we have intimated, S. Peter was still at large in Rome, we can well understand why S. Paul does not mention him in his Epistle. For, if the Epistle were intercepted, some clue might be given to his discovery and apprehension. Tradition, in fine, records that S. Peter and S. Paul were together imprisoned in the Mamertine, and that they both together received the crown of martyrdom on the same day, June 29th, A.D. 67.

We have, thus, given the only reliable historical facts which connect the Apostle S. Paul with the Roman Church and with S. Peter at Rome, viz., his celebrated Epistle to the Romans, the great work that he did at Rome in the early days of the Church there, by his preaching and teaching conjointly with S. Peter and under his Episcopate, and also his martyrdom together with S. Peter in Rome. And these we consider are substantially the data, which have merited for S. Paul the title of co-founder with S. Peter of the Roman Church, and with him, of Chief Patron and Protector of the Holy See. Since, moreover, the See of Rome is also the central See of the entire Catholic Church, the name of the great Apostle S. Paul is, from this close connection with Rome, specially joined, in the language of the ancient Fathers and of tradition, with that of S. Peter the Supreme Pastor. Thus these two Apostles are styled together the twin Rulers and Protectors of the universal Church, the Princes of all the Churches, and are distinguished by other such-like honorary titles.

We have now to consider what relation this association of S. Paul with S. Peter and the Church of Rome has to S. Peter's Roman Episcopate and universal Primacy.

We begin, then, with saying in general that, from the traditional association together of the two Apostles, it no way follows that they were in any sense united officially, or that the jurisdiction possessed by one was common to both, or that they were coordinate in authority. It is, indeed, quite true that, regarded simply as Apostles, they were co-equal: and as such they are sometimes seen to rank on the same level in the language of the Fathers. But we must remark that the same Fathers who thus speak, teach also that S. Peter was constituted by Christ to be chief of all the other Apostles and their Prince. Hence neither in the universal Church, of which S. Peter held the Primacy, nor in the Roman See of which he was Bishop, was the authority of S. Paul equal to, or coordinate in nature with, that of S. Peter.

And first with regard to the universal Church; it is of faith that the Primacy was not common to SS. Peter and Paul, but belonged to S. Peter alone.

Hence the following proposition was condemned by Innocent X., A.D. 1647:

"Sanctus Petrus et Sanctus Paulus sunt duo Ecclesiæ Catholicæ céryphæi ac supremi duces, summa inter se unitate conjuncti; vel sunt geminus universalis Ecclesiæ vertex, qui in unum divinissime coaluerunt; vel sunt duo Ecclesiæ summi Pastores et præsides qui unicum caput constituunt."

This proposition was condemned as *heretical* in the sense of asserting "an equality in all things between S. Peter and S. Paul, without subordination and subjection of S. Paul to S. Peter in the supreme power and government of the universal Church." The doctrine thus condemned was that set forth and specially favoured in France by the Jansenists.

"We do not deny," says S. Alphonsus, "that the two Apostles, SS. Peter and Paul, exercised the office of Pastors at Rome, and this is what we should infer from the testimony of S. Irenæus and S. Epiphanius; but it does not thence follow that S. Paul received the same supreme power that was conferred upon S. Peter. And as to the care which S. Paul had of all the Churches (2 *Cor.* xi. 28), S. Augustine replies that this care had respect to the Key of Science (*Clavem Scientiæ*), which was given to S. Paul in his quality of Doctor of the Nations, and not to the Key of Power (*Clavem Potentiæ*), which was given only to S. Peter. S. Paul was, then, equal to S. Peter as to the preaching of doctrine, but not as regards the exercise of power in the universal government of the Church. Thus it was S. Peter alone, who was charged with confirming his brethren the Apostles in the faith. *Et tu aliquando conversus confirma fratres tuos.*" Jesus Christ Himself declared that the Apostles were not all equal, but that there was one among them greater than the rest, and He required that this one should behave himself as the least of all from love of the virtue of humility. "He that is the greater," &c. (*Luc.* xxii. 26, 27.) By His last words here our Lord showed clearly that He was not speaking of a superiority of virtue, but of a superiority of rank in the government of the Church, that is to say, of the Primacy accorded to S. Peter, which was a supreme Primacy, as was that of Jesus Christ." (*Verità della Fede*, pt. iii. c. vii. 9.)

We need say no more with regard to the Primacy.

As to the relation of S. Paul's cooperation in founding the

Church at Rome, with any share, on his part, in the Roman Episcopate, there is some diversity of opinion and expression amongst Catholic theologians. We must admit that some of the early Fathers speak in certain passages as though S. Paul was Bishop of Rome together with S. Peter: and thence Papebroch contends that he was so really, and in the same strict sense as S. Peter, though, so to say, secondary to S. Peter. De Smedt appears to be also of this opinion.* He says:

"Duo ergo in solidum Romanæ Ecclesiæ Episcopi Petrus et Paulus: sed ita ut Petrus Collegii Apostolici caput et princeps, suam quoque dignitatem tueretur."

Amongst other passages, Papebroch cites, in support of his opinion, S. Irenæus† and S. Epiphanius. We will give the words of the latter in full, because S. Epiphanius more expressly, perhaps, than any other early writer speaks of S. Paul as Bishop of Rome, and because the whole context has an important bearing on the subject we have now in hand.

"In Rome, Peter and Paul were the first, both Apostles and Bishops; then Linus, then Cletus, then Clement, who was the contemporary of Peter and Paul, of whom Paul makes mention in his Epistle to the Romans (Philippians?). And let no one wonder that, though he lived at the same time with them, others succeeded to that Episcopate from the Apostles. Whether it was that while the Apostles were still living he received the imposition of hands as a bishop (of the Episcopate) from Peter, and then having declined that office, remained disengaged—for he says, in one of his Epistles, 'I withdraw; I go away; let the people of God be instant;' giving this advice to some (for we find this set down in certain memoirs)—or whether, after the succession to the Apostles [of Linus and Cletus], he was appointed by Bishop Cletus, we do not clearly know. Although it was possible, even whilst the Apostles were living (I am speaking here of Peter and Paul), for other bishops to be constituted, because of the Apostles frequently proceeding on journeys to other countries for the preaching of Christ, whereas the city of the Romans could not be without a bishop. For Paul went even into Spain, and Peter often made a visitation of Pontus and Bithynia. Possibly, then, Clement, who had declined the office on his first appointment (if this were really what happened, for here I am conjecturing and not deciding), later on—after the death of Linus and Cletus, who had held the See each for twelve years since the martyrdom of SS. Peter and Paul in the twelfth year of Nero—was compelled to undertake the Episcopate. In any case, the succession of the Bishops in Rome was in the following order: Peter and Paul, Linus, Cletus, Clement, ... Anicetus."‡

The opinion of Papebroch is contrary to the general teaching

* *Disputationes Selectæ in primam ætatem historiæ ecclesiasticæ.* Auctore P. Carolo De Smedt, S.J. Gandavi, 1876.
† *Hæres,* l. iii. c. iii. n. 3. ‡ *Adv. Hæres,* 27.

of Catholic theologians: and, with authors of grave authority, we hold it to be inadmissible, and even erroneous, if thereby is meant that S. Peter's episcopal jurisdiction in the Roman See was divided and shared by S. Paul, or, what comes to the same thing, that S. Paul was in any sense ordinary Bishop of Rome.

It may be readily allowed that S. Paul exercised at Rome episcopal functions, and thus acted as bishop; but if he did so, it was not as the ordinary Diocesan, but as a bishop extraordinary. And here, as Weith* remarks, two things should be borne in mind: first, that the Apostles had the right to exercise the episcopal office everywhere all over the world, with, however, due subordination to S. Peter; and, secondly, as history and tradition serve to show, that S. Peter judged it good and necessary, in the early days of the Church, to consecrate several bishops for Rome, to assist him in episcopal duties within the City, and outside in neighbouring places, and who should in his absence, by delegation from himself, administer the affairs of the Roman Diocese. This seems to have been the case with regard to SS. Linus, Cletus, and Clement, whose episcopal consecration at Rome by S. Peter is mentioned by several early writers. Still, during S. Peter's lifetime, they were not, in any proper sense, Bishops of Rome, but must be considered as Bishops in Rome, who acted by his mandate, and, especially during his absence, as his vicars. For that matter, even in the present day, the Supreme Pontiff is used to administer the Roman Diocese through another bishop, who is his Cardinal Vicar. There might, moreover, besides those mentioned, have been various others in Rome who had the episcopal order and consecration.

Papebroch is of opinion that the principle of ecclesiastical law, ruling that there should be but one bishop over each diocese, was introduced by the Council of Nice as a safeguard against dissensions; but that before that time there were several bishops in the principal Churches, one having precedence over the others. If this means that these several bishops were anything more than auxiliary, or that they had any ordinary jurisdiction as diocesans, such a view appears to us to be in direct opposition to the teaching of S. Ignatius, whose authority should be regarded as paramount in antiquity on this matter. If there is one principle upon which he insists in every one of his Epistles more emphatically than another, it is unity amongst the

* *De Primatu et Infallibilitate*, sec. i. 6.

faithful in the several Churches. And continually he puts forward the One Bishop over each Church as the symbol and source of this unity. Over and over again he urges the faithful to be united and obedient to their bishop, priests, and deacons; thus always implying that there is but one single bishop, who presides over every diocese. Frequently he speaks of the bishop as occupying the place of God, and of Jesus Christ. In the following passage he teaches expressly and most forcibly the principle of there being but one single bishop in a Church:

"Take, then, earnest heed to make use of one Eucharist: for there is one Flesh of our Lord Jesus Christ, and one Chalice for the unity of His Blood, one Altar, as there is one Bishop, with the presbytery and deacons, my fellow servants."*

Whilst, then, it would be clearly contrary to the teaching of S. Ignatius that there should be two coordinate Bishops over the Roman See, or, as Father De Smedt expresses it, that Peter and Paul should both be Bishops of the Roman Church forming a solidarity ("*Duo in solidum Romanæ Ecclesiæ Episcopi Petrus et Paulus*") it would seem not to be inconsistent with the principle of S. Ignatius that there should have been, as we have supposed, several ecclesiastics invested with episcopal order at Rome, acting as auxiliaries in the name, and by the delegation, of the one Diocesan Ordinary.

It appears evident, therefore, that the Council of Nice in this case introduced no new principle, but simply recalled the observance of what had been the primitive rule from the beginning, and is obviously inherent in the diocesan constitution of the Church; insisting on its obligation all the more, because from its violation frequent dissensions had arisen.

But if this be so, and the principle inculcated by S. Ignatius is the more excellent and primitive rule, we cannot suppose that S. Peter, the Pastor of pastors, and typical exemplar of all bishops, would have initiated in his own First See of Rome—the central source of ecclesiastical unity, and model of all the Churches—what was abnormal, and to be afterwards reprobated by the Catholic Church as an abuse fruitful of disunion.† From

* *Ad Philad.* cap. ii.
† The first example on record of two bishops in the same See is that of Alexander, coadjutor Bishop with Narcissus of Jerusalem (A.D. 205). We give the words of Eusebius, which show that such a double episcopate was considered at that time quite exceptional: "But as from extreme old age Narcissus was no longer able to fulfil his ministry, the Providence of God

the foregoing considerations we conclude as certain that S. Paul was not, in any true and proper sense, Bishop of Rome together with S. Peter.

But the most important and strongest argument for this conclusion is to be drawn from the relation that exists between the Episcopate of Rome and the universal Pontificate. According to the teaching of theology, and as we saw explained in a former Chapter by Cardinal Cajetan, these are not really two episcopates, but one and the same, and consequently the Bishop of the Roman See holds the Primacy as Supreme Pontiff of the whole Church. As then S. Paul had no share in the Primacy, which was Peter's alone, so neither had he part in the Roman Episcopate; but S. Peter was the sole Bishop of the See.

Some authors affirm that S. Paul was bishop extraordinary (*episcopus extraordinarius*) of Rome; but to say this is in complete harmony with our conclusion, since such a term at once excludes the idea of his being Bishop of Rome, properly and strictly speaking. For no one can be really bishop of a See without possessing *ordinary* jurisdiction *qua talis*.

Because S. Paul did so much by his preaching and teaching to spread the faith and to consolidate the Church in Rome, some seem to think it necessary to form hypotheses as to a division of episcopal jurisdiction between SS. Peter and Paul.

"It has, moreover, been supposed by many (says Mr. Allnatt), that when S. Paul came to Rome he undertook there a part of S. Peter's episcopal administration, exercising this office in regard to the *Gentile* converts, whilst S. Peter's local charge was that specially of the converts from Judaism. Hence Irenæus, Anatolius, Eusebius, and Epiphanius deduce the succession of the Roman Bishops from *both* Apostles; and the apparent discrepancy

called the aforesaid Alexander, who was bishop of another diocese, by a revelation which appeared to him in a vision by night, to share the sacred office with Narcissus. Admonished, then, by this vision, as by a Divine oracle, Alexander journeyed from Cappadocia, where he was first made bishop, to Jerusalem, with a view of there praying, and of visiting the sacred places. The brethren of that Church received him most cordially, and would not suffer him to return to his own country. And they, too, had another revelation by night, and a voice was most distinctly heard by those most eminent for sanctity amongst them, which signified to them that, on going outside the city gates, they should receive the bishop ordained for them by God. Having done this, with the common consent of the bishops of the neighbouring Churches, they constrained him to stay amongst them. Alexander, too, in his epistles to the Antinoites, which are still extant, makes mention of the episcopate as shared by himself with Narcissus, in the following words at the end of the epistle: 'Narcissus salutes you, the same who before me held the Episcopal See here, and is now colleagued with me in prayers, being now advanced to his hundred-and-tenth year, and who with me exhorts you to be of one mind." (*H. E.* vi. 11.)

amongst some early writers as to the order of succession of the three first is cleared up, if we suppose that, after the martyrdom of SS. Peter and Paul, the successors of S. Peter were *Linus*, *Cletus* (or *Anencletus*), whilst *Clement* succeeded S. Paul, and that Clement, after their decease, A.D. 91, was also chosen to succeed Cletus, and so joined both the converted Jews and converted Gentiles at Rome under one pastor."[*] He gives also the view of Dr. Hawarden, who "remarks that supposing SS. Peter and Paul to have together exercised an episcopal office at Rome—the one over the Jewish, and the other over the Gentile converts—' there would only have been a division of their labours, not of their jurisdiction,' and that 'it would neither injure the Pope's supremacy, nor his being the successor of S. Peter only in the government of the whole Church, though in the government of the Roman diocese he were the successor of S. Peter and S. Paul.'"[†]

We consider the several hypotheses contained in these passages to be inadmissible, as opposed to the general teaching of theology, and at variance with historical testimony, and tradition. But, independently of this, more ingenuity than wisdom is often, we think, displayed in the invention of theories which shall clear up all that is difficult or obscure in the history of the past. Such theories are, for the most part, arbitrary, very unreliable, and wide of the actual truth. In dealing with history, it is certainly better, save in some real necessity—and this no doubt may occur—to refrain from such theorising at least, as imports the origination of new matter of fact, and to take, and be content with, what we find recorded. When it is a question of antiquity, from the very nature of the case, many difficulties and discrepancies will doubtless remain unsolved. Still, however imperfect, or even obscure, the record of facts may be,—if, after being well sifted and compared one with another, they are permitted to speak for themselves in their own simplicity,—they will often be found to give an account more luminous and intelligent, than when invested with clever conjecture and plausible theory.

There is no need, we think, in the present case for conjecture at all; for the recorded facts are quite certain, very simple, and fully adequate of themselves to explain everything. S. Paul, burning with zeal for the spread of the Gospel and for the salvation of souls, finds himself in Rome, where S. Peter was Bishop. There was no sort of jealousy between the two, but complete union; they had both but one cause at heart. As an Apostle, S. Paul was invested with the fulness of Apostolic gifts and authority, and with the plenitude of the episcopal order. It was his rule to

---

[*] *Cathedra Petri*, p. 56. Burns and Oates, 1883.
[†] *Ibid.* p. 64. *True Church of Christ*, vol. ii. p. 99.

exercise his Apostolic office with prudent consideration, with a view to due order and edification, and on an entirely concordant understanding with other Apostles, and especially in subordination to S. Peter, the chief pastor. Whilst his joy is that Christ should be preached everywhere and every way*—and he had already declared his utmost readiness to preach the Gospel to the faithful at Rome†—still he was reluctant to enter into the sphere of other Apostles, and would not, uncalled for, and without sufficient reason, build upon another's foundation.‡ We may gather, hence, how cordially welcome was S. Paul to S. Peter at Rome, and how, as Bishop of the Church, S. Peter invited and rejoiced in the cooperation of S. Paul. There was room enough and work enough for both. As the special vocation of S. Paul was to evangelise the Gentiles—for to him "was committed the Gospel of the uncircumcision, as to Peter was that of the circumcision "§ —we can well understand, also, that the field of labour at Rome was thus very much *de facto* divided between SS. Peter and Paul by mutual consent; so that the work of S. Paul was principally amongst the Gentiles, as, indeed, S. Luke tells us expressly was the actual case.|| But, because of this division of labour, there is no reason whatever for supposing there was any division of diocesan jurisdiction. The great Doctor of the Gentiles was the Apostle, not the Bishop, of Rome; and whatever episcopal functions he there performed, whether by confirming or ordaining, were exercised in virtue of his Apostleship, with the consent, and in a certain sense by the delegation, of S. Peter, the Supreme Pontiff of the Church and Bishop of the Roman See.

Certainly S. Paul at Rome, in his office, position, and cooperation with S. Peter, is not to be ranked on the same level with any merely auxiliary bishops, such as SS. Linus, Cletus, and Clement are supposed to have been during the lifetime of S. Peter. S. Paul was an Apostle, and, as such, may be regarded as the greatest and most celebrated of all the Apostles. The prominent part he had in establishing the Roman Church would of itself shed an imperishable glory over that See and enhance its greatness and lustre. In virtue, moreover, of his Apostolic commission, he was also a bishop, invested potentially, by Divine right, with episcopal jurisdiction and authority, wherever he might be. The assent of S. Peter, who held the Primacy, was

---

* *Philip.* i. 18.   † *Rom.* i. 15.   ‡ *Rom.* xv. 20.
§ *Gal.* ii. 7, 8. || *Acts*, xxviii. 28.

sufficient to call these powers into actual exercise. This assent was given freely to S. Paul in Rome, so that he could carry out his Divine Apostolate to the full in the diocese of Rome as elsewhere, whilst all the while that diocese still remained Peter's See, appropriated to his Primacy, and he alone was its ordinary bishop. We marvel not, then, that in the tradition and records of Rome the Apostle S. Paul should be counted worthy of no less an honour than a throne beside that of S. Peter in his own Primatial See, nor do we marvel either that this association which he had with S. Peter, the first Bishop of the Roman Church, should have obtained for him the privilege of sharing even in some of those titles which, strictly speaking, belong by exclusive right to S. Peter, as Primate and Pastor of the universal Church, and that the peculiar glory of the Prince of the Apostles should have redounded on the Doctor of the Gentiles.

It is, then, in this sense, we hold, those Fathers are to be understood who place SS. Peter and Paul together as first Bishops of Rome. And just as we must not conclude from the fact of the Roman Pontiffs claiming, as they do, to act by the united authority of SS. Peter and Paul,[*] that S. Paul had any share in the Primacy—for all that is thereby meant is to invoke conjointly the authority of patronage of these two great Apostles—so neither can we infer, because the Popes are sometimes styled successors of the Holy Apostles Peter and Paul, that they are successors of both in one and the same sense as regards the Roman Episcopate, any more than (as, indeed, they are not) in the universal Pontificate.

We should remark, moreover, that whilst the Fathers and early writers frequently speak of S. Peter by himself as the first Bishop of Rome, and derive the succession of the Roman Pontiffs from him alone, they nowhere speak thus of S. Paul by himself alone. To style the Pope simply successor of S. Paul would be quite out of harmony with universal tradition, Catholic phraseology, and the sense of the faithful.

"During the epoch of Jansenism," writes S. Alphonsus, "appeared an anonymous book, *On the Pontificate of SS. Peter and Paul*, in which it was attempted to prove that S. Paul was equally with S. Peter head of the Church. The whole purpose of the author was, not to exalt the dignity of S. Paul, but to depreciate the primacy or supremacy of S. Peter, and, by consequence, that of the Pope. The book was submitted to examination by Innocent XI., and the doctrine contained in it was pronounced heretical by a public decree.

[*] In place of the form, "by the authority of SS. Peter and Paul," that of "by the authority of all the Saints" is sometimes similarly used.

The author grounded his argument on the ancient custom in the pontifical diplomas of representing S. Paul on the right and S. Peter on the left. But it cannot thence be inferred that S. Paul was equal to S. Peter in the supreme authority and in the government of the Church; for it was said to S. Peter and not to S. Paul: *Pasce oves meas.*[*] On this point S. Thomas says that the Apostle was equal to S. Peter in the exercise of authority—by reason of his Apostolate—but not in the authority of government. *Apostolus fuit par Petro in executione auctoritatis, non in auctoritate regiminis.*[†] If, for that matter, any argument can be drawn from S. Paul being represented at S. Peter's right, it would prove that the former was not only equal, but superior to S. Paul. . . . The same author takes his ground also on the great praises which the Fathers bestow on S. Paul. We reply that this is so, because S. Paul surpassed the other Apostles in many things, notably in his special election, and by his greater labours and sufferings in preaching the faith throughout the world, as S. Thomas remarks. But not one of the Fathers has made him superior, or equal, to S. Peter in quality of head of the Church; for the Roman Church was not founded by S. Paul, but I find it founded by S. Peter."[‡]

In saying that the Roman Church was founded exclusively by S. Peter, S. Alphonsus would be far from denying that share in the foundation of the Church of Rome, which, as we have already seen, the holy Fathers and universal tradition ascribe to S. Paul. Here, however, by the Church of Rome, he means especially its Episcopal See. Catholic writers generally, as we have before observed, when speaking of any of the Petrine facts that have relation to Rome,—as, *v.g.*, S. Peter's coming to Rome, his residence, preaching, and martyrdom there—suppose always, as a matter of course already granted, that these several facts import that one, which, being the principal and of most consequence, at the same time gives to all the other facts their real significance and value—viz., his Roman Episcopate. They do not, as is the wont of Protestants, intend, in their language regarding these facts, so to distinguish them, as though they were isolated and unconnected one with the other.

Hence the sense of S. Alphonsus' argument here is: However greatly the holy Fathers may extol S. Paul, none of them ever made him superior, or equal, to S. Peter in the supreme authority and government of the Church. And this, he implies, is evident if only from the fact, that not one of them is found to assert that S. Paul was founder of the Roman Church—confessedly the mother and mistress of all Churches—in the sense in which S. Peter undoubtedly was—viz., as the founder of its Epis-

---

[*] *John,* xxi. 17.   [†] *In Gal.* c. ii. lect. 3.
[‡] *Storia delle Eresie,* tom. ii. n. 165.

copal See, and the first bishop and ruler of what all acknowledge to be the Primatial Church. Here the premiss, from which the holy Doctor concludes that S. Peter was superior to S. Paul in the government of the Church, is the certainty that S. Peter, and he alone, was in a proper and strict sense Bishop of the Church of Rome.

CHAPTER XI.

S. PETER APOSTLE OF THE CIRCUMCISION, S. PAUL OF THE UNCIRCUMCISION.

THAT S. Peter was the first Bishop of Rome is no mere bare event of past occurrence: it is, indeed, a matter of deep historical interest; but it is much more; it is a great moral fact; and as such it necessarily involves, and is bound up with, principles and practical issues of vast and vital import. It is, we think, generally agreed on all hands, that, if the historical case be conclusively settled in the affirmative, then these principles and issues are also substantiated as true. All the constituent elements of the whole complex fact, or its qualities, both historical and moral, must stand or fall together. We mean: if S. Peter was certainly Bishop of Rome, and is succeeded in his See by the line of Roman Pontiffs; then also—on grounds of credibility quite independent of any teaching of faith—it is, morally speaking, certain that he was the divinely-appointed visible head of the whole Catholic Church; and certain, too, that the successive Bishops of Rome inherited his primacy. Or again, if, on other grounds, it be demonstrated that such a perpetual primacy as that held by the Roman Pontiffs is of Divine institution in the Church, then, morally speaking, it is also certain that S. Peter was in truth the first Bishop of Rome. Whereas, were the alleged historical fact of S. Peter's Roman Episcopate, on the one hand, proved to be absolutely untrue, it would be certain also, morally speaking, that the perpetuity of S. Peter's primacy in the Church was no institution of Christ. Or if, on the other hand, it were certain that no such primacy as that claimed by the Pope was ever instituted by Christ, it thence would follow, morally speaking, that S. Peter was certainly never Bishop of Rome.

In putting the case thus, we do not forget what we stated in a former chapter—viz., the antecedent possibility of the succession to Peter's primacy being otherwise settled by Divine appointment in the line of the Roman Pontiffs, though he himself were never Bishop of Rome at all; nor, again, the same possibility of his having been Bishop of Rome, without any consequent inheritance of his primacy by his successors in that See. But, bearing all this in mind, we have used the term, *morally speaking*, so often, because here we would purposely prescind from what is absolute, or belongs to any *a priori* hypothesis. We, therefore, take the two facts of St. Peter's Roman Episcopate and of the Roman Pontiffs' succession to his primacy, in the sense in which they are regarded all the world over, as mutually interpreting one another, and forming together one single, concrete, moral whole. Moreover, arguments and evidence the best calculated to induce conviction in matters of this sort, must themselves partake of the same moral character, and these, in point of fact, are far more practically persuasive than any abstract proofs drawn from notions of what is speculatively possible, or antecedently probable.

It is precisely because the Roman Episcopate of S. Peter cannot be divested of its moral character, that Protestants, whilst professing to controvert it simply as a matter of fact and on historical grounds, must needs go outside history into questions of doctrine and principle, in order to make out their case against Catholics: being well aware that in striking, for example, at Peter's primacy, they strike also at the historical fact of his Roman Episcopate, and by marshalling their objections against his Episcopate of Rome, they are really doing battle to his primacy as a Divine institution in the Church, and to its succession in the line of the Roman Pontiffs: since it is in this pregnant sense Catholics, and all the world besides, have ever understood the historical fact of S. Peter being Bishop of Rome.

For, after all, the bare question by itself, whether or not S. Peter was Bishop of Rome, stripped of its consequences, is hardly worth consideration except for antiquarians. But if it be taken, as it actually exists, for an alleged and largely credited fact, with numerous important results and surroundings, no reasonable investigation can be made of its truth, which should fail to take account of that doctrinal significance, and those vital principles of practical issue, with which Catholic tradition and the opinion of men in general have continually invested it. No other diagnosis or treatment of the historical question but this would be adequately proportioned to the field of thought which it occupies; and in no other way could it stand the test of examination that it might have to meet.

Hence it follows that many of the objections brought against S. Peter's Primacy lie also against his Roman Episcopate; and, consequently, the defence of our thesis must be made on the same lines as those of its attack.

We propose, therefore, in this Chapter to meet one of the principal objections of this indirect sort, which Protestants raise against the Roman Episcopate of S. Peter.

They say that S. Peter could not have been the first Bishop of Rome, at least in the sense understood by Catholics, because he never possessed a sole and universal Primacy in the Church—this, they maintain, is evident from the fact that, by a Divine appointment, to S. Paul was given the Apostolate of the Gentiles (the Gospel of the Uncircumcision), and to S. Peter the Apostolate of the Jews (the Gospel of the Circumcision), and that, consequently, the supreme jurisdiction was divided and shared by the two Apostles.

It is, no doubt, quite clear from S. Paul's own words in his Epistle to the Galatians * that at the Council of Jerusalem the evangelisation of the Gentiles was committed specially to himself and Barnabas, while that of the Jews was left especially to S. Peter and the other Apostles present.

But from this it no way follows, as some Protestants pretend, that S. Peter was divinely restricted to the Church of the Circumcision, and S. Paul to that of the Gentiles. This assertion is false, as is also the inference thence drawn with regard to the Primacy.

In order to elucidate the whole matter of the two Apostolates of S. Peter and S. Paul—so full of interest for its own sake—and at the same time to refute the afore-mentioned errors, we shall avail ourselves very freely of the learned comments on this subject of Baronius and Dr. Döllinger, from whose writings we give lengthened extracts:

"We are not to suppose," says Cardinal Baronius,† "that by this arrangement of the Apostles aught was decreed contrary to what had previously been matter of Divine appointment; as though the care of the entire flock, already committed by Christ to Peter, were in any way limited by this act of the Council; or the charge of preaching to the Gentiles, wherewith (as we have seen in the vision of the sheet let down from heaven) that Apostle was before entrusted by our Lord, were now withdrawn.

---

* ii. 9, 10.   † *Annals*, A.D. 51.

S. Peter had himself declared in the same Council that God had already* 'made choice among the Apostles, that by his mouth the Gentiles should hear the word of God and believe.'† It would be, therefore, out of all reason to suppose that what was thus of Divine appointment was set aside by the Apostles, and that any derogation of conceded right, or limitation of provinces, was made in the Council. No division of jurisdiction was effected, whereby one should abstain from the Apostolate of the other in such sense that S. Peter was to keep aloof from the Gentiles, and S. Paul from the Jews. For, were this the case, S. Paul was a most notable transgressor of the Apostolic sanction; since we find him, in the Acts of the Apostles, not merely now and then, or on occasion turning aside to the Jews, but we see him, as a rule—on his first entrance into a city, where Jews had their place of meeting—seeking them out and preaching the Gospel to them. This he did at Philippi, Thessalonica, Berea, Athens, Corinth, Ephesus—where he preached to the Jews in their Synagogue for three months—and lastly at Rome;‡ and because here he was in custody, and unable himself to go, as he was elsewhere used, to preach in the Synagogues, he at once sent for the chief of the Jews to come to his house, in order to make them partakers of the grace of the Gospel.

"We thus see that S. Paul, to whom was distinctly entrusted the care of the Gentiles, was wont, first of all, to seek out the Jews to bring them to the faith, and that in fulfilling this work, he not only, as the law allowed,§ gleaned the ears of corn that remained after the reaping, or plucked them in passing by, but of set purpose put in his sickle into the crop whilst it was still standing entire, preaching first to the Jews, and then afterwards to the Gentiles. Of this he calls the clergy of Ephesus to witness. Moreover, the Apostle frequently and forcibly insists on this same principle also in his Epistles.

'You know from the first day that I came into Asia... how I have kept back nothing that was profitable to you, but I have preached it to you, and taught you publicly, and from house to house, testifying both to Jews and to Gentiles penance towards God, and faith in our Lord Jesus Christ.' ||

"We may be quite confident that S. Peter acted in like manner

---

* *Acts*, x. 20, 28, 34, 35, 47, 48, xi. 1-18, 20, 21.   † *Acts*, xv. 7.
‡ *Acts*, xvi. 13, xvii. 1-4, 10-12, 17, xviii. 4-6, 19, xix. 8, xx. 21, xxviii. 16-31.
§ *Lev.* xix. 9, 10. || *Acts*, xx. 18-21.

with regard to the Gentiles.* For if S. Paul, to whom the ministry to the Gentiles was committed, considered himself justly entitled thus to act, by the same right, nay, with greater right, would S. Peter, who was entrusted with the government of the whole Church, do the same.

"It is hence evident that there is here no question of a divided jurisdiction, nor of a division of the peoples or races to be evangelised by the two Apostles; but that, whilst a certain charge of superintendence and patronage was given to each of them, distinct and separate, the preaching to Jews and Gentiles was alike common to both. Whence S. Jerome, in his commentary on the Epistle to the Galatians (ch. ii.), says:

> 'Here an occult question arises. Are we then to infer that when Peter met with Gentiles he did not lead them to the faith? and when Paul came upon any of the circumcision he did not exhort them to the baptism of Christ? The question may be solved by saying that each of these Apostles had given to him his own principal charge, the one for the Jews, the other for the Gentiles; so that those who stood for the law might have one to follow, and those who would put grace before the law might not be without a doctor and guide; whilst both the Apostles had this one purpose in common, to gather a Church to Christ from all nations.'

It is clearly then in this sense that those words of S. Paul are to be understood:

> 'To me was committed the Gospel of the uncircumcision, as to Peter was that of the circumcision.'†

To Peter indeed was given the ministry, ennobled with the more honourable title. For Christ Himself, Who came to save all men, and with Whom 'there is no distinction of the Jew and the Greek,' is yet called, by excellence, the Minister of the Circumcision, according to the words of S. Paul:

> 'For I say that Christ Jesus was minister of the circumcision for the truth of God, to confirm the promises made unto the fathers.'‡

And as a clear proof that this is the more august title, the same Apostle writes concerning those of the circumcision:

> 'Who are Israelites, to whom belongeth the adoption of children, and the glory, and the testament, and the giving of the law, and the service, and the promises; whose are the fathers, and of whom is Christ according to the flesh, Who is over all things, God blessed for ever. Amen.'

Whilst he says of those of the uncircumcision: 'But that the

---

* See 1 *Pet.* iv. 3.   † *Gal.* ii. 7.   ‡ *Rom.* x. 12, xv. 8.

Gentiles are to glorify God for His mercy,'* as though the Gospel of the circumcision were founded on some claim of congruous merit, and that of the uncircumcision were one of *pure mercy.*

"Since then our Lord Jesus Christ is called the Minister of the Circumcision, though He is at the same time the Pastor and Saviour of all men, so, in like manner, Peter is called the Apostle of the Circumcision, though he is also the pastor and ruler appointed by Christ of the entire flock. And hence S. Leo says:

'From the whole world Peter alone is chosen to be set over the vocation of all the nations, and over all the Apostles, and over all the Fathers of the Church; so that though there be in the people of God many priests, and many pastors, yet Peter in a true and proper sense rules all those, whom, in the first and highest place, Christ also rules.'†

"With regard to what our Lord said to Ananias of Saul on his conversion:

'This man is to Me a vessel of election to carry My name before the Gentiles, and kings, and the children of Israel,'‡

the point here of these words is not, in my opinion, that the conversion of the Jews was enjoined on him in the last place, and that of the Gentiles in the first,§ since the Apostle evidently

---

* *Rom.* x. 4, 5, xv. 9.

† *Serm. 3 de sua assumpt.* It is difficult to express adequately in English the force of the Latin words *proprie* and *principaliter*. *Proprie* may mean properly, peculiarly, ordinarily, or personally. These words of S. Leo may serve to illustrate what the Vatican Council has since defined, viz., that the Supreme Pontiff has *ordinary* jurisdiction everywhere, and over each and all of the faithful throughout the Church. "Thou art he," writes S. Bernard to Pope Eugenius, "to whom the keys are delivered, to whom the sheep are committed. There are, it is true, other door-keepers of heaven and pastors of flocks; but as much more glorious, as they differ in excellence, are both these titles which thou above all the rest hast inherited. They have each their several flocks assigned to them one by one. To thee all together are entrusted—one single flock to a single one; and not of sheep alone, but of pastors, too, art thou the one pastor of all. Whence do I prove this, dost thou ask? From the word of the Lord. To whom, too, have all the sheep, I say, not of the bishops only, but of the Apostles also, been thus absolutely, thus without exception, committed? 'If thou lovest Me, Peter, feed My sheep.' What sheep? Is it the people of this or that city, or region, or kingdom at most? *My* sheep, He says. Who sees not clearly that He did not distinguish, but that He marked out all."

‡ *Acts,* ix. 15.

§ We may compare with this passage what Simeon says of Jesus Christ Himself (*Luke,* ii. 30, 32): "Thy salvation, which Thou hast prepared before the face of all peoples: a light to the revelation of the Gentiles, and the glory of Thy people Israel." The Gentiles are first mentioned; and yet our Lord was sent, as He Himself declares, to the lost sheep of the house of Israel, and preached to them.

did not understand or act upon them in this sense;[*] for after the Council, as we have just seen, and also before it, S. Paul's invariable wont was first to enter into the synagogues and to preach to the Jews; whereof he calls the Jews of Antioch in Pisidia who had opposed his preaching themselves to witness in these words:

'To you it behoved us first to speak the word of God; but because you reject it and judge yourselves unworthy of eternal life, behold we turn to the Gentiles. For so the Lord hath commanded us,' &c.[†]

But we are to understand the words of Christ to be spoken prophetically, signifying that, through the preaching of S. Paul, there would be a great accession from among the Gentiles to the Christian religion. And this agrees with what that Apostle says himself:

'For He who wrought in Peter to the apostleship of the circumcision wrought in me also among the Gentiles.'[‡]

Since, wherever he went preaching the Gospel, he found the Gentiles ready to hear him, and submissive to his teaching, but the Jews ever in opposition to him. Hence he is called the Doctor of the Gentiles, and is said to have received an Apostleship to the Gentiles. Moreover, he himself intimates that it was from the conversion of those who believed he received the name of his Apostleship and was called the Apostle of the Gentiles; for, when writing to his Corinthian converts, he says:

'Am not I an Apostle?... Are not you my work in the Lord? And if unto others I be not an Apostle, but yet to you I am, for you are the seal of my apostleship in the Lord.'[§]

And this he says when addressing the Gentiles."

We venture to supplement what Baronius has here said by the following remarks: We may well believe that S. Paul had special gifts of illumination and persuasion, bestowed upon him for the conversion of the Gentiles, more excellent in measure and kind, together with a success in this ministry greater, than were vouchsafed to the other Apostles: whilst he himself seems to have made what was peculiarly his Divine vocation to be, at the same time, his own most cherished attrait. Thus it is, he pours

---

[*] In the same general sense S. Paul reports our Lord's words as told him by Ananias: "For thou shalt be His witness to *all* men, of those things which thou hast seen and heard." (*Acts*, xxii. 14, 15.) And again the words spoken to himself by Jesus Christ. (xxvi. 16, 18.)

[†] *Acts*, xiii. 46, 47. [‡] *Gal.* ii. 8. [§] 1 *Cor.* ix. 1, 2.

forth all his most sublime and fervid eloquence when he treats of the call of the Gentiles to the Faith, and as he contemplates himself the Apostle specially chosen to carry into effect this Divine dispensation. He speaks of it as something wholly exceptional and extraordinary in the order of Divine grace and election, as pre-eminently resulting from pure unmerited mercy; describing it as—

"The mystery which had been hidden from ages and generations, which in other generations was not known to the sons of men, but now at length was made manifest, viz., that God should make known the riches of the glory of the mystery among the Gentiles, Christ in them the Hope of Glory; and that they should be fellow-heirs and co-partners of His promise in Christ Jesus by the Gospel."

He glories that to him—

"Is given the dispensation of the grace of God towards the Gentiles, that he is the prisoner of Jesus Christ for their sakes, and that he had received his knowledge in this mystery of Christ, of which he is made a minister, according to the gift of the grace of God, which was given to him according to the operation of His power; even that on him, the least of all the saints, was bestowed this grace, to preach among the Gentiles the unsearchable riches of Christ, and to enlighten all men, that they might see what is the dispensation of the mystery which had been hidden from eternity in God, Who created all things." *

But whilst thus "he has glory in Christ Jesus towards God, because of the grace which is given him from God that he should be the minister of Christ Jesus among the Gentiles,"† it would still seem, from his whole tenor of speech, that S. Paul regarded the Apostolate to the Jews as that which was the normal, and the more excellent and noble in itself. He speaks of this ministry as the first in order, and, so to say, due by a prior claim of covenanted right: "To the Jew first, and also to the Greek."‡ Whereas he describes the vocation of the Gentiles to the Faith, as though in a sense abnormal, secondary, subservient to, and for the sake of, the conversion of the Jews. Thus the Jews, he says, are—

"The natural branches of the good olive-tree, whose root is holy, whose first-fruits are holy: whilst the Gentiles are branches of a wild olive, and, contrary to nature, are grafted into the good olive-tree, that so they may partake of the root and fatness of the olive-tree:"

and if this be so, continues the Apostle, apostrophising the Gentile—

"If thou wert cut out of the wild olive-tree, which is natural to thee, and, contrary to nature, wert grafted into the good olive-tree: how much more

---

* See *Coloss.* i. 25-27; *Eph.* iii. 1-9. † *Rom.* xv. 15-17.
‡ *Rom.* i. 14; ii. 9, 10.

shall they, that are the natural branches (broken off because of unbelief), if they abide not still in unbelief, be grafted into their own olive-tree? For God is able to graft them in again."*

S. Paul, even in the very act of glorifying his own special Apostolate to the Gentiles, recognises its, so to say, subserviency to that to the Jews:

"For," he writes, "I say to you Gentiles, as long, indeed, as I am the Apostle of the Gentiles, I will honour my ministry, if by any means I may provoke to emulation them who are my flesh, and may save some of them."†

Independently of the particular vocation the Apostle had received from heaven to evangelise the Gentiles, we cannot but think that his own extraordinary conversion and exceptional call to the Apostleship served much to influence and form the bent of his mind, and to strengthen his predilection for that ministry. He seems to draw a parallel between the grace vouchsafed to himself and the dispensation of God's mercy to the Gentiles. Thus he speaks of himself as "one born out of due time," as made a signal example of "undeserved mercy," and as having received in fulness Divine gifts and graces, though " the chief of sinners," " the least and last of the Apostles, unworthy even to be called an Apostle because he had persecuted the Church of God." ‡ He delights especially to dwell upon the absolute freedom of God's election, the unmerited liberality and munificence of His grace, and the excesses of His boundless mercy. These themes he repeatedly exemplifies; at one time by the call of the Gentiles to be partakers of the Gospel, at another by the wondrous choice God had made of himself. Hence he is all the more strongly drawn to devote himself to the conversion of the Gentiles, as being that Apostolate which, going out of the more ordinary course, most strikingly exhibits the exceeding riches of Divine mercy, and is in fuller correspondence with the entirely exceptional and extraordinary bestowal of grace he had himself received.

"S. Peter," writes Dr Döllinger, "held a preeminence among the Apostles, which none of the rest contested. He received the keys of the kingdom, and is the rock on which the Church is built—that is, the continuance, increase, and growth of the Church rest on the office created in his person. To him was the

* Rom. xi. 16-24. † Rom. v. 13, 14.
‡ Tim. i. 11-16; 1 Cor. xv. 9; Eph. iii. 8.

charge given to strengthen his brethren and feed the flock of Christ. 'The Gospel of the Circumcision,' as S. Paul says, was especially committed to him by the Lord, as to the man of Tarsus that of the uncircumcision.* Christ Himself was a minister of the circumcision; His Messianic energies were devoted to the good of Israel, so that He said Himself, 'I am not sent, but to the lost sheep of the house of Israel.'† In this S. Peter followed Him; he is peculiarly the Apostle of Israel, the head of the Church of the circumcision, and he is this in a higher and more eminent sense than S. James, who is doubly inferior to him, both as being confined to Jerusalem, while he included the whole dispersion in his labours, and as holding aloof from the Gentiles, while he was the first to incorporate them into the Church and also extended his ecclesiastical labours, though in a lesser degree, to uncircumcised converts. For there were not two Churches, one of the circumcision and one of the uncircumcision, but there was one olive-tree, one people of God, one Israel; and into this tree the Gentiles were grafted and thereby made partakers of the root and the juice, as adopted children of Abraham, whence S. Peter tells the Christian women of the communities he addresses, that they are daughters of Sarah.‡ And thus the Apostle, to whom Israel is specially entrusted by God, is necessarily the Head of the Apostolic College and the whole Church. The agreement between him and S. Paul regarded a division of labour, not of the Church; and S. Paul, who travelled to Jerusalem for the special purpose of spending fifteen days with S. Peter, knew well that he was chief among the three pillar Apostles, although he would not be dependent on him in pursuing the way shown to himself by Divine call and revelation, and opposed him at Antioch. The point on which S. Paul laid such great weight, that the Gentiles were to be converted immediately to Christ and not through the medium of previous conversion to Judaism, was first taught by special revelation, not to him but to S. Peter. Nor did S. Paul enter on his peculiar office of preaching to the Gentiles till after his fifteen days conference with S. Peter. While the Apostles remained united at Jerusalem the primacy of Peter displayed itself on all grave occasions. It was he who arranged the filling up of the Apostolic College through the election of S. Matthias; he fixed the form of election, confining it to those who had been companions

---

* *Gal.* ii. 7. † *Rom.* xv. 8; *Matt.* xv. 24, xx. 2.
‡ *Rom.* xi. 24; 1 *Pet.* iii. 6; *Cf. infra*, iv. 3, which proves that S. Peter was addressing communities, formed chiefly of Gentile converts.

of Christ, and witnesses of His teaching and acts. He takes up
the word before the people and the Sanhedrim, and works the
first miracle for confirming Christ's resurrection. The punishment of Ananias and Sapphira, the anathema on Simon Magus,
the first heretic, the first visiting and confirming the Churches
suffering under persecution, were all his acts. If he was sent with
S. John by the Apostolic College to the new converts at Samaria,
he was himself not only a member of that college, but its president. So the Jews sent their high priest Ismael to Nero; and
S. Ignatius says that the neighbouring Churches in Asia had sent,
some their bishops, some their priests and deacons.* He was at
the head, as always and everywhere else, in the assembly of
Jerusalem, which freed the Gentiles from observing the ceremonial
law; he opened it, and his motion was carried, with the conditions added by S. James.

"The sentence of S. James could not but have great weight
at that Synod, for S. Peter, like S. Paul, was in a manner a party
concerned in the question. It was known in Jerusalem that he
had ordered the Centurion Cornelius and other Gentiles with
him at Cæsarea to be baptised without circumcision, and this had
raised great opposition on his return. And when S. Paul and S.
Barnabas came to Jerusalem, and the Synod was to be held, the
converted Pharisees again urged that Gentiles must submit to circumcision and the Law.† Therefore, S. James, who with his
community was so faithful to the Law, was the best, and for
opponents the most convincing judge in this strife, and it was
obvious that the decree would be made in conformity with his
opinion. And hence S. Paul, when appealing, in his Epistle to
the Galatians, to the pillar Apostles who gave him and Barnabas
their right hand in token of fellowship, named James first, before
Cephas;‡ for in that matter, and for persons who appealed unhesitatingly to the example of the Mother Church which kept the
Law, the example of James had more weight than that of Peter,
just as afterwards the Ebionites laboured to make his authority
appear the highest in the Church. But S. James himself acknowledged that Peter was called by God's appointment to gather from
among the Gentiles a people that should bear His name, and
unite them into one Church with converted Israelites; for he confirms S. Peter's words, that God had chosen him among all to
preach to the Gentiles.§ And so it became the Apostle who had

---

* Joseph. *Ant.* xx. 7. Ignat. *Ep. ad Philad.* 10. † *Acts*, xv. 5.
‡ *Gal.* ii. 9. § *Acts*, xv. 14.

alone received the keys of the kingdom. S. Paul was the first to enter into the work S. Peter had begun, and build on his foundation; he could not have done so unless S. Peter, in consequence of their previous arrangement, had recognised him as a fellow-labourer, Divinely called, even though he derived his mission immediately from Christ. That he stood on a lower level than S. Peter is shown by his own way of describing his relations to Jews and Gentiles; he took every way of "glorifying his office," as Apostle of the Gentiles, by numerous conversions, that through the influence thus obtained he might rouse the emulation of some at least of his people and win them.[*] S. Peter had no need of this circuitous method; he wrought, by the weight of his office, equally on Jews and Gentiles, and it was his own free act that made him afterwards prefer confining his energies chiefly to Jews. S. Paul was far from concealing that, in his eyes, S. Peter was not simply one of the Twelve, but had a peculiar position and dignity distinct from the rest, and that, accordingly, an appeal to his example had peculiar weight. He is not content with saying, "Have I not power to lead about a sister, like the other Apostles?" but he adds, "like the brethren of the Lord and Cephas."[†] And if S. Peter, in mentioning the presbyters of the Churches, calls them "fellow presbyters," he was mindful of his Lord's example Who, while standing so high above the Apostles, called them "His brethren," bade him strengthen his brethren, and as greatest in the kingdom be the least and humblest.[‡] He saw in the presbyters men who, like himself, served the brethren in teaching and ministration, and who, so far, were his fellow ministers." [§]

"If S. Peter and S. Paul agreed on a certain division of labour, this was grounded on S. Peter's feeling that he and the rest of the elder Apostles were more immediately fitted and called by their whole mental training to work among the Jews, and that it was their office to bring in the Gentiles at first only where a foundation had been previously laid of converted Jews and well-instructed communities of Jewish Christians. They could only act effectively on the Gentiles through the converted Jews of the Dispersion, who were already familiar with Heathen views and morals, while S. Paul was the right man to act immediately on them with the best success. But if S. Paul designated himself the Apostle of the Gentiles, he did not mean that he was to give preference to the Gentiles over the Jews in carrying out his voca-

[*] *Rom.* xi. 13, 14. [†] 1 *Cor.* ix. 5. [‡] *Matt.* xxviii. 10; *Luke,* xxii. 32.
[§] *The First Age of the Church,* vol. ii. pp. 115-20.

tion; on the contrary, his first duty and endeavours always belonged to the Jews. But he meant that the wide domain of the Heathen provinces of the empire, where the Jews were only scattered here and there, was the special field of his Apostolical energy, while the other Apostles were still devoting themselves to the communities in Judæa and Galilee, which contained only Jewish Christians or so few Gentiles that the Jewish element gave their dominant character to these societies, and the few Gentile converts had to adapt themselves to it. On the contrary, in the communities founded or visited by S. Paul, the Gentile character predominated from the beginning, and the Jewish Christians who chanced to be there were necessarily required to act accordingly, and to renounce the separatist element of the law which forbade to eat with the uncircumcised. . . .

"S. Peter addressed his First Epistle, at a date which cannot be precisely fixed, to the communities in the north of Asia Minor, consisting partly of Jews, but chiefly of Gentile converts, to the believers living as strangers scattered among the Heathen in Pontus, Galatia, Cappadocia, Asia, and Bithynia,—communities partly founded by S. Paul, Silas, formerly a companion of S. Paul, was its bearer.[*] The word 'dispersion' in the title does not at all mean that the Epistle was only addressed to the Christians of Jewish descent in those communities—a division S. Peter never dreamt of—but it suggested itself as the natural designation for Christians who, like the Jews before, were a 'dispersion,' and felt themselves a scattered body of strangers in the Roman Empire, yet inwardly united by the closest bonds.[†] There are several expressions in the Epistle which can only be understood of those who had formerly been Heathen.[‡] . . . Its whole line, both in what it says and what it does not say, proves that the original difficulties in the way of a complete coalescing of Jewish and Gentile Christians were already overcome, at least in those regions, and that the errors S. Paul had to combat in writing to the Galatians no longer presented themselves, while the seductions of Jewish Gnosticism had not yet appeared. The date of the composition must therefore be placed several years before the Apostle's death, before, indeed, S. Paul had written his Epistles to the Colossians, to Timothy, and Titus."[§]

---

[*] 1 *Pet.* v. 12.

[†] *Cf.* 1 *Pet.* ii. 11; where the Christians are called emphatically πάροικοι καὶ παρεπίδημοι as in the superscription παρεπίδημοι διασπορᾶς.

[‡] 1 *Pet.* iv. 3, 4.   [§] *Ibid.* vol. i. p. 151-154.

CHAPTER XII.

S. PETER'S REPREHENSION BY S. PAUL AT ANTIOCH.

CLOSELY connected with the question of the two Apostolates is the episode of S. Paul's reprehension of S. Peter recorded in his Epistle to the Galatians. We have no intention of treating this matter exhaustively, or from every point of view, but only so far as its consideration may throw light on the relations existing between the two Apostles, and bears upon our main subject.

The earliest notice of this incident to be found in the Fathers is that of Clement of Alexandria, preserved by Eusebius in the following words:

> "Clement, in the fifth of his Hypotyposes, or Institutions, speaks of Cephas,—of whom Paul says, that on his coming to Antioch, he resisted him to the face,—as having the same name with Peter the Apostle, but as being one of the seventy." *

S. Jerome and S. Chrysostom mention this opinion of Clement as held also by others.†

Origen, SS. Chrysostom, Jerome, and Augustine take for granted that the Cephas here spoken of is the Apostle S. Peter. Since their time this view has been generally received, and become, so to say, traditional in the Church. The three first of these Fathers, followed by Theophylact, Baronius, and others, hold that S. Peter's reprehension by S. Paul was, by a mutual understanding, preconcerted; consequently, was not serious but feigned, and was brought about in the following way. S. Peter,

---

* *E. H.* i. 12.

† This opinion has had the support of several authors of note. In these times it has been defended with much erudition in the French periodical, *Etudes religieuses, historiques, et littéraires.* Tome vii. Nos. 30 et 32, Juin et Août, 1865; *Analecta Juris Pontif.* Serié vii. Tome iv. pp. 897-933; and in a dissertation entitled: *Lucubratio altera de Persona Cephæ ab Apostolo Paulo reprehensi distincta a Simone Petro, seu Jacobus, Cephas, et Joannes quorum mentio in Epistola ad Galatas* ii. 9, *extra catalogum Duodecim Apostolorum et Fratrum Domini collocandi,* per Prof. Aloisium Vincenzi—Romæ typis Bernardi Morini, 1872. Calmet, in his *Dissertation* on the question, maintains strongly the opposite opinion.

who at Jerusalem had been living with Jews after the Jewish manner, as was perfectly lawful, on coming to Antioch began by living with the Gentiles as a Gentile: but on the arrival there of some Jewish converts from S. James at Jerusalem,—in order not to offend them as being amongst the first called to the Faith, and having prior claims in the Church of Christ,—withdrew himself from the Gentiles, that thus he might give an opportunity to S. Paul, the Apostle of the Gentiles, to reprehend him, and that then, by his own submission to the reproof, he might, at the same time, teach the Jews a practical lesson against their Judaising, and affirm the non-obligation for Christians of the old Ceremonial Law.

S. Augustine, on the other hand, strenuously opposed S. Jerome, in his notion that the reprehension was feigned, maintaining that S. Peter was really blameable in his conduct, and was seriously rebuked for it by S. Paul: and this, he contended, was evident from the Apostle's own words.

It should be here observed, that neither S. Jerome[*] nor S. Chrysostom supposed for a moment that S. Peter was really guilty of deception, that is, of simulating by his outward conduct any such Judaising as was against his conscience, and which he condemned in his heart. The simulation they speak of, such as it was, lay not in the conduct of S. Peter at all, but in the reprehension he received. Peter, they say, was rebuked in appearance only, that thereby the error of the Judaisers might be really and more emphatically condemned.

According to S. Augustine, then, the reprehension on the part of S. Paul was real, and deserved by S. Peter for having committed a fault. That fault did not consist precisely in his living as a Jew, and observing the Ceremonial Law, for this was in itself lawful, and, as we know, the practice at times of S. Paul himself. Let us here explain. The Ceremonial Law had, it is true, ceased to be obligatory from the day of Pentecost when the New Law was promulgated and began to come in force. But the Old Law was not yet abolished, nor had it lost its force in such sense that it might not still for a time be kept; that is, until the Jews should be weaned and withdrawn from its observance by gradual and gentle disuse; and thus it would, at length, as S. Augustine says, receive at their hands a decent and honourable sepulture.

The Old Law, consequently, though dead, was not yet deadly.

---

[*] Cornelius a Lapide, whom we are here following, thinks that S. Augustine misunderstood S. Jerome on this point.

It might still be observed, especially with the view of winning the Jews more readily to the faith of Christ. Nay, it might be of obligation, through the higher law of Charity, in cases where its non-observance would cause scandal and hinder conversions. But the Old Law would be deadly if anyone observed its ceremonial precepts, thinking, or so. conducting himself, as though he were bound by them, or that their observance was obligatory on Christians for justification before God. Now, although S. Peter did not think thus himself, yet, in the judgment of S. Paul, as is clear from the Apostle's words, S. Peter acted with such want of caution as to give the Gentiles ground for thinking this. For, on seeing S. Peter suddenly withdrawing from themselves, with whom he had hitherto been living as a Gentile, and going over to the newly-arrived Jews to live as a Jew with them in observance of their legal rites and practices, the Gentiles might with good reason suppose that this Judaising was necessary for salvation, and as much binding on them as on S. Peter. S. Paul was, at the same time, very well aware that S. Peter had by special revelation understood before all others the freedom of Christians from the old Ceremonial Law, that he had been the first to preach this doctrine, and to bring it into practical effect.

There was, then, nothing that concerned doctrine in S. Peter's fault; nor did S. Paul so think. It was simply an error of judgment, in itself light and venial, and, we may say, not a formal, but only a material fault, resulting from some want of consideration, or insufficient light, or lack of precaution at the time. He judged, in good faith, that, as he was the Doctor and Apostle especially of the Jews, he ought rather to avoid giving offence to the Jews than to the Gentiles; and that this the Gentiles knew, or might easily suppose. Moreover, neither the Apostle Peter nor Barnabas intended, or adverted to, the "dissimulation" of which S. Paul speaks. Nevertheless, in this judgment, as the inspired words of the Apostle informs us, S. Peter made a mistake. And even an Apostle might thus err. On this point S. Thomas says:

"The Holy Ghost, in descending on the Apostles at Pentecost, confirmed them thenceforth in prudence and grace to avoid all mortal sins, but not all venial faults."

The short summary which S. Alphonsus gives of this question is so much to the purpose, that, at the risk of some repetition, we venture here to reproduce it:

S. ALPHONSUS—THE PROTESTANT OBJECTION BLUNTED.

"As to the reprehension of S. Peter by S. Paul, of which the latter Apostle thus speaks in his Epistle to the Galatians, ii. 11 : 'I withstood him to the face because he was to be blamed,' some, as S. Jerome,* answer that this dispute was preconcerted purposely to tranquillise the Jews ; but others, with S. Augustine,† S. Cyprian,‡ S. Gregory,§ S. Thomas,‖ and S. Jerome himself,¶ when he afterwards retracted, say more commonly, and with greater probability, that these words were a real reprehension, but that there was no question of doctrine involved—viz., as to whether, under the evangelical law, the legal observances of the Jews were to be still maintained. S. Peter was well aware that these observances were to be abolished ; nay more, before this—when S. Paul brought tidings of what the converted Jews were doing at Antioch, and how they would have the Gentiles who believed to be circumcised—it was S. Peter who severely blamed such a pretension, saying : 'Now, therefore, why tempt you God, to put a yoke upon the necks of the disciples, which neither our fathers nor we have been able to bear?'** But, in this case, the question was one only of a point of discipline and of expediance ; that is, whether it was then fitting and expedient to wholly abolish, or not, the Mosaic law. For though it was already dead, it had not yet become deadly to those who observed it. Hence, says S. Augustine, it ought to receive an honourable burial. And, in fact, S. Paul himself in those first times, to avoid giving scandal to the Jews, would have S. Timothy circumcised.†† It was with good reason, however, that S. Paul afterwards blamed S. Peter, when, from fear of displeasing the Jewish converts, he separated from the Gentiles, who did not observe the Mosaical law : for at that time it was of more importance not to shock the Gentile believers, who were many, than not to displease the Jewish converts, who were few in number, and ought to have had no reasonable grounds for scandal at seeing that the uncircumcised did not conform themselves to their usages."‡‡

This reprehension of S. Peter by S. Paul is turned to great account by Protestants in their contention against the Primacy, and thus mediately is made in their hands a strong point against S. Peter's Roman Episcopate. But the argument to be drawn from S. Paul's statement, considered in its full Scriptural context and in its patristic surroundings, tells really all the other way, and to our mind forms one of the best confirmations of S. Peter's Primacy.

In recording the two contrary views held by early Fathers regarding the person of Cephas and the simulated reprehension, we offered no opinion as to their respective merit. For ourselves we are content with that interpretation which is the more

---

* *Comment. in Gal.* ii. 11. † *Epist.* 82, n. 22, ed. Ben.
‡ *An Quint. Ep.* 71. § *Sup. Ezech. Hom.* 18.
‖ 2, 2, q. 33, a. 4, ad. 2.
¶ *Adv. Pelag.* l. i. 1 ; *Apud August. Epist. ad Ocean.*
** *Acts*, xv. 10. †† *Acts*, xvi. 3.
‡‡ *Verità della Fede*, pt. iii. c. vii. 12.

generally received in the Church, as claiming most authority from tradition and acceptance amongst the learned. But this much we will say, if either one or the other of those ancient interpretations be the true one, then the opponents of S. Peter's Primacy, on this score at any rate, have nothing more to say; they are at once disarmed, their teeth are drawn. Whereas, if those ancient interpretations are false and have no foundation in fact, then they were evidently first made for a purpose, viz., to meet what was to some a great difficulty, and they gained currency precisely because they seemed to remove or at least to lessen its force.

The difficulty would lie in the apparent incongruity or strangeness, at first sight, of S. Paul, himself lower in rank and office, thus rebuking S. Peter, the Prince of the Apostles, since, normally, a rebuke or reprimand comes only from a superior, or, at the most, from an equal; and it could never enter into the mind of antiquity that S. Peter was other than first and supreme, whilst that S. Paul was his superior or equal was altogether outside its thought. S. Peter's Primacy was to the Fathers so certain that any difficulties or objections lying in its way must be so explained as to square with what to them was evident as a first principle.

There is, however, no real incongruity at all for an inferior on an occasion of importance, and for just cause, to correct his superior in defence of the truth, provided this be done with humble charity and with due reverence for his authority. Such correction is, no doubt, exceptional and of rare occurrence. To hear of it naturally excites some surprise, and one generally needs some explaining circumstances for its justification and approval.*

The Fathers who treat of this point are full of such explanation. Thus S. Jerome tells us:†

"Origen in his comments on the Epistle to the Galatians was the first to give that explanation of S. Paul's narrative which other interpreters followed, and he himself (S. Jerome) adopted, in order especially to answer

---

* In the history of the Church there are several instances of censure, reproof, expostulation, admonition, or instruction being offered to the Popes by holy persons, who, whilst expressing themselves in very strong and earnest language, did not forget, at the same time, either their own inferiority, or the dignity and authority of him with whom they remonstrated. Amongst these we may mention S. Cyprian, S. Bernard, S. Thomas of Canterbury, and S. Catharine of Sienna.

† *Ep.* 112, *ad Augustin.* 6.

the blaspheming Porphyry, who accused Paul of forwardness in having dared to blame Peter, the Prince of the Apostles."

S. Jerome had just before said :

"If this sense please not some one—according to which it is shown that neither Peter sinned nor Paul blamed with over-presumption one greater than himself—he ought to show with what consistency Paul reproved in another what he did himself."

Again he writes :

"Of such authority was Peter that Paul has written in his Epistle:[*] 'Then after three years I went to Jerusalem to see Peter and I tarried with him fifteen days,' &c. (n. 8). . . . He went in order to see the Apostle, not with a desire of learning, . . . but to pay honour to the first Apostle."

In the incident at Antioch S. Jerome represents S. Paul as so acting—

"That he may both defer to the Apostle that was before him, and yet, compelled by truth, may 'withstand him boldly to the face.' "[†]

S. Chrysostom had already written that S. Paul, in going to Jerusalem to see Peter, went expressly to visit him in his character of chief pastor and primate.

"Jesus (he writes) saith to Simon Peter . . . 'Feed My sheep.' And why then, passing by the others, does He converse with Peter on these things? He was the chosen one of the Apostles, and the mouth of the disciples, and the leader of the choir. On this account Paul also went up on a time to see him rather than the others. . . . Christ puts into his hand the presidency over the brethren. . . . A third time He gives him the same injunction, showing at what a price He sets the presidency over His own sheep. . . . He appointed this man teacher, not of that throne (the throne of Jerusalem, given to James), but of the world."[‡]

Theodoret says :

"And this again shows the virtue of Paul's soul. For though he stood not in need of any teaching from man, since he had received this from the God of all, yet he renders suitable honour to the Coryphæus."[§]

Those Fathers who admit the reality of the reprehension and its justice are likewise full of explanations, extolling especially S. Peter's humility.

Thus S. Cyprian writes :

"For neither did Peter, whom the Lord chose as first, and upon whom He built the Church, when Paul afterwards disputed with him about circum-

---

[*] *Gal.* i. 18.
[†] In *Gal.* i.
[‡] S. Chrysost. *Hom.* 88 *in Joan*, n. 1.
[§] In *Gal.* i. 18.

cision, claim anything overbearingly, nor assume anything arrogantly, as though to say that he held the primacy, and that he ought rather to be obeyed by those newly come and after himself; nor did he despise Paul because he had been previously a persecutor of the Church, but admitted the counsel of truth and readily assented to the legitimate reasons which Paul maintained, giving us thereby an example of concord and patience that we should not pertinaciously love what is our own, but should rather account as our own the things which are at times usefully and beneficially suggested by our brethren and colleagues, if true and lawful."*

This passage of S. Cyprian is cited by S. Augustine,† who thus comments upon it:

"See how Cyprian commemorates what we have also learnt in the Holy Scriptures, that the Apostle Peter, in whom the primacy of the Apostles is pre-eminent by so excellent a grace, when led on occasion to act as regards the circumcision otherwise than truth demanded, was corrected by a later Apostle.... I think, without any contumely to himself, Cyprian the Bishop may be compared to Peter the Apostle, so far as regards the crown of martyrdom. Indeed I ought rather to fear lest I be contumelious towards Peter. For who knows not that that principality of the Apostolate is to be preferred before any episcopate whatever. But even if the grace of the Chair is different, yet one is the glory of the martyrs."

S. Augustine writes again:

"Peter himself received with the piety of a holy and benignant humility what was done profitably by Paul in the freedom of charity. And thus he gave to posterity a rarer and holier example that they should not disdain, if ever perchance they left the right track, to be corrected by their juniors, than Paul did by showing that even inferiors might confidently venture to resist superiors, if brotherly charity be maintained, for the defence of evangelical truth."‡

S. Gregory says:

"Peter kept silence, that he who was first in the height of the Apostolate might be first in humility."§

The learned Dr. Döllinger has so lucidly set forth the facts of the narrative which forms the subject of this Chapter, and has explained the whole case so admirably, that we think we cannot do better than give his exposition here at some length.

"The Apostles knew, in a general way, God's decree as to the call of the Gentiles: but they were not clear as to its precise time or conditions. Were those Gentiles only to be received who were already 'proselytes of righteousness,' that is, those who

* *Ep.* 71, *ad Quintum.* † *De Baptism.* l. ii. 2.
‡ *Ep.* 82; *Hieronymo.* n. 22. § *Hom.* 18 *in Ezech.*

had submitted to circumcision and the whole Jewish law? The law of Moses had enjoined circumcision as a permanent and constantly binding obligation; the uncircumcised was to be rooted out of the people of God. And the Apostles foresaw that to relax this condition, by admitting him to communion among born Jews, would certainly give the greatest offence, and be a serious hindrance to the further spread of the faith among them. It needed a special Divine revelation to overcome their scruples and hesitation, and accordingly one was given to S. Peter, who was destined, as head of the Church, to admit the first Gentiles.

"There were at that time many Gentiles everywhere who, in the eyes of the Jews, were half-converts, like those earlier 'proselytes of the gate,' who were not required to observe the whole law, but only to abstain from certain heathen practices. These 'God-fearing' Gentiles used to observe the hours of prayer in the Temple, and attended the service at the Synagogues, but, being uncircumcised, were regarded and treated by the Jews as unclean, and they would not eat or drink or hold any familiar intercourse with them. Such a half proselyte was the Centurion Cornelius, who belonged to the Italian cohort quartered at Cæsarea. . . . This was the man chosen out by Divine Providence to be an example and evidence of the breaking down and entire removal of the partition-wall between different nations. . . .

"If the conversion of the Gentile family at Cæsarea was an isolated event, a whole community of Gentile converts was founded at the same time in the Eastern capital of the Empire, which had also a great number of Jewish inhabitants, and thus the admission of the uncircumcised into the Church of Christ became a recognised procedure. . . . Antioch, from the size of the city and the personal standing of the men who laboured there to build up the Christian society, became the second Christian metropolis and Mother Church, which, consisting chiefly of Gentile converts, took its place beside the Mother Church of Jerusalem, consisting wholly of Jewish converts. . . .

"Several years had now elapsed since S. Paul's conversion, yet he never took more than a subordinate position in the Church, and in the rank of those engaged in the ministry. The enlightened prophets and teachers who were then in the Church at Antioch are named in the Acts of the Apostles (xiii. 1); first Barnabas, . . . and lastly, Saul. It was some time after his return from his second journey to Jerusalem with S. Barnabas that he was first raised, together with him, to the Apostolic office, according to previous announcement [from Christ Himself in the Temple,* by the prophets at Antioch]. . . . This was no conferring of Apostleship on their part: the Apostles themselves had received no power from Christ to do that. Both the vocation to the Apostolate and its bestowal could only come direct from God. . . .

"If S. Paul sought out the Apostle Peter during his short stay in Jerusalem, that was only to show honour to his primacy, not to receive instruction from him, which he needed not, or power and mission, which he already possessed.† S. Paul and S. Barnabas, though specially called to the Gentile Apostolate, always recognised the prior right of the Jews by preaching Christ first to them on their journeys. The Synagogues were the places where S. Paul appeared, the rather since a number of 'God-fearing' Gentiles, proselytes of the gate, were always among their members, who formed the bridge whereby Christ's message might reach the unbelieving Gentiles also.‡ . . .

"On the return of S. Paul and S. Barnabas to Antioch from their first missionary journey, the quarrel with the Judaizers broke out, which henceforth, through all the Apostolic age, was the sorest trial of the infant Church, and the grand difficulty especially which S. Paul had to contend with. The conduct of both Apostles in inviting Gentiles at once to enter the Jewish Christian community, without any regard to law, defilement, or separation, was something shocking and intolerable to the great body of Jews as then minded. The sons of Abraham and their lofty privileges would be swallowed up, as it were, at no distant period by the mass of Gentile believers. This anxiety was felt above all in Jerusalem, where the Temple and Levitical service were constantly before men's eyes. The affair of Cornelius was an isolated case, an exception to the rule, acquiesced in as having received the seal of Divine approval through the miraculous outpouring of the gifts of the Spirit on those Gentiles; but now that communities were being formed consisting wholly or chiefly of Gentile converts, the greatness of the danger was conspicuous. And certain 'false brethren, who had crept in secretly,' appeared at Antioch, intending to force the yoke of the Mosaic law on the new converts.

"The Ceremonial Law had its stronghold and the guarantee of its continuance in the existence of the Jewish polity. So long as this and the Temple stood, it was idle to think of abolishing the

---

* *Acts*, xxii. 17-21.   † *Gal.* i. 15-19.   ‡ *Acts*, xiii. 5-14.

law; or at least its abolition could only have come about through a general and simultaneous entrance of the Jewish nation, as well its lower as its higher classes, into the Church. For the ceremonial was also a civil law; the Jew was bound to its observance not only as an individual, but also as a member of the state and nation; nor was there any command of the Lord to the individual believer to separate from his people and its Church and State organisation. Moreover, in Judæa and Galilee it was impossible to do so without emigrating. But even the Jews of the Dispersion always regarded themselves as members of the Commonwealth which had its seat and centre at Jerusalem, and sent their contributions thither. Thus, it was not left to the caprice of believers in Judæa whether they would observe the ceremonial law or not, but was for them a necessity. Meanwhile, until the counsel of God was more broadly and clearly developed, they remained in the fullest sense Israelites, only distinguished in the one point of their believing that the Messiah had already come, but willingly conforming in all other respects to the existing order of the law.

"The Apostles on their side did not venture to do anything which might impede the grand vocation of the whole nation to become pillars and instruments of the religion of Messiah—a vocation not yet definitively rejected, nor had the interval permitted for accepting it yet expired. They did not venture to introduce or abolish anything at the risk of needlessly repelling the great body of the Jews, and were bound to sustain carefully all the fibres by which the Christian community was attached to the great national Church and State. They accordingly continued to observe the law themselves, and tolerated and approved its observance in the Jewish Christian communities.

"But the Christian zealots for the law who came from Jerusalem to Antioch declared to the Gentile converts: 'Unless you are circumcised, you cannot be saved.'* This was going beyond even the prevalent Jewish view of the period, for there was a large body of 'Proselytes of the gate' who were not required to keep the ceremonial law. But had it been announced in the name of the Synagogue that there was no salvation without being circumcised, of course no Gentile would have become a proselyte of this kind; he would either have remained a Heathen or become a 'Proselyte of righteousness;' but this class was comparatively a small one.... Here, then, was a very grave practical difficulty. It was not easy to see how a brotherly relationship and

* *Acts*, xv. 1.

healthy intercourse of common life could grow up between Gentile and Jewish Christians, the circumcised and uncircumcised. For the strict ceremonialist would not eat and drink with the uncircumcised; the law of meats prevented him. This, in fact, was a knot which could not really be untied or cut, except by the direct intervention of Divine Providence. Meanwhile, as the claims of the two parties could not be thoroughly reconciled, some temporary accommodation had to be devised.

"Paul and Barnabas, therefore, with certain others, including Titus, a learned Greek who had joined S. Paul, went to Jerusalem commissioned by the Church at Antioch to get this difficult question settled. It was S. Paul's third journey to the capital since his conversion, and fourteen years after it... It was resolved on S. Peter's proposal, in an assembly where he and S. James were present together with the presbyters of the Church, that the burden of circumcision and the law should not be laid on Gentile converts. But in order to facilitate a real fusion of Jews and Gentiles in the Church, the latter were to abstain from certain things peculiarly repulsive to the Jews, viz., from sharing in Heathen sacrificial feasts, and eating blood or the flesh of strangled animals. The Apostles felt the more bound to require the observance of these restrictions, as it was a matter causing offence to the Jews and making Christianity appear to them a religion beset with Heathen abominations. It was thought necessary in Jerusalem to add the prohibition of 'fornication,' because impurity and sins of the flesh were so common and so little regarded among the Heathen that much of this sort might also survive among converts from Heathenism.[*]

"S. Paul had communicated to the three leading Apostles at a private interview his manner of procedure in preaching to the Gentiles, probably before the public meeting; not, as he says, to gain instruction from them—for he did what he did by Divine inspiration—but to gain the confirmation and sanction of their authority. He had already successfully resisted the demands of the Christian Pharisees that his attendant, Titus, a converted Greek, should be circumcised. The Apostles had nothing to object to S. Paul's conduct and teaching, which they found all perfectly regular, and made a brotherly covenant with him, acknowledging that, as Peter had been prepared and blessed by God for the work of converting the Jews, so Paul was a chosen instrument for winning the Gentiles. They agreed, therefore, to

[*] *Acts*, xv. 1-29; *Gal.* ii. 1-10.

S. PETER'S FIRST CONDUCT AT ANTIOCH.

work according to a mutual understanding, Peter, James, and John devoting themselves principally to preaching the Gospel to the circumcised, while Paul and Barnabas worked as Apostles of the Gentiles.* But this did not hinder S. Paul from labouring with unwearied zeal to win his countrymen to faith in Christ, or withdraw S. Peter and S. John from preaching to the Gentiles when opportunity offered. All communities already founded, or now growing up beyond the limits of Judæa, were composed of both Jews and Gentiles, so that every Apostle who did not remain in Judæa, like S. James, must attend to both. At the same time whatever communities S. Paul and S. Barnabas might found were to be connected with the Church at Jerusalem, and testify their relation to it as daughters by sending contributions to the poor there.

"The worst was thus averted, and the Christian liberty of Gentile converts secured; but the main difficulty remained unsolved, and was purposely not touched upon at the Council. It was tacitly assumed that the Jewish Christians and the Apostles themselves would continue to observe the law. But how was a real Church communion to come about while the Israelite held a converted and baptised Greek for an unclean being, with whom it was defilement to eat and drink?† Without doubt the Apostles intended the requirements of the Jewish laws to yield here to the higher duties of Christian brotherly love, and the better claims of membership in the body of the Church. In Judæa, where the Christian societies were purely Jewish, there was no opportunity for exhibiting this in practice; but soon after the Apostolic Council S. Peter had an opportunity of doing so while staying at Antioch with S. Paul and S. Barnabas.‡ In that city, where the Jewish law was not the law of the land, he had no scruple about 'living as a Gentile;' *i.e.*, associating at table and in domestic life with Gentiles, until some Jewish Christians arrived there from S. James's communion at Jerusalem. And then, to avoid offending them and damaging his influence among the Jews of Palestine, he thought it right to withdraw from eating with Gentile converts. All the Jewish Christians at Antioch—S. Barnabas among them—followed his example.§ This was no violation of the rule laid down by the Council, for the whole ques-

---

* *Gal.* ii. 1-9. † *Gal.* ii. 11-14.
‡ Jungmann, following S. Augustine, is of opinion that the reprehension took place before the Council. See part i. pp. 72, 73.
§ *Gal.* ii. 11-14.

tion was left unsettled there, and whoever disregarded this part of the law was, in the eyes of all Jews, a complete breaker of the law. S. Peter, therefore, might well think that, being compelled to choose between the Gentiles and the Jews, he had better take the lesser evil of the two. As S. Paul says, he feared those of the circumcision. This was no want of moral courage, of which he had given abundant proof in more than once upbraiding all Jerusalem and its rulers with their sin against the Lord, in opening the Church's gates to the first Gentile family, and in being the first at the Council to recognise Gentile liberties. But he remembered that the Jewish Christians of Palestine belonged to the Jewish civil polity, still existing, though dependent on Rome, and based entirely on the Mosaic law; he knew that law—social, ritual, and political—to be the law of the land, from which Christians could not withdraw themselves while continuing to be citizens and residents in the country. He had rightly preferred regard for his Gentile brethren to observance of the law while living at Antioch, beyond the jurisdiction of the Jewish state. But the arrival of Jewish Christians from Jerusalem placed him in a dilemma between opposite duties and relations, his old duty to his fellow-countrymen, converted chiefly by him, and bound by the law of separation, and his new duty to brethren gained over by others. As the shepherd appointed by Christ for the whole flock, he belonged to both, but he had hitherto been peculiarly the Apostle of Israel, and was not willing to give up his labours in Jerusalem and Judæa; he wished especially to preserve his authority and influence where born Jews predominated. He had, indeed, already broken through the partition wall by the baptism of Cornelius, and maintained his right to do so against the scruples of others; but then he could appeal to the fire baptism and miraculous gifts of the Spirit, whereby God Himself attested that the Gentiles were no more unclean or inferior to Jewish believers. No such event had occurred at Antioch.

"But S. Peter had himself declared at the Council that the ritual law was a yoke neither the Jews nor their fathers had been able to bear; he had first, as S. Paul said, 'though a Jew, lived as a Gentile,' yet he now assumed an attitude which, from his position in the Church, amounted to putting on Gentile converts a moral compulsion to submit to the yoke of the law. For if he, the pillar of legitimate unity chosen by Christ as shepherd of the flock, showed by his actions that he held the uncircumcised unclean, their persons and their meats defiling, they could only infer that, to be admitted to communion with the Head of the Church, they must sacrifice the liberty guaranteed to them by the Council and adopt the Jewish law. That was intolerable to S. Paul as Apostle of the Gentiles and preacher of Evangelical freedom, and he thought, too, how the Pharisee zealots who wanted to impose the whole law on Gentiles would abuse this example of the chief Apostle. He openly and sharply censured S. Peter for building up again what he had pulled down, and after he had already by his conduct absolved Jewish Christians from the absolute obligation of the law, acting now from fear of men against his better judgment; that was 'hypocrisy.'* We are not told the reply; but there was no lasting quarrel, for in the thing itself both Apostles were agreed. S. Paul never thought of urging Jews in general, especially those in Palestine, to renounce the law altogether, of requiring them, e.g., not to circumcise their children; he acknowledged that they must keep it as long as the present State and Church organisation of the Jewish people lasted. The great separation was not yet come; the Jew who believed in Christ remained a member of his nation and shared its duties, as also its rights and privileges. When the key-stone which held all together was broken to pieces, when the national sanctuary of the Temple was destroyed by a higher interposition, then the links of the chain would be severed and the converted son of Abraham would belong only to the Church, and no more to his people and to the Synagogue. S. Paul himself, therefore, felt no hesitation about observing the law, when it did not come into collision with the higher duties of his Apostolate and his position towards the Gentile Christians, as when he had S. Timothy, the son of a Jewish mother and Greek father, circumcised, and bore the charges of a Nazarite vow.† He was only zealous against it when it was substituted for faith in Christ, and had a value given it in the conscience, as the means of man's justification before God, and when, as was only possible from this false standpoint, its yoke was to be laid on the necks of Gentile Christians. Such an attempt he thought was involved indirectly in S. Peter's behaviour. On the other hand, S. Peter and S. Barnabas thought they had full freedom of conscience to observe or neglect the ritual law as a thing indifferent in itself, and in the impossibility of doing justice to both parties they believed that they ought to give the preference to their countrymen. This

---

* *Gal.* ii. 14.   † *Acts*, xvi. 3; xxi. 23-26.

can be more naturally and easily justified in S. Peter than in Barnabas the Cypriote. For he saw in converted Israel the germ of the Church, to which the Gentile Christians belonged only as guests arrived later, and to their good all other considerations must yield; he knew that nothing could be more prejudicial to the success of his work in Jerusalem and Judæa than his being known to have broken through the fence which guarded the ritual purity of Judaism."*

* *The First Age of the Church*, vol. l. pp. 79-105.

CHAPTER XIII.

EVIDENCE OF S. PETER'S ROMAN EPISCOPATE, PRIMACY, AND RELATION TO S. PAUL FROM THE GREEK LITURGICAL OFFICES.

It is not a little remarkable that, where we might least expect it, viz., in the Liturgical Offices of the Greek Church, we should find the very strongest and most explicit testimony in confirmation of the Roman Episcopate of S. Peter, and of all that this historical fact connotes. But so in truth it is.

The Photian schism was no doubt, in effect, the practical denial of the Primacy conferred by Christ on Peter, as an institution which was to be perpetually permanent in the Church, and of its inheritance by his successors in the See of Rome. But in breaking the bonds of unity and charity by separation from the central See of Christendom, the Easterns, unlike the Protestants later on of Western Europe and of this country in particular, were not so hardy as to divorce themselves from their old Christian tradition, by denying in terms the historical facts to which that tradition bore witness; nor so bold as to attempt to shape an entirely new system of doctrinal Christianity, to innovate on the Sacraments, and to change the ancient forms of religious worship. With the exception of a few specified differences, on points rather of doctrinal explanation and discipline than of dogma, which were, without great difficulty, found capable of adjustment or concession, on the several occasions of temporary reunion, there was no divergency between Eastern and Western Christendom. The supreme jurisdiction of the Bishop of Rome, as implied in the divinely revealed doctrine of Peter's Primacy, inasmuch as this was practical and demanded submission, was the one crucial point, and alone became the stone of stumbling and rock of offence. The Greeks preserved unchanged their ancient liturgy, and other ritual offices of Divine worship, which contained all the old traditional symbolism and doctrinal expressions, handed down from former ages before the consummation of the schism; and these have generally continued in common use, as well amongst the schismatic (so-called) "Orthodox" Greeks, as amongst the Catholic Greeks in communion with the Holy See.

His Eminence, Cardinal Pitra, has appended to his learned dissertation, *Hymnographie de l'Eglise Grecque*, three Offices—(1) that of the Veneration of S. Peter's Chain, celebrated January 16th, (2) for the Feast of SS. Peter and Paul, June 29th, and (3) for the Commemoration of all the twelve Apostles, June 30th—besides other Greek liturgical hymns on the same subjects.

The testimonies to be found in them to S. Peter's Roman Episcopate, and to the Primacy assigned to him amongst the Apostles and in the Church by Catholic theology, could only be appreciated in their full force and at their right value by a perusal of the entire Offices, from which we cannot do more here than make some extracts. We may say that the prerogatives of S. Peter—in fact the whole Petrine theology—are set forth in these Greek Offices with such a fulness of expression and an explicitness of detail as are quite unknown to the corresponding Offices of the Latin rite.

We shall first make some mention of such points contained in them as will serve to confirm or illustrate our main thesis, and may bear upon other correlative matters of which we have treated in former Chapters.

1. The Apostles are represented as forming together a College essentially one; the several members of which possess coordinately their Apostolic jurisdiction which was bestowed on them by Christ Himself. They are endued with powers and gifts most sublime, and capable of being exercised throughout the whole world: they are all Coryphæi and Princes of the Church. And yet amongst them are two who tower high above all the rest, SS. Peter and Paul: these two in the Greek liturgy form a united pair, as though of a rank and style apart; they are the first Coryphæi, the twin Coryphæi of the Coryphæi, in whom all that can be said in praise of the entire Apostolic College culminates, since they are at once its base, summit, and crown, and, by consequence, form together the foundation, pillar, and capital of the whole Church of Christ. Thus they are lauded, whether both together or each by himself; and to glorify all the other Apostles, it is enough to celebrate the praises of Peter and Paul. This is strikingly illustrated in the Office for the Feast of the whole Twelve, June 30th, where, after exalting the Apostles' gifts and prerogatives in general, the Office turns to the praises of the two

chief Coryphæi, SS. Peter and Paul, followed by hardly more than the enumeration of the names of the other Apostles. Not that hereby any depreciation of them is implied, for—besides the eulogies rendered to them all in common on June 30th—at the recurrence of their own special Feasts in the course of the year their particular dignity and merits are set forth in most encomiastic terms.

2. With regard to SS. Peter and Paul, the eulogiums of the one seem continually to vie with those of the other. Successive Odes, or strophes in the same Ode, alternate in antithetically showing forth whatever may most exalt the glory of each. Their words, their acts, their virtues, their labours, their sufferings, their victories, the various incidents recorded of their lives characteristic of either, their special graces, favours, privileges, and merits—all these are so many themes of praise, and the hymnologist would seem by turns to strive at making the one outstrip the other. But this, we should well note—as appears clearly from the Hymns themselves—regards what is simply personal, or purely Apostolical, in the two Coryphæi. Herein they are, so to speak, on a level, and a match for one another. S. Paul—by reason of his special election and extraordinary vocation; his marvellous gifts of Divine illumination, knowledge, science, and wisdom; his inspired writings, whether regarded in their profundity of doctrine or in their number; the eloquence and extension of his preaching; his superabounding labours and sufferings; the sublime revelations, favours, and graces bestowed upon him; his ardent zeal and charity; his immense success; the numerous Churches he founded; his unrivalled fame—in all that was thus personal and Apostolic, is counted worthy to be in the very first rank before all the other Apostles, and to be linked together in closest union with S. Peter, their divinely appointed Chief, with whom, in the Providence of Grace, he was so intimately associated, by a specially alloted share in the evangelisation of the world at large, and by cooperation in preaching the Gospel at Rome, in founding and organising the Church there, and by their martyrdom together in that city. Hence S. Paul is made to share, as though by privilege, in the prerogative of the Prince of the Apostles; and the two are united together in patronage, as the great twin Protectors of the See of Rome, and of the Universal Church.

3. But over and above what is thus personal in SS. Peter and Paul, or common to them both as purely Apostolical,—which

forms so copious a theme for their praise in the Hymns of the Greek Offices,—something else is to be found in them for S. Peter that is official, and so appropriated to him in this sense, as to be peculiarly and exclusively his, and unshared by S. Paul or any other besides.

It cannot fail, we think, to strike those who read these Offices that—whereas the ground for the particular exaltation of S. Paul is his supernatural wisdom and illumination, his doctrine and preaching, his successful Apostolic labours, and his personal graces, as we have already enumerated them—the special ground for the praise of S. Peter is that he is the rock of the Faith, the foundation of the Church, the bearer of the keys, the door-keeper, guardian, and steward of the kingdom, the Supreme Pastor of the Church to whom Christ entrusted His entire flock. No doubt these prerogatives were shared in a certain measure by S. Paul, in common with all the other Apostles, and occasionally in the Hymns are thus attributed to them. We do not lay stress so much on the particular terms or epithets made use of, regarded precisely in themselves and apart from their context, as on the ground upon which they are made to rest and the reason for which they are employed. The former mode of appreciation is often misleading; since, when it is a question of eulogy, epithets and titles are wont to be bestowed with no niggard hand, and such frequently as are not properly, or are only partially, or analogically applicable to the person honoured. What we insist on in these Hymns is the constant and emphatic reiteration of the same titles given as distinctive of Peter, in direct antithesis to those bestowed upon S. Paul and all the other Apostles; and most especially on the ground expressly adduced for such attribution.

Now, over and over again, appeal is made in the Offices to the words of Christ Himself, recorded by S. Matthew and S. John as specially addressed to S. Peter—and in that same dogmatic sense which the Catholic Church has ever attached to them. These Divine words are made to form the ground of S. Peter's peculiar exaltation, the source whence are derived to him his titles of Rock of the Church, Foundation of the Faith, Key-bearer, Supreme Pastor of the flock, and the reason of his singular pre-eminence amongst all the Apostles. And herein, we should remark, precisely consists that Primacy conferred by Jesus Christ on Peter personally, officially, and exclusively, wherein neither Paul nor any other of the Apostles has part. They share

HIS UNION WITH CHRIST. MANIFOLD SENSE OF ROCK. 353

with him and are his compeers in all else save in that primatial jurisdiction over the whole Church, divinely bestowed, which is his alone.

4. Besides what is thus official, many personal traits and incidents in S. Peter's history which serve to portray his character and to set forth his merits find their place in the Hymns; but they are such especially as bear upon his office. Thus, what is most frequently alluded to is his temptation and three-fold denial; but this is uniformly recurred to in connection with our Lord's triple questioning of His Apostle, and with the thrice-given charge of His Church to Peter as its chief pastor. Again, several times S. Peter is spoken of as united to his Master in a most intimate and special manner, as though in equal companionship, and with the fellowship of two loving friends; or as bound up together, so to speak, in one person; their hearts knit (in the Greek it is glued) together, as we read were of old the hearts of David and Jonathan—the one the counterpart of the other. And this, we should say, bears particularly on what is official, the place, namely, which Peter was to hold in relation to Jesus Christ, as Chief Pastor, Head of the Church, and His Vicegerent on earth.

5. With regard to the famous passage from "S. Matthew's Gospel" (xvi. 17-19), it is most noteworthy that in the Greek Office Peter's confession of Christ's Divinity is always spoken of as something exclusively personal to himself, and not as though he were but the mouthpiece of the other Apostles, and giving utterance to their common belief. Again, the large breadth of interpretation is especially striking, with which the hymnologists paraphrase or illustrate those words of our Divine Lord—"Thou art Peter; and upon this rock," &c. Sometimes Christ Himself is the Rock. Again, in the very same phrase, Christ and Peter are both rocks, or together the one rock. Now, it is Peter's confession, or his faith, that is the rock; or, as recurs most frequently in the interpretation of the sacred text, it is Peter himself in person who is the one only rock upon which are founded the Church and her faith. It certainly never entered into the mind of the ancient Greek liturgical writers that these several senses clashed and mutually destroyed one another. Such an idea belongs to heresy and schism, in which collision and destruction are essentially inherent.

"Jesus Christ," writes S. Alphonsus, "is the principal Foundation of the Church, of Peter, and of all the faithful; whilst Peter is the secondary foundation, noways, however, different from the former. 'Christ,' says S. Basil (*Hom. de Pœnit.*), 'is Rock, and makes rock, communicating to His servants what belongs to Himself.' It is beyond doubt that the Lord in bestowing upon Peter the name of Rock communicated to him the vicarious power of Head. So that the edifice of the Church is built upon the double foundation of Jesus Christ and Peter, principally on that of Christ, but immediately, also, on that of Peter.... Jesus Christ was and is still the principal Head Who founded the Church, and Who governs it still by His own assistance; but since He had to leave this earth, the Church needed a visible head to whom all might have recourse, and by whose judgment they might be directed, and therefore Jesus Christ Himself appointed a Vicar on earth who should take His place as Head of the Church, whom He wills that all should obey. And just as he who obeys the Viceroy obeys the King, so he who obeys the Sovereign Pontiff obeys Jesus Christ.... The Pope is a member of the Church, as regards Jesus Christ, Who is the principal and invisible Head of all; but as regards the Church, he is the visible head who governs on the part of Jesus Christ." *

Cardinal Capellari, afterwards Gregory XVI., thus explains :

"Jesus Christ is the essential Rock, Simon the Rock instituted by Him. Jesus Christ is Rock by His own power, Simon is Rock by a communicated power." †

Again, because the Greek Hymnologists style Peter emphatically, and with a meaning incommunicable to others, the rock and foundation of the Church, the firm pillar of faith, the key-bearer, the ruler and administrator of the heavenly kingdom, and the shepherd of the flock, they had no thought of withholding from the other Apostles that share in these prerogatives to which they also were entitled by Divine right.

"Although we may say with truth," writes the holy Doctor in another place,‡ "that all the Apostles are the foundations of the Church, so that the words *Et super hanc petram*, &c., apply to all indirectly or less principally, yet it was Peter whom Jesus Christ had in view as the principal foundation, since it was to him His words were expressly and immediately addressed, as is clear from the very text of S. Matthew. For our Lord first asked all the Apostles : 'And you, whom do you say that I am?' But it was Peter alone who answered: 'Thou art the Christ, the Son of the living God.' And then it was that our Saviour spoke to him the words : 'Blessed art thou, Simon,' &c. Hence the reason why Peter was constituted the fundamental rock of the Church was because he alone had been specially enlightened and inspired to confess that Jesus Christ was the Son of God; and so he merited to hear the words from the mouth of our Lord: *Beatus es Simon*, &c. This it was that made S. Epiphanius say: 'Peter then is pronounced blessed; and well did this title become him who was to be the first among the Apostles, even

---

* *Verità della Fede*, pt. iii. cap. vii. 5, 11.

† See the Analytical Table of his work *Triumph of the Holy See and of the Church*, ch. ii. 5, 6.

‡ *Vindiciæ pro suprema Pontificis potestate*, cap. i. n. 12.

that solid rock whereon the Church is built, against which the gates of hell, that is, heresies and forgers of heresies, will never prevail.'* And S. Basil: 'Since he excelled the rest by his faith, he was made to bear the edifice on himself.'† And S. Ambrose: 'Peter is preferred above all, because he alone amongst all made his profession of faith.'‡ And S. Gregory: 'It is plain to all who know the Gospel that to Peter was committed the care of the whole Church, for to him was said: Thou art Peter, &c.'"§

Where the Spirit of truth lives and energises, there is the spirit of unity, which excludes envy, jealousy, and rivalry in matters Divine. Such a notion as that our Lord is jealous of His own Saints, and of the gifts and influence they have received from Him, or that the Saints are jealous rivals one of another, has no place in the Catholic Church which is the City of unity; it has its origin, and is bred, outside, where prevails the spirit of contention, confusion, and divorce. Hence, on the whole doctrine of S. Peter, whilst the faithful reverently accept what has been divinely revealed, witnessed to by sacred tradition, and is taught by the Catholic Church, as the will and appointment of Christ; those outside the Catholic pale strive to settle this Divine matter for themselves, by engaging in all sorts of contradictory reasonings and theories according to their private judgment of texts of Scripture, or their own views of certain past facts and events, in opposition to the teaching of God's Church, and in mutual discord with one another.

Strange, indeed, as it might otherwise appear in what belongs to Divine revelation and supernatural theology; still, under the circumstances, we can hardly be surprised that resort should be proposed to some higher human authority than that of mere individual opinion: it is thus, we observe, that an article was written, now some years since, wherein the Petrine claims are tested and adjudicated upon by what is termed the legal evidence of Scripture : ‖ and, before that, an Anglican bishop delivered a charge to his flock, in which he seems to consider that a court composed of twelve judges in law or equity would form a competent tribunal to give sentence on the question as to whether S. Peter was Bishop of Rome.¶

6. Another theme that frequently recurs in these Offices is the

---

* *Anchorat.* c. 9. † *Adv. Eunom.* l. ii. n. 4.
‡ *In Luc.* c. xxiv. l. 10, n. 175. § *Epistol.* v. Ep. 20 (*alias* l. iv. Ep. 32).
‖ "*Legal Evidence of Scripture on the Petrine Claims.*" *Church Quarterly Review*, April, 1878.
¶ *A Charge, &c.*, by *Edward Harold Browne, Lord Bishop of Ely*. See p. 195 of this volume.

wondrous and close union that existed between the two Apostles SS. Peter and Paul. They are represented as in body twain, but one through the Spirit in mind and heart; as united together in labour, the one evangelising specially the Jews, the other the Gentiles; but this by no means exclusively, for "together they convert idolatrous nations," "and bring to Christ those who believe not in God;" whilst there is no idea whatever put forth of any divided jurisdiction. They preach together in Rome, of which City they are the twin ornaments and boasts; together there they suffer martyrdom on the same day, and there together the sacred relics of both are venerated. The mode of martyrdom of either is frequently described, as universal tradition has handed it down.

7. In the Office for the Feast of S. Peter's Chain a like significance is given to his apprehension by Herod and his miraculous deliverance from prison, in connection with his going forth to preach to the world, as that given to the same event and his first going to Rome, to which, as we have seen in the Second Part of this volume, so many frescoes in the Catacombs bear witness. Several times mention is made of S. Peter's victory over Simon Magus, and as attended with those same circumstances of marvel that tradition has generally ascribed to this event.

8. In each of the three Offices it is expressly stated that S. Peter was the first Bishop of Rome, and what should be well noted is that on every occasion of this mention he is represented, in immediate connection with his Roman Episcopate, as the foundation of the faith and supreme ruler of the Catholic Church. But as S. Peter's Roman Episcopate is the one main and central point of our whole discussion, we will here at once give the several passages which explicitly testify to it.

I.—From the Office for the Feast of S. Peter's Chain.

Ἡ κορυφαία κρηπὶς τῶν ἀποστόλων, Σὺ πάντα κατέλιπες, καὶ ἠκολούθησας τῷ Διδασκάλῳ, βοῶν αὐτῷ· Σὺν σοὶ θανοῦμαι, ἵνα ζήσω τὴν μακαρίαν ζωήν. καὶ γέγονας Ῥώμης τε πρῶτος ἐπίσκοπος, τῆς ὀρθοδόξου τῶν πόλεων κρηπὶς καὶ στύλος, τῆς ἐκκλησίας Χριστοῦ ἑδραίωμα·	Thou, who art at once the foundation, base, and summit of the Apostles, didst leave all things, and didst follow the Master, calling out loudly to Him: With Thee will I die, that so I may live the life of the blessed. And thou didst become, too, of Rome first Bishop; of her, the orthodox among the cities, foundation-base and column; of Christ's Church the solidity; and the gates

S. PETER THE FIRST BISHOP OF ROME.

καὶ πύλαι ᾅδου
οὐ σαλεύσουσιν ὄντως ταύτην,
ὡς Χριστὸς ἀπεφήνατο·
ὅθεν πίστει καὶ πόθῳ
προσκυνοῦμεν σοῦ τὴν ἅλυσιν. *

of hell shall verily never move her, as Christ hath declared. Wherefore with faith and fond affection we venerate thy Chain.

II.—From the Office for the Protocoryphæi Apostles Peter and Paul.

'Ρώμης ὁ πολιοῦχος,
καὶ τῆς βασιλείας ὁ ταμιοῦχος,
ἡ πέτρα τῆς πίστεως,
ὁ στερρὸς θεμέλιος
τῆς καθολικῆς ἐκκλησίας,
ἱεροῖς ὑμνείσθω ἐν ᾄσμασιν. †

Of Rome the president, and of the kingdom the treasurer; the rock of the faith, the firm foundation of the Catholic Church, be he lauded with sacred hymns.

III.—From the Office for the Feast of all the Apostles, June 30th.

'Η κορυφαία κρηπὶς τῶν ἀποστόλων,
σὺ πάντα κατέλιπες,
καὶ ἠκολούθησας
τῷ Διδασκάλῳ, βοῶν αὐτῷ·
Σὺν σοὶ θανοῦμαι,
ἵνα ζήσω τὴν μακαρίαν ζωήν·
τῆς 'Ρώμης δὲ γέγονας
σὺ πρωτεπίσκοπος,
τῆς παμμεγίστου τῶν πόλεων
δόξα καὶ κλέος,
καὶ ἐκκλησίας, Πέτρε, ἑδραίωμα·
καὶ πύλαι ᾅδου
οὐ κατισχύσουσιν ὄντως ταύτης,
Χριστὸς ὡς προέφησεν·
ὃν ἱκέτευε σῶσαι
καὶ φωτίσαι τὰς ψυχὰς ἡμῶν. ‡

Thou, who art at once the foundation-base and summit of the Apostles, didst leave all things and didst follow the Master, calling out loudly to Him: With Thee will I die, that so I may live the life of the blessed. Of Rome thou didst become first Bishop; of the greatest of all cities the praise and glory; and of the Church, O Peter, the firm solidity: and the gates of hell shall never in truth prevail against her; for so Christ hath foretold: Whom do thou beseech to save and enlighten our souls.

We should remark that whilst in the Offices the preaching and labours of S. Paul in Rome are those most dwelt upon, it is Peter alone who is Bishop of Rome; just as he alone is styled the Rock of the Faith, and the Supreme Pastor, though the Apostolic zeal and labours of S. Paul throughout the Church at large are equally magnified with those of S. Peter.

9. What is especially worthy of notice in these Offices is, that over and over again, in the paraphrases of Our Lord's words

---

* Card. Pitra's *Hymnographie*, &c., p. lvii.   † *Ib.* p. cxx.
‡ *Ib.* p. cxxxvii.

to Peter (*Matt.* xvi. 15-19), it is not as though His founding and building the Church on Peter were something still-born, done in the past, accomplished once for all, and now over; but Peter, the rock—his firmness and solidity of faith—is represented as bound up with the whole being and continued existence of the Church, and living with her life; and is made to constitute, so to say, the very essence of her perpetual permanence and enduring immovableness. Again, with reference to these same words of our Lord and those others recorded by S. John (xxi. 15-17), Christ again and again, and most emphatically, is represented as making over His own entire Church, His own whole flock, so completely to Peter as to be Peter's own, and as though, in the very same sense, as these are Christ's own. Nothing of a like nature, or in the least approaching thereto, is found said of S. Paul or of any other of the Apostles.

From the Offices which have thus passed under our review, and from which we now make extracts, we can see clearly what was the ancient tradition amongst the Greeks concerning S. Peter's Roman Episcopate and his Primacy in the Catholic Church.

Hymn in Honour of SS. Peter and Paul.

Πέτρος, ἡ πάντων κρηπὶς τῶν πιστῶν,
ἔξαρχος τῶν ἀποστόλων, Χριστοῦ
τὸ κήρυγμα πληρῶν, πρὸς πίστιν
τοὺς ἀπίστους Θεῷ
προσκομίζων οὐ παύεται.
Παῦλος, ὁ νοῦς ὁ μέγας,
ἡ εὔλαλος κιθάρα,
ὁ πολὺς ἐν τῇ χάριτι.... P. xiii.

Peter, the fundamental basis of all the faithful, the first Prince of the Apostles, in fulfilling the preaching of Christ, ceases not to bring to the faith those who believe not in God. Paul, the great intelligence, the well-sounding lyre, the rich in grace...

Ἐβόησε Κηφᾶς
τὴν φωνὴν τῆς ἀξίας ·
Σὺ εἶ ὁ Χριστὸς ὁ Υἱὸς τοῦ Θεοῦ!
Ὅθεν τότε
κληροῦται καὶ αὐτὸς
τὴν ἐκκλησίαν τὴν σήν. xv.

Cephas cried out in that memorable word: Thou art the Christ, the Son of God. Whereupon he, too, obtains for himself the Church which is Thine own.

Πέτρος, ἡ πάντων κρηπὶς τῶν πιστῶν,
ὁ ὄροφος [πάσης] ἐκκλησίας,
ὁ τὸ πρὶν ἁλιεὺς, νυνὶ δὲ
[πρῶτος] ἀπόστολος,
ὁ σαγήνην ἀπορρήξας,
καὶ κώπας ἀπελάσας,
καὶ σύντριψας κάλαμον,

Peter, the fundamental basis of all the faithful, the roof of the whole Church, once a fisherman, but now first Apostle, after having ruptured the net, thrown away the oars, and broken the rod, when being nailed to the Cross for the faith, would not

OFFICE FOR THE FEAST OF S. PETER'S CHAINS. 359

οὐκ ἔφερεν, ἐν τῷ σταυρῷ ἡλούμενος πίστει, ὀρθίως ἀνὰ αὐτῷ παγῆναι τοῖς ἥλοις· ἀλλὰ ἐβόα τρανῶς τοῖς τολμήσασιν [αὐτὸν ἀδικῆσαι·]· Ἐγὼ θνητὸς ὑπάρχω, ἀπὸ γῆς σπεύδω εἰς τοὺς οὐρανούς· διὰ τοῦτο τὴν κάραν κάτω θέτε [ἵνα φθάσω] τὸν φανέντα, καὶ φωτίσαντα πάντα. xvii.	allow himself to be fixed upright to it, but cried out aloud to his tormentors: "I am a mortal man, who from earth am hastening to heaven; wherefore place my head downwards, that I may run to Him Who hath appeared, and Who enlightens all things."

JANUARY 16TH.—THE VENERATION OF THE PRECIOUS CHAINS
OF THE HOLY AND GLORIOUS APOSTLE PETER.

Σήμερον ἡμῖν ἡ κρηπὶς τῆς ἐκκλησίας, Πέτρος, ἡ πέτρα τῆς πίστεως, προτίθεται τὴν τιμίαν αὐτοῦ ἅλυσιν εἰς ψυχικὴν εὐδεξίαν. xx.	Lo, to-day, Peter, the foundation of the Church, the rock of the Faith, proposes to us his precious Chain for our spiritual well-being.
Τὴν Ῥώμην μὴ λιπών, πρὸς ἡμᾶς ἐπεδήμησας, δι' ὧν ἐφόρεσας τιμίων ἁλύσεων, τῶν ἀποστόλων πρωτόθρονε. xxiii.	Without leaving Rome, thou hast come to sojourn with us, by means of those precious Chains which thou didst wear, O Protothrone of the Apostles.
Πέτρᾳ στηριζόμενοι ὁμολογίας ἐνθέου σοῦ, πρωτόθρονε, καύχημα ἀποστόλων Χριστοῦ.... Τρίτον ἀρνησάμενος τοῖς θεοκτόνοις τὸν Κύριον, βροτὸν ὡς ψιλότατον οὐδὲν διήμαρτες τῆς προτέρας σοῦ θεολογίας, Πέτρε· ἐκήρυξας τοῦτον γὰρ Υἱὸν Θεοῦ καὶ Θεόν. xxv.	Made firm and secure on the rock of thy divine confession, O Protothrone, glory of the Apostles of Christ... Though thou didst thrice, before the deicides, deny the Lord, in so far as He was but a pure man, yet thou didst in nought, Peter, gainsay thy former confession of His Divinity: for thou didst proclaim the self-same to be Son of God, and God.
Ἡ Πέτρα Χριστὸς ὁ τὴν πέτραν τῆς πίστεως δοξάσας φαιδρῶς, αὐτοῦ τὸν πρωτόθρονον....	Christ, the Rock who has splendidly glorified the Rock of Faith, His own First-throne...

360 OFFICE FOR THE FEAST OF S. PETER'S CHAINS.

Τὸν κορυφαῖον
καὶ πρῶτον τῶν ἀποστόλων,
τῆς ἀληθείας
τὸν ἔνθεον ὑποφήτην,
Πέτρον τὸν μέγιστον εὐφήσωμεν·
... τὸν εὐκλεῆ
καὶ μέγαν Κυρίου μαθητὴν
... τὸν πρωτόθρονον. xxxiv. xxxv.

Let us celebrate with praise the Coryphæus and Prince of the Apostles, the Divine interpreter of the truth, Peter the greatest... that glorious and great disciple of the Lord... the Protothrone.

Ἐκ Παλαιστίνης ὁ Χριστοῦ
ἵππος καὶ ἀπόστολος Πέτρος,
ὡς ἐκ βαλβίδος προελθὼν,
καὶ τῷ κοσμῷ κηρύξας, ἐν Ῥώμῃ μὲν
τῇ προτέρᾳ κατέπαυσε,
τῇ ἕῳ δοὺς τὴν ἅλυσιν
προσκυνεῖσθαι. xxxvii.

From Palestine Peter, the courser steed and Apostle of Christ, as though now gone forth from the barriers, and, having preached through the world, came to rest in Old Rome, and gave to the East his Chain for veneration.

Νομοθέτα, ποιμὴν καὶ διδάσκαλε
τῶν θρεμμάτων Χριστοῦ, Πέτρε ἔνδοξε. xxxviii.

Lawgiver, Pastor, and Teacher of the sheep of Christ, glorious Peter.

Ὡς θεῖος κλειδοῦχος βασιλείας
τὰς ταύτης ὑπάνοιξον εἰσόδους
τοῖς πιστῶς σε τιμῶσιν ἐπὶ γῆς. xli.

As the sacred key-bearer of the kingdom, open its gates to those who faithfully honour thee on earth.

Οὐ σὰρξ καὶ αἷμα, Πέτρε, σοι,
ἀλλ' ὁ Πατὴρ ἐνέπνευσε
θεολογῆσαι τὸν Χριστὸν
Ὑιὸν Θεοῦ Πατρὸς ζῶντος·
διό σε καὶ μακάριον
αὐτὸς προεμαρτύρατο,
καὶ φερωνύμως κέκληκε
Πέτρον, ὡς πέτραν καὶ βάσιν
ἀρραγῆ τῆς ἐκκλησίας. xlii.

Not flesh and blood, O Peter, but the Father inspired to thee the Divine confession that Christ is Son of God the living Father: for which cause He both Himself was first to pronounce thee blessed, and significantly called thee Peter, as rock and basis irrefragable of His Church.

Τῷ τριττῷ τῆς ἐρωτήσεως,
τῷ· Πέτρε, φιλεῖς με;
τὸ τριττὸν τῆς ἀρνήσεως
ὁ Χριστὸς διωρθώσατο·
διὸ καὶ πρὸς τὸν κρυφιογνώστην ὁ
Σίμων·
Κύριε, πάντα γιγνώσκεις,
τὰ πάντα ἐπίστασαι,
σὺ οἶδας ὅτι φιλῶ σε.
Ὅθεν πρὸς αὐτὸν ὁ Σωτήρ·
Ποίμανε τὰ πρόβατά μου,
Ποίμανε τὴν ἐκλογάδα μου,

By the triple question: "Peter, lovest thou Me?" Christ made right again the triple denial. Therefore Simon saith to the knower of secrets: "Lord, Thou knowest all things, Thou understandest all, Thou knowest that I love Thee." Then to him the Saviour: "Feed My sheep; feed My chosen flock; feed My lambs that I have purchased to Myself for salvation with My own blood." Him do thou implore, O Apostle blessed

JANUARY 16TH.

Ποίμανε τὰ ἀρνία μου,
ἃ ἐν τῷ ἰδίῳ αἵματι περιεποιησάμην
εἰς σωτηρίαν·
αὐτὸν ἱκέτευε,
θεομακάριστε ἀπόστολε,
δωρηθῆναι
ἡμῖν τὸ μέγα ἔλεος. xliii.

of God, that on us may be bestowed
His great mercy.

Πέτρε... ἐφ' ᾧ τραχήλῳ
τὴν θείαν Χριστὸς
ἐκκλησίαν ἤδρασε
μένειν ἀκλόνητον. xlvii.

Peter, on whose neck Christ set
the Divine Church to abide unshaken.

Χριστῷ πειθαρχῶν, Πέτρε,
καὶ ἐν ἁλύσει δεσμευθείς,
παραδόξως τῆς φρουρᾶς
δ' ἀγγέλου λυτρωθείς,
μάκαρ, ἀπειθοῦντας διήλεγξας.
Τὰς κλεῖς πιστευθέντος σοῦ
τὰς οὐρανίους ἐν εἰρκτῇ
εὐχερῶς ἐκλυθεῖσαι,
δέσμαι οἷα στυππίου
φόβῳ δι' ἁλύσεις ἐξέπεσον.
Σὲ τὸν πυλωρὸν, Πέτρε,
τῶν οὐρανίων τεμένων
σιδηρᾶ πύλη φρουρεῖν
μὴ ἰσχύουσα, τρόμῳ
θᾶττον αὐτομάτη διήνοικται.
xlvii. xlviii.

Obedient to Christ, Peter, and bound in chains, miraculously set free from prison by an Angel, thou didst, O blessed one, confute unbelievers. From thee who wert entrusted with the keys of heaven, thy chains in prison easily loosed, as though but bands of tow, fell off in fear. Thee, O Peter, the Porter of the heavenly courts, the iron gate being powerless to guard, with trembling quickly opened of its own accord.

Πειράζειν ἀφρόνως οἰηθέντα
Πνεῦμα τὸ Πανάγιον, Σιμῶνα ἤλεγξας,
ὃς ἐθεολόγησας
πρῶτος τρανώσας τὸν Θεὸν, παμμακάριστε.
Ἐν πέτρᾳ Χριστὸς τῇ στερεμνίῳ,
σοὶ τῷ Πέτρῳ, τὴν ἐκκλησίαν πηξάμενος,
ἐν τῇ πίστει ἄσειστον
στηρίξοι ταύτην λιταῖς σοῦ αἰωνιζούσαν.
Ἐν τοῖς σοῖς δεσμοῖς τῆς ἀπιστίας
τὰ δεσμὰ, ἀπόστολε, κόσμου ἐκλέλυται. xlix.

Simon, when thinking in senseless folly to tempt the Holy Ghost, thou didst confute: thou who wert as theologian the first to declare openly (Christ to be) God, most blessed one. May Christ, Who founded the Church on a rock that is firm, on thee, Peter, confirm her immovable in the faith, abiding for ever through thy prayers. By thy bonds, O Apostle, the world has been set free from the bonds of unbelief.

Καταπτὰς
ἄγγελος ἀγγέλῳ
ἐπιγείῳ οὐράνιος,

The Angel from heaven coming down to the Angel upon earth, to thee, O Peter, grants deliverance

362   OFFICE FOR THE FEAST OF S. PETER'S CHAINS.

σοί, Πέτρε, τῶν δεσμῶν
δωρεῖται λύτρον
καὶ κόσμῳ σε κήρυκα
ἐξ εἱρκτῆς σωτηρίας πέμπει.
Τοπαζίου
ἡ ἐκκλησία
καὶ χρυσίου τὸν σίδηρον
ἁψάμενον σαρκός
σου, ἀπόστολε,
ὡς λίαν ὑπέρτιμον
ἑαυτῇ θησαυρίζει ὄλβον.   xlix. l.

from thy bonds, and sends thee from the prison to the world as herald of salvation. More precious than topaz and gold does the Church hold the iron that bound thy body, O Apostle, and keeps it for herself as a treasure exceeding all price.

Τῶν ἀποστόλων ὁ χόρος
σήμερον εὐφημείσθω,
τὰ ἄνω καὶ τὰ κάτω
σήμερον ἀγαλλίεσθω,
καὶ οἱ βροτοί, θεάσασθε.
Φησίν· Ὁ Ἡρώδης
κατ' ἐκεῖνον τὸν καιρόν,
τὰς χεῖρας αὐτοῦ ἔβαλε,
καὶ τὸν Πέτρον τηρεῖσθαι προσέταξε
μετὰ τῶν κακούργων,
ὤν, 'βόα ὁ δεσπότης,
ὑπέρχεις ἡ ἄσειστος πέτρα.
Αὐτὸς δὲ ὁ Χριστὸς
προσευχὴν ἀκούσας
τοῦ πιστοῦ αὐτοῦ λαοῦ,
ἐν τῇ πανσέπτῳ
καὶ ἀληθινῇ
ἐκκλησίᾳ, τοῦτο βοῶντος·
ἐξ ὧν ῥυσθῆναι ἡμᾶς καθικέτευε. lii.

Praised be to-day the Choir of the Apostles. To-day let all in heaven and on earth rejoice—ye mortals too behold and admire. It is said : At that time Herod stretched forth his hands and commanded that Peter should be cast into prison with the malefactors : For of such, cried aloud the tyrant, thou art the unshaken rock. But Christ, too, heard the prayer of His faithful people in the most venerable and true Church crying out : Make strong intercession that we may be delivered from them.

Ῥώμην σώματός σου θείου τῇ καταθέσει
καθηγιάζεις, Πέτρε,
καὶ τὴν νέαν φωτίζεις
πίστει τὴν τιμίαν σου
κατέχουσαν ἅλυσιν.
Νύκτα βαθεῖαν δεινῆς
πολυθεΐας λύεις,
τὴν οἰκουμένην διερχόμενος,
ὡς μέγιστος ἥλιος,
Πέτρε, Χριστοῦ αὐτόπτα,
τῶν ἀποστόλων κλέος.
Ἀκλονήτῳ σοῦ πέτρᾳ τῆς πίστεως
συντηρῶν ἐκκλησίας τὸ πλήρωμα. liv.

Thou dost, Peter, clean sanctify Rome by the deposit of thy sacred body, and thou dost illuminate New Rome with faith, through her possession of thy precious Chain. Thou dost dissipate the deep night of horrible polytheism, by traversing the whole world as a sun of greatest magnitude, Peter, eye-witness of Christ, glory of the Apostles. Thou who by thy unshaken rock of the faith conservest the whole fulness of the Church.

Τὸν συνάναρχον Λόγον
Πατρὶ καὶ Πνεύματι,
τὸν σάρκα γεγονότα
συγκαταβάσει αὐτοῦ,
ὡμολόγησας σεπτῶς
Υἱὸν τοῦ ζῶντος Θεοῦ,
ὡς θεολόγος μαθητής
καὶ μακάριος κληθείς,
τὰς κλεῖς ἐδέξω, πάμμακαρ,
τῆς οὐρανῶν βασιλείας,
ὡς ἀποστόλων, Πέτρε, πρόκριτος.   liv.

Reverently confessing the Word equally without beginning with the Father and the Spirit, by His condescension become Incarnate, to be Son of the living God, as the theologian disciple, and called Blessed, thou didst receive the keys, thrice blessed one, of the kingdom of heaven, as, O Peter, made prince of the Apostles.

Ἀλύσεσι δεσμώμενον
τῶν παθῶν με τὸν τάλαν
ἀπόλυσον, μακάριε,
ὡς ποτε τὰς ἀλύσεις
διέλυσεν ὁ ἄγγελος
τοῦ Θεοῦ, καὶ τῆς εἱρκτῆς
ἐξήγαγε παραδόξως
συγκλεισθέντα σε ταύτης,
ἀποστόλων κορωνίς,
μακαριώτατε Πέτρε.
Ἀλύσεις δὲ ἐφόρεσας
ὑπὲρ τοῦ διδασκάλου,
Πέτρε, Χριστοῦ ἀπόστολε,
προσκυνοῦντες ἐν πίστει,
ἀνευφημοῦμεν σε πόθῳ·
σὺ γὰρ ἅπασαν κτίσιν
εὐθέως κατελάμπρυνας
τῷ φωτὶ τῆς Τριάδος·
ἀλλὰ καὶ νῦν μετὰ τῆς
παναγνου καὶ Θεοτόκου,
σκέπε ἡμᾶς πρεσβείας σου,
ὡς πρωτόθρονος θεῖος.   lv.

Do thou, O blessed one, free me, a wretch bound by the chains of my passions, as once the Angel of God loosed thy chains, and brought thee forth miraculously from the prison wherein thou wert confined, O crown (coronet, cornice, summit, consummation) of Apostles, most blessed Peter; whilst with faith we venerate those Chains which thou didst bear for thy Master. Apostle of Christ, we raise our voices to praise thee with loving desire; for thou didst straightway illumine all creation with the light of the Trinity: and now, too, together with the most holy Mother of God, do thou protect us by thy intercession, as the Divine Protothrone.

THE FOLLOWING PASSAGES ARE FROM THE OFFICE OF SS. PETER AND PAUL, JUNE 29TH.*

Ἔδωκας καυχήματα
τῇ ἐκκλησίᾳ, φιλάνθρωπε,
τοὺς σεπτοὺς ἀποστόλους σου,
ἐν ᾗ ὑπερλάμπουσι
νοητοὶ φωστῆρες,

Thou hast given, O Lover of men, Thy venerable Apostles for boasts of glory to the Church, wherein shine above the rest those spiritual lights, Peter and Paul, as intellectual stars

* The holy, glorious, renowned Apostles and First Coryphæi (πρωτοκορυφαίων), Peter and Paul.

Πέτρος τε καὶ Παῦλος,
ὥσπερ ἀστέρες λογικοί,
τὴν οἰκουμένην περιαυγάζοντες·
δι' ὧν ἐφωταγώγησας
τὴν δυτικὴν ἀμαυρότητα,
Ἰησοῦ παντοδύναμε,
ὁ σωτὴρ τῶν ψυχῶν ἡμῶν.
Ἔδωκας ὑπόδειγμα
ἐπιστροφῆς ἁμαρτάνουσι
τοὺς διττοὺς ἀποστόλους σου,
τὸν μὲν ἀρνησάμενον
ἐν καιρῷ τοῦ πάθους,
καὶ μετεγνωκότα ·
τὸν δὲ κηρύγματι τῷ σῷ
ἀντιταξάμενον, καὶ ὑπείξωτα,
καὶ ἄμφω τοῦ συστήματος
πρωτοστατοῦντας τῶν φίλων σου,
Ἰησοῦ παντοδύναμε, κ.τ.λ.
Ἔδωκας στηρίγματα
τῇ ἐκκλησίᾳ σου, Κύριε,
τὴν τοῦ Πέτρου στερρότητα,
καὶ Παύλου τὴν σύνεσιν
καὶ λαμπρὰν σοφίαν,
καὶ τὰς ἑκατέρων
θεηγορίας ἀληθῶς
τὴν τῶν Ἑλλήνων πλάνην διωκούσας.
διὸ μυσταγωγούμενοι
παρ' ἀμφοτέρων, ὑμνοῦμεν σε,
Ἰησοῦ, κ.τ.λ.

shedding their rays throughout the world, through whom Thou hast illumined the darkness of the West, Jesus, all-powerful, Saviour of our souls.

Thou hast given an example to sinners of conversion, in Thy two Apostles, of whom the one denied Thee at the time of Thy Passion, and repented: whilst the other resisted Thy preaching, and then submitted. And now both have the first place in the College of Thy friends, Jesus, all-powerful, &c.

Thou hast given supports to Thy Church, Lord, in the firm solidity of Peter, and the knowledge and splendid wisdom of Paul; and in the Divine oracles of both that expelled by truth the error of the Greeks: therefore initiated into the sacred mysteries by means of both, we sing to Thee Jesus, all-powerful, &c.

Πέτρε, κορυφαῖε τῶν ἐνδόξων ἀποστόλων,
ἡ Πέτρα τῆς πίστεως,
καὶ Παῦλε θεσπέσιε,
τῶν ἁγίων ἐκκλησιῶν
ὁ ῥήτωρ καὶ φωστήρ,
τῷ θείῳ θρόνῳ παριστάμενοι
ὑπὲρ ἡμῶν Χριστῷ πρεσβεύσατε. lx.

Peter, Coryphæus of the glorious Apostles, the Rock of the Faith; and heaven-inspired Paul, the orator and light of the holy Churches, standing before the Divine throne, intercede for us with Christ.

Σῶσον πάντας, ἀγαθέ,
πρεσβείας τῶν σοφῶν σου
καὶ θείων ἀποστόλων
τῶν κορυφαίων, ὑπεράγαθε.

Save all, good Jesus, through the intercession of these Thy wise ones, the Coryphæi of the holy Apostles, Jesus, exceeding good.

Πέτρε, Παῦλε,
ἀποστόλων ἡ κρηπίς. lxi.

Peter and Paul, the chief foundation of the Apostles.

APOSTLES, SS. PETER AND PAUL, JUNE 29TH. 365

Ποίοις εὐφημιῶν στέμμασιν
ἀναδήσωμεν Πέτρον καὶ Παῦλον,
τοὺς διῃρημένους τοῖς σώμασι,
καὶ ἡνωμένους τῷ Πνεύματι,
τοὺς θεοκηρύκων πρωτοστάτας,
τὸν μὲν ὡς τῶν ἀποστόλων προεξ-
  άρχοντα,
τὸν δὲ ὡς ὑπὲρ τοὺς ἄλλους κοπιά-
  σαντα ;
τούτους γὰρ ὄντως ἀξίους
ἀθανάτου δόξης,
διαδήμασι στεφανοῖ
Χρίστος, ὁ Θεὸς ἡμῶν,
ὁ ἔχων τὸ μέγα ἔλεος. ...

Ποίοις πνευματικοῖς ᾄσμασιν
ἐπαινέσωμεν Πέτρον καὶ Παῦλον,
τὰ τὴν ἀθεότητα σφάττοντα
μὴ ἀμβλυνόμενα στόματα
τῆς φρικτῆς τοῦ Πνεύματος μαχαίρας,
τὰ Ῥώμης περιφανῆ ἐγκαλλωπίσματα,
τὰ πάσης τῆς οἰκουμένης ἐντρυφή-
  ματα,
τὰς τῆς καινῆς διαθήκης
θεογράφους πλάκας,
νοουμένας ἃς ἐν Σιὼν
Χρίστος ἐξεφώνησεν,
ὁ ἔχων τὸ μέγα ἔλεος ; lxii.

Τοὺς μαθητὰς τοῦ Χριστοῦ,
καὶ θεμελίους τῆς ἐκκλησίας,
τοὺς ἀληθεῖς στύλους καὶ βάσεις,
καὶ σάλπιγγας ἐνθέους
τῶν τοῦ Χριστοῦ δογμάτων καὶ πα-
  θημάτων,
τοὺς κορυφαίους Πέτρον καὶ Παῦλον,
ἅπας ὁ κόσμος
ὡς προστάτας εὐφημήσωμεν·
... ὦ Πέτρε, πέτρα καὶ κρηπὶς,
καὶ Παῦλε, σκεῦος ἐκλογῆς.
  lxiii. lxiv.

Παῦλε, στόμα Κυρίου,
ἡ κρηπὶς τῶν δογμάτων,
ὁ πότε μὲν διώκτης Ἰησοῦ τοῦ Σωτῆρος,
νῦν δὲ καὶ πρωτόθρονος
τῶν ἀποστόλων γενόμενος, μακάριε,

With what garlands of praises shall we bind together Peter and Paul, divided by bodies twain, but made one by the Spirit, the leaders of God's heralds, the one as taking the foremost rule (the first or chief governor) of the Apostles, the other as having laboured more than all the rest? For these are they whom as verily worthy of immortal glory Christ crowns with diadems, He our God Whose mercy is great . . .

With what spiritual canticles shall we celebrate the praises of Peter and Paul, whose mouths, in slaying godless impiety, were as the two-edged sword of the Spirit that may not be blunted, those two splendid ornaments of Rome, the delights of the whole world, the divinely written tables of the New Testament, which, devised in Sion, Christ has given voice to, He Whose mercy is great?

These disciples of Christ, the Church's foundations, her true pillars and bases, her trumpets, too, divinely resonant with the teachings and sufferings of Christ, the Coryphæi Peter and Paul, let us with all the world celebrate as Patrons ; ... O Peter, rock and foundation, and thou Paul, vessel of election.

Paul, mouth of the Lord, foundation of dogmas, once the persecutor of Jesus the Saviour, and now become Protothrone of the Apostles, blessed one : and, therefore, thou didst see things unspeakable, O

ὅθεν ἄρρητα εἶδες, σοφέ,
ἕως τοῦ τρίτου οὐρανοῦ ἀνάβας, καὶ
    ἔκραζες·
Δεῦτε σὺν ἐμοί,
καὶ τῶν ἀγαθῶν μὴ ὑστερηθῶμεν.

Οἱ τῆς ἄνω Ἱερουσαλὴμ πολῖται,
Πέτρος ἡ πέτρα τῆς πίστεως,
καὶ Παῦλος ὁ ῥήτωρ τῆς ἐκκλησίας
    τοῦ Χριστοῦ....
τοῦ κόσμου οἱ σαγηνευταί,
καταλιπόντες σήμερον τὰ ἐπὶ γῆς,
ἐπορεύθησαν ἐν ἀθλήσει πρὸς Θεόν.
        lxiv.

Πέτρε, ἡ πέτρα τῆς πίστεως,
καὶ Παῦλε, καύχημα τῆς οἰκουμένης,
στηρίξατε ποίμνην
ἣν ἐκτήσασθε ταῖς διδαχαῖς ὑμῶν.
        lxv.

Τοὺς φωστῆρας τοὺς μεγάλους τῆς
    ἐκκλησίας,
Πέτρον καὶ Παῦλον, εὐφημήσωμεν·
ὑπὲρ ἥλιον γὰρ ἔλαμψαν
ἐν τῷ τῆς πίστεως στερεώματι·
καὶ τὰ ἔθνη ταῖς ἀκτῖσι τοῦ κηρύγ-
    ματος
ἐκ τῆς ἀγνοίας ἐπανήγαγον·
ὁ μέν, τῷ σταυρῷ προσηλωθείς,
πρὸς οὐρανὸν τὴν πορείαν ἐποίησατο,
ἔνθα τῆς βασιλείας παρὰ Χριστοῦ
τὰς κλεῖς ἐγκεχείρισται·
ὁ δέ, τῷ ξίφει ἀποτμηθείς,
πρὸς τὸν Σωτῆρα ἐκδημήσας,
ἐπαξίως μακαρίζεται. lxvi.

Ἑορτὴ χαρμόσυνος
ἐπέλαμψε τοῖς πέρασι σήμερον,
ἡ πάνσεμνος μνήμη τῶν σοφωτάτων
    ἀποστόλων
καὶ κορυφαίων Πέτρου καὶ Παύλου·
διὸ καὶ Ῥώμη συγχαίρει χορεύουσα
ἐν ᾠδαῖς καὶ ὕμνοις·
ἑορτάσωμεν καὶ ἡμεῖς, ἀδέλφοι,
τὴν πανσεβάσμιον ταύτην ἡμέραν
    ἐκτελέσαντες.
Χαῖρε,

wise man, raised even to the third heaven, and didst cry out: Come along with me, and let us not fall short of those things that are good.

The citizens of Jerusalem above, Peter the rock of the faith, and Paul the orator of the Church of Christ ... the fishermen of the world, leaving to-day what is here on earth, have gone in combat to God.

Peter, the rock of the faith, and Paul, boast of the world, confirm the flock which you have gained by your teachings.

Let us celebrate those great luminaries of the Church, Peter and Paul, for they shone brighter than the sun, by the firmness of their faith; and by the rays of their preaching they brought out the nations from the darkness of ignorance: the one, by being nailed to the cross, made his journey to heaven, where he is put in possession by Christ of the keys of the kingdom; the other, beheaded with the sword, goes home to the Saviour, and enjoys his merited bliss.

The glad feast has shone to-day forth to the ends of the earth, the all-venerable commemoration of the most wise Apostles and Coryphæi Peter and Paul, wherefore all Rome rejoices in chorus with odes and hymns. Let us, too, hold festivity, brethren, as we keep this most sacred day. Hail, Peter, Apostle and true friend indeed of thy Master, Christ our God. Hail, Paul, most

Πέτρε ἀπόστολε,
καὶ γνήσιε φίλε τοῦ σοῦ διδασκάλου
Χριστοῦ τοῦ Θεοῦ ἡμῶν.
Χαῖρε,
Παῦλε παμφίλτατε,
καὶ κήρυξ τῆς πίστεως,
καὶ διδάσκαλε τῆς οἰκουμένης. lxvii.

well-beloved, preacher of the faith, and teacher of the whole world.

Πέτρε, τῶν ἀποστόλων κρηπὶς,
πέτρα τῆς Χριστοῦ ἐκκλησίας,
χριστιανῶν ἀπαρχὴ,
ποιμαίνων τὰ πρόβατα
τῆς σῆς αὐλῆς εὐκλεῶς,
τὰ ἀρνία σοῦ φύλαττε
ἐκ λύκου δολίου . . . .
Παῦλε, τῶν ἐθνῶν σαγηνευτὰ,
τῶν χριστιανῶν ὁ προστάτης,
τῆς οἰκουμένης φωστὴρ,
στόμα τὸ ἀσύγκριτον
Χριστοῦ τοῦ ζῶντος Θεοῦ,
ὁ δραμὼν, ὥσπερ ἥλιος,
τὰ πέρατα πάντα
διὰ κηρύγματός σου
τοῦ τῆς θείας πίστεως,
λύσον κ. τ. λ.
Πέτρε, κορυφαῖος μαθητῶν,
Παῦλε, ἀποστόλων ἀκρότης. lxviii.

Peter, foundation of the Apostles, rock of Christ's Church, first fruit of Christians, who dost gloriously shepherd the sheep of thy fold, protect thy lambs from the treacherous wolf. . . . Paul, fisher of the nations, patron of Christians, light of the world, incomparable mouth of Christ the living God, who didst run thy course as the sun to the ends of the earth, by thy preaching of Divine faith deliver us. . . . Peter, Coryphæus of disciples; Paul, summit of Apostles.

Ἀληθῶς ἀνεδείχθης
ἡ πέτρα τῆς πίστεως
καὶ κλειδοῦχος τῆς χάριτος,
Πέτρε ἀπόστολε. lxxi.

Truly wert thou designated the rock of the faith, and key-bearer of grace, O Apostle Peter.

Οὐρανόθεν τὴν κλῆσιν παρὰ Χριστοῦ
κομισάμενος, ὤφθης κήρυξ φωτὸς
πᾶσι τὰ τῆς χάριτος
καταλάμψας διδάγματα,
τὴν γὰρ τοῦ νόμου ξέσας
λατρείαν τοῦ γράμματος
τοῖς λαοῖς κατέγραψας
τὴν γνῶσιν τοῦ Πνεύματος·
ὅθεν καὶ εἰς τρίτον
οὐρανὸν ἐπαξίως
ἐπήρθης μετάρσιος,
καὶ παράδεισον ἔφθασας,
Παῦλε ἀπόστολε. lxxi. lxxii.

Having received thy vocation from heaven at the hands of Christ, thou appearedst a herald of light illuminating all with the doctrines of grace; for, taking away the worship of the letter of the law, thou hast given in writing to the nations the knowledge of the Spirit: hence thou didst merit to be raised even to the third heaven, and to anticipate paradise, O Apostle Paul.

Κορυφαίους ὀφθέντας τῶν μαθητῶν, τοὺς μεγάλους φωστῆρας καὶ φαεινούς,
Πέτρον εὐφημήσωμεν
καὶ τὸν πάνσοφον Παῦλον. lxxii.

As conspicuous Coryphæi of the disciples let us celebrate those great and shining luminaries, Peter and the all-wise Paul.

τὸν κορυφαιότατον
τῶν ἀποστόλων σήμερον,
ὡς πρωτόκλητον Χριστοῦ
θεοπνεύστοις ἐν ᾠδαῖς
ἐπαξίως ὑμνήσωμεν.
Σὲ ὁ προαιώνιος
προεγνωκὼς προώρισε,
παμμακάριστε Πέτρε,
ὡς προστάτην ἐκκλησίας
καὶ σὲ ὡς μέγαν πρόεδρον.
Οὐ σὰρξ οὐδὲ αἷμά σοι,
ἀλλ' ὁ Πατὴρ ἐνέπνευσε
τὸν Χριστὸν θεολογεῖν
Ὑιὸν Θεοῦ ἀληθινὸν
τοῦ ὑψίστου, ἀπόστολε. lxxiii.

Let us worthily laud to-day, with inspired hymns, the supreme Coryphæus of the Apostles, as first elected of Christ. Thee did He, Who knows from all eternity, foreordain, O most blessed Peter, as Chief of the Church, and her great president. Nor flesh, nor blood, but the Father inspired thee, O Apostle, to call Christ God, and true Son of God Most High.

Ὥσπερ ὄντα καλῶν τὰ ἀνύπαρκτα,
Χριστὸς τῇ θείᾳ γνώσει,
Παῦλε παμμακάριστε,
αὐτὸς ἐκ μητρικῆς
γαστρός σε ἐξελέξατο
βαστάσαι ἐναντίον τῶν ἐθνῶν
αὐτοῦ τὸ θεῖον ὄνομα,
τὸ ὑπὲρ πᾶν ὄνομα·
ἐνδόξως γὰρ δεδόξασται.
Περιτομὴν μὲν τελῶν ὀκταήμερον,
καὶ ζηλωτὴς πατρῴων,
Παῦλε, παραδόσεων,
Ἑβραίων ἐκ σπορᾶς,
φυλῆς Βενιαμίτιδος,
ἐν νόμῳ Φαρισαῖος τε δειχθεὶς,
ἡγήσω πάντα σκύβαλα,
καὶ Χριστὸν ἐκερδήσας·
ἐνδόξως γὰρ δεδόξασται. lxxiii. lxxiv.

He Who calls things that are not as though they were, Christ, by His Divine knowledge, most blessed Paul, Himself chose thee forth from thy mother's womb, to bear His Divine Name before the Gentiles, that Name which is above every name: for gloriously is it glorified. Circumcised the eighth day, and zealous, Paul, for the traditions of thy fathers, of the seed of the Hebrews, of the tribe of Benjamin, according to the law a Pharisee, thou didst count all as dung, and hast gained Christ; for gloriously is He glorified.

Μακάριον σε
τὸ γλυκύτατον στόμα Χριστοῦ τοῦ Θεοῦ
καὶ ταμεῖον ἀσφαλὲς
τῆς βασιλείας ἀνέδειξε,
διὸ ἀνυμνοῦμεν σε,
Πέτρε ἀπόστολε. lxxiv.

The most sweet mouth of Christ the God declared thee blessed, and a safe steward of His kingdom, wherefore we laud thee, Apostle Peter.

APOSTLES, SS. PETER AND PAUL, JUNE 29TH. 369

Ἐπὶ τὴν πέτραν
τῆς σῆς θεολογίας ἐπήξατο
ὁ Δεσπότης Ἰησοῦς
τὴν ἐκκλησίαν ἀκλόνητον·
ἐν ᾗ σε, ἀπόστολε
Πέτρε, δοξάζομεν. lxxv.

On the rock of thy Divine confession the Lord Jesus established the Church unshaken: in which we glorify thee, Apostle Peter.

Σὺ λίθον θεμέλιον
ταῖς τῶν πιστῶν ψυχαῖς τέθεικας,
πολυτελῆ, ἀκρογωνιαῖον,
τὸν Σωτῆρα καὶ Κύριον.
Πάντοτε τὴν νέκρωσιν
τοῦ Ἰησοῦ ἐν τῷ σώματι
εἰλικρινῶς, Παῦλε, περιφέρων,
ἠξιώθης τῆς ὄντως ζωῆς.
Παῦλε παμμακάριστε,
τῷ θεμελίῳ σοῦ πρέσβευε
τῶν ἀρετῶν ἐποικοδομεῖσθαι
εὐσεβῶν τὴν λαμπρότητα. lxxv.

For the souls of the faithful, thou didst lay as foundation-stone, costly, head of the corner, the Saviour and Lord. Always, Paul, manifestly bearing about in thy body the dying of Jesus, thou wert counted worthy of the true life. Most blessed Paul, obtain that on the foundation of thy virtues the splendour of the pious may be built up.

Πέτρε, τῆς πίστεως ἡ πέτρα,
Παῦλε, καύχημα τῆς οἰκουμένης,
ἐκ τῆς Ῥώμης συνελθόντες,
στηρίξατε ἡμᾶς. lxxvi.

Peter, the rock of the faith, Paul, boast of the universe, who together came from Rome, strengthen us.

Σταύρωσις εἷλε κήρυκα Χριστοῦ
Πέτρον·
τομὴ δὲ Παῦλον, τὸν τεμόντα τὴν
πλάνην·
ἐτλῆ ἐνάτῃ σταυρὸν Πέτρος εἰκάδι,
ἄορ ὁ Παῦλος. lxxx.

Crucifixion took away Christ's herald Peter, and the sword's stroke Paul, the striker of error. On the twenty-ninth day Peter suffered the cross, and Paul the sword.

Τὸ συμπαθὲς
θείᾳ προνοίᾳ
τοῦ Χριστοῦ παιδευόμενος
ἐκμιμεῖσθαι, συγχώρει
τὸ πρὸ τοῦ πάθους,
Πέτρε, τῆς ἀρνήσεως
ὑποστῆναι κλυδώνιον.
Σοὶ ὁ Χριστὸς
πρωτοκληθέντι,
καὶ σφοδρῶς ἀγαπήσαντι,
ὡς προέδρῳ εὐκλεεῖ
τῶν ἀποστόλων,
πρῶτον ἐμφανίζεται,
ἀναστὰς ἐκ τοῦ μνήματος.
Σοῦ τὸ τρισσὸν

Being instructed through Divine prevision to imitate the compassion of Christ, it is permitted thee, Peter, before the Passion to encounter the storm of the denial. To thee, as elected first, as loving vehemently, and as glorious president of the Apostles, Christ first shows Himself after rising from the tomb. The Lord, wiping out thy triple denial before the Passion with the triple questioning of His Divine voice, confirms thy charity. Of thy love to Christ, Peter, thou didst bear open witness, and to the Word,

τῆς πρὸ τοῦ πάθους
ἐξαλείφων ἀρνήσεως,
ὁ Δεσπότης τῷ τρισσῷ
τῆς θεοφθόγγου
ἐρωτήσεως
βεβαιοῖ τὴν ἀγάπησιν.
Τῆς πρὸς Χριστὸν,
Πέτρε, φιλίας
προετίθεσο μάρτυρα,
καὶ τὸν πάντα ὡς Θεὸν
εἰδότα Λόγον·
ὅθεν καὶ τὸ φίλτατον
ἐγχειρίζει σοι ποίμνιον. lxxxi.

knowing all things as God. For which cause, too, He entrusts to thee His most beloved flock.

Ἐχρημάτισε, Χριστέ,
σφραγὶς καὶ στέφανος τῶν ἀποστόλων σου,
ὁ ἐπ' ἐσχάτων κληθεὶς τῶν χρόνων,
σπουδῇ πάντας ὑπερβάλλων δέ,
μεθ' οὗ ὁ λαὸς
τῆς ἐκκλησίας ψάλλει σοί.
Ὁ τῶν πατέρων ἡμῶν Θεός, εὐλογητὸς εἶ.
Εἰ καὶ ἐδίωξε τὸ πρὶν
τὴν ἐκκλησίαν σοῦ Παῦλος ὁ δέσμιος,
ἀλλ' ὑπερέβη τὴν πάλαι τόλμαν
τῷ σῷ ζήλῳ τῷ ἐπ' ἐσχάτων·
συνήγαγε γὰρ
Χριστῷ τὰ ἔθνη κράζοντα· Ὁ. τ. π.

He, O Christ, became the seal and crown of Thy Apostles, who was called the latest, but he surpassed all in zeal, and with him the people of the Church sing to Thee : Thou, the God of our fathers, be Thou blessed. And even though Paul, in the chains of error, was once the persecutor of Thy Church, yet did he exceed his former daring by the zeal that he bore Thee later on, for he brought with him the nations to Christ, crying out : Thou, the God of our fathers, be Thou blessed.

Φάσμασι τὸν Σίμωνα μάγον
τὸν θεομάχον, ἐπαρθέντα
πρὸς αἰθέριον ὕψος,
καταβαλλὼν ἀρρήτῳ θείᾳ δυνάμει,
ὁ Πέτρος μακαρίζεται. lxxxiv.

In casting down by secret Divine power Simon Magus, the enemy of God, raised high in the air by his sorceries, Peter is pronounced blessed.

Σὺ ἐπαξίως πέτρα προσηγορεύθης·
ὅτε τὴν ἀκράδαντον
πίστιν ὁ Κύριος
τῆς ἐκκλησίας ἐκράτυνεν
ἀρχιποιμένα
τῶν λογικῶν προβάτων κατέστησεν·
ἐντεῦθεν κλειδοῦχον σε
οὐρανίων πυλῶν.
ὡς ἀγαθὸν ἐνεχείρισεν
ἀνοίγειν πᾶσι

Thou justly art called Rock : when the Lord made secure the unshaken faith of His Church He constituted thee chief pastor of His spiritual sheep ; moreover, He gave thee the commission as a good keybearer of the heavenly gates to open to all who keep knocking at them with faith. With good reason then were thou deemed worthy to be

τοῖς μετὰ πίστεως προσεδρεύουσιν·
ὅθεν ἀξίως
κατηξίωσαι σταυρωθῆναι,
καθὼς ὁ Δεσπότης σου.
ὃν ἱκέτευε σῶσαι,
καὶ φωτίσαι τὰς ψυχὰς ἡμῶν,
ὁ Χριστοκήρυξ, σταυροῦ καύχημα
φέρων. lxxxvi. lxxxvii.

crucified, as Thy Master. Beseech Him to save and to enlighten our souls, thou who art Christ's herald, bearing the boast and glory of the Cross.

Χριστὸς, ἡ πέτρα,
Πέτρε, τῶν ἀποστόλων πρόκριτε,
διά σε
τὴν ἐκκλησίαν ἄσειστον ἐθεμελίωσε·
ἣν πύλαι ᾅδου οὐ κατισχύσουσιν,
αἱρετικῶν γλωσσαλγίαι,
οὐδ' οὐ μὴ πορθήσουσιν
βαρβάρων φρυάγματα·
ταύτην οὖν ῥῦσαι πειρασμῶν
καὶ κινδύνων, ταῖς σαῖς ἱκεσίαις
παμμακάριστε. lxxxviii.

Christ, the Rock, through thee, Peter, Prince of the Apostles, has founded His Church unshaken, against which the gates of hell shall not prevail, and to which neither the pratings of heretics nor the insolent taunts of barbarians shall do any damage. Deliver her then from trials and dangers by thy prayers, most blessed one.

Χριστός σε πρῶτον
ἐν τῇ ἐκλογῇ, Πέτρε, κρηπίδα
τῆς πίστεως ἐστεφάνωσεν.
lxxxviii.

Thee, Peter, has Christ crowned as first in His chosen band, the foundation of the faith.

Τοὺς τῆς εὐσεβείας ἀληθεῖς κήρυκας,
καὶ τῆς ἐκκλησίας
ὑπερφαεῖς ἀστέρας
ὕμνοις ἐγκωμίων τιμήσωμεν,
Πέτρον, τὴν πέτραν τῶν πιστῶν,
καὶ Παῦλον, τὸν ἀληθῆ διδάσκαλον
καὶ μύστην τοῦ Σωτῆρος Χριστοῦ.
lxxxix.

Let us honour with hymns of praise the true preachers of religion, and stars of the Church, exceeding bright, Peter, the rock of the faithful, and Paul, the true teacher, versed in the mysteries of Christ the Saviour.

Τῆς ἐκκλησίας τὴν πέτραν
τὸν πανεύφημον Πέτρον,
καὶ ὑπέρμαχον ταύτης
τὸν πανένδοξον Παῦλον,
ἀξίως εὐφημήσωμεν, πιστοί,
ὡς ἔχοντας τὰς κλεῖς τῶν οὐρανῶν
ὑπ' αὐτῶν γὰρ ἐφωτίσθη
ἡ οἰκουμένη τῇ πίστει τῆς Τριάδος.
lxxxix. xc.

O Faithful, let us worthily celebrate, the rock of the Church, Peter most renowned, and her mighty champion, the most glorious Paul, as (both) holding the keys of heaven; for by their means was the whole world enlightened with the faith of the Trinity.

Τοὺς σοφοὺς πρωτοθρόνους τῆς ἐκκλησίας

Let us sing hymns in honour of the wise Protothrones of the Church,

καὶ ταχεῖς καθαιρέτας τῆς ἀσεβείας,
Πέτρον καὶ Παῦλον,
ἐν ὕμνοις τιμήσωμεν,
ὡς τῶν εἰδώλων τὴν πλάνην ἐξάραντας,
καὶ τὴν ὀρθόδοξον πίστιν ἱδρύσαντας. ...

and swift destroyers of impiety, Peter and Paul, as having subverted the error of idolatry, and founded the orthodox faith.

Μακαρίζω σε, Ῥώμη, καὶ εὐφημῶ,
προσκυνῶ καὶ δοξάζω καὶ ἀνυμνῶ·
ἐν σοὶ γὰρ ἀπόκεινται
τῶν κορυφαίων τὰ σώματα,
τῶν μεγάλων φωστήρων
τὰ θεῖα διδάγματα,
τῶν σκευῶν τῶν ἀχράντων
τὰ τίμια λείψανα. ...
Κορυφαῖοι ἀπόστολοι
πρευβεύσατε Χριστῷ τῷ Θεῷ. xc.

Blessed do I call thee, Rome, I congratulate, venerate, praise, and laud thee: for in thee are preserved the bodies of the Coryphæi, the Divine teachings of those great luminaries, the precious relics of the incorruptible vessels. ...
Coryphæi Apostles intercede with Christ the God.

Νωθρῶς τοὺς τῷ γράμματι τοῦ νόμου
προσπταίοντας γόνους Ἰσραὴλ
τῷ φωτισμῷ τῆς χάριτος
ὁ Πέτρος προσενήνοχε·
τὰς τῶν ἐθνῶν ἀγέλας δὲ
ὁ Παῦλος πλάνης ἐρρύσατο. xciv.

The children of Israel, dully stumbling at the letter of the Law, Peter brought to the illumination of grace, whilst Paul delivered from error the herds of the Gentiles.

Ἀποστάτην Σίμωνα, μάγον δεινὸν,
ὡς φιλοχρυσότατον ἤλεγξεν
ὁ θεῖος Πέτρος·
καὶ νῦν Παῦλος ὁ σόφος,
τὸν τρίβους διαστρέφοντα
τοῦ Χριστοῦ, Ἐλυμαν ἐπήρωσεν.
xcv.

Simon, the apostate and dreadful magician, the Divine Peter convicted as most greedy of gold: and then Paul the wise struck Elymas blind as subverting the ways of Christ.

Ὡς ὄντα στερρότατον
Χριστός σε πέτραν κέκληκε,
Πέτρε, καὶ ἐν σοὶ τὴν ἐκκλησίαν
ἣν ᾅδου πύλαι οὐ κατισχύουσι·
σὲ δέ, Παῦλε, σκεῦος ἐκλογῆς
ἔφη, τοῦτον φέρειν σε
ἐθνῶν ἔμπροσθεν τοὔνομα. xcv.

As being most firm, Christ called thee a rock, O Peter, and on thee He founded His Church against which the gates of hell shall not prevail; whilst thee, O Paul, He called a vessel of election, to bear this His Name before the nations.

Ἀκήρατον εὔκλειαν,
καὶ δόξαν τὴν ἀμάραντον,
Πέτρέ, πρὸς Χριστοῦ εὗρου σὺν
Παύλῳ·
τὰς κλεῖς ὁ μὲν τῶν οὐρανῶν πιστευθείς,

Unsullied renown and glory unfading, O Peter, thou has found from Christ, together with Paul; the one being entrusted with the keys of heaven, and the other rapt to paradise, and made to hear

ὁ δὲ εἰς παράδεισον ἀχθείς,
ῥήματά τε ἄρρητα
μυηθεὶς ὑπὲρ ἄνθρωπον. xcvi.

Νομολάτρας μὲν
ὁ Πέτρος ἐσυνέτιζεν,
ὡς προετέτακτο·
ὁ Παῦλος δὲ ἐθνικοὺς. . . .
Ὡς πανάριστος
ὁ Πέτρος τοῦ Χριστοῦ ποιμὴν,
τὴν ποίμνην εἴληφεν·
τῆς ἐκκλησίας δὲ
ὁ Παῦλος διδάσκαλος
ἔνθεος γέγονεν. xcvii.

Τῶν οὐρανῶν τὴν κλειδουχίαν ἀντηλ-
λάττετο
τῆς τῶν ἰχθύων Πέτρος σαγηνεύ-
σεως·
σκηνορραφίας Παῦλος δὲ
γνῶσιν μυστικὴν καὶ οὐράνιον. cii.

Τοὺς ἐξ Ἰσραὴλ ὁ Πέτρος
καὶ ὁ Παῦλος ἐθνικοὺς διενείματο,
ἀλλήλων διεστῶτας δὲ τοὺς λαοὺς
ἀμφοτέρους συνάψαντες,
ἑνότητι πίστεως ὁμοφρόνως
κραυγάζειν ἐδίδαξαν·
Εὐλογεῖτε, πάντα τὰ ἔργα,
Θεὸν, τὸν Κύριον, civ.

Πέτρος ἡ κρηπὶς,
σφραγὶς δὲ καὶ στέφανος
τῆς ἐκκλησίας σου,
συναρμολογούμενος
ὁ Παῦλος ὅλην,
οἱ λοιποὶ σὺν αὐτοῖς,
λίθοι καὶ στύλοι τέλειοι,
πᾶσαν συνέχοντες
ἐκκλησίαν,
ἣν πρεσβείας ἄσειστον
συντήρησον, Θεοῦ Λόγε, εὐχαῖς
τῆς τεκούσης σε. cxii.

Πέτρε, μακάριε
ἀποστόλων πρόκριτε,
ἀποστόλων καύχημα,
σῶσαι τὴν ποίμνην σοῦ. cxiv.

words unspeakable, passing what is human.

Peter instructed those who observed the Law, as was fore-arranged, and Paul the Gentiles. . . . Peter, as Christ's all-greatest shepherd, received the flock, whilst Paul was made inspired teacher of the Church.

Peter preferred bearing the keys of heaven to his fish-catching: and Paul the knowledge of heavenly mysteries to his tent-making.

Peter took for his share those of Israel, and Paul the Gentiles: joining together the two peoples divided from one another; harmoniously in the unity of faith, they taught them to cry out: Bless, all ye works, God the Lord.

Peter, the foundation, seal, and crown of Thy Church, Paul, with him, organising and uniting the whole same Church, the others with these two, perfect stones and pillars holding together the entire Church: by their suffrages, O Word of God, do Thou keep it unshaken, through the intercession of Thine own Mother.

Blessed Peter, Prince and glory of the Apostles, save thy flock.

374 THE FEAST OF SS. PETER AND PAUL, JUNE 29TH.

Ὅθεν Χριστῷ ἐκολλήθης
καὶ συνανεκράθης
αὐτῷ διαπύρῳ στοργῇ. cxvii.

Hence thou wert glued to Christ and mingled in union together with Him, by a tender love that was all on fire.

Νεφελοδρόμος ἀετὸς
ὁ πεζοπόρος ἐδείχθης·
ἐν ῥοπῇ γὰρ
ὥσπερ ὀφθαλμοῦ,
τῷ παντουργικῷ
καὶ θείῳ Πνεύματι
ἀπὸ τῆς Ῥώμης ἐν Σιὼν
διὰ νεφέλης ἐγένου,
κηδεῦσαι τὴν ἔμψυχον νεφέλην
Θεοῦ.

As a cloud-coursing eagle, thy feet still on earth, didst thou appear: for, as though in the twinkling of an eye, by the all-working and Divine Spirit, from Rome to Sion wert thou borne by a cloud, to have part with the living cloud of God.

Ἐκ τοῦ Χριστοῦ
σὺ παραλαβὼν
τὴν ἐκκλησίαν,
ἣν αὐτὸς ὁ Κύριος,
καὶ οὐκ ἄνθρωποι, ἐπήξατο,
καλῶς ἐκυβέρνησας,
ὡς ὁλκάδα, ταύτην, ἀπόστολε. cxx.

From Christ having received the Church, which the Lord Himself and not man founded, well hast thou piloted her as a ship, O Apostle.

Ἐν ᾠδαῖς πνευματικαῖς
τοὺς κορυφαίους μαθητὰς
εὐφημήσωμεν, πιστοί,
Πέτρον καὶ Παῦλον·
τὸν ἀνεξιχνίαστον τόκον Πέτρος
ὡς ἐκ τοῦ Πατρὸς προαιώνιον
μαθὼν τὸν αὐτὸν μετὰ σαρκὸς
ἐπὶ τῆς γῆς, ἐβόησε·
Δόξα τῷ εὐσπλάγχνῳ· καθόδωσον. cxxviii.

With spiritual odes let us celebrate the praises of the supreme disciples Peter and Paul : since Peter, having learnt the inscrutable generation before all ages of the Son from the Father, and that He was born incarnate upon earth, exclaimed : Glory to the Most Clement ! Direct us.

Τὸν δρόμον ἐκτελέσασα,
ἡ δυὰς ἡ ἁγία
πρὸς οὐρανοὺς ἀνέδραμεν,
ἐν σκηναῖς οὐρανίαις,
ὁ Πέτρος ὁ μακάριος,
σὺν τῷ Παύλῳ σοφῷ
καὶ τῶν ἐθνῶν διδασκάλῳ·
οὓς τιμῶντες ἀξίως
μακαρίζομεν πιστῶς,
ὡς κορυφαίους προστάτας. . . .
αὐτοὶ γὰρ ἐσαγήνευσαν
ἡμᾶς ἐκ πλάνης εἰδώλων

The holy Pair, having finished their course, winged their flight to heaven to the heavenly tabernacles, Peter the blessed one, with Paul the wise and teacher of the nations, whom in faith we bless with worthy honour as supreme patrons . . . for it was they who drew us into their net from the error of idols, presenting us to the Lord . . . preaching the cross as Apostles they enlightened the nations and taught us to glorify

προσάξαντες τῷ Κυρίῳ. . . .
τὸν σταυρὸν ἀπόστολοι
κηρύξαντες, ἐφώτισαν
τὰ ἔθνη, καὶ ἐδίδαξαν
σε Θεοτόκον δοξάζειν,
καὶ προσκυνεῖν τὸν Τόκον.
cxxviii. cxxix.

thee, the Mother of God, and to adore thy Son.

Θεὸς . . . καλῶν καὶ πέτραν,
ἐν σοὶ ἀκαταίσχυντον
ἐκκλησίας τὴν ἔδραν
ὁ θεμέλιος ἐπήξατο. cxxix.

God calling thee a rock, Himself the foundation, founded on thee the Church's seat that shall not be confounded.

JUNE 30TH.—THE COMMON FEAST (ἡ σύναξις) OF THE XII. HOLY AND GLORIOUS APOSTLES.

Ἡ κορυφαία κρηπὶς τῶν ἀποστόλων,
τὰ πάντα κατέλιπες
καὶ ἠκολούθησας
τῷ Διδασκάλῳ, βοῶν αὐτῷ·
σὺν σοὶ θανοῦμαι,
ἵνα ζήσω τὴν μακάριαν ζωήν·
τῆς Ῥώμης δὲ γέγονας
σὺ πρωτεπίσκοπος,
τῆς παμμεγίστου τῶν πόλεων
δόξα καὶ κλέος,
καὶ ἐκκλησίας, Πέτρε, ἑδραίωμα,
καὶ πύλαι ᾅδου
οὐ κατισχύσουσιν ὄντως ταύτης,
Χριστὸς ὡς προέφησεν·
ὃν ἱκέτευε σῶσαι
καὶ φωτίσαι τὰς ψυχὰς ἡμῶν.
Ὁ ἐκ κοιλίας μητρὸς ἀφωρισαμένος,
ὑλώδας ἐμφάσεως
βάρος πάσης φυγὼν,
ἀνεπτερώθης ταῖς πτέρυξι,
τῆς ὄντως θείας
Παῦλε, ἀγάπης πρὸς ὕψος ἔνθεον,
ἔνθα τὸν ὑπέρφωτον
γνόφον θείου φωτὸς
ὑπεισελθὼν, ὥς τις ἄσαρκος,
τὴν τῶν ἀρρήτων
κατεπλουτίσθης ῥημάτων μύησιν
καὶ ἀπεστάλης
τοῖς ἐν τῷ σκότει τὸ φῶς μηνύων,
Χριστὸν τὸν Θεὸν ἡμῶν. . . .

Supreme foundation of the Apostles, thou didst forsake all things and didst follow the Master, crying aloud to Him, With Thee will I die that so I may live the life of the blessed; and of Rome made first Bishop, thou wert the praise and glory of the greatest of all cities, and of the Church, Peter, the foundation, and the gates of hell shall not prevail, no never, against her, as Christ foretold: Whom, beseech to save and enlighten our souls.

Thou, who set apart from thy mother's womb, casting aside the weight of all material form, didst soar on the wings of in truth divine charity, even to the height of heaven, where, entering into the darkness of the light of God which is above all light, as one out of the flesh thou wert enriched beyond measure by mystical initiation into words unutterable, and wert sent to reveal to those in darkness the light, even Christ our God. . . .

Πέτρε καὶ Παῦλε, τοῦ Λόγου ἀρο-
τῆρες,
Ἀνδρέα, Ἰάκωβε,
καὶ Ἰωάννη σοφέ,
Βαρθολομαῖε, καὶ Φίλιππε,
Θωμᾶ, Ματθαῖε,
Σίμων, Ἰούδα, θεῖε Ἰάκωβε,
παγκόσμιε, πάντιμε
μαθητῶν δωδεκάς,
οἱ ἐν τῷ κόσμῳ κηρύξαντες
τὴν παναγίαν
Τριάδα, φύσει Θεὸν ἀΐδιον,
τῆς ἐκκλησίας
οἱ ἀλεξητήριοι ὄντως πύργοι
καὶ στῦλοι ἀσάλευτοι,
τῷ Δεσπότῃ τῶν ὅλων
πρεσβεύσατε σωθῆναι ἡμᾶς.
cxxxvii. cxxxviii. cxxxix.

Peter and Paul, husbandmen of the Word, Andrew, James, and John the wise, Bartholomew, and Philip, Thomas, Matthew, Simon Jude, and divine James, all-fair, all-honoured College of disciples twelve, after preaching in the world the most holy Trinity, by nature God eternal, do you, who in truth are the protecting towers of the Church, and her unshaken pillars, intercede with the Lord of the whole universe to preserve us in safety.

Χόρος πνευματικὸς
ἀποστόλων τῷ κόσμῳ
ἐστάλη μυστικῶς
ἐκ Θεοῦ τοῦ ὑψίστου. cxl.

The spiritual Choir of the Apostles was sent to the world in the mystery of His will by God most high.

Τοὺς μεγάλους φωστῆρας καὶ φαει-
νοὺς,
κορυφαίους ὀφθέντας τῶν μαθητῶν,
Πέτρον εὐφημήσωμεν,
καὶ τὸν πάνσοφον Παῦλον·
τῷ γὰρ πυρὶ τοῦ θείου
ἐκλάμψαντες Πνεύματος,
τὴν ἀχλὺν τῆς πλάνης
κατέφλεξαν ἅπασαν·
ὅθεν καὶ τῆς ἄνω
βασιλείας πολῖται
ἀξίως ἐδείχθητε,
καὶ τῆς χάριτος σύνθρονοι· cxlii.

Thou great and shining luminaries who appeared as Coryphæi of the disciples, Peter let us celebrate, and the most wise Paul: for illumined with the fire of the Divine Spirit they set all on flame the whole cloud of error, therefore have you merited to be received as citizens of the kingdom above, and to sit together on the throne of grace.

Θείοις δόγμασι τῆς εὐσεβείας
καταρδεύσαντες τὴν ἐκκλησίαν,
ὡς ποταμοὶ τῆς εἰρήνης, ἀπόστολοι,
τῆς εὐσεβείας τὴν χύσιν ἐξήρατε,
καὶ τοὺς πιστοὺς εὐκαρποῦντας ἐδεί-
ξατε. . . .
Τὸν Πέτρον, πίστοι,
τὴν πέτραν τῆς πίστεως,
αἰνέσωμεν νῦν καὶ Παῦλον,

Having given the Church to drink of Divine dogmas of religion, as rivers of peace, O Apostles, ye have made the effusion of piety to increase, and the faithful to abound in good fruits... Peter, O ye faithful, the rock of faith, let us now praise, and also Paul, those men after the mind of God: Moreover we call all together

COMMEMORATION OF ALL THE APOSTLES. 377

τοὺς θεόφρονας·
συγκαλοῦμεν γὰρ ἅπαντας
ἑορτάσαι πίστει καὶ τοὺς λοιποὺς
ὡς κήρυκας τῆς πίστεως,
αἰτοῦντες πταισμάτων τὴν συγχώρησιν. cxliv.

to celebrate in faith the others, too, as heralds of the faith, praying them to obtain the pardon of our sins.

Ὄντως νυνὶ ἐπέστη τοῖς πᾶσι. ...
συμφώνως ὑμνῆσαι
Πέτρον καὶ Παῦλον,
Ἰωάννην, Ἀνδρέαν, τοὺς πρωτοκλήτους,
Φίλιππόν τε καὶ Ματθαῖον,
ἀπαύστως δοξάζοντες
Σίμωνα τὸν ζηλωτήν τε καὶ Ἰούδαν,
Ἰάκωβον καὶ ἅπαντας τοὺς λοιποὺς ἀποστόλους. cxliv.

Now in truth it is incumbent on all ... to laud with harmonious voice Peter and Paul, John and Andrew, the first called; Philip, too, and Matthew; incessantly glorifying Simon Zelotes and Jude, James and all the rest of the Apostles.

Τοὺς κορυφαίους πάντες τῶν ἀποστόλων
ἐν θεοπνεύστοις ᾄσμασιν εὐφημῶμεν.
Χαίροις, Πέτρε, πέτρα καὶ θεμέλιος
τῆς ἐκκλησίας ἄσειστος,
καὶ Παῦλε, στόμα τοῦ Λόγου,
φωταγωγῶν πᾶσαν κτίσιν. cxlvi.

Let us all praise with inspired hymns the Coryphæi of the Apostles. Hail, Peter, rock and immovable foundation of the Church, and Paul, mouth of the Word, enlightening the whole creation.

25

CHAPTER XIV.

THE SUCCESSION OF THE ROMAN PONTIFFS TO S. PETER'S EPISCOPATE AND PRIMACY IN THE SEE OF ROME ILLUSTRATED FROM THE GREEK LITURGY, AND OTHER GREEK SOURCES.

WE saw in the preceding Chapter that the Greek Liturgy gives direct and clear testimony to the Roman Episcopate and Primacy of S. Peter: and we shall now see that it bears a like witness to the Roman Pontiffs as S. Peter's successors in the same Primacy and See. The Offices for several of the Popes and of other Saints whose Feasts are kept in the Greek Church plainly show this. Thus S. Leo is spoken of as 'successor of the venerable Peter and enjoying his presidency,' S. Gregory as 'the successor of the Chair of the Coryphæus and Prince of the Apostolic Choir'; and all the same supreme prerogatives which were attributed to S. Peter are ascribed also to the several Bishops of Rome. It may seem superfluous to remark—what, however, is most important—that, whilst the argument bears directly here upon the Roman Pontiffs as successors to S. Peter, it yet at the same time proves, indirectly indeed, but with equal force and clearness, our main and central thesis, that S. Peter was Bishop of Rome, since this is convertible and identical with every recurring statement that the Roman Pontiff is Peter's successor and holds his Chair or See. In addition to the passages from the Greek Offices, we have made a few extracts from the writings of Greek Saints and historians in order more fully to illustrate our subject.

THE COMMEMORATION OF S. SYLVESTER, POPE OF ROME, is celebrated January 2nd: the following passages are taken from the Office.*

Πάτερ Σίλβεστρε... στύλος ὡράθης πυρός, ἱερῶς προηγούμενος ἱεροῦ συσ-	Father Sylvester, thou didst appear as a pillar of fire, holily taking

* *Kalendarium Manuale utriusque Ecclesiæ Orientalis et Occidentalis, &c.,* Auctore Nicolao Nilles, S.J. Œniponte, 1879, p. 51.

FROM THE OFFICES OF S. SYLVESTER AND S. LEO. 379

τήματος καὶ νεφέλη σκιάζουσα, Αἰγύπτου πλάνης πιστοὺς ἐξαίρουσα, καὶ πρὸς θείαν αὐγὴν μεταφέρουσα ταῖς ἀπλανέσι διδαχαῖς ἑκάστοτε.

the lead of the sacred assembly; and, as an overshadowing cloud, delivering the faithful from Egyptian error (Arianism); and continually by unerring teachings transferring them to divine light.

Ὡς θεῖος κορυφαῖος ἱερῶν πατέρων τὸ ἱερώτατον δόγμα ἐκρατύνας, αἱρετικῶν ἀποφράξας ἄθεα στόματα.

As divine Coryphæus of the sacred Fathers thou didst confirm the most holy dogma, stopping the impious mouths.

Ἔτρεψας, Σιλβέστρε, ἐναντίων σύστημα τὸ τῶν ἀποστόλων μαχόμενον τῷ κηρύγματι.

Thou, Sylvester, didst put to rout the whole body of the enemy that was warring against the preaching of the Apostles.

Συνεχύθησαν γλῶσσαι συμφωνοῦσαι τῇ πλάνῃ ἐν τῇ δυνάμει, σοφέ, πνεύματος τοῦ θείου τοῦ ἐν σοὶ ἐνεργοῦντος· καὶ εἰς μίαν συνήφθησαν δοξολογίαν Θεοῦ πιστῶν χοροστασίαι.

Tongues that accorded together in error were confounded, O wise one, by the power of the Divine Spirit that energised in thee; and the choirs of the faithful were united in giving praise to God with one and the same doxology.

The Feast of the Pope S. Leo the Great is celebrated by the Greeks February 18th. In the *Basilian Menologium*, pp. 319-322, it is said:

"This our admirable Father Leo, for his many virtues, continence, and purity being consecrated Bishop of great Rome, did many other things worthy of his virtues, but especially in all that concerned the right faith. For in the Council of Chalcedon, where were assembled 630 Fathers against the heresy of those who said that in Christ was but one nature, when the Fathers of the Council proclaimed the truth, and still the heretics would not yield to them, it was agreed by all, that whatever Leo the most holy Pope of Rome said, should be held as settled and firm (πᾶσιν ἤρεσεν, ἵνα ὃ ἐὰν εἴπῃ Λέων ὁ ἁγιώτατος πάπας Ῥώμης θελήσωσι). At the request, therefore, of the Fathers, and after having offered prayers to God, he wrote an Epistle, wherein exposing the truth, he declared the two natures in Christ,* and the same they called a

* It is to this Epistle that the acclamations in the Council refer: "Peter, by Leo, has spoken thus... Piously and truly has Leo taught." (Πέτρος διὰ Λέοντος ταῦτα ἐξεφώνησεν... εὐσεβῶς καὶ ἀληθινῶς Λέων ἐδίδαξε. Hardouin, tom. ii. p. 305.) And: "They have brought back their vessels in due course, successfully directed to right understanding by Christ, Who in the admirable Leo shows forth the truth, and as He made use of the wise Peter, so does He use Leo as its assertor." (*Relat. ad Pulcher. Augustam, Ibid.*, p. 381.) And again: "God has provided an invincible champion against all error, and has prepared the Pope of the Roman Church for victory, girding him with the doctrines of truth in all things, that, as Peter, so he, battling with most fervent zeal, may lead to God all sense and intelligence." (*Allocut. ad Marcian. Imperatorem, Ibid.* p. 643.)

column of orthodoxy (ἣν ὀρθοδοξίας στήλην ὠνόμασαν). After this the Great Leo, having spent a most holy life, rested in peace, A.D. 461."

The following passages are from the Hymns of the Feast:

Ὄρθρος ἐκ δυσμῶν ἀνέτειλας τρισμάκαρ, τόμον εὐσεβῶν δογμάτων ὡς ἀκτῖνα τῇ Ἐκκλησίᾳ ἐξαποστέλλων.

Rising as the morning dawn from the West, thrice blessed, thou sentest forth thy volume of holy dogmas as rays of light upon the Church.

Ὁ Πέτρου νῦν τοῦ σεπτοῦ διάδοχος, καὶ τὴν τούτου προεδρείαν πλουτήσας, καὶ θερμὸν ζῆλον κεκτημένος, θεοκινήτως τὸν τόμον ἐκτίθεται.

The successor of the venerable Peter, enriched too with his presidency, and possessed of his ardent zeal, by a Divine impulse puts forth his volume.

Ὑπὸ Θεοῦ κινούμενος εὐσεβείας διδάγματα ὡς ἐν θεοχαράκτοις πλαξὶ ἐτυπώσας, Μωσῆς οἷα δεύτερος ἀναφανεὶς τῇ ὁμηγύρει τῶν σεπτῶν διδασκάλων.*

Moved by God, thou didst set down the doctrines of religion, as though on tables impressed by God; appearing like another Moses to the assembly of venerable teachers.

FROM THE OFFICE OF THE FEAST OF S. GREGORY THE GREAT, celebrated by the Greeks March 12th.

Ἱερώτατε ποιμήν, τοῦ κορυφαίου γέγονας καθέδρας καὶ τοῦ ζήλου διάδοχος, λαοὺς καθαίρων καὶ προσάγων Θεῷ.

Thou, most holy Pastor, art successor to the Chair and to the zeal of the Coryphæus, cleansing the nations and bringing them to God.

Διάδοχος τοῦ θρόνου τοῦ χοροῦ τῶν μαθητῶν τοῦ ἐξάρχοντος χρηματίζεις · ἐξ οὗ τὸν λόγον τὰς ἀκτῖνας δᾳδούχων, Γρηγόριε, καταυγάζεις τοὺς πιστούς.

Successor to the throne of the Prince of the choir of the disciples, thou dost fulfil thy office: and from thence holding forth thy word as a torch, O Gregory, thou dost illumine the faithful with rays of light.

Ἐκκλησιῶν σε κολπωσαμένη ἡ Πρώτη πᾶσαν ὑφήλιον κατάρδει τοῖς ῥεύμασι τῶν εὐσεβεστάτων δογμάτων σου.

The First of Churches, having drawn thee to her bosom, waters every land under the sun with the streams of her most holy teachings.

Χαίροις, θεοσεβείας λαμπτήρ, ὁ ταῖς ἀκτῖσι τῶν λόγων σου φωτίσας τὴν οἰκουμένην · πορσὸς τοὺς ἐν ζάλῃ τῆς ἀγνωσίας ὑπάρχοντας πρὸς λιμένα ἐκκαλούμενος καὶ θανάτου λυτρούμενος, ὄργανον ὑψηλούμενον πνοαῖς ταῖς τοῦ Πνεύματος.†

Hail, torch of religion, who enlightenest with the rays of thy words the whole world: beacon recalling to the haven those that are in the tempest of error, and ransoming them from death, organ acted upon by the breathings of the Spirit.

* See Nilles, *Ibid.* pp. 106-108. † *Ibid.* p. 121.

FROM THE OFFICE OF THE FEAST OF S. MARTIN, POPE (Nov. 12th), celebrated by the Greeks April 13th.

Τί σε, Μαρτῖνε προσφθέγξομαι; ὀρθοδόξων διδαχῶν καθηγητὴν πανευκλεῆ; κορυφαῖον ἱερῶν δογμάτων θείων, ἀψευδῶς; τοῦ ψεύδους ἀληθέστατον κατήγορον; Οὐσίας δύο καὶ δύο θελήματα καὶ ἐνεργείας διπλᾶς φέρωντα, μακάριε, τὸν ἕνα τῆς Τριάδος ἐδογμάτισας Χριστὸν τὸν ὑπερούσιον Θεόν· καὶ τοὺς μὴ οὕτως σέβοντας πάντας ἀπεκήρυξας. Ὑπάρχων ἀνάπλεος θείου ζήλου συνήθροισας ἱερὰν σύνοδον καὶ τὸ τῆς ἐκκλησίας ἐκύρωσας δόγμα... Συνόδου ἐν μέσῳ ἀπεκήρυξας Πύρρον καὶ Σέργιον καὶ τοὺς σὺν ἐκείνοις λοιδωροῦντας. Ἱερωτάτῳ σοῦ λόγῳ πανίερον σαφῶς δόγμα ἐκράτυνας καὶ τὸ στῖφος αἱρέσεων ἔτρεψας. Ῥήγνυται ὁ πονηρὸς πρὸ ποδῶν ἱερῶν σοῦ, καὶ πονηρῶν ἀνθρώπων τὰ ἀπύλωτα στόματα ἀποφράττονται, καὶ δείκνυται διαλάμπον δόγμα τὸ θεῖον ὑπὲρ ἥλιον. Ἀρχιέρεων σε ἔγνωμεν κρηπῖδα, ὀρθοδοξίας τε στήλην καὶ εὐσεβείας διδάσκαλον. Ἐπεκόσμησας τὸν Πέτρου θεῖον θρόνον, καὶ τῇ αὐτοῦ θείᾳ πέτρᾳ τὴν ἐκκλησίαν ἀσάλευτον συντηρήσας σὺν αὐτῷ δεδόξασαι.

How shall I address thee, Martin? Shall it be as all-glorious leader of orthodox teaching? As sacred Coryphæus of Divine dogmas, speaking nought but truth? As most true denouncer of error? That Christ, the Second Person of the Trinity, the supersubstantial God, has two natures, and two wills, and a twofold operation, thou, blessed one, hast set forth as a dogma, and condemned all those who otherwise worship. Being full of Divine zeal, thou didst assemble a holy Synod, and didst confirm the dogma of the Church.... In the midst of the Synod thou didst condemn Pyrrhus and Sergius, and those who blasphemed with them.

By thy most holy word thou didst openly give force to the all sacred dogma, and put to the rout the whole troop of heresies. The wicked one is shattered at thy sacred feet, the unbridled tongues of wicked men are stopped, and the Divine dogma is shown forth, shining more brightly than the sun. In thee we recognise the foundation of bishops, the pillar of the orthodox faith, and teacher of religion. Thou hast adorned the Divine throne of Peter, and since then hast preserved the Church immovable on his Divine rock, with him art thou glorified."*

In this passage is clearly expressed the Catholic doctrine that the Roman Pontiff has the prerogative of teaching infallibly, from his being Peter's successor to the Roman See.

---

* Nilles, pp. 136-8. In the Office for the Feast of the Translation of the Relics of S. Maximus C. (Aug. 13th) it is said of that Saint: "Enkindled with Divine zeal as with a fire, he went to the elder Rome, and persuaded the most blessed Pope Martin to assemble a local synod, and to anathematise the leaders of the impious teaching of those who prated of but one will in Christ." (*Ibid.* p. 244.)

THE FEAST OF S. THEODORE STUDITES (A.D. 813), the famous Hegumen of the Studium at Constantinople, is celebrated amongst the Greeks November 11th. He was a Confessor for the Holy Images, and one of the most celebrated of the Greek ecclesiastical poets. Writing to the Emperor Michael he says:

"Let your Majesty command that the declaration be received from old Rome, for so in past times and from the beginning was the custom as handed down by the tradition of our fathers. For this, O king, imitator of Christ, is the supreme (ἡ κορυφαιοτάτη) of the Churches of God, of which Peter was first Bishop (ἧς Πέτρος πρωτόθρονος), to whom the Lord said: 'Thou art Peter... against it.' To this first See even the pre-eminence of the Ecumenical Synod is referred (ᾧ καὶ τὸ κράτος ἀναφέρεται τῆς οἰκουμενικῆς συνόδου); to the Bishop of Rome legates must be sent from both parties, and thence is to be obtained the certitude of the faith (ἐξ ἑκατέρου μέρους ἀποσταλτέον πρὸς τὸν 'Ρώμης· κἀκεῖθεν δεχίσθω τὸ ἀσφαλὲς τῆς πίστεως)."*

Begging help from the Roman See against the Iconoclasts, he writes to the Pope S. Paschal, A.D. 817:†

"Come hither, then, from the West, O imitator of Christ, arise and cast not off for ever. To thee Christ our God said: 'And thou being once converted confirm thy brethren.' Now then is the time and the place: help us, for to this art thou ordained by God; stretch forth thy hand so far as is possible; thou hast the power with God, from thy holding the first place of all; and for this too thou art set. Strike with terror, we beseech thee, the heretical wild beasts with the pen of thy Divine word. O good Pastor, lay down thy life for the sheep, we implore thee."

In the next Epistle to the same Pope, after having experienced the help of the Roman Pontiff, he gratefully exclaims:

"The Orient from on high, Christ our God, hath regarded us; Who has made your Blessedness in the West as a torch divinely bright for the illumination of the whole Church, by setting you on the Apostolic first (πρώτιστον) throne. We are verily persuaded that the Lord has not forsaken our Church here, to whom the providence of God has afforded in times of trial, as our one and only help, that which comes from you up to now, and from the beginning. You then are the clear and unadulterated source, from the beginning, of orthodoxy: you are, in face of every heretical storm, the retired tranquil harbour of the whole Church; you are the city of refuge chosen by God for safety (Ὑμεῖς οὖν ὡς ἀληθῶς ἡ ἀθόλωτος καὶ ἀκαπήλευτος πηγὴ ἐξ ἀρχῆς τῆς ὀρθοδοξίας· ὑμεῖς ὁ πάσης αἱρετικῆς ζάλης ἀνψκίσμενος εὔδιος λιμὴν τῆς ὅλης Ἐκκλησίας· ὑμεῖς ἡ θεόλεκτος πόλις τοῦ φυγαδευτηρίου τῆς σωτηρίας)."

The Saint in the Epistle which he had before written to Pope Leo III.‡ (809), 'the Supreme Father of fathers' (κορυφαιοτάτῳ πατρὶ πατέρων), to implore his help, says thus:

*L. 2, Ep. 86, 129. Migne, tom. 99, pp. 1331-2; 1419-20.
†Ep. 12, ibid. pp. 1153-4.
‡L. 1, Ep. 33, ibid. pp. 1017-20.

"Since Christ our God gave to the great Peter, after the keys of the kingdom of heaven, the dignity also of the pastoral supremacy, it is assuredly to S. Peter or to his successor that every innovation in the Catholic Church, on the part of those who err from the truth, must needs be referred. For which cause we, too, in our lowliness being as we are the least of all, thus taught from our fathers of old time, when in our Church some novelty lately arose, judged that we ought to refer this to your Beatitude... O Head, most Divine of all heads (ὦ θειοτάτη τῶν ὅλων κεφαλῶν κεφαλή).... After this truthful exposition, we now make use of those words which the Coryphæus with the other Apostles addressed to Christ when the billows of the sea arose, and call on your Beatitude who is in the likeness of Christ: 'Save us, Chief Pastor of the whole Church under heaven: we perish.' Imitate thy Master, Christ, and stretch forth thy hand to our Church, as He did to Peter: except that He did so to him who was only beginning to sink in the sea, whereas thou must do so now to her who is already sunk in the depth of heresy.

"Emulate, we pray, the Pope whose name thou bearest; and as he, at the time of the Eutychian heresy, arose in spirit as a lion, as is known to all, with his dogmatic Epistles, so do thou too (I make bold thus to express myself), in accord with thy name, roar divinely, or rather thunder, against this present heresy as it behoves. For if these men, by usurped authority, have not feared to convene a heretical synod—though they had no power to assemble even an orthodox one without thy knowledge, according to the custom that has obtained from of old—how much more reasonable, nay, necessary, is it (we are making the suggestion with fear) that a legitimate synod should be convoked by thy Divine supremacy, in order that the orthodox teaching of the Church should thrust out the heretical doctrine; moreover, to prevent thy supreme dignity (ἡ κορυφαιότης σοῦ), together with all the other orthodox, being anathematised by the vain innovators.... We have made these representations in manner becoming our littleness, as the least members of the Church, and in obedience to your Divine supreme pastorate (τῇ ὑφ' ὑμῶν ὑπείκοντες θείᾳ ποιμεναρχίᾳ). For the rest, we implore your holy soul to reckon us as your own sheep (ὡς οἰκεῖα αὐτῆς πρόβατα), and to enlighten and strengthen us from afar by your holy prayers—if, too, by your instructions, it would be an act of condescension on the part of your Holiness."[*]

Two Feasts (March 13th and June 2nd) are celebrated in the Greek Church in honour of S. NICEPHORUS, PATRIARCH OF CONSTANTINOPLE, who died in exile a Confessor for the Holy Images, June 2, 826.[†]

In an Apology for the Holy Images the Saint thus writes concerning the Second Nicene Ecumenical Council:

"And indeed this Synod is of supreme authority and sufficient for the fulness of faith, for it was Ecumenical, entirely free, secure from all risk of calumny or blame, unchargeable with any alien dogma whatever, and devoid

---

[*] See Nilles, pp. 321-6.   [†] *Ibid.* pp. 121, 170-1.

Συγκεκρότητο γὰρ τοῦτο μάλιστα ἐνδίκως καὶ ἐννομώτατα ἐπείπερ ᾖδη, κατὰ τοὺς ἀρχῆθεν τετυπωμένους θείους θεσμοὺς, προῆγε κατ' αὐτὴν καὶ προήδρευεν ὅσον τε τῆς ἑσπερίας λήξεως, ἤτοι τῆς πρεσβύτιδος 'Ρώμης, μέρος οὐκ ἄσημον· ὧν ἄνευ δόγμα κατὰ τὴν Ἐκκλησίαν κινούμενον, θεσμοῖς κανονικοῖς, καὶ ἱερατικοῖς ἔθεσι νεμομισμένον ἄνωθεν, τὴν δοκιμασίαν οὐ σχοίη, ἢ δέξαιτ' ἄν ποτε τὴν περαίωσιν, ὡς δὴ λαχόντων κατὰ τὴν ἱεροσύνην ἐξάρχειν, καὶ τῶν κορυφαίων ἐν ἀποστόλοις ἐγκεχειρισμένων τὸ ἀξίωμα.

of fault: for it was convened most justly and legitimately: since from the first, according to the Divine decrees laid down from of old, the legation from the West, that is to say, from Old Rome—a no inconsiderable body in it—without whom (these, namely, from Rome) no dogma that is ventilated in the Church, even though it should have been long sanctioned by canonical decrees and ecclesiastical usage, has ever any binding force, nor is reduced to practice; because they (i.e., SS. Peter and Paul) obtained the first place (the right to rule) in the priesthood, and received the prerogative of the Coryphæi amongst the Apostles."

From the above passages of S. Theodore Studites and the Greek Patriarch S. Nicephorus we find it clearly laid down that it was the supreme prerogative of the Roman Pontiffs not only to convoke and preside over Ecumenical Councils, but also to confirm them, so that without their sanction and authority no general disciplinary enactment, nor any dogmatic definition, is to be held of peremptory force, nor to be proposed as binding on the faithful, however long before ventilated, and even sanctioned by sacerdotal use. We should here, moveover, carefully note that the originating principle of this supreme privilege, and of the sacred princedom of the Roman Church, is stated as being derived from SS. Peter and Paul.

On November 6th occurs the Feast of S. PAUL, PATRIARCH OF CONSTANTINOPLE, who—several times banished from his See by the Arians, and restored by Pope Julius—was at last exiled to Cappadocia under Constantius, and there strangled. With reference to this Saint, Socrates in his history* thus writes:

"Athanasius succeeded at length in reaching Italy: and at the same time Paul, Bishop of Constantinople, Asclepas of Gaza, and Marcellus of Ancyra in Galatia Minor, accused on various charges, and driven from their Churches, arrived in the City of Rome. When, then, they had severally laid their case before Julius the Bishop of Rome, he—for such is the prerogative of the Roman Church—(ἅτε προνόμια τῆς ἐν 'Ρώμῃ Ἐκκλησίας ἐχούσης) fortified them with frank outspoken letters, and sent them back to the East, restoring

* Book ii. ch. xv. (Migne), *Patrol. Græc.* tom. 67, pp. 211-12.

to each his own See, and rebuking those who had rashly deposed them. They then left Rome, and relying confidently upon the letters of the Bishop Julius, took possession of their several Churches, and sent the Epistles to those for whom they were written."

Sozomen also in his history,* after recording the arrival in Rome of Athanasius, Paul, and the other Bishops mentioned by Socrates, thus continues:

"Lucius, also, Bishop of Adrianople, deprived of his See on some charge or other, was then living for a time in Rome. The Roman Bishop, therefore, on learning the several charges, and on finding them all of one accord with regard to the dogma of the Nicene Council, received them to communion as of the same faith with himself. And since, on account of the dignity of his See, the care of all devolved on him (οἷα δὲ τῆς πάντων κηδεμονίας αὐτῷ προσηκούσης διὰ τὴν ἀξίαν τοῦ θρόνου), he restored to each his own Church."

ADDENDA.

"The Eastern Church continues until the present day, in spite of evasive denials, and under the eyes and with the authorisation of its pastors, to attribute always to the Bishops of Rome, in the Sacred Hymns which are sung on the Feasts of the Popes in her Calendar, the same prerogatives of Supremacy as to S. Peter: that is to say, she continues to call them *Successors to the throne of the Coryphæus of the Apostles, Coryphæi of the Church*, Presidents of the Church, Coryphæi of the Sacred System, &c., &c."†

A learned Anglican author writes as follows on the languages in which the Eastern Office Books are written:‡

"It is well known that, while, on the one hand, the vernacular tongue is not used for the Liturgy and other offices in any Oriental Church, orthodox or heretical, yet, in the Orthodox Church, for the most part, the ecclesiastical has a certain affinity with the civil language, and the former may, to a great extent, be comprehended by one well versed in the latter.

"The case is not so with most of the heretical communions. In Egypt, where Arabic is the civil, and Coptic the ecclesiastical language, the latter is not only unknown to the laity (I have said before that not more than three persons speak it in Cairo), but is understood by hardly any of the clergy. They learn the letters, and the pronunciation of the words; and they have an Arabic version at the side, which helps them to the meaning. In Ethiopia, where Amharic is the spoken, Ethiopic is the Church, language. They differ to a great extent; the latter being, especially to an Arabic scholar, very easy; the former of excessive difficulty, and possessing rules that have no affinity with the old tongue. So, in the Jacobite Patriarchate of Antioch, Syrian is

---

* Book iii. ch. viii. *ibid.* pp. 1051-2.
† *L'Eglise Orientale par Jacques G. Pitzipios, Fondateur de la Société Chrétienne Orientale*; Rome, 1855.
‡ *A History of the Holy Eastern Church*, by the Rev. John Mason Neale, M.A., General Introduction, part i. pp. 820-8; Joseph Masters, 1850.

the ecclesiastical language, whatever may be the spoken tongue, whether Turkish, or Persian, or Arabic. In the Armenian, the letters are, indeed, the same: but the language itself differs widely.

"But to come to the Orthodox Eastern Church.... The Patriarchate of Constantinople, and the countries which once composed it, employ three ecclesiastical languages—Greek, Slavonic, and Georgian.

"I.—The Greek of the Office Books makes no approach in its structure to the modern Romaic, and differs very little from the classical language, except in the employment of ecclesiastical words. It can undoubtedly be understood by educated persons, and, except where the dialect is excessively depraved, as in Crete, it is to a certain extent intelligible to the poor....

"II.—Slavonic, however, prevails over by far the greater part of the Orthodox Eastern Church. It is not only the Church language of all the Russias, but of Moldavia, Wallachia, Servia, Bosnia, Montenegro, Slavonia proper, Dalmatia, and Bulgaria. This noble language is perhaps more completely a Church language than any other. Unlike its rivals in this respect, Greek and Latin, it had no previous literature: it was adapted to ecclesiastical purposes in its full freshness and vigour, not in its decay: and it has not, like the Latin, served as the medium of works purely literary. The Church gave it its letters; and its letters, obsolete in other respects, now serve only for the use of the Church.

"In the year 863, SS. Cyril and Methodius were sent by the Emperor Michael III. into Moravia to translate the Holy Scriptures and the Offices of the Church at the instance of the Christian Princes Rotislaff and Sviatopolk. They found the Slavonic a formed language, and whether it did or did not possess characters, they introduced the Greek alphabet, with the addition of fifteen letters.

"This alphabet is known as the Cyrillic." The author goes on to say that the Uniats of Slavonian origin who make use of the Slavonian Liturgy employ not the Cyrillic, but the *Glagolita* alphabet (*Glagolita* in the Slavonic means a word), and maintains as certain that the Glagolita is not, as the Orientals assert, a more modern corruption and Latinisation of the Cyrillic alphabet, but on the contrary is the older character.

"The Slavonic language has remained unaltered in the Church books to this day; and there are Slavonian MSS. in Russia of a date as early as 1056. But the Slavonian peoples gradually lost the unity of their tongue, as they were scattered among or subjected by other nations. Five great dialects were in process of time formed from it. 1. The *Russ.*... 2. The *Polish*, also largely spoken in Lithuania and Silesia, and corrupted with many Latin and German words. 3. The *Tcheck*. This is used in Bohemia and Moravia, and a dialect of it, the *Slavack*, in Hungary; and it approaches most closely to the Cyrillic. 4. The *Illyrian*. This is subdivided into *Bulgarian*, the rudest, *Servian*, the most flowing of the Slavonic dialects, *Bosnian*, and *Dalmatian*. 5. *Croatian*: spoken in Styria, Carinthia, Carniola, &c....

"III.—*Georgian*. On the first introduction of the faith into Georgia, the Office Books were employed in Greek. In the fifth century, however, David and Stephen, who had been educated at Jerusalem under the protection of King Tatian, translated into Georgian the Holy Scriptures from the Syriac, and the Church Books from the Greek. The Georgian characters are of two kinds, ecclesiastical and civil... completely different from each other. The original Georgian, now the ecclesiastical language, differs as widely from the modern tongue as Slavonic does from Russ.... In the Georgian printing press at Moscow, and in one at Tiflis, all the Church books have been printed. Many works of the Fathers, however, and perhaps the Menology, read in Church still remain MSS."

Father Tondini, who has done so much to illustrate the whole subject of the Greek and Russian Liturgies in connection with the prerogatives of S. Peter*—and who is the founder of "The Association of Prayers for the return of the separated portions of Christendom to Catholic Unity"—which received the blessing of Pius IX. with a grant of indulgences, May 13, 1877, and also of the present Cardinal Archbishop of Westminster,—in a letter dated December, 1886, says:

"Allow me to heartily congratulate you on the subject you are treating. It is an indirect but powerful cooperation in the reunion of the Churches. ... S. Leo is called κεφαλή τῆς ἐκκλησίας (glava Esvker). The Slavonian editions have kept this passage, though it is not to be found in the Greek *printed* editions. I myself have seen it in several Slavonian Mineje. The Mineja tchetja, Mensea, or Lives of the Saints to be read in the Churches, state clearly the doctrine of S. Peter's Roman Episcopate—and the same every popular life published of S. Peter."

* *The Primacy of S. Peter demonstrated from the Liturgy of the Greco-Russian Church*, by the Rev. C. Tondini De Quaranghi, Barnabite. Richardson & Son, 1879.

CHAPTER XV.

THE TESTIMONY OF EUSEBIUS TO S. PETER'S ROMAN EPISCOPATE.

It is not unfrequently asserted by Protestants that S. Peter's Roman Episcopate cannot be proved by the testimony of Eusebius, for that nowhere does he expressly affirm that Peter was Bishop of Rome. Even if this were true, and though everything the historian says on S. Peter's position at Rome were insufficient of itself alone positively to prove his Episcopate, but yet were reconcilable with a belief and tradition of it generally prevailing at the time he wrote, and also with more direct testimony in the authors to whom he refers, we think that it would be taking a very unfair and unreasonable advantage of such want of explicitness on the part of Eusebius, therefore to decide that what he does say is of little or no weight in the argument.

The authority of Eusebius is, however, of such exceptional, not to say paramount importance, as the ecclesiastical historian of the three first centuries, in whose writings moreover we find so many words treasured up from earlier works now no longer extant, that we have thought it well to bring together the various passages which occur in his *History* and *Chronicle* on the question; so that, by their collation, the reader may see for himself what is the real truth. We shall give, at the same time, some very valuable comments from Valesius and Baronius on certain points.

In a note on *Eccl. Hist.* v. 12, where Eusebius enumerates the Bishops of Jerusalem down to 'Narcissus the thirteenth in regular succession from the Apostles,'* Valesius says:

> "The most famous Churches, especially those that were founded by Apostles, kept with the greatest care the succession of their bishops laid up in their archives, writing out their names and the day of their death in the diptychs. These books Eusebius had diligently examined, as appears from this place, and has given the order of bishops in the principal Sees from such tables alone. Consequently, the successions of bishops recorded in the *History* and in the *Chronicle* of Eusebius are to be accounted of the greatest importance, as being the most ancient and the most certain."

* See also B. iv. ch. 5.

Eusebius has given the succession of bishops in the three great Patriarchal Sees of Rome, Alexandria, and Antioch, and also in the Church of Jerusalem. We shall here treat of these successions in the chronological order of the foundation of these Churches, viz.: (1) Jerusalem; (2) Antioch; (3) Rome; (4) Alexandria.

Two main points will occupy this discussion on Eusebius. First we shall show that he distinctly records S. James, the brother of our Lord, to have been the first Bishop of Jerusalem; S. Peter to have been the first Bishop of Antioch, and afterwards of Rome; and S. Mark, by appointment of S. Peter, to have been the first Bishop of Alexandria. Secondly, we shall show that Eusebius, in giving the succession of the Bishops of Jerusalem, always includes S. James, the first Bishop; whilst in giving the succession of the Bishops of Antioch, Rome, and Alexandria, he always excludes S. Peter and S. Mark. We shall, at the same time, endeavour to account for this difference, which it will be our object to prove in no way militates against our thesis of S. Peter's Roman Episcopate, but that, on the contrary, hereby, as also in other ways, Eusebius most clearly witnesses to the truth of that fact.

I.—JERUSALEM.—In his *Ecclesiastical History*, Eusebius states expressly that S. James was the first Bishop of Jerusalem:

"James, called the brother of our Lord... surnamed the Just, was the first that received the Episcopate of the Church at Jerusalem." *

And in his *Chronicle*, A.D. 34:

"Ecclesiæ Hierosolymorum primus episcopus ab Apostolis ordinatus Jacobus, qui et habitus est frater Domini." Ἰάκωβος ὁ ἀδελφόθεος πρῶτος ἐπίσκοπος Ἱεροσολύμων ὑπὸ τῶν ἀποστόλων καθίσταται. †

ANTIOCH.—Eusebius does not explicitly record in his *Ecclesiastical History* that S. Peter founded the Church of Antioch, or that he was Bishop of that See. He clearly, however, implies this, and affirms it equivalently when he says:

"Ἰγνάτιος, τῆς κατ' Ἀντιόχειαν Πέτρου διαδοχῆς δεύτερος τὴν ἐπισκοπὴν κεκληρωμένος. Ignatius obtained the Episcopate, the second of Peter's succession at Antioch." ‡

* *H. E.* ii. 1, iii. 7, iv. 5, vii. 19.
† *Sync.* p. 328. Edit. Migne.
‡ *Eccl. Hist.* iii. 36.—Origen likewise calls S. Ignatius, "the *second* Bishop of Antioch *after the blessed Peter*." Τὸν Ἰγνάτιον λέγω τὸν μετὰ τὸν μακάριον Πέτρον τῆς Ἀντιοχείας δεύτερον ἐπίσκοπον. Hom. in Luc. vi. *Scheda Grabii.* Migne, *Patr. Graec.* tom. 13, p. 1814.

Again, he mentions:

"Theophilus in the Church of Antioch as the sixth in the succession from the Apostles."*

But in his *Chronicle*, under the year 40, we have:

"Petrus Apostolus, cum primum Antiochenam ecclesiam fundasset, Romam mittitur, ibique Evangelium prædicans XXV. annis ejusdem urbis Episcopus perseverat." Πέτρος ὁ κορυφαῖος, πρώτην ἐν Ἀντιοχείᾳ θεμελιώσας ἐκκλησίαν, εἰς Ῥώμην ἄπεισι κηρύττων τὸ εὐαγγέλιον· ὁ δ᾽ αὐτὸς μετὰ τῆς ἐν Ἀντιοχείᾳ ἐκκλησίας καὶ τῆς ἐν Ῥώμῃ πρῶτος προέστη ἕως τελειώσεως αὐτοῦ.† "Peter the Coryphæus, having first founded the Church at Antioch, went away to Rome preaching the Gospel; and he also after the Church in Antioch presided the first over that of Rome until his death."

These words of Eusebius witness equally to S. Peter's Episcopate at Antioch and at Rome.‡

So extraordinary, and, at the same time, frivolous are the cavils of certain Protestants on all matters relating to S. Peter, that we think it well at this place to make a short digression, for we should not be surprised if some one were here to object that πρῶτος προέστη did not necessarily imply that S. Peter was the first Bishop in the two Sees. We, therefore, illustrate the word προέστη, to show that it is equivalent to "was bishop of," by the following passage from Eusebius:

Κεφαλαῖον ιθ᾽. Τίνες ἐπὶ τῆς Οὐήρου βασιλείας τῆς Ῥωμαίων καὶ Ἀλεξανδρέων ἐκκλησίας προέστησαν (*Nic.*). Τῆς Ῥωμαίων ἐκκλησίας τὴν ἐπισκοπὴν ... Σωτὴρ διαδέχεται. Ἀλλὰ καὶ τῆς Ἀλεξανδρέων παροικίας Κελαδίωνος τέταρσιν ἐπὶ δέκα ἔτεσι προστάντος, τὴν διαδοχὴν Ἀγριππῖνος διαλαμβάνει.

We have had pointed out to us a critique in a religious Protestant journal on Mr. Allnatt's excellent work, *Cathedra Petri*. The anonymous writer there charges Mr. Allnatt with "deliberate bad faith," because he renders ἐνεχείρισαν in the passage of S. Irenæus,§ "committed (or transmitted)." We, for our part, are quite content with this translation, which has been common to Catholics and Protestants alike. Ἐγχειρίζω, for all that may be said as to its strict derivative meaning, as much as παραδίδωμι, μεταδίδωμι, παρεγγυάω, is used in the general sense of *giving up, handing over, transmitting, surrendering*. The middle form ἐγχει-

---

* iv. 20.   † *Sync.* pp. 539-40.
‡ *Hist. Eccl.* iv. 19. Again in his *Chronicle*, A.D. 62, *vide infra*.
§ *Hær.* iii. 3.

ῥίζομαι is frequently* used by Eusebius when recording a succession to some See, for διαδέχομαι. The sense of these two words, so to say technical, is in such passages identical. To illustrate, again, the unimportance, and entirely general meaning, of the particular word ἐγχειρίζω, when thus used, we may take the following from Eusebius:

Συμεὼν ... τῆς ἐν Ἱεροσολύμοις ἐκκλησίας κατὰ τούτους τὴν λειτουργίαν ἐγκεχειρισάμενος ἦν.†

To which passage Valesius adds this note:

"Ita quidem Codex Regius. Verum quatuor reliqui, Maz. scilicet ac Med. cum Fuk. ac Saviliano scriptum habent τὴν λειτουργίαν εἶχεν."

Thus what, according to our anonymous sapient critic any trustworthy translation must render: " Simeon had the ministry *put into his hands*"—since a word is used " denoting at once joint action, and that action not bequeathing, but entrusting "—the learned interpreters of Eusebius are content to render, or to have for it in exchange, simply εἶχεν. " Simeon *had* the ministry."

S. Irenæus and Eusebius knew Greek too; but they would, perhaps, have picked their words with greater caution and more as philologists, could they have foreseen that in after ages they would be subjected to the hypercriticism of Anglican purists, who are so often wont to make the issue of momentous historical facts affecting the faith of Catholics depend on questions of etymology, or rather on such like verbal quibbles. According to this sort of criticism, we must suppose that Eusebius meant his words in the following passages to be necessarily taken in their strict literal sense:

Λίνος ἐπίσκοπος. ... Ἀνεγκλήτῳ ταύτην (τὴν λειτουργίαν τῆς Ῥωμαίων ἐκκλησίας) παραδίδωσι (*E. H.* iii. 13). Κλήμης Εὐαρέστῳ παραδοὺς τὴν λειτουργίαν ἀναλύει τὸν βίον (iii. 34). Λούκιος ... Στεφάνῳ τελευτῶν μεταδίδωσι (strictly *gives a share of*) τὸν κλῆρον (vii. 2). Δεύτερον δὲ οὗτος (Κλαύδιος) διελθὼν ἔτος Αὐρηλιάνῳ μεταδίδωσι τὴν ἡγεμονίαν (vii. 28, *ad fin.*).

Whereas anyone with a little common sense would at once see that these various expressions are but so many forms whereby succession is implied. Nevertheless, the general sense which we have said ἐνεχείρισαν may bear does not at all exclude the more particular and proper meaning of the word, which would signify that the Apostles entrusted, personally whilst still in life, the episcopate to Linus; whether by this is implied that they gave

* As, for example, *H. E.* v. 19, 22; vi. 21.   † *H. E.* iii. 7.

him part in the episcopal duties of the Roman Church, which resulted in his being, after their death, chosen to be the Ordinary Bishop of that See; or that he was also expressly appointed by the Apostles (that is, strictly speaking, by S. Peter) to succeed as Bishop of Rome on his own death. For both these views are consonant with Catholic opinion.

It seems, indeed, to be very probable that S. Peter, in the exigencies of the time, and with the immediate prospect before him of imprisonment and martyrdom, should have provided in this way for the succession to the Primacy and the See of Rome. That he should have had an express Divine sanction in making such provision is in entire conformity with the care, we know, that our Lord has for His Church, and with the plenary powers which we might expect would be given to S. Peter under the circumstances. The action of the Prince of the Apostles in what was wholly exceptional and extraordinary would form no precedent for ordinary cases. And any appeal against it to the normal rule, or to subsequent ecclesiastical legislation of Councils made to remedy and prevent abuses, is here quite beside the mark.

Let us now return to our subject, viz., the Episcopate of S. Peter at Antioch. To further illustrate this matter, we give the following extracts from the *Annals* of Baronius, A.D. 39.

"That the Church of Antioch was this year founded by S. Peter and administered by him for seven years, Eusebius would have learnt from a no less certain source than the most ancient records of that Church, since his own See of Cæsarea was quite close to that of Antioch." (ix.)

"In the same way that Peter was sent by the Apostles to those who had believed in Christ in Samaria—as on a matter of great importance, and a mission worthy of the Prince of the Apostles [*] —so too, on the occasion of the conversion at Antioch of many Jews and Greeks to the Faith, and a Church being gathered there through the preaching of the disciples, who were dispersed abroad after the death of Stephen,[†] we may well believe that it was the opinion of all the Apostles that Peter, their chief, should preside as Bishop over that city, which was the metropolis of all Syria, and to which Palestine, with Jerusalem itself, was subject. For we know that the course adopted from the earliest times in creat-

---

[*] *Acts*, viii. 1-14.   [†] *Acts*, xi. 19-21.

ing Ecclesiastical Sees was to follow the division of the Roman Provinces, according to their respective rank of dignity. Of this there are many examples; but it will suffice here to mention one or other; and first that of Alexandria, which bears intimately on the See of Antioch. For though the See of Antioch was erected by Peter before that of Alexandria in Peter's name, yet, because the prefecture of Alexandria, styled *Augustalis* by Augustus himself, and magnificently privileged by the emperor above others, far out-stripped the prefecture of Syria—evidently for this reason it was that the See of Alexandria, erected by Mark in Peter's name, was ranked before that of Antioch, though this latter See was the first created. In like manner because the proconsulate of Syria was the first in rank of all the Eastern prefectures, the Church of Antioch, its metropolis, came to have the first place; and though the Church of Jerusalem had a claim to precedence on account of its origin and the great events accomplished in it, and its prerogatives might therefore be thought to excel those of the other Eastern Churches, yet that See was made subject to Antioch.

"It appears, moreover, that the Church of Jerusalem was not even the Metropolitan See of Palestine; but, because Cæsarea on the Sea was the Roman metropolis of the entire province, its Metropolitan See also was fixed in that city, whilst a certain honour was at the same time preserved to the Church of Jerusalem."

This, Baronius adds, is distinctly set forth by S. Jerome,[*] and attested by the Council of Nice as being of ancient tradition.[†]

"Thus it was," he concludes, "Peter, who had the primacy amongst the Apostles, undertook the charge of the Church at Antioch, being at that time the first and of most importance. From ancient time the Catholic Church has been used to commemorate this event by the anniversary celebration of the Feast of S. Peter's Chair at Antioch on the 22nd of February." (x. xi.)

"But what (asks Baronius) are we properly to understand when we say that Peter founded the Church of Antioch and held the See for seven years? For this it was not necessary that Peter should go to Antioch and constantly reside there for seven years; for if it were Peter's presence that made a Primatial Church, we should have as many Patriarchal Sees as there were Churches formed by the Apostle: and these no doubt would be very many.

[*] *Epist.* 61 *ad Pammach.*   [†] Conc. Nic. Can. 7.

Whereas the fact of the See of Alexandria—which there is no proof that Peter ever visited—being made by him the greatest of all after that of Rome shows us plainly that it was not his presence, but his authority especially that was necessary to constitute any Church a Patriarchal See.

"Now, in saying that the See of Antioch was founded by Peter, we do not mean that he was the first to preach the Gospel there, since it is notorious from the testimony of S. Luke that this was done by the disciples who were driven abroad from Jerusalem after the death of Stephen: but we are to understand the Church of Antioch to have been founded by Peter, in such sense, that from him it received its principal dignity, whereby it was reckoned the greatest of all the Eastern Sees; albeit other disciples before Peter preached the Gospel there, and so may be said to have laid the first foundation of its Church.

"Nor, again, because SS. Peter and Paul preached the Gospel at Antioch later on, in person, can they on that account be called the founders of the Church there; that is, if we are to stand by what the Apostle says in his Epistle to the Romans[*]: 'I have so preached this gospel, not where Christ was named, lest I should build upon another man's foundation.' And, even did we allow that S. Peter, because he preached the Gospel at Antioch after others, might, therefore, in some sense be said to have founded its Church, still no more could be ascribed to him, on this score, than to S. Paul, who also laboured there in the same work, and with most signal success. Nay, for that matter, Ignatius, writing to the Magnesians, does not attribute any more here to Peter than to Paul, since he affirms that the Church of Antioch was founded by both these Apostles. Consequently, the assertion that the Church of Antioch was in a special sense founded by Peter—as is the universal tradition—necessarily implies that Peter first erected or constituted that Patriarchal See: and for his so doing, we are quite at liberty to say that there was no strict necessity for his going in person to Antioch, since, wherever he was, he had this power, in virtue of the authority he possessed.

"We have been hitherto treating of S. Peter's founding and erecting the See of Antioch; let us now say a word on his own episcopate in that See.

"Since the Church of Antioch was thus made by Peter the first and most influential of all the Churches up to that time constituted, it, surely, could be the See of none other than the Prince of the

[*] *Rom.* xv. 20.

Apostles himself. For the hierarchical order, which Christ willed to be observed in His Church, seems incompatible with any other arrangement than that the Chief Apostle should occupy the principal See.* Now, in speaking of S. Peter holding the See of Antioch, we do not suppose anyone so simple as to imagine that when we say he held it for seven years (these are reckoned from its first institution until that of Rome was firmly established), we thereby mean that he never left Antioch during that space of time; any more than when he is said to have held the See of Rome for twenty-five years, it is meant that he was never absent elsewhere. For when we consider that, as supreme and universal Pastor, he had the charge not of one city only, but of the whole Christian world; and when we think how great and urgent must have been his solicitude, that he had to provide for all, and was bound, so far as he could, to visit, form, admonish, exhort, in a word, to feed and rule the entire flock entrusted to him, how could we suppose that— especially in times when the Christian faith was assailed alike by Jews and Gentiles—he would be restricted within the narrow bounds of any one single city, however great; and not rather, as in fact S. Luke records him doing this very same year, go about everywhere visiting all the Churches?† In this sense, then, we are to understand that S. Peter presided for seven years over the Episcopal See of Antioch until the erection of that of Rome, which he willed to be the greatest of all: and thus he was called Bishop successively of both these Sees." (xvi. xvii.)

ROME.—We have already quoted the passage from the *Chronicle*, A.D. 40, in which Eusebius records that S. Peter, after having first founded the Church of Antioch, went to preach the Gospel in Rome, and was the first Bishop of the Church there until his death.

See also his *History*, B. ii. 14, and v. 8.

ALEXANDRIA.—We read in the *Chronicle*, A.D. 42:

---

* We fail to understand how this principle can be accepted absolutely: since, before the erection of the See of Antioch, S. James was already Bishop of Jerusalem, when that Church was the first and the only Episcopal See: but this case, being quite exceptional and provisional, seems hardly to disturb the general and normal rule laid down by Baronius. Perhaps, however, we should understand the learned Cardinal as meaning that if S. Peter held any See at all, in such case he must be Bishop of the principal See. This is both in harmony with the Divine order, and has, moreover, been borne out by actual fact.

† *Acts*, ix. 32.

"Marcus Evangelista, interpres Petri Ægypto et Alexandriæ Christum annuntiat." Μάρκος ὁ εὐαγγελιστὴς ἐν Αἰγύπτῳ καὶ 'Αλεξανδρείᾳ τὸν σωτήριον λόγον εὐηγγελίζετο (*Sync.*).

See also his *History*, B. ii. 16.

II. We come now to our second point. Here, we will first give some passages from Eusebius, showing how, in the enumeration of the successive Bishops of Jerusalem, he always includes S. James; whilst on the contrary, in recording the successions of Bishops in the three Patriarchal Sees, he uniformly excludes both S. Peter and S. Mark. We shall then endeavour to explain this difference, and show that no argument can thence be drawn against S. Peter's Roman Episcopate.

JERUSALEM.—In the *Chronicle* of Eusebius, A.D. 62, we read:

"Jacobus frater Domini, quem omnes Justum appellabant, a Judæis lapidibus opprimitur, in cujus thronum Simeon, qui et Simon, *secundus* assumitur." Again, A.D. 111: "Post Justum [tertium] Ecclesiæ Hierosolymitanæ episcopatum *quartus* suscipit Zacchæus, post quem quintus Tobias, cui succedit sextus Benjamin, &c." *

So, too, in his *History*, Eusebius writes:

"The first Bishop was James, called the brother of our Lord: *after whom* the *second* was Simeon, the third Justus . . . and the fifteenth Judas. These are all the Bishops of Jerusalem that filled up the time *from the Apostles* until the above-mentioned date, all of the Circumcision. Last of all, Narcissus the thirtieth *from the Apostles* in regular succession." †

ANTIOCH.—In his *Chronicle*, A.D. 43, Eusebius says:

"*Primus* Antiochiæ ordinatur episcopus Evodius." The Greek (*Sync.*) is the same. Again, A.D. 69: "Antiochiæ *secundus* episcopus ordinatur Ignatius."

So also in his *History*:

"On the death of Evodius, who was the *first* Bishop of Antioch, Ignatius was appointed the *second*." "Ignatius, also, who is celebrated by many even to this day, as the successor of Peter at Antioch (τῆς κατ' 'Αντιόχειαν Πέτρου διαδοχῆς), was the *second* that obtained the episcopal office there." §

* With this the Greek ap. *Syncellum* agrees.
† *H. E.* iv. 5, v. 12.   ‡ iii. 22, 36; iv. 20.
§ "The earliest tradition," says Dr. Lightfoot, "represents Ignatius as the second of the Antiochene bishops, or (if S. Peter be reckoned) the third. Of extant authors, our first authority for this statement is Origen, who styles him 'the second after the Blessed Peter' (*Hom.* vi. *in Luc.* § 1). He, how-

Again:

"In the Church of Antioch Theophilus the *sixth from the* Apostles" (ἕκτος ἀπὸ τῶν ἀποστόλων).

"When Eusebius says that Evodius was the first Bishop of Antioch, he means," writes Baronius, "that he was the first to hold the See after the Apostle Peter. This is necessarily to be inferred from what he had already said: which, though somewhat obscure, becomes clear enough from the words of Ignatius himself, Bishop of the same See [or, we should say, from the words attributed to the Saint] in his Epistle to the Church of Antioch (12):

'Remember Evodius, your own most blessed Father, who first after the Apostles obtained the government of your Church.'

Evodius, then, was not simply the first Bishop of Antioch, but the first 'after the Apostles,' namely, Peter,—the plural being used for singular, as is of frequent custom." *

ROME.—Eusebius says in his *Chronicle*, A.D. 66:

"*Post Petrum primus* Romanam Ecclesiam tenuit Linus annis duodecim." Τῆς 'Ρωμαίων ἐκκλησίας πρῶτος ἐπίσκοπος μετὰ Πέτρον τὸν κορυφαῖον Λῖνος ἔτη ιϚ'. (*Sync.*) Again, A.D. 79: "Romanæ Ecclesiæ *secundus* constituitur episcopus Anacletus ann. xii." (*Arm.* viii.) Τῇ 'Ρωμαίων ἐκκλησίᾳ ἐπίσκοπος γέγονε β' μετὰ Πέτρον τὸν κορυφαῖον 'Ανέγκλητος ἔτη δύο (*Sync.*).

In his *History*, Eusebius writes:

"*After the Martyrdom of Paul and Peter*, Linus was the *first* who received the episcopate at Rome."——"Linus, whom Paul has mentioned in his second Epistle to Timothy, as his companion at Rome, has been before shown to have been the *first after Peter*, that obtained the episcopate at Rome. Clement also, who was appointed the *third* Bishop of this Church, is proved by him (Paul) to have been a fellow-labourer and fellow-soldier with him."——"During this time (of Trajan) Clement was yet Bishop of the Romans, who was also the *third* that held the episcopate there *after Paul and Peter*: Linus being the *first*, and Anencletus next in order."——"Enarestus was succeeded in the episcopal office by Alexander, the *fifth* in the succession *from Peter and Paul*."——"Xystus was succeeded by Telesphorus, the *seventh* in succession *from the Apostles*."——"Eleutherus, the *twelfth* in order *from the Apostles*."——"Victor, who was the *thirteenth* Bishop of Rome *from Peter*." †

ever, does not give the name of Ignatius' predecessor. This missing name, Evodius, is supplied by Eusebius [in the passages cited in the text], and in *Quæst. ad Steph.* 1, 'the second after the Apostles.' Ignatius is styled 'the third after Peter the Apostle' by S. Jerome (*Vir. Ill.* 16), and by Socrates (*H. E.* vi. 8) 'the third from the Apostle Peter.'" (*Ignatius*, vol. i. pp. 28, 29.)

* *Annal.* A.D. 39, xviii.

† *H. E.* iii. 2, 4, 21; iv. 1, 5; v. Preface to ch. i. and ch. xxviii.

ALEXANDRIA.—Under A.D. 62. Eusebius has in his *Chronicle*:

"*Post Marcum Evangelistam primus Alexandrinæ Ecclesiæ ordinatur episcopus Annianus qui præfuit annis xxii.*" (*Arm. xxvi.*) *

And in his *History*:

"In the eighth year of Nero's reign Annianus first *after Mark the Apostle and Evangelist* succeeds to the administration of the Church of Alexandria."——"In the fourth year of Domitian Annianus, the *first* Bishop of Alexandria, died after having filled the office twenty-two years. He was succeeded by Avilius, the *second* (in order)."——"Primus was the *fourth from the Apostles* who received the ministry of the Church of Alexandria." †

Now, from the above citations we see that Eusebius, in recording the succession of Bishops in the several Sees, makes use of the following terms:—(1) "After the Martyrdom of Paul and Peter;" (2) "From the Apostles;" (3) "After Paul and Peter;" "From Peter and Paul"; (4) "After Peter;" "From Peter;" "After Mark the Evangelist," or "the Apostle and Evangelist."

The term "From the Apostles," used in connection with the record of Episcopal succession, evidently means something more than, from the times of the Apostles. It points to the Apostolic origin of the Church, and to a certain relation which the Apostles had to it; but it by no means implies that Apostles (in the plural) held the Episcopal See. This is clear from this term being used not only with reference to the Patriarchal Churches, but also to that of Jerusalem, where there could be no possible question of any other being Bishop but S. James alone. Nor does it of itself necessarily imply that any one of the Apostles, strictly speaking, held the first Episcopate in the Church referred to; for it is used also with regard to Alexandria, of which See certainly none of the Apostles was diocesan bishop. Here this term, besides marking a date, doubtless connotes also the relation which that Church had with the Apostle S. Peter in its foundation, and with S. Mark its first Bishop, who is called an Apostle, as being such in a large sense. In the case of Jerusalem, the same term may have reference to the Apostles, whether as having consecrated S. James, or as having appointed him the first Bishop of that See; or again, because, according to Hegesippus, "he received the government of the Church with the Apostles." ‡ On the other hand, it may refer exclusively to S. James—since, according to

---

* It is the same in the Greek *Sync.*   † *H. E.* ii. 24, iii. 14, iv. 1.
‡ Euseb. *H.E.* ii. 23.

some, this plural form "Apostles" signifies also the singular, when the facts of the case show that one only is meant.

In connection with the Patriarchal Churches of Antioch and Rome, the term "from the Apostles,"—as also, in the particular case of Rome, "from Peter and Paul," "after Paul and Peter," and "after the martyrdom of Paul and Peter"—is not merely the notice of a date, but clearly has reference also to whatever special relation these Apostles might have had to those Churches, though it does not of itself indicate what that relation was.

The term, "After Peter," "After Mark," shows that S. Peter and S. Mark are themselves of the same official character as those recorded to succeed them are set forth to be, *i.e.*, Bishops. This term is personal and individual in contradistinction to the other terms. It is, moreover, used by Eusebius when enumerating the Bishops of Jerusalem. They are spoken of as "after James," who notoriously was the first Bishop before them.

Hence, though Eusebius does not include either S. Peter or S. Mark in his catalogues of the Bishops of the three Patriarchal Sees, yet implicitly he as distinctly affirms, both in his *History* and in his *Chronicle*, that the one and the other were the first Bishops of these Sees, as explicitly he affirms that S. James, the brother of our Lord, was first Bishop of Jerusalem. And this express testimony is over and above that which, under the head of Antioch, we before gave from his *Chronicle*, A.D. 40.

Having thus determined what, in the mind of Eusebius, was the particular relation between S. Peter and the Episcopal succession in the Roman Church when he used the foregoing terms, we are now in a position to decide with approximate certainty what he meant, or rather perhaps what he did not mean, by conjoining the Apostle S. Paul in connection with that succession. We say, then, that he evidently did not thereby intend to insinuate that S. Paul was Bishop of Rome along with S. Peter. He makes mention of them both together by name as the two great Apostles of Rome, and the founders together of the Roman Church; and the expression he uses, "from or after Peter and Paul," is, taken by itself alone, simply equivalent to "from the Apostles" (*i.e.*, those two of the Apostles who had a special relation with Rome)—a term which he also uses as much in connection with Rome as with the other Apostolic Churches. We would at the same time remark that this use of the plural and of the more general term, "from the Apostles," in speaking of Rome, no way detracts from that particular relation of S. Peter, as Bishop of Rome, which, as we have seen from other sources, Eusebius expressly affirms, but on the contrary, after such affirmation, clearly implies and confirms it. Let it, moreover, be well noted that nowhere does Eusebius, when speaking of the Episcopal succession, say "after or from Paul" as he says "after James," "after Mark," and "after or from Peter."

Here then, at length, we may give some answer to the question, why it was that Eusebius, though elsewhere affirming S. Peter to have been the first Bishop of Antioch, and afterwards of Rome, and S. Mark to have been the first Bishop of Alexandria, does not include in his catalogues of the Bishops of the three Patriarchal Sees either S. Peter or S. Mark, as he does S. James, amongst the Bishops of Jerusalem.

It is well in the first place to bear in mind that S. Irenæus, on whose authority Eusebius so greatly relied, and whom he so often quotes, had acted on the same principle in his own list of the Bishops of Rome down to Eleutherus, which list Eusebius has adopted in his *History*. So also the author of the *Poem against Marcion* of the third century, in his catalogue down to Hyginus, after expressly stating that Peter had himself held the See of Rome, speaks of Linus as the *first* Bishop—"*Linum primum.*"* S. Optatus of Milevis (A.D. 372) and S. Augustine (A.D. 400), acting on the contrary principle, include S. Peter in their catalogues, and name *Peter first* and *Linus second*.

We must not, however, omit to mention that, in a passage which Eusebius quotes† from Irenæus, the Saint twice speaks of Hyginus—whom, in his formal catalogue, he had placed *eighth* in order—as "the *ninth* that held the Episcopate in succession from the Apostles." This would give colourable ground for thinking that Irenæus, and also Eusebius, when speaking informally and simply of the Bishops of Rome as such, and when not enumerating them as the successors of the Apostle Peter in the Roman See, recognised also the other way of reckoning them. Valesius, however, appends the following as a note on this place of Eusebius:

"This passage of Irenæus is found still in his Book iii. ch. 4, where the ancient interpreter seems to have read ὄγδοος, and not ἔνατος. And this reading is more in agreement with Irenæus, as appears from ch. 3 of the same Book, where, in his list of the Bishops of Rome, he reckons Hyginus the eighth from the Apostles. The error is, however, a most ancient one; for also in Book i. ch. 28 of Irenæus we find ἔνατος, as well as in Epiphanius on the *Heresy of the Cerdonians*, and in Cyprian's *Epistle* (74) *to Pompeius*. We give here the

* See *supra*, p. 155. † *H. E.* iv. 11.

passage from Cyprian, because it seems to be a translation from Irenæus: Whose master, Cerdon, came to Rome under Hyginus, the then bishop, who was the *ninth* in the city.'"

Whatever may be the precise truth on this point is, however, of hardly any importance in its bearing on the testimony of Eusebius to S. Peter's Roman Episcopate, which, from other sources, is shown to be so ample and clear.

The reason given by Valesius and other learned commentators why S. Irenæus—as regards Rome, and after him Eusebius—did not include S. Peter and S. Mark in the list of bishops was because their dignity as Apostles raised them above the ordinary rank of the bishops who succeeded them.

We think we cannot do better than give here some notes of Valesius, which may serve to elucidate this matter and other points of our discussion.

On the words of Eusebius, μετὰ Παῦλον τε καὶ Πέτρον (iii. 21), Valesius says:

"Two things are here to be noted: first, that Eusebius places Paul before Peter; second, that he seems to make both of them bishops of the city of Rome. With regard to the first point, Eusebius does the same also in another place (iii. 2). But we must not think that he therefore sets Paul above Peter; for frequently those who are more honourable are named in the latter place.* For the matter of that, in the seals of the Roman Church Paul is always placed on the right hand and Peter on the left, as Baronius has remarked in his *Exposition of the Nicene Council.* As to the second difficulty, we would observe that Eusebius never reckons the Apostles in the number of the bishops; and, in fact, he has said already that Paul together with Peter had founded and planted the Roman Church, appealing to the words of Dionysius of Corinth, as later on he does also to those of Irenæus. When, however, he speaks of the Roman Episcopate, he attributes it to Peter alone, as is clear from his *Chronicle.* (See the learned discussion on this matter by Peter Habert in his work, *De Primatu Petri.*) It is thus, too, we must reconcile Irenæus, speaking of Hyginus (*Hæres.* L. i.) ἔνατον κλῆρον τῆς ἐπισκοπικῆς διαδόχης ἀπὸ τῶν ἀποστόλων ἔχοντος 'as holding the ninth place of Episcopal succession from the Apostles,' with what he says, L. iii. ch. 3 et 4, since Irenæus, in the same way as Eusebius, speaks of the Apostles Peter and Paul having both founded the Roman Church, though he does not reckon them in his catalogue of bishops. It is in a like sense that Epiphanius, treating of the heresy of the Cerdonians, says that Hyginus held the ninth place of Episcopal succession after James, Peter, and Paul. Now, should anyone from this passage maintain that James was Bishop of Rome along with Peter, he would simply be laughed at. And in the same way we may argue with regard to Paul."

* Thus, *v.g.*, *Luke*, ii. 16. See *supra*, p. 184.

An objection against the reason given by Valesius will here, no doubt, suggest itself, viz., that S. Mark, the first Bishop of Alexandria, was not one of the Twelve Apostles; and yet, equally with S. Peter, he is omitted from the list of the bishops of that See.

To this we reply, that this omission of the first Bishop and Founder obtains with Eusebius for all the three Patriarchal Sees alike, and for them alone: it does not extend to the See of Jerusalem. Now, the Patriarchal See of Alexandria claims for its chief Founder the Prince of the Apostles, as do the Sees of Antioch and Rome.

"For this reason, too," says Baronius, "the Church of Alexandria obtained the first place after that of Rome, because Mark erected it in the name of Peter and by his appointment; as Gelasius testifies in the following words: 'The second See at Alexandria was consecrated in the name of blessed Peter by Mark his disciple, the Evangelist; for he, being sent by the Apostle Peter into Egypt, preached there the word of truth, and accomplished his martyrdom.'" (Gelas. *in decret. de lib. apocryph.*) *

Uniformity of principle in drawing up the succession of the Bishops in the three Patriarchal Sees which derived their origin and dignity from S. Peter, may serve, then, to explain why Eusebius omits their first founders from the list of Bishops.

But we must remark, secondly, that independently of the special dignity and authority that S. Mark had in founding the Church of Alexandria by delegation of S. Peter, the Prince of the Apostles,—whom Eusebius more than once in connection with the Episcopal succession styles $\tau\grave{o}\nu\ \kappa o\rho\upsilon\phi a\hat{\iota}o\nu$,—S. Mark was himself of pre-eminent rank in the Church, as one of the four Evangelists, who, as such, have ever obtained an almost like honour, and the same rite in the Liturgy, as the Apostles themselves. In fact Eusebius, when recording the Episcopal succession at Alexandria, gives him the style of Apostle: "First after Mark the Apostle and Evangelist succeeds Annianus."† And it was, no doubt, on account of this personal dignity of S. Mark that Eusebius does not reckon him in the list of the ordinary Bishops who succeeded him.

Commenting on the words of Eusebius, "Thomas sent to King Agbarus the Apostle Thaddæus, one of the seventy,"‡ Valesius says as follows:

"The name of Apostle is here used in a large sense: much in the same way as nations and cities would call those their apostles from whom they

* *Annal.* A.D. 45. (xlvi.) † *H. E.* ii. 24. ‡ *H. E.* i. 13.

first received the truth of the Gospel. For this name is given not to the Twelve alone; but all their disciples, companions and helpers are called apostles in a general sense. And as—though our Lord chose only seventy disciples—many more are honoured with this name, as Eusebius has remarked in the preceding chapter: so also, though our Lord appointed only twelve Apostles, this title came to be shared by divers others, as S. Jerome observes in his *Commentary on the Galatians*. So, too, in the Greek Menologies, and in Metaphrastes, Mark and Luke the Evangelists, as well as Titus, Timothy, Philemon, and others of Paul's disciples, are styled Apostles."

Valesius then goes on to illustrate what he has said by the words of S. Ambrose, or rather Hilarius, on *Gal.* ch. i. On the words just quoted from Eusebius (ii. 24) Valesius says:

"Justly may Mark be called an Apostle, since he was the first to preach the faith to the people of Alexandria."

Again, on the words "Annianus the first bishop" (iii. 14):

"The first (that is) after Mark. In the same way Eusebius speaks of Linus, Bishop of Rome (iii. 2): 'After the martyrdom of Paul and Peter Linus first obtains the episcopate.' For Mark was Apostle of the people of Alexandria, as I have before said. But the Apostles were out of the usual order, and were not reckoned in the number of Bishops."

We must now endeavour to explain why it is that Eusebius, whilst excluding S. Peter and S. Mark from his catalogue of the Bishops of the three Patriarchal Sees, acts upon a different principle with regard to the See of Jerusalem, which also was of Apostolic origin, and whose succession of bishops he is so careful to enumerate; and why he includes S. James amongst the bishops of that Church. We have not been able to find an explanation of, or even allusion made to, this point of difficulty in any author.

We think then, in the first place, that some explanation of this difference may be found in the extraordinary and quite exceptional circumstances of S. James' appointment to the Bishopric of Jerusalem, as these are recorded, and were traditionally received, in the early Church. Thus it is said that S. James was designated, if not consecrated, for this office by Christ Himself after His Resurrection. More generally, and perhaps on better grounds, it is affirmed that he was consecrated, or at any rate constituted,* Bishop of Jerusalem by the Apostles, in order that with them he should rule its Church. These remarkable circumstances, added to the fact of Jerusalem being the first Mother

---

* "S. Chrysostom is of opinion that this appointment was due especially to S. Peter." *In Joan. Hom.* 87. See Baron. *Ann.* A.D. 34, cxci.

Church, and the first constituted Episcopal See in order of time, would render its episcopate quite exceptional, and give to S. James, as the first occupier, such notoriety as Bishop of a See—and such a See—amongst Christians, that his title of Bishop of Jerusalem would adhere to him as peculiarly and personally as did those other titles by which he was so universally known, of James the Just, and the brother of our Lord. We should, besides, bear in mind that the special dignity and unique character of the Church of Jerusalem were indissolubly bound up with the person and dignity of its first Bishop, S. James, as the brother of our Lord; so much so, that it was sometimes termed the Theadelphian See.*

Hence, we think, it would seem unnaturally forced and strained, had Eusebius excluded S. James, the brother of our Lord, and the first of all Christian Bishops in the order of time, from his catalogue, when enumerating the Bishops of that See.

Eusebius, in the following passages, records the circumstances of S. James' appointment to the Episcopate of Jerusalem which we have mentioned above:

"This James, therefore, whom the ancients, on account of the excellence of his virtue, surnamed the Just, was the first that received the Episcopate of the Church of Jerusalem. But Clement, in the sixth book of his *Institutions*, represents it thus: 'Peter, and James, and John, after the Ascension of our Saviour, though they had been preferred by our Lord, did not contend for the honour, but chose James the Just as Bishop of Jerusalem.'" †

"Hegesippus also, who was of the very next generation to the Apostles,‡ in the fifth book of his *Commentaries*, gives the most accurate account of him

---

* "To James belongs the title, on all hands secure and indisputable, of ὁ ἀδελφὸς τοῦ Κυρίου or ἀδελφόθεος ('the brother of our Lord,' or 'brother of God'). And hence the See of Jerusalem, to which, in the first year after our Lord's Ascension, he was ordained Bishop, came to be called *Thronus Theadelphicus* (the Theadelphian Throne), from 'the brother of God;' in the same way as the Roman See is called *Apostolic*, from Peter the Prince of the Apostles." Bollandists, 1 Maii, *De S. Jacobo*, § ii. 10. We can, moreover, see the intimate association there was between the See of Jerusalem and the brother of our Lord from what Eusebius writes (*H. E.* iii. 11). "After the martyrdom of James, and the taking of Jerusalem which immediately followed, the report is, that those of the Apostles, and the disciples of our Lord who yet survived, came together from all parts with those that were related to our Lord according to the flesh—for many of them were yet living. These consulted together, to determine who was worthy of being the successor of James. And they all unanimously declared Simeon the son of Cleophas, of whom mention is made in the sacred volume, as worthy of the Episcopal Chair there. Simeon, they say, was near kinsman to our Saviour, for Hegesippus asserts that Cleophas was the brother of Joseph." The first fifteen Bishops of Jerusalem were, Eusebius records, all of the Circumcision (iv. 5).

† *H. E.* ii. 2.

‡ Contemporary with SS. Polycarp, Anicetus, and Irenæus.

thus: 'James, the brother of our Lord, received the government of the Church with the Apostles (διαδέχεται τὴν ἐκκλησίαν μετὰ τῶν ἀποστόλων), surnamed by all, the Just, from the days of our Lord until now. For there are many called James.'"[*]

"During which times (of Vespasian) the greater part of the Apostles and disciples, and James himself, the first Bishop there, commonly called the brother of our Lord, who were still surviving, and were living in the city of Jerusalem, continued to be the greatest bulwark of the place."[†]

The last passage which we shall give from Eusebius on this point testifies, moreover, to the great honour that was paid to the See of Jerusalem, and to S. James its first Bishop—from the fact of the Episcopal Chair in which he sat being preserved with veneration down to the times of the historian:

"For the throne of James—as being the first who received the episcopate of the Church of Jerusalem from our Saviour Himself and the Apostles, and commonly called the brother of Christ, as the Divine Scriptures testify—has been preserved until the present time, and has been ever since an object of veneration to the brethren at Jerusalem in their successive generations. And thus they clearly show to all what reverence both those of old and those of our own day exhibited, and still exhibit, towards holy men on account of their love to God."[‡]

We are of opinion, secondly, that the inclusion of S. James by Eusebius in his catalogue of the Bishops of Jerusalem may be in some measure due to a doubt that he seems to have had whether James mentioned by the Evangelists as son of Mary, the wife of Cleophas, called by S. Mark James the Less, and numbered amongst our Lord's brethren,[§] was one of the Twelve Apostles, and identical with James, the son of Alphæus, recorded by the three first Evangelists as the second of the name of James in their list of the Twelve.[||] It is certainly very remarkable that nowhere does Eusebius call the first Bishop of Jerusalem an Apostle, or speak of him as among the number of the Twelve, though nowhere on the other hand does he say that he was not. There is, to say the least, considerable obscurity on this point in Eusebius, who

---

[*] ii. 23.   [†] iii. 7, iv. 5.

[‡] vii. 19.—Valesius, on this passage, says: That, according to the ancient tradition, S. James was ordained Bishop of Jerusalem by our Lord Himself; and that besides Eusebius, S. Chrysostom expressly holds this view in his 38th Homily on S. Paul (1 Cor. xv. 7), also S. Epiphanius (*Hæres. Antidic.* 8), and other early authors. Valesius, however, suspects that the source of such statements was the Clementine *Recognitions* (B. i.) and the *Constitutions* (viii. 35).

[§] *Mark*, xv. 40, xvi. 1; *Luke*, xxiv. 10; *John*, xix. 25; *Matt.* xiii. 55, xxviii. 1; *Mark*, vi. 3.

[||] *Matt.* x. 3; *Mark*, iii. 18; *Luke*, vi. 15; *Acts*, i. 13.

is generally so simple and clear. It would seem as though he had not made up his mind on the matter—which, as he could not have been ignorant, had already been brought into question —and that he would not commit himself to any definite statement one way or the other. Some words may be adduced from him which appear by turns to support both views. But we will quote all the various passages which bear on this point.

We might refer to those we have already cited on the special consecration of S. James as Bishop, whether by Christ Himself after His Resurrection or by the Apostles after the Ascension, as suggesting an intrinsic difficulty to his being one of the Twelve Apostles; since, according to the more common and probable opinion, all the Apostles were together made Bishops by Christ Himself, and immediately from Him received their jurisdiction. Suarez prefers the opinion that they were thus made Bishops on the eve of our Lord's Passion at the institution of the Holy Eucharist; for the Apostles would not have had power to preserve its perpetual memorial unless they received at the same time the power to ordain priests, which belongs to the episcopal order.*

We pass on, however, at once to other passages. In his *History* Eusebius says:

"The names of our Saviour's Apostles are well known to everyone from the Gospels; but of the seventy disciples no catalogue is anywhere given."

He then mentions Barnabas, Sosthenes, Cephas—the Cephas whom S. Paul "withstood to the face" at Antioch according to Clement of Alexandria—Matthias, who was afterwards the Apostle, and Thaddæus, as said to have been of the number of the seventy; and, after briefly commenting on S. Paul's words (1 *Cor.* xv. 5, 6) regarding "Cephas," "the eleven," and "the five hundred brethren," he thus continues:

"Afterwards, Paul says, He appeared to James. Now he was both one of those said to be the disciples of our Saviour and, more than that, one of His brethren. Lastly, since beside these there were still a great many others who were Apostles after the likeness of the twelve, such as Paul himself was, he adds the words, 'Afterwards He appeared to all the Apostles.'"†

Valesius, on this passage, after speaking of the reading he follows, says:

"Many ancient authors affirm that James, the brother of our Lord, who was ordained first Bishop of Jerusalem, was not one of the Twelve Apostles,

---

* Suarez, tom. xii. Disp. x. n. 5, sq. pp. 282-4. Edit. Paris, 1858.
† *H. E.* i. 12.

but of the number of our Lord's disciples: thus Gregory of Nyssa,* Clement,†
Dositheus,‡ and Michael Glycas.§ Certainly Paul, in his Epistle to the Corinthians, seems to favour this opinion; for, when there reviewing those to whom
Christ appeared after His resurrection, after he has named the Twelve Apostles
and the five hundred others, he straightway adds, *After that He appeared to
James and the rest of the Apostles.* Paul therefore distinguished James from the
rest of the Apostles. And it was thus Cyril of Jerusalem in his Catechism iv.
and xiv. understood S. Paul's words."

We may, moreover, remark that Eusebius, after mentioning
Matthias as having been one of the seventy, is careful to add that
subsequently he was chosen to be one of the Twelve. He also
singles out S. Paul to give him his title of Apostle; whilst, with
regard to S. James, he seems to leave him amongst those others
who might be called Apostles in the widest and most general
sense. ||

Eusebius (B. ii. ch. 1) seems to endorse a strange and erroneous
statement that S. James, the brother of our Lord, surnamed the
Just, and first Bishop of Jerusalem, was son of Joseph, the reputed
father of our Lord Jesus Christ, by a former marriage. This
opinion was shared by other ancient authors. It is refuted by S.
Jerome, who says that S. James was called our Lord's brother,
because he was son of "the other Mary,"¶ who was the wife of
Cleophas, and sister or kinswoman of the Mother of our Lord.**

In the same chapter Eusebius says:

"Now *there were two Jameses*: one called the Just, who was thrown from
a wing of the Temple and beaten to death with a fuller's club, and another
[the son of Zebedee] who was beheaded. Paul also makes mention of the
Just in his Epistles. 'But other of the Apostles I saw none, saving James,
the brother of the Lord.'"

Here Eusebius goes very near to an expression of opinion in
favour of the identity of James, the brother of our Lord, with
the second of the Twelve Apostles named James. "There were
two Jameses" is certainly very strong; and many learned authors
quote it as decisive of the question. But still the difficulty
remains that in four distinct places of the New Testament, that
is, wherever the second Apostle James is mentioned by the three
Evangelists as an Apostle, he is called the son of Alphæus.
Eusebius of course knew this well; for he had said (i. 12):

* In *Oratione 2 de Christi Resurrectione.*
† In ii. *Constitut.* c. 59, et in i. *Recognit.* sub. fin. p. 20.
‡ *Lib. de Apost. et Discip. Domini.*   § In Parte iii. *Annalium.*
|| See the previous note given from Valesius on the various senses of the
word Apostle.
¶ *Matt.* xxviii. 1.   ** *John,* xix. 25.

"The names of our Saviour's Apostles are sufficiently obvious to everyone from the Gospels."

And, consequently, it is strange if he could for a moment have held the opinion tenable that Alphæus was identical with Joseph, the foster-father of Jesus Christ (whose son he says James the Just was called), as well as synonymous with Cleophas (as is so commonly held), the husband of that Mary who appears to have been the mother of James the Just. As a set-off to the seemingly strong words on the one side, "There were two Jameses," we may cite those other words of Eusebius, "There were many called James." πολλοὶ 'Ιακώβοι ἐκαλοῦντο.*

We have by no means the intention of discussing this question on its own merits, and much less of offering any decided opinion upon it of our own.†

Our sole object in entering upon the matter at all was to try to discover what Eusebius thought about it, with a view to explain why he has included S. James in his catalogue of the Bishops of Jerusalem, contrary to the method he has adopted in the case of the Patriarchal Sees; and we incline to think that he more than suspected the right of S. James, the brother of our Lord, to a place amongst the Twelve Apostles.

We hold that it is hardly travelling out of Eusebius to record the opinion of S. Jerome, his commentator, on this point. First, then, S. Jerome does not call S. James, the brother of our Lord, an Apostle in his notice of him (*De viris Illustr.*). Secondly, in a mystical interpretation of his on the two, three, four, five, that is, in all fourteen olive-berries spoken of by Isaias (xvii. 6), he says that these are the fourteen Apostles, viz., the Twelve, James, who is called the brother of our Lord, the thirteenth, and Paul, the vessel of election, the fourteenth.

We supplement this chapter by the following extracts from Dr. Dollinger:

"In reference to the first Roman bishops, the consentient statements of the Greeks, Irenæus, Eusebius, and Epiphanius,

---

* *H. E.* ii. 23.
† The question has advocates on either side amongst learned Catholics. Baronius and Suarez hold that there were only two S. Jameses, *i.e.*, the two Apostles of that name. The Bollandists, who discuss the point *ex professo* and much more fully (*l° Maii*), maintain decidedly that there were three, and that S. James, the brother of our Lord, Bishop of Jerusalem, brother of Jude, and author of the Epistle, is a distinct person from S. James the Apostle, the son of Alphæus. Their arguments appear to us very strong. The Oriental Church in its Liturgy witnesses to this tradition.

are infinitely more trustworthy than the Latin accounts of Optatus and Augustine and the Roman catalogues of Popes. ... The statements of Optatus and S. Augustine are drawn from a common source, which is either the Liberian list or one based on it.* On the contrary, the statements of Hegesippus and Irenæus, who had both stayed in Rome, and those of Eusebius, are of the most reliable kind. Hegesippus, a Christian Jew of Palestine, having journeyed as far as Rome, stayed there till A.D. 156, in order to ascertain the state of doctrine in the separate Churches, and to examine the Apostolic succession in the principal Churches. He says that in Rome he wrote down the list of the bishops up to Anicetus. Here we perceive the authorities used by Eusebius as to the oldest Roman bishops and the duration of their episcopate; he did not go to S. Irenæus, who gives no dates, but who was enabled, from being in Rome twenty-five years after Hegesippus, to learn equally well on the best authority the succession of eleven or twelve bishops. If we consider that Hegesippus, when he came to Rome, only required for his purpose to investigate the succession of bishops there for the short period of about eighty-three years, that he certainly found persons there whose fathers could remember the beginning of that period, and that, except the short and not severe persecution under Domitian, the Roman Church had suffered no special disturbances, we must place the fullest reliance on his statements—the more so, as they are confirmed by a man who used the same authorities, and whose teacher had heard the Apostle S. John. We have, then, for the succession of the first Roman bishops two independent and accordant witnesses, Hegesippus and Irenæus. The latter certainly did not know Hegesippus's book, or he would have appealed to it against the heretics. Both of them, as well as the Roman Catalogues, make Linus the first bishop after the Apostles. ... S. Irenæus says: 'After Peter and Paul had founded the Roman Church, and set it in order, they gave over the episcopate of it to Linus' (iii. 3). This makes the regulation of the Roman Church and the appointment of Linus a common act of both Apostles, and since then the Roman bishops have been frequently regarded as successors of both. The Roman Church was viewed as inheriting alike from S. Paul his prerogative of Apostle of the

---

* There are three different Western Recensions of the Roman succession—the Roman in the Liberian list, the African of Optatus and S. Augustine, and the Gallican of Victorinus. The canon of the Roman Mass retains the original order of the Greek dyptichs, " Lini, Cleti, Clementis."

Gentiles, and from S. Peter his dignity as the foundation of the Church, and as possessing the power of the keys. Eusebius says of Linus that he was the first bishop after Peter, and of a later bishop, Alexander, that he formed the fifth link in the succession from Peter and Paul; * and he almost always reckons the others 'from the Apostles,' *i.e.*, Peter and Paul. Epiphanius calls Peter and Paul the first Bishops of Rome, which rests, indeed, on a peculiar notion of his to be mentioned presently. The Roman Church is the seat of the two Apostles; † the power of Rome founded on Peter and Paul; ‡ these and similar expressions occur frequently in later writers.

"Anencletus succeeded Linus; both, according to Eusebius, were bishops for about twelve years, so that Clement, the third, entered on his office A.D. 79 or 80. The change of the name Anencletus into Cletus, and then Anacletus, has led to one bishop being divided into two, of whom one is placed before Clement, and the other (Anacletus) after him.§ That the Greek records which give but one Anencletus, and place him before Clement, are the only correct ones is now acknowledged even in Rome. ‖

"The statement of Epiphanius about there being two bishops together in the first age stands quite alone; there is no hint or trace elsewhere of one Church having really had two bishops. But we can point to the authority from which the uncritical and credulous Epiphanius derived his view: it is the *Teaching of the Apostles.* He was the first to treat the *Constitutions* as a genuine

---

* Euseb. iii. 4; iv. 1. † Paulin. *Natal.* 3.

‡ So the Council of Arles in 314 says: "In quibus (partibus, *i.e.*, Rome) Apostoli quotidie sedant." *Ep. ad Silv. Cf.* Theodoret, *Ep.* 113 *ad Leonem.*

§ "Anacletus is no name I ever heard of. But Anencletus (meaning the same as Innocentius) is found as a man's name in a Spartan inscription.... The Greeks always have Anencletus.... The name Cletus is equally unknown, and is clearly a corruption of Anencletus, which sounded strange to Latin ears. Many things have conspired to produce an appearance of error and uncertainty in the succession of the first Roman bishops. First, there is this corruption of the second name; then, the influence of the Ebionite *Recognitions*, translated by Rufinus; Clement's *Letter to James*, from the same source, and the *Apostolical Constitutions*. The letter to S. James, which records the solemn appointment of Clement by S. Peter, was generally followed, and its chief passages were copied into the Roman Pontifical; and so Linus and Cletus were said to have been only S. Peter's assistants during life, as Rufinus had already conjectured. Then, again, Cyprian says of Hyginus, 'Qui in urbe nonus fuit,' and it was not observed that he reckoned S. Peter as first bishop, and so Anencletus was doubled to make eight predecessors."

‖ "... What makes the thing more certain is, that the Roman author of the *Little Labyrinth* (Hippolytus) knows nothing of the double Anacletus, for he reckons Victor thirteenth after S. Peter."

work of the Apostles, 'a divine discourse,' and he often uses it.*
What is said in it about the first bishops appointed by the Apostles
had accordingly full authority for him, and he found there that S.
Peter appointed Evodius and S. Paul Ignatius, in Antioch; that at
Ephesus S. Paul appointed Timothy and S. John appointed John;
whereas, of Alexandria it is said that the first ordained by S. Mark
was Annianus, and that Abilius, ordained by S. Luke, succeeded
him.† Therefore, Epiphanius says, Alexandria had not two
bishops like other cities. The element of truth in his view has
been already noticed, namely, that just at first a single bishop
distinct from the Apostles was impracticable in many Churches."‡

* "In the succession of Roman bishops he has included Cletus, whom the *Constitutions* omit, undoubtedly in reliance on the testimony of Hegesippus and Irenæus."
† Eus. iii. 22, 36.
‡ *First Age of the Church*, vol. ii. pp. 149-153, 160, 161.

CHAPTER XVI.

THE LEGENDARY THEORY OF MODERN GERMAN RATIONALISTS.

WE must now pay some attention to an entirely new system of attack that has been made within our own days against the whole tradition of S. Peter in his relation to Rome by the rationalist German school, of which Bauer, Lipsius, and Zeller are the principal exponents. These authors do not care to dispute the testimonies from early writers in behalf of the Catholic tradition on the lines of historical and positive criticism, as Protestants formerly professed to do.*

Starting with the assumption that the tradition is all pure fiction, and not matter of fact at all, they look on these testimonies as of no historical value, but rather as so many echoes resulting from, and giving voice to, a vast legend, which, they say, was formed under the influences of various very subtle and intricate causes, in, as they pretend, a pre-historic age of Christianity, and came afterwards to be believed in good faith by the early Fathers as historically true.

Hence, the professed object of these Rationalist writers is to discover and collect together the fragments of this pretended legend, to find out the conditions under which it was created, and to trace the various phases of its transformation and development.

This legendary view of S. Peter's Roman Episcopate is based on the theory that within the bosom of primitive Christianity there was a very strong and severe conflict between Petrine and Pauline tendencies, whence arose two opposite and hostile parties in the Church itself. From these two rival factions issued forth divers legendary accounts and pious frauds, which aimed at glorifying one Apostle at the expense of the other. This party spirit,

* See *La Controverse et Le Contemporain*, 15 Fevrier, 1886. " La Venue de S. Pierre à Rome," par Rev. P. Guilleux.

they say, had less influence in the Roman Church than elsewhere, since in Rome minds were more turned to what was practical than theoretical; and consequently, with a view to conciliation, the legend that S. Peter was the first Bishop of Rome was there originated and met with ready acceptance. For, say the authors of this legendary theory, since it was a matter beyond dispute that S. Paul was connected with the Roman Church by his residence, preaching, and martyrdom at Rome, the partisans of S. Paul would naturally make the most of these facts to glorify that Apostle above S. Peter, and themselves as his followers above their opponents, viz., the Judaising Christians who boasted of being the disciples of Peter. And thus it was with a view to conciliation that the Roman Church first conceived the idea of atttributing to S. Peter also a share in those events which had happened to S. Paul and made his name so famous. Hence arose the legendary and romantic accounts of S. Peter's journey to Rome, of his doings, and of his martyrdom together with S. Paul in that city. All this in course of time came to be generally believed as true, so that before the middle of the second century it was commonly regarded as a historical fact that S. Peter was co-founder with S. Paul of the Roman Church.

In order to give some historical colour to their theory, these authors invoke the authority of the pseudo-Clementines, alleging that the Simon Magus therein set forth as S. Peter's great opponent was really no other than S. Paul himself, thus personated by the party of Judaising Christians, who, for the greater and more signal humiliation of that Apostle, laid the final triumph of S. Peter over his adversary in the Capital itself: whereas the party of conciliation, in subsequent editions of the same works, with more moderation, limited the scene of conflict to the coasts of Phœnicia and Syria.

This, they say, was the original form of the legend, which was composed not merely as a romance, but with the motive of glorifying S. Peter to the depreciation of S. Paul.

The Fathers, forsooth, speak of the two Apostles as coming to Rome, if not together, at least without any mutual rivalry, and there sealing one and the same faith by a common martyrdom. And here, according to these German authors, we have the second form of the legend. But, say they, we should bear in mind that when these Fathers wrote, the conciliation had been already effected, and that—as they were evidently then unable to understand the conflicting sense of the partisan legend—they shared with good faith in the vulgar error. Still, however, their testimony bears clear trace of its mythical source, since they assign as the motive of S. Peter's journey to Rome his pursuit of Simon Magus thither.

Now the whole system of these German rationalists depends on the three following points, which they claim to be indisputable:

1. The existence of two hostile parties within the bosom of the Roman Church, and the fusion of these into a neutral party, whereby was effected the union of S. Peter and S. Paul, or, what comes to the same thing, of their alleged mutually opposing tendencies, hence termed Petrinism and Paulinism.

2. That a fictitious journey of S. Peter to Rome is to be found in the Clementines; and that the Clementine literature is of Roman origin.

3. The dependence of the Catholic tradition on this fiction.

We shall briefly expose the unreality of these three points:

1. With regard to the first, it will suffice to state what may be gathered from contemporary records as to the internal state of the primitive Roman Church.

We may well believe that the first beginnings of Christianity at Rome were amongst the Jewish community. There was, we know, since the time of Pompey, a considerable and ever increasing population of Jews in the City, who had continually active communication with the Mother country. The religious movement, excited in Jerusalem by the first preaching of the Gospel, could not pass unnoticed in Rome. We read, moreover, that there were Romans present at the preaching of S. Peter on the first great Feast of Pentecost.* Possibly some of those converted on that occasion were the first preachers of Christianity in Rome.

---

* "We cannot doubt that the original nucleus of the Church at Rome, as well as in all the other great cities of the Empire, was formed by converts (including more Gentile proselytes than Jews), who had separated themselves from the Jewish Synagogue. The name of the original founder of the Roman Church has not been preserved to us by history, nor even celebrated by tradition. This is a remarkable fact, when we consider how soon the Church of Rome attained great eminence in the Christian world, both from its numbers, and from the influence of its metropolitan rank. Had any of the Apostles laid its first foundation, the fact could scarcely fail to have been recorded. It is therefore probable that it was formed in the first instance of private Christians converted in Palestine, who came from the Eastern parts of the Empire to reside at Rome, or who had brought back Christianity with them from some of their periodical visits to Jerusalem as the 'Strangers of Rome' from the great Pentecost." (*The Life and Epistles of S. Paul*, by Conybeare and Howson, vol. ii. ch. xix. p. 167.)

FROM JEWISH AND GENTILE CONVERTS. 415

At any rate, we may be sure that the new doctrine did not meet with indifference in the Jewish circles there, but with ardent adhesion from some, and obstinate resistance from others. We must at the same time bear in mind that the heathen element had an important part in the first Christian settlements at Rome. What would especially favour the entrance of the Pagans into the Christian Church was the system of Jewish proselytism, comparatively speaking, very prevalent at that time. Evidence is found in the writings of heathen poets and moralists of a growing tendency in certain quarters to cast off the worship of the gods, and to embrace the monotheism and the religious observances of the East; and this tendency could not fail to advance the cause of Christianity. We find, moreover, that Jews were mixed up, and had intimate relations, with all classes of Roman society, with persons even of the highest rank, amongst whom were probably many proselytes *of the Gate;* the Christians of the "household of Cæsar" were, not improbably, from amongst these. The names of Domitilla, of Flavius Clemens, Pudens, and Pomponia Græcina, show the progress that Christianity was making amongst the Pagans—some even of the highest families—in Rome, at a very early period. Hence, when a number of Jews abandoned the Mosaic Law to embrace the Gospel, it was not only Jews by birth who joined the Christian ranks, but an almost equal number of Greeks and Romans.*

It would seem indeed, from S. Paul's Epistle to the Romans, that converted Pagans formed the majority of the Roman Church. This appears especially from its opening chapters. Whilst addressing his Epistle to all the Christians in Rome ($\pi\hat{a}\sigma\iota\ \tau o\hat{\iota}s$ $o\hat{v}\sigma\iota\nu\ \hat{\epsilon}\nu\ {}^{\prime}P\omega\mu\eta$, i. 7.), the Apostle begins by reminding his readers that he has received the grace and office of Apostle to bring all the Gentiles to the obedience of the faith, and that they were of the numbers of these Gentiles ($\hat{\epsilon}\nu\ o\hat{\iota}s\ \check{\epsilon}\sigma\tau\epsilon\ \kappa a\hat{\iota}\ \hat{v}\mu\epsilon\hat{\iota}s$). Later on (vv. 13-15) he expresses his desire to gather some fruit among the Romans, and the motive he gives is, that he is a debtor to Greeks and barbarians, to the learned and ignorant, and for this reason he is ready to preach the Gospel to those also who are in Rome. The Apostle addresses by turns the Gentiles and the Jews, but this is rather by way of illustrating the dogmatic questions he treats of: and no conclusion can thence be drawn as to the numerical proportion of the two elements in the Roman Church.

---

* Merivale, *History of the Romans under the Empire*, vii. 308.

So far as one can see, there is no indication whatever of any sharp conflict or division within the early Roman Church between the Jewish and Gentile converts. It was not quarrels amongst Christians, but the turbulence of the Jews themselves and their hostility to the Christians, that gave occasion to the Edict of Claudius. Amongst the victims of that proscription were Aquila and Priscilla. These Jewish converts, we know, became devotedly attached to S. Paul by a fast and enduring friendship. This would certainly seem to show that the doctrinal teaching which these Roman Jews had received did not differ from what they heard S. Paul preach at Corinth.

It is clear that when S. Paul wrote his Epistle, no important religious differences disturbed the Roman Church. He speaks of the faith of all the Christians in Rome as celebrated throughout the world (i. 8.), and of that same faith being common to himself and them (v. 12.). When referring in the later chapters to those who were weak, and to those who were strong, he by no means contemplates them as up in arms against one another.

When, later on, S. Paul went himself to Rome, we do not find that he met with opponents there. At Puteoli, where he landed, the brethren made him remain with them for a week; and, on his approach to the City, brethren went out as for as Apii Forum and the Three Taverns to meet him, "whom when Paul saw he gave thanks to God and took courage." *

The leading Jews of Rome, whom he convoked together, had never heard any harm said of the Apostle, and had, it seems, no knowledge whatever of the divisions which, it is pretended, were rending asunder the Roman Church.†

Bauer's own testimony to the internal peace enjoyed by that Church contradicts his notion that it was thus divided by Pauline and Petrine parties.

> "That Church, he says, although in great measure composed of Jews, had no immediate dependence on the Church at Jerusalem. By its Christian faith, the number of its members, as also by its position in the Capital of the Empire, the Roman Church had acquired a great renown throughout Christendom. It had moreover taken up a conciliatory position between S. Paul and his Jewish-Christian adversaries ... Nowhere was the Christian conscience so early developed as in the Roman Church."‡

Elsewhere § he acknowledges that S. Paul's Epistle to the Romans, when compared with that to the Galatians, shows a remarkable progress in the interests of conciliation. Thus, by the

* *Acts*, xxviii. 15. † *Ib.* vv. 21, 22.
‡ *Das Christenthum*, etc., p. 130. § *Paulus*, p. 353.

showing of the author of the Legend-theory himself, his Church of the Conciliation was already formed at Rome when S. Paul wrote his Epistle to the Romans, that is, long before the time when, as is pretended, the divisions within the bosom of Christendom are alleged to have reached their crisis. It is consequently absurd to set down the origin of that Church to the second century.

We have thus sufficiently shown that, as there were no hostile parties in the Roman Church when first founded, the ground there was not prepared for either the formation or acceptance of the legend.

2. *The pseudo-Clementines.*—We have now to show, first, that a record of any journey of S. Peter to Rome has no place in the Clementines, but is a fiction introduced by the authors of "the legend-theory."

Several writings under the name of Clement have come down to us, all of them more or less infected with Ebionism. The journeyings of S. Peter, his conflicts and disputes with Simon Magus on a great number of Christian doctrines and philosophical questions, narrated in the form of legendary romance, compose their principal subject-matter. The *Clementine Homilies* have more of Ebionism and of Anti-Pauline tendency than the *Recognitions*.

In the following passage of the *Homilies* S. Peter, it seems, is made directly to attack S. Paul's vocation to the Apostleship.

"If then," S. Peter says to Simon, "our Jesus appeared to you in a vision, made Himself known to you, and spoke to you, it was as one enraged with an adversary; and this is the reason why it was through visions and dreams, or through revelations that were from without, that He spoke to you. ... And how are we to believe your word, when you tell us that He appeared to you? And how did He appear to you, when you entertain opinions contrary to His teaching? But if you were seen and taught by Him, and became His Apostle for a single hour, proclaim His utterances, interpret His sayings, love His Apostles, contend not with me who companied with Him. For in direct opposition to me, who am a firm rock, and the foundation of the Church, you now stand. If you were not opposed to me, you would not accuse me, and revile the truth proclaimed by me, in order that I may not be believed when I state what I myself have heard with my own ears from the Lord, as if I were evidently a person that was condemned and in bad repute."[*]

The Ebionite author makes here, it would appear, a caricature of S. Paul under the mask of Simon Magus. But such identification of S. Paul with Simon Magus is certainly by no means the main and persistent idea of the author. This is quite an exceptional

[*] Bk. xvii. ch. xix.

passage, and stands alone. There are not perhaps more than two or three places throughout these writings in which there is found any direct allusion to S. Paul, and these are quite unimportant to the matter under discussion. The Simon Magus of the Clementine writings is in fact a very nondescript character, representing no one single person, but, chameleon-like, changing his face and colour at every moment; and meant to personify by turns all sorts of heresies, or whatever would pass as heresy in the eyes of an Ebionite. So far from any continuous and persistent identity being intended by the author between S. Paul and Simon Magus, we find in the *Recognitions* that the individuality of S. Paul is distinctly set forth as distinct from that of Simon Magus. The two are brought together: and Paul, or rather Saul the persecutor (for it is before his conversion), is represented as the enemy of Simon, as much as of S. James and S. Peter, and as entering the Temple by violence and causing a tumult in order to force away the people from the seductions of the magician.

The following is the passage from the *Recognitions* referred to, wherein Peter is made to say:

"And when matters were at this point that they should come and be baptised, some one of our enemies,* entering the temple with a few men, began to cry out, and to say: 'What mean ye, O men of Israel? Why are ye led headlong by most miserable men who are deceived by Simon, a magician?' While he was thus speaking and adding more to the same effect, and while James the Bishop was refuting him, he began to excite the people to raise a tumult . . . in the midst of which that enemy attacked James, threw him headlong from the top of the steps, and then, supposing him to be dead, cared not to inflict further violence upon him. . . . After three days one of the brethren came to us from Gamaliel . . . bringing to us secret tidings that the enemy had received a commission from Caiaphas, the chief priest, to arrest all who believed in Jesus, and go to Damascus with his letters, where, too, employing the help of the unbelievers, he was to make havoc among the faithful, and that he was hastening to Damascus chiefly on this account, because he believed that Peter had fled thither."†

In any case, even were it proved that S. Paul was really intended under the mask of Simon Magus in the romance from first to last, this would give no support whatever to the statement that the alleged fictitious journey of S. Peter to Rome has its origin in the Clementines, since there exists in them no trace whatever of S. Peter's following Simon to Rome. The legendary story of the *Recognitions* and the *Homilies* is limited exclusively to the East. The scene opens at Cæsarea Stratonis, is continued along the coast of Phœnicia, and ends at Antioch.

* A marginal note in one of the MSS. states that this enemy was Saul.
† *Recognitions*, i. 70, 71.

It is true that both in the *Recognitions* and in the *Homilies* S. Peter is represented as intending to go to Rome. Thus S. Peter says to Clement on first meeting him:

"Journey with us, and receive the word of truth which I am about to make known in all the cities, even as far as Rome."*

And in the *Recognitions*† the story is told of a deserter at Cæsarea from Simon's camp coming to S. Peter and saying:

"Then he (Simon Magus) asked me to go with him, saying he was going to Rome, and that there he would please the people so much that he should be reckoned as a god and publicly receive divine honours. . . . He set out towards Dora,‡ saying: 'You will be sorry when you hear what glory I shall get in the city of Rome.' And after this he set out for Rome. . ."

Simon, he adds, made him great promises; but perceiving that he was a magician and deceiver, he excused himself and left him.

S. Peter resolves to follow him, and thus addresses the people:

"Since, therefore, as you have heard, Simon has gone forth to preoccupy the ears of the Gentiles who are called to salvation, it is necessary that I also follow upon his track, so that whatever disputations he raises may be corrected by us. . . . In order then that you may be more and more confirmed in the truth, and the nations who are called to salvation may in no way be prevented by the wickedness of Simon, I have thought good to ordain Zacchæus as pastor over you, and to remain with you myself three months, and so to go to the Gentiles, lest, through our delaying longer, and the crimes of Simon stalking in every direction, they should become incurable."§

S. Peter ordains Zacchæus Bishop of Cæsarea, as also presbyters and deacons. He sends twelve of his disciples before him with this charge:

"Proceed to the Gentiles, and follow in the footsteps of Simon, that you may inform me of all his proceedings. You will also inquire diligently the sentiments of everyone, and announce to them that I shall come to them without delay; and, in short, in all places instruct the Gentiles to expect my coming."

Simon goes from city to city on to Tripolis, where he makes some stay. S. Peter remains meanwhile for three months at Cæsarea. On his departure thence, he announces that he will spend the winter at Tripolis. His route thither is thus traced by the romancer: Dora, Ptolemais, Tyre, Sidon, and Berytus, at which places he makes brief halts. At Tripolis, Simon, upon hearing of Peter's arrival, departs by night on the way to Syria. S. Peter,

---

* *Recogn.* i.; *Hom.* i. 16.   † B. iii. ch. lxiii.
‡ A small town on the sea coast between Cæsarea and Tyre.
§ *Recognitions*, Book iii. ch. lxiii.-lxv.

after a three months' stay at Tripolis, where he ordains Maro bishop, together with twelve presbyters and deacons, sets out for Antioch, stopping in his journey at Ortosius, Antharadus, and the island of Aradus. He at length at Laodicea comes up to Simon, who makes flight thence in the direction of Judæa. S. Peter goes on to Antioch, where the romance takes a final leave of him.

Hence it is clear that no trace of any journey made by S. Peter to Rome is to be found in the pseudo-Clementine *Recognitions* and *Homilies*.

Besides the Clementine literature still extant, other writings of a similar character are referred to, or cited by, ancient Fathers and authors under the titles of Περίοδοι, Κηρύγματα, 'Αναγνωρίσμοι, Διαμαρτύρια, &c. It is, however, now quite impossible to determine with any certainty their particular date and origin, nor can we precisely say whether each and all of these were really distinct and separate works, or were not, some of them at least, identical, though commonly known and cited under different appellations.

The German rationalists claim for the pseudo-Clementines a Roman origin, and this is of vital importance for their whole theory. Such a claim is destitute of all solid ground, since there is very clear evidence of their Eastern parentage.*

It has been already seen that the soil was not prepared at Rome, but on the contrary was most unfavourable, for either the formation or acceptance of such a legend. Besides, we know that though heresiarchs were wont to visit Rome on account of the renowned pre-eminence and authority of the Roman Church, and with the hope of obtaining there some sanction for their doctrines, yet that their heresies, whether of Gnosticism or Ebionism, were already hatched elsewhere, and for the most part in the East.

Rome was ever the great seat and centre of orthodoxy; and there is no evidence at all that these heresies had any hold on the Roman Christians. As a proof to the contrary we read that Alcibiades of Apamea came to Rome under Pope Callistus, bringing with him the book of Elchasai, or "Hidden Wisdom," in which was propounded a mystical doctrine of Ebionism, resembling very closely the teachings of the *Homilies*.

Now the author of the *Philosophumena*† remarks that this

---

* See infra, ch. xix., the opinion of Dr. Lightfoot on this point.
† ix. 3.

Elchasaism made its appearance in Rome as something *quite novel* and *before utterly unheard of.* We may hence gather that Rome was no favourable soil for the Clementine literature.

But if the doctrine contained in the Clementine legend was uncongenial to Rome, the hierarchical tendencies it revealed would not be less distasteful; for, strange to say—whilst the prerogatives bestowed by Christ on Peter are distinctly recognised in the pseudo-Clementines, as also his office and permanent succession in the Roman See—he is yet represented there as though inferior and subject to S. James, receiving his commission from that Apostle, and obliged to send a report of himself and of his doings from time to time to the Bishop of Jerusalem.

The whole contents, in short, of the Clementine books, together with the scene occupied by the romance, give clear evidence of their Eastern source. Ulhorn and other learned critics are of opinion that they had their origin in eastern Syria, at or near Edessa, where at a very early period was developed a corrupted form of Christianity of the Gnostic type, and whence came forth so many heretical sects.

We shall here, by way of digression, take notice of Dean Milman's conflicting statements and illogical reasoning on this point in the the first chapter of his *History of Latin Christianity*. The whole drift of this chapter, "Beginning of Roman Christianity," according to the evident aim of the brilliant author, represents the Church of Rome in its earliest days as distracted within itself by all sorts of doctrinal strifes and dissensions, and as a seething hot-bed of every kind of heresy. His proof of this is drawn from the fact that nearly all the Greek and Asiatic heresiarchs came to Rome seeking there to teach and propagate their errors.

But to ordinary minds Milman must, we think, appear to contradict himself by what he goes on to offer as though in confirmation of his proof:

"Not only," he writes, "do all these controversies betray the inexhaustible fertility of the Greek or Eastern imagination, not only were they all drawn from Greek or Oriental doctrines, but they must have been still agitated, discussed, ramified into their parts and divisions through the versatile and subtile Greek. They were all strangers and foreigners; not one of all these systems originated in Rome, in Italy, or in Africa. On all these opinions the Bishop of Rome was almost compelled to sit in judgment; he must receive or reject, authorise or condemn; he was a proselyte, whom it would be the ambition of all to join. No one unfamiliar with Greek, no one not to a great extent Greek by birth, by education, or by habit, could in any degree comprehend the conflicting theories."*

The inference which the author more than suggests, though he does not indeed fully express it, is that because the heresiarchs who came to Rome were Greeks or spoke Greek, and because this language was well known in Rome, and especially to the Popes, who were consequently well able to understand these different heresies; therefore, to use his own words, "in Rome every heresy, almost every heresiarch found welcome reception," that is to say, among the Catholic faithful of Rome. It is here insinuated that these heresies became more or less assimilated to, or part and parcel, for a time, of the faith and teaching of the Roman Church. Whereas history tells us that in Rome all these heresies successively met with their refutation, and that their authors were condemned and excommunicated.†

Milman himself, in the same chapter, whilst doing his utmost to incriminate several of the Popes with heresy, frequently admits this, thus:

"The Bishop Victor deposed the obstinate schismatic (Blastus, denounced as endeavouring secretly to enslave the Church to Judaism) from the Roman Presbytery."——"The feud between the Judaising and anti-Judaising parties in Rome seemed to expire with the controversy about Easter. The older Gnostic systems of Valentinus and Marcion had had their day. Montanism was expelled from Rome to find refuge in Africa."——"In Rome .... the Bishop .... had revoked his letters, denied their (i.e., the Montanist prophets) spiritual gifts, and driven out the prophets in disgrace."——"Victor condemned, indeed, and excommunicated Theodotus, who reduced the Saviour to His naked manhood."——"The first act of Callistus .... was the excommunication of Sabellius," who had "been driven into extremes by the injudicious violence of the Pope." ‡

With regard to the matter of Judaising, and the Clementine writings in particular, Milman says:

"Nowhere do the Judaising tenets seem to have been more obstinate, or held so long and stubborn a conflict with more full and genuine Christianity [than in Rome]."——"The Judaising opinions, combated by S. Paul in his Epistle to the Romans, maintained their ground among some of the Roman Christians for above a century or more after that Apostle's death." §

---

* Milman's *History of Latin Christianity*, vol. i. pp. 38, 39, Third Edition, 1872.

† From the same premisses Dr. Lightfoot draws a conclusion the very contrary to that of Milman, and one identical with our own. See *infra*, ch. xix.

‡ Milman, pp. 43, 44, 48, 49; *Note* 56, 51.   § *Ib.* pp. 38, 39.

For the truth of this assertion, the only testimony offered by the writer is his own conviction, grounded on the authority of Schlieman, Neander, Baur and Giesler, that the author of the Clementines was a Roman, or rather a Greek domiciled in Rome. The single argument expressed by himself is that of Clement being chosen as the hero of the romance:

"The whole purpose of the work," he says, "is to assert a Petrine, a Judaising, an anti-Pauline Christianity. . . . The antagonism of Simon Magus to S. Peter is chiefly urged in the Clementine homilies; but there are manifest hints, more perhaps than hints, of a second antagonism between Peter and Paul, the teacher of Christianity with the Law, and the teacher of Christianity without the Law." *

These, then, appear to be Milman's premisses from which he draws the following inference:

"Here, then, is the representation of what can scarcely be supposed an insignificant party in Rome. . . . The various forms, reconstructions, and versions in which the Clementina appear, whole, or in fragments, attest their wide-spread popularity. . . . Of the whole party it must have been the obvious interest to exalt S. Peter, to assert him as the founder, the Bishop of the true Church in Rome." And "a remarkable monument attests their power and vitality in Rome." †

We have endeavoured faithfully to set forth Milman's argument, if argument it can be called, by quoting his own words, and, indeed, exhausting nearly all that he says to the point. Most people would, we think, consider that he is reasoning in a circle, and attempting to prove *idem per idem*, viz., the asserted Judaising party in the Roman Church by the supposed Roman origin of the Clementina, and then this latter by alleging the existence of the said Roman party.

Moreover, he does not seem at all to feel the force of what he writes in the same pages, and how this must vitiate his conclusion, viz.:

"So far from ascribing any primacy to S. Peter, though S. Peter is throughout the leading personage, James, Bishop of Jerusalem, is the acknowledged head of Christendom, the arbiter of Christian doctrine, the Bishop of Bishops, to whom Peter himself bows with submissive reverence."

For how could such hierarchical teaching be acceptable and have a "widespread popularity" in the Roman Church, or square with what was "the obvious interest of the whole party, viz., to exalt Peter?" How, again, would the Roman Judaising party receive that other tenet of the Clementines mentioned by Milman,

* *Ib.* p. 89. † *Ib.* pp. 41, 89.

that "Peter is the Apostle of the Gentiles, to Peter the heathens owe their Christianity?" It was certainly safe and convenient for the historian to preface the mention of these perplexing points with the following remark:

"The views of the author as to the rank, influence, and relative position of the Apostles, are among the most singular characteristics of this work."

The decision of Rome on the Paschal question, as well under Anicetus, A.D. 109, as under Victor, A.D. 196, contrary to the ancient Jewish custom, obviously affords a very strong argument against the existence of a Judaising faction within the Church of Rome.

Milman, in treating of this question in the times of Victor, makes an observation similar in tone to the one last quoted:

"Rome, he says, *it is remarkable, now*" (just as though she had not done so before under Anicetus), "held the anti-Judaic usage of the variable feast, and in this concurred with the Churches of Palestine, of Cæsarea, and Jerusalem. These were chiefly of Gentile descent,* and probably from near neighbourhood to the Jews, were most averse to the usages of that hostile and odious race."

We must bear in mind that it was only from A.D. 136 that the Church of Jerusalem could be called of Gentile descent, when Ælia was reconstructed under Adrian on the ruins of Jerusalem. If aversion to Judaising customs caused a change in the observance of Easter in the Jerusalem Church at that time, we should hold also that the same aversion was equally the cause of the anti-Judaic observance of Easter that prevailed in Rome at a much earlier period, and was handed down to Anicetus and from him to Victor: and from this we have a clear proof that there was nothing that could be called a Judaising party within the Roman Church.†

We are of opinion that many of the misconceptions of Milman in this chapter (though, in point of fact, they serve materially to further the rationalistic tendency of his work, which is to do away with everything that is definite and positive in Catholicism, or, for that matter, in all Christianity whatsoever) arise from the inability of Protestants generally to properly understand the distinction between heresies outside, and doctrinal questions agitated within, the Catholic Church. They confound, histori-

---

* Milman soon afterwards, p. 108, speaks of Jerusalem in a different tone: "At all events, it was the capital of Judaism rather than of Christianity."

† See Dr. Lightfoot, *infra*, ch. xix.

cally, the wide field of Christianity in any shape, and its numberless floating opinions—its so-called *syncretism*—with the Church herself in her sphere of faith and dogma. It should, moreover, be borne in mind that often heretics arise from within the Church itself, and put forth their opinions at first in a mild form, sometimes with much plausibility, with a certain mixture of truth, and under a garb of sanctity. Here, in this first stage, and before any adequate examination has been made, even holy and learned men — those, too, who are in authority — may for a time be deceived as to the nature and tendency of the newly-broached opinions. This, we conceive, would have been more likely to happen in the first age of the Church, when, comparatively speaking, so few doctrines had been analysed and defined. Or, again, ecclesiastical authority might temporise and bear for a certain time with the persons who set forth the strange opinions, in hope that such indulgence would preserve them within bounds of moderation and from further extravagance, or with a view to their amendment. In the second stage, when the heretical teaching takes its full development, a formal investigation is instituted by the ecclesiastical authority, and its result at length is the condemnation of the heresy. Then the heretic, if he will not recant his errors, is excommunicated. Perhaps, however, ere this he has himself departed, and is already outside the Church's pale by his own act.

This mingling of long-suffering and severity may help to explain what to some Protestants and superficial or captious students of Church history wears the face of compromise, partisanship, or tergiversation on the part of ecclesiastical authority when dealing with heretics and their erroneous doctrines; from which they conclude that there has been some real implication of the Church with heresy. This, we need not say, is an entirely false inference. The Church of God—being the depository and guardian of revealed truth, and ever teaching under the influence of the Divine Spirit of truth—cannot hold or sanction what is opposed to that truth. She casts off and shrinks from heresy as something that would be destructive of her very life, and is incompatible with her essential nature; whilst, like her Divine Founder, she can, at the same time, "have compassion on them that are ignorant and err; and wills to have all men saved and come to the knowledge of the truth."[*]

How entirely in accord this conduct of the Church is with

---

[*] *Heb.* v. 2; 1 *Tim.* ii. 4.

Apostolic teaching is seen by the following passages from the Epistles:

> "Him that is weak in faith, take unto you." "Rebuke them sharply, that they may be sound in the faith." "Reprove, entreat, rebuke in all patience and doctrine. For there shall be a time when they will not endure sound doctrine." "Try the spirits if they be of God." "Some shall depart from the faith, giving heed to the spirits of error." "Some rejecting (faith and a good conscience) have made shipwreck concerning faith: of whom is Hymenæus and Alexander, whom I have delivered up to Satan, that they may learn not to blaspheme." "A man that is a heretic, after the first and second admonition avoid." "They went out from us; but they were not of us. For if they had been of us, they would no doubt have remained with us: but that they may be manifest that they are not of us." *

3. It remains now to show that the historical tradition of S. Peter's journey to Rome does not depend on the Clementine legend.

We have already seen that in the pseudo-Clementines mention is made of a projected journey of Simon Magus to Rome, and also of a projected journey to Rome of S. Peter; that these two journeys are there connected together, the former being spoken of as the motive of the latter, whilst, so far as the legend is concerned, neither the one nor the other was ever carried into effect. So much for the romance.

On the other hand, in the surviving notices from the first two centuries of these two events, they are represented as though unconnected and independent the one of the other. Thus, in proof that S. Peter went to Rome, we have his own testimony in his first Epistle,† the testimony of S. Clement in his Epistle to the Church of Corinth, of S. Ignatius in his Epistle to the Roman Church, of the author of the Κήρυγμα‡ cited as early as A.D. 150 by the Gnostic Heracleon; of Dionysius of Corinth, who mentions the journey to Rome of SS. Peter and Paul. None of these writers make the slightest allusion to Simon Magus, or to S. Peter's conflicts with him in Rome or elsewhere; nor has the Apostle Paul, whom they associate so intimately at Rome with S. Peter, the most distant resemblance to that Paul now alleged to be personated in the Clementine legend under the mask of Simon. Following close on these testimonies come those of S. Justin,

---

* *Rom.* xiv. 1; *Tit.* i. 9-13; 2 *Tim.* iv. 2-4; 1 *John,* iv. 1: 1 *Tim.* iv. 1, i. 6, 19, 20; *Tit.* iii. 10, 11; 1 *John,* ii. 19.

† v. 13.

‡ We learn from the anonymous author of the treatise *De Rebaptismate*, annexed to the writings of S. Cyprian, that the meeting together of SS. Peter and Paul at Rome was expressly mentioned in the Κήρυγμα Πέτρου.

S. Irenæus, and Tertullian. Now S. Justin narrates that Simon came to Rome under Claudius, where he practised his magic arts and received Divine honours; but not a word is said by him here about S. Peter. Indeed his seeming attribution of a final triumph to Simon would ill chime in with the general drift and requirements of the Clementine legend, which should naturally accord him the doom of a shameful defeat at the hands of S. Peter. From this it is plain that S. Justin's account was not drawn from any Ebionite or Judaising source, but had quite another and independent origin. This independence is, however, still more clearly seen in the testimonies of S. Irenæus and Tertullian. Both these writers speak in positive terms of the presence alike of S. Peter and of Simon Magus at Rome, but do not connect the two together there; nor do they say anything whatever to imply that the coming to Rome of one was the motive of the journey thither of the other.

The earliest known writer who connects together these two events is the author of the *Philosophumena*.* But here we should well remark the difference which separates the purely Roman tradition of the *Philosophumena* with regard to Simon Magus from the Judaising tradition of the Clementines. The latter would make S. Peter follow Simon Magus to Rome, whereas the former brings Simon to the Apostles who are already there. Again, according to the *Philosophumena*, S. Peter is there more than once engaged in conflict with Simon; but the final issue is very different from what we should suppose was required by the Clementine legend. Instead of the combat terminating with a conspicuous triumph for S. Peter by the death of his enemy in Rome, Simon is allowed to steal away quietly into some far-off solitude, where, still playing the part of a false Christ, he prevails on his disciples to bury him alive, boasting at the same time that on the third day he will rise again.

To find anything like such a combination of the journeys to Rome of S. Peter and Simon as would satisfy the exigencies of the German rationalists and their legend theory, we must go to the *Apostolic Constitutions* of the fourth century. But at that period, as all will allow, the Catholic Church was fully persuaded of the fact of S. Peter's journey to Rome, and also of his Roman Episcopate; and the certainty of this persuasion was, as we have seen, based on particular testimony of its own, apart from, and

* L. vi. i. 20.

independent of, all belief in the legendary accounts of the pseudo-Clementines.

It is worth while here to remark that although the Clementine narrative of S. Peter's pursuit of Simon Magus, of their various journeyings, and of their mutual disputes, is simply fictitious; and although any actual journey to Rome either of one or the other has no place at all in the romance, so that this legend could not be the source whence the Catholic tradition is derived, still the mere mention there of a proposed journey of both to Rome forms of itself an incidental confirmation of the Catholic tradition that both S. Peter and Simon Magus really went at some time to Rome, and were there engaged in mutual conflict of some sort at least—facts which are otherwise supported by reliable historical testimony.

S. Jerome and Eusebius say that the presence of Simon Magus in Rome was a motive or the occasion for the Apostle S. Peter's journey in order there to oppose him. Whether this circumstance of motive was an after-thought of these writers or not, whether it were rightly or wrongly affirmed, and whether the manner of conflict detailed by other authors be really true or false, in no way affects the truth of the main facts themselves, for the belief of which there is good and independent authority.

APPENDIX.

As an Appendix to this Chapter we make some extracts from the Clementine writings, and record various appreciations of them as well from a Protestant as from a Catholic point of view. First, however, we quote the following:

FROM THE PREFACE OF RUFINUS TO CLEMENT'S "RECOGNITIONS."

"The Epistle in which the same Clement, writing to James the Lord's brother, informs him of the death of Peter, and that he had left him successor of his Chair and teaching (quod se reliquerat successorem Cathedræ et doctrinæ suæ), and in which is contained the whole matter of ecclesiastical order, I have not prefixed to this work, both because it is of later date, and because I have already translated and published it. But what in it to some will appear inconsistent, if it be here explained, I do not think appears absurd. For some ask: Since Linus and Cletus were bishops in the city of Rome before this Clement, how could Clement himself, writing to James, say that the Chair of teaching was delivered to him by Peter? Now, hereof we have heard this account, that Linus and Cletus were, indeed, bishops in the city of Rome before Clement, but during the life-time of Peter: that is, that they took the care of the Episcopate, and that he fulfilled the office of the Apostolate; as he is found also to have done at Cæsarea, where, when he himself was present, he yet had Zacchæus, ordained by himself, as bishop (Zacchæum tamen a se ordinatum habebat episcopum). And in this way both statements will appear to be true, that these are reckoned as bishops before Clement, and yet that Clement after Peter's death received the seat of teaching (ut et illi ante Clementem numerantur episcopi, et Clemens tamen post obitum Petri docendi susceperit sedem)."[*]

From the Epistle of Clement to James.

"Be it known to you, my lord, that Simon, who, on account of the true faith and the most sure basis of his teaching, was ordained ($\delta\rho\iota\sigma\theta\epsilon\iota\varsigma$) to be the foundation of the Church, and for this end by Jesus Himself, with infallible mouth, had his name changed to Peter ($\mu\epsilon\tau\text{o}\nu\text{o}\mu\alpha\sigma\theta\epsilon\iota\varsigma\ \Pi\epsilon\tau\rho\text{o}\varsigma$), the first fruit of our Lord, the first of the Apostles: to whom first the Father revealed the Son, whom Christ with good reason pronounced blessed, (of Christ) the called and elect, messmate, too, and fellow-journeyer; that excellent ($\delta\ \kappa\alpha\lambda\text{o}\varsigma$) and approved disciple, who, as being fittest of all, was commanded to lighten the darker part of the world, namely the West, and was enabled to accomplish it . . . himself in person, by reason of his immense love for men, manifestly and publicly, in face of the opposition of the wicked one, in order to make known the good King that should be for the whole world, having come hither to Rome, saving men by doctrine of Divine Will, has himself, by violence, exchanged this present existence for life. Now, in the very days when he was about to die, the brethren being assembled together, suddenly seizing my hand, he rose up and said in the presence of the Church: 'Hearken to me, brethren and fellow-servants: Since as I have been taught by the Lord and Master, Jesus Christ, Who hath sent me, that the day of my death is approaching, I ordain this Clement for your bishop; and to him I entrust my Chair of discourse, even to him who has journeyed with me from the beginning to the end, and thus has heard all my homilies. . . . Wherefore, I make over to him the power of binding and loosing, so that with respect to all that he shall ordain on earth, it shall be decreed in the heavens. For he shall bind what ought to be bound, and loose what ought to be loosed, as knowing the rule of the Church. Therefore, hear ye him, knowing that he who grieves him who presides over the truth sins against Christ, and offends the Father of all; wherefore, such a one shall not live. However, it behoves him who presides to hold the place of a physician, and not to have the anger of an irrational beast.'

"While he thus spoke, falling down before him, I entreated him, begging to be excused the honour and authority of the Chair. . . . (Here follows a long discourse of S. Peter.) Having thus spoken, he laid his hands upon me in the presence of all, and to my confusion made me sit in his own Chair. When I was seated, he straightway said to me: 'I charge thee, before all my brethren here present, that whensoever I depart this life, as needs I must, to send to James the brother of the Lord a brief account of thy reasonings . . . and then at the end thou wilt not fail to inform him of the occasion of my

[*] Migne, *Patr. Græc.* tom i. pp. 1207-8.

death, as I said before. For that event will not very much grieve him, when he knows that I piously went through what it behoved me to suffer. And he will have the greatest consolation on learning, that after me no unlearned man, nor one ignorant of life-giving words, nor unversed in the rule of the Church, has been entrusted with the Chair of the teacher.'" *

THE CLEMENTINE "RECOGNITIONS" AND "HOMILIES."

In the first chapters of these works, Clement narrates how he was born in Rome, and from his earliest years was a lover of chastity. Whilst yet a youth, he was much exercised interiorly by questionings as to the immortality of the soul, the beginning and creation of the world, whether it was eternal, or what would be its end. He describes his dissatisfaction with the schools of philosophy; and how his disquiet and anxiety increased as he thought on what might be his own future state after death, and whether it were worth while to live virtuously, if there were no life after this.

In his perplexity he resolves to go to Egypt, and there consult a magician who should raise a soul for him: thereby to test whether the soul were immortal or not. He was, however, deterred by a certain philosopher from this design, as being unlawful. His distressful doubts still remain; and he thus continues:

"Whilst I was tossed upon these billows of my thoughts, and occupied with such reasonings and doings, a certain report, taking its rise in the spring-time in the reign of Tiberius Cæsar, gradually grew everywhere, and ran through the world, of what was truly the good tidings of God, rendering it impossible to stifle the counsel of God in silence. Therefore, it everywhere became greater and louder, telling forth that a certain One in Judæa, beginning in the spring season, was preaching to the Jews the kingdom of the invisible God, and saying that whoever of them would reform his manner of living should enjoy it. And in order that He might be believed as One Who spake these things full of the Godhead, He wrought many wonderful miracles and signs by His mere command, as having received power from God. For He made the deaf to hear, the blind to see, the lame to walk, raised up the bowed down, drove away every disease, put to flight every demon; and even scabbed lepers, by only looking on Him from a distance, were sent away cured by Him; the dead, too, when brought to Him were raised to life—in truth, there was nothing which He could not do. So, as time went on, and through the arrival of more persons, still greater and stronger grew—I say not now the report, but—the truth of the matter; for now at length there were meetings in various places for consultation and inquiry as to who He might be that had appeared, and what was His purpose.

* Migne, *Patr. Græc.* tom. ii. pp. 33 *seq.*

"And then in the same year, in the autumn season, a certain one,[*] standing in a public place, cried and said: 'Men of Rome, hearken; The Son of God is come in Judæa, proclaiming eternal life to all who have the will, provided they live according to the counsel of the Father Who hath sent Him. Wherefore, change your manner of life from the worse to the better, from things temporal to things eternal; for know ye, that there is One only God Who is in heaven, Whose world ye unrighteously dwell in, before His righteous eyes. But if ye be changed, and will live according to His counsel, then, being born into the other world, and becoming eternal, ye shall enjoy His unspeakable good things. But if ye be unbelieving, your souls, after the dissolution of the body, shall be cast into the place of fire, where, being punished eternally, they shall bewail their unprofitable deeds. For every one the term of repentance is the present life.'

"I therefore, when I heard these things, was grieved, because no one amongst the so great multitudes that heard such an announcement said: I will go into Judæa that I may there assure myself whether this man, who tells us these things, speaks the truth, that indeed the Son of God has come into Judæa, for the sake of a good and eternal hope, revealing the will of the Father Who sent Him. For it is no small matter which, they say, He preaches: for He asserts that the souls of some being (themselves) immortal shall enjoy eternal good things, and that those of others, being thrown into unquenchable fire, shall be punished for ever."

Clement himself embarks for Judæa, and is borne by adverse winds to Alexandria, where, being detained by stress of weather, he consorts with the philosophers, whom he tells "about the rumour and the sayings of him who had appeared in Rome. And they answered that indeed they knew nothing of him who had appeared in Rome; but concerning Him Who was born in Judæa, and Who was said by the report to be the Son of God, they had heard from many who had come from thence, and had received tidings of all the wonderful things that He did with a word.

"And when I said that I wished I could meet with some one of those who had seen Him, they immediately offered to take me to such a one, saying: 'There is one here who not only is acquainted with Him, but is also of that country, a Hebrew, by name Barnabas, who says that he himself is one of His disciples; and hereabouts he resides, and readily announces to those who will the terms of His promise.' Then I went with them, and when I came I stood listening to his words with the crowd that stood around him: and I perceived that he was speaking truth not with dialectic art, but was setting forth simply and without preparation what he had heard and seen the manifested Son of God do and say. And even from the crowd that stood around him he produced many witnesses of the miracles and discourses which he narrated.

"But whilst the multitudes were favourably disposed towards the things that he so artlessly spoke, the philosophers, impelled by their worldly learning, set upon laughing at him and making sport of him, upbraiding and reproaching him with excessive presumption, making use of the great armoury of syllogisms. But he set aside their babbling, and did not enter into their subtle

---

[*] In the *Recognitions* he is said to be Barnabas, but this, we think, must have been added by a later hand, since in the *Homilies*, from which we quote, Clement is represented as first meeting with Barnabas at Alexandria.

questions, but without embarrassment went on with what he was saying. And then one of them asked, Wherefore it was that a gnat, although it is so small, and has six feet, has wings also, while an elephant, the largest of beasts, is wingless, and has but four feet? But he, after the question had been put, going on with his discourse, which had been interrupted, as though he had answered the question, resumed his original discourse, only making use of this preface after each fresh interruption: 'We have a commission only to tell you the words and wondrous doings of Him Who sent us: and instead of logical demonstration, we present to you many witnesses from amongst yourselves who stand by, whose faces I remember as living images. These sufficient testimonies it is left to your choice to submit to or to disbelieve. But I shall not cease to declare unto you what is for your profit; for to be silent were to me a loss, and to disbelieve is ruin to you. But indeed I could give answers to your frivolous questions, if you asked them through love of truth. But the reason of the different structure of the gnat and the elephant it is not fitting to tell to those who are ignorant of the God of all.'

"When he had said this, they all, as in concert, set up a shout of laughter, trying to silence him and put him out as a barbarian madman. But I, seeing this, and seized, I know not how, with enthusiasm, could no longer keep silence with righteous indignation, but boldly cried out, saying: 'Well has God ordained that His counsel should be incapable of being received by you, for seeing you to be unworthy, as is evident to all those who are now present and have minds capable of judging. For,—whereas now heralds of His counsel have been sent forth, not making a show of grammatical art, but setting forth His will in simple and inartificial words, so that all who hear can understand what is spoken, and not with any invidious feeling, as though unwilling to offer it to all,—you come here, and, besides your not understanding what is for your advantage, to your great injury you laugh at the truth, which to your condemnation consorts with the barbarians, and will not entertain it even when it visits you, by reason of your wickedness, and the plainness of its words, and because you are not seekers after truth nor lovers of wisdom. How long will you be learning to speak, you who have not the power to speak? For all the many things that you say are not worth a single word. But if, as he affirms, there is to be a judgment, will your Grecian multitude agree together to say: Why, then, O God didst Thou not declare to us Thy counsel? Shall you not, if you be thought worthy of an answer at all, receive such as this: 'I, knowing before the foundations of the world all dispositions and characters that were to be, acted towards each one by anticipation according to his deserts, without making it known (literally, I met each one beforehand secretly: *unicuique prævius occurri*); but wishing to give full assurance to those who have fled to Me that this is so, and to explain why, from the beginning, and in the first ages, I did not suffer My counsel to be publicly proclaimed, now in the end of the world I have sent heralds to proclaim My will, and they are insulted and flouted by those who will not be benefited, and who wilfully reject My friendship. Oh, great wrong! the preachers are exposed to danger even to the loss of life, and that by men who are called to salvation.'...
(Clement continues his rebuke to the people.) 'And now give over laughing at this man and hear me with respect to his announcement, or let any one of the hearers who pleases make answer; but do not bark like vicious dogs, deafening with disorderly clamour the ears of those who would be saved, ye

unrighteous and God-haters, and perverting the way of salvation to unbelief. How shall you be able to obtain pardon, who scorn him who is sent to speak to you of the Divinity of God? And this you do towards a man whom you ought, at any rate, to have received on account of his good-will towards you, even though what he uttered were not true.'

"Whilst I spake these words and others to the same effect, there was a great excitement among the crowd; and some, pitying Barnabas, sympathised with me; but others, being senseless, terribly gnashed their teeth against me. But as the evening had already come, I took Barnabas by the hand, and by force conducted him against his will to my lodging, and constrained him to remain there, lest some one might lay hands on him. And after he had spent several days with me, and instructed me in the true doctrine, as well as he could in so short a time, he said that he should hasten into Judæa for the observance of the festival, and also because he wished for the future to consort with those of his own nation."

Barnabas departs from Alexandria: Clement following soon after, arrives at Cæsarea Stratonis, where he again meets Barnabas, who introduces him to S. Peter.*

The following is a summary of the critical remarks which Dr. Smith gives in his Introductory Notice to the *Recognitions*.† The book is, he says, a kind of philosophical and theological romance. The writer of the work seems to have had no intention of presenting his statements as facts; but, choosing the disciples of Christ and their followers as his principal characters, he has put into their mouths the most important of his beliefs, and woven the whole together by a thread of fictitious narrative. The *Recognitions* is one of a series; the other members of which that have come down to us are the Clementine *Homilies* and two *Epitomes*. The authorship, the date, and the doctrinal character of these books have been subjects of keen discussion in modern times. Especial prominence has been given to them by the Tübingen school. Hilgenfeld says:

"There is scarcely a single writing which is of so great importance for the history of Christianity in its first stage, and which has already given such brilliant disclosures at the hands of the most renowned critics in regard to the earliest history of the Christian Church, as the writings ascribed to the Roman Clement—the *Recognitions* and *Homilies*."

Some maintain that these are both the productions of the same author, and that the one is a later and altered edition of the other; and they find some confirmation of this in the Preface of Rufinus. Others think that both books are expansions of another work which formed the basis. And others maintain that the one

* Migne, *ib.* p. 57 *sq.*   † Ante-Nicene Christian Library, Edinburgh, 1868.

book is a *rifacimento* of the other by a different hand. No conclusion has been reached in regard to the author. Some have believed that in part, or in substance at least, it is a genuine work of Clement. Whiston maintained that it was written by some of his hearers and compilers.

Various opinions exist as to the date of the book. It has been attributed to the 1st, 2nd, 3rd, and 4th centuries. If we were to base our arguments on the work as it stands, the date assigned would be somewhere in the first half of the 3rd century. A passage from the *Recognitions* is quoted by Origen in his *Commentary on Genesis*, written in 231, and mention is made in the work of the extension of the Roman franchise to all nations under the dominion of Rome, an event which took place in the reign of Caracalla, A.D. 211.

Those who believe the work to be made up of various documents assign various dates to these documents. Hilgenfeld, for instance, believes that the $Κήρυγμα\ Πέτρου$ was written before the time of Trajan, and the *Travels of Peter* about the time of his reign. Nothing is known of the place in which the *Recognitions* was written. Some (as Schliemann) have supposed Rome, some Asia Minor. The Greek of the *Recognitions* is lost. The work has come down to us in the form of a translation by Rufinus of Aquileia. In his letter to Bishop Gaudentius, Rufinus states that he has omitted some portions difficult of comprehension.

Having thus given the opinions of learned Protestants, we will now say a word as to what is most generally held amongst Catholics with regard to these works.

Learned Catholic critics admit universally that the "Clementines," including the *Homilies*, the *Recognitions*, and the *Epistle to James*, are apocryphal. The *Homilies* and the *Recognitions* are substantially one and the same work, which is a historico-doctrinal romance; in the *Recognitions* the history plays the chief part, in the *Homilies* the development of doctrine. [The doctrine in the *Homilies*, especially as we have them now, is Ebionistic and Gnostic: a rendering of Christianity corrupted by Ebionism and Gnosticism, though this is less apparent in the *Recognitions*. It is disputed which was written first, the *Homilies* or the *Recognitions*. The *Epistle to James* is a letter accompanying the apocryphal work, with the object of giving weight and authority to the doctrine contained, by attributing it to S. Peter and to S. Clement. The more prevalent opinion is that these writings were composed in the latter part of the 2nd century (160-170), in Syria. It is a question on which Catholic critics appear to be not agreed, whether these writings were originally orthodox, and afterwards interpolated and falsified by heretics: it is, however, sufficiently clear that they form a historical romance, intended to set forth religious teaching under the patronage of S. Peter and S. Clement. The general opinion is that the author wished to deceive in regard to the facts and wonderful occurrences he narrates. Still, however, it may be a matter of question whether he did not write his works simply as a religious romance for the edification of the faithful.

In the judgment of the learned, these apocryphal writings contain a solid proof and confirmation of the truth of S. Peter's Roman Episcopate: since the author would certainly have taken well-known and universally admitted facts as the groundwork of his historical romance. Such was the fact of S. Peter's having been Bishop of Rome: that S. Clement likewise had been Bishop of Rome; that he was looked upon as a disciple of S. Peter, and considered the most renowned amongst that Apostle's first successors. On these facts of history the author was able to form and develop his romance. Supposing that he wished his readers to believe that all the extraordinary details and marvellous incidents of his narrative were of actual occurrence, and to accept the doctrine it contains, it was necessary for him to base their *tout ensemble* on facts of real history that were well-known and universally admitted, in order to give an air of probability to the rest with plausible effect. But if, on the contrary, his simple intention was to publish a religious historical romance which should be recognised as such—on this supposition also—he would naturally take certain well-known facts of history as his groundwork; much the same as the late Cardinal Wiseman did in his *Fabiola*.

The *Epistle to James* is, as we have said, a letter of credit accompanying the work in form of a *Proëmium*.

The notion that the persuasion of S. Peter's Roman Episcopate had its origin in these "Clementines" is utterly unreasonable and absurd: since this persuasion, already settled and fixed, as we find it to be from the Catalogue of S. Irenæus, who had been at Rome towards the close of the 2nd century, cannot be explained in this way. Besides, Hegesippus, too, before this had been in Rome, about the middle of the 2nd century, and had there drawn out his διαδόχη, or succession in order of the Roman Bishops. To set down the narrative of the "Clementines" as the source whence came the belief that S. Peter was Bishop of Rome, may be looked on as a sort of ὕστερον-πρότερον, just as though after a lapse of centuries some one should give out that the belief that S. Agnes and S. Cecilia had been Virgins in Rome took its rise in the historical romance of *Fabiola* by Cardinal Wiseman.

Before taking leave of the "Clementines," we venture to record our own thought—gathered from internal evidence in their cursory perusal—that these writings are by more than one hand. We hardly remember to have read anything that has struck us as more charming and true to life, from its natural freshness and simplicity, than the account the author gives in the opening chapters of the *Recognitions* and *Homilies* from which we have quoted, of the questionings of his soul as a youthful Pagan in Rome, of the first announcement of the Gospel in that City, and of his meeting with Barnabas at Alexandria. There is no Gnostic or Ebionistic mysticism here. All is pellucid and persuasively real. And, unless otherwise obliged by sound and learned criticism, we would fain believe that these first chapters, if not authentic as written by S. Clement, are at least substantially true as resulting from personal experience, and not, at any rate, from the same pen as the rest of the work, which to us seems darksome, tedious, and dreary indeed. In any case, whether these passages be deemed genuine or not, we can imagine nothing more like to the probably real truth, than the account they give of the first preaching of the Faith in Rome by some Christian convert from the East.

CHAPTER XVII

STATEMENTS AND VIEWS OF ANGLICAN AUTHORS.

We now propose to record opinions and statements of certain learned Anglican authors on some of those matters that have been the subject of our discussion in previous Chapters. We think it will be of interest to know what Anglicans here hold in common with Catholics, and how far some of them are prepared to go in acknowledging the Roman Episcopate of S. Peter. Amongst older authors we have chosen especially Cave and Pearson, because they have written *ex professo* on this question—so far as we know—with more erudition than others, and are generally regarded by Anglicans as authorities of weight.

Cave has treated expressly of the succession of the first Bishops of the Apostolical Churches; and Pearson has left learned dissertations on their succession in the See of Rome. The former, we shall see, accepts as facts beyond dispute that S. Peter was the first Bishop of Antioch, and S. Mark of Alexandria: facts, it will be remembered, that supplied a premiss for our argument drawn from Eusebius,[*] of which the plain conclusion was, that whenever that historian reckons Linus and his successors in numerical order as Bishops of Rome *after Peter*, he thereby implicitly declares that Peter was himself, in a true and proper sense, the first Bishop of the See, and that from him those who followed derived their succession. Pearson, indeed, sets himself to prove this identical proposition directly and formally by clear and ample patristic evidence; and, so far, on his part, there is nothing wanting to his demonstration of the very thesis that forms the main subject of our whole work.

But it is well observable, that, however convincing are the arguments, and complete the testimonies, which Pearson and Cave bring to bear against the ultra-Protestant Lutheran School, and however earnest their protests against the unhistorical novelties of Spanheim and his followers, yet, when they come face to face with the very fact they have proved, they at once start back, as

---

[*] See Ch. xv. of this work.

though afraid lest their conclusion should be accepted too seriously, and take good pains to pare it down and explain it away, to obscure, confuse, and entangle it with all sorts of difficulties on collateral issues, thereby to minimise its consequences; or they try to make what they call the abuses of the Papal system obliterate its significance.

This, of course, is a necessity for all Church-of-England historians and divines who treat of such questions at all, forced upon them by their non-Catholic position and their advocacy of Anglicanism; and we could not expect anything else at their hands. A *via media* compromise, such as Anglicanism, must needs shrink from the searching light of anything very positive and sharply defined. Itself a medley purposely formed with a view to comprehension, it deals with generalities, can live and thrive only on indefiniteness, and must ever feed on what is more or less misty and vague. It has a peculiar method of its own, which is to admit into its doctrinal circle a large number of half-way truths, on the understanding that none of them are to be very clearly defined, or to be pushed too far; whilst all of them are held liable to whatever qualification, whether by protest or partial denial, the exigencies of the Anglican position may at any time require. Anglicanism is plausible, and can obtain credit only on the hypothesis that no fixed and definite principle is discoverable in antiquity, as forming the basis of the ecclesiastical and hierarchical polity and bond of visible unity in the primitive Church; but that, on the contrary, everything relating to the Church's origin, in all matters at any rate of the highest moment, is very confused and obscure, a subject of uncertainty, one at the most of only more or less probability. And, no doubt, could it be once established that there was no one definite principle of Divine institution essentially underlying, at its origin, the whole constitution of the Apostolic Church, it would thence naturally follow that the various religious organisations at present developed over the face of Christendom, however mutually divergent in principles, have each and all an equal right to urge their several dubious claims to the heirship of, or at least to a divided heritage in, the primitive Church of Christ. Why, then, should not the "Church of England" use its right, and take its chance amongst the rest of being reckoned the best claimant, and of representing the Church of the Apostles?

Hence we can at once perceive how inconvenient and damaging to the advocacy of Anglicanism must be the historical fact, witnessed to by antiquity, that S. Peter was the first Bishop of

Rome; especially when this fact, as interpreted by the clear and definite statement of Catholic tradition, is understood to mean that the Popes, through legitimate succession, inherit by Divine right whatever prerogatives S. Peter as first Bishop of that See possessed. No one who knows history at all can safely deny—what, indeed, all the world is persuaded of—that from primitive days the several ages of Christendom have borne continuous witness that the Roman Episcopate of Peter has been held to be the historical embodiment or crystallisation of the Divine word: *Tu es Petrus*, &c., or can doubt that this same traditional belief has found its significant expression in the saying of S. Augustine, which has passed into a proverb: *Ubi Petrus, ibi Ecclesia*. Consequently S. Peter's Roman Episcopate, regarded in this light, is evidently not so much a historical fact of the past as a moral fact present in every age, and resolvable into a concrete principle of life and action, which was divinely engrafted into the original constitution of the Christian Church, a principle that must ever essentially inhere to it, grow up with its growth, and energise its development so long as that Church shall endure. Moreover, this same principle will prove a sure criterion and crucial test, whereby in all time the one true Apostolic Church founded by Christ may be discerned from all its counterfeits. A defender of Anglicanism, therefore, has no option: he is bound either to contest and deny the actuality of a fact thus universally interpreted into a definite and essential principle, which by its incisiveness cuts at the very root of his system; or, at least, he must blunt its edge, by explaining it away, and minimising its significance. Pearson and Cave have eschewed the former, to take the latter line of defence. They show, on the whole, much greater fairness and moderation than most Anglican writers; and were we to judge by three Articles on the Petrine Claims which appeared a few years since, we might well doubt whether any of the modern High Church School would go so far as these two of their old divines in the Catholic direction, and endorse all the admissions and clear positive statements made by them.

The writer of the Articles referred to seems to rejoice exceedingly, as one that findeth great spoils, over the various well-known difficulties and divergencies to be found in the early authors during the first five centuries, as to the place and succession of the first Bishops of Rome. Scrupulous critic and purist as at times he loves to appear, it matters not now what authorities he cites for any of "the eleven, or rather, twelve rival views," ingeniously strung together, which he parades as though all of equal currency. Fathers, historians, catalogues, apocryphal and heretical writers, here all alike serve his turn. His object appears to be to set Christian antiquity at loggerheads, and evidently to his own mind he has achieved a success. By exaggerating perplexed questions of minor importance, accentuating differences on side issues, some of them easily reconcilable, and by giving, in some places, a sense of his own, plainly contrary to the author's meaning, he has succeeded fairly well in throwing dust in the air, and raising a din of discordant voices, thereby to confuse and obscure the one principal point, on which all the divergent accounts are agreed, namely, that S. Peter was the first Bishop of Rome and from him is derived the succession in that See.

It may perhaps serve the purpose of certain Protestant divines in their contention against Rome to make out primitive antiquity to be a disorderly chaos, and to represent its history and traditions as a congeries of mutually conflicting statements and uncertain views. But thoughtful persons will see that controversialists of this stamp are laying down principles, and pursuing a line of argument which has no other logical issue than universal scepticism as to all objective truth, whether historical or religious. It seems to us that perhaps no writings are more calculated to sap all the foundations of rational and theological faith than some that have emanated from the school of religionists of which the Reviewer is a representative type. They teem with wild and arbitrary eclecticism, negation of all fixed principle and definite standard of truth, heedless assumptions, lawlessness, irreverent disregard, nay contempt, of authority, gross yet most artful misrepresentation, wholesale vituperation, joined to a pose of supercilious peremptoriness and overweening self-assertion that would be only ridiculous, were it not for the saddening thought of the many good simple souls that are made its dupes.

There are, thank God, many Anglicans of a very different spirit, of whom Cardinal Newman speaks, in a well-remembered passage, where he describes, from his own personal experience, the tranquil joy and satisfaction which a convert from Protestantism derives from the certainty that he is at length in true fellowship with the ancient Saints and Fathers of the Church; in feeling that Cyprian and Augustine and Jerome and Chrysostom are now his own; that he belongs to them and they to him, that his part and lot are henceforth with them. But we will give the illustrious convert's own words.

"I know the joy it would give those conscientious men, of whom I am speaking, to be one with ourselves. I know how their hearts spring up with a spontaneous transport at the very thought of union; and what yearning is theirs after that great privilege, which they have not, communion with the See of Peter, and its present, past, and future. I conjecture it by what I used to feel myself, while yet in the Anglican Church. I recollect well what an outcast I seemed to myself, when I took down from the shelves of my library the volumes of S. Athanasius or S. Basil, and set myself to study them; and how, on the contrary, when at length I was brought into Catholicism, I kissed them with delight, with a feeling that in them I had more than all that I had lost, and, as though I were directly addressing the glorious Saints, who bequeathed them to the Church, I said to the inanimate pages: 'You are now mine, and I am now yours, beyond any mistake.' Such, I conceive, would be the joy of the persons I speak of, if they could wake up one morning and find themselves possessed by right of Catholic traditions and hopes, without violence to their own sense of duty." *

A unitive sense, such as is here described, of Catholic kinship and of joint-property in all that appertains to our holy Mother the Church, whether in her early or later days, would naturally dispose a true and genuine son to seek to smooth, explain, and conciliate any difficulties and discrepancies that might occur in Christian writers of primitive times, certainly not to exaggerate and strive to render them irreconcilable.

This thought was very forcibly brought home to us after reading the Articles referred to on the Petrine Claims, where the writer sets all the Fathers and Saints by the ears, and engages them in combat one against the other, apparently with the view of persuading his readers that nothing can be gained from their Babel of strife, and that the voice of his own self-assertion is alone worth listening to. The spirit that breathes through the pages is anything but that of one who holds the Fathers and Saints of old to be his own kith and kin, fellow-citizens, and of one household of faith with himself: it is rather the spirit of one who regards them only as strangers and foreigners in whose interests and repute he has but an indifferent concern.

We have adverted to these Articles because they are reported to be the most important production of modern Anglican theological literature on the Petrine Claims. Be it so: alas, for the degeneracy of Anglicanism since the days of Bull, Pearson, and Cave!

After this digression we gladly return to matter of weightier import, the positive statements of Cave and Pearson.

* *A Letter to the Rev. E. B. Pusey, D.D., on his Recent Eirenicon;* 1886, pp. 5, 6.

CAVE.

Cave, in his *Lives of the Apostles*,* gives what is entitled his "*Diptycha Apostolica*, or an enumeration of the Apostles, and their successors in the five great Apostolic Churches," in this order: Antioch, Rome, Jerusalem, Byzantium, Alexandria. From it, and his *Historia Literaria* we make the following extracts:

"ANTIOCH.—The succession of its Bishops till the time of Constantine was as follows: (1) S. Peter the Apostle, who governed this Church at least seven years. (2) Evodius, who sat twenty-three years. In his time the disciples were first called Christians at Antioch. (3) Ignatius. . . ."

With regard to S. Peter at Antioch, he says:

"That S. Peter founded a Church at Antioch Eusebius expressly tells us;† and by others‡ it is said that he himself was the first Bishop of this See. Sure I am that S. Chrysostom§ reckons it as one of the greatest honours of that city that S. Peter staid so long there, and that the Bishops of it succeeded him in that See. The care and presidency of this Church he had between six and seven years. Not that he staid there all that time, but that having ordered and disposed things to the best advantage, he returned to other affairs and exigencies of the Church."

"ROME.—The foundation of this Church is, with just probabilities of reason, by many of the Fathers equally attributed to Peter and Paul, the one as Apostle of the Circumcision, preaching to the Jews, while the other, probably as the Apostle of the Uncircumcision, preached to the Gentiles. Its bishops succeeded in this order: (1) S. Peter and S. Paul, who both suffered martyrdom under Nero. (2) Linus. . . . (3) Cletus, or Anacletus, or Anencletus. . . ."‖

Cave holds that S. Peter went to Rome first—

"About A.D. 63, under the reign of Nero; that he organised the faithful whom he found there; and after settling and augmenting the Church, he soon annobled it with his blood, being martyred A.D. 64, about the beginning of Nero's persecution, and in the tenth year of his reign."¶

For this he invokes the testimony of Lactantius and Origen.

"That Peter was at Rome," says Cave, "and held the See there for some time (*sedemque in ea aliquamdiu tenuisse*), we fearlessly affirm with the whole multitude of the ancients. We give witnesses above all exception, derived from most remote antiquity—viz., Ignatius, Bishop of Antioch, disciple of S. Peter, certainly his successor in the See of Antioch; in his Epistle to the Romans; Papias of Hierapolis, a hearer of S. John the Evangelist;**

---

* Vol. ii. ed. by the Rev. H. Stebbing, 1834. Hatchard.
† *Chron. ad Ann. Christi.* 43. ‡ *Hieron. Comment. in 2 ad Galat.*
§ *Encom. S. Ign. Mart.* p. 503, tom. i. ‖ Cave, *Ibid.* p. 187. sq.
¶ *Scriptorum Ecclesiastic. Historia Literaria*, vol. i. *Sæculum Apostolicum*: S. PETRUS.
** *Ap. Euseb.* ii. 15.

Irenæus of Lyons, a man of Apostolic times, disciple of S. Polycarp;[*] Dionysius of Corinth;[†] Clement of Alexandria;[‡] Tertullian;[§] Caius, a Roman presbyter, an ecclesiastic of great name;[||] Origen.[¶] We have before, in another work, vindicated the testimonies of all these against the objections of Spanheim."

He cites also Cyprian, Arnobius, Lactantius, Eusebius, Athanasius, Epiphanius, Ambrose, Optatus, Jerome, and Augustine, and says there are many others whom he must needs omit. He thus concludes:

"After, then, so many venerable names, such illustrious records of primitive antiquity, who is there that will call in question a matter so clearly, so constantly handed down? Most assuredly, if so great a cloud of witnesses, so concordant a judgment of antiquity, is something to be carped at according to everyone's individual caprice, it will be all over entirely with any records of the first centuries, and no one will be able to know anything beyond his own age.[**] But though we readily allow, with the body of antiquity, that Peter was at Rome, and laid the foundation of the Roman Church, we persist in denying that he held that See for twenty-five years. This is opposed to the history of the Apostles—opposed to the Epistles of S. Paul, to the course of S. Peter's whole life—opposed by a thousand difficulties to be found in antiquity . . . opposed, in fine, to the testimonies of ancient authors, especially of Origen and Lactantius, who assert that Peter at length, towards the end of his life, and when Nero was already reigning, came to Rome, and made that city glorious by his martyrdom.[††]

"It may not without reason be doubted whether, properly speaking, Peter should be called Bishop of Rome. That he can be called Bishop of Rome in a loose sense, from his having laid the foundation of that Church and rendered it illustrious by his martyrdom, all, I think, will agree with me in asserting, both ancients and moderns. But that he was attached to the Roman See as its proper Bishop is hardly compatible with the nature of the apostolic office, and is not taught us by the records of primitive antiquity."

He then quotes Irenæus, *Adv. Hæres.* l. iii., *Ap. Euseb.* v. 6, iii. 2; and appeals for his plea, that to S. Paul are ascribed like preroga-

---

[*] *Adv. Hær.* iii. 1, 3.   [†] *Ap. Euseb.* ii. 25.   [‡] *Ibid.* ii. 15.
[§] *De Præsc.* c. xxxvi.; *De Bapt.* c. iv.; *Scorpiac. cap. ult.*
[||] *Ap. Euseb.* ii. 25.   [¶] *Ibid.* iii. 1; vi. 14.
[**] Chamier, whose words are quoted with approval by Cave, says: "All the Fathers, with great unanimity, have asserted that Peter did go to Rome, and that he did govern that Church." Grotius says: "The ancients understand 'Babylon' of Rome, where that Peter was, no true Christian will doubt." Archbishop Bramhall also says: "That S. Peter had a fixed chair at Antioch, and after that at Rome, is what no man who giveth any credit to the ancient Fathers and Councils and historiographers of the Church can either deny or will doubt." (Works, ed. Oxon. p. 629).—See Fr. Ryder's *Catholic Controversy*, p. 48.
[††] S. Petr. Alex. *Epist. Canon.* c. ix.

tives with S. Peter as regards Rome, to Epiphanius, *Adv. Carpocrat. Hæres.* xxvii. n. 5.

Cave, moreover, does his utmost to overthrow the chronological system of Emmanuel Schelstratius, Librarian of the Vatican, in his *Opus Chronologicum* (Romæ, 1692), which system he had adopted from other authors. This dates the Birth of our Lord four years before the present Vulgar Era, giving room for the twelve years, according to the tradition of Apollonius mentioned by Eusebius,[*] to elapse before the Apostles left Jerusalem, and before the second year of Claudius.

In his *Lives of the Apostles*[†] he gives the account of S. Peter's contest at Rome with Simon Magus, and seems to receive it as worthy of credit.

He holds that the Babylon of 1 *Pet.* v. 13 was in Parthia.

JERUSALEM.—" The Church of Jerusalem may in some sense be said to have been founded by our Lord Himself. . . . The Bishops of it were as followeth: I. S. James the Less, the brother of our Lord, by Him, say some, immediately constituted Bishop, but as others, more probably, by the Apostles. . . . II. Symeon, the son of Cleophas. . . ."

Cave maintains stoutly that S. James, the first Bishop of Jerusalem, was S. James the Apostle, recorded by the Evangelists as the son of Alphæus. On this point he says:

"Once, indeed, Eusebius[‡] makes our S. James one of the seventy; though elsewhere, quoting a place of Clement of Alexandria, he numbers him with the Chief of the Apostles, and expressly distinguishes him from the seventy disciples.[§] Nay, S. Jerome, though, when representing the opinions of others, he styles him the thirteenth Apostle,[||] yet elsewhere,[¶] when speaking his own sense, sufficiently proves there were but two, James the son of Zebedee, and the other the son of Alphæus; the one surnamed the Greater, the other the Less. Besides, the main support of the other opinion is built upon the authority of Clemens' *Recognitions*, a book in doubtful cases of no esteem and value."[**]

BYZANTIUM.—" That this Church was first founded by S. Andrew we have showed in his life. The succession of its Bishops as followeth: I. S. Andrew the Apostle. He was crucified at Patræ in Achaia. II. Stachys. III. Onesimus." (*Lives*, etc., vol. i.)

In proof that S. Andrew was founder and first Bishop of the Church at Byzantium, Cave gives for his only authorities, Nice-

---

[*] *H. E.* v. 18.
[†] Vol. i. pp. 140-144.
[‡] *H. E.* i. 12.
[§] *Ibid.* ii. 1.
[||] *Comment. in Isa.* xvii. 6, p. 60, tom. v.
[¶] *Adv. Heliod.* tom. ii. p. 10.
[**] *Ibid.* vol. ii. p. 160.

phorus Callistus,* and Nicephorus, Patriarch of Constantinople, A.D. 806.†

In Cave's *Historia Literaria* ‡ we read as follows:

"Nicephorus Callistus, apparently a monk in the monastery of S. Sophia (*circ.* 1333 A.D.), composed his history from the works of the ecclesiastical historians, Eusebius, Socrates, Sozomen, Theodoret, Evagrius, and others. Though written in convenient order and in a fair style for that age, he so spoilt it by intermixing almost everywhere stories which are so much 'rot and rubbish' (*fabulis putidissimis et quisquiliis*), that, in the judgment of Casaubon, it is of no more value than coltsfoot leaves (*non pluris quam folia fanfari facienda sit*)."

Of the Patriarch Nicephorus Cave only says that, because he was himself Bishop of Constantinople,

"He may be presumed to have known his predecessors in that See."

We do not here inquire whether, or how far, the sweeping criticism passed by Casaubon, and endorsed by Cave, on the *Ecclesiastical History* of Nicephorus is deserved. We can, however, well imagine what would be said of any Catholic author who should support some statement on an important point of primitive Christianity by such authority as Cave here adduces—a historical work of the fourteenth century, forsooth, in his own critical *Historia Literaria*, pronounced to be discreditable and worthless; and the single testimony of a bishop in the ninth century on a matter touching the dignity of his own See. Why, then, is not the constant attestation of so many Bishops of Rome from the earliest ages of Christianity until the present time, as to S. Peter's Roman Episcopate, at once believed, since they, too, "may be presumed to have known their predecessors in that See"? The reason is not far to seek. Protestants have no special difficulty in accepting as true whatever does not concern Rome; they have a special facility for crediting whatever to their minds seems to make at all against Rome; but they have the greatest repugnance to believe, and will combat to the bitter end, anything that they conceive makes for Rome.

We have not had an opportunity of consulting the passages either of the one or the other Nicephorus, referred to by Cave, in the original Greek. But if we are to judge from the version of them given by Baronius in his *Annals*, A.D. 44, xxxi., these

---

* *Hist. Eccles.* l. ii. c. 39; l. v. c. 6.
† *Chronographia*, a Scal. edit. p. 309.
‡ Appendix, p. 33, vol. ii. Edit. 1778.

authors do not say at all that S. Andrew was Bishop of Byzantium, but that he preached there, and appointed Stachys its bishop, as well as some other bishops in the neighbouring places. In which case, Cave's statement that S. Andrew was the first Bishop of Byzantium is simply gratuitous, and destitute of all authority.

Baronius, in opposition to the statement of the two Greek authors, asserts that it was S. Peter, and not S. Andrew, who gave to Byzantium, and other places of the same province, their first bishops. In proof of this Baronius cites the authority of Pope Agapetus in his letter to Peter, Bishop of Jerusalem, written A.D. 536, concerning Mennas, whom he had himself ordained Patriarch of Constantinople in the place of Anthimus, who, convicted of heresy, had been deposed and excommunicated. This letter was formally read out in the Fifth Ecumenical Council of Constantinople, A.D. 553. In it Agapetus says that Mennas had the singular honour of being the first bishop whom the Oriental Church had received, ordained by the hands of the Bishop of Rome since the days of S. Peter; and that a circumstance of so great significance as this would probably tend to the exaltation of Mennas, and to the subversion of his enemies by his resemblance, so far, to those bishops whom the election of the Prince of the Apostles had formally ordained for those parts. Baronius, after quoting the words of Agapetus, continues:

"We consider his authority, especially when cited in a General Council, to be of greater weight than that of the more modern Greeks, whether the Patriarch Nicephorus or others, who say that these Churches were founded by the Apostle S. Andrew, and from him received their bishops, as is reported by the more modern Greeks in the *Menologium*, by Nicephorus, the Bishop of Constantinople in his *Chronicle*, and by Nicephorus Callistus in his *History*. It is certain, moreover, that Heraclea, not Byzantium, was the See first founded of that province. And hence Pope Gelasius, when opposing Acacius, says to the Bishops of Dardania: 'Bishop of what See? presiding over what metropolitan city? Is it not the Diocese of Heraclea?' &c."*

On the same point Alban Butler says:

"We meet with no traces in antiquity that S. Andrew planted the faith in Thrace, and particularly at Byzantium."†

It is generally agreed that he suffered martyrdom at Patræ in Achaia. From this some have supposed that he was Bishop of Patræ, but this is held to be quite improbable by learned critics.

Milman—who had no love for hierarchical sacerdotalism in

* *Annals*, A.D. 44, xii. † *Lives of the Saints*: S. ANDREW, Nov. 30.

any shape, and could sneer at it by turns all round, whether Roman, Oriental, or Anglican—was, therefore, perhaps better able to speak impartially on the point, as one of simple history. He writes as follows:

"Constantinople was but a new city, and had no pretensions to venerable or Apostolic origin. It had attained, indeed, to the dignity of a patriarchate, but only by the decree of a recent Council; in other respects it owed all its eminence to being the prelacy of New Rome, of the seat of empire."*

ALEXANDRIA.—" The foundations of this Church," writes Cave, " were laid, and a great part of its superstructure raised, by S. Mark, who, though not strictly and properly an Apostle, yet being an Apostle at large, and immediately commissioned by S. Peter, it justly obtained the position of an Apostolical Church. Its bishops and governors are thus recorded: (1) S. Mark the Evangelist . . . (2) Anianus. . . ." (*Lives*, etc., vol. i.)

PEARSON.

We will now give some extracts, or rather a brief summary, of the Protestant Bishop Pearson's opinions, in his posthumous works, on the points of which we have been treating.

Pearson holds as most probable that S. James, the first Bishop of Jerusalem, was identical with the Apostle S. James, the son of Alphæus, and thus concludes:

"In any case, whether this James the Just, brother of our Lord, was one of the Apostles, viz., James the son of Alphæus, as is most probable, or related to Christ, but not one of the Twelve, it is handed down, with full consent of all, that he was made Bishop of the Church at Jerusalem by the Apostles, or by our Lord Himself. And what is said of him in the *Acts* clearly shows that he exercised a singular authority in matters relating to that Church among the Apostles, as we shall show in the proper place."†

In his first *Dissertation* on the succession of the first Bishops of Rome he thus writes:

"For although in this age a dissertation treating of this Apostolical succession (whether, namely, the first Bishop of Rome had some one of the Apostles as author and predecessor) may be called a question, yet in the primitive Church it was never looked upon as a question, but as a real and indubitable truth."‡

Then, in order to prove (1) that Peter and Paul founded the Church of Rome, he cites Irenæus,§ Epiphanius,|| Eusebius.¶

---

* *History of Latin Christianity;* third edition, 1872, vol. i. pp. 108-9.
† Pearson's *Minor Theological Works*, edited by Churton; Oxford, 1844. Vol. i. p. 348 *seq.*
‡ *Ibid.* vol. ii. c. vi. p. 323. § L. iii. c. iii. || *Hær.* xxvii.
¶ iii. 21; iv. 1.

To prove (2) that they were not merely founders, but Bishops of Rome, he quotes the words of Epiphanius. And (3) to prove that the Bishops of Rome derived their succession from S. Peter alone, he appeals to Caius as being a Greek, and to the Latin Fathers generally, v.g., Tertullian,* Cyprian,† Pope Stephen,‡ the Author of the most ancient Catalogue, *in proemio*, who says : " After the Ascension of Christ, the most blessed Peter undertook the Episcopate ; " Optatus, § S. Jerome, in his Catalogue and elsewhere ; Sulpitius ; ‖ *Auctor Quæstionum utriusque Testamenti* ; ¶ S. Augustine.**

Pearson allows that S. Peter's having been in Rome (by which he evidently means the whole fact of his Roman Episcopate) cannot be proved, nor can, on the other hand, be disproved, from Scripture. And this admission, he says, S. Jerome appears to make in his *Commentary on the Galatians*, ch. ii., where that Father writes:

" We believe Peter to have been the first Bishop of the Church of Antioch, and was thence translated to Rome : though Luke has entirely passed over this fact."

"And no wonder," remarks Pearson, "when Luke nowhere makes mention of Titus, the companion of S. Paul, of whom that Apostle himself so often speaks."

(4) That S. Peter was at Rome, Pearson proves from S. Ignatius, *Ad Romanos;* Papias ; the very ancient author of *The Preaching of Peter ;* Dionysius of Corinth, Irenæus, Caius, Clement of Alexandria, Tertullian, Origen, Cyprian, Lactantius, Eusebius, Athanasius, Epiphanius, Julian the Apostate, Augustine, Palladius. He adds :

" Since it has been handed down from almost the beginning that S. Peter preached the Gospel in Rome, and there suffered martyrdom, and since no one has ever affirmed;that either Peter or Paul was crowned with martyrdom elsewhere, I think, with full security, faith may be given to this account. For who would believe that so great an Apostle could have died in such obscurity, as that no one ever recorded the place of his death ? Who could believe that, whilst other countries have claimed for themselves their Apostle, no city, no country, no Church should have said that it had been glorified by the blood of Peter ? And since Christ Himself, with so great asseveration, spoke those words: 'Amen, amen, I say to thee . . . when thou shalt be old, thou shall stretch forth thy hands, and another shall gird thee, and lead thee whither thou wouldst not:'†† and since S. John the Apostle wrote long

---

* *De Præscriptione*, cap. 32.   † *Ep.* 55.   ‡ *Epist. Firmilian.*
§ ii. 3, and i. 10.   ‖ *De Imperio Neronis, Hist. Sac.* ii. 28.
¶ *Cap.* 110.   ** *Ep.* 145 *ad Generosum.*   †† *John*, xxi. 18.

after Peter's death that Christ signified in those words ποίῳ θανάτῳ: *i.e.*, by what sort of death he was to glorify God—who will ever suppose that none of the Christians knew by what death he suffered, but that, on the contrary, all were ignorant how he glorified God, or, at any rate, that God in His providence was unwilling that this should be known to posterity? And yet there have not been wanting learned men who have expressly denied that Peter was ever at Rome."*

According to Pearson, the Babylon in S. Peter's first Epistle was in Egypt.

We have only here to remark that the patristic evidence adduced by Pearson is one of the best apologies for the main Petrine fact of which we treat that can be anywhere found.

We refrain from touching on all the various points wherein Cave shows his Protestant bias—as well as certain conclusions and interpretations of his from which we dissent. Pearson, too, has much of this sort in his *Dissertations* which we do not reproduce. Cave lays great stress on the maintenance of the commonly received date of our Lord's birth and death against Schelstratius, in order thereby to hamper with difficulties the Catholic tradition of S. Peter's twenty-five years' Episcopate at Rome. Both he and Pearson, whilst differing amongst themselves as to where S. Peter's Babylon was, maintain stoutly that, at any rate, it was not Rome. We shall, in the next chapter, quote some passages which show that these two positions are now abandoned by learned Anglicans of the present day.

NEALE.

We give in this place some extracts from a modern Anglican writer, the late Rev. John Mason Neale, because they bear more immediately on the subject of this Chapter.

"Very shortly after this (*Acts*, xi. 19) S. Peter founded the See of Antioch, and on leaving it for Rome ordained S. Euodius his first successor, who was himself followed by the glorious martyr S. Ignatius." †

"It is the constant and unvarying tradition of both the East and the West, that S. Mark the Evangelist was the founder of the Church of Alexandria. Thus it will appear that the Gospel had already been proclaimed in more than one province of Egypt when S. Mark arrived at Alexandria. Yet this circumstance by no means forbids us to regard him as the founder of that Church, nor deprives the city of a title in which it gloried, The Evangelical See. There were many Christians both at Antioch and at Rome

---

* Pearson's *Minor Theological Works*, vol. iii. p. 341.
† Neale's *Eastern Church*, vol. i. p. 128; ed. 1850.

before S. Peter set foot in either place, yet antiquity always considered him as the founder of the Churches in each." *

"S. Peter, about the year 37, appears to have sent S. Mark into Egypt, and it would seem that he entered Alexandria in, or towards, the year 40."

Neale here follows Sollerius, whose hypothesis seems, he says, the only method of reconciling Eusebius with himself. In his *Chronicon* Eusebius states, under the second year of Claudius (*i.e.*, A.D. 42 or 43): "Mark the Evangelist preaches Christ in Egypt and at Alexandria." This, says Neale, implies that he had been there some time previously; whereas, in *H. E.* ii. 15, 16, Eusebius seems to place the mission of S. Mark after the writing of his Gospel. The *Chronicon Alexandrinum*, Anastasius, and George Syncellus are agreed in placing this event A.D. 40. A double mission, then, writes Neale, the one from Jerusalem, the other from Rome, explains the apparent contradiction:

"Having preached the Gospel," continues Neale, "with great success . . . S. Mark returned for a season to Jerusalem. From Palestine he accompanied S. Peter to Rome. It was here that, under the direction to the Apostle, he wrote his Gospel, whether, as some will have it, in Latin, or, as it seems more probable, in Greek. . . . We find him mentioned in the First Epistle of S. Peter under the affectionate title of 'Marcus, my son': but this is the only certain information that we possess with respect to the Evangelist while residing in Rome. It was apparently towards the year 49 that S. Mark returned to Egypt; and there, till the time of his decease, he laboured with great success."

Neale says the date of S. Mark's martyrdom is a question of almost insuperable difficulty. He prefers that of April 25th, 62, which agrees with Euseb. *H. E.* ii. 24; S. Jerome (*De Script. Eccl.*), and the common Martyrologies.

He holds with Sollerius, the Bollandist, that the Evangelist S. Mark was not identical with Mark the nephew of S. Barnabas.†

---

* Neale's *Eastern Church*, p. 5.   † *Ibid.* pp. 3, 67.

CHAPTER XVIII.

STATEMENTS AND VIEWS OF ANGLICAN WRITERS—
CONTINUED.

IN this Chapter we give some extracts from Anglican writers of the present day, which will serve to bring out two points especially: (1) That, whereas Protestants, almost without exception, were formerly agreed in rejecting—as we have seen did the learned Cave—the amended date of the Vulgar Era which removed certain chronological difficulties that lay against S. Peter's Roman Episcopate—now this change is generally accepted by them as a right one. (2) That, whereas the ancient and traditional Catholic interpretation of Rome for Babylon was most stoutly and almost universally opposed by Protestants of old—and as we have seen by the Anglican Cave and Pearson—this point seems now to be conceded on all hands: and the very best proofs of its truth are to be found in the writings, and—we should suppose, quasi-authoritative—commentaries of some of the ablest Anglican living divines. Had we, indeed, adverted to these Anglican writings in time, we might have spared ourselves what now appears as so much labour lost. What enhances, in some sense, the value of these admissions is, that they have not been made from any Catholic bias, nor from any love of ancient tradition—quite the contrary—but through sheer conviction as to the real facts of the case, and from purely critical and historical arguments: as the following passages tend to show:

DR. FARRAR.

"Although the date of Christ's Birth," says Dr. Farrar, "cannot be established with absolute certainty, there is yet a large amount of evidence to render it at least probable that He was born four years before our present era. It is universally admitted that our received chronology, which is not older than Dionysius Exiguus, in the 6th century, is wrong....

"Our one most certain datum is obtained from the fact that Christ was born before the death of Herod the Great. The date of that event is known with absolute certainty, for Josephus tells us* that he died 37 years after he was declared king by the Romans. Now, it is known that he was declared king A.U.C. 714, and therefore, since Josephus always reckons his years from Nisan to Nisan, and counts the initial and terminal fractions of Nisan as complete years, Herod must have died between Nisan A.U.C. 750 and Nisan A.U.C. 751, i.e., between B.C. 4 and B.C. 3 of our era.

"(2) Josephus says that on the night in which Herod ordered Judas, Matthias, and their abettors to be burnt, there was an eclipse of the moon (xvii. 6, 4). Now this eclipse took place on the night of March 12, B.C. 4, and Herod was dead at least seven days before the Passover (xvii. 8, 4), which, if we accept the Jewish reckoning, fell in that year on April 12th. But according to the clear indication of the Gospels, Jesus must have been born at least 40 days before Herod's death. It is clear, therefore, that under no circumstances can the Nativity have taken place later than February, B.C. 4."†

"It was indispensable to the safety of the whole community," writes Dr. Farrar, "that the books of the Christians, when given up by the unhappy weakness of 'traditors,' or discovered by the keen malignity of informers, should contain no compromising matter."‡ "No danger incurred by the early Christians was greater than that caused by the universal prevalence of political spies. If one of these wretches got possession of any Christian writing which could be construed into an attack or a reflection upon their terrible persecutors, hundreds might be involved in indiscriminate punishment on a charge of high treason (læsa majestas), which was their most formidable engine of despotic power. S. Paul, writing to the Thessalonians even so early as A.D. 52, had found it necessary to speak of the Roman Empire and of the Emperor Claudius or Nero in terms of studied enigma (2 Thess. ii. 3-12). S. Peter, making a casual allusion to Rome, had been obliged to veil it under the mystic name of Babylon (1 Pet. v. 13)."

"I strongly incline to the belief that by Babylon the Apostle intended Rome (so the Fathers unanimously; and Grotius, Lardner, Cave,‖ Semler, Hitzig, and the Tubingen school . . .), and we find this interpretation current in the Church in very early days. The Apocalypse was written about the same time, or not long after the First Epistle of Peter; and in the Apocalypse and in the Sybilline verses we see that a Western, and even an Asiatic Christian, when he heard the name 'Babylon' in a religious writing, would be likely at once to think of Rome. Throughout the Talmud we find the same practice of applying symbolic names. There Rome figures under the designations of Nineveh, Edom, and Babylon.... The reference to Rome as Babylon may have originated in a mystic application of the Old Testament prophecies, but it had its advantages afterwards as a secret symbol. It is therefore a mistake to suppose that the use of Babylon for Rome would be the sudden obtrusion of 'allegory' into matter of fact, or that by using it the Apostle would be going out of his way to make an enigma for all future readers.' There is, in fact, a marked accordance between such an expression and the conception which S. Peter indicates throughout his letter, that all

---

* *Ant.* xvii. 8, 1.
† Farrar's *Life of Christ*, vol. i., Appendix, "The Date of Christ's Birth."
‡ *Early Days of Christianity*, vol. i. p. 82.
‖ We are unable to understand how Cave can be cited for this opinion.

THE SPEAKER'S COMMENTARY—BABYLON MEANS ROME.

Christians are exiles scattered from the Heavenly Jerusalem, living, some of them, in the earthly Babylon. An early Christian would have seen nothing either allegorical or enigmatical in the matter. He would at once have understood the meaning and have known the reasons, alike mystic and political, for avoiding the name of Rome." (*Ibid.* vol. ii. p. 286.)

THE SPEAKER'S COMMENTARY.

The Speaker's Commentary on 1 *Peter* v. 13, says as follows:

"We have to remark (1) that the city of Babylon was certainly not the seat of a Christian community; (2) that no ancient record has the slightest trace of S. Peter's presence or work in Chaldæa; (3) that *all ancient authorities are unanimous* in the assertion that the later year or years of his life were passed in the west of the Roman Empire. On the other hand, Babylon was well known in Asia Minor during the lifetime of S. John *as the symbolical designation of Rome*, and, as was before pointed out, the whole phrase has a symbolical form or tone. Accordingly, we find *an absolute consensus of ancient interpreters that there Babylon must be understood as equivalent to Rome*. There was good reason why such a name should be given to it. All the persecutions then impending, in fact, already in progress—came from the city which succeeded Babylon as the type and centre of anti-Christian forces. . . . We adopt without the least misgiving this explanation of the word as alone according to the mind of the Apostle and the testimony of the early Church. So also Thiersch, Ewald, and Hilgenfeld very positively."

Again, in the "Introduction" to the Epistle, the learned writer, after refuting at length the opinion that the literal Babylon was intended by the Apostle, thus continues:

"In the first place, we have to encounter *the uniform, unvarying testimony of early Christian writers*. From whatever quarter their voices reach us, they affirm that Babylon is here a recognised appellation of Rome, the city which occupied the place of that ancient city as the central world-power, the head-quarters of anti-Christian influences. In fact, no other view of the passage was entertained or suggested before Calvin, who argued that the old tradition was connected with false notions as to the position of the Roman Church. . . . Papias, Clemens Alexandrinus, Jerome, Œcumenius, Eusebius, all state this as a well-known fact needing no defence. Œcumenius gives the true account of the matter: 'He calls Rome Babylon, on account of the preeminence which of old belonged to Babylon.' Renan observes that ' *Rome devint comme Babylone une sorte de ville sacramentelle et symbolique.*' (*Antichrist.* p. 118.) . . . The foregoing arguments seem to leave no alternative but to accept *the old, unvarying testimony of the Fathers*, who must have known the sense in which the statement was understood throughout Asia Minor, that S. Peter designates Rome by the title of Babylon."

BISHOP ELLICOTT'S COMMENTARY.

The writer in *Bishop Ellicott's Commentary* on the same passage from S. Peter, says:

"It may be called the established interpretation that the place meant is Rome. We never hear of Peter being in the East, and the thing itself is improbable, whereas nothing but Protestant prejudice can stand against the historical evidence that S. Peter sojourned and died in Rome. Whatever theological consequences may flow from it, it is as certain that S. Peter was at Rome as that S. John was at Ephesus. Everything in the Letter also points to such a state of things as was to be found at Rome about the date when we believe the letter to have been written. It is objected that S. Peter would not gravely speak of Rome under a fanciful name when dating a letter; but the symbolism in the name is quite in keeping with the context. S. Peter has just *personified* the Church of the place from which he writes, which seems quite as unprosaic a use of language as to call Rome 'Babylon.' And it seems pretty clear that the name (Babylon) was quite intelligible to Jewish readers, for whom it was intended. The Apocalypse (xvii. 5) is not the only place where Rome is found spoken of under this title. One of the first of living Hebraists (who will not allow his name to be mentioned) told the present writer that no Hebrew of S. Peter's day would have had need to think twice what city was meant when 'Babylon' was here mentioned. And on the mention of the name, all the prophecies of the vengeance to be taken on the city, which had desolated the Holy Land, would rush with consolation into the mind of the readers, and they would feel that S. Peter, though supporting S. Paul, was still in full sympathy with themselves. Finally, as M. Renan suggests, there were reasons of prudence for not speaking too plainly about the presence of a large Christian society in Rome. The police were still more vigilant now than when S. Paul wrote in guarded language about the Roman Empire to the Thessalonians. It might provoke hostilities if the Epistle fell into the hands of an informer, with names and places too clearly given."

Again, in the "Introduction" to the Epistle the writer says:

"The place from which the letter was written was, we may say without any hesitation, Rome. If this be not the case, we must understand the 'Babylon' (ch. v. 13) to mean the Eastern Babylon. And it is neither very probable in itself that S. Peter should have visited that city, and there have been met by S. Silas and S. Mark; nor is there any trace of a tradition, however meagre, that he ever travelled in those parts. On the other hand, were it not for the abuse made of the fact by the supporters of the Papacy, no one would ever have questioned the universal and well-authenticated tradition which affirms that S. Peter was, along with S. Paul, co-founder of the Church of Rome. The whole subject has, of late years, been sifted to the bottom by various German and other writers. . . . Though every conceivable difference may be found between these authors respecting the dates and duration of S. Peter's sojourn at Rome, very few are so hardily sceptical as to reject altogether evidence as strong, early, and wide as that on which we believe that Hannibal invaded Italy," &c.

To these Anglican testimonies on the question of Babylon we here subjoin an extract from the learned ecclesiastical historian Dr. Döllinger, which we had, through inadvertence, omitted in an earlier part of this treatise:

"S. Peter's own testimony, in his First Epistle, raises to a certainty the fact of his having been at Rome. The letter is written from a city he calls Babylon. This cannot reasonably be understood of the Egyptian Babylon, a strong fortress and station of a Roman legion, and thus the question arises, whether it is Babylon on the Euphrates, or whether, according to a method of speech very natural to the Jews of that day from the usage of the Prophets, it means Rome. The latter is the belief of the ancient Church, following a tradition of the Apostolic age to which Papias bears witness. That S. Peter had passed over the boundaries of the Roman Empire into Parthia to Babylon on the Euphrates, that there was already a Christian community there, and that from thence the Apostle salutes the believers to whom he is writing—this is more than improbable. Strabo and Pliny mention Babylon as 'a great desert,' which, chiefly from the neighbourhood of Seleucia and Ctesiphon, had become emptied of inhabitants.* The towns of Nearda and Nisibis were the principal Jewish settlements in the Babylonian Satrapy; the Jews had moved from Babylon to Seleucia several years before S. Peter could have come there, because they could not hold out against the Heathen inhabitants who were hostile to them; and soon afterwards another emigration took place on account of a pestilence. Five years later more than fifty thousand Jews were put to death in Seleucia by the Syrians and Greeks, and the remainder went, not back to Babylon, but to Nearda and Nisibis; † the only inference, therefore, to be drawn from the history of Josephus is, that at the date of S. Peter's Epistle there were no longer any Jews in Babylon, and so, too, Agrippa, in his speech at the beginning of the Jewish war, knew of no Jews to name beyond the Jordan, except those in the province of Adiabene. That S. Mark, who was in 'Babylon' with the Apostle, was at Rome at the precise time when there is every reason to believe that this Epistle was written, is clear from S. Paul's mentioning him.‡ Soon afterwards he was staying in Asia Minor, whence S. Paul recalled him to Rome shortly before his death.§ There is nothing strange in S. Peter's designating Rome in an Epistle by the name used in the poetical prophecy of the Apocalypse. A Jew, who had grown up in a country town of Galilee, with the language of the prophetic writings constantly in his ears, when he saw Rome with the abominations of Nero and the idolatry and moral corruptions prevalent there, could not but be most vividly reminded of the Old Testament description of Babylon; and thus it was natural enough that, having at the beginning of his Epistle called the communities of Asia Minor 'elect pilgrims,' he should at the close call the community, whose salutation he imparted, 'their fellow-elect in Babylon.' And lastly, there are unmistakable indications throughout the Epistle of the approaching Neronic persecution, and S. Peter had good reason for using a local designation the Heathen would not understand, in order to avoid the danger inevitable for himself and the Roman Christians if a copy of the document should fall into their hands, as it easily might."‖

* Plin. *Hist. Nat.* vi. 26; Strabo, xvi. 738.
† Joseph. *Ant.* xviii. 9.
‡ *Col.* iv. 10; *Philem.* 24. This coincidence serves as a strong confirmation of the fact of SS. Peter and Paul preaching the Faith together in Rome. (*Author's note*.)
§ *2 Tim.* iv. 11.
‖ *The First Age of the Church*, vol. i. pp. 161-164.

HOMERSHAM COX.

Mr. Homersham Cox, in his recently published volume, *The First Century of Christianity*,* professes to eschew the discussion of theological questions, and scrupulously to exclude from his treatment all religious and doctrinal topics: yet he decides very confidently and positively on two most important facts, on which, perhaps more than on any other, the whole question of doctrinal and historical Christianity depends—viz., the Primacy, and S. Peter's Roman Episcopate. With regard to the first, he affirms that S. James was Primate, and not S. Peter. 'That S. James, the kinsman of Christ," he says, "presided over this community"—that is, the Apostles and whole body of disciples acting together as a corporate society—" seems clear beyond reasonable doubt." "The Church was governed by the Apostles under his presidency." "In the Council of Jerusalem . . . he pronounces authoritatively:" is "the Primate," "first in importance?"†

This strange theory, so far as we are aware unknown to antiquity, save from its transitory recognition, to some extent, in the Clementine and other kindred Ebionite apocryphal writings, is entirely opposed to the tradition and history of the Church. Mr. Cox, indeed, invokes in its behalf the testimony of Hegesippus in Eusebius :‡ "He" (Hegesippus), writes Mr. Cox, "says that S. James 'received the government of the Church with the Apostles,' evidently implying that the Church was governed by the Apostles under his presidency." But here, as is clear from the subject and context of Eusebius's entire Chapter, Hegesippus is speaking not of the Church of Christ as a whole, but of the local Church and the See of Jerusalem, in the same sense as Clement of Alexandria spoke of it § in the passage which Mr. Cox had just before cited.

The presidency in the Church and See of Jerusalem is one thing, and the primacy amongst the Apostles and over the entire flock of Christ is another. Mr. Cox does not seem to have distinguished between these two. All the Apostles had received their co-ordinate Apostolic powers and universal jurisdiction immediately from Christ Himself. Hence, it was not within their competence, by their own act alone, to invest one of their number with any real prerogative of authority over themselves and the

---

* P. vii; Longmans, 1886. † See pp. 65-69.
‡ *E. H.* ii. 23. § Euseb. ii. 1.

Church in general. If there was a Primacy in the Apostolic College and in the Church, this must have emanated from Divine institution alone. Besides, it has been ever a moot-point, not only amongst Catholics, but amongst others also,[*] whether S. James, the Bishop of Jerusalem, was one of the Twelve at all. What they could do, and what Clement says they did, was to confer upon S. James the honourable dignity of presiding in the first, and at that time the only existing, local Church of Jerusalem. According to tradition, this, then, was done in virtue of the expressed will of Christ Himself. The dignity of S. James—commonly called our Lord's brother, and surnamed the Just—as Bishop of the holy city of Jerusalem, the cradle and Mother Church of Christendom, was doubtless very great, especially whilst the Apostles resided there, and made it their head-quarters and the centre of their apostolic labours. Indeed, for a time, Jerusalem and its sphere of action was, so to say, commensurate and identical with the Christian Church; and its Bishop was of exceptional importance, both as ordinary Diocesan, and also as being at the same time a member of the Apostolic College, which held supreme government over the whole Church. Hence this exceptional importance of the Church of Jerusalem and of its Bishop may serve well as the most probable explanation of the words of Hegesippus, that "James, surnamed the Just, . . . received the government of the Church with the Apostles"—the affairs of the Church of Jerusalem being at that time in great measure identical with those of the Church at large.

The Apostles, we may be sure, were foremost in jealously guarding and preserving the honour and dignity conferred by them on S. James. They paid all due deference to him as Bishop of the See, who by consequence took a leading and responsible part in the administration of the affairs of the then existing Church. But this episcopate of S. James, with the special honour that thence accrued to him, had nothing whatever to do with any presidency over the Apostles and over the whole Christian Church. It is quite distinct from the Primacy.

There appears, moreover, no ground for another assertion of Mr. Cox, that the Church at Jerusalem over which S. James presided, exercised, as such, supervision and authority over other Churches in Antioch, Syria, and Cilicia. These were united to the Church at Jerusalem by special bonds of charity and venera-

[*] Lightfoot, *Epistle to the Philippians*, p. 195.

tion; but were immediately dependent on the authority of the College of the Apostles at Jerusalem, or of the particular Apostles who founded them. At all events, if there were any dependence of neighbouring Churches on the See of Jerusalem, this was only provisional and informal, as on a *quasi* Metropolitan. In point of fact, it seems that the Bishop of Jerusalem had, strictly speaking, no jurisdiction outside his own diocese by ecclesiastical right, and much less by any bestowal of Christ. To illustrate this point from subsequent history, we will here quote from a learned Anglican author.

JOHN MASON NEALE.

"At the destruction of Jerusalem, Cæsarea became the civil metropolis of Palestine, and the Church, as usual, followed that arrangement. The bishops of Ælia (Jerusalem) enjoyed, indeed, a certain kind of honorary pre-eminence: as the Seventh Canon of the Council of Nicæa sufficiently proves. Yet even there, the words, 'saving the rightful honour of the Metropolis,' are carefully added. Of the right of Cæsarea over Ælia, we have many examples. Thus, in a Synod of the whole of Palestine, holden in the year 196 on the Paschal Question, Theophilus of Cæsarea presided, assisted by S. Narcissus of Jerusalem. Thus, also, Acacius of Cæsarea deposed S. Cyril of Jerusalem. So again, in one of S. Jerome's violent epistles respecting John of Jerusalem, we find the same right upheld.

"However, during the latter half of the fourth century, the See of Jerusalem, under several of its Prelates, and more especially S. Cyril, strove for the Primacy with that of Cæsarea; and the last act of supremacy on the part of the latter occurs in 398, exercised by John of Cæsarea towards Praylius of Jerusalem.

"Juvenal, the successor of the latter Prelate, a man of considerable powers, and (notwithstanding some unhappy mistakes) a worthy successor of S. James, aid the foundation of the Patriarchate. The steps by which he obtained his desire are not clear. But at the Synod of Ephesus we find him boldly declaring that the Bishop of Antioch ought 'to obey the Apostolic Throne of God in the Church of Jerusalem:' and that Apostolic order and tradition had subjected the former to the latter Prelate, in receiving instruction, and, in case of necessity, being tried by him. So at the Robbers' meeting at Ephesus, Juvenal signs before Domnus of Antioch. While St. Cyril of Alexandria lived, he yielded to these pretensions through the necessity of the times, yet without approving of them; and S. Leo strenuously, at a later period, opposed them. But Juvenal obtained letters from Theodosius which gave him the prerogative he claimed; and he even exercised the right of ordination in Phœnicia and in Arabia. After a long contention with Maximus of Antioch, the matter was compromised at Chalcedon; Maximus giving up his real or imaginary rights over the Three Palestines, on condition of retaining the rest of his diocese; while Cæsarea possessed too small a degree of influence to be able to oppose the new arrangement.

"The See of Jerusalem was happy in avoiding the great schism which afflicted Antioch and Alexandria.... At the first irruption of the Saracens,

Stephen of Dora was appointed by Pope Theodore his Vicar in Palestine... because the dying S. Sophronius of Jerusalem (the great champion of the Church against the Monothelites) had implored Rome to take cognisance of the affairs of his diocese; and the See of Jerusalem remained vacant sixty years. Thenceforward the succession continued uninterrupted till the capture of the city by the Latins. Simeon, the legitimate Patriarch, dying in the same month, the Latins elected Daimbert in his stead. The Greeks appear to have bestowed the titular honour on Agapius. At the recapture of the city by the Infidels, the Greek Patriarchs again became resident, while the Latins failed not to keep up their own titular succession.

"Syrians were almost universally elected to the Patriarchate till the elevation of Germanus in 1554. He, in his twenty-five years' episcopate, contrived so to fill up his suffragan Sees as to have a majority of Greeks; and from that time native Syrians have been scrupulously excluded from the Patriarchal throne. The Patriarchs are non-resident; they have a house, church, and gardens in the part of Constantinople called the *Phanar*. This has been the case since the time of Theophanes, in the early part of the seventeenth century. They nominate an assistant to themselves, who eventually succeeds them; and the Patriarchate is committed to the care of several 'guardians.' Should a Patriarch die without nominating a successor, the brethren of the Holy Sepulchre, the personal staff of the Patriarch, in number about 150, elect, and their choice is perfectly independent of all other authority.

"The number of parish priests in the diocese is about seventy; that of churches rather larger; and that of the 'Faithful' about 18,000." *

Reverting to Mr. Homersham Cox on the Primacy, we confess our amazement that, in deciding so peremptorily against S. Peter, and in making out so positively as he does a counter-case of his own in favour of S. James, he should have made no appeal to the Gospels, and omitted all reference to the words of Christ addressed to S. Peter, just as though he considered that the sayings and acts of the Divine Founder of the Church bearing upon its constitution formed no real part of its history in the first century of Christianity. It is of no use to plead here that this is to enter into doctrinal matters. He admits a Primacy, establishing one of his own; he discusses *ex professo* the Primacy claimed for Peter, and decides against it. Now, this is essentially a doctrinal matter. Those who maintain S. Peter's Primacy do so on no other ground than because it is a doctrine revealed by Christ in the Gospels, and was instituted by His own act. S. Peter's Primacy is of Divine institution, or it is nothing; and in treating of it at all, and, especially, in denying it to set up a rival claim, a historian who believes that the Gospel record is genuinely his-

* Rev. J. M. Neale's *History of the Eastern Church*, part i. pp. 158-160. Masters, 1850.

torical, is bound to take cognisance of that which universally purports to be the charter and title-deeds of that Primacy, if only to show that it does not bear the meaning which the assertors of Peter's Primacy put upon it.

Mr. Homersham Cox criticises a passage of Dr. Döllinger in which that historian recounts certain doings of S. Peter recorded in the Acts, as illustrating his exercise of the Primacy; and these our author pronounces to be inconclusive; but no one who upholds S. Peter's Primacy ever supposes that such examples are the direct proofs of its existence, or do more than confirm and harmonise with the exercise of it as already possessed. Nay, however conclusive they might be shown to be of its exercise, they could never of themselves form any adequate or safe title for its validity by Divine right; for this, appeal must be made to a positive act of Divine institution.

Take a case of some disputed property: One of the parties has been the reputed owner from time immemorial; has, it is averred, exercised acts of proprietorship, and can show that the unquestionably original and genuine title-deeds of the estate bear at least *prima facie* evidence in his favour—the only point on which a doubt can be here raised, is their precise meaning and force. A claim is set up for the other party on the sole ground that he, too, has exercised acts of apparent proprietorship. It is neither pretended that he has the same repute of ownership as the other, nor that there is anything whatever in the original title-deeds on which to rest his claim. Mr. Homersham Cox is a lawyer and a judge. What would he think of giving sentence in such a case simply on the more or less show of acts of proprietorship exercised by either party, without any examination of, or reference made to, the title-deeds producible? And yet in a manner still more arbitrary than this does a believer in the Gospels dispose of the Primacy and Supreme Pastorate which he admits; although on the one hand such a Primacy must affect the very constitution of the Church, and on the other hand it cannot be denied that our Blessed Lord said something in reference to a special position that should be held by His Apostle Peter in the Church which He was founding. And this, forsooth, is to write the history of the First Century of Christianity!

The writer says in his Preface * :

" Paradoxical as the statement might otherwise appear, the history of the

* P. viii.

first Christians is better understood now than it was fourteen or fifteen hundred years ago."

And again, in his chapter "S. Peter at Rome:"

"It seems almost a paradox to say that we know more about this matter than men did who lived much nearer the Apostolic age; and yet this is certainly the case."*

Leaving the author in undisturbed possession of his paradox, we will briefly summarise the conclusions at which he has thereby arrived in connection with the subject of that chapter. He concedes all the main points generally so hotly contended for by Protestants, except the Episcopate. The first who gave expression to the idea that S. Peter was Bishop of Rome was, he says, S. Cyprian, of whom he speaks very injuriously and contemptuously, indulging in such epithets as "extremely credulous," "preposterous," "silly," and "manifestly fictitious" at the Saint's expense. He has the hardihood to assert as a positive fact that Eusebius "did not consider S. Peter to be a Bishop of Rome," and his twenty-five years' Episcopate is, he affirms, "demonstrably erroneous." For this statement the only proof he offers is, that "it is quite impossible that S. Peter could have been for so long a time in Rome." Herein, at any rate, every Catholic will agree with him; but it has nothing whatever to do with the demonstration. He does not admit that "Babylon" means Rome.

Jeremy Collier says:

"If a lawyer will study divinity, examine the Scripture, read over the Fathers and Councils and other records of the earliest centuries,—if he will make himself master of this part of learning, and argue from authorities of this kind,—he ought to be believed as far as the intrinsic evidence will bear, and the proofs carry him; and so ought anybody else. But a lawyer, *quatenus* lawyer, can have no preference: he has no commission to give sentence, nor any privilege to pronounce upon the matter."†

We conclude this Chapter with the testimony to S. Peter's Roman Episcopate of the learned Anglican Controversialist, Palmer, so well-known for his strenuous antagonism to Papal claims:

"The Roman Church was particularly honoured as having been presided over by S. Peter, and was therefore by many of the Fathers called the See of Peter."‡

* P. 178. † *Eccl. Hist.* vol. iv. p. 262; ed. 1852.
‡ *Treatise on the Church,* vol. ii. part vii. chap. 3.

CHAPTER XIX.

STATEMENTS AND VIEWS OF ANGLICAN WRITERS (Continued).

Lightfoot.

In this Chapter we give some lengthened extracts from the works of Dr. Lightfoot, the Anglican Bishop of Durham. These, above all other non-Catholic writings of the present day, claim notice in a volume that treats of the first age of Christianity. The learned author deserves our respect and gratitude both for his wide erudition, and for the great services which he has rendered to the cause of historical truth by his works on the Epistles of S. Paul and the Apostolic Fathers.

Owing to the comparatively scanty and fragmentary documents of genuine authenticity that survive from the first centuries, in presence of others that are apocryphal or doubtful, there hangs, doubtless, a very thick veil over the history of the ante-Nicene Church; but, when from time to time this veil is again lifted by more profound investigation or some fresh discovery, very wonderful and even startling things are revealed, which are found to confirm and illustrate more fully the Catholic tradition. It is thus that the erudite studies and impartial criticism of Dr. Lightfoot have served so greatly to dissipate the legendary theory of the rationalist German school, and to establish the historic character of primitive Christianity; whilst the newly-recovered pages of S. Clement's Epistle to the Corinthians set the early Primacy of the Roman Church in such strong relief before the present age.

After all the multiplied assertions, so constantly dinned into our ears by Anglicans, that the present papal claims are but modern pretensions, unknown to antiquity, which have found their origin in comparatively later times, it is certainly quite refreshing to hear from Dr. Lightfoot that Gregory VII. and Innocent III. had their prototype in Pope Victor of the second century; that the historical foundation of the Primacy of the Roman Church appeared before the first century had closed; and that the authoritative tone of S. Clement's Epistle, written to the Corinthians in the exercise of that Primacy, was undoubtedly the first step towards papal aggression. The candour generally evinced by Dr. Lightfoot in his statement and recognition of facts, whatever may be their issue, merits our warmest thanks and praise; for, alas, so strong is the bias of association, that many even of those who set out to write history impartially do not attain to this candour. Still, we deeply regret that he should so much indulge in drawing wide conclusions from the particular facts which he brings out, and in building on them novel theories that are, to say the least, altogether out of harmony with history as it has been generally received. We look upon it as nothing short of a calamity, tending greatly to retard the progress of all historical science, that men who are really learned —as soon as by their studies and research they have discovered some fresh data of fact—should be so prone to make these new glimpses of truth serve as starting-points for tracing out strange and new paths away from the beaten track, and should make use of their historical discoveries—which are really so much public property, belonging to the whole commonwealth of human intelligence—as materials for building up some original theory of their own private speculation, contrary to what the world has hitherto held, and which, it is certain, others in turn—but only at the cost of much labour and pains—will make efforts to destroy.

Too often men of learning seem to make it their rule to discard what is of traditional and common belief, as though it were, on this very account, unworthy of historical credit, and to use any fresh discovered truths or facts to serve as hinges for their own self-formed hypotheses, which are generally as crude and arbitrary as they are shifting and novel. Would it not show more wisdom, though it might look more commonplace, if, instead of thus wasting their resources and energy, they pressed the results of their studies into the service of real history by making them illustrate and fit in with other already well-ascertained truths? Or, if this were impossible, and the new-found matter should seem too fragmentary and abnormal for combination with ancient certainties,—why, then, not leave it alone, at least for a while, let it tell its own tale, broken and partial though this may be, and wait on in hope that ere long fresh light may come for its fuller explanation? Why this impatience to rush at once into strange speculation and theory?

Plain common-sense, which, after all, is the true philosophy, and should guide the learned as well as the simple, would tell us that it is now too late in the day to construct a history of past antiquity that is to be fundamentally new; and that, if we feel unable to accept in general that which has come down to us, because we deem it false or unreliable, we may, indeed, reject it, but that we cannot supplant it by another of our own creation that will have any real probability. We may, moreover, hold as an axiomatic principle, applicable to history, as well as to every other science, that any theory, system, or law (so called) which is drawn from some few and isolated data only, and is not derived from such a number or range of phenomena as to be fairly exhaustive of their particular field, is entirely illusory and valueless for the sure ascertainment of truth.

Dr. Lightfoot's theories, to which we here allude, are, principally, his evolution of the episcopate from the presbyterate; that the episcopate was unequally developed in the East and West, and especially at Rome was in a low condition during the times of S. Clement and S. Ignatius; that this was recognised by these Fathers, and is evident from their own writings; that there was ever in Christendom such a Primacy as he himself describes; or, in fact, any Roman Primacy at all apart from, or other than, that of the Bishop of Rome.

These several theories do not, it is true, immediately affect the bare historical fact of S. Peter's Roman Episcopate; but the admission of their truth would at once cut the ground from under that fact, as it lies in the entire concrete form which has been ascribed to it by Catholic tradition and belief. We have been, therefore, obliged to undertake their disproof; and to show that, so far from being historically reliable, they are altogether at variance with the very facts and testimonies which Dr. Lightfoot brings forward in their support. As the passages we quote from his volumes treat on many different topics and cover a wide field, we have found it more convenient to deal with them piecemeal in disjointed detail.

But whilst strenuously opposing Dr. Lightfoot in many things —especially in his theories and the arguments and conclusions which he draws from the facts he adduces—we can find in several passages, which we reproduce, very much to illustrate and confirm certain points of our contention in the foregoing Chapters.

1. On Ebionism and Judaising Tendencies in the Roman Church—its Orthodoxy—The Clementines.

"Most of the great heresiarchs—amongst others Valentinus, "Marcion, Praxeas, Theodotus, Sabellius — taught in Rome. "Ebionism alone would not be idle, where all other heresies were "active. But the great battle with this form of error seems to "have been fought out at an early date in the lifetime of the "Apostles themselves, and in the age immediately following.

"The last notice of the Roman Church in the Apostolic writ"ings seems to point to two separate communities, a Judaising "Church and a Pauline Church. The arrival of the Gentile "Apostle in the Metropolis, it would appear, was the signal for "the separation of the Judaisers who had hitherto associated "with their Gentile brethren coldly and distrustfully. . . .

"If S. Peter ever visited Rome, it must have been at a later "date than these notices. Of this visit, far from improbable in "itself, there is fair, if not conclusive evidence; and, once ad"mitted, we may reasonably assume that important consequences "flowed from it. . . . As they (SS. Peter and Paul) had done "before in the world at large, so they would agree to do now in "the Metropolis; they would exchange the right hand of fellow"ship, devoting themselves the one more especially to the Jewish, "the other to the Gentile converts. Christian Rome was large "enough to admit two communities or two sections in one com"munity, until the time was ripe for their more complete amal"gamation. . . . At all events, the presence of the two Apostles "must have tended to tone down antipathies and to draw parties "closer together. . . . Hence, at the close of the first century, "we see no more traces of a twofold Church. The work of the "Apostles, now withdrawn from the scene, has passed into the "hands of no unworthy disciple (namely, S. Clement)." *

We must here remark, that what underlies Dr. Lightfoot's account of this joint preaching of S. Peter and S. Paul in Rome at a later date is simply gratuitous assertion, which has no warrant whatever from early writers. Neither history nor tradition afford any indication that S. Paul was in Rome, except during the time of his first imprisonment there, recorded by S. Luke, and once more before his martyrdom, when again from prison he wrote

---

* Lightfoot on *S. Paul's Epistle to the Galatians*, p. 322 *sq.*

several of his Epistles. If anything can be gathered from slight passing allusions to be found in these Epistles, the inference would be that S. Paul's second imprisonment followed shortly after his arrival in the city. Indeed, from these allusions, a recent Protestant author is led to suppose that the Apostle was arrested in Macedonia, and conducted a second time in chains to Rome.* No doubt S. Paul *may* have visited Rome and there preached together with S. Peter some time between these two imprisonments; but we deny that any trace whatever of this is to be found either in history or tradition. What is it that causes the learned writer to say that, besides the intrinsic probability, there is fair, if not conclusive, evidence that S. Peter visited Rome and there preached the faith in company with S. Paul, but because this has so much historical testimony in its support, that it cannot be rejected without doing violence to all historical truth and certainty? Let us, then, in the name and interests of truth, abide by the historical testimony, and not suffer ourselves to be led aside from it by the assertions of modern authors, who explain it away, and leave their own assumptions in its place. And let those, especially, who oppose the general tradition that S. Peter was Bishop of Rome, or that of his twenty-five years' Episcopate, be well on their guard against the strong temptation they must needs be under, to—so to say, unconsciously—manipulate or distort forthcoming testimonies and facts of history, by clothing them with gratuitous theories and other imagined facts, in order thus to make them square better with their own doctrinal contentions and religious prejudices.

"The Epistle to the Corinthians, written by Clement in the "name of the Roman Church, cannot be placed after the close "of the first century, and may possibly date some years earlier. "It is not unwarrantable to regard this as a typical document, "reflecting the comprehensive principles and large sympathies "which had been impressed upon the united Church of Rome, "in great measure, perhaps, by the influence of the distinguished "writer. . . . Belonging to no party, he seemed to belong to all.

"Not many years after this Epistle was written, Ignatius "(107) . . . addresses a letter to the Roman brethren. It con-"tains no indications of any division in the Church of the "Metropolis, or of the prevalence of Ebionite views among his

* *The First Century of Christianity*, pp. 173-4.

"readers. . . . To the Ephesians, and even to Polycarp, he
" offers words of advice and warning; but to the Romans he
" utters only the language of joyful satisfaction.*

"The Clementine writings have been assigned, with great
" confidence, by most recent critics of ability to a Roman author-
" ship. Of the truth of this view I am very far from convinced.
" The great argument—indeed, almost the only argument—in its
" favour is the fact that the plot of the romance turns upon the
" wanderings of this illustrious Bishop of Rome, who is at once
" the narrator and the hero of the story. But the fame of
" Clement reached far beyond the limits of his own jurisdiction.
" To him, we are specially told by a contemporary writer,[†] was
" assigned the task of corresponding with foreign Churches. His
" rank and position, his acknowledged wisdom and piety, would
" point him out as the best typical representative of the Gentile
" converts; and an Ebionite writer, designing by a religious
" fiction to compass his views on Gentile Christendom, would
" naturally single out Clement for his hero, and by his example
" enforce the duty of obedience to the Church of the Circum-
" cision, as the prerogative Church and the true standard of ortho-
" doxy. At all events, it is to be noticed that, beyond the use
" made of Clement's name, these writings do not betray any
" familiarity with, or make any reference to, the Roman Church
" in particular. On the contrary, the scenes are all laid in the
" East; and the supreme arbiter, the ultimate referee in all that
" relates to Christian doctrine and practice, is not Peter, the
" Clementine Apostle of the Gentiles, the reputed founder of the
" Roman Church, but James, the Lord's brother, the bishop of
" bishops, the ruler of the Mother Church of the Circumcision.[‡] . . .
" The dates assigned to the *Homilies* by the ablest critics range
" over the whole of the second century, and some place them
" even later. If the Roman authorship be abandoned, many
" reasons for a very early date will fall to the ground also.[§]
" Whenever they were written, the *Homilies* are among the most
" interesting and important of early writings, but they have no

---

* *Epistle to the Galatians*, pp. 322-324.   † Hermas, *Vis.* ii. 4.

‡ Dr. Lightfoot thinks it more probable that S. James was not one of the Twelve.—*Epistle to the Philippians*, p. 195.

§ He elsewhere expresses his own opinion more positively thus: "The Clementine Homilies cannot well be placed later than the end, and should perhaps be placed towards the beginning, of the second century . . . they emanated probably from Syria or Palestine."—*Epistle to the Philippians*, p. 209.

"right to the place assigned them in the system of a modern
"critical school, as the missing link between the Judaism of
"the Christian era and the Catholicism of the close of the
"second century, as representing in fact the phase of Chris-
"tianity taught at Rome and generally throughout the Church
"during the early ages. . . . If they were really written by a
"Roman Christian, they cannot represent the main body of
"the Church, but must have emanated from one of the many
"heresies with which the Metropolis swarmed in the second
"century, when all promulgators of new doctrines gathered
"there, as the largest, and therefore the most favourable, market
"for their spiritual wares.* There is another reason also for
"thinking that the Gnostic Ebionism cannot have obtained any
"wide or lasting influence in the Church of Rome. During the
"episcopate of Callistus (210-223), a heretical teacher appears in
"the Metropolis, promulgating Elchasaite doctrines, substantially,
"though not identically, the same with the creed of the Cle-
"mentines, and at first seems likely to attain some measure of
"success, but is denounced and foiled by Hippolytus. It is clear
"that this learned writer on heresies regarded the Elchasaite
"doctrine as a novelty, against which, therefore, it was the more
"necessary to warn the faithful Christian. If the Ebionism of
"the Clementines had ever prevailed at Rome, it had passed
"into oblivion when Hippolytus wrote. The few notices
"of the Roman Church in the second century point to other
"than Ebionite leanings. In their ecclesiastical ordinances
"the Romans seem anxious to separate themselves as widely
"as possible from Jewish practices. Thus they extended
"the Friday's fast over the Saturday, showing thereby a
"marked disregard of the Sabbatical festival. Thus, again,
"they observed Easter on a different day from the Jewish Pass-
"over; and so zealous were they in favour of their own tradi-
"tional usage in this respect (from at least as far back as the
"episcopate of Xystus, A.D. 120-129, and perhaps earlier), that, in
"the Paschal controversy, their bishop Victor resorted to the
"extreme measure of renouncing communion with those Churches
"which differed from it. This controversy affords a valuable
"testimony to the Catholicity of Christianity at Rome in another
"way.

* "At this epoch, Rome was the general meeting point of Christendom. Hither flocked Christian teachers, orthodox and heretical, from all parts of the world."—Lightfoot's *Ignatius*, vol. i. p. 435.

"It is clear that the Churches, ranged on different sides of this question of ritual, are nevertheless substantially agreed on all important points of doctrine and practice. This fact appears when Anicetus of Rome permits Polycarp of Smyrna, who had visited the Metropolis in order to settle some disputed points, and had failed in arranging the Paschal question, to celebrate the Eucharist in his stead. It is distinctly stated by Irenæus when he remonstrated with Victor for disturbing the peace of the Church by insisting on non-essentials. In its creed the Roman Church was one with the Gallic and Asiatic Churches, and that this creed was not Ebionite, the names of Polycarp and Irenæus are guarantees. Nor is it only in the Paschal controversy that the Catholicity of the Romans may be inferred from their intercourse with other Christian communities. The remains of ecclesiastical literature, though sparse and fragmentary, are yet sufficient to reveal a wide network of intercommunication between the Churches in the second century; and herein Rome naturally holds a central position. The visit of Hegesippus to the Metropolis has been mentioned already. Not very long after we find Dionysius Bishop of Corinth, whose 'orthodoxy' is praised by Eusebius, among other letters addressed to foreign Churches, writing also to the Romans in terms of cordial sympathy and respect. On the Catholicity of the African Church I have already remarked; and the African Church was a daughter of the Roman, from whom, therefore, it may be assumed, she derived her doctrine.* Cyprian,† writing to Cornelius, speaks of Rome as '*Ecclesiæ Catholicæ radicem et matricem*,' in reference to the African Churches." ‡

And yet, notwithstanding all these evidences of firm adherence to Catholic orthodoxy, and resistance to all Ebionism and Elchasaism, Dr. Lightfoot, on the sole authority of Tertullian,§ "*now become a Montanist*," and Hippolytus,|| "*no friendly critic indeed, but yet a contemporary writer*," goes on to describe the Roman Church when "assailed by rival heresies, as compromised by the weakness and worldliness of her rulers, altogether distracted and unsteady."

"One Bishop first dallying with Montanism, and then turning

* Tertull. *De Præscr.* 36. † *Ep.* 48.
‡ Lightfoot, *Ep. to the Galatians*, pp. 324-9.
§ *Adv. Prax.* 1. || *Hæres.* ix. 7 *sq.*

"round and surrendering himself to the Patripassian heresy of
"Praxeas, and, later on, two successive Bishops, one from
"stupidity and avarice, the other from craft and ambition, listen-
"ing favourably to the heresies of Noëtus and Sabellius." [*]

Dr. Lightfoot says elsewhere with regard to the Clementine writings: "Though the fictions of this theological romance have "no direct historical value, it is hardly probable that the writer "would have indulged in such statements [respecting the appoint-"ment of Bishops by S. Peter in the various towns of Palestine "and its neighbourhood] unless an early development of the "Episcopate in these parts had invested his narrative with an air "of probability." [†]

Does not the principle here suggested by the learned author apply with still more force to matters which, being of far higher and wholly exceptional importance, must have claimed for their credibility a proportionately greater probability, nay, have obtained a large antecedent general acceptance and notoriety—we mean, the Primacy of S. Peter and his Roman Episcopate so distinctly set forth in the Clementine letter to S. James? Here, too, we should take into account that it would be damaging to the Ebionite hierarchical view of the Bishopric of Jerusalem and the position of S. James for the author to exalt S. Peter at the expense of S. James—and, consequently, wholly improbable that the circumstances he narrates of S. Peter occupying the Chair of the Teacher in the See of Rome, and his presidency over the truth, should be simply matters of his own gratuitous invention.

In another place our author writes: "To Pius succeeds "Anicetus (157). And now Rome becomes for the moment the "centre of interest and activity in the Christian world. During "this Episcopate, Hegesippus, visiting the Metropolis for the "purpose of ascertaining and recording the doctrines of the "Roman Church, is welcomed by the Bishop. About the same "time, another more illustrious visitor, Polycarp, the venerable "Bishop of Smyrna, arrives in Rome to confer with the head of "the Roman Church on the Paschal dispute, and then falls in "with and denounces the heretic Marcion. These facts are "stated on contemporary authority. Of Soter (168) also, the

---

[*] *Hæres.* ix. 7 *sq.* [†] *Epistle to the Philippians*, p. 207.

"next in succession, a contemporary record is preserved. Diony-
"sius of Corinth, writing to the Romans, praises the zeal of their
"Bishop, who, in his fatherly care for the suffering poor and for
"the prisoners working in the mines, had maintained and ex-
"tended the hereditary fame of his Church for zeal in all charit-
"able and good works. In Eleutherus, who succeeds Soter (177),
"we have the earliest recorded instance of an archdeacon.
"When Hegesippus paid his visit to the Metropolis, he found
"Eleutherus standing in this relation to the Bishop Anicetus,
"and seems to have made his acquaintance while acting in this
"capacity. Eleutherus, however, was a contemporary, not only
"of Hegesippus, but also of the great writers, Irenæus and
"Tertullian,* who speak of the episcopal succession in the
"Churches generally, and in Rome especially, as the best safe-
"guard for the transmission of the true faith from Apostolic
"times." †

2. On S. Clement's Epistle to the Corinthians.

With regard to Clement himself, after a lengthened discussion Dr. Lightfoot says : " I venture, therefore, to conjecture that
"Clement, the Bishop, was a man of Jewish parentage, a freed-
"man, or the son of a freedman, belonging to the household of
"Flavius Clemens, the Emperor's cousin. It is easy to imagine
"how, under these circumstances, the leaven of Christianity
"would work upwards from beneath, as it has done in so many
"other cases, and from their domestics and dependents the
"master and mistress would learn their perilous lessons in the
"Gospel. Even a much greater degree of culture than is ex-
"hibited in this Epistle would be quite consistent with such an
"origin ; for amongst these freedmen were frequently found the

---

* Dr. Lightfoot holds that the date of the *Octavius* of Minucius Felix is most probably about 160, that he wrote before Tertullian, and that the latter borrowed from the former. He thus continues : "An objection has been raised that we should not expect to find a cultivated Latin writer in the ranks of the Christians at this early date. This objection does not seem serious. The Church of Rome unquestionably was mainly Greek and Oriental in its origin. But it was already fast emerging from this original condition. Sixty or seventy years earlier than this date under Domitian (A.D. 95) it had adherents in the imperial family itself. Thirty years later it was governed by a Latin Bishop, Victor (A.D. 189-198 or 199). The Latin element at this time, therefore, must have been very considerable, and it would comprise the more educated, or at least the more influential, members of the Christian community." (*Ignatius*, vol. i. p. 519.)

† *Epistle to the Philippians*, pp. 220-2.

"most intelligent and cultivated-men of their day. Nor is this social status inconsistent with the position of the chief ruler of the most important Church in Christendom. A generation later, Hermas, the brother of Bishop Pius, speaks of himself as having been a slave (*Vis.* i. 1), and this involves the servile origin of Pius also."* . . .

Treating of the Epistle of S. Clement, Dr. Lightfoot says: "The newly-recovered portion of the First or genuine Epistle of Clement consists of about one-tenth of the whole. . . . It stands immediately before the final prayer, commendation of the bearers, and benediction, which form the two brief chapters at the close of the Epistle. It contains an earnest entreaty to the Corinthians to obey the injunctions contained in the letter, and to heal their unhappy schisms; an elaborate prayer which extends over three long chapters, commencing with an invocation, and ending with an intercession for rulers and governors; and then another appeal, of some length, to the Corinthians, justifying the language of the letter, and denouncing the sin of disobedience. The subject is not such as to admit of much historical matter; but the gain to our knowledge, notwithstanding, is not inconsiderable.

"In the first place, we are enabled to understand more fully the secret of Papal domination. This letter, it must be premised, does not emanate from the Bishop of Rome, but from the Church of Rome. There is every reason to believe the early tradition which points to Clement as its author, and yet he is not once named. The first person plural is maintained throughout, 'We consider,' 'We have sent.' Accordingly, writers of the second century speak of it as a letter from the community, not from the individual. Thus Dionysius, Bishop of Corinth, writing to the Romans, about A.D. 170, refers to it as the Epistle, 'which you wrote to us by Clement;'† and Irenæus soon afterwards similarly describes it: 'In the time of this Clement, no small dissension having arisen among the brethren in Corinth, the Church in Rome sent a very sufficient letter to the Corinthians, urging them to peace.'‡ Even later than this, Clement of Alexandria calls it in one passage, 'the Epistle of the Romans to the Corinthians,'§ though elsewhere he ascribes it to Clement." ||

---

* Lightfoot's *S. Clement's Epistle to the Corinthians*, p. 265.
† Euseb. *H. E.* iv. 23. ‡ *Ibid.* iii. 33. § *Strom.* v. 12. || *Ibid.* pp. 252 *sq.*

What else does this prove, but that Clement of Alexandria considered it a mere matter of form, and quite indifferent, whether the letter were called the Epistle of Clement, Bishop of Rome, or the Epistle of the Church of Rome? Dionysius of Corinth, too, whilst calling it the Epistle of the Romans, speaks of it expressly as "written by Clement;" and because it was written personally by the saintly Bishop, and had his authority, it was so long reverenced and read in the Church, as full of "instruction and admonition" to the Corinthians. Eusebius, from whom we learn this, in the same chapter,[*] says of Dionysius' letter, which was in answer to a second Epistle from Rome, that it was written to "the Romans, and addressed to Soter, the Bishop of that city." Hence, then, we may with reason gather that the Roman letter to Corinth had been in like manner written by Soter, the Bishop of the Church of Rome, to the Corinthians, and addressed to Dionysius, their own Bishop; and was called indifferently a letter, sometimes of the Church, at other times of the Bishop, of Rome, to the Bishop, or to the Church, of Corinth. Dionysius, speaking generally of his own letters to the Churches (*l. c.*), says that they were all written "at the requisition of the brethren." In his account of them, Eusebius records the name of the Bishop of the Church to which each was addressed, as mentioned by Dionysius in some of them, but not in all. So very careful is the historian to treasure up local details, especially on this matter of the succession of bishops, that it is unlikely he would have passed over the names of any, had they been given in the letters. The same remark applies also to the letters of Alexander, Coadjutor-bishop of Jerusalem (A.D. 204). In one of these to the Antiochenes, Asclepiades is mentioned as their Bishop in the third person, but at the end Alexander styles those to whom he writes, as "My lords and brethren." This is quite consistent with the letter being written and addressed particularly to the Bishop, as was that of Dionysius to Soter, though bearing the name of a letter to the Antiochene Christians.[†] This view receives stronger confirmation from another letter of the same Alexander, respecting Origen, which is described as

"Written to Demetrius, Bishop of Alexandria, by Alexander, Bishop of Jerusalem, and Theoctistus, Bishop of Cæsarea."[‡]

From this letter, Eusebius gives an extract beginning thus:

"He (*i.e.*, Demetrius) has added to his letter, that this was never before either heard or done," &c.

[*] *H. E.* iv. 23.   [†] *Ibid.* vi. 11.   [‡] *Ibid.* vi. 19.

Such mention of Demetrius in the third person, in a letter ostensibly written to himself, is certainly strange, but it is well explained, if it were usual in these earlier times to address to the Bishop of a See letters that in form were written to a Church collectively.* And this, to judge at least from the history of Eusebius, seems to have been the most ancient custom; since, with the exception of S. Ignatius' Epistle to S. Polycarp, which soon in its course merges into an address to the faithful of Smyrna, we can find no trace of bishops writing letters in a personal form to other bishops, until the middle of the third century, when we meet with several examples in the Epistles of Dionysius of Alexandria, and of the Bishops of Rome and Carthage, &c.† Eusebius records, also, the letter written by the Church of Smyrna to the Churches of Pontus,‡ and the letters from the Churches of Lyons and Vienne addressed alike to Eleutherus, then Bishop of Rome, and to the brethren in Asia and Phrygia.§

"Still it might have been expected," continues Dr. Lightfoot, "that somewhere towards the close mention would have been "made (though in the third person) of the famous man who was "at once the actual writer of the letter and the chief ruler of the "Church in whose name it was written. Now, however, that we "possess the work complete, we see that his existence is not "once hinted at from beginning to end. The name and person-"ality of Clement are absorbed in the Church of which he is the "spokesman.

"This being so, it is the more instructive to observe the urgent "and almost imperious tone which the Romans adopt in address-"ing their Corinthian brethren during the closing years of the "first century. They exhort the offenders to submit 'not to "them, but to the will of God' (§ 56). 'Receive our counsel,' "they write again, 'and ye shall have no occasion to repent'

---

* We see some traces of this custom in the Epistles of S. Paul. Thus, in his Epistle to the Philippians, written to the Church at Philippi collectively, the Apostle addresses some one personally without naming him; and he was probably the Bishop. "And I entreat thee also, my sincere companion," &c. (iv. 3). Referring to this passage, Döllinger says: "It was he who received the Epistle, and was to communicate or read it to the rest." (*The First Age of the Church*, vol. ii. p. 135.) So also S. John addresses his Apocalypse to the Seven Churches in Asia collectively (i. 4); whilst there are in it, at the same time, words spoken personally to the several Bishops of those Churches. (*Apoc.* ii. and iii.)

† *H. E.* vi. and vii. *passim.*   ‡ *Ibid.* iv. 15.   § *Ibid.* v. 1-4.

"(§ 58). Then shortly afterwards: 'But if certain persons should be disobedient unto the words spoken by Him (i.e., by God) through us, let them understand that they will entangle themselves in no slight transgression and danger, but we shall be guiltless of this sin' (§ 59). At a later point again they return to the subject and use still stronger language: 'Ye will give us great joy and gladness if ye render obedience unto the things written by us through the Holy Spirit, and root out the unrighteous anger of your jealousy, according to the entreaty which we have made for peace and concord in this letter; and we have also sent unto you faithful and prudent men, that have walked among us from youth unto old age unblameably, who shall be witnesses between you and us. And this we have done that ye might know that we have had and still have every solicitude that ye may speedily be at peace' (§ 63).

"It may seem strange to describe this noble remonstrance as the first step towards papal aggression. And yet undoubtedly this is the case. There is all the difference in the world between the attitude of Rome towards the Churches at the close of the first century, when the Romans as a community remonstrate on terms of equality with the Corinthians in their irregularities, strong only in the righteousness of their cause, and feeling, as they had a right to feel, that these counsels of peace were the dictation of the Holy Spirit, and its attitude at the close of the second century, when Victor the Bishop excommunicates the Churches of Asia Minor for clinging to a usage in regard to the celebration of Easter which had been handed down to them from the Apostles, and thus foments instead of healing dissensions.* Even this second stage has carried the power of Rome only a very small step in advance towards the pretensions of a Hildebrand, or an Innocent, or a Boniface, or even of a Leo: but it is nevertheless a decided step." †

In another place Dr. Lightfoot says: "With Victor (A.D. 189), the successor of Eleutherus, a new era begins. Apparently the first Latin prelate who held the metropolitan See of Latin Christendom, he was, moreover, the first Roman Bishop who is known to have had intimate relations with the imperial court, and the first also who advanced those claims to universal dominion, which his successors in later ages have always consistently and often successfully maintained. 'I hear,' writes

---

* Euseb. *H. E.* 23, 24.   † *S. Clement's Epistle, ibid.*

"Tertullian scornfully, 'that an edict has gone forth, aye, and
"*that* a peremptory edict: the chief pontiff, forsooth, I mean the
"bishop of bishops, has issued his commands.' At the end of
"the first century the Roman Church was swayed by the mild
"and peaceful counsels of the Presbyter-bishop, Clement; the
"close of the second witnessed the autocratic pretensions of the
"haughty Pope Victor, the prototype of a Hildebrand or an
"Innocent."*

"The substitution of the Bishop of Rome is an all-important
"point. The later Roman theory supposes that the Church of
"Rome derives all its authority from the Bishop of Rome, as
"the successor of S. Peter. History inverts this relation, and
"shows that, as a matter of fact, the power of the Bishop of
"Rome was built upon the power of the Church of Rome. It
"was originally a Primacy, not of the Episcopate, but of the
"Church. The position of the Roman Church, which this
"newly-recovered ending of Clement's Epistle throws out in such
"strong relief, accords entirely with the notices of other docu-
"ments. A very few years later, from ten to twenty, Ignatius
"writes to Rome. He is a staunch advocate of Episcopacy. Of
"his six remaining letters, one is addressed to a bishop as bishop,
"and the other five all enforce the duty of the Churches whom
"he addresses to their respective bishops. Yet, in the letter to
"the Church of Rome there is not the faintest allusion to the
"episcopal office from first to last. He entreats the Roman
"Christians not to intercede, and thus, by obtaining a pardon or
"commutation of sentence, to rob him of the crown of martyr-
"dom. In the course of his entreaty he uses words which
"doubtless refer in part to Clement's Epistle, and which the
"newly-recovered ending enables us to appreciate more fully.
"'Ye never yet,' he writes, 'envied any one,' *i.e.*, 'grudged him
"the glory of a consistent course of endurance and self-sacrifice.
"Ye were the teachers of others (οὐδέποτε ἐβασκάνατε οὐδενί·
"ἄλλους ἐδιδάξατε),' § 3. They would, therefore, be inconsistent
"with their former selves, he implies, if in his own case they
"departed from those counsels of self-renunciation and patience
"which they had urged so strongly on the Corinthians and
"others. But, though Clement's letter is apparently in his
"mind, there is no mention of Clement or Clement's successor
"throughout. Yet at the same time he assigns a Primacy to

* *Epistle to the Philippians*, p. 222.

"Rome. The Church is addressed in the opening salutation as "'she who hath the presidency (προκάθηται) in the place of the "region of the Romans.' But immediately afterwards the nature "of this supremacy is defined. The presidency of this Church is "declared to be a presidency of love (προκαθημένη τῆς ἀγάπης). "This, then, was the original Primacy of Rome—a Primacy, not "of the Bishop, but of the whole Church—a Primacy, not of "official authority, but of practical goodness—backed, however, "by the prestige and the advantages which were necessarily "enjoyed by the Church of the Metropolis.... When, some "seventy years later than the date of our Epistle, a second letter "is written from Rome to Corinth during the Episcopate of Soter "(about 165-175), it is still written in the name of the Church, "not the Bishop of Rome, and as such is acknowledged by "Dionysius of Corinth. 'We have read your letter' (ὑμῶν τὴν "ἐπιστολήν), he writes in reply to the Romans. At the same "time he bears a noble testimony to that moral ascendency of "the early Roman Church which was the historical foundation "of its Primacy: 'This hath been your practice from the beginning, "to do good to all the brethren in the various ways, and to send "supplies (ἐφόδια) to many Churches in divers cities, ... thus "keeping up, as becometh Romans, a hereditary practice of "Romans, which your blessed Bishop Soter had not only main- "tained, but also advanced,' with more to the same effect."*

We can well imagine the consternation that would have been excited amongst Protestants had the learned Anglican Bishop decided that S. Clement, who wrote the letter, must himself, as the ruling pastor and the chief in the executive government of the Roman Church, be held personally responsible for the authoritative language and imperious tone in which it is couched. That S. Clement, as Bishop of Rome, should assert his right to adjudicate on the question in dispute amongst the Corinthians, whether their own Bishop and certain of the presbytery were to be deposed or not, and should actually pass judgment on this

* Eusebius—*H. E.* iv. 23, whence this account is taken—says expressly that this letter, in reply to the second Roman one, was written by Dionysius and addressed to Soter, the then Bishop of Rome. Ἔτι τοῦ Διονυσίου καὶ πρὸς 'Ρωμαίους ἐπιστολὴ φέρεται, ἐπισκόπῳ τῷ τότε Σωτῆρι προσφωνοῦσα. We here supply the few concluding words given of the letter "to the same effect" which Dr. Lightfoot has omitted: "Both by administering the abundant supplies sent for the saints, and by encouraging the brethren who came from abroad, as a tender, loving father his children, with blessed words."

matter; that he should lay claim to the submission and obedience of the Corinthian Church, on the ground that his will was the Will of God, and that his words were dictated by the Holy Ghost; that he should, after making a most solemn appeal to the Three Divine Persons, promise, on the one hand, benediction on the part of God to those who were obedient, and threaten, on the other hand, with the Divine displeasure those who resisted his sentence; that he should, in fine, send his own legates to Corinth in order to secure the acquiescence of its Church to his will; such conduct as this would be branded as ultramontane usurpation and Papal aggression on the part of Clement; whilst the submission given by the Corinthians, which the peace that ensued in their Church makes evident, would be held up to reproach as an unworthy surrender of their independent rights through tamely yielding to the dictation of a foreign prelate—especially when it is borne in mind that Corinth was an ancient See, itself too founded by the Apostles. That S. Clement was responsible for all this was quite inadmissible, and could not be allowed for an instant; since it holds as a first principle amongst Protestants, and one of vital importance to the position of Anglicans in particular, that there was no assertion of supremacy on the part of the Bishop of Rome, at any rate in the first two centuries, but that this had its origin and growth in after times. Hence, when Rosmini says:

"Lastly, unity was, above all, due to the authority of the Supreme Pontiff, the chief stone of the Episcopal edifice," &c.

Canon Liddon, the Anglican editor, as though by instinct of self-preservation, at once gives the death to a statement so dangerous, by saying in an appended note:

"This is inaccurate. In the earliest times no such authority as the Papacy existed in the Church," &c.[*]

Still, explain it as you will, the Primacy, nay, the supremacy of Rome is there, and there is no way of getting away from it; it stares us in the face before the first century has closed, through the Epistle of S. Clement: and, at the commencement of the second century, S. Ignatius bears witness to it, as recognised at Antioch and in the Eastern Churches. This is too palpably plain for denial, and Dr. Lightfoot acknowledges the fact. Moreover,

[*] *The Five Wounds*, edited, with an Introduction, by H. C. Liddon, D.D., Canon Residentiary of S. Paul's. Rivingtons, 1883.

it is not a Primacy of mere name, of rank, and honour, for it appears in active and very critical operation; it passes definitive sentence, and exercises an act of supreme jurisdiction with regard to another Church of venerable and Apostolic foundation, possessed of its own constituted rights. To ascribe this Primacy to S. Clement would, as we have seen, be out of the question and impossible; for it would be to say, that the Bishop of Rome did in the first century the very same that Pope Julius did in the fifth, when, in the case of S. Athanasius and other Eastern Bishops who went to Rome to appeal to him against their deposition, he, by his own authority, after he had examined the matter, restored them to their respective Sees;* and what other Popes in subsequent times have done all the world over. But this would not square with the Anglican theory that "in the earliest times no such authority as the Papacy existed in the Church."

In what way, then, is this Roman Primacy to be interpreted? how is it to be accounted for? to whom is it to belong? S. Clement must have nothing to do with it; that is clear; it must be shifted from his shoulders, and the body of the Roman Church must be made to bear the charge. For, from what we can gather from the principles of Dr. Lightfoot, this primitive Primacy of the Roman Church was one entirely distinct from, and independent of, its Bishop; who, so far from having personally any Primacy as Bishop of the Church, is represented as occupying a lower grade of authority in his own See than other Bishops of that period did in theirs. In fact, so immaturely developed was Episcopacy in Rome at that time, compared with its condition elsewhere,—though the learned author considers it "as certainly existing at Rome in some form or other,"—that not only the authority, but "the very name and personality of the Bishop Clement was absorbed" in the body of the Roman Church, and, consequently, he is more fitly styled a "presbyter-bishop" than a normal bishop. This Primacy of the Roman Church had, moreover, nothing to do with S. Peter; for Dr. Lightfoot peremptorily cuts off the Roman Primacy—as he sees it set forth in the *Inscription* of S. Ignatius—from all connection with that of Peter, supposing that that Apostle had himself any sort of Primacy at all. "The idea of the *Cathedra Petri*," says the learned commentator, "has no place here."

* Socrates, *Hist.* ii. 15.

480 A PRIMACY, WHEREIN PETER'S CATHEDRA HAS NO PLACE,

We are somewhat at a loss to understand what precisely Dr. Lightfoot would mean here by the *Cathedra Petri*—whether it is S. Peter's Episcopal Chair at Rome, or his Primatial Chair. If the former, and supposing that S. Peter was not Bishop of Rome at all, it is no doubt true, or rather a truism, to say that his Episcopal Chair is out of place at Rome; since a bishop's cathedra or chair can have place only where is his Episcopal See; and it follows as a matter of course that, if S. Peter was not Bishop of Rome, his Episcopal Cathedra could have no place there. But if by the *Cathedra Petri* is meant the Primatial Chair, it is equally self-evident that this, so far as Peter is concerned, could have no place in such a Roman Primacy as Dr. Lightfoot asserts. For it is quite clear that, if S. Peter had any Primacy at all, it was one bestowed upon himself in person by our Lord Jesus Christ: and it stands to reason that, if such Primacy was intended by Christ to be permanent in His Church, it must have devolved after Peter's death on some one individually who was to be personally Peter's successor as Primate and Chief Pastor, and could not find its place in the collective body of any particular Church. In whichever sense, then, the *Cathedra Petri* is taken, we fully agree that in the hypothesis of Dr. Lightfoot its very idea is quite incongruous and out of place.

But here, we may ask, whence did this alleged Primacy of the Roman Church, as such, abstracted, as it was, from its Bishop, and cut off from S. Peter, derive its origin? And what was its sanction? Certainly no Divine sanction can be claimed for it as coming directly from Christ. For if He did not bestow it on Peter, there is not the faintest shadow of ground for holding that He bestowed it elsewhere. But had this Roman Primacy of Dr. Lightfoot's indirectly a Divine sanction through some act of the whole Christian Church? Or had it any ecclesiastical sanction at all? If so, where is the proof? Can any Council or act of the Church be pointed out during the first century whereby this Primacy over the other Churches of Christendom was conferred on the Church of Rome? Certainly not. And yet, undeniably, that Church had a Primacy, and asserted its claim to the obedience of the Church of Corinth under a Divine sanction. But then it is urged, as though a justifying plea: There is all the difference in the world between such a claim when made by the Roman Church, and the same claim if made by the Roman Bishop. In the latter case it would, no doubt, be a simply gratuitous act of Papal aggression: whereas, in the former case it is justifiable and righteous, and euphemistically it is described as "a noble remonstrance" of a community with brethren on terms of equality. For though, as Dr. Lightfoot goes on to explain, there is certainly an assertion of authority and a summons to obedience, set forth in an urgent and almost imperious tone, yet, in point of fact, this Primacy is "not one of official "authority at all, but of love and practical goodness, an entirely "moral ascendency—backed, however, as it is, by the prestige and "the advantages which were necessarily enjoyed by the Church of "the Metropolis." Such is all we can glean from Dr. Lightfoot of the origin and sanction of this active Primacy of the Roman Church.

Here, however, we find ourselves wholly at a loss to understand the learned author's argument, and as little able to discover the logical connection between his premisses and conclusion, as we are to admit their truth. In default, then, of any direct answer to his reasoning, we deem it sufficient simply to ask one or other question. Would such a Primacy as is described bear with it any righteous and justifiable claim to obedience and submission on the part of others? Is not the correction of fraternal charity, and its claims, of a nature wholly distinct from that of legitimate authority, and its rights,—this latter belonging to the virtue of justice? Could we conceive for a moment that a Primacy of love and good example, whose recognition by others must necessarily be voluntary, would be efficaciously operative to obtain their submission in religious and ecclesiastical differences, wherein, as experience shows, self-will, jealousy, and ambition have generally so much part? Does an act—which, if done by the Bishop of Rome, would be one of unjust aggression—change its nature and become justifiable, righteous, and of a binding character, because done by the Church of Rome?

In another passage Dr. Lightfoot seems to hold that the local prestige and advantages enjoyed by Rome as the Metropolis were not only "the backing up," but the very foundation of its ecclesiastical Primacy; and this is the view of most Protestants; but we may dismiss such purely human and adventitious circumstances from any serious consideration. These doubtless may, through Divine Providence, contribute something. The religious sense in man belongs, however, to another order quite distinct from what is merely secular. Nothing but the conviction that a Divine and supernatural cause is at work, is adequate to produce a strong religious faith. The prestige of Rome did not originate the Christian belief in the Roman Primacy, nor was this necessary to preserve its influence. When the imperial capital was changed for Constantinople, and Rome had lost her former prestige, the Primacy of Rome was unaffected, and could in vain be transferred with the throne of the Cæsars.

"Constantine," writes Mr. Allies, "meaning to found a new empire, instinct with Christian life and unity, withdrew from Rome, and gave it a new capital. And then, just in proportion as old Rome decayed, new Rome, a second birth, . . . from the fourth century onwards, rose out of its very ruins into a spiritual empire. . . . In Rome, the Apostolic Throne became more eminent as the Cæsarean Throne was fixed at a distance. But had it not been the Apostolic Throne from the beginning, no absence of the emperor could have made it what it became, just as no presence of the emperor could make Byzantium Apostolic." *

Later history records the futile attempts made to remove the Popes from Rome to Paris. Even the "holy city" of Mecca illustrates the natural principle which we assert.

Had we to express our opinion on the whole transaction which forms the subject-matter of S. Clement's Epistle, according to Dr. Lightfoot's showing, and looking at it from the principles and standpoint of a non-Catholic, we should set it down as an act of very impertinent and unwarrantable interference on the part of the Roman Church, thus claiming the right to settle with a high hand the domestic disputes of the Church of Corinth—an ancient Church of Apostolic foundation, as independent, and as much *sui juris*, as herself—in matters, too, of only a disciplinary and non-essential nature, about which the Corinthian ecclesiastical authorities might well be supposed themselves best able to judge. It is all very well to water down such exercise of supreme jurisdiction on the part of Rome to "a noble remonstrance of a community on equal terms." We have only to read the Epistle for ourselves to see that this is not its true account, but that there is a formal summons to obedience, under grievous threats, to be followed up by the vigorous measure of sending legates to Corinth to see that the will of those who command is practically carried out. Now, what right had the Roman Church to act in this way? Evidently none but what itself assumed. Consequently it was an act of unjust usurpation. But what here greatly aggravates the injustice is its glaring hypocrisy; for, whilst thus claiming the submission of the Corinthians, they say,

---

* *The Throne of the Fisherman*, pp. 248, 249, 274. See the entire ch. vi.

forsooth, that it is not to themselves this obedience is due, but to God Himself, inasmuch as their command is the word of God—putting forth a pretension to act in God's name and to interpret His will, or rather, we should say, making out the utterances of their own counsel and will to be the word and will of God, whereas they know all the while that they have no Divine sanction either for this supremacy they assume or for setting themselves to be the authoritative exponents of God's word and will. What else is this but the very head and front of every Pope's offending? for who knows not that, from the days of the "haughty" Victor down, no Pope ever claimed submission or assumed to speak with binding force save on the plea that he did so by Divine authority. Well, then, may Dr. Lightfoot regard this affair "as the first step towards Papal aggression." He calls it, indeed, "a noble remonstrance;" but, to our view, from the standpoint we have taken, there is much shabby cowardice in it. Those who claim this supremacy and Divine sanction do not speak out and say who they are. Is it the whole body of the Roman faithful that has this Primacy? or the entire clergy? or a knot of the leading presbyters? or, may be—who knows?—some clique of forward Roman clerics and laymen, busy-bodies of extreme—what now-a-days would be called ultramontane—party views, that makes this pretension? Whoever were the real authors of the Epistle—for, though written by Clement, it "did not emanate from the Bishop, but from the Church of Rome"—who thus claim to represent that Church, they do not declare themselves, but screen their own personality all along under the indefinite terms of *we* and *us*.* What at any rate is clear, they make a tool of S. Clement; and this we consider a very shabby part of the procedure. Dr. Lightfoot speaks of him, indeed, elsewhere as "the illustrious Bishop of Rome, whose fame reached far beyond the limits of his jurisdiction;" of "his rank and position, his acknowledged wisdom and piety." But from what the learned author says of him in immediate connection with the See of Rome, and especially in his dealing as Bishop with this Corinthian affair, we should take him to be a man of very simple and gentle nature; unobtrusive, quietly accepting a

---

* "*We* consider."—"*We* have sent."—"If certain persons should be disobedient unto the words spoken by God through *us*, let them understand that they will entangle themselves in no slight transgression and danger, but that *we* shall be guiltless."—"Ye will give *us* great joy and gladness if ye render obedience unto the things written by *us* through the Holy Ghost." (See *supra*, pp. 474-5.)

place in the background, and a less active and prominent share in ecclesiastical administration; perhaps rather wanting in force and decision of character, and hence liable to be too easily led and imposed upon by men of more shrewdness and diplomacy. Certainly he is not represented by Dr. Lightfoot as a Bishop disposed to take the initiative in a business so intricate and critical as that of settling the angry disputes in the Corinthian Church; for he was a man of "mild and peaceful counsels," and, "belonging to no party, he seemed to belong to all." But whatever might be the energy of his will, and his real force of character, there seems to have been hardly any room for its exercise in Rome; for, though holding the See and styled its Bishop, he was after all no more than a "presbyter-bishop," and a mere nobody—"his existence not once hinted at" in the Epistle, "his name and personality absorbed in the Church from which it emanated." Whatever precisely this "Roman Church" may be supposed to be, poor Clement is made its "spokesman" and scape-goat, and prevailed on, evidently against his own leanings and sentiments, to write an Epistle couched in "almost imperious tone" and backed with an assumption of Divine authority which he was well aware neither he nor the Roman Church really possessed. Hereby both the purity of the Roman Church and the sanctity of Clement are seriously compromised. The whole transaction, moreover, wears the mark of double-dealing shiftiness. Clement is on the one hand responsible for the Epistle, since he is its author, and it will ever bear his name; on the other hand, he is not responsible, since it "emanated not from the Bishop, but from the Church." Such is the opinion we should form of the matter on Dr. Lightfoot's showing, as regarded from a Protestant standpoint. But we cannot agree thereto.

Dr. Lightfoot, as we have seen, maintains that the Roman Primacy was originally not one of the Roman Episcopate, but of the Roman Church, and that, so far from its power being derived from the Bishop of Rome, as successor of Peter, the Bishop of Rome, on the contrary, derived all his authority from the Church of Rome. This, he says, is a matter of fact demonstrable from history; whereas the substitution of the Bishop of Rome for the Church of Rome, is the secret of that subsequent Papal domination, which gained its first step through the autocratic pretensions of the haughty Pope Victor, at the close of the second century.

We have a right to expect that what the learned author

claims to be a clear historical fact—so important in its issues to all future Christianity—and which he so largely develops into a vast polemical armoury, would be shown to rest on a very sure and solid foundation. The sole basis, however, which we can discover in his writings for this supposed historical superstructure, is his own allegation that episcopacy at Rome was quite in an embryo state, as compared with its development in the East, at the period when S. Clement and S. Ignatius wrote their Epistles; and this he says, "there are grounds for surmising." It is well, indeed, to call that a "surmise" for which the evidence forthcoming is very uncertain and slight; but it is over-hazardous to attempt to rear on the strength of a surmise an edifice of certainty, bearing with it the fortunes of the Church of Christ: and, to our mind at least, not a little overweening for any one, out of his mere individual surmise, to think to construct a whole fabric of fact, which is to determine the measure, whether of truth or falsity, of all historical Christianity.*

But let us examine a little the grounds of this "surmise." From history, properly speaking, no grounds at all are offered. The only evidence adduced is altogether of a negative character, drawn from what is commonly called "the fallacy of silence," which, singularly, with Dr. Lightfoot assumes the form of positive "notices from other documents."

First, as regards this Roman Epistle to the Corinthians, Dr. Lightfoot urges that it does not emanate from the Bishop of Rome, but from the Church of Rome. Clement, who wrote it, is not once named; the first person plural is maintained throughout, &c.

Over and above what we have said on this point in another comment, we would here observe that there seems an especial fitness in this letter being written in the name of the Roman faithful collectively, that, by the example of their own union and obedience, the Corinthian brethren might be more persuasively led to cease from their unhappy schism, and peacefully to submit themselves to the legitimate ecclesiastical authority. But it is further objected, that no mention is made in the letter of any Episcopate at all in Rome. We reply, that neither is there anything said of any presbyterate and diaconate, nor, for that matter, of any ecclesiastical rule whatever in Rome, so that, for this objection of silence to have any force, it would tell as much against these, as against the Episcopate. But if the letter does not speak of a matter so obvious, it treats of what is far more to

* *Ignatius*, vol. i. p. 381.

the point. The Corinthian faithful are exhorted by arguments, derived from many sources, to submit to that ecclesiastical rule which has been divinely constituted in the Church. The threefold order of bishops, priests, and deacons is explicitly mentioned (xlii., lvii.). An analogy is drawn from the submission commanded in the Jewish Church to the triple gradation of the High Priest, the Priests, and the Levites (xl.), and the still weightier obligation of obedience enjoined on Christians. The Apostles are recorded as ordaining bishops and deacons in all the Churches. The Apostolic rule for electing bishops is appealed to, and of not depriving of their office those who were legitimately elected, and had lived in a manner befitting their state (xliii.). Any one who attentively studies this Epistle to the Corinthians will, we think, find the doctrine of Episcopacy, according to the Ignatian type, quite as clearly and forcibly inculcated by the Scriptural arguments and mystical analogies of S. Clement, as it is in the more simple, sententious phraseology of S. Ignatius: and whilst there breathes throughout, with singular unction, a spirit of Divine charity and respectful gentleness towards the brethren at Corinth, its closely-reasoned and didactic exposition of Apostolic order, ecclesiastical authority, and the duty of obedience, couched in more grave and solemn style, forms a dignified justification of the energetic measures employed to restore peace and union in the Corinthian Church.

Now, is it not quite unreasonable to suppose that the Roman Church would have addressed such a letter as this to the Church of Corinth, urging the obligation of submission to the Episcopate legitimately constituted there, as of Apostolic institution, if episcopal rule was at that time amongst themselves merely nominal, and at so low an ebb, that "the very name, personality, and authority of the Bishop of Rome were absorbed in the body of the Roman Church"? Simply to ask this question, is we deem a sufficient answer to the objection made as to silence on the episcopate at Rome in the Epistle of S. Clement.

In support of this argument of Silence in S. Clement's Epistle, Dr. Lightfoot appeals to "the notices of other documents," where, again, we are met with similar phenomena, *i.e.*, the same latent phenomena of silence. These documents are the Epistle of S. Ignatius, the *Pastor* of Hermas, and the letter of S. Dionysius of Corinth: we deal with them in later comments, though we are unable to discover any of the "notices" affirmed to be contained in them.

He says, moreover, that this silence in the letters of S. Clement and S. Ignatius would be an anachronism later on in the days of Hegesippus or S. Irenæus, and even earlier than that time in the second century. From this Dr. Lightfoot seems to imply that the substitution of the authority of the Bishop of Rome for the original authority of the Roman Church, had come about some time between the episcopate of Evaristus (100-108) or of Alexander (108-117)—within which dates the martyrdom of S. Ignatius certainly took place—and that of Anicetus (157-168), in whose time Dionysius of Corinth lived, and Hegesippus came to Rome. This marvellous change cannot be placed later, since, in the pontificate of Anicetus, the succession of the Roman Bishops was deemed of the highest importance as "the chief guarantee of the transmission of the orthodox doctrine," and then to make "no mention of the Bishop of Rome would be an inexplicable anomaly, a stark anachronism." Moreover, we find several notices of the exercise of personal authority on the part of Eleutherus (176-190) and Soter (168-176), the immediate predecessors of "the haughty Pope Victor" (190-200), in trustworthy contemporary and later authors.*

As the non-mention of the Bishop of Rome is the evidence offered of the Primacy of the Roman Church, in contradistinction to that of the Roman Bishop, and of the absorption of the name, personality, and authority of the latter in the former, we must hold that the prominent mention of the Bishop marks the epoch when the Roman Bishop emerged from his obscurity, or rather nonentity *qua* bishop, recovered his name and personality, and substituted his own episcopal authority for that of the Roman Church. There can be no doubt, we say, that this had been already effected in the time of S. Anicetus, since, besides what was said of Hegesippus, we find that the aged S. Polycarp came all the way from the East to Rome, expressly to see and to consult, not the Roman Church, but S. Anicetus in person, who was then its Bishop. Here we should remember, that it was from Smyrna, whilst the same S. Polycarp was Bishop there, that S. Ignatius wrote his Epistle to the Romans, whose then Bishop, according to Dr. Lightfoot, was still in the swathing-bands of a "presbyter-bishop." S. Polycarp, of course, would have been aware of this circumstance were it really the case, and have known, too, which Bishop of Rome it was, who had been the first to develop into a

* Euseb. *H. E.* v. 4-21; S. Hieron. *Script. Eccl.* IRENÆUS; Ven. Bede, *Hist.* i. 4; *Catal. Felic.*; Tertul. c. *Prax.* i. 1.

full-grown and normal Bishop like himself at Smyrna, and such as he found Anicetus to be when he afterwards visited Rome. This is the more evident, because, as Hermas, the brother of Pope Pius (142-157), informs us, it belonged to the special office of the Bishop of Rome to keep up correspondence with the Churches abroad. But, did we need any positive evidence to refute such a theory as this, based only on the fallacy of silence, but which is set forth by Dr. Lightfoot, as though a matter of actual fact, "shown by history in notices of contemporary documents," we might find it in the testimony of S. Irenæus, who, in his letter to S. Victor, speaks of the Roman Bishops during the first half of the second century as personally holding the same rank and official authority in the Roman Church; exercising the same right of jurisdiction abroad, though not with the same mode of application as the "haughty" and "autocratic" Victor himself; and practising the same episcopal usages as anciently prevailed amongst all the Bishops of Christendom, and in particular amongst those of Asia. The words of S. Irenæus are as follows:

> "And those presbyters who governed the Church before Soter, and over which thou now presidest, I mean Anicetus, Pius, Hyginus, Telesphorus, and Xystus (who immediately succeeded Alexander, A.D. 117), neither themselves observed it (*i.e.*, the Paschal custom of the Asiatic Churches), nor permitted those with them to observe it. And yet, though they did not keep it themselves, they were none the less at peace with those who came to them from Churches in which it was kept; albeit its observance, in the very face of those who did not observe it, was an act of still greater opposition. Neither were any cast off on account of the said custom. But those very presbyters before thee who did not observe it, sent the Eucharist to the presbyters of other Churches who observed it."*

Surely there would be no point, sense, or meaning at all in this remonstrance of S. Irenæus, and in his contrasting the conduct of these early Bishops of Rome, under the same circumstances, with that of Victor, unless these were reckoned to have had equal power, discretion, and authority with Victor himself.

"Another point of special interest," continues Dr. Lightfoot, "in the newly-recovered portion of Clement's Epistle, is the link "of connection which it supplies with the earlier history of the "Roman Church. In the close of the Epistle, mention is made "of the bearers of the letter, two Romans, Claudius Ephebus and

* Euseb. *H. E.* v. 24.

THE TWO LEGATES SENT FROM ROME TO CORINTH. 489

"Valerius Bito, who are sent to Corinth with Fortunatus—the
"last mentioned being apparently a Corinthian (though this is
"not clear), and perhaps the same who is named in S. Paul's
"First Epistle (xvi. 17). In the newly-discovered portion, these
"delegates are described, in the words which I have already
"described, as 'faithful,' &c. Now, the date of this Epistle, as
"determined by internal and external evidence alike, is some-
"where about the year A.D. 95, and as old age could hardly be
"predicated of men under sixty, at least, these persons must have
"been born about the year 35, or earlier. Thus they would be
"close upon thirty years of age when S. Paul first visited Rome
"(A.D. 61-63). They must, therefore, have had a direct personal
"knowledge of the relations between the two Apostles, S. Peter
"and S. Paul (supposing that S. Peter also visited the Metropolis,
"as I do not doubt that he did), and of the early history of the
"Roman Church generally; for the description obviously implies
"that they had been brought up in the Christian faith from their
"youth. If we couple this notice with the fact that in an earlier
"passage of the Epistle these two Apostles are held up together
"as the two great examples for the imitation of the Christian, we
"see a new difficulty in the way of the Tübingen theory, which
"is founded on the hypothesis of a direct antagonism between the
"teaching of the two Apostles, and supposes an entire dislocation
"and discontinuity in the early history of the Christian Church,
"more especially of the Church of Rome. To this theory, the
"Epistle of Clement, the one authentic document which has the
"closest bearing on the subject, gives a decided negative."

The learned author conjectures as probable that Claudius and
Valerius were connected with the imperial household.* He says:
"This becomes still more probable now that we know them to
"have been old men in the closing years of the first century. On
"the supposition that they were freedmen or children of freedmen,
"they would probably have obtained their names somewhere
"about the time when a Claudius was seated on the imperial
"throne with a Valeria as his consort (A.D. 41-48).† Thus,

* *Philip.* iv 22.
† The coincidence of what is here conjectured, with the date assigned by antiquity to the first preaching of S. Peter in Rome, when the two legates would have been boys, will not fail to be remarked by the reader. What is further said in relation to S. Paul will equally well agree with the chronology of Jüngmann, which places his imprisonment in Rome at A.D. 56-58, as with that of Dr. Lightfoot.

"when S. Paul wrote from Rome to Philippi (about A.D. 62),
"they would be young men in the prime of life, their consistent
"course would mark them out as the future hope of the Church
"in Rome; they could hardly be unknown to the Apostle, and
"their names (among many others) would be present to his mind
"when he dictated the words, 'They that are of Cæsar's house-
"hold salute you.'" *

We will here group together a few items on S. Paul in Rome from Dr. Lightfoot's commentary *On the Philippians.*

S. Paul probably arrived in Rome in the early spring of 61, when Burrus and Seneca still lingered at the head of affairs. S. Paul must have been liberated before July, 64, the year of persecution, if liberated at all (pp. 2, 3). The abode of S. Paul at Rome, not improbably, was in the great camp, the head-quarters of the Prætorians without the walls to the north-east of the city (p. 9). "In no Church are the antipathies and feuds of the Jewish and "Gentile converts more strongly marked than in the Roman. "Long after their junction the two streams are distinctly traced, "each with its own colour, its own motion; and a generation at "least elapses before they are inseparably united. In the history "of S. Paul they flow almost wholly apart" (p. 14). [Döllinger holds the direct contrary of this last statement. See above, Ch. ix. p. 300, note; and Ch. x. p. 307, note.] "Gentile Christian-"ity was not less fairly represented in Rome than Judaic "Christianity" (p. 18). Pomponia Græcina, Flavius Clemens and his wife, Flavia Domitilla, are recognised as Christian converts (p. 19). The Church of Rome was not insignificant at this time (p. 25). "On the whole, therefore, it must be confessed "that no great stress can be laid on the direct historical links "which might connect Seneca with the Apostle of the Gentiles." (p. 300).

3. ON THE EPISTLE OF S. IGNATIUS TO THE ROMANS.

"Though the Epistle to the Romans was written and de-
"spatched from Smyrna probably about the same time with the
"Epistles to the Ephesians, Magnesians, and Trallians; though
"it closely resembles them in style and expression, yet the main
"topics are wholly different. The subject-matter is changed with

* *S. Clement of Rome*, pp. 252-256.

S. IGNATIUS' LETTER TO THE ROMANS—ITS TOPICS. 491

"the change in the relations between the writer and the readers.
There is no direct allusion to the Judæo-Gnostic heresy, which
occupies so large a place in his letters to the Asiatic Churches.
The Roman Church is complimented in the opening as 'filtered
clear from every foreign colouring,' and, from first to last, the
Epistle contains no reference to false doctrine of any kind. On
the correlative topic, also, the duty of obedience to the Bishop,
and other officers of the Church, which shares with the denunciation of heresy the principal place in the other letters, he is
equally silent here. Indeed, we might read the Epistle from
beginning to end, without a suspicion that the episcopal office
existed in Rome at this time, if we had no other grounds for
the belief."*

"It is plain," writes Dr. Lightfoot, "that Ignatius is apprehen-
sive lest influence of the Roman Christians should procure a
mitigation or a reversal of his sentence, so that he will be
robbed of the crown of martyrdom.† How was this possible? Who were these powerful friends who might be expected to rescue him from his fate? Twenty years earlier, or
twenty years later, than the assumed date of Ignatius, it is not
probable that any persons possessing sufficient influence would
have been found in the Roman Church. At least we have no
evidence of their existence at either date. But just at this
moment Christianity occupied a position of exceptional influence
at Rome. During the last years of Domitian's reign the new
religion had effected a lodgment in the imperial family itself.‡
The Emperor's cousin-german, Flavius Clemens, is stated to
have been converted to the Gospel: the same also is recorded
of his wife Flavia Domitilla, who, besides her relationship by
marriage, was herself also own niece of Domitian. The evidence of the Catacombs in the *Cœmeterium Domitillæ* suggests
that other members of the imperial family likewise became
Christians. These facts betoken a more or less widely spread
movement among the upper classes in the direction of Christianity. In his last years Domitian stretched out his hand to
vex the Church. Flavius Clemens was executed, others, in-

---

* Lightfoot, *S. Ignatius*, vol. ii. p. 185.
† Dr. Lightfoot is of opinion that the martyrdom of S. Ignatius most probably took place in the month of October, "within a few years of A.D. 110 before or after." The commonly received date is 107.
‡ See also Hefele, *S. Ignatii Epistolæ*, Prof. i., v. 1, g.

"cluding Domitilla, suffered banishment for their faith. Further
"persecutions were prevented by his death. On the accession of
"Nerva (A.D. 96) the victims of Domitian's cruelty were restored,
"and their penalties remitted. Nerva himself only reigned
"sixteen months, and was succeeded by Trajan (A.D. 98). Thus,
"in the early years of Trajan's reign there was a certain number
"of Christians moving in the highest circles of society at Rome;
"and, if they chose to bestir themselves, it would not be a very
"difficult matter to rescue one poor victim from the tortures of
"the arena. We do not hear of Christians in such high place
"till the reign of Commodus (180-190), when the influence of
"Marcia with the Emperor was exerted to alleviate the sufferings
"of certain Christian confessors.* But this is not the only point.
"There are also incidental allusions to the previous history of
"the Roman Church, which deserve notice. When S. Ignatius
"writes, 'I do not command you like Peter and Paul' (§ 4), the
"words become full of meaning, if we suppose him to be alluding
"to personal relations of the two Apostles with the Roman Church.
"In fact, the back-ground of their language is the recognition
"of the visit of S. Peter as well as of S. Paul to Rome, which is
"persistently maintained in early tradition; and thus it is a
"parallel to the joint mention of the two Apostles in Clement of
"Rome (§ 5), as the chief examples among the worthies of his
"time. The point to be observed, however, is not that the writer
"believed in the personal connexion of S. Peter and S. Paul
"with the Roman Church (this he might do, whether a genuine
"writer or not), but that in a perfectly natural way this belief is
"made the basis of an appeal, being indirectly assumed but not
"definitely stated. Again, he writes to the Romans (§ 3): 'Ye
"never grudged any one, ye instructed others,' where the context
"shows that the 'grudging' and the 'instructions' refer to their
"attitude towards Christian athletes striving for the crown of
"martyrdom. The bearing of the passage, however, is at first
"sight obscure, and certainly does not explain itself. But a clear
"light is thrown upon it by the Epistle of Clement, written in
"the name of the Roman Church, which appears to have been in
"the writer's mind when he speaks of the Romans as instructors
"of others."†

Though this interpretation of S. Ignatius' words here may be
true, yet we must not forget what Dionysius of Corinth himself

---

* Hippol. *Hær.* ix. 12.   † *S. Ignatius*, vol. i. pp. 435 *seq.*

says, when writing to the Romans, with regard to this letter of Clement, and another which he had lately received from Rome, to the Corinthians :

"To-day we have spent the holy day of the Lord, when we read your letter; in reading which, as also that former one written by Clement, we shall always find ourselves continually admonished."*

And again :

"In this way, by so great an admonition [as that contained in your Epistle], you too have united closely together that planting which had its origin from Peter and Paul, viz., of the Romans and the Corinthians; for both of them came to our city of Corinth ... and together taught us."†

This surely points to instruction in a more proper sense, more general and authoritative than that simply of example spoken of by Dr. Lightfoot.

We here give, with some abridgment and curtailment, Dr. Lightfoot's interpretation of part of the Inscription of S. Ignatius in his Epistle to the Romans,‡ and then make our comments :

"Προκάθηται. Has the chief seat, presides, takes the prece-
"dence. The word is used for preeminence or superiority generally
"in writers about this time.—Ἐν τόπῳ χωρίου Ῥωμαίων. These
"words probably describe the limits over which the supremacy or
"jurisdiction extends, just as Jerusalem might be said to preside
"in the region of the Jews. It might be thought that there was
"here a reference more especially to the presidency of the Roman
"See over the Suburbicarian bishops, who formed a sort of college
"under the Bishop of Rome as their head, of which some have
"seen distinct traces at least as early as the beginning of the
"third century; but such a reference would be probably a great
"anachronism.§ If, however, the words describe not the range
"of the supremacy, but the locality of the supreme power itself,
"προκάθηται would be used absolutely of a certain precedence
"assigned to the Church of Rome as situated in the metropolis of
"the empire and the world over the other Churches of Christen-
"dom, akin to the *potentior principalitas* of Irenæus, though the
"term here used is not so strong. But if this were so we should
"expect ἐν Ῥώμῃ rather than the expression actually used.

We are unable to see the point here, for the learned author

---

* Euseb. *H. E.* iv. 23.   † *Ib.* ii. 25.   ‡ *S. Ignatius*, vol. ii. pp. 190, 191.
§ Döllinger, *Hippol. u. Kallistus*, p. 108 *sq.*

lays down in another place that neither S. Ignatius nor other Bishops had at that time any jurisdiction outside the city or place of their Sees; and he would, we presume, hold that a particular "Church" was conterminous with its episcopal See; hence the words employed by S. Ignatius should be equivalent to "in Rome."

"The idea of the 'Cathedra Petri,' therefore, has no place here.—Προκαθημένη τῆς ἀγάπης. There is doubtless here a reference back to the foregoing words, meaning that the Church of Rome, as it is first in rank, is first also in love."

Here Dr. Lightfoot ignores the common grammatical rule for the construction of the genitive with verbs signifying authority or preeminence. This is the more remarkable, as in the immediate context he calls attention to a similar expression in *Clement's Epistle to James* ii. 17, where προκαθέζεσθαι ἀληθείας is applied to Clement as the successor of Peter, and where surely the ordinary rendering of the phrase is the true one: "To preside over the truth." To refer the word ἀγάπη primarily and principally to the abundant almsgiving of the Roman Church is certainly quite out of harmony with the dignity and general tenor of this Epistle, and with the use of the word in the other Epistles of S. Ignatius. We entirely concur with those who interpret the word here as equivalently meaning "the Church," which is the union of Divine charity; and in this sense the German Protestant Professor Harnack translates the phrase: "The president, whether it be in the confederation of love, or in the union of doing the works of love." We think that the words of S. Ignatius at the close of this Epistle may serve to illustrate it: "Pray for the Church of Syria, whose only pastor now is God. Jesus Christ will be its bishop. He and your love:" and with this we may also compare the other passages in which S. Ignatius uses the same expression: Ἀσπάζεται ὑμᾶς ἡ ἀγάπη Σμυρναίων καὶ Ἐφεσίων (*Trall.* xiii.). Ἀσπάζεται ὑμᾶς ἡ ἀγάπη τῶν ἀδελφῶν τῶν ἐν Τροάδι (*Philadelp.* xi.), and the same (*Smyrn.* xii.). Lastly, and still more remarkably: Ἀσπάζεται ὑμᾶς τὸ ἐμὸν πνεῦμα καὶ ἡ ἀγάπη τῶν Ἐκκλησιῶν τῶν δεξαμένων με (*Rom.* ix.).*

"One point," says Dr. Lightfoot,† "especially calls for a

---

* See article in *Dublin Review*, April, 1887.   † *S. Ignatius*, vol. i. p. 383 *sq*.

THEORY OF AN UNDEVELOPED EPISCOPATE IN ROME. 495

"notice when we are considering the unequal development of
" the episcopate in the different parts of Christendom. Of the
" seven letters bearing the name of Ignatius, six are addressed to
" Asia Minor, the remaining one to Rome. The six are full of
" exhortations, urging obedience to the bishops; the letter to
" Rome is entirely free from any such command. Indeed, if
" Ignatius had not incidentally mentioned himself as 'the Bishop
" of, or from, Syria,' the letter to the Romans would have con-
" tained no indication of the existence of the episcopal office.
" It is addressed to the Church of Rome. It assigns to this Church
" a preeminence of rank as well as of love (*Insc.*). There are
" obviously in Rome persons in high quarters so influential, that
" the Saint fears lest their intervention should rob him of the
" crown of martyrdom. With all this importance attributed to
" the Roman Church, it is the more remarkable that not a word
" is said about the Roman Bishop. Indeed, there is not even the
" faintest hint that a Bishop of Rome existed at this time. To
" ourselves the Church of Rome has been so entirely merged in
" the Bishop of Rome, that this silence is the more surprising.
" Yet, startling as this omission is, it entirely accords with the
" information derived from other trustworthy sources. All the
" ancient notices point to the mature development of episcopacy
" in Asia Minor at this time. On the other hand, all the earliest
" notices of the Church in Rome point in the opposite direction.
" In the Epistle of Clement, which was written a few years
" before these Ignatian letters purport to be penned, there is no
" mention of the Bishop. The letter is written in the name of
" the Church; it speaks with the authority of the Church. It is
" strenuous, even peremptory, in the authoritative tone which it
" assumes; but it pleads the authority not of the chief minister,
" but of the whole body. The next document emanating from
" the Roman Church, after the assumed date of the Ignatian
" Epistles, is the *Shepherd* of Hermas. Here, again, we are met
" with similar phenomena. If we had no other information, we
" should be at a loss to say what was the form of Church govern-
" ment at Rome when the *Shepherd* was written."

In another place Dr. Lightfoot says as follows: "An anonymous
" writer,* treating on the Canon of Scripture, says that the *Shep-
" herd* was written by Hermas 'quite lately, while his brother Pius
" (A.D. 142) held the See of the Church of Rome.' This passage,

---

* In the Muratorian fragment, Westcott, *Canon*, p. 480, 2nd ed.

"written by a contemporary, besides the testimony which it bears to the date and authorship of the *Shepherd* . . . is valuable in its bearing on this investigation (that is, of the Episcopate at Rome), for the use of the 'Chair' or 'See' as a recognised phrase points to a more or less prolonged existence of episcopacy in Rome when the writer lived." *

To resume our former quotation from *S. Ignatius*: "Thus the contrast between Asia Minor and Rome in the Ignatian letters exactly reproduces the contrast to be found elsewhere in the earliest and most authentic sources of information. As S. Jerome said long ago, the episcopal government was matured as a safeguard against heresy and schism. As such it appears in the Ignatian letters. But Asia Minor was, in the earliest ages, the hot-bed of false doctrine and schismatical teachers. Hence the early and rapid adoption of episcopacy there. On the other hand, Rome was at this time remarkably free from such troubles. It was not till the middle of the second century that heresiarchs found it worth their while to make Rome their centre of operations. The Roman Church is described in the Ignatian letters 'as strained clear from any foreign colour of doctrine.' Hence the Episcopate, though doubtless it existed in some form or other in Rome, had not yet, it would seem, assumed the same sharp and well-defined monarchical character with which we are confronted in the Eastern Churches. But what explanation could be given of this reticence, if the Ignatian letters were a forgery?† What writer, even a generation later than the date assigned to Ignatius, would have exercised this self-restraint? The Church of Rome is singled out by Hegesippus and Irenæus, in the latter half of the second century, for emphatic mention in this very connection. The succession of the Bishops of Rome is with them the chief guarantee of the transmission of the orthodox doctrine. Much mention of the Church of Rome, and yet no mention of the Bishop of Rome—this would be an inexplicable anomaly, a stark anachronism in their age."‡

"Though there are grounds for surmising that the Bishops of Rome were not at the time raised so far above the presbyters as in the Churches of the East, yet it would be an excess of scepticism, with the evidence before us, to question the existence

---

* *Epistle to the Philippians*, p. 220

† The subject of the chapter from which this extract is taken, is their genuineness.

‡ *S. Ignatius*, vol. i. p. 383 *sq.*

"of the episcopate as a distinct office from the presbyterate in the Roman Church."*

We fail to see in the *Pastor* of Hermas "a document emanating from the Roman Church." Such description suggests that the book was put forth as coming from that Church, and with its formal or public authority; whereas it was a work written by a holy man, claiming for its sanction his own private revelations and mystical visions. Being an ascetical treatise composed in allegorical style, on penance and the virtues, together with certain particular points of morality and doctrine, we should no more expect to find in it any mention of Church government, than in the *Revelations of S. Gertrude*, or the *Imitation of Christ*. Curiously, however, it does contain an incidental reference to this subject, which is very significant. In *Vision*, ii. 4, it is said to Hermas:

"Thou shalt, therefore, write two copies of the book, one thou wilt send to Clement, and the other to Grapte. Clement will send it to the foreign cities, for this appertains to his own proper charge. (*Illi enim permissum est.*) Whilst Grapte will (with it) admonish the widows and orphans. Thou, on thy part, wilt read it here in the city, together with the ancients (presbyters) presiding over the Church."

Here we find precisely the same form of government as the Ignatian letters describe in the Churches of Asia Minor—the Presbytery presiding in the Church with the Bishop.† Mention is made of Clement's name apart; thus denoting that his rank and office in the Church was of another and of a higher order than that of the presbyters, and that thus he presided over them, and the whole Roman Church. Had Hermas had us of the nineteenth century in his mind, he would doubtless have explained that this Clement was the Bishop; but for Roman Christians of his own day, mention of anything so obvious was clearly superfluous. Clement, it is added, had another office peculiarly his own, distinct from the jurisdiction and administration proper to the Roman Episcopate, and this was to com-

---

* *S. Ignatius*, vol. i. p. 381.

† The impression sought to be conveyed by Dr. Lightfoot's description of the Episcopate in the Eastern Churches as of "a sharp and well-defined monarchical character," jars unpleasantly on the memory that recalls the beautiful words of S. Ignatius, in which he compares the union of the Ephesian Presbytery with their Bishop to the harmony of chords on the harp, or to the melody of a chorus in unison; and the concordant rule over the Magnesian and Trallian faithful of the Bishop and his Presbyters, to the Divine government of Jesus Christ and His Apostles. (*Ephes.* iv.; *Magnes.* xiii.; *Trall.* iii.)

municate with the Churches abroad. On this we make no further remark, than that what is here said accords well with the Catholic doctrine of the Primacy, and with the uniform practice of the Bishop of Rome as Pastor of the universal Church. We maintain, then, in opposition to Dr. Lightfoot, that from intrinsic evidence of the *Pastor* itself, we might gather what was the form of Church government at Rome when Hermas wrote, as well as the preeminence of Clement the Roman Bishop.

We inserted, at once, after Dr. Lightfoot's comment on the *Pastor*, the passage containing the *Muratorian fragment*, because it is a contemporary testimony, bearing immediately on Hermas, which confirms our contention. We think it will be difficult for our learned author to convince ordinarily intelligent minds, that, at a period when now "the use of 'Chair' or 'See' was a recognised phrase pointing to a more or less prolonged existence of episcopacy in Rome," the Chair of the Church of Rome was, on the one hand, distinct from the primatial presidency of the Roman Church, which he admits to be then existing, and that the same Chair of the Church of Rome had in it, on the other hand, no idea of the *Cathedra Petri*, when the author of the Clementines— writing about the same date, and who, to render his story anyway plausible, would reflect current belief of the day on the main point—represents Clement as S. Peter's successor in the Roman Episcopate, and seated in the identical Chair, or "Cathedra," of the Prince of the Apostles.

Dr. Lightfoot speaks of the silence of S. Ignatius, with regard to the Bishop of Rome and the Episcopate in that Church, as "surprising and startling." We fail to see any reason for such great astonishment at what might be only naturally expected, if, as he alleges, it appears from notices in other contemporary documents that episcopacy in Rome was at that period in a very undeveloped state compared with what it was elsewhere, and especially in the East;—so that, in fact, the Bishop of Rome was but a "presbyter-bishop," his existence ignored, his name, personality, and authority absorbed in the Roman Church. This, as we have already shown,* is a theory based only on "the fallacy of

---

* *Supra,* pp. 485 sq.—However startling the alleged silence, reticence, and omission may appear to Dr. Lightfoot, and however adequate he may deem these as grounds of his own surmise, we must, in the interests of historical truth, earnestly protest against their being on that account foisted upon his readers as though they were positive evidence, and "information" of quite phenomenal importance, derived from a series of "the earliest and most authentic documents, and other ancient trustworthy sources."

silence," and a mere "surmise" which has no foundation in history, since whatever contemporary records survive go to prove the contrary fact. If then the silence here is to any a matter of surprise, it should be so to those who deny the theory of the low condition of the Roman Episcôpate at the date of S. Ignatius. For us, however, it is no matter of surprise, though, indeed, it is one worthy of note, and of interest to examine, with a view to its explanation.

We have then to keep in mind how different was the object which S. Ignatius had in view when writing his Epistles to the Churches of Asia on the one hand, and his Epistle to the Romans on the other. What the Saint had most at heart in writing the six other letters was to preserve these Churches in purity of faith and to keep them from heresy. He saw how much the faithful in the East were exposed to this danger, and, consequently, he insists so strongly on their being united and obedient to their orthodox Bishops as the great means to prevent their being led away by teachers of false doctrine. On this account, too, he lays such great stress on episcopacy and its Divine institution. Thus, he says that the "faithful should see God Himself in their Bishop;"* that "where the Bishop is seen, there is the congregation of the faithful, just as where Christ is, there is the Catholic Church,"† whilst "without the Bishop and the Presbyters it is not called a Church;" ‡ that those who act in religious matters "independently of the Bishop are not Christians" in any true sense,§ whilst "return to communion with the Bishop is the way to obtain pardon from God."‖ For the same reason he admonishes and exhorts the Bishops to constant zeal and watchfulness, and recommends them to their flocks, with words of praise for each, according to their several merits. To the Ephesians, he speaks of Onesimus as a man of incomparable charity, whom he desires that they should love, and to whom he would have them all become like; to the Magnesians of Damas, their "worthy (God-worthy) Bishop;" to the Trallians of Polybius, a model of charity, whose whole bearing is a lesson to them; to the Philadelphians, he praises their Bishop, without mentioning his name, for his modesty and gentleness, and as gaining much by his reticence; he salutes "the worthy (God-worthy) Bishop" of Smyrna without naming him; but to Polycarp himself, that

---

* *Ephes.* vi.   † *Smyrn.* viii.   ‡ *Trall.* iii.   § *Smyrn.* viii.
‖ *Philadelph.* viii.

same Bishop, he writes as a Saint to a Saint. With him he has no reserve, but pours out to him his heart in full confidence. He praises Polycarp as a good Bishop, and exhorts him to still greater perfection in the discharge of his pastoral duties, speaking as a father to a son. In all these letters there is a paternal tone; indeed one can hardly fail in reading them to recognise that they come from one who is of superior dignity and influence, and who has a right to speak with the accents of a father and with authority, notwithstanding his disclaimer of this, and his repeated words of humility. And justly he might have urged such a claim, as a disciple of the Apostles, and as successor to S. Peter, the prince of the Apostles, in his own See of Antioch, the first and the greatest Church in Eastern Christendom.

Though the name of Patriarchate dates from the Council of Chalcedon, the power and prerogatives which belonged to the three chief Sees of Rome, Alexandria, and Antioch had their origin long before.

"At the Nicene Council," writes Mr. Allies,* "the bishops of these Churches were seen in possession of a higher authority than the rest, an authority which had come down to them from the first origin of their sees, and which the Council did not create, but recognise. Though their sees were the most renowned cities of the empire, the higher authority of these bishops was carried back to the Apostle Peter, who had sat in person, first at Antioch and then at Rome, and had placed his disciple Mark at Alexandria. The name of Peter stood at the head of the episcopal catalogue in these three sees;† and the local tradition in all of them gave constant witness afterwards to Peter in many various ways. The Nicene Council knew only these three superior metropolitans, recognising their special rights in the Sixth Canon, which runs thus : ‡ 'Let the ancient custom continue in force which subsists in Egypt, Libya, and Pentapolis, by which the bishop of Alexandria possesses authority over all these, since the like custom subsists also with the Roman bishop. In like manner, also, their privileges should be preserved to the Churches, as to Antioch and the other provinces.'. . ."

"In these terms the Council admitted what were afterwards called the patriarchal rights of the bishop of Alexandria. . . . It admitted a similar right in the see of Antioch over the metropolitans subject to it, in which patriarchate both metropolitans and bishops were much more numerous than those subject to the Alexandrine bishop. The Council, in this Sixth Canon, justified the prerogatives which it thus admitted in the see of Alexandria, by reference to a similar right existing and exercised at Rome, and then by force of the same principle recognised the prerogative of Antioch and of metropolitans in general. In the previous history of the Church, these three

---

* *The Throne of the Fisherman*, p. 49.   † Hergenröther, *Photius*, i. p. 26.
‡ Hergenröther (*Photius*, i. pp. 26-30) shows that the Sixth Canon speaks of the rights of the great Metropolitans over a complex of provinces.

named sees, which were often called in a special sense 'the Apostolic Sees,' exercised a sort of hierarchical triumvirate, which the Roman see, ever strenuous in its grasp of tradition, firmly maintained. They were the chief leaders of ecclesiastical matters, as to which they referred in the first instance to each other. Thus, in the judgment deposing Paul of Samosata, the Synod of Antioch, in 269, directed its letter to Dionysius of Rome and to Maximus of Alexandria.* Before that, in the Novatian schism, and in the contest upon heretical baptism, these sees had carried on active correspondence with each other." "So strong was this hierarchical order, that, before the middle of the third century, Heraclas, the bishop of Alexandria (A.D. 238-244), could depose Ammonius, bishop of Thmuis, for disobedience, and consecrate a new bishop."†

It seems worthy of notice that S. Ignatius calls himself the Bishop not of Antioch, but of Syria,‡ and speaks of his Church as that of Syria.§ When he uses the term, "the Church of Antioch of Syria "‖ this is in connection with the cessation of the persecution in that city. We are inclined to think that such a territorial designation of his Episcopate, in place of the local one of Antioch, which would be more obvious, is not without meaning, as denoting the preeminence of that See, and the wide range of its influence. Syria, in which were many other Christian Churches besides that of Antioch, was at that period the most important province in the East; and under its name was sometimes signified the East in general, since Antioch, its metropolis, ranked next after Rome and Alexandria as the third city of the empire, and was not unfrequently the residence of the imperial Court. And here we hazard a conjecture that the periphrasis employed by S. Ignatius, which has given much trouble to interpreters, ἥτις καὶ προκάθηται ἐν τόπῳ χωρίου ‘Ρωμαίων (Rom. Inscr.), is parallel to this territorial designation of the See of Antioch, denoting the West in general, and the great metropolitan Church that presided in that part of the empire. An Asiatic would not unnaturally look upon the West as identical with the home territory of the Romans and the more adjacent European provinces, in contra-distinction to the East. Moreover, in the passage where S. Ignatius describes himself as the Bishop of

* Euseb. *H. E.* vii. 30.
† *The Throne of the Fisherman*, pp. 49 sq., p. 75. The chapters ii. and iii., "From S. Peter to S. Sylvester," of the work from which we here cite, form an admirably luminous exposition of the hierarchial order in the ante-Nicene Church, and especially of the historico-doctrinal significance of the triple Petrine Patriarchate.
‡ *Rom.* ii. ix.; *Trall.* xiii.
§ *Ephes.* xxi.; *Magnes.* xiv., twice; *Trall.* xiii.; *Rom.* ix.
‖ *Philad.* x.; *Smyrn.* xi.; *Polycarp*, vii.

Syria, he says that he is being sent over from the East to the West—εἰς δύσιν ἀπὸ ἀνατολῆς μεταπεμψάμενος.* What a later author says of the Church of Antioch, as presiding over the East, προκαθημένη τῆς ἀνατολῆς,† is to the point here,—whilst, at the same time, it illustrates that other expression of S. Ignatius (*Rom. Inscr.*) προκαθημένη τῆς ἀγαπῆς, which Dr. Lightfoot has so strangely translated—and confirms our own view, viz., that by the territorial designations of the Sees of Antioch and Rome is not improbably denoted the preeminence of these two Churches in the East and West respectively. In any case, by the last-mentioned expression is certainly signified the Primacy of the Roman Church over the whole congregation of the faithful throughout the world. What here, however, is simply our own conjecture, we submit to the judgment of the learned.

This Eastern part of S. Ignatius' journey Romewards, as he sent for the Bishops to meet him on his way, and wrote his letters to their Churches, was, so to say, a visitation in germ by a Metropolitan of his Suffragans. By his own paternal recommendations of them in his letters—to use an expression of Cardinal Newman, when writing on this same subject—"he took them under his wing," that so he might the better secure for them the union and obedience of their several flocks, and thus hinder these latter from listening to the heretical teachers in their midst.

But with his *Epistle to the Romans* all this is changed. He has now quite another object in view. It is no longer to teach and to exhort others, but to receive a personal favour for himself at their hands; and this was, that they would do nothing to hinder his martyrdom in Rome, now so near, and for which he so ardently longed. It would have been going out of his way to speak of aught else save what was the sole burden of his letter. Besides, why should he treat of episcopacy, or urge upon the Romans the obligation of shunning heretical teaching, and of being united and obedient to their Bishop, when writing to a Church which he feels he cannot too highly praise for its wondrous enlightenment and purity from every taint of foreign error? Had not, moreover, its own sainted Bishop himself, only a few years before, addressed that celebrated *Epistle to the Corinthians*, wherein he dealt so profoundly with the whole subject of ecclesiastical authority, and so luminously set forth the Divine institution of the Episcopate, and the Apostolic practice? Add to this that S. Ignatius was now addressing a Church altogether

---
* *R/m.* ix. † See *Joan. Antioch.;* ed. Oxon, 1691, p. 278.

outside his own influence as the chief Bishop in the East, and one, too, which he recognises as having the Primacy in Christendom.

Dr. Lightfoot considers the purity of faith and absence of false doctrine in the Roman Church to be a confirmation of his theory that its Bishop was as yet of but minor importance, whose office was one of subordinate influence and authority. For this view he cites S. Jerome, as though that holy Doctor meant to say that the first appointment of Bishops was due to heretical teaching as its original occasion and principal cause. S. Jerome, no doubt, speaks of the Episcopate as instituted to be a safeguard against heresy, but he says of it many things besides. He teaches, with S. Clement and S. Ignatius, that it belongs to the Divine constitution of the Church, and is the succession of the Apostolate; that the Bishop is set by Christ in the Church to be the shepherd and ruler of the flock, not only to keep the faithful from strange pastures, but to feed them with the doctrines of truth; that he is *lumen Ecclesiæ, condimentum mundi*, meaning thereby that it is especially by means of the orthodox and holy teaching, the good example, and wholesome instruction of a zealous and pious Bishop, that a people is to be preserved in the light of the true faith, and in sound Christian morality. So far, then, from deducing Dr. Lightfoot's inference from the teaching of S. Jerome, we hold, on the contrary, that the purity of faith and the sanctity ascribed by S. Ignatius to the Church of Rome were due especially to the holy influence, active zeal, and prominent authority of its Bishop, seconded by the exemplary submission of the faithful to the rule of their pastor.

To return to the holy Martyr. Who can brook with any patience, even for a moment, the thought that from Smyrna itself—the See of Polycarp—Ignatius, whilst in close confidence with its model Bishop, should be writing letters to the Churches of Asia, wherein he insists with such earnest force on the importance and Divine institution of the Episcopate; and should at the same time be penning one to the Romans, wherein he is supposed, of set purpose, to suppress all mention of their Bishop and of submission to episcopal authority, because, forsooth, he knew that his uniform teaching on this point would clash with the ideas of the then existing ecclesiastical authority at Rome, and be unacceptable to the Roman Church? For nothing short of this is involved in Dr. Lightfoot's theory.

Or, again, can we conceive that S. Ignatius, the type and champion of episcopacy, the chief Bishop of the East, who held his own See in succession from S. Peter, should regard with favourable eyes a See in the West wherein episcopacy was in no repute? How could he address the Church of Rome in terms of such deep veneration and high praise, as divinely enlightened and bearing the Primacy in Christendom, if in that Church the Episcopate existed in a condition so abnormal that the Bishop was held of no account, and his very name, personality, and authority were, as is alleged, entirely ignored?

If such were the real truth of the matter, we should have to say that S. Ignatius, in six of his letters to Churches in the East, laid down as the Divine rule that every Church was to be governed by its Bishop: whilst in his letter to the Roman Christians he most highly commended a Church wherein this same Divine rule was inverted and its Bishop was a mere subordinate. Nay more: we must say that he held up to universal veneration this Church, *de facto* presbyterian, as bearing the Primacy amongst all the really episcopal Churches throughout Christendom, and his own East in particular.

Had, then, the Saint two views of Christianity—for it comes to this—one for the East and another for the West? Or had the Apostles S. Peter and S. Paul left two traditions of Church government, one for use at Antioch, and another at Rome—analogous to what some Anglicans hold nowadays, as regards communion with Rome abroad and here in England? S. Irenæus, however, tells us—and he knew well the Apostolic traditions both in the East and the West—that still in his own time, though two generations later, the preaching of these Apostles was ringing in the ears of all Rome and of its Bishop too. But away from us the very thought of such truckling economy and suppression of truth derogatory to the character of S. Ignatius, the intrepid and noble Martyr-Bishop.

The one desire of S. Ignatius was that the Christians of influence in Rome should not seek to procure a reversal of his sentence to death. If the Saint does not mention any of these by name, still less reason would there be for mentioning the name of the Bishop of Rome, who was not amongst their number. In addressing the faithful of Rome, there was no need, as there might be in other Churches, to commend the Bishop by name, in order to secure to him the dutiful and united obedience of his flock. Moreover, the Saint's humility and deference towards the Bishop of the First See would forbid such mention, and thus seeming " to take Clement under his wing."

The fact is the Saint salutes no one in particular. Perhaps he did not know personally any of the Christians in Rome, and makes special mention of Crocus as with him at Smyrna, because he was a Roman, or was known to some of the faithful in Rome. This would be his reason for saying, that those whom he had sent on before him were, he believed, known already to the Roman Christians. We have already remarked that letters written to Churches by Bishops seem always to have been addressed to the Bishop of the See; so that if S. Ignatius had anything to communicate specially to the Bishop of Rome, he would have an opportunity of doing this either by sending it in writing, or by word of mouth of the bearers.

Near the close of his letter, the Saint speaks some very touching words which seem to discover the sentiments he had in his heart of deep veneration and filial attachment towards the Apostolic See, and the entire confidence that he reposed in the charity and zeal of the Roman Bishop, to whom Christ had entrusted His entire flock, and given the care of all the Churches. We offer a literal translation of the whole passage, as in it is illustrated another point also to which we have before adverted.

He had previously (in chapter ii.) spoken of himself as the Bishop of Syria, sent over in the providence of God from the East to the West; and in chapter ix. he says:

"Remember in your prayer the Church in Syria which, in my place, will needs have God for pastor. Jesus Christ will alone be its bishop, and your charity. But I am ashamed to be called of their number (*i.e.*, of bishops), for I am unworthy, as being the last of them, even an abortion. But I have received mercy to be some one, if I obtain God. My spirit salutes you, as doth also the charity of the Churches that have received me in the name of Jesus Christ, not as one passing through (*i.e.*, not as a stranger merely passing by these Churches on my way); for even Churches that did not belong to me* furthered me on my earthly journey from city to city."

The charity of the Roman Church, to which the Bishop of Syria commends his own widowed Church, is evidently the episcopal charity of the Roman pastor,—joined, as the expression is so closely, to the mention of Jesus Christ the Divine Pastor and Bishop. This conjunction, in which S. Ignatius seems to have before his mind the words of S. Peter (1 *Ep.* ii. 25), is very

---

* Which were outside my jurisdiction (*Pearson*).

significant. The same thought of the universal pastorate of Rome, which S. Ignatius had in the hour of his Church's bereavement, also was present, some five centuries later on, to the mind of S. Sophronius, who, when near his death, sent to implore the then Roman Pontiff, in his paternal charity, to take care of his own Church of Jerusalem, and of the neighbouring Churches, in the circumstances of great trouble and imminent peril with which Palestine was at that time beset. Pope Theodore responded to the appeal, by appointing Stephen of Dora to be his own Vicar in Palestine. The insertion of the name of S. Ignatius in the Roman Canon of the Mass before that of S. Alexander, the immediate successor of S. Evaristus, in whose pontificate the Bishop of Antioch was martyred, shows that his memory was cherished, and his recommendation of his own Syrian Church was not forgotten by S. Evaristus.

CHAPTER XX.

THE ROMAN EPISCOPATE OF S. PETER AND HIS SUCCESSORS, THE CHIEF MONUMENT OF HISTORICAL CHRISTIANITY, AND THE REALISATION OF THE DIVINE IDEA IN THE TWO DISPENSATIONS.

In the course of this work on S. Peter's Roman Episcopate we have discussed many particular questions; and our object in this last Chapter is to treat of something more general and comprehensive, which may, so to say, cover our whole thesis. The subject which we have chosen is profound; and, we confess, so much beyond our depth, that we can do little more than skim upon its surface, or, at the most, attempt its shallows. We trust, however, holding fast to old established truths and certainties, and keeping Peter's bark ever well in sight, not to lose ourselves, whilst on our venture, in any idle speculations.

So far as we can anticipate the matter of this Chapter, and formulate it into a definite proposition, it will run thus: The fact of S. Peter's Roman Episcopate, and of its perpetual succession in the Holy See, is to the world a historical monument, and an external symbol, of the realised Divine idea and purpose in the two Dispensations, and of the union of the Old and New Testaments in the Person of Jesus Christ, and in His Church:—that historical fact being to the Roman Pontiff's Primacy, as Christ's Vicar on earth, what the setting is to the jewel, or the shell to the kernel—its casket and shrine.

As the ostrich, it is said, buries her egg in the warm sand of the desert, and then, going away, returns after some time to find it come forth to life; so we, having laid down our proposition, here leave it for a while, hoping that when we take it up again after somewhat lengthened digression, we may present it under the form of manifest truth.

The various religions that have appeared in the world may, we think, be broadly divided into two classes, historical and non-historical.

RELIGIONS HISTORICAL AND NON-HISTORICAL.

A historical religion is, we conceive, one that is built up of facts and objective truths purporting to be divinely revealed and proposed to man's belief. Its basis is historical: it dates from some event of the supernatural order, or Divine interposition, alleged and believed to have taken place on earth at some particular epoch of the world's history. It is distinctly recognisable to the world by a historical continuity of its own, and is perpetuated amongst men, especially by means of its external monuments or institutions. These serve as memorials and symbols of its Divine origin, and of the supernatural facts and truths that form its subject-matter. Being a religion, it must needs have its own (so-called) speculative theology and its own moral teaching. But these, so far as they are proper to itself, flow from, are based upon, and intimately bound up with, the Divine objective realities and supernatural events contained in its revelation. Consequently, viewed in this connection they are definite, circumscribed, incapable of human alteration by addition or diminution, and themselves objective and absolute. On the other hand, inasmuch as the religion—which is revealed for men—meets the action of human thought, and is assimilated to man's mind and heart, it has its subjective side also.

A non-historical religion is to be looked on as rather a system of subjective philosophy or theodicy, evolved from reason, and from that religious sense which is natural to the human soul. Other influences may bear their part too,—whether traditions surviving from original revelation, or elements derived from some prevalent positive and historical religion—but this regards the subject-matter rather than the process of elaboration.

If a religion of this class claims for itself some particular date of origin, this is not, properly speaking, any historical event of Divine interposition, but merely the fact of its author at such a time putting forth his views and teaching—it may be under more or less extraordinary religious influence—analogously to Plato, Locke, or Hegel, inaugurating their systems of philosophy. A non-historical religion does not take its start from what professes to be positive revealed truths or supernatural facts. These do not, at least as such, form its subject-matter. It is, rather, a subjective process of speculation, wrought in a religious and reverential spirit,—on philosophical ideas and humanly conceived theories, with regard to the nature and order of the whole universe, material and spiritual, Divine and human, temporal and eternal, doctrinal and moral, on causes and effects, on good and evil, on the origin and end of being, on everything, in fact, that is contained *in natura rerum*—which gathers itself into a system whence may be drawn formulas, principles, and motives, directive of human thought and of practical conduct.

It is evident that a religion thus humanly evolved is, of its nature, capable of indefinite development, modification, and change. It might wear an appearance of more or less perfect form in various circumstances of place and time, according as a higher or lower type of religiousness was prevalent, or some more special "Divine influence" shed abroad at particular epochs of the human race. But such subjective religion, in whatever form, having its origin in the mutable, and depending on circumstances of change, must be always passing and transitional. Hence, we can easily conceive how a religion more or less philosophical would—from the natural tendency in the human mind to express abstract principles in a concrete form—popularly come to clothe itself in outward symbol. We can understand, too, how ere long, and by degrees—from that instinctive craving there is in man's soul to seek and feel after a real and personal God, if haply he may find Him, even though still unknown,*—the ruling forces of physical nature would be severally deified; how, around such symbolical divinities fabulous stories would gather, and these legends would hold the place of historical facts in the minds of a credulous people. Thus may we see how the surviving traditions of original revelation, and religious systems, born of reason and philosophy, degenerated, in course of time, into the deification of material objects—the worship of the sun, or the stars, or fire, —or into the mythological idolatry of Heathenism, as we find it, for example, in Greece and Rome.

Such religions as these are not to be ranked as historical, since their legendary records served to express externally, and their religious monuments and institutions to symbolise, not any really historical facts, nor any Divine objective truths alleged to be revealed, but only what was itself symbolical, and subjective theories and ideas of purely human genesis. Rather, we should class these various forms of mythology, idolatry, and of creature-worship generally, as so many gross religious expressions of Pantheistic and Materialistic philosophy. The Indian religions of Hinduism and Buddhism, which, perhaps, more than most others of Paganism, have preserved their first philosophical and

---

* *Acts*, xvii. 23-28.

idealistic character, are also, in our opinion, to be ranked as non-historical.

In the foregoing reflections on idolatry, we have purposely kept aloof from the consideration of any of its other causes—whether diabolical agency, or the depravation of the human mind and heart,—as this does not come within our present scope.

Besides Christianity and Judaism, Mahomedanism alone has held its own as a historical religion. This, like the two former, claims for itself positive facts of Divine intervention for the date of its alleged supernatural origin, professes to be expressly revealed, and to be based upon historical events.

It would be superfluous to verify Christianity as essentially an objective and historical religion, built up, as it is, on Divine positive facts and supernatural events, which are the foundation of its credibility, the cause of its effects, and the source of its doctrines, spirit, and life. Taking it in its widest signification—since its credibility at all depends on the reality of these facts,—the religion of all who bear the Christian name may be said to be historical. But it is, nevertheless, true that the Christianity of large numbers of professing Christians outside the Catholic Church has lost very much of its historical character, and is become rather a system of doctrines and ethics, independent of those Divine facts, which are, in truth, the only real rational basis for the credibility and authority of Christianity in any form.

We are not speaking here of those who professedly treat Christianity as only one of various forms of religious thought that have appeared in the world, or as an evolution of a higher kind from lower types of religiousness, and itself in process of development to the still more perfect "religion of the Future." Such men must deny point-blank the Divine revelation of Christianity. For it evidently stands to reason that a religion, so far as it is revealed by God, is a Divine quiddity, a Divine integral whole, complete and perfect in itself, which is, and must continue to be, what it is, as it came forth from, and was revealed by, God its Author. So far as it is divinely revealed, it is extrinsic to man, beyond his power and right of jurisdiction, save that, being revealed to him, it must be accepted and believed by him when it comes to his knowledge. It is given to be carefully treasured and faithfully guarded as a Divine deposit committed to man's trust, to be kept pure, uncorrupted, and without alloy. Hence, it cannot be subject to any human action, nor be liable to change, development, addition or diminution, on man's part. It is immutable of its own nature, for it is the incorruptible seed, the Word of God, which abideth for ever. And were Christianity other than what we have thus described, it would not be in any true sense a religion revealed by God to man at all.

In saying that Christianity is historical, we mean not only that it starts with, and is based upon, certain events and facts that took place in the world's history which any secular and even anti-Christian historian might record—such as the Birth and Crucifixion of Jesus Christ, the preaching of the Apostles, the writing of the Books of the New Testament, their genuineness and authenticity, &c.—but also, and principally, that it is built up of, and relies upon, Divine facts or truths of the eternal and supernatural order expressly revealed by God Himself as objective verities, such as the Mysteries of the Divine Unity and Trinity, the Creation of the World, the Fall of Man, the Incarnation of the Eternal Word in the womb of the Blessed ever-Virgin Mary, His Redemption of mankind, His institution of His Church endowed by Him with the Sacraments, supernatural powers, and Divine prerogatives,—to which Church, moreover, He delivered doctrines and precepts which she was to proclaim to the world with the right to be believed and obeyed by all who should hear her voice—the Personal descent, too, on earth of the Holy Ghost.

We say that to recognise in a vague sort of way the truth of Christianity, and to hold some of its doctrines apart from all those facts and realities that essentially adhere to it as revealed by God, is not to believe in it at all, properly speaking, as a historical religion,—since, as we have before shown, its teachings, as such, are credible only inasmuch as they are based on the reality of these facts—but is, rather, to turn Christianity into a sort of philosophy, subject, like every other product of human thought, to individual elaboration, eclecticism, and change.

Now, this is what is actually done with Christianity everywhere amongst the sects outside the Church: and the work of disintegration is more or less complete just in proportion as the historical character of Christianity is lost sight of. The Protestant Reformation in this country, and wherever it prevailed abroad, broke off the continuity of Christianity as a historical religion, and made a divorce between its history and its doctrines. This was effected in various measures; and in proportion to its thoroughness was the corruption and loss of Christian doctrine. In Scotland and some parts of the Continent, where the divorce was most complete and the historical element wholly ignored, the great objective truths of the Gospel revelation are, for the most part, practically effaced from the religion of the people, and what goes for Christianity is really no more than some human phase of religious thought derived from Luther, Calvin, or John Knox, as the case may be.

With regard to Scotland in particular, a personal observation of several years tells us that, whilst amongst religious-minded Presbyterians there is much talk of "the Saviour's finished work," "election by grace," &c., there exists hardly a notion of Who that Saviour Himself is, of His Divine Nature as Incarnate God, or of His historical character here on earth; so that the very idea of His having really been once an Infant—as set forth in our traditional Christmas commemoration of His Birth—is not only strange to them, but when proposed, is positively abhorrent to their thoughts, as much so as would be the sight of a great Crucifix with the title attached to it, "The All Holy and Most Merciful God," to a London crowd, if set up at Charing Cross. The historical Saviour being only an abstraction, of course it fares the same with His Blessed Mother, and the Saints most nearly associated with Him in His life on earth. The history of the Jewish nation has, in fact, a far greater place in Scotland's religion, and attraction for its people, than the history of Christianity; and the Saints and worthies of the Old Covenant are much more familiar to them than those of the New Testament.

In England, religion presents a more historical aspect: and this especially from two causes. In the first place, the retention to some extent of the ancient ecclesiastical calendar, with the commemoration of the Holy Seasons and certain Saints, year by year, in the public worship, has helped to keep alive in the minds of the English people the memory of the great historical mysteries and events of Christianity. Secondly, there was a semblance kept up of historical continuity between the Anglican Establishment and the Catholic Church, as it existed in this country before the Reformation, by means of the imitation, or rather we should say, at least in some points, the parody which the former made of the latter.

When the ancient Catholic Church was ousted on the pretended charge that she was an usurper in the land, a State-creature was set up, decked with much of the old paraphernalia and borrowed ornaments of Catholicism. The new Anglican Establishment was at once put into possession of the temporal goods of the Catholic Church, of her ancient episcopal Sees, benefices, Cathedrals, parish churches, glebes, revenues, titles, and dignities; to these was added a Protestantised adaptation of her rites and ceremonies, episcopal consecration, priesthood, Sacraments, Divine Office, and Sacred Liturgy. The Divine institution of the Roman Pontiff's Primacy and universal jurisdiction was parodied by the Royal Supremacy of the Sovereign, thenceforth styled, over all persons and in all causes, whether spiritual or temporal, within his dominion, supreme; whilst the form of the old ecclesiastical courts, now placed under the paramount and central authority of the Crown, still remained. Thus was attempted a semblance of continuity between the old and the new religions: but it is no more than a semblance. Anglicanism, however, by the preservation of its institutions received at its first start, can show a continuity of its own during the three centuries and more of its existence. Hence, it is really historical, and its religious monuments, institutions, and formularies distinctly proclaim its historical character: for they are all standing witnesses to, and symbolical of, the events of its origin and the continuity of its career. They tell of its supplanting the old Church and the old religion, of ruin done to the Catholic Faith in this land, and of sacrilegious spoils; they loudly testify that "the Church of England," as such, is essentially and historically Protestant and anti-Catholic, and has no continuity, whether in the order of time or of religion, with the Church of Christ as it existed in England before the so-called Reformation.

But we have already allowed that more of true historical Christianity is preserved amongst Anglicans than in any other of the Protestant sects. This can hardly be attributed to the authoritative standards of Anglican doctrine, since, for that matter, there is not very much to choose between the Thirty-nine Articles and the Homilies of the Church of England, and the Westminster Confession of the Presbyterian Kirk. It is partly due to the cause which we first assigned, and also to the fact that the Anglican Establishment was originally founded to be a counterfeit of the Catholic Church—a human imitation or adaptation of that which is Divine; and such it continues still to be. It pretends to the rights and authority of the Church of Christ; and what with its pompous assertion and imposing exterior, many may, through ignorance or simplicity, honestly take the phantom for the reality. Here we should not forget that Anglicanism, from its elastic and comprehensive nature, is tolerant of every manner of religious thought and opinion, so it be not "Romanising," and teems with divers schools of doctrine—"Catholic," too, and free-lances—which interpret its standards as they please, or do not care to trouble themselves about them at all, and so can make out the teaching of the "Church of England" to be what they will.*

* There are certain religious principles and truths so very plain and obvious that most persons can hardly understand their non-recognition; and certain inconsistencies so strange that it is almost inconceivable how they should ever be entertained. Such of these as exist in religion outside the Catholic Church a convert who knows both sides can better appreciate than another, and is, perhaps, best able to set forth. The following thought, which bears upon our present subject, has always very forcibly struck the writer. He must be allowed to express it in his own way.

A Catholic looks upon *his* Church—*i.e.*, the Holy Catholic and Roman Church—of which he is directly and personally a member, and whereon, as a child on his mother, he immediately depends for teaching, guidance, and support—as absolutely perfect, because he knows that she is the one only true Church of Jesus Christ, and that all her doctrinal and moral teaching is pure and holy, coming as it does from His revelation. In *his* Church, then—in the whole complexus of her faith and religion as actually proposed to him—he has that Divine ideal of truth and sanctity described by S. Paul, 'the glorious Church of Christ, not having spot or wrinkle or any such thing, holy and without blemish—sanctified and cleansed by Him, the Saviour of the Body, Who delivered himself up for it—that Church which He loves, nourishes, and cherishes as His own flesh,' even as His most fair and perfect Bride (*Ephes.* v. 23-30). This one Church of Christ is the Catholic's *only* Church, the one alone that he knows, and on her, be it observed again, he is immediately dependent for all his teaching and support—there is no other Church between him and her. To have a better Church, one more perfect, to seek to make her, or to wish her, better than she is, this is an absurdity that would never cross his mind. The very thought would be a sacrilege. She is perfect, the very ideal of excellence. She is *the Church of Christ*; she is *Divine*, and all that she has and communicates is Divine. This is enough and more than enough. What more will he have? If her members are defective and imperfect in practice, if some party in the Church is so, they have but to go to her, to listen to her teaching, to receive again of her fulness, and they will find in her a remedy and supply.

How different are the thoughts of non-Catholics about *their* several Churches, and the attitude they bear to their immediate teachers. Every one will of course profess that *his* Church is the true Church of Christ, or belonging to it as its part. But how does he treat it? He speaks of it, perhaps, as the Church of his Baptism, as though there were some distinction between it and Christ's one Church, wherewith it is not every way identical, and as though there were several Churches for Baptism into Christ. He sees not in it any ideal of sanctity or purity of doctrine—and yet it is his immediate teacher, he calls it his Mother, and bears the name of a "Churchman," because he is its member. On the contrary he laments his Church's doctrinal shortcomings, her defective, ambiguous, perhaps—so he deems—her partially erroneous teaching; he strives to bear with, and make the best of, her, to interpret her well, to improve and teach her better, to catholicise her more fully from ideas of his own which he has formed of Catholicism, derived from outside her doctrinal pale. *His* Church is evidently no perfect ideal, no Divine Mother on whom to depend, no unerring Teacher from whom safely to learn, no perfect spotless Church, and consequently no true Church of Christ at all. Poor orphan! he is his own chief-pastor and teacher, his own self-sufficient guide.

There is yet another cause well worthy of note, and that is the *Book of Common Prayer* and its appointed use in the Sunday and week-day public worship. This two-fold institution has served as a standing monument to mark the historical continuity of Anglicanism; whilst the recital or chanting of the Psalter and Canticles, the Creeds, Collects, and other prayers, clothed in the traditional language of the Church, the prescribed forms of reverential posture, &c.—all derived, in the main, from ancient Catholic sources—have been probably more influential than anything else in preserving amongst the people Christian truths, feeding their hearts with sentiments of Christian piety, and staying their downward progress to the excesses of religious innovation elsewhere prevalent.

We say, then, that Anglicanism, as such, is distinctly a historical religion. This character is, moreover, emphasised, and stands out more clearly from the very abrupt severance of the historical continuity of the Catholic Church in England at the Reformation—a break which serves to date precisely the first real start of the new Church, and the beginnings of its own proper history in Parker's succession.

But thus to affirm the historical character of Anglicanism clearly implies the denial of its being historical Christianity in any proper and true sense. Whilst it is the historical religion of the Church of England, it is by no means the historical religion of the Church of Christ; and this we have already shown. Still to say this does not contradict the admission we made that the Church of England,—without having any continuity with the one true original Church of Christ,—has from its adoption or adaptation of Christian institutions and other causes, been especially the means of preserving to English Protestants the knowledge of many truths of historical Christianity; but this is by accident, and is incident also in various degrees to all Christian sects.

It may appear to some quite idle here to remark that the history of Christianity, taken as a syncretism in its widest sense —whereof the history of Anglicanism forms a part—is a totally different thing from the history of that Church which was originally founded by Jesus Christ Himself. We, for our part, are of a contrary opinion; being persuaded that the idea of the very self-same Church which Christ first founded being still in existence, as such—in the identity of her original visibility and divinely constituted external organisation, with a continuous history of her own apart—is a notion foreign to the minds of Protestants and Anglicans generally, though here and there a high-Churchman seems hazily and very inadequately to conceive it.

We shall here illustrate our thought by something personal. We allow that it is not well as a rule for an ordinary person, and without some very good reason to speak of his own individual experience in the leadings of truth. When, however, it is a case of a mind acted upon, and not of one itself acting, and when the effect of truth is rather *ex opere operato* than *ex opere operantis*, there seems to be less objection to such disclosure. And since one man's mind is of like nature to another's, and since the human mind in general is connatural to truth; and truth may be said normally to act upon, and assimilate itself to, men's several minds pretty much in one and the same way; there is some ground, at least, for thinking that a case of this sort is a typical one, showing the direct action of truth of its own nature and according to the common law of its operation, and not so much due to the subjective character or circumstances of the individual.

It chanced then one day in an idle hour, that the writer, then some 18 years of age, fell in with one of the *Tracts for the Times*, the subject of which bore on our present matter. After reading a little in a desultory way, the idea—but as though quite independently of what he was reading—suddenly flashed across his mind that perhaps the original Church of the Gospel, founded by Christ, was really an external body, with its own Divine organisation, still visibly existing on earth. The idea that presented itself was distinctly not the Catholic Church, as the writer had learned to conceive that to be, composed of various branches, of which the Anglican Church—whether derived from the old British Church, or from S. Augustine—formed a part; but the *ipsissima Ecclesia Christi* first founded by Jesus Christ, whatever and wherever that might actually be. The idea was definite, tangible, concrete, personal, not any mere abstract, floating notion. It was to him as though a new revelation. He had, of course, often heard it expressed in terms before, but the realised idea was quite other than that conveyed by those outward terms. He does not mean that he weighed it, or assented to it, or followed it up. The time for that had not yet come. But there it was; and, for the nonce, it looked him full in the face. What, indeed, became of it he could not well say. Whether it was laid aside, docketed in some pigeon-hole of the brain; or whether it fell silently into his heart, as the seed in the Gospel, and as he slept and rose night and day for many a long year, the seed was all the while springing and growing up, and he knew it not—he cannot say.* However this might have been, it was not until after a decade more of years of manifold wandering had passed by, that he arrived at the Catholic Church by another way. Then this same fragmentary idea appeared again, but now verified as an integral portion of the whole sum of Christian truth.†

And now to return to our subject. If Anglicanism, in the sense we have noted, is a historical religion, much more so is the Eastern schism. We speak of this, for our present argument, collectively, as though it were one, though it is really manifold.

By an ecclesiastical schism, in its strict and proper sense, is meant the severance, and consequent excommunication, of an organised constituent portion of the Church from the one true visible Body of Christ, and from its divinely appointed head on earth. A schism does not of itself necessarily import heresy, except so far as by implication it denies the divinely constituted authority of the Head, and the unity of the Church itself. As a matter of fact, schism is generally found to have its origin or result in doctrinal error, and thus to be more or less heretical. But principally it is schism: this is substantial, and heresy is its predicated quality. Schism, then, as such, is always historical. It has borne away with it, in its origin, the historical religion; that is, the complexus of those revealed doctrines which are based on Divine supernatural facts and events. It retains all the historical institutions of Christianity, not by way of imitation or adaptation, as does Anglicanism, but in their integral identity

---

* *Mark*, iv. 26, 27.

† We should be very curious to see a universal History of the Catholic Church on such a scale as that of Rohrbacher and in somewhat of Bossuet's philosophical spirit, from the pen of an able High Church Anglican. It seems to us that from a high Anglican standpoint, hardly any of the whole bulk of acts and events which is generally held to be the subject-matter of ecclesiastical history, could be regarded as, in the Divine mind, belonging to the real history of Christ's true Church, if these repose upon an utterly false assumption, viz., that Peter had by Divine right a universal Primacy in the Church, and that this Primacy is inherited by the Bishops of Rome who succeed to his See. It is plain that facts which, if weighed in the balance of Christian philosophy, are themselves false—inasmuch as they are based on a figment—cannot form the genuine subject-matter for any true history of Christ's Church, which is nothing at all if it be not divinely true, and itself the pillar and ground of the truth. Such a historian must needs seek for other facts wherewith to compose his history than those which ordinarily purport to belong to historical Christianity. We should be equally curious to see written from the same standpoint, not a mere summary, or a monograph relating to a particular epoch, but something like an exhaustive and detailed history of the Catholic Church in England from its first beginning until the present day.

of unbroken succession; for example, valid Orders and Sacraments, the Catholic Liturgy and rites—everything, in fact, save that jurisdiction and spiritual life which must needs be derived from intercommunion with the mystical Body of Christ, and participation from its supreme visible Head. Unlike Anglicanism, the several schismatical Churches of the East have a real ecclesiastical fabric of their own: they are not mere phantom Churches, as is the Church of England. They consequently form, in a different sense from what it does, a part of historical Christendom.

Anglicanism, on the contrary, is, strictly speaking, a heresy rather than a schism, though, of course, its adherents, so far as they are baptised, are individually schismatics. It is, in truth, nothing more than a particular, localised phase of the wide-spread and multiform heresy of Protestantism. This—whatever its schismatical character in its first genesis—has resulted into a general heresy, containing the germs of every principle subversive of Catholic truth and of genuine historical Christianity.

That Anglicanism—no matter what it may appear in its varied outward trappings—is really and essentially but part and parcel of English Protestantism, and homogeneous as a whole with all the multitudinous sects environing it, and to which it has given birth, is most evident. This is shown from the fact that the various religious opinions peculiar to those several sects, during its history of three centuries, have found, and still find, their place within its ample bosom, and their representative advocates amongst its bishops and clergy.

It is, indeed, more to the taste of some English Protestants to create or to join a particular denomination, which will crystallise, so to speak, their own favourite doctrines. Still all are free to remain in the Church of England, there to profess and teach them, and to communicate with those who hold their direct contrary. For here all diverging doctrines meet. Here, diametrically opposing schools of religious thought—High and dry, Broad and Low, Evangelicals, Rationalisers, and Ritualists, whether of the æsthetical or Catholic type—may dwell together with equal rights in brotherly union as a happy family. True, there may be some occasional sparring; but this is soon and easily arranged or compromised. And, after all, what are doctrinal inconsistencies compared with the grand principle of religious comprehensiveness, and the large maxim of "Live and let live"? This, to the genuine Anglican mind, is true Catholicity—"the unity of spirit in the bond of peace" of a common, albeit motley, Christianity.

We have said that the religion of the Oriental schismatical Churches is historical, inasmuch as of their own nature, and in a true sense, they hand down historical Christianity, imperfect and marred though it be. These Churches are also historical in regard of their schism. For, whereas heresy, simply as such, is a product rather of the human mind and will; schism is at once an overt act, and an external fact, determining the origin of any Church's independent existence and schismatical condition, whereby it distinctly marks out the beginning of its history to the world. Whatever justifying pleas the Greeks bring forward for their schism, at any rate they do not allege that it was due to any positive act of Divine interposition, or to a revelation from heaven. Whereas, the world at large attributes it, for the most part, to the jealousy and ambition of the Byzantine Patriarch, joined to the influence of the Imperial Court. Hence, the history of the Greek schismatical Church, as such, takes its rise, not in any Divine fact at all, but in an event brought about by purely human causes. Hence, just as water cannot rise above its source, so the whole historical course of that Church, as existing in its assumed independent state, can be no more than human.

Having made a survey of Christianity in its historical aspect outside the Roman Communion, let us now speak of that form of the Christian religion which is universally known as Roman Catholicism. It would be superfluous to prove that this is a historical religion, and that the Catholic and Roman Church is historical. In manifold ways it preserves the memory of all the Divine facts and supernatural events on which Christianity is based: of these so many external institutions bear ever visible witness—its holy seasons and festivals, its Liturgy, sacred offices, and rites, its ecclesiastical hierarchy, its relics of Saints, holy images, and pictures. In fact, it is from Roman Catholicism that all the rest of Christendom has derived its historical commemorations. This same Church, together with her religion, has had an uninterrupted historical continuity in the world since the days of the Apostles. This is an indisputable matter of fact, patent to Protestants and Eastern schismatics, as well as to all others, whatever these may allege as to her usurped authority, or her change of doctrinal Christianity. This is witnessed to especially by the unbroken line of her Pontiffs from Apostolic times. All historians, whether ecclesiastical or secular, attest that hers is historical Christianity, and that whatever share with her in this is claimed for other Churches or sects comes, in one way or other, from their relation to her—that she is the original trunk from which the now separated branches in Christendom were broken off. If looked on as one out of the several Christian Churches, and compared with the Greek or Anglican communions, she alone claims, and has ever claimed, for the fontal-fact of her first being and existence as a Church, an event of Divine institution, viz., the Roman Episcopate and Primacy of S. Peter. She, moreover, has ever, not so much asserted, as—with calm, dignified consciousness that she is in possession of it—exercised, her right to hold, in the enduring succession of her Bishops to Peter's See, the primacy and supremacy throughout Christendom—a right that all the Churches within her communion, with unbroken uniformity, have gloried in upholding against assailants, and honoured by their reverent submission; a right that those only have rejected whose very existence, as separated from her unity, is bound up with its denial.

Herein is a fact that her children can point to, which has its witness in every age of Christianity. Of itself, it forms the strongest monumental evidence to the whole world of her historical continuity. It proves that she, the Catholic and Roman Church, is in truth what she has ever claimed and still claims to be—the Church of Christ's original foundation, the primatial Church of universal Christendom. This fact alone is the surest guarantee of her Divine and exclusive right to be called, and to really be, the Mother and Mistress of all the Churches.

So much, then, for historical Christianity. Outside Christendom there are two religions which are distinctly historical—Judaism and Mahomedanism—the one divinely instituted to be the precursor of Christianity, the other set up by the false prophet in direct antagonism both to the Jewish and Christian religions. Here we note certain phenomenal characteristics which are common alike to these three historical religions, *i.e.*, Roman Catholicism, which we claim to be, properly speaking, historical Christianity; Judaism; and Mahomedanism.

1. Each alike claims for its Divine origin definite supernatural facts, and positive acts of interposition on the part of God.

2. Each alike claims in its Divine origin, the institution by God of a sacred office of chiefdom or primacy, committed to one whom He Himself chose; which office, passing on to others in a line of perpetual succession, marks the historical continuity of the religion, and is also both the symbol and the safeguard of its unity.

3. To each of these religions belongs a city which it looks upon as holy—because typical and representative of itself, having part in its own Divine origin, and enshrining all its most cherished historical associations. To this, as to a centre and source of sacred influence, all who profess the religion are instinctively attracted—Jerusalem, Rome, and Mecca.*

We have mentioned Mahomedanism, both because we wished to give a fairly exhaustive view of our subject, and also because Islamism, as a religion, bears to Christianity, as well in its nature as in its history, a special relation of opposition. We may now dismiss it.

Our immediate object here is to bring out to view some of the points of connection, similarity, and contrast that exist between Judaism and that form of Christianity—since so, for the sake of argument, we must express it—or Christian ecclesiastical organisation which is known as Roman Catholicism.

They are both of them, then, historical religions claiming a Divine origin. All Christians will at once concede such an origin to Judaism, and also to Christianity in some sense, and re-

* We here note, by the way, the tendency there evidently is in the different historical sections of Christendom outside the Catholic Church to some sort of centralisation, and to union under one personal head—as though this tendency were inherent in a historical religion. Thus we see the various groups of Oriental Churches ranged under their several patriarchs, Orthodox Greeks, Nestorians, *et hoc genus omne*—the Russian Church under the Tsar. The Abbé Gerbet, in his *Esquise de Rome Chrétienne*, treating in the second chapter of "Rome, the centre of Christendom," describes her as quite unique amongst all cities, from the universality of her holy relics, the multiplicity of her churches, and the reunion found in her of all Christian Rites—of the entire East as well as of the Latin West. This he contrasts with the Greek Church, which has utterly failed to preserve any central city of unity. He illustrates the fact by the Russian Church, which has been successively compelled to have three representative cities of its religion, Kiew, Moscow, and St. Petersburg—Kiew the city of its relics, Moscow of its churches, and St. Petersburg the central seat of its pastoral—*i.e.*, imperial authority. We observe in the work we have mentioned, that the learned, pious, and profound author treats of many points closely connected with the whole subject of this Chapter, to which we had not before adverted. The same tendency to centralisation and to union under a personal headship is manifest also in the Anglican communion. The idea would seem to be in favourable ventilation of making the Archbishop of Canterbury a Patriarch, or an Exarch, nay, of giving him the title of *Papa alterius orbis*. Successful efforts have been already made towards affiliating and taking under the Anglican wing certain Nestorian and Monophysite Churches in various parts of the East. What, however, appears to be most significant in this direction is the idea already broached, of forming the Pan-anglican communion into a new sort of Catholic Church—co-extensive, at any rate, with the dominions of the British Crown and English-speaking peoples. This, it is expected, will, to a great degree, take the place of the original Catholic Church of Christ—considered to be now decidedly in a state of decay—and is to be henceforth the rallying point for the reunion of all the Churches of divided Christendom.

34

garded *in abstracto*. But here the agreement ends. For, confessedly on all hands, Christendom is, well-nigh hopelessly, religiously divided. Hence it is impossible to ascribe a Divine origin to this divided Christianity taken as a whole, and as it is found *in concreto*. If, then, we would verify Christianity as of Divine origin, we are forced to look at the various sections of Christendom distributively. But, as we have already seen, the Roman Catholic Church, alone of all these, claims for herself, as such, a directly Divine origin—and this she does most distinctly. Consequently, she alone can profess to compare and meet with Judaism on equal terms.

The national Jewish Synagogue was in the Divine idea, as set forth in the Inspired Word, the type and figure of that more excellent, world-wide visible Church on earth which Christ Himself was to found. This Church was to fully realise—but after a higher order and a heavenly type—all that the other imperfectly, though adequately, according to the then Divine dispensation, foreshadowed and imaged forth. This Christian Church was to be the perfect accomplishment of that for which the Synagogue was but the preparation. The one was passing, the other to remain until the consummation of the world. Hence the divinely-appointed Mosaic rites and institutions, whether of doctrine, government, or worship, were figures of what should find their perfection, and obtain their true significance, in the Christian Church. Hence, too, because Judaism stood to Christianity in the relation of type to antitype, all that was prominently distinctive of the former must appear—set forth in strong relief, whether by contrast or more excellent resemblance—contained in the latter. For where both the type and the antitype are Divine —as they are in the case before us of the Jewish and Christian Churches—they will be seen adequately to correspond with one another. Thus, what is most traceable in the type will be seen shining forth with full perfection in the antitype. On the other hand, all that is most characteristic of the Christian Church will be found adumbrated in the Synagogue.

Such being the case, it must be evident to all reasonable men that Christendom, taken as a whole and in its widest sense and name, cannot be the Divine antitype of the Jewish Church, since this is conspicuous for its unity and homogeneousness, whereas Christendom at large is equally conspicuous for whatever tells of disunion and contradiction. Hence, if Christianity is the antitype of Judaism—as all revelation proclaims it to be—we must look for it as such, not in its widest denomination, but in one of its particular forms or sections.

Now it would be vain to look for this antitype anywhere in Christendom save in the Catholic and Roman Church. It is there and there only, or it is nowhere. Indeed the very proof we give that it is there will serve at the same time as an evident demonstration that it is not elsewhere.

Consider, then, well some of the more obvious marks of correspondence—for to draw out all the points in detail would of itself fill a volume—between the Jewish Synagogue and the Roman Catholic Church as type and antitype.

Judaism had a Divine origin. The Roman Catholic Church, alone of all Christian Churches, distinctly claims the same for herself. Both one and the other have a historical continuity since their first origin. Judaism formed one homogeneous kingdom in this world, with a rule of Divine sanction. The Roman Catholic Church, too, is essentially a kingdom here on earth, one also and homogeneous, appealing to the institution of Christ Himself for her authority throughout the world. The divinely-appointed Aaronical high-priesthood—held in the hands of one alone and transmitted in lineal succession from father to son—which, united to the office of teaching God's truth and explaining His law, was in the Synagogue the fountain-head of all other priesthood—this, together with the divinely instituted leadership and royalty over the people, was typical, in the first and most excellent sense, of Jesus Christ, the great Antitype of Aaron, as well as of all priesthood and sacrifice anterior to the Mosaic law.

In the fulness of time He was to come, the "Priest for ever, after the order of Melchisedech," who should unite in His own Person the triple office of Prophet, Priest, and King in the kingdom of His Church. He, by the one oblation of Himself, as Redeemer of the whole human race, was to do away with the multiplicity of Aaronical sacrifices, even by bringing them to their perfect fulfilment and consummation in Himself, and to replace but "weak and needy elements"*—the figurative rites and ceremonies of the former Dispensation—by the sacraments and life-giving ordinances of the New Law, quickened and informed with His own Divine grace. As the crown of all the rest, He was to institute the Most Holy Eucharist of His own Body and Blood, wherein is summed up and

* *Gal.* iv. 9.

fulfilled all that was of ancient figure and type. Here Jesus Christ Himself, the great Antitype, verily is in person, God and man, with all the saving merits of His Passion and Death. This most Divine gift of His love He has left to His Church, to be daily offered up by her priests as a true sacrifice in mystical oblation, and to be received by the faithful; to be a perpetual memorial of Himself, and an everflowing fountain of grace—the means and symbol of her continuous life in union with Himself until He shall come again.

And as everything in the Old Law was typical of the great Antitype, so was it also in a secondary, but real and true, sense of him whom Jesus Christ appointed in His Church to be His Vicar. Hence, he holds from Christ, both by likeness and by participation, His own threefold office—of Teacher of God's truth and interpreter of His law, of Supreme Pontiff in His new priesthood, of Chief Ruler in His kingdom and Pastor over His whole flock.

"God, says S. Cyprian, is one, and Christ one, and the Church one, and the Chair one, founded by the voice of the Lord upon a rock. Another altar cannot be set up, nor a new priesthood made, besides the one altar and the one priesthood. Whosoever gathereth elsewhere, scattereth. It is adulterous, it is impious, it is sacrilegious, whatsoever by human madness is instituted so as to violate the Divine appointment. *

"If any one will consider and examine these things, there is no need of lengthened proof and arguments. There is easy proof for faith in a short summary of the truth. The Lord says to Peter, 'I say to thee,' saith He, 'that thou art Peter, and upon this rock . . . loosed also in heaven.' † And to him, again, after His resurrection, He says, 'Feed My sheep.' Upon him being one He builds His Church, and to him commends the sheep to be fed. And although to all the Apostles, after His resurrection, He gives an equal power, and says, 'As the Father sent me . . . they are retained;' ‡ yet, in order to manifest unity, He constituted one Chair, and by His own authority disposed the origin of that same unity as beginning from one. And they all are shepherds, and the flock is shown to be one, such as to be fed by all the Apostles with unanimous agreement, that the Church of Christ may be manifested as one. Which one Church also, in the Canticle of Canticles, does the Holy Spirit design and name in the Person of the Lord, 'One is My dove, My perfect one, the only one of her mother, the chosen of her that bare her.' § He who holds not this unity of the Church, does he think that he holds the faith? He who strives against and resists the Church, who deserts the Chair of Peter, upon whom the Church was founded, does he feel any confidence that he is in the Church?" ||

* *Ep.* 40 *ad Pleb.*   † *Matt.* xvi. 18, 19.   ‡ *John,* xx. 21.   § *Cant.* vi. 9.

|| *De Unit. Eccl.* If any one objects to the Benedictine text, as represented above, we here give that adopted in the *Oxford Translation:* "The Lord saith to Peter, 'I say unto thee,' saith He, 'that thou art Peter,' &c. To him,

"The Chair of Peter, and (Rome) the principal Church, whence the unity of the priesthood took its rise ... the same Romans, whose faith was praised in the preaching of the Apostle, to whom faithlessness cannot have access." *

As the Aaronical high-priesthood, in its appointed succession, was the central institution of Judaism, marking the unity of its religion and polity, and also its historical continuity, so is it with the Supreme Pontificate in the Catholic Church. And as the Jewish Pontificate had its seat in the holy city of Jerusalem, to which the whole religion of the Synagogue and its people converged; thus, too, is it with the Holy Roman See. Hence the very names of Jerusalem and Rome might each stand, with Jews and Roman Catholics, for the integral faith and the aggregate body of both one and the other people.

We have hitherto been comparing Judaism as it was of old with the Roman Catholic Church. Judaism, however, as it now exists, is no longer the true religion, but an apostacy from the Messiah, Who, as the end of the Mosaic Law, has, by His coming, brought it to its perfect fulfilment. It will, then, be interesting now to consider some points of analogy or antithesis that Judaism, in its present condition, bears with the same Catholic and Roman Church.

Judaism—Divine in its first origin, the religion of God's revelation, once His true religion—is, in its present condition, like some fallen angel who still bears many marks of his lost high-estate, preserving much of its original supernatural type, and characteristic traces of its former dignity. Remark, by the way, with what a sort of reverent tenderness S. Paul speaks of it in his Epistle to the Romans—as "the holy first-fruit," "the holy root," "the natural branches of their own good olive-tree, broken off therefrom because of unbelief,"—intimating, at the same time, that the future of God's ancient people is still within

---

again, after His resurrection, He says, 'Feed My sheep.' Upon him, being one, He builds His Church, and though He gives to all the Apostles an equal power, and says, 'As the Father sent Me,' &c., yet, in order to manifest unity, He has, by His own authority, so placed the source of the same unity as to begin from one. Certainly the other Apostles were what Peter was, endued with an equal fellowship both of honour and power; but a commencement is made from unity, that the Church may be set before us as one; which one Church, in the Song of Songs, doth the Holy Spirit design and name in the Person of our Lord, 'My dove, My spotless one, is but one; she is the only one of her mother, elect of her that bore her.' He who holds not the unity of the Church, does he think that he holds the faith? He who strives against and resists the Church, is he assured that he is in the Church?" (Waterworth, *A Commentary, &c.*, p. 29. *sq.*)

* *Ep.* 55 *ad Cornelium*, n. 18.

the designs of His mercy, and setting forth "their fulness," "the receiving of them again," "their grafting in once more into their own olive-tree," and at length "all Israel's salvation," as a glorious object of Christian hope.[*]

The very existence of the Jewish people—with all their peculiar and distinctive characteristics of religion and race, persevering in every country of the world, through so many centuries, amongst such great calamities and persecutions as have befallen them—is in itself one of the world's greatest prodigies. It forms, so to speak, a perpetual miraculous standing-monument in witness of the supernatural order, of the Divine revelation and authenticity of Sacred Scripture, of the truth of the history of the Jewish people, and, by moral consequence, of all else that is contained in its pages. This prodigious fact has no parallel save in the ever-living monumental evidence that has from the beginning been borne to the truth of Christianity by the historical continuity of the Roman Catholic Church and religion: and most conspicuously, through the Roman Episcopate of S. Peter, and the unbroken succession in his See.

But Judaism—besides giving forth this testimony to its own identity with its former self, as the historic religion of Divine revelation—under its present condition, and by what we may speak of as its very change from its former self, bears loud witness to, and proves with moral certainty, the truth of Christianity that has supplanted it, or, we should rather say, of that form of Christianity which, as such, alone can claim on equal terms to be its divinely-ordained antitype and completion.

Besides the points of comparison, which we have already drawn out between Roman Catholicism and Judaism of old, there are several analogies and contrasts between the former and Judaism as it now exists.

Jews, like Roman Catholics, are found in every part of the world: they are citizens of all nations, but their religion, as such, is not national. Both alike look to a central city of their religion outside the country of their residence. In the Divine worship of both the language of their city is used normally, and serves to each as a token and bond of their religious unity. The religion of Roman Catholics and that of Jews are marked off by lines so incisive, that those who profess them are ranked, amongst other denominations, as though castes apart. Take Anglicanism for

---

[*] See *Rom.* xi. 16-24, 12, 15, 25-32.

example: some of this sect will make hopeful efforts towards union with Constantinople, Antioch, Alexandria, or Moscow—others, again, with Wesleyans, Presbyterians, or Independents. Hence it is plain that the extreme borders of Anglicanism, in one and the other direction, are vague and undefined. But they all know that it is fruitless to seek for communion with Rome without acknowledging her claims and submitting to her authority. Again, the creeds of these two religions, Judaism and Roman Catholicism, are homogeneous; those who belong to either know what they must believe, and all believe alike.

But in comparing present Judaism with Roman Catholicism it is rather the points of contrast than of resemblance that are the most remarkable. The universal dispersion of the Jews is analogous to the Catholicity of the Roman Communion. But, whereas the Roman Catholic Church is, as her name implies, everywhere diffused, the joyful Mother of many children, having for her heritage the whole world; one family, knit together by ties of spiritual brotherhood, finding its home in every land; a kingdom ruled over by many princes, with one universal priesthood, all united under the paternal rule of one Sovereign Pontiff, Supreme Pastor and Teacher:—the once favoured Synagogue, by the Crucifixion of her Lord, and on account of her unbelief, has, as was predicted by David and the Prophets, since the destruction of Jerusalem, become a widow, sterile, desolate, and abandoned, and her children have become orphans and vagabonds, no longer forming together one family, one people, one kingdom,—but so many separate units scattered amongst strangers, without king or leader, Prophet or teacher, high priest or any priesthood whatever, without altar or sacrifice—even a very by-word among the nations of the earth.*

The two cities which represent these two historical religions have between them several points of analogy well worthy of note.

Jerusalem, the city of peace, with its temple on Mount Sion—chosen and beloved of God; a type of the true Church of Christ on earth and of the heavenly Jerusalem; so highly favoured even by the Divine Messiah Himself; that city which was the joy of the people of Israel and the theme for the inspired songs of the Prophets—that once holy city of God, still survives in her desolate ruins, but now branded in the Apocalypse " as spiritually called Sodom and Egypt, where the Lord also was crucified:—" †

* *Ps.* cviii. 7-16; *Osee*, iii. 4; *Jer.* xxiv. 9; xxix. 18.   † *Apoc.* xi. 8.

Whereas Rome, formerly, on account of her iniquities and idolatry, styled the Mystical Babylon, has become the Holy City, consecrated with the blood of the two great princes of the Apostles and of countless martyrs of Christ—its Church founded by those two Apostles, its Episcopal Chair that of S. Peter, chosen by our Lord to be the rock whereon is built His Church, and of his successors in perpetuity—Rome, the seat of Peter's Primacy, the primatial See, wherein is to be found the sceptre of Divine authority, the unity of the Christian pastorate and priesthood, the rule of doctrinal teaching for all the faithful—Rome, the Mother and the Mistress of all the Churches.*

* We hear, whilst writing these pages, echoes of a sermon preached on a recent important occasion, by an Anglican bishop, in which he quotes the following words from S. Bernard: "Consider above all things, that the holy Roman Church, over which by God's authority thou presidest, is *the Mother of all Churches, not their Mistress;* that thou, too, art not the lord of bishops, but one of themselves: the brother, moreover, of those who love God, and partner with those who fear Him." (*De Consid. ad Eugen.* III. L. iv., c. viii.) Now, most fairly instructed Catholics, and Anglicans, too,—at any rate, those who are controversially inclined,—know that in the Catholic Church it is, as though, a common-place, that "the Roman Church is the Mother and Mistress of all Churches," that this is defined in Councils, and forms part of the profession of faith of Pius IV., which is made by all converts. Hence, this episcopal denial, whatever might have been the preacher's immediate purport, was held in the mind of the public to mean the pitting of S. Bernard against the Church of Rome, as much as to say: "Here you have the Roman Church distinctly affirming what a Doctor of the same Church flatly denies." To reconcile the two apparently contradictory statements, we must go behind their English translation to the original Latin of the profession of faith, and of S. Bernard. For the single English word *Mistress,* there are in Latin two words, *Magistra* and *Domina,* which, as any Latin scholar knows, represent in their proper sense two ideas essentially different. *Dominus* means a lord and master who has dominion, or even rights of property over another, frequently implying the exercise of unjust and despotic power. Hence the English, to "domineer," or "lord it over." Whereas *Magister* means a superior, indeed; being of the same root as *magis* and *magnus,* but without any idea of dominion. This word is used in the sense of a director, chief leader, conductor, and, especially, a teacher or instructor. It never of itself implies abuse of superiority. Now, the word used by S. Bernard is *domina.* "Considera ante omnia Sanctam Romanam Ecclesiam, cui Deo auctore præes, ecclesiarum matrem esse, *non dominam;* te vero *non dominum* episcoporum, sed unum ex ipsis." Whilst the word employed in the profession of faith of Pius IV. and in definitions of Councils is *magistra.* "Romanam Ecclesiam omnium Ecclesiarum Matrem et *Magistram* agnosco." We may remark also that the Definitions of Sacred Councils, in speaking of the Bishop of the Roman Church, call him *Pater* et *Doctor,* Father and Teacher—correlative terms with *Mater* and *Magistra.* To Catholics, then, there is nothing strange in S. Bernard's exhortation. He implicitly reminds Pope Eugenius, formerly his disciple, of the teaching of our Lord Jesus Christ Himself to Peter (*Luke,* xxii.). Christ there intimates to His Apostles, that one amongst them would be greater than the rest, viz., Peter, who was to confirm his brethren—not to lord it over them, as is the manner of this world's princes, but to follow His own example, Who, though their Lord and Master, came not to be ministered unto but to minister. He also implicitly

Aptly indeed may Jerusalem be contrasted with Rome—Jerusalem, once the holy city, the city of peace, now called the spiritual Sodom, that loathed city of abomination, and Egypt the place of her people's slavery—for such, in truth, writes S. Paul, is "the Jerusalem that now is which is in bondage with her children."* Thus is Jerusalem in her destruction and desolation made typical of the execrable crime of Deicide committed within herself, and of the rejection by God of her people.

See, in contrast, Rome, once the proud Capital of the Heathen world, that mystical Babylon of the Apocalyptic vision, wherein met the confusion of all idolatrous religions and of every abomination, now become the Capital of the Christian world, synecdochically, and by excellence, styled the Holy See and the Eternal City, in token that Christ has been given "the Gentiles for His inheritance and the utmost parts of the earth for His possession; that the kingdom of this world is become our Lord's and His Christ's; that He shall reign for ever and ever. Amen. And that of His kingdom there shall be no end." †

Another point calls for some remark. Other Christian systems and communions—as the Oriental Schismatics, Anglicanism, and other forms of Protestantism—compare themselves with the Roman Catholic Church: she never compares herself with any. As impossible would it be for any reasonable man to deny his own personality, and to doubt his own identity, that he is what he is—a certainty whereof he has from inner consciousness of the

---

reminds Eugenius of the teaching of that same Peter whose successor he is. For Peter,—following his Lord's counsel and example, albeit the head and rock of the Church, and universal pastor,—when speaking to the clergy (1 Pet. v. 1-3), calls himself their fellow-presbyter, and specially exhorts them not to lord it over their flocks. What strikes one in Protestant controversialists is how constantly they make the issue of some momentous question turn on a single word, and how they are ever finding antagonism where to Catholics all is concordant or easily reconcilable. But what else can we expect from a system bred of divorce and fostered in disunion?

* Gal. iv. 25.

† Ps. ii. 8; Apoc. xi. 15; Luke, i. 33. The Abbé Gerbet, in his Esquisse de Rome Chrétienne, chap. vii. § 8, "De la ville Papale," notes several other symbolical analogies between Jerusalem and Rome. Speaking of the Providential choice of Rome as the capital of Christendom, he quotes the following words from Seneca: "Nullum non hominum genus concurrit in Urbem, et vitiis et virtutibus magna præmia ponentem. Jube nos omnes ad nomen citari, et unde domo quisque sit quære: videbis majorem partem esse, quæ, relictis sedibus suis, venerit in maximam quidam ac pulcherrimam urbem, non tamen suam." (De consol. ad Helv. Matr.) And from S. Jerome: "Urbs potens, urbs domina, urbs Apostoli voce laudata, interpretare vocabulum tuum: Roma aut fortitudinis nomen apud Græcos est, aut sublimitatis apud Hebræos." (Adv. Jovin. ii. 38.)

continuity of his thoughts and memory, which finds its outward expression in the visible course of his life and actions,—as for the Catholic and Roman Church to doubt her own identity, as herself being the one only true Church of Christ, which He Himself founded. This full assurance of certainty in believing is a complement of the gift of Divine faith, and is therefore shared in measure by every thorough Catholic. Hence it is that, whereas conversions from the sects to the Catholic Church, from all classes, often at the cost of much personal sacrifice, are frequent; Catholics are very rarely seen to go over to the religion of the sects, or, should they do so, other influences than conviction of truth are for the most part apparent, whether compulsion, religious ignorance, or some temporal and worldly interest. In point of fact, Roman Catholic converts are largely gathered from those who were most conspicuous for zeal and piety in their former religion, and they often prove most fervent and exemplary Catholics. Those, on the contrary, who abandon the Roman Catholic Church for a sect, are drawn generally from such as lived in neglect of their religious duties, and frequently come to be reckoned amongst those members of whom the communion of their adoption can be but little proud. Consequently, if a Roman Catholic has the misfortune, through some intellectual difficulties or other cause, to give up his faith and abandon his religion; as a rule, he doubts of the truth of Divine revelation altogether, and becomes a sceptic or infidel; since it can hardly come into his thoughts that the religion of any of the sects deserves his consideration. With him, failing the Pope and the Roman Catholic Church, it is all over with Christianity.

Looking at things objectively, and in the logical order of ideas, the only real independent foe, within the whole circumference of Divine revelation, that the Church of Christ has to encounter, is Judaism, which, like Heathenism, is beyond her own sphere of jurisdiction. As for schismatics and heretics, these are by right subject to her power. She regards them as rebellious or erring children, who have forfeited their family rights and privileges. They are under her displeasure, and she is used to treat them with a rigour, more or less mingled with compassion and lenity, according to their knowledge, malice, and obstinacy, or their ignorance and other circumstances of excuse. She invites and longs for their return to her maternal embrace, but she can never treat with them, so to say, as independent and on equal terms.

It is otherwise with the Jews—they have never yet belonged to her, they were never her children, but are recognisable foes, who have, at the same time, a certain claim to respect on account of their origin and former rank in the Divine dispensation. Thus, S. Paul speaks of them, in his Epistle to the Romans, as enemies, from the Gospel point of view, and taking Christians into account; but, considering their election, as most dear, on account of the fathers.* Hence, from the beginning the Church has meted to them a toleration of their worship, which, on principle, under normal circumstances at any rate, she would not accord to heresy and schism. And whilst she ever keeps in horror their obstinate unbelief and that heinous crime which still brands their race, she spreads forth her hands all the day long, as did her Lord, to that people that believed Him not and contradicted Him,† if haply she may win them to the Christian faith.

We say, then, that although in the actual life of the Catholic Church here on earth, and especially in these later times, her warfare is engaged with heresy and schism, yet, objectively, and in the order of thought and ideas, the real and logical issue is, as of old in Apostolic times, with Judaism—the Old Dispensation pitted against the New. This commends itself, moreover, as more befitting what is Divine, viz., that the revealed Law of the Old Dispensation should be the typical antagonist of the Gospel of the New Testament, rather than its formal opposition should be found in some merely human, base-born system of corrupted Christianity. ‡

---

* Rom. xi. 28. † Rom. x. 21; Is. lxv. 2.

‡ That the chief battle-field of the Catholic Church is still the same as in S. Paul's days may be gathered from an Article in the *Dublin Review*, October, 1887—"The Jews in France." The writer cites from several recently-published works, and in particular from M. Drumont's *La France Juive*, many passages of past and current Jewish literature, which show the bitter and undying hatred of the Jews to Christianity. The following points are extracted from that Article, and, for the most part, are in the reviewer's own words.

1. There lives not a Jew, whether he has given up the exterior practices of his religion or not, even though he professes to be a sceptic or freethinker, who does not firmly believe that he belongs to a superior race, the destiny of which is to rule over all the races of mankind, and to become the arbiter of all the other nations. They say, that if they are scattered over the surface of the whole earth, it is because the whole earth is to be their possession. The faith in this destiny is not of to-day or yesterday—it has never forsaken the Jew. It has come down from the time of Titus, and S. Jerome bears witness to it. 2. The aim and purpose of the Jewish race is the ruin and breaking up of Christian society, the conquest of the world, and the triumph of Israel. 3. But, knowing, as they do, that historical Christianity is identical with Catholicism, and that the Catholic Church is the one strong citadel

532 BY THE JOINT RELATIONS OF PETER AND PAUL TO ROME

It is here of significance to note that these two chief rival forces, within the pale of Divine revelation, meet with their fullest exposition both as regards their points of repulsion and cohesion, in an Epistle to the Roman Church, which was composed of Christian converts from Judaism and Paganism in such equal proportion that it would be hard to say which element was predominant. In that Epistle the doctrinal teaching for either class is alike evenly balanced. It is addressed to the Roman Church by S. Paul; who, whilst continually glorying in being a Jew and a "Hebrew of the Hebrews,"* is, nevertheless, the great Apostle of the Uncircumcision, and never tires in rendering thanks and praise to God for having been chosen out, by an exceeding and exceptional grace, for the special ministry of evangelising the Gentiles.

of Christ's religion, they regard that Church as their great enemy, and the great obstacle to the realisation of their object and hopes. They understand very well that if once the Catholic Church could be ruined and destroyed, it would be but short and easy work with the rest of Christendom, which would soon fall to pieces and crumble away. Hence they entertain against the Church the fiercest hatred, and seek by open and secret means to undermine her influence. Whenever they see the Church humbled and down-trodden their exultation and insolence know no bounds. 4. From one end of the world to the other, the Jews are bound together by the strongest ties of solidarity and brotherhood in their aim and object, which is everywhere the same—the triumph of Israel, the destruction of Christian society, in particular and above all of the Catholic Church. Everywhere they band themselves with her avowed enemies, and are aided in their war against her by all those who with them curse Christ and His Church, by those who are in rebellion, open or secret, against legitimate authority, and are like themselves watching for their opportunity for destroying existing institutions; they find especially faithful and willing allies in the secret societies, foremost in that of Freemasonry, which is their own invention and offspring, in the machinations and government of which they have the chief share. They make common cause with Protestants in their rebellion against the Catholic Church, and with them gratefully cherish the memory of the Reformation, which they class with the French Revolution, as a movement which for more than three centuries has been shaking and for eighty years has upset the old state of society. The orthodox Jews everywhere look upon the revolutions and political catastrophes that agitate the world as the hope and the forerunners of their freedom and triumph. 5. The Jew has no country. He is a stranger everywhere. France, Germany, England, or Austria is to him but a dwelling-place, which he uses for his commerce. Such a thing as patriotism is altogether unknown to him. He is essentially a cosmopolitan, and settles where he can make most money. He has no other interests but those of his sect. The whole Jewish race is but one great clan, regarding every creature outside of itself as a stranger and a legitimate prey. The Jew wields the most powerful twofold sceptre of tyranny that exists in the world, that of gold and the press. (We pass over here his exercise of the former and its results.) Through the press he disseminates all those modern principles of infidelity, scepticism, religious indifference, godless education, false liberty, lawlessness, and socialism which pervert the Christian conscience, and tend to the utter destruction of Christian civilisation and of Christian society.

* See *Rom.* ix. 3-5; xi. 1-14; 2 *Cor.* xi. 22; *Philip.* iii. 4-6; *Acts*, xxi. 32; xxii. 3; xxiii. 6; xxvi. 4-7.

It is remarkable, again, that S. Peter, to whom first was divinely revealed the vocation of the Gentiles to the faith, who was the first to preach the Gospel, not only to Jews but also to Gentiles, and to form Christian communities from both—the first also to preside over the earliest Gentile Church of Antioch—should yet be, in a most special and emphatic sense, the Apostle of the Circumcision.

It is remarkable, in fine, that S. Peter, the Apostle of the Circumcision, should be ever traditionally regarded in the mind of the Church—and history bears witness to the truth of the fact—as the first founder of the Church in the Capital of the Gentile world, and the first Bishop of its See—and, at the same time, that S. Peter, the Apostle of the Circumcision, should be associated in joint labour with S. Paul, the Apostle of the Uncircumcision, and that by their united efforts, from the two elements of Judaism and Paganism, that Church should be founded whose Roman Catholic faith has ever since been celebrated throughout the whole world, which has claimed ever to be the Mother and Mistress of all Churches, and to be under the special joint-patronage of SS. Peter and Paul, whilst she derives the enduring succession of her Bishops from S. Peter alone. This was very congruous, and meet indeed—since Jesus Christ, the Divine Founder of the Church, and the Rock whereon she is built, is called in the inspired words of S. Peter, her "Bishop,"[*] and of S. Paul, the "Minister of the Circumcision,"[†]—it is meet, we say, that he who was made by Christ the rock together with Himself, S. Peter, the Apostle of the Circumcision, should, as Christ's Vicar, alone have the preeminence of Bishop of that Church, which, by the twofold element of Jew and Gentile in its foundation and members, typically connotes the universal Christian Church : "Where there is neither Gentile nor Jew, circumcision nor uncircumcision, Barbarian nor Scythian, bond nor free: but Christ is all, and in all."[‡]

All this reads like a living drama. The finger of God is here: for it is an epitomised realisation of the Divine idea in His two revealed Dispensations—showing forth their originally projected end and actual accomplishment—whereby, in the Eternal City of Rome, through Peter's Episcopate and the never-failing succession of Bishops to his See, are fulfilled our Lord's own Divine words: "They shall hear My voice, and there shall be one fold, and one shepherd."[§]

[*] 1 *Pet.* ii. 25. [†] *Rom.* xv. 8. [‡] *Coloss.* iii. 11 ; *Rom.* x. 12.
[§] *John*, x. 16.

APPENDIX TO CHAPTERS VII. AND VIII.

FROM CARDINAL FRANZELIN.

IT was not until this work had well-nigh passed through the press that our attention was directed to the recently published posthumous *Theses de Ecclesia Christi*[*] of the lamented Cardinal Franzelin. Anything coming from the pen of this eminent theologian must carry the greatest weight. We have, therefore, thought it well to add here some lengthened extracts from such of his Theses as bear upon the relation of the Roman Episcopate to the universal Pontificate. These have been very fully and most lucidly developed; and the extracts we give from them will serve as a most valuable appendix to Chapters vii. and viii., which treat of that matter.

THESIS X.

On the Institution of Jesus Christ's Kingdom on Earth in the form of a Monarchy in His Third Apparition.

"Christ Jesus so instituted His kingdom on earth that, both in the "proximate preparation (*Matt.* xvi.; *Luke*, xxii.) and in the corresponding "execution (*John*, xxi.), He chose *one* Simon Peter from the rest, and over "the rest, of the Apostles, and furnished him with supreme and universal "power, as well over the several parts and every member of the Church as "over its whole body—a power which was to be vicarious, derived from Christ, "immediate in its direct influence over the whole and the parts, and plenary in "regard to the proper object of the kingdom of God on earth. Consequently "this power constitutes the principle that forms and contains the visible "unity of the Church according to the express institution of Christ its "Founder, and is therefore of Divine right."[†]

THESIS XI.

On the Propagation of the Ecclesiastical Monarchy, or on the Perpetual Succession in Peter's Primacy.

"1. As Christ the Lord Himself instituted the Primacy in Peter, so, "equally *jure divino*, did He institute the same Primacy ever to remain in "His visible Church, in such wise that there should be a perpetual series of

---

[*] Romæ, 1887.　　　　[†] *Theses de Ecclesia Christi*, pp. 124-162.

"successors one after the other; and this institution of perpetuity and suc-
"cession, set forth in the Gospels, is to be believed with Divine faith.
"2. After Peter, bearing in his own person the Primacy committed to him
"by Christ, founded and took to himself the Episcopate or See of Rome, and
"in dying left this See vacant with the necessity of filling up the succession
"both in the Primacy and in the Roman Episcopate,—the mode itself of
"succession in the Primacy became determined, so that legitimate succession
"in the Roman Episcopate is at once succession in the Primacy over the
"universal Church. For so the Church universal has always and everywhere
"understood the Divine right of succession to be determined, as is proved by
"the consentient teaching of Councils, of the Roman Pontiffs, and the rest
"of the Fathers, which declares the self-same evident and perpetual fact of
"the union of the Primacy with the Roman See of Peter."*

"This perpetual succession in Peter's Primacy, which we have shown is contained in the words of Christ's promise and institution (*Matt.* xvi.; *Luke,* xxii.; *John,* xxi.), has ever been a common and well-known theme in the faith and profession of Christian antiquity; nay, what is here our special point, the *mode itself of the succession* has been recognised as certain and indefectible both by the common profession and by positive acts of all ages. For as the power instituted in Peter, as we described it in the last thesis, has been ever believed and proclaimed to be in full force in the several successors of Peter; so no other succession of Peter was ever heard of or recognised than succession in the Roman See of Peter, which he took to himself for his own special Episcopate, consecrated by martyrdom. He thus by his own now unalterable act raised the See and Episcopate of a particular Church to a See and Episcopate of 'more powerful princedom,' according to the words of S. Irenæus. And hence in the heirs to this Roman See Peter is acknowledged and proclaimed as ever living—in virtue, namely, of the plenary power instituted in his person—by the Councils, the Roman Pontiffs themselves, and by the rest of the Fathers."†

"In like manner the Roman Pontiffs, not only without contradiction, but with the willing consent of the Bishops and Churches to whom they wrote, have been used to claim the whole power instituted by Christ in the person of Peter as conferred upon themselves as much as on Peter, and that this was always recognised and to be acknowledged by the entire Church for no other reason than because they are Peter's successors in the Roman See, in that particular Church, namely, which Peter specially adopted as his own."‡

"We meet constantly the same topic in other Fathers, viz., the union of the Church or See of Rome with succession to the power, that is, to the See, of Peter; for this same Roman See, and never any other, is acknowledged and celebrated as Peter's See, having all the prerogatives instituted in the person of Peter. 'Cornelius,' says Cyprian, 'has been made Bishop ... since the place of Fabian, that is, *since the place of Peter and the rank of the sacerdotal chair was vacant.*' (*Ep.* 52 *ad Anton.*) Thence he calls the Roman Church 'the root and womb of the Catholic Church.' (*Ep.* 42 and 45 *ad Cornel.*) ..."§

"All that has been shown forth in this thesis may be thus summarised:
"Christ the Lord Himself, by words and facts recorded in the Gospel, instituted in Peter the supreme and universal power of rock and head of the

---

* *Theses de Ecclesia Christi*, pp. 163-191. † *Ib.* p. 166.
‡ *Ib.* pp. 168-9. § *Ib.* p. 185.

Church—which power was to continue in perpetuity—and therefore instituted it to be propagated for each and all of Peter's successors and heirs. For the words of the promise and institution, 'Upon this rock I will build My Church; I will give to thee the keys of the kingdom of heaven; Confirm thy brethren; Feed My sheep,' were said indeed to Simon; but inasmuch as he was made that *Peter*, who was always to live by reason of the charge and perpetual office and power instituted by these same words, they consequently in their whole significance and force equally belong to each and all of Peter's successors who should follow one another in perpetual line.

"The perpetual succession in the supreme power is, therefore, as much set forth and instituted by the words in the Gospel as the power itself; but the mode of succession *in particular* (*in individuo*) is not signified by these same words; it is, however, contained in the very nature of the visible office which was to endure by succession in the visible Church, that the mode of succession must be visible, that is, easily recognisable and manifest to all; and so far the mode of succession *generally* (*in genere*) may be said to be really determined by the same Divine institution. But it is determined individualities and not undetermined generalities, that have their concrete existence in the nature of things (*non genera indeterminata sed determinata individua concrete existunt in rerum natura*); and, therefore, from the very institution of the Primacy and of its perpetual succession, it appertained to the Divine Institutor's supernatural providence over His Church built upon a rock, that the mode itself of the succession, whereby this rock perpetually endures, should be determined in its individuality, so as to be manifest and certain, and, thus, not fluctuating but abiding. Now, from the testimonies above cited, it is evident that this was the one only mode of succession, and never any other—that was always, everywhere, and by all recognised, and publicly set forth in the Church.

"(a) That the Bishop of Rome succeeds to all the rights of the sacred magisterium and government, which, as instituted by Christ in Peter, are perpetual, and to be carried on to each and all Peter's successors,—so that *with regard to these rights and offices* all the several Roman Bishops *are one moral person with Peter*—is witnessed to by the following: 'In Julius the memory of Peter is honoured, whereby the priests of the Lord refer to the head, that is, to the See of the Apostle Peter.' 'In Siricius the blessed Apostle Peter bears the burdens of all.' 'Innocent, Theodore, are the summit and crown of prelates in the honour of the most blessed Peter.' 'Such as is the authority of Peter, equal is the rank of power in Zosimus.' 'The solicitude of the universal Church awaits blessed Peter in Boniface.' 'The most blessed Peter lives and exercises judgment in Celestine.' 'Christ has granted to Celestine in the Apostle Peter the obligation of treating on all matters.' 'Peter has spoken by Leo, by Agatho.' 'Peter has not abandoned the government of the universal Church in Leo.' 'The blessed Peter has ever held the princedom he received through the voice of the Lord, and he holds it in Gelasius.'*

"(b) This succession to Peter's whole power divinely instituted is asserted and believed from the very fact alone, of any one legitimately succeeding to

---

* For the Councils, &c., from which the above extracts are taken, see pp. 161-187, where the passages, and many others besides, are given in their full context.

that particular Episcopate which Peter, the prince of the Apostles, took to himself as Bishop. That is to say, Peter, ennobled by Christ the Lord with a power *primatial, apostolic,* and *ordinary* (that is, supreme, universal, to remain perpetually in his legitimate successors), in assuming to himself the Roman Episcopate or the See of Rome—by this very fact of his—made that See apostolic, primatial, that is to say, Petrine, and left it at his death vacant, not only *negatively* in the sense that now no one occupied it, but, *with the right and positive obligatory necessity*, that another—and that other according to the way of Divine appointment—should in perpetuity succeed to that same *ordinary Petrine power*. Hence there is not a double succession, one to the Roman Episcopate instituted by Peter, and another to the Primacy instituted by Christ; but by the very fact of Peter's leaving at death his whole power, primatial, as well as episcopal over the city, included in the former, in his own Apostolic Roman See now vacant,—that is, necessarily requiring a successor to the Primacy and to the included Episcopate of the city,—it is clear that the succession is one, not separated but distinct for a twofold reason."

"On this point we shall say more later on. We have already sufficiently confirmed this doctrine by the universal profession of the Fathers. 'When the place of Fabian is vacant the *place of Peter* is vacant, and Cornelius succeeds to *the place of Peter*.' 'Siricius *heir* to Peter's administration.' 'The Africans knew what is *due to the Apostolic See in which place* Innocent is set." Here follow many other testimonies to the same effect.

"... The Roman See is therefore the Apostolic See, not only historically, as that of other Apostles, for example S. James, because its first Bishop was an Apostle, who was unable to leave the *extraordinary* prerogatives of the Apostleship to his See; but is *the primatial Apostolic See*, because the Primacy, or princedom, or more powerful principality in Peter, was an *ordinary* office of equally valid force for his successors...."

"(c) On account of this union of succession to the plenitude of the power divinely instituted in Peter with succession to the particular Church, that is to say, to the Roman See; *the Primacy of the Roman Church itself* over the universal Church is everywhere spoken of by the Fathers. For since Peter, in reserving to himself the Episcopate of the particular Church of Rome, kept it, as it were, included in his Divine Primacy over the universal Church; by reason, and only by reason, of this inclusion of the Roman Episcopate in the universal Divine Primacy, is the Roman Church itself most truly said to hold the Primacy over the universal Church. It is this union, then, of the Roman Episcopate with the Primacy, and nothing else, that the Fathers teach, when they speak so frequently of the Primacy of the Roman Church over the universal Church. Hence, on the ground of such union brought about by the Petrine fact, it is clear that he who succeeds Peter in the Roman Church, which holds the Primacy, thereby at once succeeds to the Primacy; and, on the other hand, no one can succeed Peter in the Primacy without at once thereby succeeding to the Roman Episcopate, which is already included in the Primacy."

"Because the Roman Church founded by the Apostles Peter and Paul has for its Bishops the successors of Peter in perpetual line, for this cause in it is the more powerful principality: 'With this Church, on account of its more powerful principality, every Church, that is, the faithful on all sides, must needs be in accord (in faith and communion).' 'It is the Chair of

Peter and the principal Church, whence sacerdotal unity took its rise'—'the root and womb of the Catholic Church'—'the Roman Church, whence to all flow forth the rights of venerable communion.'..."

"The sum, then, of what we undertook to prove from the teaching of all Christian antiquity is, that the perpetual succession to the Primacy, which succession Christ Himself instituted, has been always understood and set forth in the Church in the sense that Peter's Roman See is at the same time the Apostolic Primatial See over the universal Church; and, therefore, legitimate succession to the Roman Episcopate in the See of Peter is succession to the divinely-instituted Primacy of Peter."*

Thesis XII.

A further explanation of the Doctrine of the Union of the Primacy with the Roman See.

"1. The same truth of the union of the Primacy over the universal Church with the Roman Apostolic See is demonstrated from the definitions of Councils and from professions of faith. 2. From the above teaching, it follows that the mode of union is such that, by a distinction of reason, succession in the Roman See is the visible sign of succession in the Primacy; but really, in actual fact, the one Roman See has been raised to the dignity and power of a primatial See over the universal Church. 3. Then follows, as a theological truth, that the Primacy can never, not even by the supreme power of Peter's successor himself, be separated from the Roman See and transferred elsewhere. 4. But to say that such a translation can be made by any other power, whether ecclesiastical or secular, is a condemned doctrine, and one connected with errors essentially opposed to the Divine constitution of the Church."

"I. Up to this we have seen the doctrine that has always and everywhere been asserted and proclaimed concerning the union of Peter's Primacy and its perpetual inheritance in Peter's Roman See; but, in order to give a still clearer and more precise proof, and, at the same time, more sure ground for the solution of the further question, whether the Primacy is separable from the Roman See, we shall consider the formal definitions and professions of faith, so far as the union of the Primacy with the Roman Church, and the perpetual succession of the Bishops of Rome, both in Peter's Primacy and in his Episcopate, are contained in them."

"(a) The definition of the Council of Florence is as follows: 'We also define that *the Holy Apostolic See and the Roman Pontiff* hold the Primacy over the whole world, and that *the same Roman Pontiff is the successor of blessed Peter, prince of the Apostles*, and the true Vicar of Christ, and the head of the whole Church, and the father and teacher of all Christians; and that *to himself in blessed Peter* has been delivered, by our Lord Jesus Christ, the plenary power of feeding, ruling, and governing the universal Church; as also is contained in the acts of Ecumenical Councils and in the Sacred Canons.'

"Here, consequently, is defined not only, in general, the Roman Pontiff's right of primacy over the whole world, but, in particular, the right and mode of his succession. He who succeeds in the holy Apostolic See of Peter, and thus is Roman Pontiff, or Peter's successor in the Episcopate of Rome, is, by

---

* *Theses de Ecclesia Christi*, pp. 187-191.

the very fact, not only successor to Peter as Bishop, but, at the same time, successor to Peter as prince of the Apostles, and, therefore, the true Vicar of Christ and head of the whole Church; for to the Roman Bishop himself, that is, to each and all of the legitimate Roman Bishops, has been delivered by our Lord Jesus Christ the plenary power of feeding, ruling, and governing the universal Church, in the person of blessed Peter, who, as though the first root, represented the whole series of his successors; the series, I say, at least for the present order, composed of all—and of those alone—who are his successors in the Apostolic Roman See."

"The definition of the Vatican Council is explicit: 'The holy and most blessed Peter ... *even to the present time, and always*, lives and exercises judgment *in his successors, the Bishops of the holy Roman See, founded by him, and consecrated with his blood. Hence, whoever succeeds in this See of Peter, he, according to the institution of Christ Himself, obtains the Primacy over the universal Church.* ... If any one, therefore, shall say that it is not from the institution of Christ the Lord Himself, or by Divine right, that blessed Peter has successors in the Primacy over the universal Church; *or that the Roman Pontiff is not the blessed Peter's successor in the same Primacy*, let him be anathema.' (Const. *Pastor æternus*, cap. ii.)"

"(*b*) This unity of succession in the Episcopate of the particular Roman Church of Peter, and in the plenary power of Peter over the universal Church, is no less expressly declared whenever *the Roman Church itself is defined to have received and to hold the Primacy over the Catholic Church*, namely, through its Bishop, who is successor of Peter, the prince of the Apostles."

"Thus we find, in the profession of faith prescribed by Clement IV. and Gregory X., and accepted by the Greeks at their union with the Catholic Church in the second Council of Lyons: 'Also, the same Holy *Roman Church* holds the supreme and plenary Primacy over the universal Catholic Church, which she truly and humbly acknowledges *she has received with the plenitude of power from the Lord Himself, in blessed Peter, the prince or head of the Apostles, whose successor is the Roman Pontiff.*' In the Council of Constance was condemned, by Martin V., the XLI. Proposition of Wickliff: 'It is not of necessity to salvation to believe *that the Roman Church is supreme amongst other Churches*.' In the form prescribed by Pius IV. 'for making an orthodox profession of faith according to the ordinance of the Council of Trent,' and in the same words as those of another form prescribed by the Holy See for the Greeks, all Catholics solemnly declare: 'I acknowledge the holy Catholic and Apostolic *Roman Church to be mother and mistress (magistram) of all Churches*, and I promise and swear true obedience *to the Roman Pontiff, the successor of blessed Peter, prince of the Apostles*, and the Vicar of Jesus Christ.' Finally, in the Vatican Council (Const. *Pastor æternus*, cap. iii.) it is defined : 'We teach and declare that *the Roman Church, by the Lord's disposition, holds the princedom of ordinary power* * *over all other Churches, and that this power of*

---

* "The same dogma was already set forth, in the same words, in the Fourth Lateran Council (cap. v.): 'We decree, with the approbation of the whole Sacred Synod, that after the Roman Church, which, by the Lord's disposition, holds the princedom of ordinary power over all others as being mother and mistress of the whole of Christ's faithful (*mater universorum Christifidelium et magistra*), the Church of Constantinople (whose Patriarch at that time was of the Latin rite) holds the first place, that of Alexandria the second, of Antioch the third, of Jerusalem the fourth.' (Hard. tom. vii. p. 23.) That the

jurisdiction of the Roman Pontiff, which is really episcopal, is immediate in regard to which pastors and faithful of whatsoever rite and dignity, as well individually as collectively . . . are held bound.'"

"From these definitions and professions of faith, this same *Roman Church* holds the Primacy, or princedom of power over all other Churches, over the universal Church, and is Mother and Mistress of all Churches. But she has all this in her Bishop, because he is successor of Peter the prince of the Apostles, that is, successor in his own princedom itself. And hence we see, in the Vatican definition, that the Roman Church's princedom of ordinary power is spoken of as no other than the Roman Pontiff's power of jurisdiction; and in the profession of Lyons and Trent, the Roman Church's supreme and plenary Primacy, maternity, and magisterium, of all Churches is founded in the fact of the Roman Pontiff being the successor of blessed Peter, prince of the Apostles, and, therefore, the Vicar of Jesus Christ. The subject of supreme authority is solely the Bishop of the Roman Church, who, by the very fact of his succeeding Peter, the prince of the Apostles, in the Episcopate of this Church, succeeds him also in the princedom over the universal Church. On account of this unity, for two distinct reasons, 'the same Holy Roman Church, in truth and humility, acknowledges that she has received the supreme and plenary Primacy and princedom from the Lord Himself, in blessed Peter, prince of the Apostles, whose successor is the Roman Pontiff:' that is to say, through the same Roman Pontiff who is her own Bishop, as successor of the prince of the Apostles, she has received the Primacy—not only by reason of its *end* (*non solum rations* finali) whereby the Primacy is instituted for the good as well for the whole Church as for the Roman Church in particular—but also —in regard of what may be considered the *formal* reason (*sed quodammodo* formaliter)—inasmuch as the Primacy is united to the Roman Episcopate, and thus the succession to the Primacy is by the continuous series of her own Bishops ingrafted into the Roman Church herself. 'Thou oughtest to know that the Bishop is in the Church, and the Church in the Bishop.'" *

"II. From all that has been set forth in this and the two preceding theses may be inferred how the union of the Primacy with the Episcopate, in other words, with the Roman See or Church, ought to be understood."

"(a) As the Church of Jesus Christ is a visible institution, and, therefore, easily recognisable by sure and stable marks, amongst all the sects that bear the Christian name, as the one and true Church of Christ; so, too, all the elements which belong to the visibility of the Church, and render her visible, certainly ought to be visible. Now, amongst these elements the visible head itself holds the first place, as being the visible foundation instituted by Christ, viz., Peter, from rock in perpetual succession (*Petrus de petra in perenni successione*). Consequently, in this same institution of a visible head of the Roman Church is *mother* of all Christ's faithful, and *mistress* (*magistra*) (by her supreme power of *ruling* and *teaching*), we may see from what is said in the Florentine definition of the proper subject of that power, viz., that the Roman Pontiff himself is the *father* and *teacher* of all Christians. And what is termed her princedom of ordinary power *over all other Churches*, as being the mother and mistress of all Christ's faithful—all this is contained in the Tridentine profession: 'I acknowledge her mother and mistress *of all churches*.'"

* Cyprian. *Ep.* 69 *ad Flor. Pupian.*

Church, who is to remain in perpetuity and in continuous succession, is involved the necessity of the succession itself being visible, that is with certainty easily recognisable by constant and manifest outward sign. But, as a matter of fact, that which has always, ever since Peter's glorious martyrdom, been universally held and believed in every age of the Church, to be the certain, constant, and manifest sign of succession to Peter's Primacy, is succession in Peter's Roman See, which, by his own death, he left (to use the expression of S. Cyprian) *vacant*, that is, to be occupied by his several lineal successors to all his own rights. Therefore, just as by antecedent Divine institution a visible sacrament avails for perpetual succession to the visible Episcopate and priesthood, so, by Divine ratification, consequent at least after the whole Petrine fact (*divina ratihabitione saltem consequente post factum Petri*), the visible sign of succession in the *Roman* See of Peter avails for perpetual succession in the visible Primacy. 'The blessed Peter, who *first presided over the Apostolic See*, left the princedom of his apostolate *to his successors, who are to sit uninterruptedly* (perenniter) *in his most holy See*, to whom also he himself, *by Divine command, consigned and delivered, as the Pontiff's who should succeed him*, the power of authority, in the same way as that power was conferred on him by the Lord God, our Saviour.'"

"To this explanation, derived from all the above cited ecclesiastical documents, we have the agreement of eminent theologians. 'As we have shown the necessity,' says Suarez, 'from reason and from the institution and the end of the Church, of her being visible individually and in particular, *so is it necessary, from the institution and end of the office of the Vicar of Christ, that this should be visible to the Church in particular, and by a determined See and succession.*' (Suarez, *Contra Reg. Aug.* l. iii. c. 13.) 'The Primacy of Peter, that is, the universal pontificate or the government of the whole Church, was bound to be attached to a certain See. For, though this Primacy did not *per se* (that is, antecedently, and of its own intrinsic nature) require any particular episcopal See to which it should be fixed, still *the succession in the Primacy certainly required it* (since the succession itself, together with the Primacy, was divinely instituted to last in perpetuity), *in order that it might persevere, as it was bound to do, for the good of the Church, and be easily put in execution.* . . . Hence Peter necessarily chose some particular episcopate, to which the person of Primate should be attached. He was, indeed, founder of the See of Antioch, and its ruler for some years; but when he thence passed on to Rome, he transferred thither the Primacy inseparable from his own person, and retaining the same Roman Episcopate until death, transmitted the Primacy to his successors in the same See.' (Laurent. Veith. *de Primat. Rom. Pontif.* Posit. viii. § 18; Pet. Ballerini, *de vi et ratione Primat. R. P.* tom. i. c. 1, n. 2; Theol. Würzeburg, tom. i. *de Primat. R. P.* § 170, n. iii.; Franc. Ant. Zaccaria, *de S. Petri Primat.* c. 5, n. 7)."

"(*b*) It follows further from those documents especially, in which is taught the princedom of the Roman Church itself, that is, of the Apostolic Roman See, not only that there is a *union* between the Primacy and the Roman Episcopate as between two separate things in some one third, but that there is in fact *one Roman See* with princedom over the universal Church, which princedom contains in it the Roman Episcopate, as the particular is contained in the universal. We are not, in truth, to distinguish two Sees of Peter, of which one may be understood as instituted by Christ and given to Peter for supreme pastoral power over the universal Church, and the other be the See of the particular Roman Church of Peter's institution, separate from the former See, having an actual existence of its own, and only joined to the other by reason of the one person who should administer both; but we are to regard the action of Peter—who had been instituted by Christ pastor of the whole Church, not for himself alone, but also for each and all his successors in a perpetual series—as choosing for himself and constituting this Roman Church as his *episcopal See*, and so making it the Apostolic Petrine See. Hence by this very fact there was constituted the one Roman See, and this in Peter's death was consecrated, with perpetual hereditary right,* the Primatial See in the dignity and power of the princedom which Christ instituted over the universal Church. I will say the same in the words of Bellarmine. 'We should observe,' he says, 'that the Roman Episcopate and the Pontificate of the universal Church are not two Episcopates nor two Sees, save potentially (*in potentia*). For Peter, instituted by Christ Pontiff of the whole Church, did not annex to himself the Episcopate of the city of Rome, as a Bishop of a certain place annexes to himself some other Episcopate, or a Canonry, or Abbacy; *but he raised the Episcopate of the city of Rome to the supreme Pontificate of the whole world*, just as when a simple Bishopric is raised to an Archbishopric or to a Patriarchate; for an Archbishop or a Patriarch is not twice or thrice Bishop, but once only ... and the supreme Pontiff, although he is Bishop, Archbishop, Patriarch, and supreme Pontiff, yet all these things are one actually, and only potentially many (*hæc omnia sunt unum actu, et tantum in potentia multa*). And from this it follows that whoever is chosen to be the Bishop of Rome is, by that very fact, supreme Pontiff of the whole Church, even though the electors did not happen to express it.' (Bellarmine, *de Rom. Pont.* l. ii. c. 12.) What this great theologian says of 'many things potentially and of their actual unity' must be rightly understood; that is to say, it was not necessary from the nature of the case, and as though *a priori*, that Peter should appropriate to himself, as pastor of the whole Church, this definite See of Rome. Hence, absolutely speaking, the Episcopate of the city of Rome might have been instituted existing independently, and without being thus raised to the supreme Pontificate of the world; but this once done (*sed posito facto*), the particular inferior power of the Roman Episcopate is thereby included in the one supreme and universal power. And no less were the metropolitan rights over the ecclesiastical Roman province and the patriarchal rights over the patriarchate of the West thereby contained in the supreme universal power, when the Pope specially reserved these to himself,† to the exclusion of others, or rather by not con-

---

* "See former documents wherein the Roman Pontiffs are called *heirs of Peter* so frequently that the term seems in a manner to have passed into a proper name. 'Since Peter placed his See at Rome, and conferred on it his whole Primacy and power, and did not in his lifetime change this institution, the Church, when afterwards without a head (*acephala*) by Peter's death, had no power to change this institution, and, therefore, Peter's successor in the Roman Episcopate necessarily at the same time succeeded to the Primacy.'" (Suarez, *Contr. Reg. Angl.* l. iii. c. 13.)

† "Hence we see why the Council of Nice (*Can*. vi.) was able expressly to *confirm* the patriarchal rights (as afterwards, perhaps, from the 5th century they began to be called) of the Bishops of Alexandria and Antioch, and of other Exarchs (of Pontus, proconsular Asia, Thrace), for they were of merely

ceding these rights to any other Metropolitan or Patriarch; for we have already seen that such Metropolitan Sees and Patriarchates, not being of Divine but only of ecclesiastical institution, had their origin from the grant direct or indirect of the Roman See of Peter, and can only have their actual existence in communion with, and in dependance on, this See. Moreover, as the Pope does not always act with the whole intensity of his supreme power, so also he can exercise more restricted acts of jurisdiction, whether episcopal, archiepiscopal, or patriarchal, within the limits which he has specially reserved and marked out for these same rights. It is in this way 'the many things *in potentia*,' as well of exercise and *a posteriori*, as *a priori* by exclusion when of absolute necessity, whilst they are 'all actually one' (*omnia unum actu*) in the divinely instituted universal power."

"III. From our whole disputation some one may perchance think it follows, as a consequence, that the union of the Primacy with the Roman Episcopate is such, that it is a dogma of Catholic faith, that a separation and transfer of the Primacy to another See cannot be made even by the supreme power of the Roman Pontiff himself."

"1. The three following points are without doubt of Catholic faith: (a) That Christ instituted in Peter a power of Primacy over the universal Church; (b) that He instituted this Primacy to remain in perpetuity as the visible foundation and rock placed by Christ the principal Rock (*et petram a Christo petra principali positam*); and so, essentially belonging to the Divine constitution of the Church, as long as she remains indefectible till the consummation of the world; and that, consequently, together with the Primacy, was instituted *in him a perpetual succession*, so that always (by a series morally continuous) *one* should be in the visible Church a visible and recognisable successor of Peter; (c) that these successors in the Primacy are the Roman Pontiffs, to whom alone the legitimate succession to Peter actually belongs and has ever belonged. See above, the definition of the Vatican Council.

"That the first and the second dogma are contained in the very words of the promise and institution made in Peter by Christ, as those words have always and everywhere been understood in God's Church, and that they are deduced from these same words by simple analysis without assuming any proposition which is not revealed—this we have demonstrated in foregoing theses. The third is no other than the concrete expression and application of these first two dogmas. The words of Christ the Lord, whereby He promised and instituted the Primacy, and a perpetual succession therein by a

ecclesiastical right; but it neither could nor had the will to *confirm* the patriarchal rights of the Roman Bishop, included as these were in the Primacy divinely instituted over the whole Church, but only to *acknowledge* and bring them forward as though the *norma*, and as an argument whereby it might be shown to be congruous, to grant similar patriarchal rights to those other Sees, and for the synod to confirm them. . . . 'The Nicene Council did not presume to constitute anything with regard to him (the successor of Peter), for it knew well that to him all things were granted by the words of the Lord.' (Bonifacius, 1 *Ep.* 14, and others above cited.) 'Privileges given to this holy Church by Christ, not given by synods, but therein only celebrated and venerated, whereby not honour so much as burden is laid upon us, although we have received this same honour, not by our own merits, but by the appointment of God's grace through the blessed Peter and in the blessed Peter.' " (Nicol. I. *Ep.* 8 *ad Michael. imperat.*; Hard. tom. v. p. 162.)

continuous series (Thou art Peter . . . I will give to thee the keys . . . Confirm thy brethren; Feed My sheep) do not set forth a merely abstract truth, nor have respect to persons indeterminate, but are said and directed *in concreto* to the person of Peter, and to each and all of his successors in their entire series; they are not words merely theoretical and speculative, but they are practical words, and efficacious of what they signify in Peter and in his successors, each and all of whom Christ had in His mind, and to them He spoke them. Well, now, these successors in Peter's Primacy are either non-existent, in which case the words of Eternal Truth would not be true, or they always were, and, in the present order, alone are successors of Peter in the Apostolic Roman See. For, as a constantly enduring matter of fact, evident through most universal tradition, they alone were always practically acknowledged, and are still acknowledged, and were theoretically published abroad, and are thus known—from the very fact of their succeeding Peter in the Roman See—to be the successors in that Primacy which Christ, by efficacious Divine words, instituted in Peter, together with a perpetual succession thereto. Therefore, the words of Christ, at least for the present order, *implicitly* comprehend and set forth as the successors in the divinely instituted Primacy all the Roman Pontiffs and these alone, and this truth is *explicitly* applied and proposed as credible, and to be believed, the fact being evident from most universal tradition. Therefore, as we believe with Catholic faith, the divinely instituted Primacy, and its perpetual conservation, and the succession therein of one Pontiff after another (*et in eo singulorum successio*),—so no less is to be believed, at least for the present order, the succession in the same *of the Roman Pontiffs*. 'For the Church to know certainly,' says Suarez, 'that in such a See the institution made by Christ and revealed in Scripture has been fulfilled, and till now is being fulfilled, it is enough that the application, so to speak, of that institution and dignity to such an Episcopate should be most sufficiently proposed to the same Church by evident tradition, and continuous and most notorious use. . . . As, therefore, the visible Church, not only with human but also with Divine faith, is believed to be the Church (the true Church of Jesus Christ), not because the sensible signs whereby she is seen, are the reason for believing, but because they propose, as evidently credible, that she is the true Church; so not only with human, but also with Divine faith, is it to believed that the *Roman Pontiff* is the visible head of this Church in Christ's place, because those signs whereby we show this head, make it evidently credible, that it is he whom Christ, by virtue of His institution, constituted His Vicar. In this way, then, we say that the assertion laid down is of faith, and is sufficiently contained in Scripture, taken in conjunction with the Church's tradition (*in Scriptura, adjuncta Ecclesiæ traditione*)." (Suarez, *cont. Reg. Angl.* l. iii. c. 13.) Nay, this same dogma of the succession of the *Roman Pontiffs* in the Primacy divinely conferred on Peter for himself and his successors, is expressly declared and defined in the decrees and professions of faith given before in this thesis (No. 1). . . ." [The Cardinal goes on to show this conclusively from the Florentine definition.]

"2. Now, then, if all this be so, is not the fourth point we mentioned also a dogma simply to be believed as of faith—viz., that the union of the Primacy with the See and Church of Rome is so absolute, and belongs so essentially to the unalterable constitution of the Church, that by no power, not even the supreme power of the Roman Pontiff himself, can the Primacy be separated and transferred elsewhere? We answer that this hitherto at least is not a defined dogma *of faith*; but that it is a theological truth. . . ."*

As this point is rather a corollary resulting from the main thesis of the union of the Roman Episcopate with the Primacy, which it was our object to illustrate; having given the opinion of the learned Cardinal, we here leave it: and must refer the studious reader to the work itself, where the author extends his proofs of this part of his thesis over many pages. †

* *Theses de Ecclesia Christi*, pp. 192-202. † *Ib.* pp. 202-220.

INDEX.

INDEX.

Authors are either quoted or referred to on the pages indicated.

A

ACTS, 83, 308.
Alexander I., Pope, 100, 109, 506.
Alexander, Bishop of Jerusalem, A.D. 205, the first Coadjutor-bishop on record, 314; his letters, 473.
Alexandria, the second See, founded by S. Mark, its first Bishop, in S. Peter's name, 393, 395, 398, 447, 449, 500, 539.
Allard, Paul, 118, 163, 168, 308.
Allen, Cardinal, on hatred of the Roman See, 248.
Allies, 87, 144 sq., 162, 167, 169 sq., 482, 500.
Allnatt, 315 sq., 390.
Alphonsus, S., 189, 192, 213, 214 sq., 226, 243, 258, 259 sq., 285, 289, 311, 318 sq., 336 sq.
Ambrose, S., 132, 158, 224, 289, 403.
Anatolius, S., of Alexandria, 19.
Andrew, S., claimed as first Bishop of Byzantium, 261, 444; this disproved, 445 sq., 245.
Andronicus and Junias, 163.
Anger, 79.
Anglican authors, statements and views of, bearing upon S. Peter's Roman Episcopate: Cave, Pearson, Neale, Ch. xvii. 437-450; Farrar, *The Speaker's Commentary*, *Bishop Ellicott's Commentary*, Homersham Cox, Neale, Ch. xviii. 451-461; Bishop Lightfoot, Ch. xix. 462-506.
Anglicanism, topics connected with, xiv.-xvii., 178 sq., 195 sq., 211, 227, 234, 238-243, 272-274, 438 sq., 477 sq., 504, 511-519, 521, 528-530.
Anicetus, Pope, 101, 469, 470, 487, 488.
Annianus, the first Bishop of Alexandria after S. Mark, 398, 402, 447.
Antioch, the See of, S. Peter its founder and first Bishop, 13, 16, 245, 250, 253, 389, 392 sq., 396, 442, 449, 500; it does not inherit the Primacy, 280, 289, 341, 541.
Apocryphal writings appreciated, 201-205.
Apollonius, S., Martyr, 44, 444.
Apostolate, the, compared with, and how related to the Primacy, 251-260, 263, 329; its relation to the Episcopate, 252 sq., 261-268.
Apostolical, gifts and jurisdiction purely, 253, 255, 258 sq., 263.
Aquila and Priscilla (Prisca), 38, 73, 75, 164 sq., 167, 308.
Armellini, 110.
Arnobius, 62.
Athanasius, S., 384 sq., 479.
Augustine, S., 61, 72, 132, 139, 158, 246, 311, 334, 335, 336, 340, 400, 409.

B

BABYLON (1 Pet. vi. 13), 9, 37 sq., 56 sq., 65, 139, 443, 444, 449, 451 sq. See also 232, 528 sq.
Baptistery, the, in the Vatican, 152 sq.

Baratier, 32.
Baronius, Cardinal, 46, 60, 118, 323 *sq.*, 392-395, 402, 445 *sq.*
Baur, 416.
Bede, S., 38, 43, 487.
Beelen, 55.
Bellarmine, Cardinal, 279, 542.
Bernard, S., 135, 215, 225, 326, 528.
Boldetti, 133.
Bollandists, the, 404, 406.
Bosio, Antonio, 109, 117.
Bossuet, 226.
Bramhall, 443.
Browne, E. H., the Anglican Bishop, 195, 234, 355.
Brutius, Gens Brutia, 116, 117.
Burrus, 75, 490.
Butler, Alban, 446.
Byzantium, the See of, 444, 482.

C.

Caius, 23, 92, 443.
Cajetan, Cardinal, 286-295, 315.
Callistus I., Pope, 424.
Capellari, Cardinal (Gregory XVI.), 354.
Cassiodorus, 41.
Catacombs of the Apostolic age: the Cemeteries of the Vatican, 106; of S. Paul, 107; of Priscilla, 108; the Ostrianum and Basilica of S. Emerentiana, 109 *sq.*; of S. Domitilla, 114 *sq.*, 491; of S. Sebastian, the temporary resting-place of the bodies of SS. Peter and Paul, 125 *sq.*; value of their evidence, 112 *sq.*, 128 *sq.*, 160, 176 *sq.*; the losses they have sustained, 181 *sq.*
Catalani on the Pallium, 174 *sq.*
Catalogues of early Popes: the Liberian (Bucherian), 40, 41, 45, 91, 93, 409; the Felician, 40, 41, 90, 91, 93, 97, 156, 487; Fragment, 3rd century, 41, 42.
Catholic Church, the, a city of unity, outside of it discord, 297 *sq.*, 355 (see Anglicanism); variety in its unity, 297; one only, built exclusively on Peter, 287, 330; the Catholic and Roman Church ever asserts her claim to be exclusively the one true Catholic Church of Christ, 514, 529 *sq.*; the unity of its priesthood in the Vicar of Christ, 524 *sq.*
Cave, 39, 437, 442 *sq.*, 449.
Ceadwalla, his visit to Rome, 151, 154.
Censure, the denial of the Petrine facts subject to manifold, 276.
Cephas, as distinct from S. Peter, 334, 337, 406.
Chair, S. Peter's, in the Ostrianum, 109 *sq.*; oil from, 109, 124, 116; in the Vatican, 38, 148 *sq.*; the two Feasts of, 156-9; his Chair at Antioch, *ibid.*, 393; *Cathedra* used not only in a metaphorical but also in a material sense, 152 *sq.*, 498. The Chair of S. James at Jerusalem, of S. Mark at Alexandria, 156, 404.
Chaldee Office, 57.
Chamier, 443.
Charles V., 247 *sq.*
Chronology, 66 *sq.*, 206; mistake in the Vulgar Era of the date of our Lord's Birth, U.C. 754, the true date December 25th, U.C. 747, A.C. 7; His Crucifixion, March 16th, U.C. 782, A.D. 29, 40, 67; Patrizzi's Chronology of the *Acts of the Apostles*, 67 *sq.*; S. Paul's Conversion, A.D. 31, 71; S. Peter, Bishop of Antioch, A.D. 35-42, 71; Conversion of Cornelius, A.D. 40 or 41, 44, 72; S. Peter's imprisonment by Herod, deliverance, and journey to Rome, where he founds the Roman Church and undertakes the Episcopate, A.D. 42, the second year of Claudius, 44, 55, 72. — Dispersion of the Apostles, A.D. 41 or 42, 28, 44, 72; SS. Paul and Barnabas set apart for the Apostolate, A.D. 42.—S. Paul's first Apostolic journey, A.D.

INDEX. 551

42, return to Antioch, and some abode there till A.D. 47, 72.—S. Peter writes his First Epistle, and S. Mark his Gospel, at Rome, whence the latter is sent by S. Peter to Alexandria, A.D. 43, where he dies A.D. 61 or 62, 44, 45, 72, 450; S. Peter leaves Rome, A.D. 46, for Antioch and Jerusalem; his reprehension by S. Paul; Council of Jerusalem, A.D. 47, 70-72.—S. Paul's Second Apostolic journey with Silas, A.D. 47; he is soon joined by SS. Timothy and Luke; he arrives, A.D. 48, at Corinth, where he remains 18 months with Aquila and Priscilla; with whom, in the spring of A.D. 50, he sets sail for Syria, leaving them at Ephesus, and reaches Jerusalem by Pentecost, A.D. 50, whence he goes to Antioch, 72.— S. Paul's Third Apostolic journey, A.D. 50; he is at Ephesus two years and three months with Aquila and Priscilla; he leaves Ephesus in the summer of A.D. 52, and in December arrives at Corinth, whence early, A.D. 53, he writes his *Epistle to the Romans*, with salutations to Aquila and Priscilla, already returned to Rome. It was then probably that S. Peter came to Corinth, and preached there with S. Paul, both Apostles leaving Corinth at the same time, S. Peter for Rome, S. Paul for Syria; the latter reaches Jerusalem by Pentecost, A.D. 53, 52, 73 sq., 77-81.—S. Paul's imprisonment at Jerusalem, Pentecost, A.D. 53, 68-70, 77-80; he is detained in prison at Cæsarea for two years, till A.D. 55; in October that year he arrives shipwrecked at Malta, and in the early spring of A.D. 56 reaches Rome, 75, 308, where he remains in free custody till the earlier part of A.D. 58, 75, 206 sq.; his return to Rome and second imprisonment there, probably A.D. 67. The Martyrdom of SS. Peter and Paul, June 29th, A.D. 67, 40, 45, 46. See also 285, 447, 451 sq.

Chrysostom, S., 13 sq., 224, 253, 254, 334, 339, 345, 408.

Claudius, the two Edicts of, against the Jews, A.D. 46 and 48, 56, 72, 73, 74, 84, 307.

Clement I., Pope, his pontificate, 92-97; quoted or referred to, 83-86, 90, 151, 156, 205 sq., 313, 316, 397, 465, 467, 471, 497; his *Epistle to the Corinthians*, its authorship and date, 83-86, 52, 94-96, 466, 472 sq., 492 sq.; its newly-recovered portion, 462, 472, 488; his parentage, 93; according to Lightfoot, 471.

Clement IV., Pope, profession of faith of, 539.

Clement of Alexandria, 31, 37, 44, 58, 334, 472.

Clementines, the, 22, 156, 202, 271, 410, 413, 417 sq., 423; not of Roman, but of Eastern origin, 420, 467. No journey of S. Peter to Rome recorded in them, 426 sq.—*Epistle to S. James*, 204, 205, 429, 434.—*Recognitions* and *Homilies*, 430 sq.; their date, 434, 435, 467. Critical remarks on the Clementines, 433 sq.

Cletus (Anacletus, Anencletus), Pope, 91, 92, 106, 107, 156, 205, 206, 316, 317, 397, 410.

Collier, Jeremy, 461.

Columbier, Père, 92.

Constant, 95.

Conybeare and Howson, 414.

Cornelius a Lapide, 335.

Cornelius, the centurion, 44, 143, 144, 161, 166, 170, 341, 342. The Gens Cornelia, 166, 167.

Councils: Jerusalem, A.D. 47, 331, 334 sq.; Arles, A.D. 314, 410; Nice, A.D. 325, 86, 313 sq., 393, 500, 542 sq.; Synods of Antioch, A.D. 269 and 341, 501, 85; Fourth Carthage,

A.D. 398, 172; Chalcedon, A.D. 451, 500; Roman Synod, A.D. 494, 87; Fourth Lateran, A.D. 1215, 539; Second Lyons, A.D. 1274, *ibid.*; Constance, A.D. 1414, *ibid.*; Florence, A.D. 1434, 2, 277, 283, 538 *sq.*; Trent, ratified by Pius IV., A.D. 1564; Vatican, A.D. 1870, 1, 276, 277, 284, 539.
Cox, Homersham, xiv., 456 *sq.*
Cyprian, S., 19 *sq.*, 138, 140, 155, 215, 259, 339 *sq.*, 401, 461, 469, 524 *sq.*, 535.

D.

DAMASUS, Pope, 112, 121, 124, 126, 153, 156.
Darby, 36, 76.
De excidio Hierosolymarum, the Author of, 46.
De Lugo, 279.
De Rossi, 92, 106, 110, 116, 117, 120, 121, 124, 132, 133, 138, 149, 165.
De Smedt, S.J., 92, 312, 314.
Dio Cassius, 55, 72, 93, 115, 116.
Dionysius, Bishop of Corinth, 29-31, 59, 250, 469, 471, 472, 473, 492 *sq.*
Dionysius Exiguus, 66.
Dispersion of the Apostles, 28, 44, 72.
Döllinger, 162, 221-227, 234 *sq.*, 249 *sq.*, 262-268, 300, 301, 304, 307, 329-333, 340-348, 408-411, 455, 460, 474, 493.
Dressel, 32 (misprinted Bressel, *ibid.*).
Drumont, 531 *sq.*
Dublin Review, 494, 531 *sq.*

E.

EASTERN CHURCHES, testimony of, to S. Peter's Roman Episcopate, 17 *sq.*, 57, 193 *sq.*, 288, 849 *sq.*, 378 *sq.*; their Liturgical languages, 385 *sq.*
Ebionism, 465, 467 *sq.*, 491.
Elchasaism, 420, 468.
Eleutherus, Pope, 106, 377, 471, 487.
Ellicott's Commentary, 453 *sq.*
Ennodius of Pavia, 152.
Epiphanius, S., 45, 206, 265, 311, 312, 400, 410.

Episcopate, the, in relation to the Apostolate, 252 *sq.*, 261-268; its development in the Apostolic age, 262 *sq.*
Epistles of Churches one to another, anciently written by, and addressed to, their respective bishops, 52 *sq.*, 478 *sq.*
Era, Vulgar (Dionysian), mistake in the, 66 *sq.*
Errata, xx.
Eucherius, S., 214.
Eusebius, 15 *sq.*, 23, 29, 37, 41, 44, 47, 60, 75, 76, 89, 93, 97, 101, 116, 132, 314, 334, 428, 444, 477, 487, 493; his *Chronicle* and S. Jerome's version, 16, 41; his testimony to S. Peter's Roman Episcopate examined, 388-408, with frequent quotations.
Evaristus, Pope, 97-100, 106, 377, 505 *sq.*
Evodius, or Euodius, Bishop of Antioch, next after S. Peter, 396, 397, 442, 449.

F.

FARRAR, 451 *sq.*
Fermilian, S., 20, 21.
Fisher, the B. John, 5, 244-248.
Flavii, the, 94, 108, 114, 120; T. Flavius Sabinus, 114, 118; T. Flavius Clemens, the martyred consul, 93, 94, 115, 121, 415, 490 *sq.*; Flavia Domitilla, the elder and the younger, 115, 116; St. Flavia Domitilla, 93, 94, 116 *sq.*, 415, 490 *sq.*
Foggini, 5, 55.
Fons Petri (*Ad Nymphas Petri*), 109 *sq.*, 166.
Franzelin, Cardinal, 28, 534-545.
Funk, 35, 36, 95.

G.

GALLIO, proconsul of Achaia, elder brother of Seneca, 73, 308.

Gavazzi's impudent assertion, 17.
Gelasius, Pope, 87, 226, 402.
Gerbet, 521, 529.
Gibbon, 115.
Gilded glasses in the Catacombs, 131 sq.
Greek Liturgical Offices, 112, 349 sq.; SS. Peter and Paul the protocoryphæi, 350; their rival eulogiums, 351; those of S. Paul personal, of S. Peter official, 352; his union with Christ, manifold sense of "Rock," the due share in prerogatives given to the other Apostles, the union of SS. Peter and Paul, 353-356; the significance of S. Peter's apprehension by Herod, 356; S. Peter the first Bishop of Rome, the principle of the Church's permanence and solidity, 356-358; passages cited from these Offices, 357-359, the Feast of S. Peter's Chains, 359-363, of SS. Peter and Paul, 363-375, of all the Apostles, 375-377; from the Offices of Popes SS. Sylvester, Leo the Great, Gregory the Great, and Martin, testifying to the succession of the Roman Pontiffs in S. Peter's See and Primacy, 378-382; this confirmed from the writings of Saints and historians of the Greek Church—*v.g.*, S. Theodore Studites, S. Nicephorus, Patriarch of Constantinople, Socrates, and Sozomen, 382-385.
Greek schism, the, 349 sq., 517 sq.
Gregory, S., the Great, 109, 122, 124, 127, 340; his Office in the Greek Church, 380.
Gregory X., Pope, Profession of faith prescribed by, in the Second Council of Lyons, 539.
Grotius, 443.
Gueranger, 157, 172.
Guilleux, Père, xx., 413.

H.

HARNACK, 494.

Harwarden, 316.
Hefele, 96.
Hegesippus, 42, 94, 102, 378, 404, 409, 456, 470, 498.
Herbst, 5, 39, 47, 61.
Heresy, the Church's dealing with, 425 sq., 531; distinguished from schism, 517 sq.
Hergenröther, 500.
Hermas, 103, 472; his *Pastor*, 486, 488, 495, 497.
Hippolytus, 410, 468, 469.
Historical and non-historical religions, 507-510; Christianity is a historical religion, but outside the Church it is not, as such, properly speaking historical, 510-512; Anglicanism is historical, but not historical Christianity—the different senses in which the Greek schism and Anglicanism are historical, 512-519; Roman Catholicism, Judaism, Mahomedanism, as historical religions—the first of these is historical Christianity, 510, 519 sq.; Jerusalem, Rome, Mecca, the tendency of historical religions to centralisation and to union under one head, 521.
History, topics connected with the writing of, xi. sq., 50, 113, 129 sq., 179 sq., 194 sq., 201, 208 sq., 272, 316, 435, 459 sq., 463 sq., 465 sq., 470, 498, 517.
Holy Scripture: Objections raised against S. Peter's Roman Episcopate from passages in the *Acts* and *Epistles*, 37 sq., 53-56; from the silence found in these, 50-52, 74, 448, 452, 454, 455; S. Luke's scope in the *Acts*, 51.—The teaching in the Gospels prophetic of what was to be characteristic of Christ's Church—*v.g.*, devotion to the B. V. Mary, the Evangelical counsels, the Holy Eucharist, Penance, and especially an intimate relation of Christ's Church with S. Peter, 206-228.—*Matt.* xvi. 18, 212-214, 221,

245, 286, 353-355; *John*, x. 16, 214, 533; *Luke*, xxii. 24-32, 216-218, 222-228, 245, 293, 311.—The special union of Peter with Christ, the tribute money, *Matt.* xvii. 26, 216.—The "Stone," *Dan.* ii. 34 *sq.*, *Isa.* xxviii. 26, *Luke* ii. 34, 35, 1 *Pet.* ii. 6-8, 230 *sq.*—Rome in the Apocalypse as Babylon, *ibid.*; Jerusalem as Sodom, *ibid.*, 527-529.—*John*, xxi. 15-22, 233 *sq.*, 293.—The exercise of S. Peter's Primacy in the *Acts*, 254, 330 *sq.*, 460.—The title of the Roman Pontiff to be Peter's successor in the Primacy not discoverable in the Gospels, 288, 544.—The numerical unity, or unicity, of Christ's Church in Scripture, 237 *sq.*—Scripture, not history, the point for Protestants in contending against the Petrine claims, 273 *sq.*

Hyginus, Pope, 92, 100, 106, 400, 401, 488.

I.

IGNATIUS, S., the second Bishop of Antioch after S. Peter, 81 *sq.*, 100, 313 *sq.*, 396, 442, 487, 497.—His *Epistle to the Romans*, 81-83, 476, 490-506; its object, 491, 499, 502 504; its "Inscription," 83, 493, *sq.*—His Epistles to the Asian Churches, 499 *sq.*; his preeminent dignity as Bishop of Antioch, the territorial title of his See, 500 *sq.*; he is not silent about Clement, and episcopacy in Rome, for Lightfoot's reasons, 502 *sq.*; he commends his Syrian Church to the Bishop of Rome, 100, 505 *sq.*

Innocent I., Pope, 85, 139.
Innocent III., Pope, 175.
Innocent X., Pope, 311.
Innocent XI., Pope, 318.
Inscriptions, 85, 90, 107, 108, 111, 112, 120, 121, 123, 126, 131, 132, 138, 142, 152, 153, 164.

Irenæus, S., the weight of his authority, 24-29; quoted, *ibid.*, 17, 59, 60, 62, 92, 100, 101, 167, 250, 311, 312, 400, 409, 427, 443, 472, 488, 496, 535.

Isidore Hispalensis, 41, 43.
Isidore of Pelusium, 172.
Itineraries, old, of Christian Rome, 106, 109, 125.

J.

JACOBSON, 32.
James, S., first Bishop of Jerusalem, 253, 261, 263, 264, 330, 331, 333, 389, 396, 398, 403 *sq.*—The doubt as to whether he was one of the Twelve Apostles, 405 *sq.*, 444, 447, 457, 467.—A false notion that he had the Primacy, 456 *sq.*—His dignity as Bishop of Jerusalem, 457.

Jerome, S., 14, 16, 29, 38, 45, 75 *sq.*, 90, 98, 101, 117, 258, 325, 334, 335, 338 *sq.*, 393, 403, 408, 428, 444, 496, 503, 529, 531.

Jerusalem, the See of, its honorary preeminence and history, 393, 396, 424, 457-459; called the Theadelphian See, 404.—The succession of its Bishops, 389, 444.—Analogy between the city of Jerusalem and Rome, 525, 527-529.

John, S., the Evangelist, who records the Divine bestowal of the universal pastorate on Peter, and the prophecy of his crucifixion, bears witness to his martyrdom at Rome, 26, 198, 233 *sq.*, 448 *sq.*

John of Antioch, 502.
John, the abbot, 109, 111.
Josephus, 44, 46, 68, 69, 78 *sq.*, 331.
Judaism, the parallel between, and Christianity, 145 *sq.*; it has its true antitype alone in Roman Catholicism, 522-529; points of analogy between the two, *ibid.*; still the typical foe of Christianity, 523 *sq.*, 530-532.

Julius, Pope, 479.
Jungmann, xviii., 101, 345, 489.
Justin, S., 59, 60, 61, 101, 427.

L.

LACTANTIUS, quoted, his meaning and authority discussed, 47-50.
"Legal Evidence," Articles in the *Church Quarterly*, 180, 355, 439-441.
Legates, the two, sent from Rome to Corinth by S. Clement, 488 sq.
Legendary theory of German rationalists, the, xii., 64, 412 sq.
Leo, S., the Great, 48, 57, 107, 137, 147, 175, 225, 231, 244, 259, 326; his Office in the Greek Church, 379; letter of Gallic Bishops to him, 86.
Leo XIII., Pope, 242.
Liberatus on S. Mark's Pallium, 173.
Liber Pontificalis, the, 93, 97, 100, 106, 151.
Liddon, Canon, 180, 478.
Lightfoot, the Anglican bishop, xiv., 116, 180, 396, 422, 457; his writings quoted and examined, Ch. xix. 462-506.—On Ebionism and Judaising tendencies in the Roman Church, its orthodoxy, the Clementines, 465-471; his theories of a primacy of the Roman Church in the first two centuries, apart from its Bishop and the *Cathedra Petri*, one not of official authority, but of love, practical goodness, and local prestige; of the unequal development of episcopacy in the East and West; of the Roman Bishop being but a presbyter-bishop—his name, person, and authority absorbed in the Roman Church—examined and refuted, 472-488, 493-505.
Linus, Pope, 40, 89 sq., 107, 156, 205 sq., 309 sq., 313, 317, 397, 409.
Lipsius, 3, 64, 65.
Literature, controversial, the, on S. Peter's Roman Episcopate, 3-5.

M.

MACARIUS, S., 135.
Marchi, Padre, 110, 126.

Mark, S., his Gospel written in Rome under S. Peter, by whom he was sent to Alexandria, A.D. 43, as first Bishop of that See, 15, 31, 37, 44 sq., 389, 393, 395, 398 sq., 447, 449 sq., 500; styled an Apostle, 402 sq.
Marsilius Patavinus, the first assailer of S. Peter's Roman Episcopate, 4.
Martin, Pope, his Office in the Greek Church, 381.
Martin, Père, 18.
Matthew, S., the writing of his Gospel, 28.
Mazzella, 279.
Menander, 60, 89.
Metropolitan Churches, 86, 87, 543.
Milman, 7, 9, 13, 196, 421 sq., 446 sq.
Minucius Felix, the date of his *Octavius*, in connection with Tertullian's writings, 471.
Monica, S., 132.
Muratorian fragment, the, 495.
Murray, 251, 280.

N.

NEALE, J. M., 385 sq., 449 sq., 458.
Nereus and Achilleus, SS., their Acts, 118-122, 167; their Basilica, 122 sq.
Nestorian Office, 18.
Newman, Cardinal, xvi. sq., 242, 440 sq.
Nicephorus, S., Patriarch of Constantinople, 383, 445.
Nicephorus Callistus, 445.
Nicodemus, the Gospel of, 204.
Nilles, S. J., 378.

O.

ŒCUMENIUS, 38, 453.
Onophrius Panvinius, 109.
Optatus, S., 154, 286, 400, 409.
Origen, 21, 46, 47, 234.
Orosius, 43.

P.

PAINTINGS in the Catacombs, 120, 123; S. Peter as Moses with the

rod striking the rock, 134 *sq.*, 139; the Good Shepherd, 141; S. Peter's denial, *ibid.*; their symbolism, *ibid.*
Paisius Ligarides, 137.
Pallium, the, 172 *sq.*; of S. James, of S. Mark, *ibid.*
Palmer's *Early Christian Symbolism*, 131 *sq.*, 137, 14 *sq.*
Palmer (Anglican writer), 461.
Papal aggression in the 1st and 2nd centuries, 462 *sq.*, 472, 474 *sq.*, 479 *sq.*, 482 *sq.*
Papebroch, 312, 313.
Papias, 38, 58.
Patriarchal Churches, the three great, founded by S. Peter, 86 *sq.*, 396 *sq.*, 402, 500 *sq.*, 542 *sq.*
Patristic testimony to S. Peter's place in the Church, and Roman Episcopate, dogmatic not polemical, 41; indirect, implicit, fragmentary, 190 *sq.*, 199 *sq.*
Patrizzi, 28; his chronology, 67 *sq.* (wrongly called Cardinal, 69), 89.
Paul, S., the Apostle: chronology of his life, his Apostolic journeys, 68-81; sketch of his character, vocation, gifts, labours, success, 301 *sq.*, 350, 358-377 (extracts from Greek Offices), *passim*—not a diocesan bishop, 253; his association with the Roman Church, 82, 299, 300, 307, 310, 490; his *Epistle to the Romans*, 37, 52, 74, 532; his work in Rome during his imprisonment, A.D. 56-58, subsequent labours, return to Rome and martyrdom, A.D. 67, 46, 308-310; S. Paul, bishop-extraordinary in Rome, 313, 315 *sq.*; parallel between his own election and the vocation of the Gentiles to the Faith, 327 *sq.*; this his most prominent doctrine, *ibid.*, 51. See also Peter and Paul, SS.
Paul, S., Patriarch of Constantinople, 384.
Pearson, the Anglican Bishop, 189, 437, 447 *sq.*, 505.

Persecutions under Nero, 34, 87-89; Domitian, 93 *sq.*; Trajan, 97.
Peter, S., the Apostle, first came to Rome under Claudius, A.D. 42, founded the Roman Church, was the first Bishop of Rome, 14 *sq.*, 43, 161 *sq.*, 249 *sq.*, 390, 395, 397, 442, 448, 454, 461, 489; notices of his pontificate and of his successors down to S. Anicetus, 82-102; Bishop of Rome 25 years until his death, not all the time continuously in Rome, 2, 46 *sq.*, 189, 270, 277, 289, 461; he alone ordinary Bishop of Rome, 250, 313 *sq.*, 319 *sq.*; head of the Apostles and of the entire Christian Church, 263, 326, 329-332, 339 *sq.*, 346, 534 (see Greek Offices *passim*, 348-385); disciples sent by him abroad to preach the Faith and to preside over Churches, 85 *sq.*; martyred in Rome June 29th, A.D. 67, 18 *sq.*, 45 *sq.*, 193, 233-235. See also Peter and Paul, SS.
Peter and Paul, SS., how represented, and their relative position in works of art, 132-135, 138, 319; their striking contrasts and intimate union, its providential meaning, 298 *sq.*, 303-305, 308, 310, 316, 330-332, 338-344; subordination and deference of S. Paul to S. Peter as his superior, S. Peter's affection for S. Paul and testimony to his Epistles, 53, 304 *sq.*, 399 *sq.*—S. Paul not equal to, nor coordinate with, S. Peter in authority, 332; not Bishop of Rome, 263, 310-320, 399; divided jurisdiction untenable, 315 *sq.*, 323 *sq.*; a practical division of labour in Rome very probable, 316 *sq.*, 332; S. Paul with S. Peter joint-founder and patron of the Roman Church, both Apostles the chief protectors of the universal Church, 25, 298 *sq.*, 310, 317-319, 399, 442; their both preaching together at Corinth and Rome,

29-31, 74, 465 sq., 492 sq.—S. Peter the Apostle of the Circumcision, S. Paul of the Uncircumcision, how this is to be understood, 323 sq., 829 sq., 344 sq.; the former title the more honourable, *ibid.*, 533; both Apostles evangelised alike Jews and Gentiles, 324 sq., 333; S. Peter's reprehension by S. Paul, 334-348; various views of Fathers on the matter, 334 sq.; no doctrinal difference between the two Apostles, 336, 344 sq.—By the joint relations of SS. Peter and Paul to Rome is realised the Divine idea in both Testaments, 532 sq. See also the Greek Offices, 348-379.

Petrinism, Paulinism, and Petri-Paulinism, 64 sq., 412 sq., 465 sq., 489.

Petronilla, S. Aurelia, 82, 118; not a martyr, 123.

Philo with S. Peter in Rome, 15 sq., 43.

Philosophumena, the author of the, 22, 60, 62, 63, 420, 427.

Phœbe, 53.

Pitra, Cardinal, 350, 357.

Pitzipios, 385.

Pius I., Pope, 101, 106, 472, 488, 495.

Pius IV., Pope, the Profession of Faith of, 290.

Pliny's letter to Trajan, the emperor's reply, 98 sq.

Podogoritza, the glass plate from, 142.

Polycarp, S., 24, 26, 100, 101 sq., 468, 470, 487, 499 sq.

Pomponia Græcina (Lucina), 82 sq., 94, 168, 415, 490.

Prætextatus, the author of, 89.

Primacy, the Divine institution of S. Peter's, over the universal Church, and of its indefectible permanence by a perpetual succession to him therein, as well as the appointed mode of this perpetual succession, viz., by legitimate succession to the Roman Episcopate—these are three dogmas of Catholic Faith, the third being the concrete expression and application of the first two, 1, 269, 288, 534 sq., 543 sq.—The Church has ever professed and believed this mode of succession to the Primacy, and attested it in definitions of Councils and professions of Faith, 535 sq., 538-40; and that the Bishops of Rome, forming one moral person with Peter, inherit the plenitude of power divinely bestowed upon him, which was ordinary; and that the Roman See is the primatial Apostolic See over the whole Church, the Mother and Mistress of all Churches, the subject of this supreme authority being solely the Roman Pontiff, *ibid.*—It was necessary that succession to the divinely instituted office of visible head of Christ's visible Church should itself be also visible, and this it is through succession to Peter's Roman See, 540 sq.—This Petrine, Roman, primatial See, containing in it the Roman Episcopate, forms but one supreme Pontificate of the whole world, 541 sq.—The union of the Primacy with the Roman See is so absolute that it is not separable by any power in the Church, 544 sq.—The Primacy and its succession in the Roman See the crucial note which marks off the Catholic Church and Faith from all other communions and religious beliefs, 290.

Proselytes, *justitiæ* and *portæ*, 84, 341, 343, 415.

Prosper, 41.

Protestant arguments and objections, vii., ix. sq., 58, 65, 113, 129, 178-181, 193, 196, 201, 206, 235, 241 sq., 272-275, 294, 298 sq., 329, 337 sq., 390-392, 424, 438 sq., 445, 459 sq., 465 sq., 511-519.

Prudentius, 135.
Pudens, 38, 82, 164-167, 309 sq., 415; related to the Cornelii, 144.
Pudentiana and Praxedes, SS., 164 sq., 309 sq.

R.

Reumont, 88.
Roma Sotterranea, Northcote and Brownlow, xix., 105, quoted *passim*, in Part II.
Roman Episcopate, S. Peter's, the constant and universal belief of Christendom, 8-11, 187 sq., 272; of the Eastern Churches, 17, 194 (see Greek Liturgical Offices); never denied till 13th century, 4; Patristic testimony thereto, 11-36, 188 sq., 199 sq., 271 sq.; the Apostle's going to Rome, preaching, and martyrdom there are so connected with his episcopate as to form one Petrine fact, viii., 2, 11 sq., 191; which is not to be confounded with its duration of 25 years, 11, 39 sq.; not only a historical event, but a great moral fact, with most important issues, x. sq., 3, 11, 321 sq.; a dogmatic fact in a wide sense, infallibly certain, 3, 188; it alone adequately fulfils S. Peter's Apostolic career, 198, 229-232, 285; it, with its unbroken succession in the Roman Pontiffs, is the only bond of union in Christendom, 287-241; the actual verification in all time of Christ's promise, vii., 219; the visible sign, and notification to the Church and to the world, of the divinely instituted Primacy, 295 sq., 540 sq.; the monumenial fontal-fact of historical Christianity, and the realisation of the Divine idea in the two Dispensations, 507-533.—The historical fact of S. Peter's Roman Episcopate is not intrinsically and antecedently connected with his Primacy and its succession in the Bishops of Rome, viii., 270, 321. Hence the disproof of the fact would not avail Protestants in combating the Petrine claims, these rest on revelation, 272 sq.; the essential relation between the Roman See and the Primacy, 270 sq., 286 sq.; the unity of the Episcopate of that See and the universal Pontificate, 286 sq., 290, 294 sq., 315, 535, 537 sq., 541 sq.; whether the Bishops of Rome, as such, succeed to the Primacy *jure divino*, 278 sq.; they are, *de facto*, the *de jure divino* successors of S. Peter, 294; on the transfer of the Primacy from Rome to another See, 284; whether S. Peter's choice of Rome for his Episcopate was by his own act alone or also by a Divine decree, 280 sq.

Rome, the first preaching of the Gospel in, 161 sq.; condition of Jews and Christians in, the number of Roman Christians in S. Peter's time, 83 sq., 91, 116, 162 sq., 168-170, 308, 414; the union and purity of the Roman Church in early times, composed alike of Jewish and Gentile converts, some of high rank, its freedom from party strife, 82, 93 sq., 100, 116, 120, 300, 307, 414 sq., 420 sq., 466 sq., 490-492; ever held as the centre of Christendom, because its Bishop was believed to be successor of St. Peter, 6 sq., 100, 102, 192, 470; the Roman Church regarded in its head, the Mother and Mistress of all Churches, 290, 292, 317, 469, 520, 528; the only Apostolic See, 245, 253, 264, 288, 291 sq., 537, 538; its Primacy is independent of local prestige or secular aid, 247 sq., 481 sq.—The first Bishops of Rome down to S. Victor exercised the same primatial authority as that Pope, 487 sq.—The appellation of the Roman Church in relation to the Catholic Church, 287, 292.— Roman Catholicism alone is historical Christianity, 519 *sq.*; the analogy between Rome and Jerusalem, 523, 526-529.

Rufinus, his Preface to the *Recognitions*, 205 *sq.*, 428, 434.

S.

SAMARIA, S. Peter's mission to, 250, 260, 331, 392.

Sanguinetti, 5, 16 *sq.*, 21, 49, 54.

Sarcophagi, sculptures on the Christian, 109, 135 *sq.*; S. Peter as Moses with rod striking the rock, his apprehension by Herod, 133, 136-138, 143 *sq.*; his threefold denial, 136, 138; the symbolism of these representations, 135, 137, 139, 140-147.

Schelstratius, 444.

Scotland, Christianity in England and in, 511 *sq.*

Seneca, 75, 490, 529.

Simon Magus, 22, 58; his history and statue, 59-63; in the Clementines, 413, 417 *sq.*, 426 *sq.*

Sixtus I. (or Xystus), Pope, 100, 101, 397, 468, 488.

Socrates, A.D. 429, 334.

Sollerius, 450.

Sophronius, S., 459, 506.

Soter, Pope, 470, 487.

Sozomen, A.D. 445, 385.

Spanheim, 4, 58.

Speaker's Commentary, the, 453 *sq.*

Stenglein, 61.

Suarez, 252 *sq.*, 256, 258, 406, 541, 544.

Succession, the, of the Bishops of Rome after S. Peter, by whom probably the three first were consecrated, 25, 40, 90 *sq.*, 156, 205 *sq.*, 313, 400, 406-411, 442; the line of Roman Pontiffs unbroken, 242 *sq.*, 246-248, 519.—The succession and its conditions, 2, 279; the former of Divine faith, the latter not so, 279, 288 *sq.*; opinions of theologians, 281-288.—S. Peter's action in settling the succession was divinely directed, 295.—The succession of the Roman Pontiffs was from S. Peter alone, 315, 318.

Suetonius, 62, 84, 88, 116.

Syllabus of Pius IX., 285.

Sylvester, Pope, his Office in the Greek Church, 378.

T.

TACITUS, 34, 62, 69, 77, 82 *sq.*, 87 *sq.*, 114.

Telesphorus, Pope, 100, 101, 106, 397, 488.

Tertullian, 21, 56, 59, 60, 90, 99, 115, 155, 156, 206, 427, 469, 471, 476.

Theodolinda, 109, 111, 124.

Theodore, S., Studites, 382.

Theodoret, 61, 224, 329.

Theophilus, 293.

Theophylact, 334.

Thomas, S., Aquinas, 336.

Tillemont, 63, 95, 116, 118.

Tondini, 387.

Traditional belief of S. Peter's Roman Episcopate, the, 7-9, 179-181, 187 *sq.*, 196 *sq.*, 204, 250, 447-449; it results from the reality of the fact, 10; is fraught with consequences most important to society, 201; its pretended origin, 58, 63.

U.

ULPIANUS, a Pagan lawyer, 99.

V.

VALESIUS on Eusebius, 23, 42, 400-407.

Veith, 313, 541.

Velenus, 63.

Verdun, the Codex of, lines from, 152.

Victor, Pope, 92, 101, 106, 397, 410,

www.ingramcontent.com/pod-product-compliance
Lightning Source LLC
Chambersburg PA
CBHW031934290426
44108CB00011B/553